THE DEMOCRATIC DEBATE

American Politics in an Age of Change

Sixth Edition

Bruce Miroff
State University of New York–Albany

Raymond Seidelman
Sarah Lawrence College

Todd Swanstrom
University of Missouri–St. Louis

Tom De Luca
Fordham University

CENGAGE
Learning·

Australia • Brazil • Japan • Korea • Mexico • Singapore • Spain • United Kingdom • United States

CENGAGE Learning®

The Democratic Debate: American Politics in an Age of Change, Sixth Edition
Bruce Miroff, Raymond Seidelman,
Todd Swanstrom, Tom De Luca

Senior Product Director: Suzanne Jeans

Product Team Manager: Carolyn Merrill

Content Developer: Wendy Langerud

Content Coordinator: Eireann Aspell

Product Assistant: Abigail Hess

Media Developer: Laura Hildebrand

Art Director: Linda May

Senior Rights Acquisition Specialist: Jennifer Meyer Dare

Manufacturing Planner: Fola Orekoya

Marketing Director: Michelle Williams

Marketing Manager: Valerie Hartman

Marketing Development Manager: Courtney Wolstoncroft

Art and Design Direction, Production Management, and Composition: Cenveo Publisher Services

Cover Image: Shutterstock

Cover Designer: Riezebos Holzbaur/Tim Heraldo

Photo Composite: Riezebos Holzbaur/Yvo Riezebos

For product information and technology assistance, contact us at
Cengage Learning Customer & Sales Support, 1-800-354-9706

For permission to use material from this text or product,
submit all requests online at **www.cengage.com/permissions.**
Further permissions questions can be emailed to
permissionrequest@cengage.com.

Library of Congress Control Number: 2012943550

ISBN-13: 978-1-133-60439-6

ISBN-10: 1-133-60439-0

Cengage Learning
200 First Stamford Place, 4th Floor
Stamford, CT 06902
USA

Cengage Learning is a leading provider of customized learning solutions with office locations around the globe, including Singapore, the United Kingdom, Australia, Mexico, Brazil, and Japan. Locate your local office at:
international.cengage.com/region.

Cengage Learning products are represented in Canada by
Nelson Education, Ltd.

For your course and learning solutions, visit **www.cengage.com.**
Purchase any of our products at your local college store or at our
preferred online store **www.cengagebrain.com.**

Instructors: Please visit login.cengage.com and log in to access
instructor-specific resources.

Printed in the United States of America
1 2 3 4 5 6 7 17 16 15 14 13

CONTENTS

Contents

13 Presidential Leadership and Elite Democracy 297

14 Bureaucracy: Myth and Reality 321

PREFACE

When we wrote the first edition of *The Democratic Debate*, we were convinced that many students and professors were looking for a different kind of textbook—one that covered the conventional topics in American politics but in an unconventional way. Instead of taking our critical standard from European socialism or utopian democratic theory, we wrote a point-of-view text that draws its standard from the homegrown traditions of participatory democracy in America. These traditions are rich and deep, stretching from the Anti-federalist critics of the Constitution to the Populists, the progressive unions, the civil rights movement, and more recent struggles, including the women's rights, gay rights, environmental, fair-trade, and peace movements. The positive response to the first five editions has convinced us that our initial intuition was right.

Students can easily become overwhelmed and confused by the sheer volume of facts presented in most textbooks on American politics. They need a framework to make sense of the facts. We have developed a simple yet powerful framework for analyzing American politics. In *The Democratic Debate*, the facts of American politics are organized around the theme of democracy. Specifically, each chapter examines the debate between what we call elite democracy and popular democracy, showing how that debate has impacted the particular institutions, processes, or policies covered in the chapter. The overall goal is to assess the prospects and possibilities for the extension of democracy in the United States.

Our thematic framework leads us to treat the conventional topics of American politics differently from other textbooks. Many texts, for example, treat the framers as a brilliant group of men who gave the country a Constitution that created a consensus about democracy that has persisted to this day. Because they lost the debate on the Constitution, the Anti-federalists are viewed by most textbooks as backward-looking opponents of progress who were relegated to the dustbin of history. *The Democratic Debate* takes the arguments of the Anti-federalists seriously. In our view, the founding period did not end debate but began a debate about American democracy between the tradition of elite democracy, as founded by the Federalists, and popular democracy, as founded by the Anti-federalists.

Although the basics of the democratic debate were laid down at the founding, both the elite and popular democratic positions have evolved over the years. We define *elite democracy* as a system in which elites acquire the power to rule by a free competition for the people's votes; between elections, the elites are given substantial autonomy to govern as they see fit. Elites stress that inequalities of power and economic resources are justified if they reflect real differences in ability, knowledge, and ambition. Over the years, the elite justification for rule has been buttressed by claims of knowledge and expertise in an increasingly complex, dangerous, and competitive world.

We define *popular democracy* as a system of government in which people participate as much as possible in making the decisions that affect their lives. Popular democracy does not just mean majority rule, however, because it requires rules of the game that ensure basic equality, tolerance, and respect for individual rights. That's why the Constitution cannot be changed just with a majority vote. Although elites have successfully buttressed their authority with claims of expertise, popular democrats have not been without resources. Since the first ten amendments to the Constitution were added, partly at the insistence of the Anti-federalists, popular democrats have succeeded in amending the Constitution in a more democratic direction, including winning the vote for women and African Americans. The inclusionary logic of democracy, based on the language of equal rights and equal participation, has been used to revive the spirit of protest that began the American Revolution, as well as to build popular democratic movements throughout American history.

In addition to organizing the facts of American politics, the theme of the democratic debate helps students to become personally engaged with the material. The book challenges students to examine their own beliefs about democracy. At the most basic level, the democratic debate revolves around different conceptions of human nature. Elite democrats view most people as private and self-interested; with the exception of a well-educated elite, they argue, people are not well suited to make public policy decisions. Popular democrats, on the other hand, view people as political beings by nature; once involved in democratic participation, they are capable of transcending their narrow parochial interests and becoming responsible, public-spirited citizens. *The Democratic Debate* challenges students to devise their own democratic philosophy based on their view of human nature.

Although we make every effort to present both sides of the democratic debate, we make no pretense of impartiality. In the pages ahead, we develop a popular democratic critique of American politics. Our values are clear. We constantly ask the question: How is it possible to increase democratic participation in American politics and create a more democratic society?

We are sad to report that on October 30, 2007, Ray Seidelman, our coauthor and dear friend, died after a four-year battle with cancer. An award-winning teacher at Sarah Lawrence College for twenty-five years, Ray was a driving force behind *The Democratic Debate* from the moment it was conceived on a camping trip in 1988. Involved in all aspects of the book, he took primary responsibility for the chapters on public opinion and political culture, nonvoting, campaigns, political parties, and the media. These chapters still reflect Ray's incisive intelligence—his hard-hitting exposés of elite manipulations and democratic distortions. He always pushed us to deepen our analysis and challenge students to think more critically.

Ray was not just an insightful political observer; he was also a passionate political actor. Encouraging his students to get involved in the political fray, he did likewise. He loved political debate. In many ways, Ray was the model popular democrat—politically engaged and passionate about his beliefs—but tolerant of those he thought were wrong. He will be missed—not just by his coauthors and his students—but by friends of democracy everywhere.

We are very fortunate to have added Tom De Luca for the fifth and sixth editions. Tom has had productive careers as both an academic and a political advocate and organizer. He has been an activist on issues ranging from nuclear arms, apartheid, and political reform to the quest for equality in meeting basic human needs. He teaches and directs the International Studies Program at Fordham University at Lincoln Center in New York City, where his courses include democratic theory, American politics, civil rights, and an annual field study in China. Engaged in the study of democracy in both the United States and China, Tom is a prolific author who brings theory and practice together, especially in the area of political participation.

New to the Sixth Edition

The sixth edition has retained the most successful features of previous editions while adding extensive discussions of new developments in both popular and elite politics. Highlights among the new developments and controversies covered in the sixth edition include:

- Full coverage of the 2012 elections
- Impact of the Great Recession on American democracy

- New voter-identification laws
- The *Citizens United* decision and its impact
- Government secrecy and media independence in the Internet age
- Role of the Internet in interest-group politics
- The Tea Party, Occupy Wall Street, and protest politics
- A Congress and political parties more polarized than ever
- The Obama presidency
- A new section: "How Well Does Government Work?"
- Progress in gay and lesbian rights
- Partisan polarization in U.S. foreign policy

Organization of the Book

The Democratic Debate covers all of the conventional topics treated in mainstream texts. One of the main purposes of a textbook, we believe, is to cover every important institution and process of American politics that should be addressed in an introductory course, thus freeing the instructor to lecture on themes of particular interest that supplement the text. We do not sacrifice coverage to develop the theme but rather use the theme to draw the reader along, examining the essential facts and concepts that are covered in other texts.

We also discuss a number of unconventional topics that are not covered in most mainstream texts. We believe, for example, that a book with democracy as its central theme must have a chapter on political participation that highlights the issue of nonvoting, probably the most serious flaw in American democracy. Hence, Chapter 6 examines why so many Americans don't vote and how voters might be mobilized. Chapter 4 examines the political economy, showing why corporations cannot be viewed as just another interest group, and Chapter 11 explores mass movements—their history, tactics, and importance to American democracy.

The book is organized in four parts. Part One deals with the foundational rules and structures of American politics. After a short introductory chapter that lays out the theme of the democratic debate, we go on to examine the Revolution and the struggle over the Constitution. In this book, the chapter on the founding is not presented as merely of historical interest in explaining the Constitution, as it is in most texts, but instead, it defines the basic contours of the democratic debate that have persisted to this day. Chapter 3 treats the historical dilemma of federalism in the democratic debate. Chapter 4 analyzes the political economy, showing how the private system of wealth formation affects the public system of democratic governance. Part One concludes with a chapter on public opinion and political culture.

Part Two covers the basic processes of participation in American politics. As befits a book that is focused on the issue of democracy, this section is longer than in most texts, spanning six chapters. Part Two is designed to acquaint students with the basic patterns of participation, as well as with the political science literature that helps explain why some people are well represented in the political system and others are not. In the absence of strong political parties, we argue, other institutions—such as the mass media and interest groups—take over important political functions, with questionable results for democracy. While fully documenting the phenomenon of nonvoting and other obstacles that lie in the path of democratic participation, Part Two ends on a hopeful note by examining the ability of mass protest movements to level the playing field of American politics.

Part Three covers the basic institutions of American politics—Congress, the presidency, bureaucracy, and the judiciary. In Chapter 2, we show how the original Constitution set up institutions that were highly elitist in nature, with the House of Representatives the only institution directly elected by the people. Since then, democratic struggles have made the major institutions more responsive to popular pressure, although they still contain many elitist elements. A theme of Part Three is that institutions have an independent effect on political outcomes and on the democratic debate.

Part Four explores the democratic debate further by looking at three policy areas: civil rights and civil liberties, economic and social policy, and foreign policy. The democratic debate concerns not just processes and rules but the distribution of rights, resources, and services. Part Four examines contemporary public policy debates through the lens of democracy, concentrating on a question usually ignored by policy analysts: Does a particular policy enhance or undermine democratic participation?

Special Features

We have included a number of special features to help students learn from the book and deepen their understanding, but we have tried not to clutter the text with too many distractions from the central theme.

To give students a road map through the book, we have included an outline at the beginning of each chapter. Important terms are boldfaced and defined at the end of the chapter. Our online website contains a guide to further reading and a list of Internet resources.

The boxed feature "A Closer Look" provides students with vivid examples of the democratic debate. "Making a Difference" boxes profile extraordinary individuals and groups, famous and not so famous, who have made a difference in popular democratic struggles. "New Reform" boxes offer short descriptions of practical reforms that have been proposed to further the goals and values of popular democracy. In guest op-ed boxes, prominent authors take stands on controversial issues in contemporary American politics.

We have illustrated our book with cartoons and photographs. We think that the cartoons we have selected are eye-opening as well as funny.

Supplements for Students and Instructors

Online PowerLecture with Cognero® for Miroff et al.'s *The Democratic Debate*, 6th Edition ISBN-13: 9781285775678

This PowerLecture is an all-in-one online multimedia resource for class preparation, presentation, and testing. Accessible through login.cengage.com with your faculty account, you will find available for download: book-specific Microsoft® PowerPoint® presentations; a Test Bank in both Microsoft® Word® and Cognero® formats; an Instructor's Manual; Microsoft® PowerPoint® Image Slides; and a JPEG Image Library.

The Test Bank, offered in Microsoft® Word® and Cognero® formats, contains multiple-choice and essay questions for each chapter. Cognero® is a flexible, online system that allows you to author, edit, and manage test bank content for Miroff et al.'s *The Democratic Debate*,

6th edition. Create multiple test versions instantly and deliver through your LMS from your classroom, or wherever you may be, with no special installs or downloads required.

The Instructor's Manual contains for each chapter: an outline and summary; critical thinking questions; in-class activities; lecture launching suggestions; a list of key terms with definitions; and suggested readings and web resources.

The Microsoft® PowerPoint® presentations are ready-to-use, visual outlines of each chapter. These presentations are easily customized for your lectures and offered along with chapter-specific Microsoft® PowerPoint® Image Slides and JPEG Image Libraries. Access your Online PowerLecture at login.cengage.com.

Free Companion Website for Miroff et al.'s *The Democratic Debate*, 6th Edition ISBN-13: 9781285058573

This free companion website for *The Democratic Debate*, 6th edition that is accessible through cengagebrain.com allows access to chapter-specific interactive learning tools including flash-cards, quizzes, glossaries, and more.

The free, password-protected website for instructors features all of the free student assets plus an instructor's manual, book-specific PowerPoint® presentations, and a test bank. Access your resources by logging into your account at login.cengage.com.

Acknowledgments

Like democracy itself, this text has benefited from the participation of many people. We were fortunate to have a series of dedicated professionals to guide this project over the years at Houghton Mifflin: Gregory Tobin, Margaret Seawell, Jean Woy, Janet Young, Tracy Patruno, Fran Gay, and Katherine Meisenheimer. We especially want to acknowledge the work of our editor for the first edition, Ann West, who improved the book immeasurably with her suggestions. Naomi Kornhauser helped select appealing cartoons and photos for the first edition. Our editors for the second edition, Ann Torbert and Melissa Mashburn, did an excellent job working under extremely tight deadlines. Mary Dougherty, our editor for the third edition, also gave us wise guidance and support. Christina Lembo was a careful and attentive editor for the fourth edition, and Nancy Benjamin at Books By Design did an excellent job of handling the day-to-day production. Julia Giannotti and Jane Lee worked diligently on the fifth edition. And finally, thank you to Wendy Langerud, our development editor, Carolyn Merrill, product manager, and Chris Schoedel, the production manager, for their meticulous detail-oriented work in this sixth edition.

Our friends and colleagues Walter Balk, Susan Christopherson, Peter Dreier, Marty Edelman, Anne Hildreth, and Steve Wasby provided insightful feedback on a number of chapters. A number of graduate students at SUNY–Albany, including Martin Shaffer, David Filbert, Christopher Price, Yong-Hoo Sohn, and Paul Alexander, helped us with research on various editions of the text.

At Saint Louis University, Mamoun Benmammoun and Scott Krummenacher provided valuable research assistance, as did Jeremy Main and Isaiah John at the University of Missouri–St. Louis. Michael Parrott, a former Fordham student and now a doctoral candidate in political science at the University of Maryland, continued his collaboration from the 5th to the 6th edition, providing essential research, updating, and sharp critical ideas to a number of chapters and generating a number of graphics. At Fordham University, Juanita John also provided excellent research assistance and ideas to a number of chapters.

At Sarah Lawrence College, students Joni Ang, Asia Friedman, and David G. Hill provided outstanding research assistance for the second edition. Amanda Slagle, Claire Landiss, and Brooke DeRenzis provided indispensable help with research and with the themes and writing of many feature boxes for the third edition. Laura Ann Pechacek was a great help in preparing the fourth edition. The staff of the Esther Raushenbush Library—especially Charling Fagan, Bill Haines, David Nicholls, Judy Kicinski, and Barbara Hickey—showed how patient librarians can be with impatient scholars. Grants from the Julie and Ruediger Flik Travel Fund and the Hewlett-Mellon Fellowship Fund helped provide the time needed to meet publishing deadlines.

Charles Tien at Hunter College and the Graduate Center of CUNY helped with analysis of class patterns in voting participation. Michelle Lin provided expert help in editing for grammar and grace. John Buell is a lifelong collaborator in ideas.

The book benefited greatly from the comments of many political scientists across the country. Fortunately, these outside reviewers did not spare us in their criticisms, and although we squirmed, the book was ultimately much better because of their efforts. Our thanks go to Gordon Alexandre, Glendale Community College; Stephen Amburg, University of Texas–San Antonio; Theodore S. Arrington, University of North Carolina at Charlotte; Judith A. Baer, Texas A&M University; Horace Bartilow Jr., University of Kentucky; Gerald Berk, University of Oregon; Jim Bromeland, Winona State University; John P. Burke, University of Vermont; Michael John Burton, Ohio University; Richard Bush, Southern Illinois University; Allan J. Cigler, University of Kansas; Sue Davis, University of Delaware; Jeffrey Edwards, Roosevelt University; Henry Flores, St. Mary's University; Dennis J. Goldford, Drake University; Richard Herrera, Arizona State University; Herbert Hirsch, Virginia Commonwealth University; Steven Hoffman, University of St. Thomas; James Hogan, Seattle University; Kenneth Kennedy, College of San Mateo; Robert Kerstein, University of Tampa; Virginia G. McClamm, City College of San Francisco; James Meader, Augustana College; Jerome O'Callaghan, State University of New York at Cortland; Mark P. Petracca, University of California–Irvine; George Pippin, Jones County Junior College; Jerry Pubantz, Salem College; Ted Radke, Contra Costa Community College; Leonard Ritt, Northern Arizona University; John S. Robey, University of Texas–Brownsville; Pamela H. Rodgers, University of Wisconsin–La Crosse; Melissa Semione, SUNY Jefferson; John Squibb, Lincoln Land Community College; Deborah Tompsett-Makin, Norco College; M. Elliot Vittes, University of Central Florida; and Mitchell Weiss, Charles S. Mott Community College.

Finally, we want to thank our families and friends for their love, support, and patience: Melinda, Nick, Anna, Fay, Eva, Rosa, Katie, Jessica, Madeleine, Eleanore, Tom Sr., Karen, Amelia, Giovanna, and always Bob.

ABOUT THE AUTHORS

Bruce Miroff (PhD, University of California–Berkeley, 1974) is professor of political science at the State University of New York–Albany, and he is the past president of the Presidency Research Group of the American Political Science Association. He is the author of *Pragmatic Illusions: The Presidential Politics of John F. Kennedy, Icons of Democracy: American Leaders as Heroes, Aristocrats, Dissenters, and Democrats,* and *The Liberals' Moment: The McGovern Insurgency and the Identity Crisis of the Democratic Party,* as well as numerous articles on the presidency, American political theory, and American political development. Along with Seidelman and Swanstrom, he is coeditor of *Debating Democracy: A Reader in American Politics.*

Raymond Seidelman (PhD, Cornell University, 1979) was a professor of politics and the Sara Exley Yates Professor of Teaching Excellence at Sarah Lawrence College in Yonkers, New York. Seidelman was the author of *Disenchanted Realists: Political Science and the American Crisis,* and the coeditor (with James Farr) of *Discipline and History: Political Science in the United States.* He taught courses in American electoral politics, the mass media, and urban and suburban history and politics. He taught in China and South Korea and lectured extensively in many East Asian countries. He died in 2007.

Todd Swanstrom (PhD, Princeton University, 1981) is the Des Lee Professor of Community Collaboration and Public Policy Administration at the University of Missouri–St. Louis. Specializing in urban politics and public policy, he is the author of *The Crisis of Growth Politics: Cleveland, Kucinich, and the Challenge of Urban Populism* and coeditor of *Justice and the American Metropolis* (2011). His coauthored book, *Place Matters: Metropolitics for the Twenty-First Century* (rev. ed., 2005) received the Michael Harrington Award from the New Politics Section of the American Political Science Association. Using the resources of his endowed professorship, he supports the Community Builders Network of Metro St. Louis (http://www.community-buildersstl.org), a coalition of thirty-four community-based nonprofits working to build great neighborhoods where everyone, regardless of income or race, can access all the opportunities necessary for a good life.

Tom De Luca (PhD, University of Massachusetts–Amherst, 1983) is professor of political science and the director of the International Studies Program at Fordham University at Lincoln Center in New York City. He is the author of *The Two Faces of Political Apathy* (1995) and coauthor of *Liars! Cheaters! Evildoers! Demonization and the End of Civil Debate in American Politics* (2005), and *Sustainable Democracy: Individuality and the Politics of the Environment* (1996). He was Honorary Professor of Political Science at Sun Yat-sen University (Guangzhou, People's Republic of China), 2010–2012, and China University of Political Science and Law (Beijing, People's Republic of China), 2008–2010. He was also the Thomas Jefferson Distinguished Fulbright Chair in American Social Studies at the University of Amsterdam in 2006. He is currently writing on political equality. Before beginning at Fordham in 1991, he spent ten years as a community organizer, trying to help stop the nuclear arms races and to support economic justice and human political rights.

Introduction:
The Democratic Debate

Men, by their constitutions, are naturally divided into two parties: 1. Those who fear and distrust the people, and wish to draw all powers from them into the hands of the higher classes. 2. Those who identify themselves with the people, have confidence in them, cherish and consider them as the most honest and safe, although not the most wise, depository of the public interests.... The appellation of Aristocrats and Democrats is the true one, expressing the essence of all.

Thomas Jefferson, *Writings*, vol. XVI, p. 73

Most Americans view the United States as a democracy, pure and simple. Certainly, there are flaws in our government, but most people agree that the foundation for a democratic society was secured by the Constitution and later laws. The great debates about the rules of the game are settled. Consider elections. We began as a nation that excluded African Americans, women, and people without property from voting. But property requirements were struck down early in the nineteenth century, women got the vote with the adoption of the Nineteenth Amendment in 1920, and African Americans finally won full voting rights with the passage of the civil rights laws of the 1960s. In 2008, Barack Obama, the son of a black man from Kenya and a white woman from Kansas, shocked the political world by capturing the presidency. The election of an African American as president suggests that there are few barriers to the realization of a fully democratic nation.

But true democracy requires more than free and fair elections. It requires having a democratic economy and society. More than 200 years after the founding, we still lack many of the economic and social requirements of a fully developed democracy. Economic inequalities between rich and poor are greater than at any time since the Gilded Age of the late nineteenth century. More and more citizens find themselves trapped in dead-end jobs with low pay and few benefits. Working multiple jobs or struggling to care for children and aging parents, many citizens lack both the time and the resources to participate effectively in American democracy. Meanwhile, large corporations and wealthy elites exercise disproportionate power. In a much-criticized 2010 decision (*Citizens United v. Federal Election Commission*), the Supreme Court ruled that spending money to influence elections was protected by the First Amendment prohibition against government regulation of free speech. As a result, in the 2012 election, so-called "Super PACs," funded mostly by wealthy elites and large corporations, spent massive amounts of money attacking candidates running for office. How can we have a democracy in which everyone's voice is heard when those at the top shout loudly with the help of expensive amplifiers, while others can only speak in whispers?

The war on terror has also violated basic democratic principles. Following the 9/11 terrorist attacks, President George W. Bush stampeded the nation into invading Iraq based on false information. America's moral standing in the world was severely damaged by revelations of the use of torture at Abu Ghraib in violation of international treaties and the violation of the civil rights of prisoners at Guantanamo Bay in Cuba. Abuses of power in war contracting became rampant, and the soaring costs of the war weakened the ability of the nation to respond to domestic issues, such as our crumbling infrastructure and high unemployment. Although it is less expensive in lives and treasury, the war in Afghanistan has many of the same problems. Following a Bush-era policy, President Obama has asserted the power to assassinate American citizens abroad without a trial if intelligence agencies determine that the person was involved in terrorist activities. Throughout the war on terror, Congress, cowed by the politics of fear, has failed to provide the checks and balances against the executive that are necessary in a democracy.

Most textbooks treat American politics as based on a consensus. According to the consensus interpretation, Americans agree on the basic rules of the game. What they disagree about is who will win and who will lose, that is, how to divide up the spoils in the "game" of democratic politics. We take a different approach. We present American democracy as a work in progress. Americans disagree not just about policy, but also about the fundamental rules of the game—about how far democracy should be extended into American society. Democracy means more than the ability to vote for president every four years. It means building a democratic society and economy that support the maximum possible participation by citizens in the decisions that affect their lives. The struggle for democracy is never ending. In the pages ahead, we introduce you to the democratic debate.

What Is Democracy?

The central idea of democracy is quite simple. Democracy originated in the fifth century BCE in the small city-states of Greece. The word *democracy* comes from the Greek words *demos*, meaning "the people," and *kratein*, meaning "to rule." Therefore, democracy means simply "rule by the people." Defined as "rule by the people," democracy, Americans agree, is the best form of government. Americans disagree, however, about what democracy means in practice and how far democratic decision making should be extended.

One of the fundamental disagreements is over who is best suited for democratic decision making—the masses or political elites. *Elites* are small groups of people who possess extraordinary amounts of power. Throughout history, advocates of elite rule have argued that ruling is too difficult for ordinary citizens. Elites dominate many political systems—including communist, aristocratic, and even formally democratic ones. Elitism comes in various forms, with different justifications for elite rule. A totalitarian regime, for instance, is ruled by an elite few with unlimited power to control the daily lives of the citizens; a theocracy is a system run by religious elites.

Few Americans are classical elitists, however; a strong democratic impulse pervades American culture and politics. Anyone who argued that family background, religious training, or even wealth automatically qualified a person to rule would not be taken seriously in the United States. Americans believe in the democratic principle that political power should ultimately stem from the people. Americans also agree on certain basic principles of democratic government, including the importance of a written constitution, representative government, and basic rights such as freedom of speech and press. Throughout American history, political movements have risen to extend democratic citizenship to blacks, women, and other excluded groups. Political equality is a strong value in American politics.

A deep elitist strain, however, also pervades our politics. Americans support elitism not because they believe elites are inherently superior to the common people, but because they believe elites have the specialized knowledge and experience to make the best decisions. In a technologically complex and dangerous world, democracy must often defer to specialized expertise, whether in government or in private corporations. Democracy is a fine ideal, many people argue, but to be realistic and effective, "the people" must cede much of their decision-making power to elites. Americans, for example, often cede power over war and peace to an executive elite on the grounds that "the president knows best."

The thesis of this text is simple: American politics is characterized by a fundamental conflict between elite democracy and popular democracy. **Elite democracy** is a political system in which elites acquire the power to decide by a free and fair competition for the people's votes.[1] Once elected, elites are given the freedom to rule as they see fit. If the people do not like the results, they can vote these elites out at the next election and put different elites into office. Under elite democracy, the people are not expected to participate in the day-to-day affairs of governing.

The alternative to elite democracy is **popular democracy**, which can be defined as a political system in which the people are involved as much as possible in making the decisions that affect their lives.[2] Popular democracy has its roots in **direct democracy**, in which all citizens gather in one place to vote on important matters. In the Greek city-states, where democracy originated twenty-five hundred years ago, democracy meant face-to-face debate and decision making by all citizens, with offices rotating among the citizens. Some examples of direct democracy still exist in the United States, such as the New England town meeting, where all town citizens gather in one hall to debate and decide important issues.[3]

Popular democracy is the adaptation of direct democracy to a large country with a modern economy and society. Popular democrats maintain that ordinary citizens should be closely involved in governing and that, in the long run, they will govern more wisely than elites. In a large country, popular democrats admit, everyone cannot meet in one place to make decisions. Political representatives are needed, but they should remain as close as possible to the people who elected them, accurately reflecting their values and interests. Between elections, citizens should be involved in political affairs, holding representatives accountable and making sure that experts, who are necessary in a complex modern society, serve the needs of the people and not the needs of elites. And the right of people to engage in extra-electoral peaceful protests in order to dramatize their issues and influence decision makers should be protected as much as possible.

At the heart of American politics lies an essential tension between two different conceptions of democracy. We are not the first to present a conflict interpretation of American politics. Marxists have long focused on the "contradictions" of capitalism, particularly the conflict between workers and capitalists. Although class inequalities have often caused deep divisions in American politics, we believe that the fundamental conflict in American democracy is not between workers and capitalists but between elite and popular democrats.

Origins of the Democratic Debate: The Founding

Normally, the founding period is treated as a celebration of the American consensus on democracy as embodied in the Constitution. Chapter 2 shows, however, that the U.S. Constitution was born in conflict, not in consensus. The ratification of the Constitution did not end debate but began a new debate about the meaning of democracy. The terms of this debate, which were laid down over two hundred years ago, continue to influence American politics to this day.

Our Constitution was not written by lofty statesmen who offered their eternal truths to a grateful nation. The men who wrote the Constitution were practical politicians with pressing political objectives. The framers distrusted popular democracy, especially the power of the majority. (Read James Madison's *Federalist No. 10*.) The supporters of the Constitution in the late 1780s, known as **Federalists**, were the founders of elite democracy in the United States. The Constitution they wrote and ratified was mixed, containing elements of both elitism and democracy. The original Constitution placed severe limits on majority rule and contained many elitist elements; neither the president nor senators, for example, were to be elected directly by the people. (In the original Constitution, senators were chosen by state legislatures and presidents were elected by an elite, the Electoral College, appointed under procedures chosen by the state legislatures.)

The ratification of the Constitution was bitterly opposed by a group known as the **Anti-federalists**. The Anti-federalists were the founders of popular democracy in the United States.[4] The Anti-federalists denounced the proposed Constitution as a betrayal of the democratic spirit of 1776 and of the American Revolution itself. The new Constitution, they protested, took too much power away from the states and localities and gave it to the central government. In the long run, they charged, the Constitution would erode the face-to-face participation necessary for a healthy democracy. The Anti-federalists were not a marginal group; many state conventions ratified the Constitution by only the narrowest of margins.

Federalists and Anti-federalists disagreed about the most basic questions of human nature, society, and politics (see Chapter 2). In the eyes of the Federalists, the mass of Americans were passionate and selfish creatures. In a small republic, where simple majority rule prevailed, nothing would stop this mass from taking away the rights or the property of the minority. The Anti-federalists had more faith in the common people. They believed that most people could be educated into civic virtue, overcoming their selfish inclinations and learning to pursue the common good. According to the Anti-federalists, the main threat to democracy came not from majorities but from selfish and powerful elites.

Evolution of Popular Democracy: The Logic of Inclusion

The Anti-federalists are frequently viewed as losers who had little impact on American politics. This is false. Although the Anti-federalists lost the initial struggle over the Constitution, their perspective has had a tremendous influence on American politics.

If the founding document of elite democracy is the Constitution of 1789, the founding document of popular democracy is the Declaration of Independence of 1776. With its bold statement that "all men are created equal" and are "endowed by their Creator with certain unalienable Rights," the Declaration laid down the basic principles of popular democracy. The Declaration of Independence proclaimed a radical idea: if the government violates people's rights, they have a right "to alter or abolish it." This "Spirit of '76"—based on political equality, rights, and rebellion—has inspired popular democrats ever since.

The democratic faith of Americans, as expressed in the Declaration of Independence, has given popular democrats an ideological advantage and has frequently placed elite democrats on the defensive. In 1791, for example, two years after the Constitution was ratified, the first ten amendments—the Bill of Rights—were added, mostly at the insistence of the Anti-federalists, who wanted to ensure protection of their political rights. (Chapter 16 discusses the importance of civil rights and civil liberties for popular democracy.) Nearly all the amendments to the Constitution since then have moved it in a popular democratic direction, including the Fifteenth Amendment (1870), which extended voting rights to African American men; the Seventeenth Amendment (1913), which required the direct election of senators; the Nineteenth Amendment (1920), which extended the right to vote to women; and the Twenty-sixth Amendment (1971), which gave the vote to eighteen- to twenty-year-olds.

Popular democratic influence, however, has not been limited to amending the Constitution. It has also affected how we interpret the Constitution. Elected in 1800, Thomas Jefferson, who shared many of the beliefs of the Anti-federalists, was our nation's first popular democratic president. As such, Jefferson could have proposed writing a new constitution. Instead, he decided to infuse democratic content into the Constitution of 1789 by expanding the participation of common people in governmental decision making.

A Muslim woman casts her ballot—her right to vote protected by the Constitution and the courts.

Although politicians at the top of the political system, like Jefferson, sometimes championed popular democracy, more often such impulses came from ordinary citizens. Throughout American history, popular democrats have mobilized the masses to expand democratic decision making. Periods of elite dominance have given way to periods of mass participation and popular democratic upsurge, such as the 1890s, the 1930s, and the 1960s–1970s.[5]

In mobilizing people for mass movements, popular democrats have appealed to the ideas of political equality and rights found in the Declaration of Independence. In 1848, for example, Elizabeth Cady Stanton used the language of the Declaration of Independence to write a women's declaration of independence. Her Declaration of Sentiments is considered the founding document of the women's rights movement, which won the right to vote in 1920 and flowered into a modern feminist movement in the 1960s. In the 1950s and 1960s, Martin Luther King Jr. used the popular democratic language of rights and equality to energize the civil rights movement and appeal successfully to a broad, white audience.

In American politics, popular democratic methods do not always line up with popular democratic goals. The methods used by the Tea Party protests fit squarely in the popular democratic tradition but their goals do not. By invoking the Tea Party in Boston Harbor that helped to launch the American Revolution, Tea Party protestors fit squarely in the popular democratic tradition. They are channeling the anger many people feel toward a government they think has become too big, too expensive, and too powerful. The movement has a dynamic grassroots component and many people actively participated in politics for the first time through it. The aims of the Tea Party movement, however, do not fit the inclusionary logic of past popular democratic protests. The antipathy of Tea Party partisans toward immigrants; their willingness to suspend the Bill of Rights for suspected terrorists; and their opposition to programs to help the poor, minorities, or those facing foreclosure all point in the direction of greater exclusion, not inclusion.[6] In addition, the close ties of the Tea Party to wealthy corporate elites and the Republican party conflict with past patterns of popular democratic protests. How recent protests such as the Tea Party and Occupy Wall Street fit into popular democratic traditions is discussed at greater length in Chapter 11.

Evolution of Elite Democracy: The Logic of Expertise

Elite democrats have not stood still while popular democrats pushed for extending democracy. Throughout American history, elite democrats have been immensely resourceful, devising new arguments for limiting democracy. In the early years of the republic, many openly defended elite values. However, the democratization of American values soon rendered such naked appeals to elitism illegitimate. Elitism is no longer defended on the grounds that elites are inherently superior to the masses or that certain people are destined to rule. In contemporary American society, elites profess democratic values but maintain that elite rule is necessary in many spheres of modern society. Elite democrats would not admit they are elitist; they would simply say they are realistic.

The elite democratic position cannot be easily dismissed. When we ride on an airplane, for example, we do not take a vote to see how high the plane will fly or who will serve as pilot. Everyone acknowledges that democratic decision making must defer to rule by experts, or technical elites, in particular situations. But where do we draw the line? Elite democrats believe that in a rapidly changing, technologically complex, and dangerous world more and more power must be ceded to elites—elites whose power is justified not by birth or wealth but by their knowledge, expertise, and experience. Democracy is viewed as a kind of luxury that we cannot "afford" too much of, especially given our desire for economic growth and the necessity to compete with other nations for economic, political, and military advantage.

"We can't come to an agreement about how to fix your car, Mr. Simons. Sometimes that's the way things happen in a democracy."

The New Yorker Collection.

J.B. Handelsman/The New Yorker Collection/Cartoonbank.com

In the late nineteenth century, a popular democratic movement called *populism* emerged, challenging the control of corporate elites over the economy. In the crucial election of 1896, however, the populist candidate, William Jennings Bryan, was defeated by the candidate of big business, William McKinley. Drawing on huge corporate contributions, McKinley is credited with having pioneered the first modern campaign using mass-media techniques of persuasion. McKinley's victory ushered in a long period of weak party competition and declining voter turnout.[7] Chapters 6, 7, and 8 document the power that money can exert over the electoral process when parties decline and their functions are taken over by the mass media.

The Federal Government and Popular Democracy

From the time of the founding, popular and elite democrats have reversed their positions on the importance of a strong federal government. At the time of the founding, elite democrats favored a strong federal government to protect the property of elites and filter the passions of the masses. Popular democrats feared an aristocratic federal government and wanted most power placed in the hands of the states, which were closer to the people. Over time, the positions have reversed: popular democrats now generally look to the federal government to protect common people from economic exploitation, and elite democrats generally favor states rights and less government regulation of the economy.

At the time of the debate over the Constitution, few private corporations existed; those that did were small and family owned. Elite democrats like Alexander Hamilton favored a strong national government that could aid in the development of manufacturing and the accumulation of wealth. Popular democrats like Thomas Jefferson feared a strong federal government as too removed from the common man and likely to aid in the accumulation of large fortunes that could corrupt democracy. As president, Jefferson supported giving more power to the states, not as a general principle, but as a means to promote the wide distribution of productive property in the hands of small farmers and businessmen.

The process of industrialization and the creation of huge national corporations completely changed the attitude of popular democrats toward the federal government.[8] Throughout the nineteenth century, industrial fortunes swelled and economic inequality grew. A strong federal government was needed to rein in the power of national corporations and ensure a minimum level of equality necessary for a vibrant democracy. It became clear to popular democrats that tyranny can come from private abuse of power as much as public abuse. In 1913, progressives passed the Sixteenth Amendment, which allowed for a progressive income tax and enacted an estate tax to break up the huge fortunes that were corrupting democracy.

Over the same period, elite democrats increasingly argued in favor of states' rights and against federal regulation of the economy. The principle of states' rights was used by southern elites to prevent the federal government from intervening to guarantee African Americans the right to vote. Corporate elites have argued that economic regulations stifle the free-market competition that produces innovation and economic growth. Chapter 4 examines the argument for free-market capitalism that is so important for contemporary elite democrats, as well as the popular democratic response that corporations exert power over the marketplace and thus must be held democratically accountable.

It is too simple, however, to say that popular democrats favor the federal government and elite democrats favor state and local governments. Neither side is entirely consistent.

Elite democrats, for example, support a smaller federal government—except in military and foreign affairs. In Chapter 18, we discuss the effort to insulate foreign and military policy making in the hands of an executive elite. Similarly, popular democrats have not uniformly supported federal power. The need to expand the federal government has placed popular democrats on the horns of a dilemma: although a more powerful federal government is necessary to address inequalities and curb the power of corporations, national laws too often remove government from popular democratic participation. Chapter 3 examines the efforts of popular democrats to devise federal programs that help empower local citizens.

Summarizing the Democratic Debate

This consensus view of American politics fundamentally distorts reality. Americans disagree about the rules of the game. In particular, Americans disagree about the meaning of democracy and how far democratic decision making should be extended into the economy and society. This text argues for a conflict, not a consensus, approach to American politics. American politics is best understood as embodying an essential tension, or conflict, between two different conceptions of democracy: elite democracy and popular democracy. The differences between these two approaches can be summarized in six points.

ELITE DEMOCRACY

1. With the exception of an educated, largely white male elite, most people are uninterested in politics and uninformed about issues; most people are more interested in their own private lives than in politics.

2. When the masses do get involved in politics, they tend to be highly emotional and intolerant; ironically, the main threat to democracy comes from the masses, not from elites.

3. Democracy basically means free and fair elections in which elites acquire the power to rule by competing for people's votes.

4. The main goal of democracy should be to protect the rights of individuals to pursue their own interests, especially the acquisition of property. Because of varying talents and ambitions, democracies must tolerate substantial inequality.

POPULAR DEMOCRACY

1. People are naturally inclined to participate in the decisions that affect their lives; if they don't participate, something must be wrong with the democratic system.

2. Through democratic participation, people can overcome their parochial interests and become public-spirited citizens. When their powers and privileges are threatened, elites often respond by curtailing democracy; the main threat to democracy comes from selfish elites, not from ordinary citizens.

3. Democracy means more than fair elections; it means the participation of ordinary citizens in the decisions that affect their lives in an atmosphere of tolerance and trust.

4. The main goal of democracy should be to strengthen community; inequalities that divide the community should be minimized.

(Continues)

9

ELITE DEMOCRACY	**POPULAR DEMOCRACY**
5. Political representatives should filter the views of the people through their superior expertise, intelligence, and temperament.	5. Representatives should stay as close to their constituents as possible, accurately reflecting their views in the political system.
6. Reforms in America almost always come about gradually, through the actions of elites.	6. Meaningful reforms in American politics have almost always come about because of political pressure from below by ordinary citizens.

Interpreting Political Facts: The Problem of Participation

It is easy to become confused by the complexity of American politics. Magazines, newspapers, radio, and TV bombard us with facts about political negotiations in Congress, interest-group bargaining, maneuverings of the political parties, the state of the economy and its effect on political fortunes, key decisions by the Supreme Court, and the actions of foreign countries. The sheer volume of political facts threatens to overwhelm our ability to comprehend them. Students of American politics need an organizing framework to make sense of these facts—to identify patterns, decide which facts are important, and evaluate political outcomes.

The ideas of elite and popular democracy can serve as an interpretive framework to help make sense of American politics. To understand how this framework is used in the text, we apply it here to one example: the different ways that people interpret basic facts about political participation in American politics (a topic covered in Chapter 6).

The facts of political participation in the United States are well known. Voting is the most common political act, yet less than 60 percent of the eligible electorate votes in most presidential elections (the turnout in 2012 was 57.5 percent); only about one-third of voters turnout for off-year congressional elections.

Although these facts are straightforward, making sense of them is more difficult. For example, how do we assess the simple fact that only a little more than half of the eligible electorate normally votes in presidential elections? Is the glass half full or half empty? What you see depends as much on your interpretation of the facts as on the facts themselves.

For elite democrats, the glass of democratic participation is half full. According to this view, the fact that only about half the people participate in elections is a sign of a healthy democracy. People are not inclined to participate in politics; most prefer to spend their time in private pursuits: making a living, raising children, watching TV. The fact that many people do not participate in politics is a sign of satisfaction. After all, nothing is stopping them from voting—legal barriers to voting (property qualifications, poll taxes, literacy tests) have been eliminated. If the masses of nonvoters felt their interests were threatened by government, they could mobilize their slack resources, including the vote, and influence the system. Moreover, because we know that nonvoters tend to be less educated, we should be happy that many do not participate in politics. As *Newsweek* columnist George Will put it, "The reasonable assumption about electorates is: smaller is smarter."[9]

Popular democrats contest the elite democratic interpretation of the facts of participation on every count. For them, the glass of democratic participation is at least half empty. They see low levels of political participation as a sign of a sick democracy. Popular

Figure 1.1 Do you see an old woman or a young woman?

democrats believe that people are naturally inclined to participate in the governance of their societies. When they don't participate, something must be wrong. Although there are no legal barriers preventing Americans from participating in the political process, popular democrats argue, many people feel so alienated from politics that they view their own participation as meaningless. They see the decisive role of money in elections and conclude that ordinary citizens have little influence. Moreover, when they see the limited choices on the ballot, they think that it doesn't matter who wins. In short, those who fail to participate in politics are not satisfied; they are *discouraged*.

Who is right? As the example of participation shows, political facts do not speak for themselves. The same facts can be seen from radically different perspectives. Interpreting the facts of American politics is like viewing Figure 1.1; what you see depends on how you look at it. Do you see an old woman or a beautiful young woman? You can see one or the other, but you cannot see both at the same time. As with this image, we must interpret the facts of American politics to give them meaning. Elite and popular views of democracy are the two frameworks we will use to interpret the facts of American politics.

There is an important difference, however, between interpreting Figure 1.1 and interpreting political facts. What you see in the figure does not affect anyone's interest. In politics, interpretations of the facts are hotly contested because they directly affect people's interests. Consider the different interpretations of nonvoting. If nonvoting is an expression of satisfaction, then the system is legitimate—those in power are viewed as having the right to rule. On the other hand, if nonvoting is an expression of alienation, then the government loses legitimacy and political protests outside of normal channels, such as street demonstrations and civil disobedience, would be justified. Our interpretations of political facts shape our evaluations of right and wrong, and what should and should not be done.

Conclusion: Joining the Democratic Debate

We must end this introduction with a warning: the authors of this text are not neutral observers of the democratic debate. Although we present both sides, we defend popular democracy and develop a popular democratic critique of American politics. We do so to redress an imbalance that is unconsciously embedded in most treatments of American politics, both in scholarly texts and in the mass media.

Finally, we invite readers not to accept our bias but to critically examine their own views toward democracy. In short, we invite you to join the democratic debate.

Reader's Guide

Critical Thinking Questions

1. The term *elite* has almost universal negative connotations but elites could be viewed simply as people who are better at something than ordinary people. Olympic athletes are elites, for example. Has American culture become too democratic and therefore unwilling to recognize special talents and abilities?

2. Does the invention of the Internet favor elite or popular democracy? Why?

3. In your college or university, which decisions should be left to experts and which decisions should be made by the students? What distinguishes the two types of decisions?

Key Word Definition

elite democracy   A political system in which the privileged classes acquire the power to decide by a competition for the people's votes and have substantial freedom between elections to rule as they see fit.

popular democracy   A political system in which the citizens are involved as much as possible in making the decisions that affect their lives.

direct democracy   The face-to-face meeting of all citizens in one place to vote on all important issues.

Federalist   Supporter of the Constitution during the Constitutional Convention of 1787 and the ratification debates of 1787–1788.

Anti-federalist   Opponent of the Constitution during the ratification debates of 1787–1788.

The Revolution and the Constitution: Origins of the Democratic Debate

FROM COLONIALS TO REVOLUTIONARIES

FROM REVOLUTION TO CONSTITUTION

THE CONSTITUTIONAL CONVENTION

RATIFICATION STRUGGLE AND THE DEMOCRATIC DEBATE

THE BILL OF RIGHTS

CONCLUSION: BEGINNING THE DEMOCRATIC DEBATE

When modern American politicians hope to establish their noble aspirations and to provide their policies with the sanction of higher authority, they invariably turn to the founders of the republic—even to those whose ideas seem very different from their own. Proclaiming a new national beginning after the dark days of Watergate, President Gerald Ford, a conservative, quoted radical Thomas Paine on our revolutionary beginnings. President Bill Clinton, an advocate of an activist national government, was fond of citing Thomas Jefferson, who favored local action and feared national power. Republicans or Democrats, conservatives or liberals, American political leaders speak in hushed tones of the founders as our political saints.

Presidents draw on assumptions that most Americans hold: that the founders agreed among themselves about the fundamental premises of politics and government; that they believed in the same kind of democracy that we profess; and that they were above the desires for power and wealth that seem to drive most present-day political leaders. All of these assumptions are essentially false. The founders of the republic did not agree among themselves; they argued vehemently about fundamental issues of human nature, society, and government. Many were skeptical about democracy and its values and held to an elitist conception of government that no contemporary American politician would dare to profess openly. Struggles over power and wealth were as central to their politics as to our own.

This chapter demonstrates that the American political system was born not in consensus but in conflict. American political life at the time of our founding was characterized by a debate between popular and elite democracy—a debate that has driven our politics ever since. The two sides differed on six basic political issues:

1. Human nature
2. The proper scale of political life
3. Representation

4. Separation of powers and checks and balances

5. The purpose of government

6. Stability and change

Popular democratic answers to these questions produced a hopeful brand of politics that extended self-government to ordinary citizens. Elite democratic answers left ultimate sovereignty to the people but placed actual governance in the hands of a political and economic elite.

The American founding did not produce a final victory for either elite democrats or popular democrats. In studying the Revolution and the Constitution, we witness the origins of an ongoing democratic debate. Particularly in the argument over the new Constitution, which pitted Federalists against Anti-federalists, the democratic debate was launched with a depth and passion that still echo in today's politics.

From Colonials to Revolutionaries

In 1763, the idea that the American colonies of Great Britain would declare their independence, start a revolution, and shape a political system unlike any then known would have seemed absurd. The colonists enjoyed their status as outposts of a glorious empire. England, their "mother country," was nurturing and permissive. The colonies flourished economically and possessed a considerable degree of liberty and self-government under the relatively lax British administration. Colonists not only thought of themselves as English people but also resembled them in many respects. Americans felt a strong allegiance to the king and liked to celebrate his birthday with rousing toasts.[1]

Beneath the surface, however, elements of a distinct American identity were detectable. Immigrants from many European countries—Scots, French Protestants, Germans, and others—made the colonies far more heterogeneous than their "mother country." And the emerging American brand of religious freedom gave the colonists a spiritual diversity found nowhere else in the world. Even as they continued to think of themselves as English, Americans were becoming a separate people.[2]

By 1763, the British had defeated the French and Spanish in the Seven Years' War and established their dominance in the New World. They needed revenues to pay off the debts incurred in this war. As beneficiaries of the British efforts, the American colonists seemed the obvious targets for new taxation. However, this assumption proved to be disastrous for the British. Colonial America responded to the first British tax levies, the Sugar Act and the Stamp Act, with spirited resistance. While American writers denounced taxes imposed by a Parliament in which the colonies were not represented, American "patriots" formed organizations known as the Sons of Liberty and mobbed stamp-tax collectors until they resigned their royal commissions.

For the next decade, a political dynamic developed that led the Americans toward independence. When the British eased their attempts at taxation, peace returned. But every time they tried to reassert their authority, the American spirit of resistance grew stronger. The increasingly bitter conflict wore away old loyalties and crystallized an independent American identity.[3]

Two events epitomized the colonists' growing radicalism. One was the famous Boston Tea Party in 1773, where Boston patriots, disguised as Indians, dumped a shipload of tea into the harbor in protest of a tax on the beverage. Notable here was the colonists' militancy, their reliance on direct popular action to redress a grievance. Fascinated today by the handful of brilliant leaders whom we honor as our founding fathers, we too often forget that

After listening to a reading of the Declaration of Independence, a New York crowd of soldiers and civilians pulls down a statue of King George III. The picture dramatizes the overthrow of monarchism (rule by one) by republicanism (popular rule).

the American revolutionary cause required uncommon dedication from "common" people as well. As historian Gary Nash observes, it was the "backcountry farmers, urban craftsmen, deep-blue mariners, female camp followers, and food rioters . . . who did most of the protesting, most of the fighting, most of the dying, and most of the dreaming about how a victorious America might satisfy the yearnings of all its peoples."[4]

A second landmark event was the fiery rhetoric of the most widely read pamphlet calling on Americans to declare their independence: Thomas Paine's *Common Sense*, published early in 1776. Paine poured scorn on a monarch whom Americans had customarily revered. By sending his troops to enforce his taxes with bayonets, wrote Paine, George III deserved to be called the "Royal Brute of Britain." Monarchy itself, Paine thundered, was a crime; if we could trace the origins of kings, he wrote, "we should find the first of them nothing better than the principal ruffian of some restless gang."[5] A decade of resistance and protest had undermined much of the hierarchical thinking of colonial Americans; reading Tom Paine, many of them became filled with a bold and hopeful spirit that was ready to launch a grand revolutionary experiment in popular democracy.

The Birth of Republicanism

To understand this revolutionary experiment, we need to look beneath questions of taxation and representation. Contemporary historians have identified a deeper level of thought that transformed loyal colonials into defiant revolutionaries. This body of thought shaped the

15

political activities of Americans and infused them with the revolutionary "Spirit of '76." The name historians have given to this body of thought is **republicanism**. (The republicanism of the Revolution should not be confused with the ideas of the Republican Party, formed in the 1850s.[6])

What were the central ideas of republican ideology, and how did they shape the thinking of the American revolutionaries? We focus on four interrelated ideas: liberty versus power, legislatures versus executives, virtue, and the small republic.

Liberty versus Power. Eighteenth-century republicans saw the struggle between liberty and power as the core of political life. *Power* meant dominion or control. Although necessary for the maintenance of order, power's natural tendency was to exceed legitimate boundaries and to invade the sphere of liberty. By *liberty*, republicans meant both private liberty—such as property rights—and public liberty—the right of the people to have a collective say in government.

Legislatures versus Executives. Republican theory identified power largely with executives. Executives were entrusted with enforcing the laws, but they had a natural inclination to arbitrary rule and self-aggrandizement. Thus, executives were seen as the most likely threats to liberty. Legislatures, on the other hand, were the most likely defenders of liberty. Closer to the people, mirroring the people's desires, cherishing the people's liberties, the legislature was the natural adversary of the executive.

Virtue of the American People. Why were republicans so optimistic about the people and their representatives in the legislature? Might not the people, under some circumstances, also prove dangerous? Republicans conceded that liberty could go too far and become anarchy. But they hoped for a people characterized by virtue rather than lawlessness. By *virtue*, they meant the willingness of individuals to subordinate their private interests to the common good. Virtue was a passion for the public good, superior to all private passions. Americans believed that the British effort to introduce tyranny into the colonies showed that the British government and even the British people had become corrupt; selfishness had destroyed their traditional commitment to liberty. But America—peopled by those who had fled the Old World in search of liberty—was a land where virtue still resided.

The Small Republic. What conditions encouraged virtue? As good republicans, the American revolutionaries stressed such things as simplicity and frugality. But the single most important condition necessary for republican virtue was the small republic. In a large republic, diverse economic interests and dissimilar ways of life would produce factional conflicts, encouraging selfishness and eroding virtue. In a small republic, however, a genuine common interest could be found, for the people would be more homogeneous and united.

Thus, the revolutionary assumptions of 1776 were the danger of power and the need to safeguard liberty, the threat of executives and the confidence in legislatures, the hope for a virtuous people, and the stress on small republics and political decentralization. On the basis of these popular democratic assumptions, Americans began shaping their own independent governments in 1776. However, each of these assumptions would be challenged in the decade that followed and debated at length in the struggle over the Constitution.

The Spirit of '76

The American Revolution exploded in 1776 with political energy and creativity. The institutions it first shaped were soon replaced by others, but the ideals it espoused were to form the base of America's democratic creed. Both the successes and the failures of revolutionary creativity are evident in the Declaration of Independence, the constitutions of the new states, and the Articles of Confederation.

The Declaration of Independence. When the Second Continental Congress finally decided that the moment had arrived for the definitive break between America and Britain, it appointed a small committee to prepare a justification for such a revolutionary act. This committee of five wisely turned to its best writer, the young Thomas Jefferson of Virginia. The **Declaration of Independence**, the document that Jefferson drafted and that the Congress adopted with some revisions on July 4, 1776, has become, along with the Constitution, the most hallowed of all American political texts. Its opening words are very familiar, so familiar that we usually do not read them with the care and reflection they deserve.

> When in the course of human events, it becomes necessary for one people to dissolve the political bands which have connected them with another, and to assume among the powers of the earth the separate and equal station to which the Laws of Nature and of Nature's God entitle them, a decent respect to the opinions of mankind requires that they should declare the causes which impel them to the separation.
>
> We hold these truths to be self-evident, that all men are created equal, that they are endowed by their Creator with certain unalienable rights, that among these are life, liberty, and the pursuit of happiness. That to secure these rights, governments are instituted among men, deriving their just powers from the consent of the governed. That whenever any form of government becomes destructive of these ends, it is the right of the people to alter or to abolish it, and to institute new government, laying its foundation on such principles and organizing its powers in such form, as to them shall seem most likely to effect their safety and happiness.

Scholars argue about the sources of Jefferson's ideas in the Declaration of Independence. The most common view is that he was influenced by an English philosopher, John Locke. Several of Locke's central themes are evident in the Declaration: that the primary objective of government is the protection of life, liberty, and property, and that all legitimate political authority derives from the consent of the governed and can be taken away from rulers who betray the will of the people. Locke's ideas are considered central to the political philosophy of liberalism.

If Locke's liberal philosophy is found in the Declaration, the democratic Jefferson gives it a more revolutionary interpretation than the English philosopher intended. The Declaration of Independence establishes equality as the basis for American political thought and makes "life, liberty, and the pursuit of happiness" universal rights. It dethrones government as a higher power and renders it subject to the consent of the people. In its argument, and even in its form, it transforms the nature of political life, supplanting the commands of a king with the discussion and debate suitable to a free people.[7]

Like most great documents, the Declaration of Independence bears the marks and limits of its time. Its words about equality and rights were not meant to include women or African Americans. The American revolutionaries used universal terms but restricted them in practice to white males. Still, the Declaration created a standard to which later popular democrats would appeal in efforts to include those who had originally been excluded from its promises. Battling the spread of slavery, Abraham Lincoln grounded his opposition on the words of the Declaration, proclaiming in 1859 that the "principles of Jefferson are the definitions and axioms of free society."[8] Feminist and African American movements for emancipation have also rested their cases on the Declaration of Independence.[9]

The Revolutionary State Constitutions. The revolutionary ideas of 1776 were also embodied in the first state constitutions. In 1776, ten states established new constitutions to replace their old colonial charters. These constitutions reflected both the struggle with Britain and the core ideas of republicanism. They provided popular democratic answers to the basic questions at issue in the democratic debate—answers that would be rejected a decade later by the elite who drafted the U.S. Constitution.

Three features of the new constitutions were noteworthy: the inclusion of a bill of rights, the weakening of executive power, and the enhancement of legislative power.[10] After years of fighting against British invasions of their rights, Americans wanted to make it clear that these rights were sacred and inviolable, beyond the reach even of the governments that they themselves were establishing. So, most of the new constitutions contained a bill of rights; several, including Virginia's influential one, began their constitutions with such declarations.

Colonial experience and republican theory had identified executive power as the chief threat to liberty. Therefore, the revolutionary constitution makers sought to guard against the return of executive despotism. Revolutionary executives were, by intention, weak executives. In the first state constitutions, executives were chosen by the legislature and held office for a term of only one year. They were stripped of the executive powers traditionally exercised by the British monarch and were left with only modest duties of law enforcement.

The revolutionary mistrust of executives did not extend to legislatures. In the eyes of the constitution writers of 1776, the legislature was not likely to threaten public liberty because it would be an embodiment of the people. The revolutionaries attempted to make the state legislature, particularly the more popular lower house, genuinely representative. This required annual elections so that legislators would frequently be returned to live among the people and feel the effects of the laws they had passed. It also required a large and equal representation so that all areas of a state would be fairly reflected in legislative deliberations.

The Articles of Confederation. The states, not the nation, were seen as the centers of political life in 1776. More than a holdover from colonial experience, the primacy of the states reflected the belief that republics were workable only in a small territory. Consequently, the first American system of national government was a confederation, a loose association of states that agreed to join in a compact for common ends (especially foreign relations and the conduct of war). In a confederation, the individual units remain sovereign, so each state had supreme power within its borders. The **Articles of Confederation**, adopted by the Continental Congress in 1777 but not finally approved by all thirteen states until 1781, put little power in the hands of a centralized authority.

Congress under the Articles of Confederation was an assembly of delegates from the states, each of which had one vote. It had the authority to levy taxes and raise troops but had to requisition each state to supply its assigned quota; should a state fail to meet its duty, the central government could do little about it. The suspicion of the states toward national authority was displayed most dramatically in the provision of the Articles of Confederation regarding amendments: No alterations in the Articles could be made until the legislature of *every* state agreed to them. There was no provision in the Articles for either an executive or a judiciary. All of this government's limited and closely watched powers were left in the hands of the Congress.

The deficiencies of the Articles of Confederation became apparent once it was put into practice. Supporters of the 1787 Constitution based their strongest arguments on the inadequacy of the Articles of Confederation to meet America's need for an effective national government. Yet it should be remembered that the Articles of Confederation were not designed to create a strong national government. The framers of the Articles, adhering to the revolutionary spirit of '76, believed that local liberty—and not national power—was the true source of republican strength and virtue.

A CLOSER LOOK

A Revolutionary Experiment in Popular Democracy

All of the state constitutions written in 1776 reflected the revolutionary desire to restrict the power of rulers and to place government more directly in the hands of the people. No state carried this impulse further than Pennsylvania. The Pennsylvania Constitution of 1776 was the boldest revolutionary experiment in popular democracy.

In most states, the struggle for independence created a coalition between the social and economic elite and "common" folk. In Pennsylvania, however, the elite clung to the hope of reconciliation with Britain. Encouraged by champions of independence in the Continental Congress, middle-class and working-class Pennsylvanians—small merchants, shopkeepers, and artisans—shouldered aside this elite. Aiming to shift political control to the people and to prevent wealthy "gentlemen" from resuming their traditional rule, they drafted a constitution whose character was, for its day, remarkably democratic.

The principal institution in the new government was a unicameral (one-house) legislature. Pennsylvania democrats saw no need for an "upper" house, which would be dominated in any case by the elite. To ensure that this legislature would represent all the people, the constitution established the easiest suffrage requirement in any of the states. To ensure that it did what the people wanted (and did not become a new elite with interests of its own), it provided for annual elections and prohibited any representative from serving for more than four years out of every seven. Even more fearful of executive despotism than constitution writers in the other states, popular democrats in Pennsylvania eliminated

the office of governor, putting in its place an Executive Council of twelve, elected directly by the people and holding very limited powers.

Critics complained that this simple form of government placed no checks on the power of the unicameral legislature. Defenders of the constitution responded that it was designed to make the people themselves the check. The constitution made government in Pennsylvania more open to public knowledge and involvement than in any other state. It required that the doors of the legislature be open for public attendance and votes be published weekly for public scrutiny. Once the legislature passed a bill, it could not become law until the next session, allowing the people time to consider it and, if they chose, to reject it through their election of new representatives.

Was this popular democratic experiment in government workable? What makes the question hard to answer is that the experiment never had a clear trial. Opponents of the constitution, many from the old social and economic elite, fought from the beginning to obstruct and overturn it. Their powerful resistance gained ground as the revolutionary spirit of 1776 faded. In 1790, Pennsylvania adopted a new constitution, setting up a government similar to those in other states, and ended its revolutionary experiment in popular democracy.

Sources: The Pennsylvania Constitution of 1776; David Hawke, *In the Midst of a Revolution* (Philadelphia: University of Pennsylvania Press, 1961); Gordon S. Wood, *The Creation of the American Republic, 1776–1787* (New York: Norton, 1972).

From Revolution to Constitution

Why did the spirit of '76, the hopeful experiment in liberty and virtue, give way to a more somber spirit a decade later, as reflected in the Constitution and in the arguments that upheld it? To answer this question, we must look at the years between the Declaration of Independence and the Constitution, some of the most fateful years in American history.

In 1776, the American revolutionary cause attracted a broad coalition. The struggle for independence and self-government united wealthy merchants, slave-owning planters, and lawyers with yeoman farmers, urban artisans, and unskilled laborers. But during the war for independence, and even more so in the years immediately following the war, major economic and social tensions emerged in the revolutionary coalition. The result was a sense of crisis in the new American republic that engendered a move to reconstitute American politics on a different footing than that of 1776.

Conflicts within the revolutionary coalition that had begun during the war with England grew much worse after the fighting stopped. As a depression spread from commercial areas to the countryside, prices for both manufactured and agricultural goods fell. Money became scarce, especially specie or "hard money" (gold and silver). Hardest hit during this depression were the small farmers, who constituted the majority of Americans at the time. With falling prices and a shortage of specie, farmers could not pay off their creditors. Because many states were levying taxes to pay off wartime debts, the farmers also faced demands for payments from the tax collector. The combination of debt and taxes threatened many small farmers with foreclosure—the loss of their tools, livestock, or land. Some faced prison, for in this period one could be jailed for a failure to pay debts.

Not surprisingly, small farmers faced with such dire losses became the main source of political agitation in the mid-1780s. They wanted their state legislatures to relieve their distress. They petitioned for "stay laws" to postpone foreclosures and "tender laws" to allow payment of debts and taxes in agricultural commodities. Most of all, they sought paper money—a new and inflated currency that would make paying their debts and taxes easier.

In Massachusetts, the legislature, dominated by the merchants and moneylenders of the coastal cities, ignored the debtors' pleas. By the fall of 1786, conditions were ripe for rebellion. Under the leadership of Daniel Shays, a former revolutionary army officer, farmers in the western counties banded together to close down the local courts and prevent further foreclosures. When Shays and his followers marched on the state armory in Springfield, they were dispersed by the state militia. **Shays's Rebellion**, as this event came to be called, was hardly a revolution; it was a disorganized campaign by desperate farmers who felt they were losing everything that the American Revolution had promised them.

To the more conservative and propertied American republicans, Shays's Rebellion was a disturbing yet familiar phenomenon. Just as republican theory had warned that power, if not properly checked, led to despotism, so it had also maintained that liberty, if not properly contained by power, led to lawlessness. But in the 1780s, what most troubled the conservative and the propertied was not the people's rebellions against the state governments. Rather, they were troubled that the majority of the state governments, with their strong legislatures and weak executives, *were* responding to popular grievances. For example, seven states passed paper-money legislation; stay and tender laws were also put into effect.[11]

Why were the legislatures in the majority of the states so responsive to mass grievances? One reason was the popular democratic nature of these revolutionary governments. With annual elections and with large and equal representation, the legislatures were quick to grant their constituents' requests. A second reason was the character of the representatives themselves. Before the Revolution, colonial assemblies had been dominated by an upper class of merchants, lawyers, and large landowners. But the Revolution had brought new men into politics from the middle class, and the composition of the legislatures had changed. Now, when yeoman farmers petitioned their state legislatures, they were heard in many states by people like themselves.[12]

To conservative and propertied republicans, the new state laws (such as paper-money legislation) and the new state legislators called into question the assumptions about politics that had been shared by all republicans in 1776. These men, looking fearfully at developments in the states, no longer believed the core ideas of 1776. Condemning the "Vices of the Political System of the United States," the young James Madison, soon to play the leading role at the Constitutional Convention, attributed them to "the representative bodies" and "the people themselves." To Madison, the heroes of 1776 had become the culprits of 1787.[13]

The Constitutional Convention of 1787 assembled largely in response to these developments in the states. The delegates who came to Philadelphia agreed that efforts in the states to block what was happening had been unsuccessful. They also agreed that the weak national government under the Articles of Confederation, with its dedication to state sovereignty, provided no recourse. These delegates were still republicans, but they no longer hoped to base the American republic on the virtue or public spirit of the people. As they saw it, if republicanism was to survive in America—without subverting either order or property—only a proper constitution could save it.

The Constitutional Convention

The Constitutional Convention of 1787 was a lengthy affair, lasting from May 25 to September 17. For nearly four months of a sweltering Philadelphia summer, fifty-five delegates from twelve states (Rhode Island refused to send a delegation) orated, debated, and negotiated the creation of a new American political system. Their proceedings were secret, and our knowledge of what took place rests mainly on notes of several delegates—particularly James Madison.[14]

A Strong National Government

Forging a new national government was a complex process whose eventual outcome no one really anticipated. Many of the principal figures at Philadelphia—the delegates who took leading roles—wanted a far stronger national government than the Articles of Confederation provided. Some, however, were tenacious defenders of state interests. The actual features of the new government emerged gradually through the debates, votes, and compromises of four months.[15]

As the debates commenced, the delegates were subject to conflicting pulls. On one hand, these mostly propertied and conservative men were representatives of the tradition we call elite democracy, and they were eager to end the upsurge of popular democracy that had been manifested in paper-money legislation and Shays's Rebellion. Furthermore, they hoped that a new national government, elevated high above local democracy, would be dominated by people like themselves rather than by the more ordinary folks who had gained prominence in the state legislatures. On the other hand, they knew that whatever they might consider the best plan of government, the new Constitution would have to obtain the approval of the American people. Frequent references were made during the proceedings to the values or "genius" of the American people, which could not be ignored or overridden.[16]

The initial agenda for the convention was set by the **Virginia Plan**, introduced on May 29 by that state's governor, Edmund Randolph, but principally the handiwork of James Madison. This plan envisioned the United States as a large republic—the kind of centralized political order that the American revolutionaries had opposed as inconsistent with liberty. Under the Virginia Plan, representation for each state in *both* houses of the bicameral legislature was to

The Architect of the Capitol.

An artist's rendition of the Constitutional Convention.

be based on either taxes paid to the national government or the number of free inhabitants—provisions that would favor the large states. The provision that most strongly indicated how authority was to be shifted from the state governments to the national government was one crafted by Madison that empowered the national legislature to veto state legislation.

Although the Virginia Plan dominated the initial debate, it leaned so far in the direction of the large states that the smaller states took alarm. On June 15, they countered with an alternative framework, introduced by William Paterson of New Jersey and thus known as the **New Jersey Plan**. The New Jersey Plan was essentially a reform of the Articles of Confederation rather than a wholly new constitutional order. It retained from the Articles a unicameral legislature in which each state would have equal representation. It strengthened the Articles by bestowing on Congress greater powers over revenues and commerce and by establishing a plural executive and a national judiciary. The New Jersey Plan never had enough support to gain serious consideration, but the concerns of the small states that it raised had to be addressed if the convention was to arrive at sufficient agreement to present a new constitution to the nation.

The quarrel between large and small states over representation was finally settled through a compromise proposed by the delegation from Connecticut and known as the Connecticut Compromise, or **Great Compromise**. Under the terms of this compromise, the House of Representatives would be apportioned according to the populations of the various states, whereas each state would have two members in the Senate. Senators would be selected by their state's legislature. The origination of revenue acts would be an exclusive right of the House.

The delegates who were most eager to build national power at the expense of the states had to accept compromises that pained them. Equal representation for the states in the Senate was one blow to the "nationalist" position; another was the defeat of Madison's plan for a national veto power over state legislation. Rather than drawing clear lines of national dominance and state subordination, the constitution that began to emerge by midsummer drew uncertain boundaries between national and state powers. The Constitution of the United States is celebrated for creating a novel system of **federalism**, under which power is divided between the central government and the states. Alexander Hamilton and especially James Madison applauded the virtues of this federalism in *The Federalist Papers*, considered later in this chapter. The irony is that this system of federalism was not what Hamilton, Madison, or their allies wanted. If they had not needed to compromise on representation and had not lost on the veto over state laws, the United States would have a far more centralized government today.

National Institutions

The Articles of Confederation had provided only a single legislative branch. But the Constitutional Convention intended to create a more complex government, possessing a bicameral legislature, a national executive, and a national judiciary. Molding these institutions and determining the appropriate relationships between them occupied much of the convention's time. In framing new national institutions, most of the delegates rejected the assumption that had dominated constitution making a decade earlier: that the legislature—the branch closest to the people—should be entrusted with the most power. Recent actions of the state legislatures had soured most of the men at Philadelphia toward the virtues of the people's representatives and made them look more favorably at the executive and courts as organs of power and stability.

The Legislature. The House of Representatives proved to be the least complicated of the institutions to fashion. The delegates were clear that this branch would directly reflect the people's opinions and interests. But they were also clear that a legislative body so closely representing popular democratic sentiments would need strong checks. The House was seen as the most democratic part of the new system—and for that very reason the part most feared and constrained.

The nature of the second legislative body, the Senate, occasioned greater controversy. Many delegates envisioned the Senate as an elite assemblage, a forum where the nation's economic, political, and intellectual aristocrats would constrain the more democratic House and supply wisdom and stability to the process of lawmaking. Those who wanted a cool, deliberative, elite legislative body fought hard against making the Senate a forum for state interests. Even though the Great Compromise disappointed them, the Senate was still seen as more selective, conservative, and stable than the House. As a consequence, it was given deliberative functions and prerogatives denied to the House: Senate consent was required for treaties and for presidential nominations to the executive branch and the judiciary.

The Executive. If the fashioning of a Senate gave the convention its share of pains, the shaping of the executive was a continual headache, not relieved until the closing days of the proceedings. The Virginia Plan had left open the question of whether the United States would have a single or a plural executive. To some delegates, the idea of a single man exercising executive powers over so vast a country as the United States conjured a disturbing likeness with the king of Great Britain. Thus, when James Wilson of Pennsylvania proposed on June 1 that "the Executive consist of a single person" who would provide "energy, dispatch, and responsibility to the office," Madison's notes observe "a considerable pause ensuing." Attacking Wilson's proposal, Governor Randolph of Virginia claimed that a single or "unitary" executive would be the "fetus of monarchy" and suggested instead that the executive consist of three men.[17]

After vigorous debate, Wilson's proposal for a unitary executive carried, but another of his proposals—election of this executive by popular vote—failed. For most of the remainder of the convention, the prevailing view was that the national executive should be selected by Congress. But the convention was moving, gradually and fitfully, to strengthen the executive office. Revolutionary fears of executive power were waning, especially among conservative and propertied republicans; a more favorable view of executives as pillars of order and stability was gaining ground. The willingness of the delegates to create the kind of powerful

American executive that would have been unthinkable in 1776 was furthered by the universal assumption that George Washington would be the first president. The final key decision of the convention on the executive—selection by electors rather than by Congress—added greatly to executive independence and strength.

The Judiciary. The third branch of the new national government provoked surprisingly little debate. The idea of "judicial review"—that federal courts have the authority to judge a law by the standard of the Constitution and to declare it null and void should it be found incompatible—was not stated in the Constitution but was discussed by the delegates. Although they did not agree universally on the subject, their comments about judicial review suggest that most delegates did assume that the federal courts would have this authority.

Values, Fears, and Issues

The Constitution was gradually shaped by the convention as institutions were formed, their powers defined, and their relationships to one another determined. In this process, a number of issues preoccupied the framers.

Property. Ever since historian Charles Beard charged in 1913 that the Constitution of the United States was written for the economic benefit of its authors, a debate has ensued about the role of property in the Constitutional Convention.[18] Although Beard's specific arguments about the framers' personal economic gains have been refuted by other historians, considerable evidence remains in the record of the convention debates that the general protection of property was an objective for many of the framers. The new national government was designed to make property far more secure than it had been under the state constitutions. The convention bestowed on the national government new powers that holders of substantial property desired, such as the means to pay off public debts, disproportionately held by the wealthy. Equally important, it prohibited the state governments from coining money, issuing paper money, or "impairing the obligations of contracts," thus putting an end to the popular democratic efforts of the 1780s to aid the many at the expense of the few.

The "Threat" of Democracy. In the eyes of most of the framers, democracy was the chief threat to property. When the framers talked about democracy, they usually meant the lower house of the legislature, where the people's interests and feelings were directly represented. Some delegates assailed democracy on the grounds that the people were ignorant, subject to fits of passion, and prone to pursuing their own economic interests at the expense of a minority of the most industrious, successful, and propertied citizens. Others feared the people less because of their inherent flaws than because they were so easily duped by demagogues, selfish leaders who stoked the flames of popular passion to gain power. Given this perspective, it is not surprising that the delegates aimed many of the checks and balances they were writing into the Constitution at democracy. Only the House of Representatives would be directly democratic, and it would be restrained by the Senate, president, and judiciary, all of which would be selected in an elite rather than a popular fashion.

Slavery. The delegates at Philadelphia concurred on the importance of promoting property and averting the dangers of democracy. But they were sharply divided on another issue: slavery.
Many northern delegates resisted giving slavery any support in the Constitution. However, delegates from South Carolina and Georgia insisted that slaves were indispensable to their economies, and they warned the convention that if slavery was not given special protection, their states would not join the Union. Delegates from New England, who expressed dislike for slavery but suggested that the convention should not meddle with this topic, proposed compromises that would keep the most southerly states in the Union. In accordance with

their position, slavery was given three special safeguards in the Constitution: (1) to apportion direct taxes and representation in the House, slaves would count as three-fifths of free persons, thereby enlarging southern representation; (2) the slave trade could not be banned for at least twenty years; and (3) fugitive slaves would be returned to their owners.

The framers of the Constitution compromised in this case for the sake of union. They justified their moral lapse with the belief that slavery would gradually die out without any forceful effort against it. The Civil War would show this pious hope to have been their greatest error.[19]

Table 2.1 summarizes the chief features of the Preamble and seven articles of the Constitution. The final article stated that ratification by conventions in nine of the thirteen

Table 2.1	Preamble and Articles of the Constitution
Preamble	"We the people"—and not the states—establish the Constitution to "form a more perfect union" and to secure justice, domestic tranquility, national defense, the "general welfare," and "the blessings of liberty...."
Article 1	Provides for the selection of representatives and senators, with a two-year term for representatives and a six-year term for senators. Grants seventeen explicit powers to Congress, including the powers to levy and collect taxes, to regulate interstate and foreign commerce, and to declare war. Also grants to Congress the power to make laws that are "necessary and proper" for executing its enumerated powers.
Article 2	Establishes the office of the president. The president is to be selected by electors, with each state choosing as many electors as it has representatives in the House and Senate. Serves a four-year term with no restrictions on reelection. The president is to be "commander in chief" of the armed forces and chief of the executive branch. The president is to have a say in legislation by informing Congress of "the state of the Union" and by recommending measures that he deems "necessary and expedient." The House can impeach and the Senate can remove the president (and all other civil officers) for "treason, bribery, or other high crimes and misdemeanors."
Article 3	Creates a federal judiciary, who hold their offices "during good behavior"—until they resign, die, or are impeached and convicted by Congress. Vests the judicial power in a Supreme Court and in lower courts to be established by Congress. Although the Supreme Court is made the highest court of appeals, Congress retains the power to alter its jurisdiction.
Article 4	Governs relationships between the states. Each state must give "full faith and credit" to the acts and records of the other states. Citizens traveling to another state are entitled to the same "privileges and immunities" as its own residents.
Article 5	Establishes two methods for proposing and two methods for ratifying amendments to the Constitution. Amendments can be proposed either by a two-thirds vote in both houses of Congress or by a convention requested by two-thirds of the states. Ratification of an amendment requires a favorable vote in the legislatures of three-fourths of the states or in special conventions in three-fourths of the states.
Article 6	The Constitution and the laws and treaties made pursuant to its authority are "the supreme law of the land...."
Article 7	Ratification by conventions of nine states establishes the Constitution as the new national authority.

original states would be sufficient to put the Constitution into effect. It began one of the most important contests in American history—a political and philosophical struggle to determine nothing less than the basis on which American politics would be conducted.

Ratification Struggle and the Democratic Debate

Most contemporary Americans assume that the greatness of the Constitution under which we have lived for more than two hundred years must have been obvious from the start. In reality, the ratification of the Constitution required a long and sometimes bitter struggle whose outcome was by no means certain. Although some states ratified the Constitution swiftly and with little dissent, in a number of the larger states the contest was close. In Massachusetts, the vote in the ratifying convention was 187 to 168 in favor of the Constitution. Virginia ratified by the narrow margin of 89 to 79; New York endorsed the Constitution by a vote of 30 to 27.[20]

The closeness of these votes becomes less surprising when we recall that the Constitution largely reversed the political verdict of 1776 by ending the revolutionary experiment in state-based popular democracy. Its supporters had to overcome strong resistance. Historian Saul Cornell notes that "contemporary observers on both sides of the ratification debate were struck by the intensity of popular opposition to the Constitution."[21] If the Constitution was a defeat for popular democracy and a victory for an elite democracy (moderated by concessions to the democratic spirit), how did its supporters, who called themselves Federalists, win in the face of such opposition?

The Federalists enjoyed a number of political advantages over opponents of the Constitution, who came to be known as Anti-federalists. Perhaps most important, they were united around a common and positive program. With a solution in hand to the nation's distresses (which they often exaggerated for rhetorical purposes), they possessed the political initiative. The Anti-federalists, on the other hand, could not agree among themselves either about what was wrong with the Constitution or about what should take its place. The Federalists also had an advantage in disseminating their ideas. Based largely in the cities and supported by most of the wealthy, they had better access to newspapers than the Anti-federalists.

The Federalist cause was also blessed with exceptional intellectual talent. A majority of the distinguished, learned, and articulate men in America argued for the ratification of the Constitution. Among them, none presented the case for the Constitution so brilliantly as Alexander Hamilton, James Madison, and John Jay in *The Federalist Papers*.[22]

Although a number of able writers opposed the Constitution, no single Anti-federalist writing was comparable to *The Federalist Papers*. Moreover, the Anti-federalists can be said to have lost the intellectual debate because their side lost the political contest. *The Federalist Papers* thus have overshadowed Anti-federalist thought. Yet both sides were important in the debate over the Constitution. As political theorist Herbert J. Storing has written, "If . . . the foundation of the American polity was laid by the Federalists, the Anti-Federalist reservations echo through American history; and it is in the dialogue, not merely in the Federalist victory, that the country's principles are to be discovered."[23]

The dialogue that Storing mentions is what we call the democratic debate. In the following discussion, we pay equal attention to both voices in the debate—Federalist and Anti-federalist, elite democrat and popular democrat. We consider six issues on which the two sides differed: human nature, the proper scale of political life, the character of representation, separation of powers and checks and balances, the purpose of government, and stability and change. These issues are at the core of the democratic debate.

Human Nature: Its Dangers and Its Possibilities

The basic issue of the democratic debate is human nature. The Federalists held a pessimistic view of human nature. In the most famous of *The Federalist Papers*, number 10, James Madison wrote that people were "much more disposed to vex and oppress each other than to cooperate for their common good."[24] Although Madison could also write that "there are other qualities in human nature which justify a certain portion of esteem and confidence,"[25] the Federalist view was that good government could not be founded on the idea of goodness in its participants.

Any goodness in human nature, the Federalists believed, was most likely to be found in elites. Madison argued that the new national government would bring to power the relatively few citizens who are both wise and public spirited. Hamilton claimed that his favorite institution, the presidency, would be filled by men "preeminent for ability and virtue."[26] The Federalists recognized that the dangerous qualities in human nature might also show up in the governing elite. But their greater fear was the raw human nature of the masses. The history of experiments in popular democracy had, in the eyes of the Federalists, demonstrated that most ordinary people were prone to passion, selfishness, and disorder. To the Federalists, any attempt by the people to assemble and debate affairs in a face-to-face or direct democracy would inevitably degenerate into mob rule.

The Anti-federalists were not naive optimists who held a rosy view of human nature. They, too, wrote vividly of the ambition and greed that could disfigure the human character. Yet they differed profoundly from the Federalists on where virtue and vice were most likely to be found. Ordinary individuals, most Anti-federalist writers believed, had modest aspirations; they wanted to live a life of comfort, decency, and dignity. Moreover, whatever natural tendencies existed toward selfishness and quarreling could be counteracted through instruction in morality and religion. Virtue could be supported by republican institutions, laws, and customs.[27]

The Anti-federalists feared human nature among elites. Power, they claimed, was intoxicating, especially when the connection between governors and citizens grew distant and the instruments for abuse and corruption were nearby. Human nature at its worst was not a lawless people, the Anti-federalist Patrick Henry of Virginia proclaimed. Rather, it was "the tyranny of rulers."[28]

Scale of Political Life

From this initial difference between Federalists and Anti-federalists over human nature flowed a further difference over the proper scale of political life. Federalists favored a large republic (national government); Anti-federalists favored small republics (state governments).

In the view of the Federalists, the small republic brought out the worst in human nature. In the face-to-face political space of the small republic, a majority of selfish but like-minded individuals would form a "faction" or political group and try to oppress a minority, such as those who owned large amounts of property or those who held unorthodox religious beliefs. Politics in the small republic would degenerate into turbulence, injustice, and misery.

But in the large republic, the Federalists claimed, the selfish passions of the people could not have this unhappy result. There would be so much diversity in the large republic that a powerful and unjust majority faction was unlikely to form. James Madison explained the logic of the large republic: "Extend the sphere and you take in a greater variety of parties and interests; you make it less probable that a majority of the whole will have a common motive to invade the rights of other citizens; or if such a common motive exists, it will be more difficult for all who feel it to discover their own strength and to act in unison with each other."[29]

Given their view of human nature, the Anti-federalists favored the small republic and feared the large republic. The Anti-federalists saw the small republic as the home of liberty rather than oppression. It was only in the small republic, they argued, that citizens were close enough to their representatives in government to have confidence in them and to hold them accountable for their actions. Further, only in the small republic could citizens participate in political affairs and, through the practice of active citizenship, develop a broader and less self-ish understanding of the common good.[30]

The Anti-federalists saw the large republic as bringing out the worst in human nature. Above all, they mistrusted the national elites on whom the Federalists were banking their hopes. As a New York Anti-federalist who used the pseudonym of Brutus (killer of the tyrant Caesar, who had destroyed the Roman republic) put it, "In so extensive a republic, the great officers of government would soon become above the control of the people, and abuse their power to the purpose of aggrandizing themselves, and oppressing them."[31]

Representation

Federalist and Anti-federalist understandings of representation also followed from their differing views of human nature. Because ordinary people were prone, the Federalists believed, to selfish, factional, and even violent passions, the task of the elected representative was to filter out these bad impulses and seek the people's true welfare. In a large republic, James Madison argued in *Federalist No. 10*, the process of representation would "refine and enlarge the public views by passing them through the medium of a chosen body of citizens, whose wisdom may best discern the true interest of their country and whose patriotism and love of justice will be least likely to sacrifice it to temporary or partial considerations."[32] The Federalist claim was that representatives, forming a small elite, would both know better and do better than the people themselves.

The Anti-federalists denied that representatives should act the part of the people's superiors. Representatives, they argued, should not filter out what the people wanted; they should mirror the people's exact hopes and goals. In the words of New York Anti-federalist Melancton Smith, "The idea that naturally suggests itself to our minds when we speak of representatives is that they resemble those they represent; they should be a true picture of the people; possess the knowledge of their circumstances and their wants; sympathize in all their distresses, and be disposed to seek their true interests."[33]

Separation of Powers and Checks and Balances

Although the Federalists entertained high hopes for a talented and virtuous elite to run the new national government, they were aware that concentrated power could be abused. Their remedy was to separate the powers of government into three branches—legislative, executive, and judicial—each of which would have the constitutional weapons to check the others. Thus, the president could check the legislature with his veto, the Senate could check the executive with its power over appointments, and the judiciary could check the other two branches by its authority over the meaning of the Constitution and the laws. Members of each branch were expected to defend their rightful powers against the others, James Madison explained, less out of virtue than out of a regard for their own interests. To guard against an oppressive concentration of powers within government, he wrote in one of his most famous sentences, "ambition must be made to counteract ambition."[34]

The Federalists did not see all branches as equally dangerous. They worried most about the popular democratic body, the House of Representatives. The more elite institutions were expected to hold the House in check and thereby ensure wiser and more stable governance.

The Anti-federalists viewed the institutions of government in a different light. Most of them accepted the idea of separation of powers and checks and balances but complained that the Constitution was checking the wrong people. It was not the democratic House that needed most closely to be watched, but rather the elite branches. Patrick Henry warned that Hamilton's vaunted executive "squints toward monarchy."[35] Several Anti-federalist writers denounced the constitutional alliance between a monarchical president and an aristocratic Senate in making treaties and appointing civil officers, judges, and ambassadors.

Purpose of Government

What was the purpose of government? Both Federalists and Anti-federalists agreed that government must protect and promote the liberty of the people. Yet they meant different things by *liberty*. To James Madison, liberty was primarily a private possession— private property or private convictions. Liberty in this sense needed to be protected from oppressive majorities that would take away property or force the same religious faith on everyone. If liberty was protected, individuals would, Madison believed, succeed or fail in accordance with their own abilities. A free society would inevitably be marked by a substantial amount of economic inequality that resulted from the natural differences between people.[36]

Alexander Hamilton thought of liberty in slightly different terms—as the freedom to acquire greater property and power. He wanted a powerful national government that would promote the economic growth and develop the military potential of the United States. The purpose of government was to steer the United States in the direction of national greatness. In the right hands, he suggested in *The Federalist Papers*, this bold young nation "might make herself the admiration and envy of the world."[37]

To the Anti-federalists, liberty was equally precious. But they emphasized the political rights of the people as much as the people's right to private property. Understood in this way, liberty was endangered less by oppressive majorities than by oppressive rulers. The most common Anti-federalist complaint against the Constitution—that it contained no bill of rights to safeguard the people against government oppression—is considered in the next section.

The Anti-federalists also disagreed with the Federalists about how liberty related to economic life and national defense. Although desiring a prosperous America, they hoped for a more egalitarian society than the Federalists. If wealth became highly unequal and Americans began desiring luxurious goods, they feared, the republic would lose its anchorage in the civic virtue of the people. The public good would be neglected once Americans cared only about getting rich. Anti-federalists also worried about the rise of a powerful military that might be used by rulers for domestic tyranny or foreign aggression. The Anti-federalist view of the purpose of government looked back to the vision of popular democracy that had fired the hopes of American revolutionaries in 1776. They protested against turning America away from its original democratic dream and making it more like the undemocratic governments of Europe.[38]

Stability and Change

The final critical area of difference between the Federalists and the Anti-federalists involved their perspectives on stability and change in American politics. Responding to the upsurge of popular democracy in the Revolution and its aftermath, Federalists looked for sources of stability in a new constitutional system. Their chief answer to the danger of radical economic and social change through popular democracy lay in the complex mechanisms of the Constitution itself. In the vastness and diversity of a large republic, majorities desiring radical change were unlikely to form; should they overcome the problem of distance and gain power in the democratic branch—the House of Representatives—the more elite branches would check their progress and protect the status quo. Federalists were not averse to all change—witness Hamilton's program for economic development—but they wanted change guided by an elite.

Among the Federalists, James Madison was particularly insightful in recognizing a more profound basis for stability. He saw that if the Constitution could prevail over its initial opposition, its status as the foundation of American politics would eventually cease to be questioned. It would gain "that veneration which time bestows on everything, and without which perhaps the wisest and freest governments would not possess the requisite stability."[39] Madison foresaw that Americans would come to worship the Constitution. Forgetting the original debate over it, they would revere the document—and the ideas—produced by the winning side.

What the Federalists desired as stability looked to the Anti-federalists like the most dangerous form of change: political corruption and decay. The Anti-federalists were not worried that the people would become unruly; they feared that the people would become apathetic about public affairs. Under the new constitutional order, they predicted, arrogance and corruption would grow among ruling elites, while the people would become preoccupied with the scramble for riches.

The Anti-federalist view continued the spirit of popular protest that had marked the American Revolution. No one expressed this spirit so strongly during this period as Thomas Jefferson. Strictly speaking, Jefferson was neither Federalist nor Anti-federalist; as the American minister to France during the years in which the Constitution was written and debated, he stood at a distance from the conflict over it. Yet his support for popular protest, expressed in letters to friends in America, dramatically opposed the Federalist dread of popular action. Whereas the Federalists reacted in horror to Shays's Rebellion as a signpost of impending anarchy, Jefferson wrote to Madison that "I hold it that a little rebellion now and then is a good thing, and as necessary in the political world as storms in the physical."[40] Jefferson, like the Anti-federalists, believed that only an alert and active citizenry could preserve the democratic values of the American Revolution (see Table 2.2).

Table 2.2	Differences Between the Federalists and Anti-federalists	
Issue	*Federalists*	*Anti-federalists*
Human nature	Ordinary people basically selfish; capacity for virtue greater among elites	Ordinary people moderately ambitious and capable of virtue; dangerous ambitions found among elites
Scale of political life	Favored a large republic (national government)	Favored a small republic (state governments)
Role of representatives	To refine the public views	To mirror the people's hopes and goals
Separation of powers	Favored checks and balances, with particular eye on the House of Representatives	Believed in checks and balances, with particular eye on the president and Senate
Purpose of government	To protect liberty, especially private rights; expected inequality as just result	To protect liberty, especially political rights; sought to prevent large inequalities that threatened values of a republic
Stability and change	Stability found in complexity of Constitution and in public reverence for it	Feared political decay and corruption; favored spirit of protest embodied in the Revolution

The Bill of Rights ★ ★ ★ ★

When farmers in the back country of South Carolina heard that their state had ratified the Constitution, they "had a coffin painted black, which borne in funeral procession, was solemnly buried, as an emblem of the dissolution and interment of public liberty."[41] Anti-federalist fears that the Constitution would become a monstrous mechanism for oppressing the people strike us today as absurd. Yet in one crucial respect, the fears of the Anti-federalists were fortunate. Without them, we would not have gained the Bill of Rights.

Among the Anti-federalists' objections to the Constitution, none was as frequently voiced, as popularly received, and as compelling in force as the complaint that the Constitution lacked guarantees of the people's basic liberties. Most of the state constitutions, Anti-federalist writers and debaters pointed out, expressly protected the fundamental personal and political rights of the people against arbitrary and invasive government. Yet this new national constitution contained no such guarantees of liberty. Anti-federalists at the state ratifying conventions thus began to propose various amendments to the new Constitution as safeguards of the people's fundamental rights.

Some Federalists resisted the call for amendments, fearing that they would weaken the new political system. But the more moderate supporters of the Constitution increasingly recognized that amendments that guaranteed the rights of the people would conciliate opponents of the Constitution and thus give the new system a better chance to survive and flourish. The leader of these moderates was James Madison, who became the principal drafter and legislative champion of what became the Bill of Rights.[42]

The Bill of Rights adds to the original Constitution a commitment to the personal and political liberties of the people. It safeguards the rights of religious conscience, free speech, a free press, and political activity; it protects the people against an invasion of their homes and papers by an intrusive government; it guarantees a fair trial and a freedom from excessive punishment. If the Constitution proved to be the great charter of American government, the Bill of Rights was the great charter of American liberty. It stands as an enduring testament to the vision and values of the Anti-federalists. Today, when Americans think of the U.S. Constitution, the Bill of Rights seems as much a part of its original composition as the seven articles drafted at the Philadelphia convention of 1787. The original democratic debate had made the Constitution a better—and a more democratic—document.

Conclusion: Beginning the Democratic Debate ★ ★ ★

The ratification of the Constitution was a victory for elite democrats in the original democratic debate. Not only did this victory lie in the creation of lofty national institutions in which elites would control most of the offices, but even more, it lay in the impediments to popular democracy that the constitutional system established. The growing size of the national republic tended, as Madison had argued, to fragment potential popular democratic movements and encourage in their place the narrower struggles of interest group politics. The complexity of national institutions tended to stalemate democratic energies for social change. The remoteness of national institutions tended to undermine the civic virtue nourished in local, face-to-face political participation.

Elite democrats also won a philosophical victory in 1787. Embodied in many of the clauses of the Constitution and brilliantly argued in the pages of *The Federalist Papers*, the premises of elite democracy have come down to Americans with the sanctity of the highest political authority.

Yet the victory of the Federalists, the original elite democrats, was far from complete. Historian Saul Cornell observes that the "ideas of the Anti-Federalists, the Other Founders of the American constitutional tradition, continue to provoke, inspire, and complicate our understanding of what the Constitution means."[43] When Americans today discuss the Constitution, their assumptions about the document's democratic character reflect many of the Anti-federalists' central arguments.

Popular democrats thus were not really vanquished in the era of the American founding. Later generations of popular democrats have looked back to the founding for authority and inspiration—though more often to the Revolution than to the Constitution. The American tradition of popular democratic protest and struggle finds its roots in the Sons of Liberty, the Boston Tea Party, and the revolutionary war militia. The popular democratic vision of equality and self-government rests on the opening paragraphs of the Declaration of Independence. Echoing the revolutionaries of 1776 and the Anti-federalists, popular democrats balance their fears of remote and unaccountable power with hopes for democratic community and public-spirited citizens.

Today's popular democrats not only can claim the revolutionary heritage, but they can also point to concessions obtained from elite democrats in the constitutional system itself. The framers of the Constitution had to include elements of popular democracy in order to win ratification. Soon after ratification, popular democrats won an even larger victory when the Bill of Rights was added to the Constitution. Later amendments have also made the Constitution more compatible with popular democracy. The Thirteenth, Fourteenth, and Fifteenth Amendments, products of the Civil War and Reconstruction era, established the rights of African Americans to participate in the American political system. The Nineteenth Amendment established women's right to suffrage. Products of long struggles by popular democratic movements, these amendments opened doors that the founders had kept shut. They established the equal right of all Americans to exercise the political rights and enjoy the political rewards that had originally been reserved for white males alone.

The Revolution and Constitution engendered a great democratic debate, but they did not resolve it for all time. Throughout this text, we point out how the democratic debate continues to enliven American politics. As we study its contemporary expressions, we need to recall the fundamental terms of the debate set down by the creators of the American republic.

Reader's Guide ★ ★ ★

Critical Thinking Questions

1. How did the American Revolution express popular democratic ideals? Which of these ideals have endured?

2. Why did the hopeful political mood of 1776 give way to the more somber outlook of 1787?

3. Were the framers of the U.S. Constitution more concerned to advance democracy or to hold it in check?

4. What were the strongest arguments of the Federalists? Of the Anti-federalists? If you had been an American citizen at the time of the ratification debates, which side would you have supported?

Key Word Definition

republicanism   The eighteenth-century body of political thought, based on the ideas of liberty versus power, legislatures versus executives, civic virtue, and the small republic, that shaped the political activities of colonial Americans and infused them with the revolutionary "Spirit of '76."

Declaration of Independence   The document written by Thomas Jefferson and adopted by the Continental Congress on July 4, 1776, in which the American colonies announced themselves to be free and independent from Great Britain and set forth the revolutionary principle of democracy.

Articles of Confederation   The first written U.S. Constitution, ratified by the states in 1781, establishing a loose confederation among the former colonies under a weak national government.

Shays's Rebellion   A 1786 upheaval by desperate small farmers in Massachusetts that alarmed conservative republicans and thereby set the stage for the Constitutional Convention of 1787.

Virginia Plan   The proposal submitted by the Virginia delegation at the Constitutional Convention of 1787 to create a strong national government.

New Jersey Plan   The proposal submitted by the New Jersey delegation at the Constitutional Convention of 1787 to reform the Articles of Confederation but maintain most governmental power in the states.

Great Compromise   An agreement, also known as the Connecticut Compromise, in which the Constitutional Convention of 1787 resolved that Congress would be bicameral, with the Senate composed of two members from each state and the House of Representatives apportioned according to each state's population.

federalism   A system in which power is divided between the central government and the states.

3

The Dilemma of American Federalism

FEDERALISM AND THE CONSTITUTION

THE FAILURE OF DUAL FEDERALISM

INTERGOVERNMENTAL RELATIONS

DEVOLUTION: FROM REAGAN TO GEORGE W. BUSH

THE OBAMA ADMINISTRATION: HYBRID FEDERALISM

THE SURPEME COURT, FEDERALISM, AND DEMOCRACY

CONCLUSION: IS THERE A WAY OUT OF THE DILEMMA?

The United States has a system of government called *federalism*, which divides power between a central government and state and local governments. Federalism has had a profound effect on the way the game of politics is played in this country by creating what has been called a "double battleground": as in all nations, political interests battle over whether the government should act to address a public problem, but in American politics there is *also* a second battle over which level of government, the federal government or the states, should have the power to act.[1] Where decisions are made makes a difference because it influences who wins and who loses. State governments are not just smaller versions of the federal government. They are different. And states often have constraints on what they can do that the federal government does not.

Political actors often talk as if they have a principled stand on federalism, based on a careful reading of the Constitution, favoring states rights or the federal government. As we will see, however, the Constitution is exceedingly ambiguous on the division of powers between the federal government and the states. As a result, there has never been a neat separation of powers into the different levels of government. Instead, there has been a constant political battle over which level of government has the authority to act. Federalism has always been a political football. Stands on federalism have been shaped more by political expediency than by principle because where decisions are made affects who wins and who loses. Federalism gives losers at one level of government another place where they can continue the fight. As a result, political battles (with the exception of the fight over slavery) are rarely finally settled. In sports, athletes are often told never get too high after a win or too low after a loss; there is always another game. This is true of federalism and the game of American politics. Consider the recent case of the fight over national health care.

In 1994, President Clinton was defeated in his effort to pass national health care legislation. Riding the wave of their defeat of Clinton, the Republicans took control of both houses of Congress that year and it looked like national health care was dead. Stymied at the national level, however, proponents of universal health care turned to the states. In 1997, the Clinton administration began a children's health insurance program, later termed CHIP, which provided funds to states to insure children in families who were low-income but did not qualify for Medicaid. Millions of children got health insurance that way. The Clinton administration provided waivers to states to allow them to experiment in other ways to expand health insurance coverage. In 2005, the Bush administration gave Massachusetts a waiver that enabled it to creatively use federal funds to expand coverage. In 2006, Massachusetts passed a law that required everyone have health care coverage or face tax penalties. The most radical state effort to achieve universal coverage was signed and endorsed by Governor Mitt Romney. The Massachusetts law helped build momentum for an individual mandate at the national level.

In the 2008 campaign, Barack Obama made reforming health care one of the top four priorities of his presidency. In 2010, Congress passed the Patient Protection and Affordable Health Care Act without a single Republican vote. The act has many features, including an array of taxes and charges that will be used to subsidize expanded coverage. The most controversial part of the law, however, is the "individual mandate" that requires everyone, with the exception of people who are members of certain religious sects, to have health insurance or pay a fine. When fully implemented, an additional 30 million people will be covered by health insurance. Supporters argue that without the mandate only sick people will purchase health insurance, and it will be prohibitively expensive. Opponents call it an unwarranted intrusion of the federal government into personal freedom.

After losing at the federal level, opponents turned to the states in an effort to nullify the law. In 2010, eight states passed laws barring state government from implementing individual or employer insurance mandates. Eventually, twenty-eight states filed lawsuits challenging the constitutionality of the individual mandate. In 2011, the Supreme Court agreed to hear the case on health care reform. On June 28, 2012, the Supreme Court issued its decision in *National Federation of Independent Businesses v. Sebelius*, the most important ruling on federalism since Supreme Court decisions in the 1930s that upheld the expansion of federal power under the New Deal. In a close 5–4 decision, the Supreme Court upheld the constitutionality of the linchpin of Obama's health care reform, the individual mandate that imposes a tax on most people who refuse to purchase health insurance. The key swing vote was conservative Chief Justice John Roberts, who ruled that the law did not command people to purchase health insurance, it simply imposed a tax if they did not. Congress clearly has the power to tax and therefore the individual mandate is constitutional. The ruling removed a key obstacle to the most extensive reform of the American health care system since the creation of Medicare and Medicaid in 1965.

National Federation of Independent Businesses v. Sebelius was a short-term victory for Obama's health care reform, but it may represent a long-term defeat for those who want an expansive role for the federal government in regulating the economy and addressing inequalities. First, a majority in the case ruled that the individual mandate was not constitutional under the Interstate Commerce Clause. Even though the health care system clearly influences interstate commerce, the justices ruled that Congress could not require people to purchase health insurance. Potentially, the power of the federal government to regulate economic activity could be greatly curtailed. A majority also ruled the section of the law unconstitutional that denied states Medicaid funding if they refused to expand coverage as required in the act. This could set a precedent that the federal government cannot use its expenditure powers to promote desirable outcomes, such as requiring colleges that receive federal funding to give girls equal opportunity to play sports. We will not know the effects of *National Federation of Independent Businesses v. Sebelius* for many years, but it laid down arguments that could be used in future cases to turn back federalism to the pre–New Deal period, when the federal government was not constitutionally permitted to act in many areas of domestic policy.

The recent history of health care reform illustrates the importance of federalism in American politics. When President Clinton failed to enact his health care reform in 1994, it looked like the dream of universal health care was dead. Experiments at the state level, however, kept the issue alive and laid the groundwork for Obama's 2010 health care reform law. When Obama succeeded in passing legislation, it looked like universal coverage was finally a reality, but opponents shifted the battle to the states, where they succeeded in undermining implementation and initiating a lawsuit that challenged its constitutionality. Many, including then 2012 Republican presidential candidate Mitt Romney, based their opposition to Obama's health care reform law on federalism grounds, stating that the federal government lacked the authority in the Constitution to mandate health insurance but that states do have this power. These same critics know that shifting the battle to the states will give them an advantage. Many states are threatening not to expand coverage of Medicaid. Following the Supreme Court ruling in *National Federation of Independent Businesses v. Sebelius*, if they do so, they will lose only the expanded Medicaid funding under the law, not all of their Medicaid funding. The battle over health care reform has, once again, shifted to the states.

Federalism is more than a political football to be manipulated for political advantage. Federalism raises the question of what sort of mix of powers between the federal and state government is best for the expansion of popular democracy. As with so many other questions, there is no one neat answer to this question that is valid for all times and places. The mix of federal and state powers must adjust to the demands of the times. At the founding, popular democrats clearly favored state and local powers over the national government. As many decisions as possible should be made by governments that are closest to the people. Citizen participation is more meaningful in small governments where citizens can more easily make themselves heard. That made sense in a largely agrarian society, where many important decisions were still made at the local level and citizens were not dependent on the ups and downs of a national market economy.

With the rise of industrial capitalism, popular democrats increasingly turned to the national government to protect citizens against the power of national corporations and the disruptions of capitalism. The failure of the states to respond adequately to the Great Depression of the 1930s opened the way for major expansion of federal power. In addition, as popular democratic rights expanded, it became clear that states could not be relied upon to guarantee them. "States rights" had been used as a shield by southern states to deny African Americans the right to vote—a right that had supposedly been guaranteed to them with the passage of the Fifteenth Amendment in 1870. Following passage of the 1965 Voting Rights Act, the federal government intervened into the administration of elections by southern states, finally guaranteeing African Americans the right to vote.

As a result of the need for strong national action, popular democrats find themselves on the horns of a dilemma: Governments closest to the people maximize participation, but they often lack the power and the resources necessary to protect citizens and provide them with the tools they need to participate fully in the political life of the nation. On the other hand, federal agencies, captured by experts and elite interests, often leave little room for citizen input.

As we will show in the pages ahead, in many ways the dilemma of American federalism is a false choice: It does not need to be *either/or*. The two levels of government can work together to maximize popular democratic participation. State and local governments can operate as laboratories of democracy, experimenting with new policies to address the challenges of the twenty-first century. The federal government can take up the best experiments of state and local governments and support them with federal laws and resources. Instead of undermining the efforts of state and local governments, the federal government can empower them. Organized in a popular democratic fashion, a strong federal government can help empower people in states and communities.

Federalism and the Constitution

The debate over federalism began with the controversy over ratification of the U.S. Constitution. Under the Articles of Confederation, the state legislatures held great power that the framers feared would be used by envious majorities to confiscate the wealth of the rich. The framers of the Constitution favored moving power from the states to a national government with a strong executive. In his famous "extended republic" argument in *Federalist No. 10*, James Madison argued that a large democracy like the United States would be less vulnerable to majority tyranny than a small democracy because of the greater obstacles to coordination and communication. Moreover, by electing representatives from larger districts, Madison maintained, voters in an extended republic would favor educated and wealthy elites.

Led by Madison and Alexander Hamilton, the framers of the Constitution initially favored a **unitary government** in which all significant powers would rest in the hands of the central government and state and local governments would derive their authority from the central government. (Over 90 percent of all countries in the world today, including France and the United Kingdom, are governed by unitary systems.) However, the founders knew that most citizens, and especially the rank-and-file soldiers who had fought in the Revolution, would not vote for a unitary government that reminded them of their subservience under the British monarchy. To aid in ratification, the Federalists were forced to compromise with Anti-federalist sentiment, creating a mixed system that gave some powers to the federal government and left others to the states. Federalism was born in compromise.

Reluctant to admit that one of the primary characteristics of the new Constitution was the result of a tactical political compromise, the framers put their best "spin" (as we would say today) on the new Constitution in order to boost its chances of ratification. They argued that the federalism of the new Constitution arose not from a compromise but from a general theory of government that carefully balanced the powers of the central government and the state governments. Protection for the states, the Federalists argued, would come from the way that the new Constitution divided power into two spheres, a theory that we have come to call **dual federalism**. Under dual federalism, the national government and the states each have separate spheres of authority, and "within their respective spheres the two centers of government are 'sovereign' and hence 'equal.'"[2] Each level of government relates directly to the citizens, and no level of government can interfere within the legitimate sphere of authority of another level.

Under dual federalism, the federal government has only those powers specifically granted in the Constitution, called **enumerated powers** (see Table 3.1). Seventeen such powers are given to the national government, or Congress, in Article I, Section 8, including the power to "regulate commerce with foreign nations and among the several States," "coin

Table 3.1 Principles of Dual Federalism

Power	Definition	Example
Enumerated	Powers specifically granted to Congress	Coin money, national defense
Concurrent	Powers exercised by both Congress and the states	Taxation
Reserved	Powers not mentioned in the Constitution and therefore left to the states	Police powers (for example, land use regulation)

money," and "provide for the common defense." All powers not given to the national government are **reserved** to the states by the Tenth Amendment. (Dual federalism is sometimes called *Tenth Amendment federalism*.) With the powers of the federal government clearly spelled out in the Constitution, Federalists maintained, the Supreme Court would act as a neutral umpire, making sure that the federal government does not go beyond its enumerated powers and invade the powers reserved to the states. In cases where both levels of government possess the power to act—so-called **concurrent powers**—the **Supremacy Clause** (Article VI) states that national laws supersede state laws.

Anti-federalists opposed the Constitution primarily because it gave too much power to the national government. The Anti-federalists argued that Madison's extended republic was a contradiction in terms; democracy was possible only in small, homogeneous republics. The principal threat to our liberties, they asserted, came not from tyrannical majorities in the state legislatures but from selfish elites in the national government. And they did not trust that the Constitution narrowly defined the powers of the federal government. Vague language in the Constitution, such as the so-called Necessary and Proper Clause (Article 1, Section 8), they warned, would be interpreted by the Supreme Court, which was itself a federal institution composed of elites.

On the surface, the debate between the Federalists and Anti-federalists was based on principle: Each side claimed it was only trying to create a more perfect representative democracy. In fact, however, both had practical political purposes behind their positions. Fearing the radicalism of the state legislatures, the Federalists thought that they would be able to dominate a national government with a strong executive that could protect their property from radical movements by the poor and propertyless. Conversely, the power base of the Anti-federalists was in the state legislatures, and they feared that the new Constitution would weaken them politically.

Throughout American history, federalism has been a political football. Political conflicts over federalism are not surprising because the division of powers between levels of government is not politically neutral. *Where* decisions are made determines the scope of conflict, and the scope of conflict, in turn, helps determine who wins and who loses. From the beginning in the American republic, struggles over policy have been transformed into struggles over federalism.

Whether you favor popular or elite democracy, understanding federalism is essential for understanding American politics. In our political system, disagreements over *what* policies should be enacted are frequently played out as disagreements over *where* policy decisions should be made—at the national, state, or local level. The reason for this is that state and local political systems are not simply miniature versions of the national political system; the various levels of government differ in important ways.

The Slavery Issue: Reaffirming National Authority

After the Constitution was ratified, elite democrats continued to champion a powerful national government while popular democrats emphasized states' rights. John Marshall, chief justice of the Supreme Court from 1801 to 1835, was a brilliant Federalist advocate of national power. Perhaps his most important decision, *McCulloch v. Maryland* (1819), used the Necessary and Proper Clause to expand the powers of the federal government. In 1836, the popular democrat Andrew Jackson appointed Roger B. Taney, a strong advocate of states' rights, to succeed Marshall as chief justice. Led by Taney until 1864, the Court chipped away at federal powers by upholding state laws that probably would have been struck down by the Marshall Court.

Popular democratic support of states' rights came up against a contradiction with the issue of slavery. Southern states used states' rights to defend the institution of slavery. Led by South Carolina's John C. Calhoun, southern states resisted tariffs that protected northern industries and raised prices for manufactured goods. They also opposed efforts by the federal government to restrict slavery. Calhoun argued for the doctrine of **nullification**—that states have the right to nullify, or refuse to obey, federal laws they consider unconstitutional. In the infamous *Dred Scott* decision (1857), the Supreme Court under Taney ruled that the federal government had no power to prohibit slavery in the territories.[3] (This case is discussed in more detail in Chapter 15.) By striking down the Missouri Compromise as unconstitutional, the *Dred Scott* decision helped precipitate the Civil War. The Civil War finally settled the federalism issues raised by slavery: The federal union is indissoluble, and states do not have the right to declare acts of the federal government unconstitutional or secede from the union.

Federalism and Corporations

During the period of rapid industrialization after the Civil War, a new threat to popular democracy arose: giant national corporations and the wealthy elites who ran them. Popular democrats had power in many state legislatures, and they used that power to regulate corporations. These efforts were frustrated by the Supreme Court, however, which often ruled against the states when they threatened property rights. Angry about rate discrimination in areas not served by competing railroads, for example, in the early 1870s popular democrats passed laws setting maximum rates. In 1886, however, the Supreme Court ruled that the Constitution placed power to regulate railroad rates exclusively in the hands of the federal government, even for segments of the journey lying entirely within one state.[4]

The Court's blocking of state action provided an impetus for Congress to create the Interstate Commerce Commission (ICC) in 1887, the first attempt by the national government to regulate the economy through means other than general control over money and credit. Additional support for the ICC came from the railroads, which feared the rising power of popular democrats in the state legislatures. The railroads saw federal railroad regulation "as a safe shield behind which to hide from the consequences of local democracy."[5]

In short, elite and popular democratic forces tried to shift policy-making authority to the federal or state level, depending on where they saw their advantage. In the late nineteenth and early twentieth centuries, the Supreme Court generally acted to protect property rights and was suspicious of governmental efforts, at all levels, to regulate private property. From today's viewpoint, the Court construed the powers of the federal government quite narrowly. For example, it struck down the federal income tax,[6] restricted the powers of the ICC to set railroad rates,[7] and declared federal laws to regulate child labor unconstitutional.[8]

For almost the first 150 years of the U.S. Constitution—until the New Deal in the 1930s—something like dual federalism prevailed in American government. The powers of the federal government were construed narrowly, and Congress did not legislate in many domestic policy areas that we now take for granted, such as transportation and social welfare. In domestic policy, state and local governments raised more revenues, spent more money, and provided more services than the federal government. There were important exceptions to this pattern of federal reluctance, particularly the assertion of federal power following the Civil War during Reconstruction in the South and federal regulation of corporations during the Progressive era. Nevertheless, until the New Deal the federal government was the junior partner in domestic policy. The Great Depression of the 1930s exposed the glaring weaknesses of state and local governments and popular democrats turned to the federal government for protection.

The Failure of Dual Federalism

It is difficult for Americans today to imagine the depth of the economic and political crisis that the nation faced during the Depression. It began with the stock market crash on October 24, 1929—Black Thursday. The effects of the crash rippled out from Wall Street to paralyze the entire nation. The unemployment rate soared from 3 percent in 1929 to more than

Unemployed men waiting in line during the Great Depression.

one-quarter of the workforce in 1933. Those who were lucky enough to have jobs saw their average incomes fall 43 percent from 1929 to 1933. The collapse of the economy spread to the financial system; by the end of 1932, more than 5,000 commercial banks had failed. The political situation was tense. Frequent and violent street confrontations broke out between police and Communist-led demonstrators, as well as workers trying to organize unions.

The initial response of the political system to the Depression was halting and inadequate. Under the system of dual federalism, almost all social welfare functions were left to the states and localities. In 1929–1930, local governments bore 95 percent of the costs of general relief for the destitute.[9] The American welfare state was incredibly fragmented; the state of Ohio, for example, had 1,535 independent poor-relief districts.[10] Burdened by a crazy quilt of jurisdictional responsibilities, welfare was poorly administered and inadequately funded. Local welfare policies had other weaknesses: Able-bodied men were generally excluded from receiving any aid, strict residency requirements excluded many others, and those who did qualify for help were usually required to live in almshouses under wretched conditions and were forced to work at menial jobs with no pay.[11]

Even though donations to private charities increased when the Depression hit, the system was incapable of keeping up with soaring needs. In 1932, less than a quarter of the unemployed got any relief at all. For those who did, relief payments were usually inadequate. In New York City, families received an average grant of $2.39 per week.[12] The cities with the worst problems had the fewest resources to deal with them. With nearly one-third of its industrial workforce unemployed, Detroit made a heroic effort to provide relief, spending more per capita than any other city in the country. However, Detroit's compassion soon surpassed its tax base. Under pressure from the city's creditors, Detroit was forced to cut already inadequate relief appropriations in half in 1931–1932.[13]

Adhering to the principle of dual federalism, President Herbert Hoover refused to expand federal relief efforts. Speaking in 1932, Hoover asserted:

> I hold that the maintenance of the sense of individual responsibility of men to their neighbors and the proper separation of the functions of the Federal and local Governments require the maintenance of the fundamental principle that the relief of distress rests upon the individuals, upon the communities and upon the states.[14]

Holding steadfastly to the position that capitalism would right itself, as long as the federal government did not interfere, Hoover remained in office until 1933.

Roosevelt's Dilemma

When Franklin Delano Roosevelt assumed the presidency on March 4, 1933, he faced a difficult dilemma. The situation cried out for decisive federal action, but he knew that any attempt to expand federal power into areas that had previously been reserved for the states would meet crippling opposition in Congress, which strongly represented local interests. More important, the Supreme Court would simply declare such expansions of federal powers unconstitutional.

A Supreme Court veto was no idle threat because the Court was dominated by conservative justices who accepted the tenets of dual federalism. In 1935, for example, the Supreme Court struck down the National Industrial Recovery Act, asserting that the regulation of wages and hours fell outside the powers of Congress to regulate interstate commerce.[15] Emboldened by Supreme Court rulings, by late 1935 lower court judges had issued 1,600 orders to prevent federal officials from implementing acts of Congress.[16] In perhaps the biggest blow to the New Deal expansion of federal power, in 1936 the Supreme Court struck down the Agricultural Adjustment Act, which would have enabled the federal government to restrict production in order to increase the prices that farmers received for their crops. Rejecting an expansive definition of the General Welfare Clause, Justice Owen Roberts gave a classic reaffirmation of dual federalism:

> From the accepted doctrine that the United States is a government of delegated powers, it follows that those not expressly granted or reasonably to be implied from such as are conferred, are reserved to the states or to the people....None to regulate agricultural production is given, and therefore legislation by Congress for that purpose is forbidden.[17]

Frustrated by the Supreme Court's opposition, Roosevelt attempted to "pack the court" by adding justices friendly to the New Deal. He failed. Although most Americans opposed Supreme Court limitations on the New Deal, they also opposed tampering with the checks and balances of the Constitution. Roosevelt was caught on the horns of a dilemma: Congress and the Court prevented him from using the federal government to address the problems of the Depression, but if the federal government did nothing, the people would continue to suffer (as would Roosevelt's reelection prospects). How Roosevelt resolved this dilemma would revolutionize federalism in the United States.

Roosevelt's Solution: Grants-in-Aid

Roosevelt gradually embraced a compromise approach that slipped between the horns of the dilemma of federal versus state action: the New Deal used the powers of the federal government to initiate action but gave the states and localities considerable leeway in running the programs. This solution was advocated by Louis Brandeis, a Roosevelt supporter on the Supreme Court. In a famous dissenting opinion in 1932, Brandeis praised the federal system for allowing a state to "serve as a laboratory, and try novel social and economic experiments without risk to the rest of the country."[18] Brandeis recommended to Roosevelt that the federal government encourage the states to assume more active policy roles in addressing the crisis. The Brandeis approach was essentially a "third way" that attempted a compromise between federal domination and state inaction.

Roosevelt implemented the Brandeis approach through **grants-in-aid** that combined federal funding with state administration. Grants-in-aid are funds provided by one level of government to another for specific purposes. Usually, states are required to put up some of their own money (these are called **matching grants**), and they have to meet minimal federal standards for the program. Grants-in-aid had been in existence for many years, and as early as 1923 the Supreme Court had declared them constitutional on the ground that they were not obligatory but simply offered "an option which the state is free to accept or reject."[19] Federal grants-in-aid expanded rapidly during the New Deal, from $217 million in 1932 to $744 million in 1941.[20]

The Death of Dual Federalism

In 1937, the Supreme Court, with no change of membership, approved the New Deal's expansion of the federal government into areas previously reserved for the states. The Anti-federalist fears of federal expansion turned out to be well founded, but in ways they would have found ironical: Vague words in the Constitution, such as the Necessary and Proper Clause and the Interstate Commerce Clause, were used to justify expansions of federal power, but these expansions were opposed by elites and favored by masses of common people who needed help from the federal

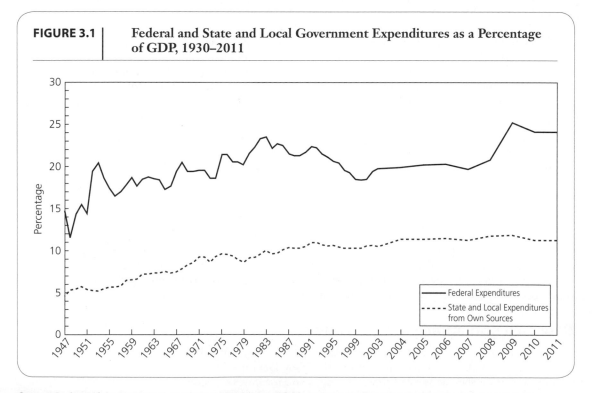

FIGURE 3.1 | **Federal and State and Local Government Expenditures as a Percentage of GDP, 1930–2011**

Source: Budget of the United States, Historical Tables; available at: http://www.gpo.gov/fdsys/search/pagedetails .action?granuleId=BUDGET-2013-TAB-15-3&packageId=BUDGET-2013-TAB&fromBrowse=true.

government against the ravages of the Great Depression. Expanded federal powers were used to redistribute wealth and opportunity from elites to the common people. Supreme Court decisions in 1937 signaled the demise of dual federalism. Within a few years, the federal government was allowed to legislate in almost all areas of domestic policy.

The New Deal revolutionized American federalism, moving the federal government into domestic policy functions previously reserved for the states. At the same time, state and local governments retained a great deal of power over these functions because they controlled the details of policy and who was hired to run the programs. As Figures 3.1 and 3.2 show, although federal spending has soared, most public employees work for state and local governments.

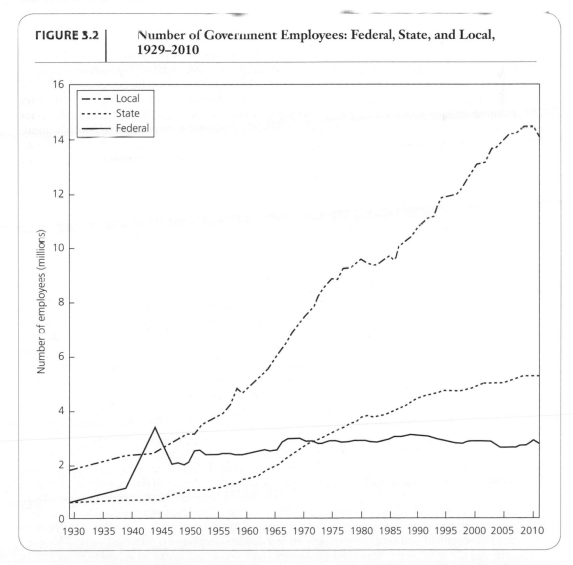

FIGURE 3.2 | **Number of Government Employees: Federal, State, and Local, 1929–2010**

Source: "Number of Government Employees: Federal, State, and Local, 1929–2001," from *Vital Statistics on American Politics, 2005–2006* by Harold W. Stanley and Richard G. Niemi. Copyright © 2006 CQ Press, a division of Congressional Quarterly Inc. Reprinted by permission of CQ Press; United States Census Bureau, *Government Employment and Payroll;* available at: http://www.census.gov/govs/apes/.

▬▬▬ Intergovernmental Relations ★ ★ ★

Beginning with the New Deal, dual federalism was replaced with a new federal system called **intergovernmental relations**. Under the new system, relations among federal, state, and local governments are worked out by specific legislation and negotiations, not by judicial rulings establishing separate spheres of authority. Two aspects of the system help preserve a balance of power between the national government and state and local governments: (1) The states remain as separate governments with independent taxing and spending powers, and (2) the states play a crucial role in the selection and orientation of federal officials.[21] Members of Congress are elected from individual states and congressional districts, imparting a "local spirit" to the national government. In addition, state and local governments lobby the federal government vigorously. Under intergovernmental relations, the powers of states and localities are protected more by political processes than by the courts.

The system of grants-in-aid put in place by the New Deal expanded slowly until the presidency of Lyndon Johnson (1963–1969). Between 1960 and 1970, grants-in-aid more than tripled, from $7 billion in 1960 to $24.1 billion in 1970. During his presidency, Johnson created hundreds of **categorical grant** programs—which required recipients to apply for funding under specific categories, detailing how the money would be spent and subjecting themselves to strict federal guidelines. Johnson's expansion of categorical grants was motivated both by a desire to make sure the money was targeted to social problems and by a political desire to cement the loyalty of urban blacks to the Democratic Party.

The Backlash Against Federal Grants

The huge growth of federal grants during the administration of Lyndon Johnson provoked a backlash among conservatives who thought that federal grants-in-aid had become intrusive, distorting local decision making and imposing burdensome regulations on state and local governments. Red tape, it was called. Implementation became complicated because each program required the cooperation of different agencies and governments. One study of a federal program in Oakland, California, concluded that it required seventy separate agreements among different agencies, making successful implementation nearly impossible.[22]

The expanding system of federal grants was also criticized for undermining democratic accountability. With hundreds of grants, each involving numerous actors at the federal, state, and local levels, the voters had difficulty pinpointing responsibility. Complex federal grant programs, critics argued, took power away from elected representatives and gave it to staff experts, issue specialists, and bureaucrats. *Grantsmanship*—the ability to write successful grant applications—biased the allocation of funds away from those who needed them the most to the most skillful grant writers.

Johnson's creative federalism provoked a backlash among suburban whites, who viewed federal grants as biased toward inner cities and blacks.[23] Republicans took advantage of this backlash, beginning in the 1960s, by appealing to working and lower-middle-class white voters who perceived that their hard-earned tax monies were going, under Democratic-sponsored federal grants, to inner-city poor and minorities. Direct opposition to the objectives of these programs, however, risked alienating traditional Republican voters who would be repelled by any taint of racism. Richard Nixon found a brilliant way out of this dilemma that helped him win the presidency in 1968: He supported the goal of racial equality but opposed federal intervention to achieve it in education, employment, and voting rights. Advocating decentralization of power to states and localities provided a way for Republican (and sometimes Democratic) politicians to appeal to white voters, who felt threatened by African Americans without explicitly voicing racist views.[24]

Nixon's **new federalism** shifted the grants-in-aid system from categorical grants to grants giving more discretion to state and local governments. In 1972, Nixon won passage of

general revenue sharing, which provided for the distribution of about $6 billion per year in federal grants to state and local governments, with few strings attached. Nixon also proposed a series of **block grants**—grants in which federal involvement is midway between the tight controls of categorical grants and the minimal controls of general revenue sharing. Under this method, a number of related categorical grants are consolidated into one block grant. Instead of competing for the funds, governments are allocated monies according to a formula based on need. The recipients spend the grant as they see fit within the broad purposes of the block grant.

Devolution: From Reagan to George W. Bush

President Nixon did not try to do away with the system of intergovernmental grants that had expanded so much under President Johnson. Nixon restructured federal grants to give states, where Republicans had greater political power, more of a say on how the federal funds were spent. Beginning with President Reagan, who assumed office in 1981, conservatives supported a more radical idea, **devolution**, turning the powers and responsibilities of the federal government back to the states. The main reason Republicans and many Democrats have supported devolution is simple—devolution is popular with the voters. Since the 1960s, confidence toward all levels of government has declined, but the drop in confidence has been more severe for the federal government than for state or local governments. In 2010, only 38 percent of respondents viewed the impact of the federal government on their lives as positive; 42 percent viewed state governments positively, and a majority (51 percent) reported a positive view of local government.[25]

Although politicians give lip service to devolution, for the most part the reality of devolution has fallen far short of the rhetoric. When Republicans were out of power in Washington, it was easy for them to call for returning power to the states. But it was far different once they controlled the presidency and Congress. Once in control of the federal government, they saw that it could be used to pursue conservative goals as well as liberal goals. For the most part, both liberals and conservatives practice "situational federalism": Their stance on federalism depends on their situation—what their political goals are and where their political strengths lie.

President Ronald Reagan (1981–1989) had a firm ideological commitment to the market as a better allocator of goods and services than government. He thought that decentralizing power to states and localities would achieve his goal of shrinking government. Three reasons were cited for this belief: (1) Liberal lobbies, which had been centered in Washington, D.C., for a generation, would be less influential in state capitols and city halls; (2) because they were closer to the voters, state and local governments would be less inclined to increase taxes to pay for social programs; and (3) economic competition among states and localities for mobile investment would force them to cut taxes and limit spending.

Reagan's basic approach to federalism was to cut federal grants, especially grants to state and local governments. The Reagan cuts in intergovernmental grants hurt poor people the most, especially minorities and those living in cities.

When the Reagan administration's new federalism goals came in conflict with its goals of enhancing private decision-making power, however, the federalism goals were sacrificed. Businesses have trouble keeping track of regulations in fifty different states and thousands of local governments. Moreover, states sometimes pass more-restrictive regulations than the federal government. As John Kincaid puts it, "Many businesses engaged in interstate commerce would rather be regulated by one 500-pound gorilla in Washington than by 50 monkeys on steroids."[26] To forestall state and local limits on business, the Reagan administration implemented pro-business federal regulatory expansion in many areas, including trucking, nuclear power, offshore oil exploration, and coastal zone management.

In contrast to Reagan, Bill Clinton won the presidency in 1992 with a reputation for supporting an expanded federal government, but, in the face of political pressure, Clinton became a supporter of devolution. After President Clinton lost decisively on a health care proposal that opponents smeared as a massive federal intrusion into people's lives, he declared that "the era of big government is over." In fact, during the Clinton administration the number of federal employees fell in absolute numbers to the lowest level since the Kennedy years (see Figure 3.2).

The most controversial federalism issue during the Clinton presidency was welfare reform. Clinton ran for office in 1992 promising to "end welfare as we know it," and in 1996 Clinton signed a bill passed by the Republican Congress that ended the sixty-one-year federal entitlement to welfare. In place of a federal guarantee that everyone who met certain criteria would receive cash assistance under programs administered by the states, the federal government now turns the money over to the states in the form of block grants. Welfare reform was touted as a devolution revolution, but in fact it imposed a number of regulatory requirements on the states motivated by conservative values. For example, it denied aid forever to any children born when the mother was on welfare. Despite these regulations, states now have a great deal of discretion on how the money is spent. Welfare reform was touted as a great success during its first ten years. Welfare caseloads were slashed. Helped by a booming economy, many former welfare recipients found jobs. During the recent economic downturn, however, many states have diverted money away from the poor to cover budget deficits. As a result, only one in five poor children receives cash aid, the lowest level in nearly fifty years.[27] By contrast, the food stamp program, which is administered by the federal government, increased the number of recipients significantly during the recent recession, reducing the poverty rate substantially.[28] (For more on welfare reform, see Chapter 17.)

The Bush Administration: The Rise of Coercive Federalism

As a former governor of the state of Texas, President George W. Bush came into office in 2001 with the expectation that he would shrink the federal government and enhance the power of the states. Instead, he did just the opposite: The federal government grew tremendously in size, fueled by large deficits, and the Bush administration repeatedly overruled decision making in the states. The federal government almost always expands its powers in times of crisis, like the 2001 terrorist attacks and Hurricane Katrina. But President Bush also used the federal government to push his social agenda and his preference for free markets, even when states resisted. One scholar characterized Bush's intergovernmental approach as "coercive federalism."[29]

Some of Bush's expansion of federal power fit with conservative ideology. After the 9/11 attacks, Bush pushed Congress to pass the Patriot Act, which greatly increased the surveillance powers of the federal government. Bush created the Department of Homeland Security, establishing one of the largest centralized bureaucracies in government.

Although Bush paid lip service to limited government, he came into office as a social conservative and did not hesitate to use the federal government as a means to enact his conservative agenda. In the 2005 reauthorization of welfare policy, the Bush administration succeeded in enacting stricter work requirements, taking away federal funds if states did not meet the new goals. Having already cut welfare rolls by more than 60 percent, states complained that the new rules took away their ability to experiment with innovative programs for supporting former welfare recipients in jobs. The new rules, for example, reduced the amount of time people could spend in job training and education. The Bush administration also required that sex education programs funded under Title V use an abstinence-only approach. As of January 2008, sixteen states had opted out of the federal program in order to offer a more comprehensive curriculum, including contraception.[30]

Like the Bush administration, the Republican-controlled Congress, which declared its commitment to devolution in Gingrich's 1994 Contract with America, frequently supported expanding federal power when it served its ends. A good example is the Terri Schiavo case.[31] Terri Schiavo was a young woman who suffered sudden heart failure in 1990 that caused severe

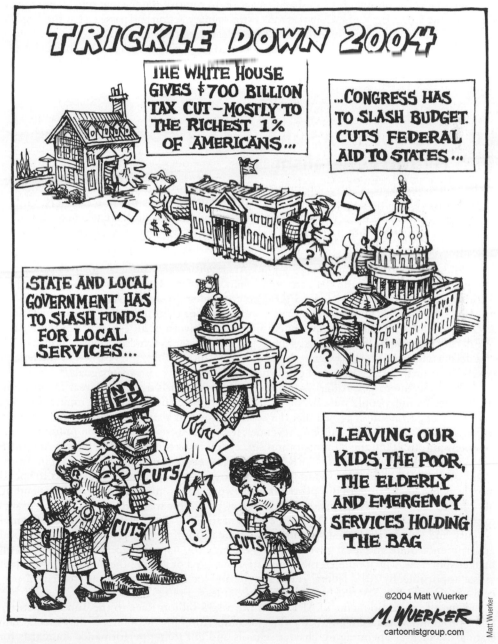

Trickle Down 2004.

brain damage. A feeding tube was inserted to keep her alive, and she remained in a "persistent vegetative state" for fifteen years. Schiavo had left no written instructions about her wishes, but her husband maintained that she had made it clear before her collapse that she would never want to be sustained on life support. Under Florida law the husband has the right to make these decisions, and Schiavo's husband decided to have the feeding tube removed despite strenuous objections by Schiavo's family. The issue was finally settled by the courts after a seven-year legal battle at all levels, approving the husband's decision to remove the feeding tube. Under pressure from the Christian Right, Congress took extraordinary action and passed a law that applied only to the Schiavo case (traditionally, only courts decide individual cases), ordering the federal courts to review the decisions of the Florida courts to see if Schiavo's rights had been violated. The federal courts quickly showed their deference for the state court proceedings and refused to intervene. Terri Schiavo died thirteen days after the feeding tube was removed.

The Obama Administration: Hybrid Federalism

Trillion dollar deficits, government control of health care, federal ownership of banks and auto companies, taxpayer-funded bailouts of irresponsible homeowners, and attempts to control energy consumption have combined to push a nation conceived in liberty and devoted to free markets to bankruptcy, down what F. A. Hayek called the road to serfdom.[32]

The above opinion expressed by Dick Armey, former House Majority Leader and prominent spokesmen for the Tea Party movement, is typical of the anger many conservatives feel toward the growth of the federal government under President Obama. In fact, Obama has followed a much more nuanced path on federalism than polarized political rhetoric suggests. Although Obama has expanded the federal government, especially in the area of health care, overall, he has not been as much of a centralizer as Lyndon Johnson nor as much of a decentralizer as Ronald Reagan. In pragmatic fashion, Obama has turned to the federal government or the states, depending on which level best serves his policy goals.[33]

Obama came to power during the worst economic crisis since the Great Depression. Banks were failing, people were losing their homes to foreclosures, and unemployment was soaring. Most economists agreed that the economy needed a stimulus. Unable to engage in deficit spending and facing shrinking revenues, the states were in no position to fund stimulus spending. In 2009, the administration succeeded in passing the $787 billion American Recovery and Reinvestment Act (ARRA). The largest economic stimulus program in American history, ARRA did not expand federal employment by much. The goal was to spend money as fast as possible to put people back to work and to jumpstart consumer spending in order to feed business expansion. The best way to do this was through tax cuts or grants to state and local governments. About one-third of the stimulus was delivered in the form of tax cuts, and about half of total spending was in the form of flexible grants to state and local governments. State and local governments were only too happy to accept the money to fill budget shortfalls, which fulfilled the administration's goal of getting the money on the street as fast as possible. By 2010, federal grants to state and local governments represented 4.2 percent of GDP (Figure 3.3), the highest level since at least 1940.[34]

One of the components of ARRA was the $4.35 billion Race to the Top competitive grant program. States were awarded points in competition for the money if they met certain standards, such as encouraging charter schools and enforcing performance standards for principals and teachers. Strapped for cash, many states altered their educational systems in order to make themselves more competitive for the grants. Although critics called it excessive federal intrusion into an area of state responsibility, the Obama approach was less coercive than Bush's No Child Left Behind Act that mandated performance standards without providing much money to achieve them. Participation in Race to the Top was completely voluntary, with the state of Texas under Governor Rick Perry early on deciding not to participate.

In a number of areas, the Obama administration engaged in partial preemption. **Preemption** is the ability of the federal government to nullify state laws that conflict with federal authority or laws. Partial preemption under the Obama administration meant that federal laws preempted state laws in some cases, but in other cases states were allowed to supersede federal standards. For example, as part of the 2010 Dodd-Frank financial regulatory reform law, states are permitted to engage in consumer protection and bank regulation alongside the newly expanded federal powers. During the Bush presidency, some state consumer and banking laws were preempted by the federal government. Currently, some states enforce regulations that are tougher than the federal government's laws. In effect, federal regulations form a regulatory floor instead of a ceiling, providing extra protection to prevent a replay of mortgage abuses and the 2008 financial meltdown.

The Patient Protection and Affordable Care Act, or Obamacare, represents one of the most significant expansions of federal power in history. For example, the federal government will encourage states to greatly expand Medicaid coverage to all persons up to 133 percent of the federal poverty line. Although the federal government will pay for most—if not all—of the costs, this represents a new responsibility states will be required to assume or risk losing huge amounts of federal funding. The individual mandate also represents an expansion of federal power, although it is worth noting that expanded health insurance is not provided

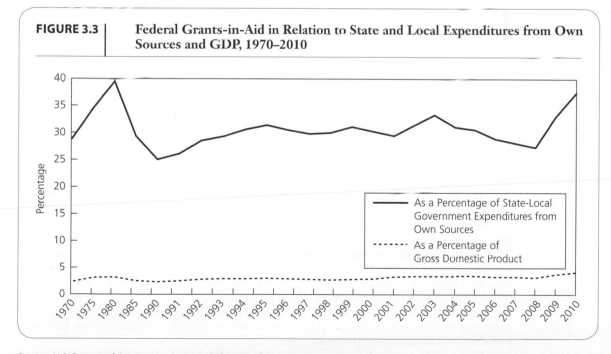

FIGURE 3.3 | **Federal Grants-in-Aid in Relation to State and Local Expenditures from Own Sources and GDP, 1970–2010**

Source: U.S. Bureau of the Census, *Statistical Abstract of the United States 2008* (Washington, D.C.: U.S. Government Printing Office, 2008), Table 418; http://www.census.gov/compendia/statab/2012/tables/12s0431.pdf.

by the federal government, the so-called single-payer plan. Instead, states have a great deal of latitude to manage health care marketplaces where individuals will purchase insurance from private companies. President Obama has even offered to allow states to opt out of the individual mandate and establishing health exchanges if they can achieve universal participation without raising costs.[35]

The Supreme Court, Federalism, and Democracy

For popular democrats, the standard for judging federalism issues should be what division of powers best enhances democracy. Appealing to the advantages of local democracy, many conservatives have called for a return to the era of dual federalism, when the courts ruled that the federal government could not legislate on a range of domestic functions. This would turn back the clock to a time, for example, when disadvantaged people, such as the poor, disabled, and homeless, had to rely almost entirely on private charity for help. Organizations such as the Tenth Amendment Center have sprung up to make the case that if the federal government simply stepped aside, state and local governments would be empowered.[36] The reality, however, is not so simple; often, federal action is needed to empower state and local governments to address pressing problems.

The most obvious area where federal action is needed to support state and local democracy is in the area of voting rights, where the rhetoric of states' rights and local control has often been a cover for racist practices. Southerners criticized the 1965 Voting Rights Act as interference by the federal government in the internal affairs of states. However, the act precipitated a democratic revolution in southern politics, enabling millions of African Americans to vote for the first time. In this case, federal "interference" clearly increased freedom and democracy. In fact, federal courts have repeatedly intervened to guarantee citizenship rights against mean-spirited state and local majorities. Although popular democrats believe in empowering local majorities, they also believe in setting limits on what local majorities can do. In a true democracy, basic rights, like the right to vote and speak freely on issues, should be protected by the courts and not be subject to a vote.

The case of *Bush v. Gore* (2000) represents a particularly embarrassing departure of the Supreme Court from its customary role of protecting voting rights. In this case, the Rehnquist Court intervened, by a five-to-four majority, to stop the hand-counting of ballots in Florida in the disputed 2000 presidential election. By stopping the count, the Supreme Court effectively gave the presidency to George W. Bush, taking the decision out of the hands of the voters (even though a valid recount might have shown Bush the winner anyway). Declaring that a state supreme court could not interpret state election law, the majority seemed to acknowledge the shaky ground on which it stood when it declared that its decision would establish no precedent for future cases. *Bush v. Gore* is a particularly egregious example of "situational federalism," where the five justices knew what outcome they wanted and then created arguments to justify their decision—even if the decision contradicted their loudly proclaimed adherence to states' rights in earlier decisions.[37]

In a series of earlier decisions, a slim majority on the court signaled an intention to restrict the powers of the federal government on the grounds that they are reserved to the states under the Tenth Amendment. In 1995, the Court declared the Gun-Free School Zone Act of 1990 unconstitutional, the first decision in sixty years ruling that Congress had exceeded its authority under the Interstate Commerce Clause of the Constitution.[38] In 1997, the Court struck down a provision of the Brady Handgun Violence Prevention Act that required state or local authorities to do background checks on buyers of handguns

(*Printz v. United States*). On the face of it, this frees local governments from a federal directive not of their choosing. However, many cities, especially poor central cities, find themselves the victims of rampant gun violence. Their ability to keep guns out of the hands of criminals is limited by surrounding jurisdictions with lax gun control laws. Suburban jurisdictions, for example, can sell assault weapons with few controls. These weapons are then imported into central cities, which are forced to spend substantial amounts of money on police protection. Without a federal law to keep guns out of the wrong hands, the actions of some governments can impose costs on other governments. Instead of undermining local democracy, federal gun control laws can empower local governments to spend their money on other, more needed programs.[39]

The 2012 decision that approved Obama's national health care legislation, *National Federation of Independent Businesses v. Sebelius*, is viewed as a major expansion of federal power. In fact, it approved the Patient Protection and Affordable Health Care Act ("Obamacare") on narrow grounds and, as discussed earlier, the majority made arguments that could be used in the future to strike down other federal laws. The Patient Protection and Affordable Health Care Act does increase the power of the federal government but not nearly to the extent that exists in most other "single-payer" national health care systems.

How Federal Policies Undermine Democracy in the States

Federal actions have powerful effects on the ability of state governments to meet their financial responsibilities. State revenues are linked to federal tax laws. When the federal government cuts taxes, invariably state revenues decline as well. Unlike the federal government, however, states are required to balance their budgets each year. When Congress repealed the estate tax, states suddenly found themselves with less revenue. Federal law currently forbids state and local governments from taxing transactions over the Internet, denying these governments an estimated $45 billion in revenue in 2006. Instead of revenue sharing, which Congress ended in 1986, recent actions by Congress would be more accurately termed "revenue shrinking."

On the spending side, the federal government often requires states and localities to provide services but does not provide them with the money to cover the cost. These requirements are called **unfunded mandates**. The National Conference of State Legislatures estimates that Congress shifted more than $131 billion in costs to state and local governments from 2003 to 2008.[40] One example is the 2001 No Child Left Behind (NCLB) act that President Bush called "the cornerstone" of his domestic policy. NCLB requires that each school administer annual standardized testing, and if they do not show sufficient improvement in the scores of eight categories of students, including low-income and minority students, the school will be labeled "low performing" and risk reorganization and losing federal funding. Besides attacking what they say is an unwarranted intrusion of the federal government into an area traditionally left to the states, critics of NCLB argue that the act does not provide enough money for implementation.

The greatest pressure for state spending is generated by the federal Medicaid program, which provides medical insurance for the poor with the cost shared by the federal and state governments. In 2010, spending on Medicaid totaled $429 billion, with states and localities spending $156 billion of that total. States now spend more on Medicaid than they do on elementary and secondary education.[41] States find themselves in a bind: Federal funds encourage them to provide Medicaid coverage, but constantly increasing costs strain state budgets. As a result, states have begun to shred the social safety net for poor people.

Cooperative federalism, where the federal, state, and local governments partnered to address domestic policy needs, has been largely replaced by a kind of "fend-for-yourself" federalism in which governments must compete with each other to survive the fiscal pressures.[42] This means that the ability of state and local governments to meet their responsibilities varies tremendously across time and space. In the wake of the economic crisis of 2008–2009, states (and cities) faced the most severe fiscal crisis since the Great Depression. The credit freeze is locking many states out of the bond market, and many states and cities have requested emergency loans from the federal government to meet expenses. According to one study, twenty-nine states faced a combined shortfall of $48 billion in the 2008–2009 fiscal year.[43]

The ability to cope with fiscal stress and provide services varies significantly from state to state because the taxable resources of states vary. As Figure 3.4 shows, per capita

---

FIGURE 3.4 | **Personal Income Per Capita in Current Dollars by State, 2010**

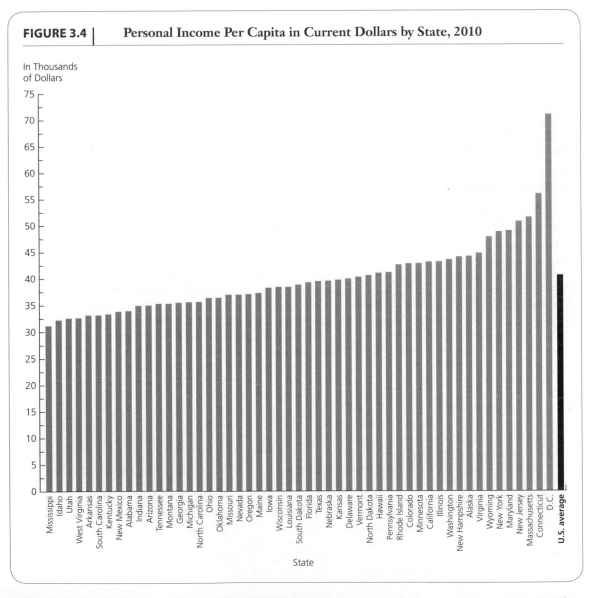

Source: U.S. Bureau of the Census, *Statistical Abstract of the United States 2008* (Washington, D.C.: U.S. Government Printing Office, 2008) p. 439; http://www.census.gov/compendia/statab/2012/tables/12s0681.pdf.

incomes vary tremendously across the states. In order to raise the same revenue, states such as Arkansas or Mississippi must tax incomes at almost twice the rate of states such as New Jersey or Connecticut. Perversely, poor states not only have the fewest resources but also the greatest need for social spending. The United States is the only federal system in the world that does not systematically redistribute financial aid to the poorest sub-units.[44] In the American federal system, resources are divorced from need. Because of their different resources and different political traditions, social policies vary tremendously across the states.

Supporters of dual federalism argue that if the federal government would simply step out of the way and stop telling state and local governments what to do, they would be empowered to act on their own, and all the advantages of decentralized decision making would be realized. However, this view that the two levels of government are locked in a zero-sum conflict—that if one level asserts power, the other level loses power—is simplistic and misleading. It ignores what one legal scholar calls the "baseline problem," the idea that state and local governments are shaped by their relations with each other and their ability to act is inextricably linked to the actions of the federal government.[45] As we have seen, state fiscal viability is linked to the policies of the federal government (and local law enforcement costs are linked to federal gun control laws). To realize their democratic potential, state and local governments do not need to just be left alone by the federal government; they need help from the federal government.

States as Laboratories of Democracy

Although states are hobbled by fiscal pressures, a survey of state policies shows that there are enough exceptions to elite rule to keep our hopes for popular democracy alive. In the present period, in fact, much like the period before the New Deal, state governments have often led the federal government in experimenting with popular democratic policies.

We would expect little room for democratic choice if states were tightly constrained by competition for investment. However, research has demonstrated that state policies are not completely constrained by economic forces; there is room for variation. State elections and policies reflect the distinctive political beliefs of their citizens. Based on surveys of 170,000 individuals over thirteen years, researchers classified states according to the liberalism or conservatism of their voters.[46] They found that even after controlling for socioeconomic factors, such as class and race, public opinion made a significant difference in policies: States with liberal voters enacted more liberal policies than did states with conservative voters. For example, Oregon and Oklahoma are similar socially and economically, but Oregon has liberal policies, whereas Oklahoma has conservative ones. States have different political cultures that are expressed through elections. Although states are hardly model popular democracies, public opinion and elections do make a difference.

Political institutions also make a difference. States without party competition tend to be unresponsive to public opinion. For many years, the one-party Democratic South enabled a minority of whites, especially wealthy planters, to dominate state politics and kept blacks and many poor whites powerless.[47] The political polarization of the country and the division of the country into "red" (Republican) and "blue" (Democratic) states raises the fear that one-party rule could disable democracy again.

Nevertheless, states have shown a surprising ability to innovate and fill the vacuum created by federal inaction. Consider the case of minimum wage laws. A minimum wage was first enacted in the United States in 1938, but over the years it has not kept up with inflation. Goaded by states and localities that required minimum wages above the federal level, in 2007 the Democrat-controlled Congress finally passed a modest increase in the national minimum wage to $7.25 over a two-year period. But there is no provision for it to increase with infla-tion. As of 2012, eighteen states had stepped in to set their minimum wage above the federal level, with Washington state having the highest at $9.04.[48] Many cities also passed "living wage" laws that exceed the federal minimum wage. By 2007, more than 150 cities had passed living wage laws, but usually these laws apply only to those who work for companies that do business with city government. Living wage campaigns have also been successful on college campuses.

In the absence of action by the federal government on global warming, states have stepped in to fill the policy void. In 2004, California adopted tougher rules on automobile tailpipe emissions than the federal government. Eleven other states soon followed suit. At a signing ceremony for an agreement to reduce greenhouse gases between California, the United Kingdom, and Northern Ireland, Governor Arnold Schwarzenegger declared: "We cannot wait for the United States government to get its act together on the environment. We have to create our own leadership."[49] Increasingly, states recognize that environmental policies not only do not harm the economy but they have great potential to stimulate economic growth by reducing imported oil and creating green jobs.

Conclusion: Is There a Way Out of the Dilemma?

Which way should popular democrats turn? Is there a way out of the dilemma of federal-ism? First, popular democrats recognize that the federal government has a responsibility to guarantee basic rights that are necessary for a well-functioning democracy. The right to vote, to speak, to protest peacefully should not vary across the states. The majority does not have right to take away a citizen's right to vote, as southern states did before the Voting Rights Act of 1965 was enforced by the federal government.

Moving beyond basic political rights to economic rights it is more difficult to determine if something should be guaranteed by the federal government. Take the example of health care. Is health care a right or a commodity? If you think it is a commodity, you will be uncom-fortable with the federal government guaranteeing everyone access to it—thus, the argument of some Supreme Court justices that the individual mandate opens the door for the federal government to require people to eat broccoli. If you think health care is a right, however, then you do not want access to health care to to vary from state to state. Only the federal government has the resources and the reach to guarantee everyone access to health care. We believe a good case can be made that not having access to basic health care undermines the ability of citizens to fully participate in the political process. (The United States is the only developed country that does not have national health insurance.) You cannot participate in politics if you are too sick to go to the polls or you are constantly anxious about an illness wiping out your life savings.

Having concluded that health care should be a national right, how much health care the federal government should provide beyond a basic minimum will be the subject of debate. The federal government should not guarantee everybody access to expensive plastic surgery, for example. There is still plenty of room to debate how much coverage people should be entitled to and who should pay for it. Therefore, there is room for state variation—not just on health care coverage above a basic minimum but also on all the preventive programs that are so necessary to improve health care outcomes.

When you turn from basic rights to political decisions about policies and programs, federalism presents a dilemma for popular democrats. Ever since the Anti-federalists criticized the Constitution for putting too much power in the hands of a distant central government, popular democrats have favored decentralizing power as much as possible. At the same time, popular democrats recognize the limits of localism. State and local governments lack the resources to tackle important issues such as economic inequality and environmental pollution, which cross jurisdictional boundaries.

First, popular democrats must understand that concentrations of power in the marketplace require countervailing concentrations of power in government. As we will see in Chapter 4, multinational corporations are not controlled by markets but have acquired huge amounts of power over markets and governments. Until corporations are made more democratically accountable to shareholders, workers, consumers, and especially their communities, we will need powerful federal bureaucracies, such as the Environmental Protection Agency (EPA) and the Securities and Exchange Commission (SEC), to regulate them in the public interest.

For the most part, however, federalism should not be framed as an either/or issue: Either give power to the federal government or turn power over to states and communities. An active federal government can bolster democracy at the state and local level. The federal government, for example, publishes information that empowers citizens and by requiring citizen participation in federal grant programs, the right of citizens to be heard is protected. Good examples are the Home Mortgage Disclosure Act (HMDA) of 1975 and the Community Reinvestment Act (CRA) of 1977. HMDA requires banks to provide information on where and to whom they are making loans. CRA requires lenders to "meet the credit needs of their communities"; that is, when banks take deposits from a community they must also lend back to that community. Community groups have used these laws to challenge redlining, the practice of banks refusing to lend in minority neighborhoods. As a result, community groups have signed lending agreements with local banks that have resulted in billions of loans for disadvantaged communities. CRA loans have also been found to have a low default rate. In this case, action by the federal government helped to empower local communities to stop discrimination and devise innovative programs to lift up their neighborhoods.[50]

Federal programs to promote greater equality among jurisdictions would also go a long way toward empowering state and local governments to address their own problems. Overall, federal grants do just the opposite, giving more money to wealthier states.[51] Other federal systems, including Germany, Australia, and Canada, have well-funded national laws designed to equalize the tax capacities of subnational governments.[52] A federal program to reduce economic inequalities among regions and between central cities and suburbs would invigorate local democracy.

Finally, we need to think more creatively about federalism. Some have proposed new regional institutions, modeled on the European Union, that would enable governments to meet together to forge intergovernmental agreements to take into account the effects of their actions on other governments.[53] Others have developed a new theory about how central governments should relate to local governments called "democratic experimentalism."[54] Under this arrangement, state and local governments would be free to set goals and choose the means to attain them so long as they were consistent with national objectives. Instead of a central bureaucracy monitoring adherence to federal goals, the local governments would set the standards of evaluation themselves by pooling information about best practices, using local knowledge to solve local problems.

Federalism is the great American contribution to political theory. By holding out the promise of diversity within unity, federalism provides a way for popular democracy to flourish in a large nation like the United States with so much economic and social diversity. In this chapter, we have outlined a series of obstacles that hinder our federal system from realizing its democratic potential. But the theory and practice of federalism are still evolving, holding out the promise that our state and local governments can someday realize their potential as true laboratories of democracy.

Reader's Guide ★ ☆ ★

Critical Thinking Questions

1. If you had been alive in 1789, would you have been a Federalist or an Anti-federalist?
2. Which level of government do you trust the most to side with the common people? Why?
3. In times of crisis, such as Hurricane Katrina, people turn to the federal government for help. Do you think that we need to create a stronger federal government to respond to crises, or should we rely more on state and local governments and nonprofits?
4. Which level of the government do you know the most about: your local government, your state government, or the federal government? Which level of government is covered most by the media? Why?

Key Word Definition

unitary government   A system in which all significant powers rest in the hands of the central government.

dual federalism   The system created at the founding of the Constitution in which the national and state governments each have separate spheres of authority and are supreme within their own sphere.

enumerated powers   The authority specifically granted to the federal government in the Constitution under Article I, Section 8.

reserved powers   The authority not given to the federal government and left to the states by the Tenth Amendment.

concurrent powers   The constitutional authority granted to both the federal and state governments, such as the authority to tax.

Supremacy Clause   Article VI of the Constitution, which states that when the national and state governments conflict, the national laws shall supersede the state laws.

nullification   The doctrine that the states have the right to declare invalid any federal legislation that they believe violates the Constitution.

grants-in-aid   Money provided by one level of government to another to perform certain functions.

matching grant   Money given by the federal government to lower levels of government to fulfill certain functions, requiring that the recipients put up some of their own money and meet minimal federal standards for the program.

intergovernmental relations   The modern system of federalism in which relations between the different levels of government are worked out by specific legislation and negotiations, rather than through the formal distinction of separate spheres of authority that characterized dual federalism.

categorical grant   Federal money to state and local governments that requires recipients to apply for funding under specific categories, detailing exactly how the money will be spent, and subject themselves to strict monitoring.

new federalism   The attempt by President Richard Nixon to weaken the power of liberal political lobbies in Washington and reverse the trend toward centralization of authority and control in Washington by placing more power, monies, and responsibility for government programs in the hands of the states.

general revenue sharing   Federal grants to states and localities without the stringent requirements associated with categorical grants.

block grant   The consolidation of a number of related categorical grants into one larger grant that provides recipients with the ability to spend the money as they see fit within the broad purposes of the grant.

devolution   The movement of decision-making authority down the federal ladder from the federal government to state and local governments.

preemption   The ability of the federal government to nullify state laws that conflict with federal laws.

unfunded mandates   Laws passed by higher levels of government that force lower levels of government to spend more money without providing them with additional resources.

4

The American Political Economy

WALMART: THE FUTURE POLITICAL ECONOMY?

THE DEMOCRATIC DEBATE ON THE POLITICAL ECONOMY

UNACCOUNTABLE CORPORATE POWER

RISING ECONOMIC INSECURITY

THE EROSION OF CIVIL SOCIETY

CONCLUSION: CHOOSING DEMOCRACY AND PROSPERITY

At President Obama's State of the Union Message on January 24, 2012, there was a surprising guest sitting next to First Lady Michelle Obama—Debbie Bosanek, a secretary from Omaha, Nebraska. Later in the speech, when President Obama got to the issue of taxes, it became clear why she was given a front-row seat. "Right now," the president said, "… a quarter of all millionaires pay lower tax rates than millions of middle-class households. Right now, Warren Buffett pays a lower tax rate than his secretary." Buffett, head of multinational conglomerate Berkshire Hathaway, is one of the richest men in the world. Debbie Bosanek is his secretary.

President Obama went on to recommend tax reform along lines recommended by Buffett. "Tax reform should follow the Buffett rule: If you make more than a million dollars a year, you should not pay less than 30 percent in taxes." Obama's speech provided more evidence that economic inequality and the alleged unfairness of the tax system would play a prominent role in the 2012 election.

Clearly, part of the reason is that economic inequality has widened significantly since the 1970s. Between 1979 and 2007, for example, the Congressional Budget Office found that the incomes of the top 1 percent grew by 275 percent, while the incomes for the bottom 20 percent increased by only 18 percent.[1] Historically, however, Americans have been quite tolerant of high levels of income inequality so long as they feel the system is fair and everyone has an equal chance to move up the economic ladder.

Increasingly, however, Americans sense that the system is rigged against them. Wall Street firms that behaved recklessly and plunged the economy into a recession are bailed out by the federal government at the same time that families who saw their homes plummet in value through no fault of their own get little help. Americans don't mind some people getting rich, but they do mind if those people are able to use their riches to buy political influence that will make them even richer—creating a reinforcing cycle of economic and political inequality. In a democracy, the economic and political spheres are supposed to be separate. In fact, they are intertwined in all sorts of ways that are dangerous for democracy.

Walmart: The Future Political Economy?

With more than 2 million employees and a net income of $16.39 billion in fiscal year 2012, Walmart has become the most successful retailer in history.[2] The basic reason for its phenomenal growth is that Walmart has focused like a laser on one and only one goal: lowering prices. And it has been remarkably successful at achieving this goal, saving American consumers billions of dollars each year. When it enters a product category, Walmart typically undercuts the competition by 10 percent or more. With 70 percent of its shoppers being blue-collar, unemployed, or elderly, Walmart caters to lower-income groups, concentrating its stores in small towns or working-class suburbs.[3] Consumers love Walmart because it saves them time shopping and provides them with incredible deals and friendly service. Walmart employees who find themselves within ten feet of a customer are supposed to smile and offer assistance. The firm is known for offering advancement opportunities to non-college graduates and a stock option plan to all employees.

But there are also costs, many hidden, to Walmart's remarkable success. Walmart can offer very low prices because it pays very low wages. In the early twentieth century, Henry Ford paid his workers handsomely so they could afford to buy his cars. Sam Walton, the charismatic founder of Walmart who died in 1992, basically turned Ford's approach on its head: Walmart pays its workers very little so the only place they can afford to shop is Walmart. The average full-time Walmart wage is $10–$12 an hour,[4] close to half of what workers earn in unionized chains such as Costco.[5] By hiring professional union busters and firing union supporters—even though that is illegal—Walmart has ensured that no U.S. store is unionized. Its health care benefits are meager, and, mostly as a result of low wages and high turnover, fewer than one out of fifty Walmart workers ever accumulates as much as $50,000 in Walmart stock.[6]

Although Walmart treats its women customers well, it often treats its women employees poorly. A remarkable 11 percent of all women workers in the United States work for Walmart. In 2001, the average female Walmart employee earned $5,000 less annually than the average male employee, even when they both had the same position. Women make up 72 percent of the chain's hourly workforce but only 34 percent of its salaried managers.[7]

In 2001, Barbara Ehrenreich traveled to Minneapolis as part of a journalistic experiment to see if a single, low-skilled woman could make ends meet in today's labor market.[8] Posing as a recently divorced homemaker entering the labor force after several years as a stay-at-home mom, Ehrenreich allowed herself one concession: a working automobile that was paid for. After submitting to a demeaning drug test, Ehrenreich quickly landed a $7-an-hour job at Walmart sorting clothes in the women's section. She found the work surprisingly demanding—and her fellow workers surprisingly devoted to Walmart.

Try as she might, however, Ehrenreich could not find an apartment she could afford on her Walmart wages. The best she could find was a $245-a-week room at a motel a twenty-minute drive from the store that smelled of mouse droppings and lacked air conditioning and even window screens. (Minnesota summers can be surprisingly hot.) One day raw sewage backed up through the drains and flooded her room. Admitting defeat, Ehrenreich later acknowledged that she might have been able to make it in Minneapolis if she had been willing to live in a $19-a-night "dormitory."

Ehrenreich's story illustrates a basic fact about the current American political economy: A single person—let alone an entire family—cannot live with dignity on the low-wage, service-sector jobs that are available today at companies like Walmart. In 2002, Walmart surpassed General Motors as the largest U.S. company. In 1997, the *Wall Street Journal* contrasted the average wage of a GM assembly-line worker ($19/hour) with the average at Walmart ($7.50/hour). When benefits such as health insurance are included, the GM wage jumps to $44 an hour, while the Walmart wage increases only to $10 an hour.[9]

How does Walmart get away with paying near poverty-level wages? Part of the answer is that the taxpayers are forced to pick up the tab. Documents show that Walmart encourages its workers to apply for food stamps and other social welfare benefits. A study by a Democratic congressman found that each Walmart employing 200 people costs taxpayers $420,750 per year in public assistance.[10] Walmart also pits communities against one another to garner tax abatements and other subsidies from local governments. Hungry for sales and property tax revenue, local governments are put in the perverse position of subsidizing the largest corporation in the world in order to drive down wages in the local economy, giving new meaning to the term **corporate welfare**.

Another reason Walmart can offer such low prices is because its products are made with cheap overseas labor. Walmart is a prime example of the globalization of American businesses. Although it exudes patriotism with its "Made in America" slogan, 85 percent of Walmart's products are made overseas. (Ironically, Sam Walton's autobiography is titled *Made in America*.[11]) Its biggest overseas supplier is China. In her book *Selling Women Short*, Liza Featherstone states, "If Walmart were a country, it would be China's fifth largest export market."[12] Independent unions are illegal in China, and workers are forced to endure deplorable working conditions. Walmart has a code of conduct concerning working conditions for its suppliers, but like most retailers it does little to monitor and enforce the code. Apparel workers in Guatemala work fifty-four hours a week, and many are paid less than the country's minimum wage of $2.80 a day. Also, there is evidence that Walmart has imported products made with prison labor in China.[13] In relying on products produced in Third World sweatshops, the company is little different from most American retailers. With its huge volume, however,

Citizens protesting dangerous Walmart working conditions.

Walmart has more leverage to force its suppliers to lower their prices, thus putting further downward pressure on wages.

Finally, Walmart stores erode local civic life. Walmart requires its managers to work seventy to eighty hours per week, leaving little time for civic commitments. When a Walmart moves into an area, family-owned businesses that often support Little Leagues and Kiwanis clubs are forced out of business. The old mixed-use town square where people would gather for conversation and major civic events is replaced by a huge, windowless box surrounded by a sea of asphalt.

Walmart likes to portray itself as a popular democratic institution that caters to working-class individuals and communities. (One of its Three Basic Beliefs is "Respect the individual.") Its founder, Sam Walton, drove a pickup truck all his life and abhorred those who flaunted their wealth. Beneath the populist rhetoric, however, is an elitist and hierarchical institution. Walmart has become so big it can dictate terms to suppliers as well as entire communities. The claim of free-market ideologists that individual workers can negotiate labor contracts on an equal footing with one of the largest companies in the world is absurd. Workers need unions to level the playing field. Corporations as large as Walmart do not support popular democracy; they contradict it.

Does Walmart represent the future of American political economy? The country's rule of law and popular democratic resistance to elites make this unlikely. As a result of workers' struggles during the Great Depression, in 1938 Congress passed the Fair Labor Standards Act, which established a minimum wage and overtime pay for working more than forty hours per week and on the weekends. Walmart has been successfully sued several times for not paying overtime when it was justified. (Lacking such laws, workers in Third World countries are forced to work fifty and sixty hours per week with no extra pay.) In communities around the nation, local activists are challenging Walmart's demands for tax subsidies and zoning changes, often successfully.[14] In January 2011, at the urging of Michelle Obama and her staff, Walmart announced a program to improve the nutritional values of its store brands over the next five years, gradually reducing the amount of salt and sugar, and eliminating trans fat.

Unquestionably, Walmart is a remarkably efficient and successful corporation, but it did not achieve this success solely through its own efforts in the private market. Without the massive government expenditures on streets and highways, Walmart would not be able to bring together the goods and the customers that make it so profitable. Walmart's success is rooted in dedicated working-class employees and social welfare policies that help them to make ends meet. Because Walmart depends on society, it should in turn be responsible to society. The company should be judged not only on low prices but also on its contribution to a democratic society based on equal rights and respect for the individual.

The Democratic Debate on the Political Economy

Throughout our history, Americans have engaged in heated debates about how our economy should be organized, who should make key decisions, and what effects the economy has on the quality of democratic life. These debates have not been between advocates of communism—government ownership of the means of production—and free-market capitalism. Even Americans who are critical of the economic system have shunned state ownership of factories and advocated that private goods and services be produced and distributed by markets, not by governments. Within the American consensus about markets, however, there has been plenty of room for debate about how the economy should be structured.

The main difference between elite and popular democrats is how they view the relationship between economics and politics. Elite democrats view the economic and political systems as largely operating in separate spheres (and they want to keep them that way); popular democrats view them as interconnected (and they want to improve those connections). For elite democrats, markets operate on the principle of freedom—no one can tell you what to do; all market exchanges are voluntary. Inequalities reflect the different talents, work effort, and willingness of individuals to take risks. Talented individuals who work hard or are willing to risk their savings starting new businesses are rewarded with high incomes. Those who lack the traits that contribute to economic growth fall behind. According to elite democrats, large corporations are held accountable by the marketplace; if a corporation is inefficient or makes products that nobody wants, they will soon be forced out of business. Government regulations only stifle the innovation and risk-taking that are essentially for a prosperous economy.

Popular democrats view markets as inherently political. Small businesses—think of local restaurants or dry cleaners—are controlled by market competition. But large corporations shape the market as much as the market shapes them. True, corporations lack the coercive powers of government, but they can charge monopolistic prices, engage in deceptive advertising, or threaten to pull their investments out of a community if they do not get their way. Above all, corporations and wealthy elites can use their control over economic resources to influence the political process. The result can be a vicious cycle of economic and political inequality, which can bias the political process further in favor of the haves and against the have-nots.[15] Popular democrats do not believe in absolute equality, but they oppose extremes of wealth that invade and corrupt the political process. Finally, popular democrats worry that **corporate capitalism** accentuates the acquisitive side of human nature at the expense of our social or political side. Slick ads teach that fulfillment comes from possessing commodities, not from participating in society.

In this chapter, we develop the popular democratic perspective on the American political economy, a perspective largely overlooked by mainstream media. Unlike most American politics textbooks, we do not treat large corporations such as Walmart as just another interest group. With their global reach and control over investment and people's livelihoods, the contemporary corporation possesses levers of power that no other group can duplicate. Charles Lindblom calls this the **"privileged position of business."**[16]

The example of Walmart shows the two faces of modern American capitalism. As an engine of prosperity and innovation, American capitalism delivers a dazzling array of goods and services. At the same time, it imposes tremendous costs, not only on individuals but on whole communities. The modern U.S. economy has four characteristics that raise troubling questions for American democracy: unaccountable corporate power, growing inequality, rising economic insecurity, and the erosion of civil society.

Unaccountable Corporate Power

According to market theory, corporations are held accountable by the marketplace. Citizens may have little direct control over corporations, but they have indirect control through the dollars they spend. Consumers "vote" with their dollars for the products and services they want. In effect, they have delegated the production process to corporate elites who are held accountable by the market. All market exchanges are voluntary; in the free market you never have to do anything you don't want to do. According to free market theorist Milton Friedman, markets produce "unanimity without conformity." "On the other hand, the characteristic feature of action through explicitly political channels is that it tends to require or to enforce substantial conformity."[17] According to this viewpoint the less government we have, the freer we are.

Foreclosures and the Financial Meltdown of 2008

An examination of the foreclosure epidemic that led to the financial meltdown and recession beginning in 2008 gives lie to this simplistic view that we are always better off with less government. As the British social critic R. H. Tawney once wrote, "Freedom for the pike is death for the minnows."[18] In the absence of protections for the weak and the vulnerable, markets can lead to oppression just as surely as unjust governments. As the mortgage crisis shows, when markets run amok, it is not just the weak and vulnerable who are hurt. Whole communities, indeed, even the whole national and global economies, can be harmed.

Consider the case of Tommy Meyers and his wife Marcia.[19] A hardworking couple from Dayton, Ohio, Tommy worked as a delivery man and Marcia as a cafeteria worker. In 1995, they paid $60,000 for a modest home that, nevertheless, with three bedrooms and a nice backyard, felt like a small palace to them. In 2001, however, Marcia was diagnosed with a congenital heart problem that required surgery. This meant she would not be able to work for about a year. In their newly perilous financial situation, they suddenly found themselves carrying over $10,000 in credit card debt. A salesman from Household Finance kept calling, offering to refinance their home and consolidate all of their debt under one loan at 7.2 percent. With the interest rates on his credit cards as high as 10 percent, Tommy thought refinancing sounded like a good idea. One Friday night he was rushed to sign the papers for the loan. All Tommy paid attention to was the 7.2 percent interest rate and his wife. "She was fixing to have her operation and I wanted to get these obligations out of the way so I could pay attention to her," Tommy said.

The loan Tommy got, however, was nothing like the loan he thought he was getting. Household Finance engaged in classic predatory lending practices. For example, Household charged the Meyerses 8 percent in points and fees and threw in an insurance policy that would pay off the loan if Tommy died. Most insurance policies are paid for month-by-month but the Meyerses had to pay the entire policy in one lump sum, $7,600. Instead of a simple loan for $80,000 at 7.2 percent interest, the Meyerses actually borrowed $95,000 at 13.9 percent. Tommy expected a monthly payment of less than $600; instead the monthly payment was $1,400. Five months after taking out the loan, the Meyerses walked away from their home and mortgage and moved into a trailer park. Household was eventually sued for mortgage fraud and agreed to pay $484 million in fines. The Meyerses got their own settlement, but it was not nearly enough to make up for the damage. When the trailer park raised its rates, they were forced to move into an even cheaper place. At the age of 74 and still working packing boxes in a warehouse, Tommy feels as though he has let Marcia down.

Of course, some of the people who lost their homes were not innocent victims like the Meyerses. They got greedy and borrowed more than they could afford to pay. Some people deserved to lose their homes. But the main cause of the foreclosure epidemic was not individual greed. According to a Report to Congress by the U.S. Department of Housing and Urban Development based on a thorough review of the research, the main cause of the foreclosure epidemic was the proliferation of high-cost, predatory loans that were aggressively marketed to unsuspecting borrowers.[20]

Foreclosures have not just had a negative impact on the families involved but also on surrounding communities—on families who were themselves not involved in a foreclosure. Research has shown, for example, that foreclosures have a negative effect on the market value of properties located within 1/8 of a mile. According to one estimate, by 2012 92 million neighboring property owners will have suffered losses totaling $1.2 trillion.[21] Declining property values mean less tax revenues for local governments at the same time that they face increased expenditures from foreclosures—from increased paperwork to cutting the grass to even having to demolish abandoned properties. When children are pulled out of school, their ability to learn is undermined, and the stress on families leads to higher rates of divorce, child abuse, and addictive behaviors.[22] Foreclosures are also associated with rising crime rates.

In short, even if you think that homeowners who went through a foreclosure are to blame for getting in over their heads, there is no way to blame those who did not engage in risky borrowing yet suffered from the foreclosure epidemic. In reality, almost everyone suffered from the irresponsible actions of mortgage lenders and Wall Street investors whose actions caused the 2008 financial meltdown and subsequent recession.

Who Is to Blame?

Who is to blame for the foreclosure epidemic that has caused so much economic hardship? Some people blame government. The argument is that markets are self-correcting. If too many bad mortgages had been issued, investors would soon refuse to buy them and the money for more bad mortgages would dry up. Government interfered with the natural self-correcting processes of free markets by forcing bankers to lend to people who were not ready to be homeowners.

There is almost no evidence to support the claim that government regulation was a significant cause of foreclosures.[23] Government did encourage homeownership but bankers did not need to be pushed; they were eager to jump into the market for high-interest, risky mortgages during the run-up in housing prices. Deregulation of the mortgage industry, under both Republican and Democratic presidents, unleashed the foreclosure epidemic. A key act was the repeal of usury laws, beginning in 1980, that enabled **subprime mortgage lenders** to charge higher interest rates for riskier loans. They responded by creating a range of new loan products, such as adjustable rate mortgages (ARMs) and interest-only loans, that they aggressively marketed to consumers. These mortgages were highly profitable because they were issued at higher interest rates and they piled on fees, as we saw in the case of the Meyerses. Mortgage originators loosened the requirements for getting a loan. So-called "liar loans" enabled borrowers to report any income they wanted in order to get a loan. So long as housing prices kept rising, driven by loose lending requirements, the problems of these risky mortgages were covered up. If borrowers could not make the payments, they could just sell the home and pay off the mortgage. Once the housing bubble burst in 2006–2007 and housing prices plummeted, the house of cards came falling down.

But if these mortgages were unsustainable, why did investors keep buying them year after year in violation of market theory? Part of the answer is that the originators bundled the mortgages into **mortgage-backed securities** (MBSs) and Wall Street eagerly bought them because they paid a high interest rate. Investors were assured that MBSs were safe, but in fact they were so complex and combined so many different kinds of mortgages that investors did not know what they were buying. Moreover, ratings agencies gave them triple-A ratings. With no government oversight, the rating agencies ignored warnings by independent analysts that the loans were unsustainable. Hired by the companies that were selling MBSs, the ratings agencies were corrupted by the desire to please their clients and get more repeat business.

Wall Street went one step further. It invented all sorts of ways that investors could invest in mortgages through new instruments, such as "credit default swaps," which were essentially insurance for MBSs. Being entirely unregulated, this new form of insurance did not require the insurers to have any reserves so they could actually pay up if the mortgages went bad. The credit default swaps were essentially gambles that the MBSs would not go bad. The mortgages were "leveraged" into all sorts of new wealth many times the value of the mortgages themselves. When the mortgages went bad, the loss in value ricocheted through the economy, destroying investment capital many times the original value of the mortgages. The sudden destruction of trillions of dollars of wealth tipped the U.S. economy into the worst economic crisis since the Great Depression of the 1930s.

Although the government did not directly cause the crisis, its response was slow and uneven. The government did much more to help the big banks than the ordinary homeowners and communities that bore so much of the damage from the foreclosure epidemic and financial meltdown.[24] Deeming Wall Street banks and investment firms "too big to fail," the government stepped in to bail them out with the $700 billion Troubled Asset Relief Program (TARP). Citizens resented Wall Street firms paying large bonuses to their executives at the same time that taxpayers were bailing them out. This may help explain the odd outcome that more citizens blame the government for the crisis rather than the corporations.[25] To be sure, government failed to take action when it should have to stem the crisis. But to blame government for the financial crisis would be like blaming government for causing the pollution coming out of a factory smokestack because it failed to regulate it. Irresponsible corporate behavior directly caused the crisis. Until corporations are brought under greater democratic control, corporate abuse of power will be a common occurrence.

Corporate Organization: Special Privileges

The modern multinational corporation is often viewed as simply a series of individual contracts that are the natural outgrowth of the marketplace. In fact, the modern corporation is a powerful institution that has been given huge grants of power by state governments (Chapter 15), the federal government (Chapter 17), and the Supreme Court (Chapter 14). As developed in American law, the modern corporation has three legal characteristics that set it apart from the mom-and-pop grocery store:

1. *Joint stock ownership*. Corporations pool the resources of a number of investors, called stockholders. The stock can be freely bought and sold. The owners of any company can, in short, change on a daily basis.

2. *Limited liability*. Corporations can attract investment more freely because no single owner is financially responsible for more than his or her own investment.

3. *Continuous legal identity*. Corporations do not dissolve with the death of any owner. Like the Energizer Bunny, they just keep going, no matter what.

The law has established that corporations are like artificial persons. But these persons are giants who can traverse the globe in a few steps. And unlike real persons, these artificial persons have the best of both worlds: They have the *rights* of real individuals but few of the *responsibilities*. In a seminal Supreme Court decision, *Santa Clara County v. Southern Pacific Railroad* (1886), the Court declared that private corporations are "persons" for constitutional purposes. Thus, corporations have the right under the Fourteenth Amendment to "equal protection." Since then, courts have given corporations eleven separate rights that we normally think of as reserved for persons under the U.S. Constitution.[26]

Unlike real people, however, corporations can live forever, and no individual person is responsible for corporate actions. In contrast to individual citizens, corporations are not born with rights; they are licensed and, in effect, created by governments. There is an even greater difference: Corporations are composed of individuals in a hierarchy. With certain restrictions, the people who work for this legal fiction can be hired and fired at will and, within the limits of law, can be made to pursue the corporation's real interest: profits for stockholders. Even though corporations possess a wide array of rights, ironically, when individuals go to work for a corporation they check their constitutional rights at the door. Your employer has the right to search your person, require you to take a drug test, and stop you from speaking or handing out literature. Sometimes, you even need permission to go to the bathroom. As Barbara Ehrenreich, the author discussed earlier who tried to make ends meet in a low-wage job, states:

> When you enter the low-wage workplace—in many of the medium-wage workplaces as well—you check your civil liberties at the door.…We can hardly pride ourselves on being the world's preeminent democracy, after all, if large numbers of citizens spend half their waking hours in what amounts, in plain terms, to a dictatorship.[27]

According to political scientist Charles Lindblom, "The corporation fits oddly into democratic theory and vision. Indeed, it does not fit."[28]

The Myth of Shareholder Democracy

According to economic theory, corporations are held accountable by their owners, the shareholders. In theory, the shareholders elect the board of directors, who in turn hire management. Because so many people own stock today, the system is said to be legitimated by **shareholder democracy**—or "people's capitalism." There are two fundamental problems with shareholder democracy: First, the ownership of stock is much less widespread than generally believed, and second, even those who do own stock have very little control over corporations, which are run by a self-selected oligarchy of top executives.

The idea that a diverse nation of shareholders keeps corporate power in check is not supported by the facts. First, less than a majority (48.6 percent) of American households own any stock at all. The distribution of stock ownership is heavily skewed toward those at the top. The richest 10 percent of Americans own about 78 percent of all stock.[29] Moreover, owning small amounts of stock hardly gives individual investors much power. Workers who own stock through their

Gay marriage rally.

Matt Wuerker

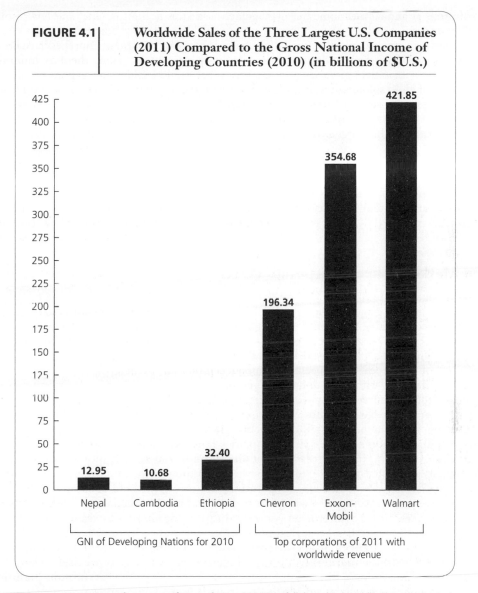

FIGURE 4.1 | **Worldwide Sales of the Three Largest U.S. Companies (2011) Compared to the Gross National Income of Developing Countries (2010) (in billions of $U.S.)**

GNI of Developing Nations for 2010 | Top corporations of 2011 with worldwide revenue

Sources: money.cnn.com/magazines/fortune/fortune500/2011/full_list/; data.worldbank.org/indicator/NY.GNP.ATLS.CD/order=wbapi_data_value+wbapi_data_value-last&sort=asc

pension funds have little control over corporate behavior. Pension-fund managers control these stock funds.[30]

Even if you individually own stock, your ability to influence corporate policy is practically nil. In theory, the shareholders choose the managers of the corporation and set broad policy. But in reality, management tightly controls shareholder meetings. Usually management is able to get enough proxy votes to control the meeting. The election of the board of directors resembles elections under Soviet communism, with voters having only one slate to choose from, handpicked by management. Shareholders can introduce resolutions at annual meetings, but management can strictly limit debate, and few resolutions ever pass.

For years, several orders of Catholic nuns and groups of Protestant churches have introduced resolutions at shareholder meetings of military contractors, asking them to limit sales to countries with violent histories or to countries that would enable the weapons to fall into the hands of child soldiers. Their resolutions have lost every time. "Sometimes," said Sister Mary Ann of the Sisters of Loretto in St. Louis, "it feels like I'm the only one concerned."[31] Nevertheless, these shareholder resolutions do create publicity for their cause, and in recent years management has agreed to at least sit down with these shareholders and talk about their concerns.

From the viewpoint of popular democracy, boards of directors of private corporations should represent not just shareholders but all the stakeholders that are affected by corporate policies, including workers, consumers, and the communities in which corporations are located.[32] But as we have seen, even the more limited idea of shareholder democracy is a myth. Corporations are controlled by executive oligarchies that rule in a top-down fashion.

Do Markets Check Corporate Power?

Even though private corporations are highly undemocratic institutions, run in a top-down manner by an elite group of managers, defenders of corporate capitalism argue that they are ultimately accountable to ordinary consumers through the marketplace. Citizens may have little direct control over corporations, but they have indirect control through the dollars they spend. In effect, consumers have delegated the production process to corporate elites, but the end goals of that process, the specific commodities produced, are determined by the consumers when they vote with their dollars. To respond to ever-changing consumer preferences, companies must be free from governmental interference. Any corporation that engaged in lengthy democratic consultations with shareholders, workers, consumers, and governments would soon be left in the dust in the competitive race.

Popular democrats agree that companies must compete and respond to consumers. Yet corporations have a great deal of discretion in *how* they respond, and this gives them unaccountable corporate power. As we saw in the case of the foreclosure epidemic and financial meltdown of 2008, corporations are often not held accountable by markets. Markets are justified by their "informality" and by the freedom of both producers and consumers, and they are often contrasted to the "deadening bureaucratic hand" of government. But there is a great deal of bureaucracy inside corporations, which allocate huge amounts of resources inside the corporation according to a centralized plan, rather than according to the market. Ironically, modern corporations do precisely what free-market economists don't like about government: They engage in **economic planning** trying to dominate markets and control their environment.[33] Corporate managers must decide long in advance what to do with their investments—where to build factories, what workers to hire, and how much to pay the CEO. None of these decisions are dictated by the market.[34]

It seems as though consumer demand determines what items are produced, but this isn't strictly true. The advertising and marketing industries discovered long ago that consumer demand does not grow by itself but must be created, even manipulated. Most advertising is designed not to inform consumers about the product but to create demand for the product or establish brand identities. Spending on advertising was projected to reach an astounding $280 billion in 2007 (up from $33 billion in 1976).[35] The average American is exposed to a mind-numbing 100 commercial messages each waking hour.[36] By celebrating the upper-class lifestyle, ads encourage us to consume beyond our needs. One study found that each additional hour of television watched per week caused consumption to go up by $208 per year (or savings to go down by that amount).[37]

The Challenge of Globalization

In recent decades many American corporations, such as General Electric, General Motors, Ford, and RCA, have moved their manufacturing operations abroad in search of cheap labor and lax environmental and health and safety regulations. More and more companies have shed their national identities because their capital, their production, and their marketing have what Richard Barnet has called a "global reach."[38] By the mid 1990s, these global companies had become so large that 40 percent of U.S. exports and half of U.S. imports were actually goods that big global companies bought from and sold to one another.[39]

The globalization of corporations represents new challenges for democratic accountability. As the example of Walmart shows, the movement of production to low-wage countries has brought advantages to consumers in the form of lower prices. But for U.S. manufacturing workers—the backbone of the middle class in the 1950s and 1960s—the rise of the global corporation has generally been bad news. In the 1980s, the United States lost more than 1.3 million manufacturing jobs, devastating such towns as Youngstown, Ohio, and Schenectady, New York. Job growth has instead shifted to service workers, that broad swath of workers from hamburger flippers to paralegal assistants who make far less than manufacturing workers on average.[40]

The U.S. government has promoted globalization by signing on to international trade agreements that lower tariffs and other barriers to world trade. The most prominent of these are the **World Trade Organization (WTO)** with 153 members worldwide[41] and the **North American Free Trade Agreement (NAFTA)**, a trade agreement involving the United States, Mexico, and Canada. Free trade has many benefits for consumers and potentially even for workers, but truly free trade requires more than just cutting tariffs (taxes on imported goods). Labor unions should be free to organize and environmental regulations should not be eroded by free trade. Under NAFTA, for example, a U.S. waste disposal company, Metalclad, sued the Mexican government for stopping the construction of a waste dump because it would have polluted the local water supply. Arguing that this regulation interfered with its ability to compete in the global marketplace, a NAFTA tribunal awarded Metalclad $16.7 million from the Mexican government.

The fact is, international trade organizations are undemocratic bodies. They operate behind closed doors with little transparency, using economic jargon to create an aura of technical rationality that suppresses democratic debate. In Chapter 11, we discuss the international mass movement that has emerged in opposition to globalization. Contrary to how they are portrayed by the mass media, global activists are not against free trade; they are against the way globalization gives multinational corporations the power to undermine workers' rights and environmental protection.

Labor Unions: Checking and Balancing Corporate Power?

It is hard to imagine a vibrant democracy without strong labor unions. Labor unions provide a necessary counterweight to the power of large corporations. Unions are important not just to fight for better wages and working conditions, but to give workers dignity and encourage participation in the political process. Isolated individuals feel powerless. When joined together in a union, workers are emboldened to participate in the political process.

Before the 1930s, unions had a difficult time organizing in the United States. Corporations frequently responded to union organizing drives with violent repression, often aided by the police. As part of Franklin Roosevelt's New Deal, in 1935 Congress passed the **Wagner Act**, which guaranteed workers the right to organize unions and bargain collectively. Union membership soared, reaching a peak of 31.8 percent of the nonagricultural workforce in 1955 (Figure 4.2). Union contracts negotiated with management often gave workers valuable rights within the corporation—for example, to take work breaks and refuse to work overtime. And unions played a key role in supporting social welfare policies that aided those at the bottom.

As Figure 4.2 shows, union presence in the U.S. workforce has been declining steadily since the 1950s. Today, less than 12 percent of American workers belong to a union, one of the lowest rates among all the capitalist democracies.[42] The major reason for the decline of unions, some argue, is that unions drive away jobs in the global economy. But many advanced countries around the world, such as Germany, that face the same global competition as the United States, have much higher unionization rates than the United States. Another argument is that unions are simply unpopular among workers, but since the 1980s there has been growing support for unions among workers. By 2002, 50 percent of nonunion workers said they would prefer to be represented by a union.[43]

The main reason unions have declined is that rights to organize have eroded in the hands of judges and administrators appointed by pro-business Republican presidents. Since the election of Ronald Reagan in 1980, workers who want to unionize have been deprived of many of the legal protections they once had.[44] It is illegal for companies to fire workers simply for supporting a union, but they do it anyway, knowing that at worst the courts will force them to pay back wages many years later. The ability of companies to fire anyone who even talks about joining a union has tilted the playing field strongly against unions.[45]

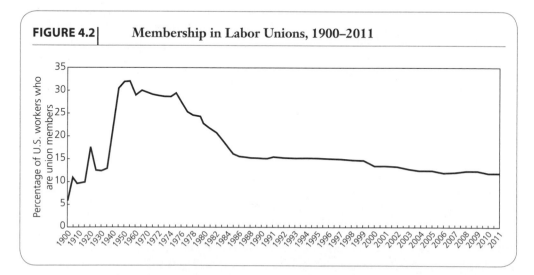

FIGURE 4.2 | Membership in Labor Unions, 1900–2011

Sources: Harold W. Stanley and Richard G. Niemi, *Vital Statistics on American Politics, 1999–2000* (Washington, D.C.: Congressional Quarterly Press, 2000), p. 401; U.S. Bureau of the Census, Statistical Abstract of the United States 2008, Table 642, downloaded from www.census.gov; data for 2007 from www.bls.gov/opub/mlr/2008/10/art3full.pdf; 2008 from www.bls.gov/opub/ted/2009/jan/wk4/art05.htm; 2009 from http://www.bls.gov/news.release/archives/union2_01222010.htm; 2010 from http://www.bls.gov/opub/ted/2011/ted_20110125.htm; 2011 from http://www.bls.gov/news.release/union2.nr0.htm.

As Figure 4.3 shows, unions don't come close to matching the contributions of corporations—and that is a major reason they have not been able to pass laws to level the playing field of union organizing.

Unions are stronger in the public sector, but even here there is an assault on union organizing rights. In 2011, under the leadership of Governor Scott Walker, Wisconsin passed a bill that took away most collective bargaining rights of government employees. The law polarized the state and resulted in a campaign to recall Governor Walker. A similar law to repeal bargaining rights by government workers was overturned in a statewide initiative in Ohio.

Unions are the weakest they have been for more than a century, and if they decline much further, there will be devastating consequences for popular democracy. Research has shown that states with higher rates of unionization also have:

- Higher wages
- Greater income equality
- Higher minimum wage laws
- Stronger social safety nets (e.g., unemployment benefits)
- More health insurance coverage
- More progressive taxes[46]

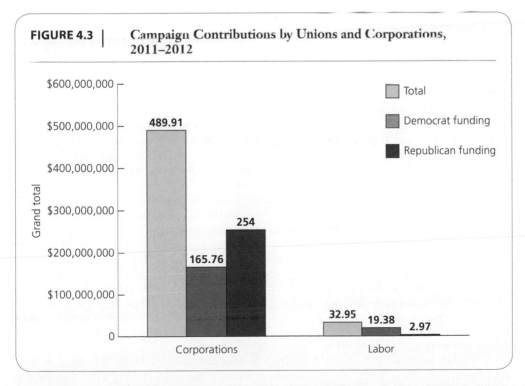

FIGURE 4.3 | Campaign Contributions by Unions and Corporations, 2011–2012

Note: The corporate category is a sum of the Financial/Insurance/Real Estate, Misc. Business, Communications/Electronics, Energy/Natural Resources, Construction, Agri-Business, Transportation, and Defense sectors.

Source: www.opensecrets.org/industries/index.php.

Besides these economic benefits, unions promote democratic participation. States with higher rates of unionization have significantly higher voter turnout rates. According to one estimate, if unionization had been 10 percentage points higher during the 2008 presidential election, between 2.6 and 3.2 million more Americans would have voted.[47]

Part of the weakness of labor unions must be attributed to the unions themselves. Too often they have been undemocratic, bureaucratic, and parochial—concerned only with the wages of members and not fighting for a broader economic and social agenda. Many unions, however, have started to reach out to the community and form broad regional coalitions. The Service Employees International Union (SEIU) in St. Louis, Missouri, for example, played a key role in passing a transit tax in 2011 that raises about $75 million a year for buses and light rail. Without the tax, the bus system would have suffered massive cuts that would have fallen heavily on the African American community. SEIU recognized that public transit was important for its members but it was also crucial to the well-being of the entire region. As Robert Reich, former Secretary of Labor, observed, "Organized labor is an aging, doddering prizefighter still relishing trophies earned decades ago. But it's the only fighter in that corner of the ring. There's no other countervailing political force against the overriding power of business and finance."[48]

Growing Inequality

A political economy composed of hierarchical corporations aided by a largely pro-business government limits the ability of citizens to control the forces that shape their lives. Yet many people reason that the loss of control is worth it if economic prosperity is secured for large numbers of Americans. Indeed, the United States has one of the most productive and prosperous economies in the world. The problem, however, is that the United States also has the greatest inequality—the gap between the rich and poor—of any developed nation. Besides signaling that the economic system is not working for many people, severe inequalities threaten the health of our democracy.

Historically, American society has been held together by an implicit social contract: "If you work hard, you will get ahead." Economic prosperity, Americans believe, benefits everybody. In President Kennedy's memorable words, "a rising tide lifts all boats." As Figure 4.4 shows, between 1947 and 1979 this was true: Those in the bottom 20 percent of the income range saw their incomes rise faster than those above them.

After 1979, however, the trend toward greater income equality reversed itself. Between 1979 and 2010, those in the bottom 20 percent (families making less than $25,636 in 2000) actually saw their incomes decline on average every year (after controlling for inflation). Every group above them saw their incomes increase annually, with the top 20 percent (families making over $97,460 in 2000) enjoying a healthy 1.2 percent increase on average every year. The very rich, those in the top 1 percent, did even better. Between 1974 and 2007 the top 1 percent saw their share of national income increase from just over 9 percent to 23.5 percent.[49] The super-rich, those in the top 0.01 percent (the richest one in ten thousand households) increased their share of national income during that same period from less than 1 percent to over 6 percent. This is the largest share of income going to the super-rich since data began to be collected in 1913.

Wealth inequality is even greater than income inequality. (*Wealth* is defined as people's assets in homes, stocks, bank accounts, or other possessions, minus what they owe to creditors.) In the 1950s and 1960s, wealth inequality remained fairly steady; a rising economic tide lifted most boats. Since the 1980s, however, economic tides have only lifted the

[MAKING A DIFFERENCE]

Unions and the New Economy

Graciela Diaz never dreamed where she would end up when she illegally crossed the border from Mexico into the United States in 1991. Eventually, she won U.S. citizenship, but life was tough at first. She began by working in a sweatshop in Los Angeles, earning about $30 a day. Three years later she met her future husband, Manuel, who persuaded her to move to Las Vegas where he had heard life was better. She began by taking backbreaking housekeeping jobs at various hotels, but her luck changed when she landed a unionized job at the La Salsa restaurant. After passing the course at the union's Culinary Training Academy, she was promoted to waitress, with wages and tips totaling about $20 an hour and generous health insurance. Meanwhile, Manuel landed a unionized construction job that paid $23.66 an hour, with substantial overtime. Now they own their own home and have big ambitions for their daughter, Cecilia: college and maybe law or architecture school.

The story of the Diazes is the story of the American Dream, but for many people, the American Dream is receding as dead-end, low-wage jobs lock them in poverty. For those with popular democratic institutions on their side, such as progressive unions, however, the American Dream is very much alive.

Progressive unions, like those to which the Diazes belong, have had to change in order to survive. Consider the following: Las Vegas, with 1 million residents, is America's fastest-growing big city. Some call it the "Pittsburgh of the Twenty-first Century" because of the large numbers of workers in new factories there. But instead of making steel, today's workers make the beds, clean the toilets, shuffle the cards, and dig the ditches that make for a new service economy. In Las Vegas, service jobs mean gaming jobs.

All over America, but especially in Las Vegas, the new face of this service workforce is increasingly female, often Hispanic, African American, Asian American, and young. But until recently, organized labor has primarily been composed of male workers in declining manufacturing industries, such as autos and steel. That's one reason why union membership has been declining and, with it, the wages, working conditions, and job security of millions of new service workers.

For a long time, the leadership of American unions didn't pay much attention to organizing new workers. But back in 1994, the Culinary Workers Union, Local 226, began to fight for recognition at the MGM Grand Hotel—with 2,000 rooms, Las Vegas's biggest. MGM, like many companies, had wanted to outsource many of its restaurant jobs to subcontractors who paid their workers low wages and provided no medical insurance. After three years of struggle with MGM, the 4,000 workers won management recognition of their union and also a contract that paid a living wage and provided important benefits.

The Culinary Workers Union is now locked in a battle to organize Station Casinos, owned by the billionaire Fertitta brothers, who are determined to keep unions out. An administrative law judge has issued a cease-and-desist order against Station Casinos and forwarded 87 charges to a full three-member panel of the National Labor Relations Board, including charges that the casinos fired and disciplined workers for being involved in the union drive. The union regularly writes letters to guests and performers at Station Casinos denouncing the casino for being unfair to its workers. With the tight job market and the well-funded anti-union campaign of the Fertitta brothers, the union will have to use all of its organizing skills to win.

Clearly, unions have begun to reform themselves internally, shaking up rigid bureaucracies to make them more responsive to the members. The leadership has been revamped to include more women and people of color—those with the lowest wages in the U.S. workforce. The AFL-CIO has urged all the member unions to spend up to 15 percent of their dues on new organizing activities. Unless unions make organizing a top priority, they will not be able to maintain their present members, let alone grow. Above all, they must shift away from business unionism, which focuses only on better wages for the members, to embrace social movement unionism where unions form alliances with environmentalist, civil rights, and consumer groups. One new labor strategy has been to reach out to students through "Union Summer," where college students work with union organizers on boycotts, strikes, and political campaigns.

Unions can be successful. Culinary Local 226, the one that Graciela Diaz joined, grew from 18,000 members in the late 1980s to approximately 60,000 today. And since becoming one of the most unionized cities in the nation, Las Vegas has prospered, contradicting corporate claims that unions choke off economic growth. Speaking of his unionized workers, the chairman of the MGM Mirage, which owns the largest hotel in the world in Las Vegas, said that happy workers make for happy customers. "Is it perfect? No. But it's as good as I've seen anywhere."

Sources: Steven Greenhouse, "Local 226, 'the Culinary,' Makes Las Vegas the Land of the Living Wage," *New York Times* (June 3, 2004); Jon Ralston, "Much at State Economically in Station, Culinary Fight," *Las Vegas Sun* (January 22, 2012); Margaret Levi, "Organizing Power: The Prospects for an American Labor Movement," *Perspectives on Politics* 1, 1 (March 2003): 45–68.

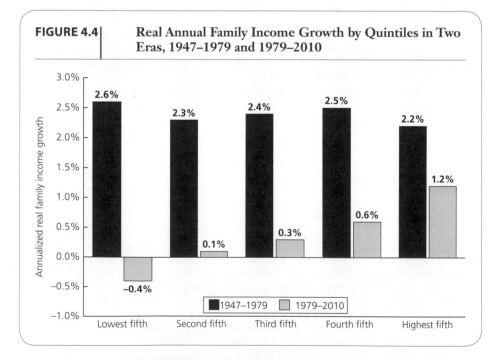

FIGURE 4.4 | Real Annual Family Income Growth by Quintiles in Two Eras, 1947–1979 and 1979–2010

Sources: *EPI analysis of U.S. Census Bureau, Income, Poverty and Health Insurance Coverage in the United States: 2010—Historical Income Tables*, Table F3: Mean Income Received by Each Fifth and Top 5 Percent of Families; http://stateofworkingamerica.org/charts/real-annual-family-income-growth-by-quintile-1947-79-and-1979-2010/.

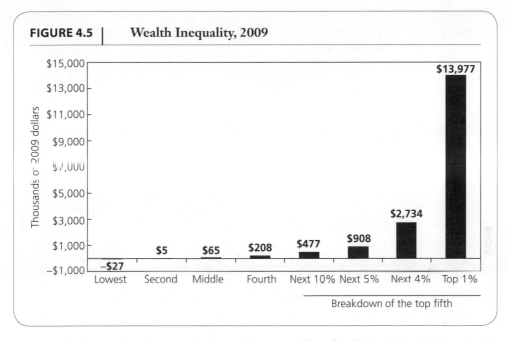

FIGURE 4.5 | **Wealth Inequality, 2009**

Breakdown of the top fifth

Sources: Federal Reserve Board, Survey of Consumer Finances and Flow of Funds; http://stateofworkingamerica.org/charts/average-wealth-by-wealth-class-in-2009/

yachts, while swamping the small craft. As Figure 4.5 shows, in 2009 the top 1 percent had an average net worth of almost $14 million, whereas those in the bottom 20 percent actually had negative net worth (the value of assets minus debt). Whether looking at income or wealth, the United States has levels of economic inequality not seen since the Gilded Age of the nineteenth century or the Roaring Twenties (just before the Great Depression of the 1930s). As Figure 4.6 shows, the share of income going to the top 1 percent increased in most countries between 1990 and 2007. But the United States had the highest share going to the rich and that percentage increased more than in any other country. The United States stands out in its degree of inequality, and the political power of the rich has a lot to do with it.

Defenders of corporate capitalism argue that we should not be concerned with inequality; the only thing we should be concerned with is whether those at the bottom are better off than they were before.[50] From the viewpoint of sheer consumption, those at the bottom of American society have done well. Indeed, the consumption of the poor in American society would place them at the very top in many Third World countries. (In 2008, the World Bank revised its poverty cutoff upward to $1.25 per day.) But poverty is not just a matter of inadequate consumption; it is about living a life with dignity and being able to participate fully in society.[51]

It is more difficult to be poor in an affluent society than in a society where most people are also poor. In American society, the rich bid up the cost of living, especially for housing and education.[52] American life is structured so that almost everyone needs to own a car to be a fully functioning member of society. (According to the American Automobile Association, the average cost of owning a car in the United States was $8,773 in 2011.)[53] Inequality does not just harm those at the bottom, it pulls down the quality of life for everyone. Countries with greater levels of economic inequality have worse outcomes on a wide range of health and

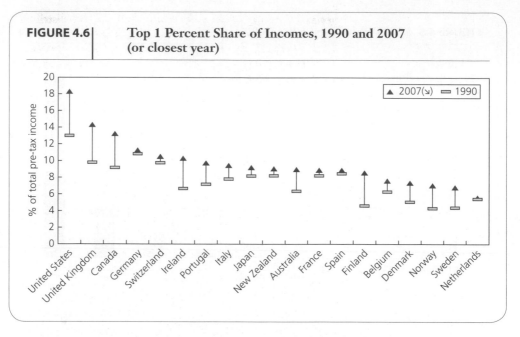

FIGURE 4.6 | Top 1 Percent Share of Incomes, 1990 and 2007 (or closest year)

Source: *An Overview of Growing Income Inequalities in OECD Countries: Main Findings;* accessed at www.oecd.org/els/social/inequality.

social problems, including physical health, mental health, drug abuse, education, imprisonment, obesity, social mobility, trust and community life, violence, teen pregnancies, and child well-being.[54]

Are Inequalities Fair?

Elite democrats do not deny that inequalities are widening, but they argue that inequalities are justified because they represent different levels of ability, skill, work, and risk. Ultimately, you are rewarded based on how much you contribute to production.

The evidence shows, however, that rising inequality cannot be explained by people's contribution to production. The reason why American workers are lagging further behind the rich is not because they are lazy. In fact, Americans work more hours than workers in just about every other industrialized nation—and take much shorter vacations. Since enactment of welfare reform in 1996, welfare rolls have fallen by more than 60 percent. American workers are among the most productive in the world. But, as Figure 4.7 shows, since the late 1970s family incomes have not kept pace with rising productivity. The problem is essentially a political one: How does a society distribute its rewards? Increasingly, in the United States, the answer has more to do with your wealth and power, not with your willingness to work. As Felix Rohatyn, a Wall Street investment banker, put it, "What is occurring is a huge transfer of wealth from lower-skilled middle-class American workers to the owners of capital assets."[55]

Another problem with the productivity explanation of rising inequality is that the people whose incomes have surged the most are not research scientists, brain surgeons, innovative inventors, or others who have played major roles in the innovation that drives the American economy. Much of the wealth has gone to **paper entrepreneurs**, people who reap huge salaries from Wall Street investments, mergers, acquisitions, and other such deals.

FIGURE 4.7 | **Productivity and Real Median Family Income, 1947–2010**

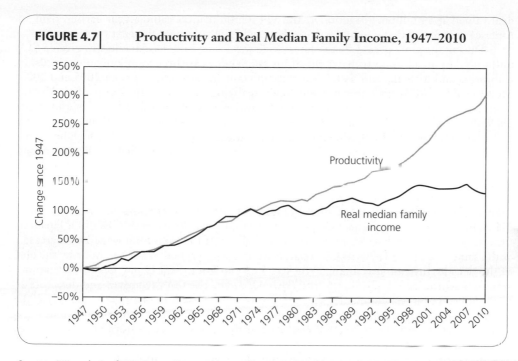

Sources: EPI analysis of U.S. Census Bureau, *Income, Poverty and Health Insurance Coverage in the United States; 2010—Historical Income Tables*, Table F 5: Race and Hispanic Origin of Householder—Families by Median and Mean Income; U.S. Bureau of Labor Statistics, *Productivity—Major Sector Productivity and Costs* Database; http://stateofworkingamerica.org/charts/productivity-and-real-median-family-income-growth-1947-2009/.

One example of the "rewards" of "jobs well done" can be seen in the compensation received by **chief executive officers (CEOs)** of U.S. corporations.

In March 2008, Angelo Mozilo was one of three mortgage industry executives brought before a congressional committee to defend their exorbitant pay packages at a time when the mortgage industry was reeling from the foreclosure crisis.[56] At the time, Mozilo was CEO of Countrywide Financial Corporation, one of the largest home mortgage lenders in the nation. Countrywide was a phenomenally successful corporation based on sales of subprime mortgages, generating a 23,000 percent return on its stock between 1982 and 2003.[57] But this profitability was based on pushing people into loans they could not afford. Congressional figures show that Countrywide lost more than $16 billion in the third and fourth quarters of 2007, and its stock fell 80 percent between February and the end of the year. Approximately 11,000 employees were let go. In July 2008, Countrywide was purchased by Bank of America in an all-stock

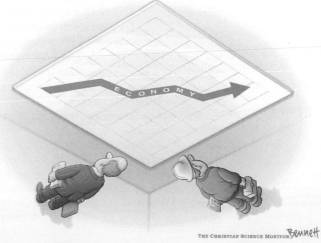

THE CHRISTIAN SCIENCE MONITOR

Clay Bennet/Christian Science Monitor

deal valued at $4 billion, a fraction of the $24 billion market value a year earlier. Bank of America announced that it would cut an additional 7,500 jobs over the next two years.

During the same period that Countrywide was losing billions, Mozilo was given a $1.9 million salary in addition to payment of his annual dues at three swanky country clubs in California and Alabama and $44,454 for use of company aircraft. Between 2005 and 2007, Mozilo sold most of his Countrywide stock, realizing $291.5 million in profits. Mozilo dumped Countrywide stock at the same time he was touting its value to shareholders. In 2009, the Securities and Exchange Commission (SEC) charged Mozillo with insider trading and securities fraud. In 2010, Mozillo reached a settlement with the SEC in which he promised to pay $67.5 million in fines and was banned from serving as an officer or director of any corporation. Given his estimated net worth of $600 million, the fine was nothing more than a slap on the wrist.

CEOs in the United States are paid much more, relative to the average employee, than CEOs in other countries. The average CEO of a large corporation in the United States makes 531 times the pay of the average employee; the average CEO of a Japanese firm makes 10 times what the average worker makes.[58] If the minimum wage had increased at the same rate in the 1990s as CEO pay, it would have reached $25.50 an hour by the end of the decade. Instead, it remained stuck at $5.15 an hour.[59] CEO pay has little relationship to performance. According to the *Financial Times*, the top executives and directors at the twenty-five largest companies that went bankrupt between January 2001 and July 2002 made off with $3.3 billion in compensation. During that same time, their companies were going bankrupt, more than 100,000 workers lost their jobs, and investors lost hundreds of millions of dollars.[60]

How can U.S. companies get away with paying huge salaries to executives who perform poorly? The answer is corporate governance. CEO compensation is determined by corporate boards of directors, based on the advice of "compensation consultants" who are often hired for lucrative contracts by the very same CEOs whose compensation they are recommending. A 2008 study of 22,000 directors found that more than half made over $100,000 a year.[61] The time commitment is minimal—mostly, attending a few meetings a year. For the most part, boards of directors seem happy to rubber-stamp CEO pay packages recommended by compensation consultants. The process for setting CEO compensation is fraught with conflicts of interest—if not outright corruption.

The Political Causes and Effects of Economic Inequalities

Elite democrats believe that the economic and political spheres are, and should be, separated. Popular democrats view them as inextricably connected—and argue that these connections should be democratically controlled. Americans tolerate unequal outcomes in the marketplace, but they oppose economic inequalities that reinforce political equalities.[62] Americans oppose using wealth to acquire political power, especially when that political power is used to acquire more wealth, setting in motion a vicious cycle that violates democratic principles of justice and fairness (Figure 4.8).[63]

The elite democratic tendency to view rising economic inequality as a natural and inevitable outcome of economic processes does not stand up to the facts. We have seen how the failure of labor laws to guarantee the rights of workers to join unions has led to a precipitous drop in the proportion of unionized workers. The weakening of unions is a major cause of widening economic inequality.[64]

Tax policies have also played a major role in widening economic inequality. President George W. Bush's tax cut provided an estimated $477 billion in tax breaks over a 10-year period for the top 1 percent ($34,247 per household per year). By contrast, the bottom

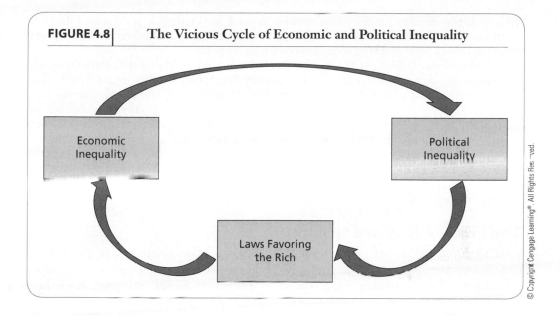

FIGURE 4.8| The Vicious Cycle of Economic and Political Inequality

Economic Inequality

Political Inequality

Laws Favoring the Rich

60 percent of households received an average tax break of only $325 per year.[65] Although polls at the time showed that a majority of voters favored the Bush tax cuts, there was also clearly a great deal of confusion about who would benefit. When offered more egalitarian tax cuts or spending alternatives, a majority favored those over the Bush tax cuts.[66] In fact, the voices of the rich often drown out the voices of the majority in congressional deliberations. Although it is difficult to prove that money buys political power, there is no doubt that it buys political access. One study found that a $6,400 contribution by an interest group buys on average twenty-five minutes of access to the office of a member of Congress; $72,300 buys an hour-long meeting.[67] According to one analysis of Senate roll call voting, "the opinions of millions of ordinary citizens in the bottom third of the income distribution have *no* discernible impact on the behavior of elected representatives."[68]

Economic inequalities generate political inequalities in other ways. The poor do not participate at the same rate that the middle class and the rich do. They lack the money to contribute to campaigns, and most lower-paid workers don't acquire the skills on the job that aid political participation, such as how to run a meeting or find information. The result is what a major study of civic participation called "participatory distortion."[69] As a Task Force of the American Political Science Association concluded, "Citizens with lower or moderate incomes speak with a whisper that is lost on the ears of the inattentive government officials, while the advantaged roar with a clarity and consistency that policymakers readily hear and routinely follow."[70]

Another way economic inequalities disadvantage the poor in the political system is through economic segregation.[71] In most American metropolitan areas, suburbs enact exclusionary zoning regulations to keep out the poor. Zoning laws forbid the construction of apartment buildings, for example, or require single-family homes to be built on large two- or three-acre lots. Poor people, especially minorities, are prevented from moving closer to where the jobs are, thus hurting their job prospects. In addition, the poor are relegated to central cities and inner-ring suburbs with weak tax bases and expensive service needs. As a result, participation in local government is less meaningful because the resources just aren't there.

Rich suburban districts can spend up to twice as much per student as poor school districts. With education being crucial for success in our high-tech economy, these educational inequalities have profound effects on economic inequalities.[72]

Philosophers from Aristotle to Thomas Jefferson have stressed that stark economic inequalities are dangerous to democracy. A healthy democracy needs a strong middle class that can function as a moderating force between the potentially divisive demands of the rich and the poor. Great inequalities undermine social solidarity—the idea that we are all basically in the same boat. Rising inequality makes blatant class legislation—laws that benefit one group at the expense of another—more likely. A huge gap between the rich and the poor makes it possible for the rich to dominate, even buy off, the poor. If the gap between the rich and the poor continues to widen, it is unlikely that even carefully crafted campaign finance reform laws will protect elections from the corrupting influence of concentrated wealth.

The Prism of Race and Gender

Economic inequalities fall particularly hard on women, African Americans, and Latinos (Figure 4.9). Most people in these groups are not poor, but they bear, if for somewhat different reasons, a disproportionate share of poverty's burdens. Moreover, each group lags behind in wage levels, even when they work at jobs comparable to those of white males.

Since the late 1970s, women have made significant wage gains relative to men. In 2010, fulltime working women earned 77 percent of what men earned—up from just 57 percent in 1973.[73] Unfortunately, part of the reason for the reduction in the gap is that men have

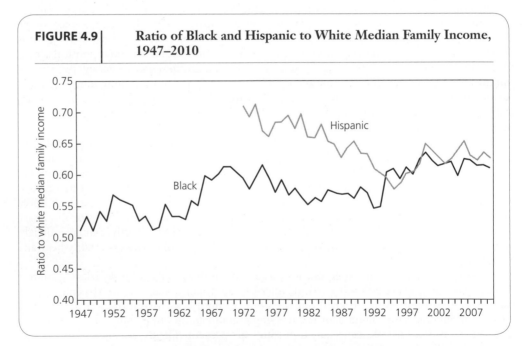

FIGURE 4.9 | **Ratio of Black and Hispanic to White Median Family Income, 1947–2010**

Sources: EPI analysis of U.S. Census Bureau, *Income, Poverty and Health Insurance Coverage in the United States: 2010—Historical Income Tables*, Table F 5: Race and Hispanic Origin of Householder—Families by Median and Mean Income; http://stateofworkingamerica.org/charts/ratio-of-black-and-hispanic-to-white-median-family-income-1947-2010/.

been more vulnerable to layoffs and have seen their earnings stagnate. Black family income improved significantly relative to whites in the 1990s, but when the labor market softened in 2001, the gap widened again. In 2010, black and Hispanic family incomes were still less than two-thirds that of white family income. Hispanic incomes have actually fallen significantly relative to whites in the past thirty years, partly due to the influx of poor immigrants.

What factors account for these economic inequalities? Defenders of corporate capitalism respond that these inequalities fairly reflect differences in education and skill. Besides, economic growth will take care of the problem in the long run. Both explanations are flawed.

Economic growth has not changed the ratio of white to black and Latino earning levels, and a large gap between men and women still remains. Moreover, all three groups have made great strides in educational and skill levels since the 1970s. If skills and education were rewarded equally in the marketplace, then the racial and income gap should be closing for African Americans and Latinos. Instead, it is widening for Latinos and not improving much for blacks.

African Americans have been especially disadvantaged in the marketplace, despite generally rising education and skill levels. For African Americans with college degrees or high school degrees in the 1980s and 1990s, earnings were 17 percent less than for whites with similar education. Working-class blacks have been disproportionately harmed by a number of other factors. The decline in union membership, combined with the downsizing of many manufacturing industries, has caused much pain in the black community. Jobs are moving to the suburbs, but discrimination in housing markets often leaves African Americans stuck in central cities, unable to reach the new jobs. And finally, outright racism persists in the job market. An Urban Institute study sent testers of both races with equal qualifications and similar ages to apply for the same 476 jobs in the Washington, D.C., metro area. Black applicants were rejected more often than whites, and the study concluded that "discrimination against blacks appears to be highest in types of jobs offering the highest wages and future income potential."[74]

Thanks to federal laws and the women's movement, gender inequalities have been significantly reduced, but racial economic inequalities have proven to be surprisingly resistant to change. Racial economic inequalities are especially dangerous in a democracy, because they threaten to create a permanent underclass that is alienated from democratic politics. Since the victories of the civil rights movement (Chapter 11), legal discrimination has largely ended. But left to itself, the market will not redress racial inequities based on centuries of slavery and discrimination. Affirmative policies will be needed to bring African Americans and other minorities into full participation in our democracy.

Rising Economic Insecurity

As we saw earlier in the case of Tommy and Marcia Meyers, many families are only a layoff or a health emergency away from economic free fall. Unfortunately, stories like the Meyerses' are becoming more and more common. Jacob Hacker calls this "the great risk shift."[75] At the same time that the United States has become a more prosperous nation, we have also become a riskier nation. The American economy behaves more and more like a casino: Some people are lucky and become fabulously wealthy but the majority of people struggle to stay afloat. Increasingly, we are becoming a "winner-take-all" society with a "winner-take-all" politics.[76]

The underlying cause of the "great risk shift" is increased income volatility. As Figure 4.10 shows, the chance of a person experiencing a 50 percent or greater income drop in a given year more than doubled, from 7 percent in the 1970s to over 16 percent by

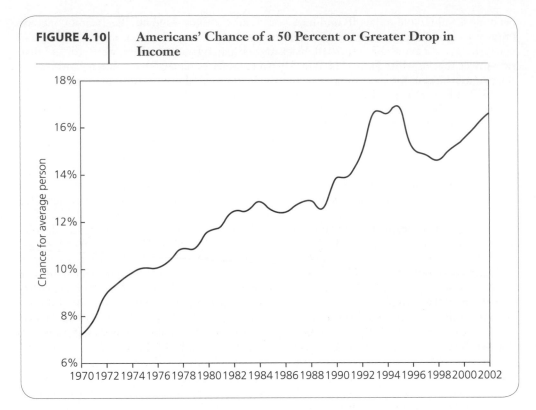

FIGURE 4.10   Americans' Chance of a 50 Percent or Greater Drop in Income

Source: *Panel Study of Income Dynamics.* Results are from a logistic regression predicting drops in household-size-adjusted family income among individuals aged 25–61; Jacob Hacker, *The Great Risk Shift* (New York: Oxford University Press, 2006), p. 31.

2002. If you are less educated or low income, the chances of a 50 percent drop in income are much higher, but rising economic insecurity has affected Americans of all economic classes. The reasons for the increased income volatility are not entirely understood, but globalization, the decline of unions, and increased reliance on outsourcing and part-time workers have played a role. Corporations are less loyal to their employees. A survey of business leaders in the 1980s found that 56 percent agreed with the statement that "employees who are loyal to the company and further its business goals deserve an assurance of continued employment." A decade later the number had dropped to 6 percent.[77]

What is most disturbing is that the consequences of a loss in income have become much more serious. As one author put it, "If you take a fall, the resulting losses can include career, house, saving, pension, and the ability to provide educational and other opportunities for your children."[78] The reason sudden drops in income have become more damaging has largely to do with the erosion of the public and private protections that were previously in place. Since the 1970s, economic elites have argued, successfully, that if society takes care of families that experience trouble, it will create a "moral hazard"—reducing the incentives for them to act responsibly and increasing the likelihood they will get into trouble in the future. Welfare causes poverty, they argue, or health insurance causes people to seek unnecessary health care. The problem with this reasoning is that many of the causes of financial trouble are beyond the control of individuals, and, lacking protections, they can suddenly lose all of the assets they had accumulated over the years.

As part of Franklin Roosevelt's New Deal, the United States enacted a series of programs that protected those who worked from economic insecurity, most prominently the Social Security retirement system and unemployment compensation. They were later supplemented by Medicaid and Medicare, guaranteeing health care for the very poor and the elderly. In addition, private corporations provided lifetime employment for many Americans and guaranteed pension benefits that ensured a comfortable retirement. In the past thirty years, however, the fabric of public and private obligations that protected families from high levels of risk has developed gaping holes. As a result, families are now forced to bear larger and larger risks.

Below are some of the areas where policies of the government and private corporations have contributed to economic insecurity.

1. **Pensions:** In 1980, 62 percent of private-sector workers belonged to defined-benefit retirement plans so that they could count on a certain monthly pension when they retired. By 2005, that number had dropped to 10 percent. Now, 63 percent belong to defined *contribution* plans, which means they know how much they put in each month, but what they get in retirement will depend on how well their investments do.[79] Private pension plans require workers to become shrewd investors. Even Nobel Prize winners in economics, it turns out, have made huge mistakes investing their retirement funds.[80] President Bush wanted to "privatize" Social Security by creating private retirement accounts controlled by each investor. The danger of his proposal, which the public largely rejected, was exposed in the stock market collapse of 2008.

2. **Unemployment Insurance:** Part of the Social Security Act of 1935, unemployment insurance creates a fund that pays people at about 50 percent of their salary for six months. However, workers tend to be unemployed for longer stretches now and it does nothing to provide health insurance, an increasing burden on family budgets. For higher-income workers, unemployment insurance does not come close to 50 percent of their previous salary, and, in 1979, the federal government and most states began taxing benefits. Unemployment insurance does not provide the same protection it once did.

3. **Insurance:** In 1752, Ben Franklin helped to found the Philadelphia Contribution for Insurance Against Loss by Fire so that homeowners who suffered a fire would not be wiped out financially. The Contributionship is still in business today. The basic idea behind insurance is the pooling of risk: If everybody contributes a small amount to a fund, they can be protected in the unlikely event of a loss, such as a fire, accident, or illness. Insurance companies now slice and dice people using sophisticated computer techniques that place people in different risk pools to ensure higher profits. Allstate sorts its auto and home policyholders into 384 categories.[81] At the extreme, such policies undermine the very idea that insurance is a way to spread risk over a wide range of people with different risk levels.

4. **Mortgages:** During the New Deal of the 1930s, the federal government helped create the standard thirty-year, fixed-rate mortgage with a 10 percent to 20 percent down payment, putting homeownership within reach of millions of Americans.[82] As we discussed earlier, deregulation of the mortgage market has led to the creation of new types of mortgages that have been aggressively marketed to people who cannot sustain them. The predictable result has been a rash of foreclosures that have had ruinous effects on families, communities, and governments.

Economic insecurity damages not just individuals but the broader political system. People lose faith in government and withdraw from participation. Communities are disrupted by foreclosures, losing the social capital and trust that is necessary for effective government. The result is an erosion of civil society, the soil needed for democracy to grow and prosper.

The Erosion of Civil Society

Democratic theorists have long recognized that a healthy democracy requires a strong civil society.[83] **Civil society** encompasses the voluntary associations that lie between the private realm of the family and the public sphere of politics. Alexis de Tocqueville, the French democratic theorist who visited the United States in the 1830s, argued that the great strength of American democracy lay precisely in the character of its voluntary associations. Voluntary associations, from food banks to labor unions, from Boys and Girls Clubs to arts associations, act like informal schools, enabling citizens to develop the civic skills that are necessary to participate effectively in a democracy. Civic associations can help to take the rough edges off of American individualism, with its tendency to worship personal wealth and competitiveness. Such associations help people realize that they are part of a community and that a meaningful life is found not in possessions but in building a shared life with others.

Since the days of Tocqueville, Americans have continued to be joiners. A 1990 national survey found that 79 percent of Americans were affiliated with at least one organization. Americans are still more likely to be members of voluntary associations than are citizens in other democratic countries.[84] On the other hand, evidence is mounting that civil society in the United States has deteriorated in the past thirty years. Robert Putnam titled his book on this issue *Bowling Alone* for good reason. Even though Americans are bowling more than ever, because of the rapid decline of bowling leagues, more people are doing it alone rather than as part of a group. Putnam surveyed a wide range of data to document the decline of associations of all types, including the League of Women Voters, which is down 61 percent in its membership rate (actual members per eligible members) since its peak in 1965, and parent-teacher associations (PTAs), down 60 percent from their peak in 1966.[85]

The decline of civil society is a major cause of the decline in civic participation. Putnam documents that despite increases in education, since peaking in the 1960s Americans have become 15 percent to 20 percent less likely to be interested in politics, 35 percent less likely to attend public meetings, and roughly 40 percent less engaged in party politics.[86]

The deterioration in civil society is clearly related to changes in the economy. Putnam shows that there is a strong correlation between equality of income in states and an index of social capital. States that are more egalitarian have stronger civil societies, with citizens joining more associations and participating more in politics.[87] Ironically, the associational life of some people is harmed by having too little work, while for others the problem is too much work. The poor are increasingly concentrated with other poor people in so-called "underclass" neighborhoods that suffer from severe social problems, including high crime rates, drug abuse, and family breakdown. Lacking strong institutions and voluntary associations, underclass residents experience social isolation and deep feelings of powerlessness and despair.

Economic pressures to withdraw from associational life affect the working poor as well. In general, the poor are underrepresented in voluntary associations. Only 52 percent of the poor are involved in a nonpolitical organization, compared to 89 percent of the rich.[88] The economic pressure to work overtime and "moonlight" eats up the time available for civic commitments.

The middle class has not emerged unscathed from the corrosive effects of the economy on civil society. During the 1950s and 1960s, middle-class households didn't generally suffer from declining wages, sudden drops in income, or constant insecurities about how to balance work life with raising a family and participating in civic life. Many families could achieve homeowner status with only one wage earner, usually the male. Most of all, most families could expect to have stable job prospects and thus could make solid plans for their children's future. Yet in the last thirty years, middle-class insecurity has risen on all these counts. In the past, women who stayed home or worked part-time were a backbone of civic organizations, such as the League of Women Voters and the school PTA. Since the 1960s, many women have sought equality with men by entering the workforce and building their own professional careers. But for many women, working full-time was not a choice but an economic necessity. Survey research shows that three-quarters of women who work full-time do so to meet financial pressures, not to gain personal fulfillment. And it is precisely women who work full-time out of necessity (the largest, fastest-growing group) who are least inclined to be involved in the community.[89]

Indeed, the economic pressures on free time have negatively affected participation in civil society for all classes, even those at the top. A main culprit is the work demands of "lean and mean" corporations. In 2004, the average American middle-income family with children was working 539 more hours, or 13.5 more full-time weeks of work, than in 1979.[90] Because their husbands still do relatively little of the housework, employed mothers average about 65 hours of work a week on the job and at home.[91] With this kind of harried schedule, it is not surprising that many women have withdrawn from participation in voluntary associations.

The decline of civil society has been especially severe among the young. A survey has been conducted each year since 1966 of college freshmen, documenting declining interest in politics and community involvement. Taken just before the hotly contested 2004 presidential election, the survey reported that 34.3 percent of freshmen think it is important or essential to "keep up-to-date with political affairs." This marks a substantial increase from the low point in 2000 at 28.1 percent, but it is still way behind the high point in 1966 when 60.3 percent said it was important to keep up with political affairs.[92] Clearly, a major cause of the declining interest in politics has been a rise of materialistic values, with the number of freshmen reporting that "being very well off financially" was either "essential" or "very important" soaring since the 1960s.

Consumerism has permeated American life to the extent that it is driving out social and political commitments. Americans are exposed to thousands of commercial messages every day.[93] Have you seen any ads lately trying to persuade you to participate in local politics as a way to become more prestigious or sexually attractive? Americans now spend three to four times as much time shopping than do Western Europeans. As Cornel West put it, "The fundamentalism of the market puts a premium on the activities of buying and selling, consuming and taking, promoting and advertising, and devalues community, compassionate charity, and improvement of the general quality of life."[94]

Finally, it is not just that civic commitments and involvements have declined but that the organizations have changed as well. Tocqueville was enamored with voluntary associations because they had the potential to bridge the divides between citizens of different regions, ethnicities, and occupational backgrounds. But the modern political economy divides people into segregated groups that have little interaction with one another. Increasingly, the professional class is less oriented to membership in local associations and more oriented to national networks through which they can advance their careers.[95] We lack not just community involvements, but, in particular, community involvements that bridge the economic, racial, and religious divisions that bedevil American society.

New Reform

New Reform New Reform New Reform New Reform New Reform

Individual Development Accounts

In 1991, Michael Sherraden published a path-breaking book arguing that we should look at poverty not just in terms of income but also in terms of assets. The research shows that ownership of assets makes a difference in the lives of the poor. Owning assets makes people more likely to plan for the future, to take care of their property, to have healthy relationships, and to participate more politically and civically.

Asset poverty is widespread in the United States. Defined as not having enough savings for the family to survive at the poverty level with no outside source of income for three months, more than half of all families with children were "asset poor" in 2007. In 2009, the bottom 20 percent of households actually had negative assets. By contrast, that same year the top 1 percent averaged $14 million in assets.

Sherraden recommended what he called Individual Development Accounts (IDAs), which would provide a match, for example, $2 for every $1 a poor person saved. These monies could then be used for specific purposes, such as buying a home, going to college, or starting a business. There are now more than 83,000 IDAs in the United States, run by hundreds of community-based organizations. Thirty-three states have IDA programs and the federal government has demonstration programs to provide funding for IDAs.

The "I Can Save" program in St. Louis, Missouri, provided an initial deposit of $500 and then a one-to-one match for all dollars saved by elementary school children from poor families. After four years, the average child had saved $377 for a total accumulation of more than $1,200. The money could be used for college. Research has shown that children who have savings are more likely to work hard in school and plan for a college education.

Asset building is catching on as a strategy to attack poverty. Some have gone even further and recommended that every young person receive an $80,000 "stake" that they could use like an IDA. Expensive as this would be, it would also, advocates argue, provide young people a stake in society, which would motivate them to work hard to succeed. So far, the federal support of IDAs has been paltry. Do you think the federal government should fund a program to give every child a stake or to provide matching funds for savings by the poor? Do you think direct deposits of taxpayers' money into the bank accounts of the poor balance out tax expenditures for upper-income households or are they an unfair giveaway?

Rising economic inequality is not inevitable; something can be done about it. Popular democrats agree with the old saying that money is like manure: If you let it pile up in one place, it stinks to high heaven, but if you spread it around, it makes things grow.

Sources: Michael Sherraden, *Assets and the Poor: A New American Welfare Policy* (Armonk, NY, M. E. Sharpe, 1991); Bruce A. Ackerman and Anne Alstott, *The Stakeholder Society* (New Haven, CT, Yale University Press, 1999); Center for Economic Development, "Individual Development Accounts: Providing Opportunity to Build Assets" (January 2007); Yumiko Aratani and Michelle Chau, *Asset Poverty and Debt Among Families with Children*, National Center for Children in Poverty (February 2010).

Conclusion: Choosing Democracy and Prosperity

Elite democrats would have us believe that a prosperous economy requires a limited democracy. Democratic decision making is slow and inefficient. Corporations should be run in a top-down fashion by managerial elites, held accountable by consumers, who vote with their dollars on which products and services they want. Ever since James Madison warned in *Federalist No. 10* that "pure democracy" was incompatible with the "rights of property," elite democrats have warned that too much democracy could lead to the leveling of wealth and income, eliminating the incentives to work hard and invest that fuel economic prosperity.

Throughout American history, ordinary citizens have ignored these warnings, struggling to shape the political economy to democratic ends. During the Progressive era in the early twentieth century, popular democrats succeeded in passing the 26th Amendment to the Constitution (1913), which allowed for a progressive income tax and a tax on large estates (1916). During the New Deal of the 1930s, the right of workers to join a union was safeguarded by the Wagner Act (1935), and that same year unemployment insurance and Social Security were created to protect workers against loss of income due to layoffs and old age. In the 1960s and 1970s, two important institutions were created to protect the environment and worker safety: the Environmental Protection Agency (1970) and the Occupational Safety and Health Administration (1971).

In each case, elites predicted dire economic consequences if these popular democratic reforms were passed. In fact, there is no convincing evidence that these reforms significantly harmed the economy's ability to grow or to produce new wealth. Indeed, greater equality and economic security benefit the economy by stimulating consumer spending and giving workers more of a stake in society, increasing their motivation to work. There is no steep trade-off between equality and economic efficiency and growth. We can have *both*.

Reader's Guide

Critical Thinking Questions

1. Extreme economic inequalities are clearly a problem in a democracy, but where do we draw the line between acceptable and unacceptable levels of inequality?

2. Do you believe in progressive taxation; that is, should we tax the rich at a higher rate than the middle class and the poor?

3. "If you work hard and play by the rules, *anyone*, regardless of race, religion, education, or income, can achieve the American Dream." Agree or disagree. Be sure to define what you mean by the American Dream.

4. Do you think you will be better or worse off economically than your parents? What are the main policies today that affect the opportunities of young people to get ahead?

Key Word Definition

corporate welfare   Government subsidies, tax breaks, and tax expenditures that directly aid corporations.

corporate capitalism   The developed or advanced stage of capitalism in which large corporations dominate the means of production and often the political system as well.

privileged position of business   The idea that business has the advantage in most political disputes because of its power to threaten "disinvestment" when government proposes regulations and/or taxation.

subprime mortgage lenders   Financial institutions that give loans at higher interest rates than conventional mortgages because the borrower is viewed as higher risk.

mortgage-backed securities   Collections of mortgages that are bundled together and sold to investors.

shareholder democracy   The idea that corporations are held accountable to the public through the power of shareholders over corporate policies.

economic planning   Long-term decisions by either government or corporations about what and how much to produce.

World Trade Organization (WTO)   An international organization with 153 members that promotes international trade and enforces trade agreements.

North American Free Trade Agreement (NAFTA)   An agreement between the United States, Canada, and Mexico designed to reduce barriers to trade between the countries.

Wagner Act   A federal law passed in 1935 that protects the right of American workers to join a union.

wealth inequality   The gap in net worth among various population groups.

paper entrepreneur   A person who makes his or her fortune by managing mergers or speculating in stocks.

chief executive officer (CEO)   The person, hired by the board of directors, who runs the day-to-day affairs of a private corporation.

civil society   The public space between the formal realm of government and the private realm of the family in which people form voluntary ties to each other.

asset poverty   The lack of enough savings for a family to survive at the poverty level with no outside source of income for three months.

5

Public Opinion and Political Culture: Can the People Be Fooled?

Ordinary people's beliefs and expressions about politics and policies are called **public opinion**. Today, public opinion seems to reign supreme. Dozens of polling organizations investigate and report minute changes in the public's mood, while social movements and interest groups compete to gain its attention and support. Political candidates and their organizations track it, while think tanks, lobbyists, and advertisers try to shape it. In a democratic society where the public's thoughts and beliefs should matter, all this is hardly surprising. Yet this apparent respect for public opinion may disguise deep elite skepticism about the public's capacity to understand, reason, or judge public policies.

Beneath the constant monitoring of opinion may be the worry that unless the public is educated in the right way, and carefully contained, it might surge out of control. From the perspectives of some elites in politics, business, and intellectual life, the public may be ignorant, yet potentially passionate. This, they fear, is a dangerous combination.

Public Opinion and the Democratic Debate

More than two centuries ago, Alexander Hamilton is reputed to have called public opinion "a great beast" prone to "sudden breezes of passion." In the 1920s, the first systematic student of public opinion, Walter Lippmann, observed that the public was "a bewildered herd" driven by "manufactured images." More recently, one prominent student of contemporary public opinion argued that on many important questions the public is so ill-informed and indifferent that opinions might just as well be decided by a coin toss.[1]

These days, elite doubts about the public are rarely voiced so bluntly. Still, skeptics have provided evidence to validate their doubts. Despite rising levels of formal education, most Americans are ignorant of key political facts. Although 85 percent of Americans today know what Twitter is, almost three-quarters cannot identify the Chief Justice of the United States Supreme Court, and most cannot name their representative in the House of Representatives. The public's knowledge is even worse when it comes to foreign affairs: In 2004, six in ten Americans *still* believed that Iraq either had weapons of mass destruction (WMD) or had a major program to develop them.[2] Another problem skeptics point to is that public opinion is sometimes volatile, inconsistent, or even irrational. The billions of dollars spent to influence, test, and understand public opinion may be better used, from this elite perspective, to manage and control what elites see as its potential excesses. Political scientist Ben Ginsberg calls this modern apparatus of public opinion management a huge effort to create a "captive public."[3]

But *is* the public "captive" and is public opinion as ignorant and volatile as some claim? According to popular democratic views of public opinion, the answer is no. Jefferson saw public opinion as the fount of republican government. Lincoln's famous belief that "you can fool some of the people all of the time, and all of the people some of the time, but you cannot fool all the people all the time" lives on.

In the 1920s, philosopher John Dewey argued that it was government and corporate propaganda—not ordinary people—that posed a problem for democracy. Granted, most people would have a difficult time separating fact from fiction when the media, government, and corporations were all centralized and information became an elite dominated resource. Yet, Dewey believed, vigorous democratic debate among the public could be the antidote to private and public propaganda. After all, ordinary people had to live with the consequences of war, inequality, and injustice in a way that expert elites usually didn't. Therefore, the challenge for democrats would be to build strong communities and free spaces, a vibrant civil society, where people could talk, debate, learn, interact, and thereby fulfill the promise of democracy. For popular democrats like Dewey, public opinion should be freed to do more, not less.[4]

The Vietnam War era provides one of the best examples of the emergence of active and informed public opinion. Although during the early stages of U.S. troop involvement, popular majorities supported U.S. engagement as the patriotic thing to do, the initial drive to go to war came from elites rather than the public. It was a top-down process of elites winning public support, often by depriving the public of essential facts about the nature of U.S. involvement.

As the war escalated, public opposition and anti-war protest grew in tandem with new facts that revealed a pattern of government dishonesty and propaganda about the war's origins, consequences, and results. As public opinion matured, and as media coverage expanded beyond cheerleading for the government, the war became the subject of a protracted national debate. Many were slow to respond, of course, and the war dragged on for years. Yet, in popular democratic terms, public opinion played a significant role in exposing, and then curbing, elite claims about what was at stake in Vietnam and about the war's progress.[5]

American flag and American money being used as protest symbols at an Occupy Wall Street demonstration in New York. What is the protestor trying to say? Is it effective?

The democratic debate about public opinion raises fundamental questions about democracy itself. If the public is as ignorant, fickle, and dangerous as elite democrats believe, then control of public opinion by "responsible" elites

David Grossman/Alamy

in government, corporations, and the media can be justified. If, on the contrary, these same elites distort democratic politics through propaganda, manipulation, and even intimidation, then popular democratic ideas stressing the independent and intelligent democratic role of public opinion can be supported.

Is the public as ignorant and irrational as many elite democrats believe? Or is there democratic promise in a public opinion that has more information and is freer, probing, and more deliberative as popular democrats hope?

American Political Culture

As a multiracial, multicultural nation of immigrants, Native Americans, and descendants of slaves, the United States' survival as a nation depends on the quality and scope of its democratic values. Common values of toleration, mutual respect, and national community must work to forge bonds among people of diverse races, national origins, religions, cultures, and political views. When these fail, the darkest dimensions of American politics emerge, whether in the form of slavery and racism, the subjugation of Native Americans, or the demonization of nonconformist dissent as unpatriotic and "un-American." Alternatively, the brightest moments in U.S. history are those times when more and more people become included in the expanding democratic promise of American life.

What do citizens today understand about what it means to be an American? The set of common rituals, stories, symbols, and habits that Americans share might be called American **political culture**. Our democratic political culture is not just a set of abstract values. It is more like a common political language that we speak with a set of reference points that we share—even when we otherwise profoundly disagree. Table 5.1 details some of the essential elements of our common political culture.

Patriotism, Democracy, and the National Community

Democracy became an honored idea in the United States soon after the founding debates. Even in periods of crisis and upheaval, such as the 1960s, public support for the basic forms and procedures of democratic government has remained extremely strong and widespread. Today, the common language of democracy still stands as the essence of American political culture.

The vast majority of Americans agree, at least in the abstract, on many fundamental tenets of democratic life. More than nine in ten citizens support the ideas that public officials should be chosen by majority vote in regular elections, and that minorities and individuals maintain rights to freedom of speech, press, expression, and religion. The idea that defects in the American system should and can be changed through legal processes and not through violence is also very strongly supported. Not surprisingly, so are the Constitution and the Bill of Rights.

Democratic values are accompanied by extraordinarily high and resilient levels of patriotism and pride. Even during uncertain economic times in 2012, nearly nine in ten Americans said they were very patriotic—a level identical to that of the far rosier days of the late 1980s. Although pride in America cuts across all demographic, regional, and political lines, its perception can vary. When asked if they are more patriotic when compared to other Americans, men, whites, and especially Republicans, older Americans, and Tea Party supporters were somewhat more likely to answer yes.

A consensus also exists on the "special" character of U.S. history, society, and institutions in comparison with other nations, and on an American "destiny" to set a democratic example while helping expand freedom in the world. Often referred to as **American Exceptionalism**,

---

Table 5.1   The Essentials of American Political Culture

At Least Eight in Ten Americans Agree to the Following:

1. Free speech should be granted to everyone regardless of how unpopular their opinions are.
2. A party that wins an election should respect the rights of opposition parties to criticize the way things are being run.
3. Forcing people to testify against themselves in court is never justified.
4. Our elected officials would badly misuse their power if they weren't watched and guided by the voters.
5. A minority family that wants to move into a particular neighborhood shouldn't have to check with anyone before doing so.
6. Our society should do what is necessary to make sure that everyone has an equal opportunity to succeed.
7. Children should have equal educational opportunities.

Are Some Values Changing?

Religious Freedom: In 1984, McClosky and Zaller reported that over eight in ten agreed with the statement: "Freedom to worship as one pleases applies to all religious groups, regardless of how extreme their beliefs are." Asking a similar question in 2011, the First Amendment Center found that only 67 percent agreed, with 22 percent saying it does not "apply to religious groups that most people would consider extreme or fringe."

The Economic System: In 1984, McClosky and Zaller reported that eight in ten agreed that "The private enterprise system is generally a fair and efficient system." And in 2012, Gallup, indeed, found that nine in ten Americans had a positive view of free enterprise; support for "capitalism" was lower at 61 percent. When it asked about "socialism," a surprising 39 percent responded positively, while 54 percent viewed it negatively. A Rasmussen poll that year found that 49 percent of likely voters thought the American economy was *unfair*, while 47 percent called it "fair," including only 9 percent who believed it to be "very fair."

Sources: Adapted and reprinted by permission of the publisher from *American Ethos* by Herbert McCloskey and John Zaller (Cambridge, MA: Harvard University Press). Copyright © 1984 by the Twentieth Century Fund; Survey by The Freedom Forum and Center for Survey Research and Analysis, University of Connecticut, June 12–July 5, 2002. Survey by Pew Research Center for the People & the Press and Princeton Survey Research Associates International, December 12–January 9, 2007. Survey by The First Amendment Center, "State of the First Amendment 2011: Final Annotated Survey," www.firstamendmentcenter.org/sofa; Frank Newport, "Democrats, Republicans Diverge on Capitalism, Federal Gov't," Gallup, November 29, 2012, www.gallup.com/poll/158978/democrats-republicans-diverge-capitalism-federal-gov.aspx. "47% Say U.S. Economy is Fair, 49% Disagree," Rasmussen Reports, December 12, 2012, www.rasmussenreports.com/public_content/politics/general_politics/december_2012.

this set of beliefs is basic to American political culture. Eight in ten Americans, for example, think our history and constitution give our nation "a unique character that makes it the greatest country in the world." Feelings of general *cultural* superiority may be declining, however, with only half of Americans now viewing their culture as "superior to others," down 10 percent from ten years ago and lowest among the young.

Nevertheless there is little doubt that the national community's image is still strongly positive. It is often experienced symbolically as reverence for the flag—nearly six in ten Americans display it at home, in their office, or on their car—for our great public buildings such as the Capitol, Washington Monument, and Lincoln Memorial, and for U.S. holidays

CAGLECARTOONS.COM

#1 MANNED SPACE FLIGHT

#1 AUTO MANUFACTURING

#1 MASS TRANSIT INFRASTRUCTURE

#1 ENERGY TECH

#1 EDUCATION

#1 HEALTH CARE

#1 AIRLINE MANUFACTURING

Prigge 11-7
www.MILTPRIGGE.com

Milt Prigge/Caglecartoons.com

What is this cartoon trying to say about American Exceptionalism?

such as the Fourth of July and Thanksgiving. Out of thirty-three countries, ranked by pride in 2004, the United States came in first (tied with Venezuela), although there may be some evidence that its self-image in comparison to others may have slipped a little since then.[6]

Throughout American history, some elites and populist demagogues have often sought to use patriotism as a way of repressing dissent as "un-American." However, both support for, and dissent from, the status quo are equal parts of the American tradition. Professions of faith in democracy and patriotism can be found all across the political spectrum.

Individualism and Liberty

Since the beginning of the republic, foreign observers have noted that American culture is distinctively individualistic. Individuals are thought to be the authors of their own destinies, endowed with the capacity—even the duty—to define beliefs, thoughts, and aspirations for themselves. Where some other nations most highly value the society in general or even the national state, pride of place in America is reserved for the individual.

Individualism is often associated with the idea that U.S. citizens are born with rights to liberty and freedom. No institution, and especially not government, can arbitrarily command us to think, speak, or act against our will. Therefore, American political culture favors limits on government power. Government use of power must follow strict procedures and be only for legitimate purposes such as protecting the rights and security of others. Public support for freedom and liberty, especially of speech and religion, is virtually universal in surveys taken since the 1930s.

To whom should the rights of liberty extend? The idea that all "men" are created equal is as old as the Declaration of Independence. That promise has taken years to fulfill, and there is still some more work to do. Perhaps there will always be more to do as our ideas about freedom and rights develop further. Nevertheless, when it comes to the basic ideas of legal and political equality—to civil and political rights such as the right to vote in fair and free elections, to free speech, to freedom of association, to a fair trial—Americans strongly believe that all citizens should be treated in the same way before the law. They also believe that such basic human rights should be available to everyone across the globe.[7]

Community: A Country of Joiners

Although Americans believe in individualism, they also value community. Even in the 1830s, the French aristocrat Alexis de Tocqueville wrote that American individualists tempered their isolation by joining numerous associations and groups. Today, when Americans care for sick relatives, work with others on a common project, vote, or attend a demonstration they are showing their willingness as individuals to come together for a larger purpose.

Although most Americans no longer live in small towns, they still value the face-to-face relationships among family and friends to be found in them. That's why the New England town meeting remains an icon of American democracy, and why, in spite of modern pressures, and mobility, many Americans try to reproduce neighborhood virtues in their cities and suburbs.

One way they do so is through voluntary participation in civic associations of many types and purposes. Another is to participate in religious worship and affiliated activities. Organized religion and churchgoing remain more popular in America than in other rich countries, as do associations that help the needy, aid local schools, or organize community events such as youth sports leagues and community cleanups. Americans also join groups of a more self-interested nature. State and national clubs and associations that bring together people of common lifestyles, political beliefs, or economic interests are more common in the United States than elsewhere. Thus, even in a country that highly prizes liberty, more than eight in ten Americans have said that the pursuit of the public good should be of equal or greater priority than individual freedom alone. Overall, Americans still think of themselves as a nation of participants and joiners.[8]

However, some believe this tradition of participation is now in great jeopardy. Robert Putnam gives the whimsical example of people "bowling alone" rather than in leagues in spite of the fact that they go "bowling today more than ever before." His study suggests that fewer people now are joining associations, clubs, and organizations than they once did. As a result, they are missing "social interactions and even occasionally civic conversations" that are very important to civic life, community, and democracy.[9] Other analysts raise a different concern about community. They contend that many citizens now live in "gated communities"—some estimates put the figure at one in ten occupied U.S. households—perhaps trying to separate themselves from the broader public and the problems they perceive to exist there.[10] Finally, some analysts find that although people often express preference for diversity, there is evidence that American communities are becoming more politically and economically homogeneous than even several decades ago. Whether this clustering is a result of conscious choices or demographic trends or some combination of the two is harder to tell.[11]

These sets of problems, however, may be less indicative of the diminished power of community as an ideal than they are of pressures against achieving community, given changes in culture and technology, and the transformation of our economy (see Chapter 4). The explosion of social and even political networking on the Internet suggests that the quest for community continues, and that it may be taking unanticipated forms.

Political and Economic Equality

Not surprisingly, a culture that values individualism is also inclined to have generally favorable beliefs about private property, especially if it is acquired through individual work and effort. Yet favorable views of property ownership are associated with the broader social and political goals that it supposedly helps to further. Thomas Jefferson believed, for example, that a nation of independent farmers would be the kind best able to resist arbitrary authority, and Alexander Hamilton believed that property ownership would build the nation's power and wealth. Today, property ownership, especially in moderate amounts, is still seen both as a badge of achievement and a mark of character. Even most Americans who own neither a home nor a business seem to share in the political culture of property ownership—they aspire to own their own homes or to run their own businesses, even though many have difficulty doing either, especially as home ownership has become more difficult in recent years.

Most Americans rank small-business entrepreneurs as one of the most respected groups in U.S. society. Fully three quarters of Americans—Republicans, Democrats, and Independents alike—believe that small businesses have a positive impact on the country.

Widespread cultural support for private property doesn't mean, however, that most Americans favor large gaps in wealth or income. Neither does the public simply accept all practices and consequences of the corporate economy. While a majority of Americans think "Wall Street makes an important contribution to the American economy," roughly three-quarters believe "there is too much power concentrated in the hands of a few big companies," and Wall Street "only cares about making money for itself." In fact, in some ways strong belief in private property ownership is accompanied by ideas that ownership should be spread throughout the population and not concentrated in a few hands: Everyone should have *some* property, perhaps the way small business owners do, but no one should have so much that it deprives others of the chance to get their fair share too. Still, in comparison with the views of people in other wealthy countries, Americans are remarkable for how little they believe in **equality of condition**—distributing income and wealth so that nobody is either very rich or very poor. Instead, Americans generally support the idea of **equality of opportunity**—all people should begin their lives with an equal chance to succeed or fail on their own merits.

However, equality of opportunity can mean very different things to different people. For some, it means simply creating the legal right to compete without discrimination. For others, it *also* means that government should help make the start of the race in life as fair as possible so that success is determined by an individual's merit alone.[12]

Interpreting Divides within the Political Culture

Americans may not know all the issues or all the players involved in public affairs, but they do share a common vocabulary of political culture. This shared heritage helps protect the republic during times of stress. When it comes to the basics of political culture, the consensus among Americans is solid, especially when compared to some other nations. Faced with a presidential election as disputed as the one in 2000, decided by an ideologically divided Supreme Court, or faced with elections as divisive as those in 2004, 2008, and especially 2012, other democracies might have plunged into serious turmoil. Here the norms were strong enough to withstand bitter divisions and afford the winners sufficient legitimacy to govern.

Political Polarization

Although we share a common belief in democracy, we don't all interpret our political heritage in the same way. In fact, U.S. history has been filled with periods of conflict and division, underscoring the fragility even of American political life. We may be in one such period now. In an exhaustive study of **political polarization** the Pew Research Center concluded that over the last twenty-five years "and particularly over just the past decade—the country has experienced a stark increase in partisan polarization"—a growing gap between a more conservative Republican party and a more liberal Democratic party.[13]

What is striking about the Pew study, however, is it suggests that, except for becoming more liberal on issues such as race, the rights of women and their roles in the family, and the rights of homosexuals, and more skeptical regarding the effectiveness of government, American values are pretty much the same now as they were back in 1987. What has changed is how differences of opinion now distribute themselves. Today, more than at any time in the Pew study, people with a cohesive set of ideas on a broad range of issues are likely to wind up in the same political party. Because each party is more homogeneous than before, the differences between Republicans and Democrats is at its widest point in memory. The views and values of Americans, however, haven't changed nearly as much.[14]

Civil Liberties and Political Tolerance

One of the most important sets of values in a democracy is that regarding civil liberties and political tolerance. Ordinary people may profess support for these values in the abstract, but what about in practice?

There is a lot of evidence that Americans today are more tolerant of unpopular ideas and groups than in the past. Over the last six decades or so, however, some studies have also found that rhetorical support for civil liberties doesn't always translate into popular toleration for disfavored cultural, racial, and political minorities at particular points in time. These studies conclude that ordinary Americans are intolerant of people who are culturally, politically, and racially different. In contrast, highly educated and affluent people are said to be more tolerant, expressing much firmer support of the Bill of Rights and its guarantee of free speech, religion, and nonconformity. In political science, the ironic notion that the uneducated masses are quite authoritarian, whereas elites are the real defenders of democratic values, is part of a concept that has been labeled **democratic elitism**.

Public intolerance is generally strongest when there is a perceived threat to security or to cherished beliefs. It seemed to run particularly high at the beginning of the Cold War, the so-called McCarthy era of the late 1940s and early 1950s. One study conducted during that era found levels of popular support of only 38 percent for freedom of speech for atheists and only 28 percent for Communists. Only 6 percent believed that Communists should be allowed to teach in colleges (see Table 5.2). Again, support for freedom of speech rose proportionately with level of education: Among "opinion leaders," levels of toleration were almost half again as high as they were for those with only high school diplomas.[15]

It is true that elites often tell pollsters that they are tolerant, whereas a higher proportion of ordinary citizens say they are willing to restrict the speech of certain groups. Yet in practice, ordinary people have not been the instigators or participants in most of the acts of recent political repression. Even during the McCarthy era hysteria of the early 1950s, surveys revealed that the public was not as concerned about Communism in the United States as government leaders were. In an important study, political scientist James Gibson found no evidence that the mass public favored repression of American Communists. Rather, Gibson discovered that political elites in state governments were likely to push repressive legislation even when they weren't urged to do so by the public.[16]

A similar pattern was evident in the 1960s and 1970s. At that time, the federal government and some state and local political agencies initiated secret plans of repression against antiwar activists, the Black Panthers, and the Native American movement. The COINTELPRO (short for Counter-Intelligence and Propaganda) program during the Nixon years deployed federal agents from the FBI and CIA as plants in numerous political organizations. All of these operations were conducted secretly. They were neither initiated nor caused by an authoritarian majority. In fact, public opinion polls taken at the time recorded widespread public opposition to such measures when they were revealed.[17]

What about the public's reaction to measures taken after the 9/11 terrorist attacks on the United States? After September 11, 2001, the Bush administration and Congress passed a number of measures, including the USA Patriot Act, giving new authority to various government agencies, and providing guarantees of secrecy for their actions.

Under the USA Patriot Act, the FBI can secretly monitor both Internet communications and library records. It can also secretly search homes without immediately notifying the occupants that it has done so, a practice referred to as "sneak and peek," if they are suspected of terrorist activity. The Bush administration also proclaimed that citizens suspected of terrorist acts could be held without access to counsel and without charges, and that noncitizens could be held indefinitely if they are suspected of aiding terrorism. It created a new category—"enemy combatants"—under which it held hundreds of prisoners in Guantanamo Bay, Cuba, and elsewhere without charge or trial and, initially, without access to legal counsel. And, most notably, it authorized the use of torture, by claiming that the Geneva Conventions did not apply to the "war on terrorism." Through the "extraordinary rendition" program, the CIA whisked away uncharged "suspects" to friendly countries such as Egypt and Jordan for interrogations, knowing full well that such countries would torture these suspects, out of sight, and in ways that clearly violate U.S. law. Some of these measures, most especially the treatment of prisoners at Abu Ghraib prison in Iraq, were deeply embarrassing, and a few were rebuffed by the Supreme Court. President Obama has since renounced torture, although he decided not to hold legally accountable those responsible for it, and has continued some provisions of the Patriot Act that were set to expire in 2011. When he signed the National Defense Authorization Act of 2012, he condemned the power of indefinite military detention of citizens given to him in it. However, his administration has defended this prerogative in court even after it was ruled unconstitutional in U.S. federal district court. How has public opinion, reacted to these questionable practices?

Initially after 9/11, public opinion provided wide support for government "antiterrorism" measures. Respondents claimed they were willing to give up many civil liberties to prevent future terrorist acts. But over time, this support diminished. By 2003, a slim majority opposed the preceding provisions of the USA Patriot Act, and eight in ten opposed the idea that Americans detained under suspicion of terrorist acts should have no right to legal counsel or a speedy trial. When it came to torture at Abu Ghraib prison in Iraq or elsewhere, the public had turned against the government position. A majority blamed government higher-ups for the torture scandals at Abu Ghraib, and an overwhelming 92 percent said that detainees—"illegal combatants" in the Bush administration's terms—had a right to a hearing and access to inspection of their condition by the Red Cross.[18]

Two lessons can be learned from these experiences. First, during crisis periods elites have unrivaled ability to shape public opinion. But once citizens are more fully informed and have a chance to discuss diverse points of view, they are in a better position to shape their opinions for themselves.

Table 5.2 shows that Americans are still somewhat divided about the rights of specific political and cultural minorities, yet it also reveals growing and, in many cases, strong support for increased tolerance since the 1950s. The most striking example of this, although not in this table, is the changing attitude toward gay marriage: In 2012, for the first time, support for marriage equality exceeded opposition, a dramatic change from even four years earlier. Support was far from uniform, however—it was weakest in the south, and among conservatives, evangelicals, and older Americans.

Hostility toward immigrants that accompanied 9/11 also has dissipated, in spite of heated debate in recent years over illegal immigration. Attitudes are complex, and predictably more negative toward illegal than legal immigrants. A majority of Americans support the provision of the 2010 Arizona immigration law (a provision upheld by the Supreme Court in June 2012) requiring that police, when they suspect people they stop or arrest are in the

Table 5.2 Public Tolerance for Advocates of Unpopular Ideas, 1954–2010						
	1954	*1972*	*1998*	*2002*	*2006*	*2010*
Person Should Be Allowed to Make a Speech						
An admitted communist	28	52	67	69	68	64
Someone against churches and religion	38	65	75	77	78	77
Admitted homosexual	*	62	81	83	82	86
Someone who believes that blacks are genetically inferior	*	61	62	63	62	59
Person Should Be Allowed to Teach in College						
An admitted communist	6	39	57	60	60	61
Someone against churches and religion	12	40	58	60	61	62
Admitted homosexual	*	50	74	78	78	84
Someone who believes that blacks are genetically inferior	*	41	46	52	47	49
Person's Book Should Remain in Library						
An admitted communist	29	53	67	69	69	69
Someone against churches and religion	37	60	70	73	72	75
Admitted homosexual	*	55	70	75	75	78
Someone who believes that blacks are genetically inferior	*	62	63	66	65	66

Sources: 1954 data from Samuel Stouffer, *Communism, Conformity, and Civil Liberties* (New York: Wiley, 1954); 1972 and 1998 data from the General Social Survey; 2002 to 2010 data from Richard Niemi and Harold Stanley, *Vital Statistics of American Politics* (Washington, D.C.: Congressional Quarterly Press, 2012), 140–142. *Question not asked in 1954.

Changing Demographics.

country illegally, verify their legal status. However the proportion of Americans thinking immigration is a good thing for the country (66 percent) is back to pre-9/11 levels, and the number who wants to see *less* immigration is at its lowest level since 1965. In exit polls during the 2012 presidential election, 65 percent of voters polled said that illegal immigrants should be offered a chance to apply for legal status, while 28 percent opted for deportation.[19]

So to sum up, is the mass public likely to be intolerant, whereas elites strive to uphold democratic norms? The answer is not simple. Tolerance has grown over time. Nevertheless, when the nation is thought to be in crisis, public opinion will often initially support repressive government policies. The public rarely initiates these measures, however, and as events unfold and more facts about the policies and their consequences are brought to light, public opinion may change—sometimes even to oppose government policy.

National Security and the Example of the Iraq War

High levels of patriotism, belief in America's unique mission in the world, reverence for the symbols of U.S. nationhood, and deference to the President's role as Commander-in-Chief suggest that public opinion about American national security issues should spark few divisions—especially when there is a perceived external threat. This is all the more true because most Americans are dependent on the government and the media for information, and for analysis, of what is going on abroad. Perhaps unsurprisingly, therefore, when President Bush used the attacks of 9/11 as one of the justifications to invade Iraq, the public (and the Congress) too easily went along.

Figure 5.1 shows a time line charting the public's support for the war in relation to events. Initially, the overall case about WMD was more or less accepted as uncontroversial

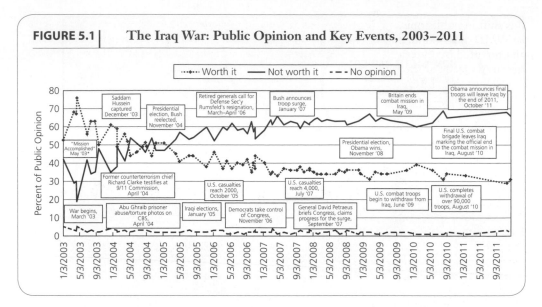

FIGURE 5.1 | The Iraq War: Public Opinion and Key Events, 2003–2011

Sources:

- January 2003–March 2007: CNN, *USA Today,* Gallup Poll retrieved from iPOLL Databank, The Roper Center for Public Opinion Research, University of Connecticut, www.ropercenter.uconn.edu.
  Question: "All in all, do you think it was worth going to war in Iraq, or not?"

- April 2007–December 2008: ABC News/*Washington Post* Poll retrieved from "Polling—Iraq," Pollingreport.com, www.pollingreport.com.
  Question: "All in all, considering the costs to the United States versus the benefits to the United States, do you, think the war with Iraq was worth fighting, or not?"

- January 2009–December 2011: CNN/ORC Poll retrieved from "Polling—Iraq," Pollingreport.com, www.pollingreport.com.
  Question: "Do you favor or oppose the U.S. war in Iraq?"

*On May 1, 2003, President Bush dramatically landed on the flight deck of the aircraft carrier USS Abraham Lincoln. In a televised speech he declared: "Major combat operations in Iraq are over." Behind him was a giant banner declaring: "Mission Accomplished." The banner and the speech became a major embarrassment as casualties multiplied and the fighting lasted for years.

by the mainstream media, perhaps most egregiously by Judith Miller of the *New York Times*, whose erroneous reporting actually helped make the case for war. On February 5, 2003, a month and a half before the war began, Secretary of State Colin Powell went before the UN Security Council to lay out the case, also later shown to be false, that the Iraqi regime was hiding WMD, and that it had ties to Al Qaeda. In a television interview the previous September, National Security Advisor Condoleezza Rice had already warned that the United States wouldn't wait for "the smoking gun to be a mushroom cloud." In December 2001, Vice President Dick Cheney indicated that Iraq had important ties to Al Qaeda. Over time, both President Bush and Vice President Cheney continuously and deliberately talked about the "war on terror" and the war in Iraq as if they were the same thing.[20]

Dissent to the push for war was strong. The largest antiwar demonstrations in the nation's history (and the world's) took place in February 2003. Nevertheless, when the war started, and especially after early victories, Americans were firmly behind it; by April 2003, supporters outnumbered dissenters by more than three to one. By mid-2005, however, opinion had swung permanently against the war. Why? There were a series of factors that led to this shift in public opinion, including the growing insurgency, the revelation that there were *no* WMD of *any* kind, photographs of Iraqi prisoners in Abu Ghraib prison being humiliated and tortured by Americans, and the 9/11 Commission report that Saddam Hussein had no ties to Al Qaeda or the 9/11 attacks.

Does this shift in public opinion demonstrate that the public can be an independent judge of events as new facts are revealed and more deliberations take place? It's not clear.

Against evidence to the contrary, surveys conducted in October 2004 showed that more than half of Americans still believed that WMD had been found, and one-quarter still believed that Saddam Hussein's connections to Al Qaeda had been verified. The early overwhelming support for the war demonstrates the enormous capacity of government and the media to shape public opinion during crisis and under war conditions, and the willingness of the public to go along, especially when danger is perceived, and once American troops are deployed abroad. Public opinion changed primarily *after* the Iraq War began to turn into a quagmire with increasing American casualties. Yet it is also true that as new facts emerged, as the mainstream media began to do its job, and as a debate was thrust on the public agenda by the antiwar movement and some candidates in the 2004 presidential election, the public responded. By 2008 Senator Barack Obama was able to best Hillary Clinton for the Democratic nomination for president, in part because of his early opposition to the Iraq war. By October 2011, 75 percent of Americans supported his decision to remove all remaining troops.[21]

Equal Opportunity and Elite Power

The idea of a society based on opportunity—where everyone has an equal and fair chance to be able to succeed based only on merit, motivation, and hard work—is central to the American Dream. Americans also strongly ratify the general outlines of the free enterprise system, which in theory is based on merit, but which in practice can produce and reproduce inequalities that make equal opportunity more difficult to achieve. How do Americans view the relationship between the facts of economic power and inequality and the ideal of equal opportunity?

Americans overwhelmingly share the core belief that people with drive and ambition who work hard should and can get ahead in America. They take the idea of equal opportunity to succeed so seriously that nine in ten have consistently—over time—either completely or mostly agreed with the idea that "society should do what is necessary to make sure that everyone has an equal opportunity to succeed."

Although U.S. political culture does provide more uncritical support than any other rich country for free-enterprise capitalism as an ideology and economic system, many people are also wary of some of its consequences regarding equal opportunity and for their daily lives. They have the sense that *corporate* America is out of touch with the decline in middle-class economic security and the rise in economic inequality since the early 1970s (see Chapter 4). They fear that the American Dream of increased social mobility, home ownership, and education and job opportunities is a goal that fewer people could realize in today's economy.

This strong support for and wariness about the economic system is reflected in public opinion. While six in ten "likely voters" in 2012 believed that equal opportunity exists, all Americans—whether likely to vote or not—thought by a similar margin that "an economic system that results in continuing inequality and poverty" is the "primary cause of America's problems," and that too many gains "going to big companies and the richest Americans" were a "major obstacle in the way of people getting ahead." Not surprisingly, therefore, two-thirds of the public thinks major corporations, banks, and financial institutions have too much power and almost that many would like to lessen corporate power. As they left the polls after voting in 2012, only 39 percent of Americans surveyed said they thought the economic system was "fair." Perhaps that's why in spite of very strong support for free enterprise, and skepticism about government solutions, six in ten Americans nevertheless thought that government has the responsibility "to make sure that everyone has an equal opportunity to get the skills they need to succeed in life."

Public attitudes such as these, and about corporate power and corporate-friendly tax and regulatory public policies, suggest concerns about the levels of class inequality that exist and government attention—or lack there of—to them. One response to perceptions of government and business indifference to growing inequality was the development of the Occupy Wall Street movement in 2011 (see Chapter 6).

How active do Americans think government should be in solving such problems? During recent presidential elections voters were asked which statement more closely reflects their view: "Government should do more to solve problems" or "Government is doing too many things better left to businesses and individuals." Support for government activism rose from 43 percent in 2000, to 46 percent in 2004, and then peaked at 51 percent in 2008. By 2012, however, it slipped back to its 2000 level, as we witnessed growth in anti-government sentiment symbolized most significantly by the Tea Party movement (see Chapter 6). Voters' attitudes, however, are complex and can change. Our understanding of them also depends on how opinion questions are worded. For example, despite skepticism about government, nearly six in ten Americans also believed that "it's the government's responsibility to take care of people who can't take care of themselves." That response, however, was itself down ten points from 2007, pointing back again to growing concern about the capability and legitimacy of government. Views on government activism, however, are drawn sharply along politically partisan lines and have become even more so since Barack Obama became president.

What economic issues and concerns does the average person now face? In their broad survey of the political views of the working class, Ruy Teixeira and Joel Rogers have written of the "new insecurity" felt by working-class Americans. By large majorities, ordinary Americans worry about the insecurities provoked by the new "flexible" corporation. For many it means decreasing health insurance coverage, loss of retirement pensions, no job security, and a significant increase in work hours.

Another source of anxiety, directly related to corporate change and development, is the phenomenon called "globalization"—the centerpiece of which is greater integration of the world's capital, financial, and labor markets. While Americans generally welcome globalization as an idea with great potential, according to Teixeira and Rogers, "they are convinced...that globalization today is primarily benefiting business and that trade policy making is driven by business interests." Consequently, Americans are split over trade policy: Generally middle- and low-income Americans believe that protecting jobs and improving the global environment ought to be the chief goals of trade policy. Upper-income citizens are more interested in promoting U.S. business and helping the economy grow, without regulations on trade. Overall, attitudes are complex. Americans strongly believe that globalization has hurt job creation and job security, and are concerned for the next generation. They also think it helps them as consumers, is "mostly good" for the United States, and, by a slim margin, has even helped their own standard of living.[22]

As a people, Americans strongly support their free enterprise economic system. However, that support is based partly on the belief that everyone will have an equal opportunity to succeed within it. It is how to achieve that goal of giving everyone a fair chance that divides America's people. Republicans are far more likely than Democrats to believe equal opportunity already exists. Democrats are far more likely than Republicans to seek government action to redress unfairness and inequality. As with other important issues, answers to questions about elite power and equal opportunity tend to be organized around partisan lines.

Ideologies and Public Opinion

Specific worldviews that are used to form opinions about political issues are called political **ideologies**. Sometimes, we use this term to refer simply to coherent and consistent ways of seeing what's valuable and worthwhile and how to achieve it. Today the term also has a more negative connotation, as being "ideological" is often seen as adhering to rigid and intolerant dogmas that ignore facts and enforce conformity. In political history, ideologies have often taken root in social and economic groups as a way to express broad political goals.

Conservatism and Liberalism: Ideology in America

In Europe, politics has long been divided along broad ideological lines among socialists, communists, social democrats, aristocratic conservatives, greens, religious advocates, economic laissez-faire liberals, and even neofascists and monarchists. At least since the 1950s, scholars have claimed that these large differences in **ideology** don't divide Americans. While there is some truth to that claim, it would be a mistake to see American political culture as a bland consensus bereft of difference.[23]

In place of the apparently larger ideological divides of European politics, Americans have long been portrayed as divided over lesser differences between contemporary **liberalism** and **conservatism**.

For a long time, pollsters have been asking Americans whether they see themselves as liberals, conservatives, or moderates. The responses are summarized in Figure 5.2. Except for a few dips and rebounds, they haven't changed too much in recent years with moderates and conservatives outpacing liberals since the late 1970s. What, however, do these terms mean?

Liberals and conservatives share some very important beliefs, while also having very significant differences. Both support the broad outlines of the American economic system of private property, and the private ownership of certain kinds of basic assets and services that are public in some other democratic nations. They also both agree on the legitimacy of the system of American political democracy as the way to determine who has the authority to govern, and in the general idea that government should be limited and prevented from intruding on individual rights. Over time most conservatives have come to accept the broad outlines of the liberal programs of Social Security and Medicare, just as most liberals have come to accept the

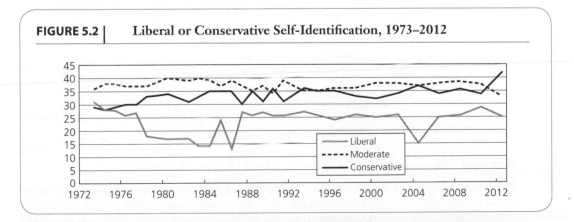

FIGURE 5.2 | Liberal or Conservative Self-Identification, 1973–2012

Sources: Data for 1973–2010 taken from the General Social Survey, National Opinion Research Center, University of Chicago. Data after 2010 taken from the NBC/WSJ Poll, October 7–9 2012.[24]

conservative argument that economic health requires limiting if not eliminating federal government budget deficits. The differences between them, however, are quite profound.

Liberals advocate government action to stimulate economic growth and produce jobs, provide national health insurance, and regulate some of the negative consequences of the market economy. They support a serious government role in reducing racial, class, and gender inequities, and in defending civil rights, whether of cultural and political nonconformists, or of women, ethnic and racial minorities, and gays and lesbians. Liberals tend to favor international solutions in foreign policy, and are supportive of the United Nations. They also seek to control military spending, in part to free up resources to solve domestic problems.

In contrast, conservatives resist governmental programs that seek to redress inequalities that they believe stem from differences in motivation, merit, or ability. They oppose governmental regulation and other programs that they believe interfere with business growth, market efficiency, profit making, properly rewarding people for their hard work, and liberty. Many also call for precise standards for private conduct, such as banning abortion and discouraging homosexuality. Most support a very large military budget, a willingness to intervene unilaterally abroad, and many also harbor deep suspicions regarding the United Nations.

Each category, however, has its own complexity. All conservatives are economically conservative in some sense. Many, however, are also social conservatives, often quite religious, and opposed to abortion and gay rights and supportive of more traditional gender roles. Although in the clear minority, some conservatives are more liberal on these social issues. Some economic conservatives are pro-big business, while others are wary of Wall Street, including its perceived complicity with government, for example, during the financial bailout of 2008. Some conservatives, although clearly a small minority, are even thoroughgoing libertarians, opposing a large military establishment and an interventionist foreign policy, as well as government intrusion of any kind in personal liberties at home.

What does it mean to say someone is liberal? Most liberals support both an activist government to achieve both a vibrant economy, and also social justice. As with conservatism, however, we can distinguish this ideology in terms of its economic and its social characteristics. While the majority of liberals are both economically and socially liberal, not all are. Some are very liberal when it comes to defending the rights of individuals and minorities, but also suspicious of an overweening government. Others support strong, activist government economic policy, but may not support gay rights, and/or abortion rights, and/or immigration. Some are more isolationist in foreign affairs, and others more willing to use American power, albeit multilaterally. Liberals tend to be less religious than conservatives, but some are religious and this too can affect their ideology.

What about the "moderates"? Many moderates favor government health insurance guarantees (a "liberal" position) but also strongly favor the death penalty for murder (a "conservative" position). Being a "moderate" may, but doesn't necessarily, mean that one is "in the middle" or is "centrist"; it may mean instead that people simultaneously hold conservative views about some matters and liberal views about others. Nor does it necessarily mean one's views are lukewarm. In fact, some so-called moderates are quite strong in their beliefs regarding the issues about which they care the most.[25]

Beyond Liberalism and Conservatism: New Ideologies

Does this complexity in trying to make sense of how Americans identify themselves mean that the political belief systems of people are not very coherent, or that people don't think very systematically about politics? Or, are the beliefs people hold on various issues really no more than a set of prejudices without much substance? Either view would confirm elite democratic fears about the nature of public opinion.

There is, however, an alternative, popular democratic explanation of the same phenomena. Perhaps the choices being offered don't meet the needs and concerns of many citizens.

In *Why Americans Hate Politics*, E. J. Dionne argues that elite ideologues pose "false choices…that make it extremely difficult for the obvious preferences of the American people to express themselves." In his view, rather than being idea oriented, our politics has become "either/or based on ideological preconceptions" because elites prefer to appeal to citizens' fears and cynicism through broad and largely meaningless clichés or code words like "family values," "freedom and liberty," or "national strength."[26]

Many ordinary people may simply have views that aren't captured adequately by elite definitions of liberalism and conservatism, yet those categories are the only ones that seem available for political self-expression. Contrary to elite democratic criticism of the public for not being articulate and deliberative, this overall point suggests that elites share some responsibility for any deficiencies in the public's ability to express the full complexity of its opinions.

Some critics of the elite view also point to what they consider to be ingredients of latent alternative ideologies. They believe there is a **populist** and **communitarian** strain in American public opinion. Such beliefs, for example, are particularly strong in the middle and working classes. They include hostility to all concentrations of economic and political power and a belief that institutions work best when they are simple, understandable, and accountable to the basic needs of people who work hard and play by the rules. There is also some resistance to cultural nonconformity, a desire to defend "middle-class values," and belief that religious and ethical questions, and issues of community, ought to become more important in political dialogue and public policies.[27] This is just one example of the fact that there may be alternatives to traditional conservatism and liberalism that are out there to be developed. If there are, they might just provide the basis for a different kind of public opinion that weighs in on a different kind of democratic debate.

Where Does Public Opinion Originate?

We are not born with a ready-made political culture, or a distinct political ideology. Opinions develop through complex interaction between people's life experiences—in their families, at school, at church, at work, and at leisure—and their experiences as citizens, as women or men, as gay or straight, and as members of racial or ethnic groups or distinct religious communities. Public opinion is also forged in response to critically important national and international events. The formation of individual opinions is thus the result of a lifelong process.

Political Socialization

People develop their basic sense of identity early in life. So too are basic views of the political and social order and of other people. In the impressionable years through age eighteen, political orientations are developed that help to shape opinions later on about specific government actions and policies. By the time people reach their twenties, many of their political preferences are already formed. The overall process by which basic political orientation is developed is called **political socialization**.

The family is an important shaper of a child's basic orientations. Learning is sometimes indirect: Observing a parent struggling with tax forms or unemployment probably has important if subtle effects on later political attitudes. Family also directly influences the later choice of a political party. Six in ten adult Americans develop the same allegiances to a political party or to being an independent as their parents. Religious life at home as well as family norms also may teach forms of morality that are later applied by children to society.

However, there is reason to believe that the political views of parents do less to shape the political views of the young than they once did. Many parents nowadays have less time to spend with their children, and consequently exert less influence on future political orientations. In many families, politics has never been much of a discussion topic anyway, and the increased role of media in its many forms in the lifestyles of the young may further erode parental influence.[28]

Schooling is the second shaper of political orientations. The specific political effects of schooling on pre-college-age children are not always clear. However, schools do help teach students the core beliefs of the American creed and basic civic rituals such as the Pledge of Allegiance, as well as a sympathetic review of U.S. history. They also provide initial exposure for many children to people of different races, creeds, and religions, and to new ideas. In recent years, multicultural curricula have been designed to teach that America is a land of racial and ethnic diversity. Schools also provide political socialization in another way. Numerous studies confirm that teachers and school authorities treat non-college-bound students differently. Sometimes their school routines resemble the kind of workplace environment teachers believe these students will face. Such differential treatment, whether subtle or not, reinforces their working-class status.

People also learn from direct experience. They are not just passive receptacles of authority. Critical events—depressions, wars, financial crises, social protests, and cultural change—have a deep impact on each generation. These **generational effects** can have profound consequences on later politics. People who were adolescents or in their twenties during the onset of the Great Depression sometimes broke with their elders and became the most loyal Democrats in the electorate identifying strongly with Franklin Roosevelt's "New Deal." Some students who attended college in the 1960s distanced themselves from many of the views about race, culture, and politics of their parents' generation.[29]

What about young people today? In his massive study of U.S. civic life, Robert Putnam reports that Generation X (roughly those who reached the age of eighteen between the mid-1970s and mid-1990s) were socialized by their mostly baby-boomer parents, television, and other factors to have a "personal and individualistic view of politics. They came of age in an era that celebrated personal goods and private initiative over shared public concerns." More materialistic, Xers are less likely to trust other people, contribute money or volunteer time to charity or advocacy work, or engage in political discussions and actions. However, the situation may be changing for Generation Y (roughly born between the mid-1970s and late 1990s), the so-called Millennials. In the late 1990s, surveys of college freshmen began to detect an increase in political interest among eighteen-year-olds. Millennials are also more engaged in direct volunteer and advocacy work than their immediate predecessors and are more concerned with questions of economic equity and security, environmental causes, and civil liberties. They were also quite active in recent presidential elections, even comprising a slightly higher share of the overall electorate in 2012 than they did four years earlier.

This overall discussion indicates how it is that change across generations is possible—although the core values of each generation may be in place by the age of eighteen, the specific responses people make to politics are also shaped by learning and events.[30]

Social Differences and Public Opinion

Political socialization occurs *in* families and schools, but it is also linked to people's social class, race, gender, and religion. Position in the social hierarchy, and common or different conditions, histories, and experiences generate opinion similarities and divisions on how people perceive the political world. They help define people's identities.

Social Class Differences. Since the advent of democratic governments in many Western countries, class difference has often been the major dividing line both in public opinion and in politics. Differences exist, however, over the definition of social class. Is it simply a group with higher or lower income and wealth? Or should it include major collective experiences relevant to being fully empowered, such as where and how people work and are educated, and how much control they have over their lives? How the upper classes use their power in economic and political institutions has enormous effects on democracy, culture, and the life chances and choices of others in society. The majority of citizens neither own nor control these institutions. That important fact influences the way they think about politics and other aspects of life.[31]

Class matters in public opinion. People with incomes below the median, who have not completed college, and who labor in nonprofessional blue- or white-collar jobs feel more vulnerable in the new global economy than do wealthy professionals and managers. They are more likely to favor governmental programs that create jobs, raise the minimum wage, establish standards of occupational safety and health, and prevent corporate downsizing and outsourcing and workplace shutdowns. They are more dissatisfied with conditions in the workplace and are generally in favor of measures that promote government aid to education and tax rates based on the ability to pay. People with incomes and levels of formal education below the median are more concerned about high unemployment than about high inflation. They are also more likely to think favorably about labor unions and unfavorably about corporate behavior than are people with the highest incomes. The gap between working-class and upper-class respondents is particularly large when it comes to support for government-run programs to guarantee universal health care; pensions, including Social Security; and unemployment insurance. In Table 5.3, some important policy differences are displayed.[32]

Still, class doesn't make as much of a difference in American opinions as one might expect given growing inequality. Nor does it make as much a difference as it does in many other wealthy capitalist democratic countries. Working-class people elsewhere might be

---

Table 5.3   Class Differences in U.S. Public Opinion

Wanting to spend more government money on	Working Class (%)	Middle Class (%)	Upper–Middle/Upper Class (%)
Health care	80	74	63
Public education	71	71	61
Social Security	69	54	39
Aid to large cities	47	51	38
Aid to the poor	54	49	37
Child care support	60	49	45
Research on AIDS	60	51	38

Note: Respondents determine which social class they are in.

Source: Adapted from Robert S. Erikson and Kent L. Tedin, *American Public Opinion: Its Origins, Content, and Impact,* Updated 8th Edition (New York: Longman, 2010), 192.[33]

surprised at the relatively high numbers of low-income Americans who oppose many measures that would redistribute wealth and power downward and regulate corporate behavior. If American wage earners don't always think like a class, the upper classes often do. Among owners and managers, there is little support for measures to redistribute wealth and income.

Racial Differences. The prominence of racial divisions, often exploited for political advantage, has served to dilute awareness by economically vulnerable people of all races of their potential common interests. This is one reason that American public opinion is less divided by social class than it is elsewhere. While some progress has been made, whites and African Americans differ on some important political questions. Although the divisions between whites of European origin, Latinos, and Asian Americans are also significant, the black-white split remains more pronounced than any other in public opinion.[34] At one level, great strides have been made over the last three or four decades. On questions concerning equal treatment of blacks and whites in the major public spheres of life, public opinion registers a strong and steady movement of white attitudes from denial to affirmation of racial equality. Today, less than 5 percent of whites favor racial segregation in neighborhoods, workplaces, schools, or other public facilities, and they reject racist organizations like the Ku Klux Klan in numbers as high as African Americans do. Very few whites say they oppose sending their own children to schools where black children attend, working in the same office as blacks, or eating in the same restaurants as blacks. Today, 84 percent of whites approve of interracial marriage, up from 17 percent in 1968. Even before the election of Barack Obama, 95 percent of whites had said they would vote for qualified African Americans for the presidency and lesser offices. And although Obama failed to win a majority of the white vote in both his presidential campaigns, back in 2008, he did better than all but two Democratic candidates for president going as far back as 1968.

However, significant differences remain about the sources and remedies for racial inequality, and the degree to which it exists. In spite of bipartisan passage of welfare reform in 1996, many whites continue to associate the idea of being on "welfare" with African Americans, for example by thinking that African Americans are more likely than whites to prefer welfare to work. While whites almost unanimously find no problem with schools, neighborhoods, and workplaces where some blacks are present, white support for integration decreases when blacks equal or outnumber whites, especially in residential neighborhoods.[35] A majority of whites support affirmative action. However, that support evaporates when programs are described as "special preferences," even for qualified applicants to help overcome past discrimination. African Americans, on the other hand, are strongly supportive. Whites and blacks also seem to experience a different daily reality. Eighty percent of African Americans believe that racial discrimination is an everyday occurrence, not just a historical curiosity. Unsurprisingly, therefore, half of African Americans think not enough attention is paid to race and racial issues, compared to only 15 percent of whites.

Apart from opinions about race and race relations, African Americans and whites differ most in their opinions about policies to reduce economic inequalities, the responsibility of government, and about aspects of foreign affairs. For example, a majority of African Americans and Latinos opposed the Iraq War, when whites were still in support of it. African Americans of all incomes are also much more likely than whites to believe that many features of the U.S. economy are unjust for everyone. Unique in the American population, high-income and low-income earners among African Americans express similar opinions about economic equality, and high-income African Americans are as likely as low-income whites to challenge economic inequalities. However, in terms of support for egalitarian public policies that stress greater government benefits, Latinos actually surpass African Americans (see Table 5.4).[36]

One aspiration of popular democrats has been to bridge racial gaps through fairer sharing of the nation's economic resources. Yet the above difference of public opinion

Table 5.4   Opinions of Whites, African Americans, and Latinos (of Any Race) on Various Issues

	Non-Latino Whites (%)	African Americans (%)	Latinos (%)
Federal government's responsibility to make sure that:			
Minority jobs are equal to those of whites	30	73	66
Minority schools are equal to those of whites	50	79	79
Minority treatment by the courts and the police is equal to whites	58	83	79
Other political views:			
Prefer high taxes to support government with more services to low taxes and fewer services	35	43	60
Believe blacks "almost always" or "frequently" face job discrimination	20	67	36
Government rather than private organizations does best job in providing services to people in need	31	36	52
Government should see that people have good jobs and standard of living	42	76	*
Iraq War increases U.S. national security**	54	22	44
Immigrants are a burden on country (Democrats only[37])	53	56	36

Sources: Pew Hispanic Center and Kaiser Family Foundation, 2002 National Survey of Latinos; Steven Tuch and Lee Sigelman, "Race, Class, and Black-White Differences," in *Understanding Public Opinion,* ed. Barbara Norrander and Clyde Wilcox (Washington, D.C.: Congressional Quarterly Press, 1996), 48–49; *Washington Post*/Univision/TRPI Election Survey of Latinos, 2004; Joint Center for Political and Economic Studies, Focus, November–December, 2004; Pew Hispanic Center, "America's Immigration Quandary," April 6, 2006; Richard Morin, "Do Blacks and Hispanics Get Along?" January 31, 2008, Pew Research Center, www.pewsocialtrends.org; 2010 Blair-Rockefeller Poll http://blairrockefellerpoll.uark.edu/6107.php.

* Not surveyed separately.

** Surveyed before public opinion turned decisively against the war. Included here because it highlights important attitudinal differences

may stand in the way. Many poor and working-class whites may be less supportive of such goals because they sometimes associate them with favoritism toward blacks. However, when it comes to social programs that seem to benefit people of all races, low-income whites, blacks, and Latinos often do express similar views.[38]

Gender Differences. Since the early 1970s, the **gender gap** in public opinion and in voting behavior (see Chapter 8) has sparked much commentary. The feminist movement clearly has something to do with the gap, but much research indicates that the increasing economic independence of women and the perceived economic vulnerability of both genders have also widened it. The changing role of parenting, and different expectations about obligations to children, home, and the workplace have also contributed to the gender divide.

Perhaps surprisingly, the gender gap is least evident in opinions about gender equality and women's rights. Women and men have very similar views both on the legality and the morality of having an abortion. Nor were there differences between men and women over the proposed but unratified Equal Rights Amendment (ERA) in the 1970s and 1980s. The opinions of men and women do differ on some feminist issues, however: Women express more support for Affirmative Action, equal pay in the workplace, and legislation regarding sexual harassment.

The gender gap widens over policies on the use of force and violence by the military, the state, against criminals, or in the family. Women are much more likely to oppose the use of military force. While a solid majority of women are in favor of the death penalty for murder, men are even more supportive. Women favor stricter gun laws more so than men. And while both by sizable majorities think "a good hard spanking" is sometimes necessary to discipline a child, more men think so than do women.

Women are also somewhat more likely to favor increased support for the weaker members of society, whether they be the ill, the elderly, the homeless, the working poor, or, most particularly, children. They are more inclined than men to favor higher governmental spending for education, the environment, health care, and social welfare. And they are more likely to favor laws that curb the use of pornography.

Significant differences exist among women as well. Single, working women tend to be much more "liberal" and "populist" in their political views than are married women who don't work outside the home. The former provide almost bloc support for Democratic candidates, for instance, while married women are just about evenly divided in their partisan preferences. Single women favor more egalitarian public policies and are much more likely to support the right to choose, equality for gays and lesbians, and equality in the workplace.[39]

Religious Differences. Views both stemming from religious beliefs and about religion's public role have for some years been important divides in U.S. public opinion and in political discourse. Although there is some evidence that this central role of religion in politics has recently begun to lessen, its influence will continue to be important because religion remains such a central part of American society.

Overall, the United States is far more religious than other wealthy nations. Eight in ten Americans say that religion is "very" or "somewhat" important in their lives, with a little over half reporting that it is "very important"; half of Americans say that they pray at least once every day; and more than 40 percent say they go to religious services weekly. Nevertheless, religious observance varies with generations, and Millennials are the least observant Americans, with one-quarter unaffiliated with any religion. While religious affiliations haven't changed very much in recent years, the United States today contains a greater diversity of religious faiths than at any previous time in its history. For the first time, Protestants comprise less than half of the population, and those professing no formal religious affiliation is growing rapidly, now at one in five Americans.

Religion has played an important part in American political life over the last thirty years, particularly with the political coming of age of white evangelical Protestants, who have been at the center of a number of conservative causes, and have been strong supporters of the Republican Party. Seculars and those who attend church only occasionally, on the other hand, have become increasingly Democratic and identify with liberal positions on many social issues. Catholics and mainline Protestants are generally in between these poles or find fewer of these issues as being relevant to their political orientations.[40]

When it comes to economic issues, such as health care and policies to counteract income inequality, white fundamentalist and evangelical Protestants, even those with low incomes, are more likely to take conservative positions. They seem to place a higher priority on "moral" issues than economic questions. Here religion acts to reduce class divisions in public opinion and class-focused understandings of political and economic power. Catholics seem the most torn over questions of traditional family values and toleration, and remain generally more liberal on both cultural and economic questions than are evangelical Protestants.[41]

The extreme views of many evangelical white Protestants sometimes can, however, be overstated. Even evangelical Protestants are considerably more tolerant of aspects of gay rights than they were only a quarter century ago. There is also a growing environmental awareness among some Evangelicals, and even a developing progressive minority.

Although Americans are united over many issues, their gender, class, race, religion, family, experiences, and efforts to understand their world do result in important differences. Contrary to elite democratic views, these differences are not simply driven by sudden and irrational shifts in mood. They are rooted in how people interpret their identity, experiences, and values, and where people are located, and how they locate themselves, in society and its structures of values and power.

How Public Opinion Is Organized: Polls

No matter how rational, public opinion goes unheard if it is not expressed and is powerless if it is not organized. But who does the organizing? If opinion is organized only by elites, then public opinion is merely an echo. On the other hand, if the public has the means to deliberate, then it fulfills the promise of popular democracy. In Chapters 6 through 11, the important roles of electoral campaigns, political parties, the media, interest groups, and social movements are discussed with these questions in mind. Here we discuss the most obvious way in which public opinion is measured and even shaped: polling.

The Potential Tyranny of Polls

We are a poll-driven society. We poll everything from the softness of toilet paper to the quality of marriages to what candidates should do on vacation. A reasonable question, then, is whether polls express or distort public opinion. George Gallup, the founder of systematic public opinion polling, believed that polling was like bringing the entire nation into a big "town meeting." Like many of his successors, he assumed that good surveys are a scientific tool to discover what the public really thinks and wants.

To be sure, some polls don't merit this confidence. Some can be superficial, and some are simply not very objective. When polls merely tap short-lived or dramatic events, they may miss the deeper views of the public. Some polls even are advocacy or push "polls" sponsored by interest groups and political candidates, and are designed to influence the person being surveyed or to push—support—a particular political agenda in the paid or unpaid media. Most surveys conducted by academics and by reputable national organizations, however, do strive to use neutral, professional scientific methods, which is ever more challenging in the era of the Internet and cell phones.

Yet there is a broader problem with surveys that goes beyond their scientific rigor. The very act of asking certain questions of separate and distinct individuals and then pooling the responses together might create public opinion where it otherwise wouldn't exist on its own. As such, polling is a way not only of recording opinions but also of shaping what issues and concerns are on the political agenda.

Gallup was also wrong to think of polling as a town meeting. Unlike town meetings, the people interviewed don't know one another, nor can they engage in discussion before they answer questions put to them. They have no influence on the questions asked, nor can they control how their responses are recorded and used. In most polls, they can't warn the poll's sponsors that the questions being asked are not the right ones or that the situation is more complex than the surveys allow. Consequently, respondents are limited in their ability to give the kind of thoughtful answers that public opinion needs in a democratic society.[42]

Polls, therefore, are an inadequate stand-in for the real discussion that should be characteristic of the democratic debate. By asking some questions and not others, polls may artificially increase what scholars call the salience, or priority, of those issues they do ask about, and may reduce potentially important views to marginal ones. In doing so, they can be useful, not just in political competition, but also in efforts by elites to control and dominate the political agenda itself.

New Reform   Can the Public Deliberate?

What if people did have time to think and converse? A Stanford University political scientist, James Fishkin, has tested this idea through what he calls a "**deliberative poll.**" The idea is simple: Take a national poll based on a representative sample of the entire U.S. population. Ask about many issues. Then bring a scientific sample of voters to one place, and hold weekly discussions together. Let them question experts, read carefully prepared materials on the issues, and talk among themselves with a neutral moderator present. Make sure that everyone has a chance to talk and ask questions. Then survey them again. After they'd become more informed, would their opinions be any different than they were before?

In 2004, his research center and PBS cooperated in both online meetings and in face-to-face encounters in seventeen cities for an hour and fifteen minutes every week for five weeks. The general results? The knowledge of participants increased substantially from that of the mass public in the control group. Moreover, people became much more tolerant of one another. Racial, ethnic, and regional stereotypes broke down. While people didn't switch their views entirely, some views did change on a number of issues. Most importantly, participants gained an interest in politics and a renewed respect for its possibilities.

In their book *Deliberation Day*, Fishkin and fellow political scientist Bruce Ackerman have even proposed that millions of citizens could be brought together in election years to discuss, debate, and educate themselves before they vote. They argue that "Deliberation Day will require presidents to rethink their relation to this steady stream of polling data, and in ways that promise a more reflective relation to the public good." It would be very expensive to do, costing several billion dollars, and its chances of taking place are extremely remote. But it is worth thinking: *what would the election in 2012 have felt like if it had?*

Sources: Bruce Ackerman and James Fishkin, "Righting the Ship of Democracy," *Legal Affairs*, January–February 2004; Bruce Ackerman and James Fishkin, *Deliberation Day* (New Haven, CT: Yale University Press, 2005); "Online Deliberative Poll Gives Picture of Informed Public Opinion," Center for Deliberative Democracy, Stanford University, October 2004; Steve Berg, "Reaching Common Ground on Volatile Issues," *Minneapolis Star Tribune* (January 26, 1996), A1.

Conclusion: The Sensible Public

Elite democracy thrives on passive public opinion; popular democracy thrives on an active and informed citizenry. U.S. public opinion is not always right, is frequently ill informed about policy details, and is especially subject to "sudden breezes of passion" when aroused by dramatic events and rapid presidential responses to them. Yet how strong is the evidence to support the elite democratic view of the public as a bewildered herd? Most of the public holds coherent beliefs, many of which are rooted in institutions such as families and schools, as well as in personal and collective experiences. Moreover, public opinion can respond to new information, new events, and new movements for change, and modify its views. Public opinion reveals its best qualities when it is free to organize and is exposed to many sources of information about politics.

Perhaps most significantly, public opinion can change for the better. In a little over fifty years the United States went from a nation in which racial segregation was the law in many places to one that elected and re-elected an African American to be its president. That's something many Americans thought they would never live to see. That it took so long illustrates the dangers to democratic values of a public opinion that is shaped without free and full debate based on the equal worth of all its citizens. That it did happen is a monument both to the courage of individuals and movements that pressed for equality, and of the ability of the public itself to change.

Reader's Guide

Critical Thinking Questions

1. As you think about your friends, how would you describe their political ideology? Is it liberal, moderate, or conservative? Do these categories adequately capture their views? Do they capture yours?

2. What have been the most important influences on the development of your own political views? Family, teachers, or friends? Did some event or series of events have a great impact? Do you remember at what age you started to think of yourself as a person with definite political views?

3. How would you characterize your socioeconomic status and education level? Do you think your perception of where you fit in the American social pyramid influences your political views? In what ways?

4. There has been a lot of talk in recent years about American politics being highly polarized, with Red states and Blue states and divides over policy and values. How deep do you think the divisions within America are? What about among the people you know best? How has the 2012 election had an effect on polarization in America?

5. We've talked in this chapter about individualism, liberty, community, and equality. Do you think these are the values that are important to your friends and family? In what ways? Are there other values that you see them exhibit that also should be considered as fundamental to American political culture?

Key Word Definition

public opinion   The average person's ideas and views on political issues.

political culture   The political values shared by the vast majority of citizens in a nation despite disagreements about their precise meanings.

American Exceptionalism   The idea that America's history, beliefs, and character make it a unique nation whose destiny is to guide others. It is often traced to John Winthrop's 1630 sermon, "A Model of Christian Charity," in which he suggests the new colony of Massachusetts would be "a city upon a hill" that the world would watch.

equality of condition   The idea that income and wealth should be leveled so that nobody is either very rich or very poor.

equality of opportunity   The idea that there should be no discriminatory barriers placed on an individual's access to economic success.

political polarization   The idea that differences within the public's opinion and between the political parties on issues and policies have grown larger than before.

democratic elitism   The idea that responsible, well educated, and experienced political, cultural, and economic elites protect democratic values and institutions more than ordinary citizens do.

ideology   A specific set of beliefs for making sense of issues and actions; a consistent pattern of opinion used to justify political behavior.

liberalism   A political ideology that stresses promoting government action to regulate some of the negative consequences of the corporate economy, and to achieve some measure of social and economic equality. Liberalism stresses the preservation of individual and group rights and liberties, and toleration for social change and ethnic, religious, and cultural diversity. Historically, American liberals have usually placed a priority on social over military spending.

conservatism   A political ideology emphasizing streamlined government, low taxes, and a business sector generally free from government regulation and interference. Conservative ideology also stresses traditional social values and a priority for military spending over social spending.

populism   A political view advocating the regulation of excessive concentration of economic and political power, and the redistribution of power and wealth toward ordinary people. Populists often stress the importance of a common social morality over the claims of social and cultural minorities.

communitarianism   A political doctrine emphasizing the mutual obligations between individuals, society, economy, and government. Communitarians limit individual rights to property and to nonconformity in the name of the larger collective good, emphasizing instead government's and society's duty to regulate individual behavior and to impose a minimal standard of social and economic well-being on the capitalist economy.

political socialization   The ways in which individuals obtain their ideas about human nature, politics, and political institutions.

generational effects   The idea that public opinion is shaped primarily by the collective experience of particular generations in their early adulthood; this concept suggests that distinctive ideas of politics came from the generation that fought World War II, that lived through the Vietnam War, and that experienced the "postmodern" politics of the 1980s and later.

gender gap   Distinctions between the attitudes, voting behavior, and political outlooks of men and women.

deliberative poll   A new type of survey in which a representative selection of the population is brought together, presented with objective information about certain public questions, discusses the issues, and is then surveyed for its opinions.

6

Democracy and Voting

INTRODUCTION: POLITICAL EQUALITY AND DEMOCRACY
DEMOCRACY AND ELECTIONS: THEORY
POLITICAL EQUALITY AND THE PROBLEM OF NONVOTING
OBSTACLES TO VOTING—AND SOME SOLUTIONS
GRASSROOTS POLITICS MATTERS
MOBILIZING NONVOTERS: WOULD IT MAKE A DIFFERENCE?

Introduction: Political Equality and Democracy

One of the most important and enduring features of American political culture is the idea that when it comes to political voice and representation all Americans "are created equal." While we seem willing to accept the logic of "one dollar, one vote" in the arena of economic competition, when it comes to politics we believe the rule should be "one person, one vote." This principle, in turn, guides our broader democratic belief in political equality, in which each citizen is entitled to an equal opportunity to have one person's worth of *political* influence.

In democratic theory, a nation is a representative democracy if, and only if—at a minimum—all of its citizens have a right to cast a vote of equal weight in choosing their representatives. Even though it took years of struggle to bring a universal right to vote almost to fruition—the task is not quite complete—there is no doubt that the idea of **political equality** is at the heart of the democratic ideal.

Democracy and Elections: Theory

In the modern world, elections are so central to the democratic ideal that we sometimes assume that democracy and holding elections are one and the same thing. However, in societies as diverse as ancient Athens and America's own New England, people believed in representing themselves. The Athenians viewed elections as an aristocratic device. Some New Englanders to this day still hold town meetings to have a direct say in how they're governed. The famous French philosopher Jean Jacques Rousseau, writing in the mid-1700s, even argued that representation doomed democracy, preventing the kind of civic participation and knowledge that would lead to the people's real interests being discovered and acted on.

Although it is highly unlikely a society the size of the United States can ever be governed by a system resembling direct democracy—even considering the potential of the Internet and modern communication—concerns like these about representative democracy and elections are still relevant to elections today. Are elections elitist? Can they be made more democratic, to better represent what the public wants—and to help it discover what it needs?

Types of Political Participation

For the rest of this chapter, we will analyze the relation of elections to democracy quite closely. Before we do, however, let's take a moment to consider that elections are not the only way people can legitimately influence public policy in a democracy. What other forms of legitimate political participation are there and how do they relate to the theory of democracy?

In fact, there are many forms political participation can take. Some are more controversial than others. While writing a letter to a Congress member, or blogging to convince and organize voters are considered legitimate participation by most, are public demonstrations? Are pickets or sit-ins? Is civil disobedience—the intentional breaking of laws for a higher moral purpose—a legitimate way to try to influence policy in a democracy? Not everyone will agree on the democratic legitimacy of all these forms of participation. Some oppose direct action—whereby you try to remediate a grievance yourself without going through normal political channels. Examples include participating in demonstrations, strikes, picketing, workplace takeovers, or joining with others to physically block some legal activity you consider to be morally unacceptable. They contend these have little place in a society like ours that allows free elections. Proponents of direct action often respond that it is illusory to think that voting actually influences policy. Instead they argue that taking direct action is a better way of expressing one's view and gaining results than are voting and lobbying. For them, civil disobedience and demonstrations should be considered more legitimate forms of participation than voting. Still others would accept some forms of direct action but reject others, or support direct action *and* voting and lobbying.

What this debate tells us is that the very question of what types of activities should count as *legitimate* democratic political participation is itself a *political* question. People with different political outlooks may have different answers to this question. A full theory of democracy, therefore, should consider the legitimacy of a full range of participatory activities.

So far we have discussed the type of participatory activity, but we haven't talked about the goal of the participation itself. However, before we can say an activity constitutes legitimate political participation we must not only approve of the *form* of participation but also decide that the *goal* of the participation is appropriately "political."

Ask yourself this: If a group were to picket a corporation to try to get it to improve safety conditions at work, should this count as legitimate *political* participation? The answer to this question depends not just on whether you consider picketing to be a legitimate *form* of political participation. It also depends on whether you believe that worker safety, the *goal* of the group's participation, is the kind of issue the public has any right to influence at all, regardless of whether through legislation or protest. Or is it instead an issue that should be considered part of private economic activity and not subject to public review? In other words, should we think of the goal of worker safety as a legitimate political issue? If we believe it is *and* if we believe picketing to be a legitimate way to participate, then we are likely to consider picketing for worker safety to be legitimate political participation. On the other hand, if we think such workplace issues should be left to the private contractual relationship between worker and business owner, then such protest would be viewed as illegitimate intrusion into the private realm, even if we approved of picketing in other circumstances.

In thinking through what should count as legitimate political participation in a democracy, therefore, we need to consider at least two things. First, what kinds of activities are legitimate forms of participation? Second, what is the scope of issues that we believe should be counted as legitimate goals of participation? In each case, there will be disagreements between different people depending on their political views and philosophies. Debating these differences is itself part of the democratic debate. Analyzing these differences is part of the process of developing theories of democracy.

Voting and Democratic Participation

Elsewhere in this text we will consider a broad array of types of political participation including participation through political parties, interest groups, and mass movements. In this chapter, we focus on elections and campaigns for two very important reasons. They are the most potentially democratic of all available forms of participation. They help set and reinforce the nation's political agenda—those issues that are on the table for discussion and debate and those that are kept off—sometimes for many years into the future. It matters a great deal who wins elections.

Joe Raedle/Getty Images News/Getty Images

Long lines of voters waiting to vote early in North Miami, Florida on November 1, 2012.

Some critics of the contemporary political system, however, question whether elections are the primary way in which important decisions are made, and also whether they are an authentic expression of participation. One argument is that electoral activity is a kind of pseudo-politics. While the public is diverted by the spectacle of elections, the important decisions in society are made by elite economic and political actors with access to the information and power necessary to rule in modern society. Therefore, focusing on the existence of elections as a sure sign that a robust democracy exists legitimizes elite rule by giving us the mistaken impression that "the people" are in charge. Critics like these might favor instead a variety of forms of direct action.[1]

Others think that while there is some truth to these assertions, elections and representative institutions are nevertheless essential to modern democracy. To offset the unfair and unequal tendencies that exist in these institutions, they believe that they must be supplemented with engaged, active political participation of varied kinds and at the local as well as national level.

Whatever you decide about these issues, consider that democracy seems to require that its citizens be able to develop two important qualities valuable for meaningful participation: they must both have enhanced *voice* and be capable of enhanced *receptivity* to the needs and concerns of others.[2]

Enhanced voice—the ability to formulate your ideas and interests, and the personal and institutional capacity to have them heard—is needed to level the playing field of politics. Receptivity—the ability to put on hold your own needs and interests in order to really hear the voices of others and experience their presence—is important both ethically and politically in a democracy. It enables people with differences, whether of political party, religion, class, race, sexual orientation, ethnicity, gender, or other distinctions, to expand their horizons and to become more generous in democratic spirit. People with differences, thereby, get to know each other better, to think through how significant their differences really are, and perhaps even to rethink their ideas and political views. When people are more receptive to each other, it becomes harder to manipulate them through the use of stereotypes designed to divide them politically. For example, race has often been manipulated as an issue in order to divide people with similar economic interests. This was done both in the old

Pinch Me, by Chan Lowe

agrarian South as well as in the modern industrial North. Authentic political participation, in which both voice and receptivity are enhanced, can serve to offset undemocratic tendencies in our current system of representative government, and help make that system more genuinely democratic.

What about elections themselves? Can they play an important role today as a key vehicle of *authentic* political participation? We believe they have in the past and that from a democratic perspective they must. The reason is that elections are far and away the most democratic and egalitarian of all forms of political participation.

This point becomes clearer through a comparison of who votes with who participates in politics and public affairs in other ways. First, who are the activists? Sidney Verba and Gary Orren report that the United States has a higher proportion of citizen activists than do comparable democracies. However, unlike in other nations, activists here tend to "come disproportionately from the better educated and more affluent."[3] Steven Rosenstone and John Hansen provide some comparisons: "The prosperous are two and a half times more likely than the poor to attempt to influence how others vote and over ten times more likely to contribute money to campaigns…the best-off are around twice more likely than the worst-off to sign a petition, to attend a public meeting, and to write a letter to Congress."[4]

This problem for democracy is especially deep because political inequalities such as these persist across generations. Just as the equal opportunity to compete in the economic marketplace depends on family background, so too does the opportunity to have equal political voice. According to a comprehensive study of political inequality completed in 2012: "In neither economy nor politics does equality of opportunity obtain. The transmission of class advantage across generations implies that we are not even equal at the starting line." This is particularly troubling for us as Americans, Schlozman, Verba, and Brady contend, because while we are willing to accept inequality of condition in wealth and income, "the promise of democracy requires equal voice for all." Yet our chances of participating and being heard are heavily influenced by whom our parents are.[5]

We saw in the last chapter Robert Putnam's concern that ordinary Americans are not joining voluntary associations to the degree they once did. Yet, these associations form the bedrock of a vibrant **civil society** so necessary to democratic life, and are important to the ability of average working people to organize themselves politically.

What about those associations and organizations that do exist? Modern associational life is also biased toward the affluent and educated. Whether in phone books or online, there are few listings for organizations of janitors, daycare workers, home health aides, restaurant workers, Walmart-type workers, or other members of the **new working class**. Many of today's associations also tend to be organized from the top down, managed by professionals, and composed mostly of middle- and upper-class people, whose main form of participation is in writing checks to support the institution. Such mail order politics means that credit cards and checkbooks stand in for face-to-face conversations between ordinary people. "Mail order politics," one study concludes, means "money is fast replacing time as the most valuable commodity in political campaigns."[6]

This quick survey of various types of political participation in today's world reinforces the idea that voting is the political activity *least* affected by social, educational, or economic disadvantages. It is far more democratic than contacting a public official, giving money to campaigns, working on a political campaign, or even working with others to solve community problems.[7] For many citizens, it is the *only* important public political participation in which they will ever engage.

Political analyst Ruy Teixeira once remarked that voting should provide democratic balance to offset other forms of participation that are far less egalitarian. Teixeira had his doubts that elections were effectively playing this role because "Widespread nonvoting makes it less likely that electoral participation by ordinary citizens will be that counterweight."[8]

Two Facts About Nonvoting

There are two basic facts about nonvoting that lie at the heart of the problem it causes for American democracy. First, as Table 6.1 shows, the United States ranks near the bottom in voting participation in comparison with other advanced democracies. In fact it ranks very poorly among all countries that hold democratic elections.[9]

Table 6.1	Voter Turnout (in percentage) in Some of the World's Wealthiest Democracies, National Presidential or Parliamentary Elections, 2008–2013		
Belgium	93.3	Italy	68.3
Sweden	82.6	Germany	64.6
Australia	81.0	United Kingdom	61.1
Austria	75.6	Japan	59.7
Norway	74.7	**United States**	**55.8***
France	71.2	Canada	53.8
Netherlands	71.0	Switzerland	40.0

Note: For purposes of cross-national comparison, all figures are percentage of voting age population (VAP). In discussing American elections elsewhere in the chapter we use voter eligible participation (VEP). For an explanation of the difference see box feature "How Should We Measure Voting Turnout?"
*Average of the 2008 and 2012 elections.

Source: The International Institute for Democracy and Electoral Assistance, www.idea.int.

Hard as it is to believe, voter turnout was at its highest during the second half of the nineteenth century when it averaged over 78 percent, levels never approached since. As Figure 6.1 shows, voter turnout in America declined sharply in the early twentieth century, recovered somewhat with the onset of the Great Depression, peaking in the 1960s, with a modern high of almost 64 percent in 1960. It then declined again roughly for thirty-two years, until 1992 when it increased to a little over 58 percent. Since then it has dipped and then risen again to 61.6 percent by 2008. Although not shown in the figure, it fell back to 58.9 percent in 2012. However, even the turnout of 2008, which was the highest in forty years, ranks poorly against almost all comparable democracies or against our own nineteenth-century standards.

The problem of low turnout is even worse during federal elections when there is no race for president (called midterm or off-year elections)—depicted by the dotted line in Figure 6.1—and in state and local races. It is worse still in the primaries, when parties choose their nominees. For example, turnout in the 2012 Republican New Hampshire primary for president was a little over 30 percent of eligible voters—yet it was by far the *highest* turnout of any Republican contest that year.[10]

The second fact is that voting turnout in most of the twentieth and twenty-first centuries has been highly associated with a person's income, occupation, education, race and ethnicity,

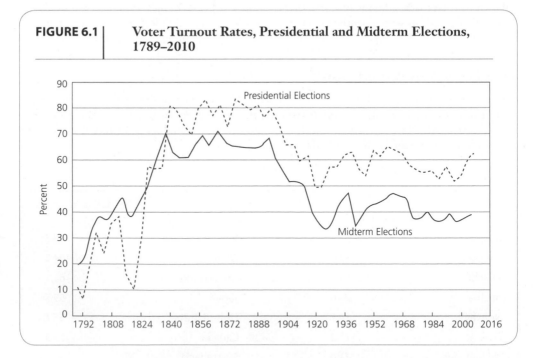

FIGURE 6.1 | **Voter Turnout Rates, Presidential and Midterm Elections, 1789–2010**

Source: "Voter Turnout Rates: Presidential and Midterm elections, 1789–2010." In H. W. Stanley and R. G. Niemi (eds.), *Vital Statistics on American Politics 2011–2012*. (Washington, D.C.: CQ Press.) See also Table 1-1 "Voter Turnout Rates: United States, South, and Non-South, 1789–2010 (percent)." As far as possible, these figures represent the percentage of the eligible electorate that cast votes. Retrieved from http://library.cqpress.com/vsap/vsap11_fig1-1a.

and age. It wasn't always this way. As you read the discussion below, it is important to know that in the nineteenth century—although race, ethnicity, and gender discrimination disenfranchised millions—socioeconomic status by itself had a far less significant impact on voting turnout among those allowed to vote than it does today. Being of modest means didn't mean you were less likely to vote.[11]

Now, however, things are quite different. Table 6.2 illustrates some of the biases at work by looking specifically at the 2008 presidential election. In 2008 turnout for those making less than $20,000 per year was 28 percent *lower* than those making $100,000 or more per year. Although not shown in the table, those in the middle, making the median income of $52,000 per year, were about 10 percent less likely to vote than those in the high income group. The disparity is most stark, however, when considering education. Those with an advanced degree were more than *twice* as likely to vote as those without a high school diploma.

What about race, ethnicity, and gender? In 2012, whites voted at a rate more than 16 percent higher than Latinos and Asian Americans, showing that ethnicity remains very relevant to voter participation. Historically, black turnout has trailed that of whites—in 2004 the difference was a little more than 7 percent. However, in 2012, for the *first* time, African American turnout exceeded that of whites—by about 2 percent in that election. Years ago, women typically voted at rates lower than men. Since 1980, however, female turnout has exceeded that of males in every presidential election, including approximately a 4 percent difference in 2012.[12]

Table 6.2 Which Groups Vote the Most and Which the Least? The 2008 Presidential Election

Groups Most Likely to Vote	Percent Turnout	Groups Least Likely to Vote	Percent Turnout
$100,000+ annual income	75.3	<$20,000 annual income	47.4
People with advanced degrees	78.2	No high school diploma	34.9
People ages 65–74	67.9	People ages 18–24	44.0
Homeowners	63.3	Renters	47.1
People currently employed	61.4	Unemployed	50.2
Non-Hispanic whites	61.6	Hispanics,	45.4
African Americans	60.2	Asians	43.1
Native citizens	59.9	Naturalized citizens	49.5
Married, living with spouse	65.4	Never married	49.0
Five years or more at same address	73.3	Less than one year at same address	52.5

Note: Percentages are of voting eligible citizens. Because some respondents to surveys like the one used to compile this table sometimes say they voted when they didn't, we have subtracted 4.5 percent from Census data to calculate turnout in each category of turnout above. Census data on the 2012 election will be released in 2014.

Source: U.S. Census Bureau, "Voting and Registration in the Election of 2008: Population Characteristics," May 2010.

Political Equality and the Problem of Nonvoting

We have just reviewed *two basic facts* about nonvoting in America—the low *overall* rates of voting, and the *class bias* in voting turnout. Do these facts pose a challenge to American democracy? In particular, does the large class voting gap raise questions about the degree of political equality that now exists in America?

The Class Voting Gap

The difference in voting turnout between people from different socioeconomic groups gives us important information about political equality in a society. The bigger the gap in turnout, the greater the inequality. We see variations of this gap in some of the comparisons of turnout in Table 6.2. One important example is the difference based on educational level—where the gap is very large.

Let's now look at the class voting gap regarding income. Here we create an "index of voting equality" to compare turnout differences between income groups. The index tells us how likely a person of relatively low income is to vote compared to a person of relatively high income. To find the answer, we divide the percentage of voter turnout among the bottom one fifth of income earners by the turnout of those who are in the top one fifth. For example, if 40 percent of low earners voted in an election in which 80 percent of higher earners also voted, the index would be: 0.40 ÷ 0.80 = 0.50. In our example, low income voters were only *half* as likely to vote as high income voters. Since a score of 1 would indicate full equality, this is not a very good score. In Figure 6.2 we graph the index of voting equality for all presidential elections from 1964–2008. We can see that in these elections quite

often the index is not too much better than in our example. In 2008, however, voting equality was the *highest* it has been since at least 1964. Nevertheless, even in the 2008 election, low income citizens were *only* 69 percent as likely to vote as high income citizens.

Figure 6.2 also compares the index of voting equality to the turnout percentage of all citizens eligible to vote. As we can see, when overall turnout is relatively low (1988, 1996), equality is too. Conversely, when turnout is higher (1968, 1992, 2008), voting equality is as well, largely because of increases in turnout among the less affluent.[13] Improving voter participation, therefore, is important not just for a more participatory democratic process, but also to make our electoral system more equal, and therefore fairer too.

Figure 6.2 also shows a hypothetical "future" year in which 80 percent turnout and perfect equality occur. Higher turnout with greater equality occurs in much of Europe. What would it take to make it happen here?

Note: Data needed to calculate the index for 2012 are not yet available from the U.S. Census Bureau. The data used in Figure 6.2 are not included in Table 6.2.

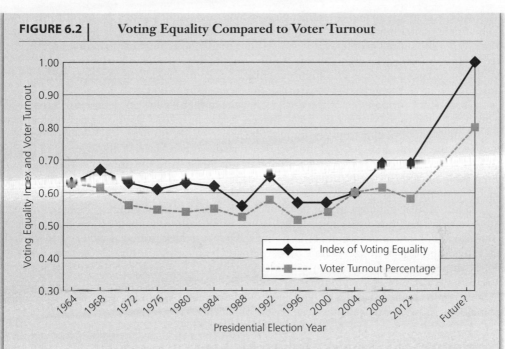

FIGURE 6.2 | **Voting Equality Compared to Voter Turnout**

*The Index of Voting Equality for 2012 is an approximation. Data needed to calculate the index are not yet available from the Census Bureau.

Sources: Tom De Luca and Charles Tien, "Political Inequality and the Class Voting Gap: A Persistent and Growing Problem." Paper presented to the American Political Science Association Annual Conference, August 28–31, 2008. 2008 income turnout data from: Thom File and Sarah Crissey, "Voting and Registration in the Election of 2008," July 2012, United States Bureau of the Census, www.census.gov. Overall voter turnout data from: Michael P. McDonald, United States Election Project, "Voter Turnout," http://elections.gmu.edu/voter_turnout.htm; McDonald and Samuel L. Popkin, "The Myth of the Vanishing Voter," American Political Science Review Vol. 95, No. 4, December 2001, Table 1, 966.

Nonvoting: The Elite Democratic View

Elite theorists of democracy have argued that since overt legal discriminatory restrictions on voting have now been largely eliminated, high levels of nonvoting should not be viewed with alarm. Many people don't vote, they contend, because they lack the interest or knowledge that is necessary for politics, or they are too busy with personal affairs, or too easily confused by the complexity of modern issues and politics. Nonvoting might even be evidence that they are content with things as they are. From this perspective, nonvoting reflects attributes of *individual* citizens rather than a deficiency in the political system. Some elite theorists even argue that nonvoting actually benefits a democratic polity by protecting it from an "overload" of demands by a highly energized and participatory mass electorate.[14]

ABC commentator and columnist George Will quite bluntly states the overall elite view. "The fundamental human right," Will claims, is not to the vote, but to "good government." Why, Will asks, should people who are more interested in watching TV soap operas, and who are likely uninformed, be urged to vote at all? Why should we be distressed if they don't vote? Will also fears the passions of a highly mobilized citizenry, recalling the high turnout and polarization in Germany that led to the rise to power of the Nazi Party.[15]

In general, proponents of the elite view believe that American democracy fares well when compared to the democratic ideal. Indeed, it may be a good thing that nonvoters leave the voting to others—elite thinkers argue, with views reminiscent of the Federalists—because they lack the talent, interest, and independence to do so wisely. In Will's words, "Thought must be given to generating a satisfactory (let us not flinch from the phrase) governing class. That there must be a class is, I think, beyond peradventure." High levels of nonvoting allow such a "governing class" to form.[16]

Some scholarly studies appear to support aspects of the elite argument. They report that nonvoters are less interested in political issues, don't follow campaigns, have less formal education, and less information about politics. They also lack **political efficacy,** the belief that they can have an impact if they do participate. Nonvoting can thus be seen as the tendency of people who have certain individual attributes. For such people, voting just isn't worth the effort.[17] Instead of emphasizing the structure of political organization and power in which individuals' attributes develop, and within which people must operate, these studies emphasize the psychological and social profile of *individual* nonvoters.

Nonvoting: The Popular Democratic View

Theorists of popular democracy disagree with the elite view on two major counts. First, they argue that *broad* voter participation is fundamental to the ideal of representative democracy. Therefore our low participation rates are unacceptable. Second, because nonvoting is correlated with certain groups and classes of people—those with less income, those with less education, the young, and racial and ethnic minorities—they believe we need to look to *structural inequalities* rather than individual attributes in our explanation of nonvoting.

Popular democratic thinkers buttress this second argument by pointing to the facts that class inequalities in voting participation didn't exist during the second half of the nineteenth-century in America, nor do they exist today in comparable democracies in the way they do here. To illustrate, they cite studies such as those by Mark Franklin who concludes that, except in the United States, "whether people vote is hardly at all affected by their socioeconomic status (SES) and hence the resources they bring to the political world." Popular democrats Frances Fox Piven and Richard Cloward put the point this way: It is the "political system [that] determines whether participation is predicated on class-related resources and attitudes." Indeed, a very prominent study of political participation concludes that "when it comes to political participation, class matters profoundly for American politics."[18] Therefore, rather than labeling nonparticipants as "apathetic," thereby subtly placing the entire blame on them for their disengagement, we need to investigate precisely the sources and types of structural inequalities that keep so many from voting.

In summary, most popular democratic theorists concede to elite democrats that many nonvoters could choose to vote if they wanted to. Unlike elite thinkers, however, they believe that the choice of whether to vote or not takes place within a structure of political, economic, and social inequalities and power arrangements that inhibits the participation of many citizens in a multitude of ways. If they are right, widespread nonvoting and disparate levels of participation between different social groups reflect *political inequalities* that diminish the quality of American democracy.

How Should We Measure Voting Turnout?

There are two primary ways to calculate participation in elections. The traditional way is to divide the number of people who vote by the voting age population (VAP)—all *persons* living in the United States of voting age regardless of whether they are eligible to vote. Another way is to divide the number of people who vote by the voter eligible population (VEP)—the number of *citizens* who are eligible to vote. In either case, the resulting fraction is turned into a percentage—this percentage is what we refer to as the *voting turnout*.

What are the advantages and disadvantages of each? The VAP method has been and continues to be widely used here and abroad. It also gives a better sense of the proportion of people in a country that are making important electoral decisions in relation to *all* the people affected by those decisions because they are living in that country. This is significant for the United States because we have extremely large noncitizen and prison populations—each of which can't vote but live under leaders chosen by those who can. The VEP method, on the other hand, by excluding these ineligible populations, is a better measurement of the *motivation* of those Americans who actually can vote.[25] Michael McDonald strongly argues for the use of VEP. He believes that use of VAP has led to the false conclusion that turnout significantly declined from 1972 to 2000. Instead he points out that the lower turnout picked up using VAP during that period is entirely attributable to the increase in the number of persons living here of voting age but who were ineligible to vote because they were immigrants or in the prison population.[26] See Figure 6.3.

FIGURE 6.3 | **Presidential Turnout Rates, 1948–2012**

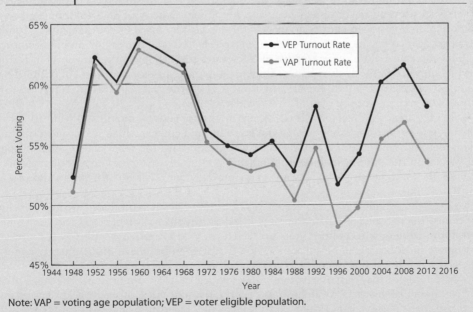

Note: VAP = voting age population; VEP = voter eligible population.

Source: Michael McDonald, United States Election Project, "Voter Turnout," http://elections.gmu.edu/voter_turnout.htm.

The Cycle of Bias: Agenda, Mobilization, Rules of the Game

The famous political scientist E. E. Schattschneider argued over fifty years ago that there was a "bias" to the existing political debates and issues that dominated the American political agenda, what he called the "bias of conflict." This bias, in which certain debates (or conflicts) were on the political agenda, while others were excluded, discouraged the less well-off from voting because issues of greatest relevance to them were not *even* debated in politics. More recently, Rosenstone and Hansen have added that "the class biases in political involvement derive as well from class biases in political mobilization."[19]

Think about how this might happen. If you are an activist trying to get other people involved, say in an electoral campaign, you might reasonably conclude that you are most likely to be successful if you recruit people who have been active in the past and/or have similar backgrounds to others active now. In this way, as Schlozman, Verba, and Brady suggest, political activists reproduce the class and other biases of who gets mobilized, and thereby who participates. While this scenario is most true in the recruitment of campaign contributors—those who then of course have significant influence over the political agenda—it is also true of all forms of participation, including voting itself.[20]

Taking these authors together, then, we can see that a biased agenda discourages many from voting and participating in other ways, and the fact that they don't participate gives political leaders little incentive to mobilize them. This, in turn, reinforces their nonparticipation and ensures that the political agenda will not change to meet their needs and spark their political interest in the future. And as we have seen, these biases are intergenerational, with families of nonparticipants, over time, tending to be among those lower on the socioeconomic scale, ethnic minorities, and the less educated. In this way, a vicious cycle is created in which the bias in the agenda is reproduced by the bias in efforts at mobilization, which then serves to reproduce a biased agenda. And so on.

Rosenstone and Hansen also apply this question of bias to the subject of political equality across borders and over time. They conclude: "The capacity of political mobilization to promote participatory equality is no mere supposition. The more intense exertions of political parties and labor unions to include citizens in the electoral process are an important reason why voters are more representative of electorates [that is, the entire citizenry] in Europe that [*sic*] they are in the United States. Similarly, the more passionate efforts of political parties to get people to the polls are an important reason why class equality in American voter turnout was greater a century ago than it is today."[21]

To get a hands-on feel for why politicians might not actively mobilize all who are potentially eligible to vote, including poorer and less educated citizens, think like a successful politician does. Why *not* do things in the same ways—and with the same voters—that brought you success in the past? Why bother mobilizing potentially troublesome and unpredictable nonvoters?[22] Who knows if they'll vote? Who knows who they'll vote for? Who knows what they'll demand?

Given the overall bias of conflict and how it is systemically reproduced, we may conclude that nonvoting may be less a symptom of political apathy than a "silent vote of no confidence" by millions of people to politics in its present form.[23] Many citizens with few resources to participate in politics—and even some who are not so poor—have unfortunately come to believe that "politics is for someone else."[24]

The cycle of bias has at least one other feature of great importance: the rules of the political game themselves. Which groups do the present laws, procedures, practices, and dominant institutions favor? Which do they disfavor? The American historical record is full of frank attempts—from blatant violence to discriminatory law—to limit the kinds of people who vote and to limit voters' choices. What kinds of *structural* obstacles in the rules of the game, however subtle, remain today?

Obstacles to Voting—and Some Solutions

With the exception of laws in a number of states that prevent former felons from voting even after they have served their time, there are virtually no legal restrictions on voting by citizens.[27] Legally residing aliens are not permitted to vote, although there were times and places in our history when they were.

Let us define *structural inequality in participation* as that relationship between laws, institutional practices, political agenda, and mobilization efforts that unfairly disadvantage some Americans. We have already considered agenda and mobilization. Now let us pinpoint some institutional and legal rules of the game.

The Registration Problem

Almost alone among the citizens of Western nations, each American is personally responsible for the sometimes complicated process of registering to vote. In many other countries, government is responsible for ensuring that eligible voters are registered. Because the great majority of people in the United States who are registered to vote actually *do* vote, there is little doubt that duplicating European methods here would raise levels of turnout, although just how much is hard to predict.

Personal voter registration was introduced in the United States in the late nineteenth and early twentieth centuries to decrease voting participation. In the South, it was used in conjunction with much more draconian **Jim Crow laws** to prevent African Americans (and some poor whites) from voting. In the North, it was used to prevent fraud in urban areas. But the motive was also less honorable: Registration laws and other means were used to "cleanse" the electorate of urban immigrants and other working-class voters. More recently, some jurisdictions have continued to make registration unnecessarily difficult. After a study of the 2000 election, the Caltech-MIT Voter Technology Project concluded that voter registration problems topped the list of causes of "lost votes," costing some 2 million to 3 million people their ballots in that extremely close election.[28]

In 1993, Congress finally passed and President Clinton signed into law the so-called "motor voter" bill. It mandated that registration forms and voter assistance be available in motor vehicle and other government offices and that mail-in registration be allowed in all states. In order to get majority support, the original provision calling for the *automatic* registration of all people who apply for driver's licenses or public assistance was dropped. The new law added a modest but still significant estimated 11 million new registrants by the 1996 election. Registration surged again before the 2000, and 2004 election, then also partly as a result of the 2002 Help America Vote Act (HAVA). Among other reforms, HAVA urged but did not require states to establish uniform standards for registration lists. There is little doubt that overcoming voter registration obstacles makes a difference. In 2008 Barack Obama became the first Democrat to carry North Carolina since southerner Jimmy Carter did so back in 1976. Obama carried the state (a feat he failed to repeat in 2012) by only 14,000 votes in a year in which heightened registration by the young and among African Americans had added 400,000 voters to the voting rolls in that state. Across the nation that year, increased voter registration was largely responsible for the fact that almost 10 million more voters were eligible to vote in 2008 than in 2004. Unfortunately, starting in 2011, a half-dozen states began passing laws that make it more difficult to register to vote, which will likely keep otherwise-qualified voters from voting.[29]

Even with "motor voter," HAVA, and strong mobilization efforts, our system of individual voter registration dampens voter turnout, and does so disproportionately by socioeconomic group, race, ethnicity, and age. Automatic voter registration would boost turnout across the board, but especially among those now least likely to vote.[30]

Voting on a Workday

In 1845, Congress established the first Tuesday after the first Monday in November as the day to choose members of the Electoral College. That particular day was chosen because it didn't interfere with the Sabbath on the weekend and allowed people to travel by horse and buggy long distances to the county seat and return in time for Wednesday, often the market day. Tuesday has been the federal Election Day ever since.

Modern democracies in Europe with far greater turnout hold their major national elections on weekends or holidays. Political scientists generally believe that voting on a nonworkday would boost turnout here as well. Martin Wattenberg asks those who think it makes no difference when elections are held "to consider whether they would recommend that Iraq or Afghanistan hold their elections on Tuesday like we do….if Americans wouldn't recommend Tuesday elections to other countries, why should the United States continue this practice?"[31]

A number of bills have been presented to Congress, either to move Election Day to a weekend, or to make it a federal holiday (it is now a partial holiday in a number of states). Any of these proposals would make it easier for those people with long hours of work and family and other obligations to get to the polls.

Lack of National Election Standards

Individual state laws and procedures largely determine how all elections are conducted in the United States, including election for federal offices. Outside of setting the day for elections, prohibitions against discrimination, such as those codified in the Fifteenth, Nineteenth, Twenty-fourth, and Twenty-sixth Amendments, the **Voting Rights Act of 1965** and its amendments, and the "motor voter" and HAVA laws, the states have very wide latitude in determining election rules and procedures. This means that there are few universal national standards in existence that ensure that the rules—even in federal elections—are the same in one state as in another, or even within different counties of the same state. The result is a crazy patchwork quilt of different ballot designs, voting machines, registration forms, polling hours, absentee ballot procedures, vote-counting processes, guidelines for allocating voting machines across a state, and other important elements such as whether to have early or mail-in voting.

Much state law also gives wide discretion to state officials responsible for administering election law, and often these officials, whether Democrat or Republican, are partisans in the elections they are administering. For example, in the recounting of votes after the razor-close 2000 election in Florida, Katherine Harris, the Republican secretary of state in charge of administering Florida's election laws, was also serving as cochair of the Bush-Cheney election effort. Among other problematic acts, she'd hired a private company to create a list of former felons, who under Florida law had lost their right to vote. The list they delivered, however, also included eligible voters who had the same name as felons. It likely purged from the voter rolls and thereby disenfranchised more than 40,000 registered voters, the vast majority of them African American or Hispanic and many of them likely Gore supporters. To many observers, Harris's actions cost the Democrats the election in Florida and therefore in the nation.[32]

Today, new trouble is brewing. On June 25, 2013, the Supreme Court declared unconstitutional a key provision of the Voting Rights Act. This provision required states and jurisdictions with discriminatory histories to "pre-clear" changes in their election procedures and laws with the Justice Department. The goal was to protect against new efforts at, or forms (see

New Voter Identification Laws, below) of, discrimination. Since 1982, the Justice Department has objected to 2,400 such changes. Now that the Court has struck down the law, unprincipled politicians in states and jurisdictions with a history of discrimination will have greater leeway, and greater temptation, to reintroduce discriminatory practices.[33]

No doubt, most officials try to conduct elections fairly. Still, when state and county officials, often partisan, are given free rein to interpret and administer a complex set of state laws, questionable practices, distortions and even fraud are bound to occur.[34]

This lack of clear *national* standards undermines fairness. Arbitrary application of rules undermines trust, especially when it discourages, intimidates, or even disenfranchises those citizens with the least ability to navigate the process. Clear, enforceable, and universally applicable national standards would make our elections fairer, build greater trust in them, and help increase voter participation.

No Constitutional Right to Vote?

As hard as it is to believe, there is no explicit guarantee of the right to vote in the U.S. Constitution. As a result, election laws—with the critically important exceptions mentioned above—are left to the states.

For example, although all states now have the people elect delegates to the Electoral College, they are not constitutionally mandated to do so. Nor are those electors who win constitutionally required to vote for the person to whom they were pledged on Election Day. Even in national elections the rules of the game can be very different depending on which state you are in. For example, although many states allow former felons to vote, some states continue to disenfranchise almost four and one half million of them—even though they have served their time.[35] What about those people whose votes were "spoiled" because of nonfunctioning voting machines, confusing ballot designs, or other idiosyncrasies of state law? There were some estimated two to four million people in that category in the 2000 election. What kind of constitutional right to vote did they have? And what impact did those particular state laws and practices have on the election results for national offices that affect us all?

What is needed is an explicit federal constitutional right to vote that covers all the states and is backed up by clear national standards. Otherwise our *national* elections, and therefore all of us, will be affected by important rules that vary state by state—with some of those rules, at the least, being very questionable.

The Question of Citizenship

With immigration at record highs, an increasing share of the American population consists of people who have no say over the laws and rules that govern them, even though they obey the law, pay taxes, and participate in American life in many other ways. For example, Latinos are now 16.7 percent of the U.S. population, representing more than half of the nation's population growth from 2000 to 2010. Yet they comprise only 11 percent of the eligible voters and accounted for only 10 percent of the electorate in 2012. Why? Undocumented workers and even long-term legal residents face significant obstacles to the acquisition of citizenship and voting rights. Making the path to citizenship as fair as possible is the humane thing to do, and it would also improve the democratic process.[36]

Proud to be an American.

Rod Anderson/Christian Post

New Voter Identification Laws

Back in 2005, Indiana passed a law requiring all voters to present a valid state or federal photo ID. Beginning in 2011, nine states jumped on board passing new strict photo identification requirements, while two-dozen state legislatures have bills before them requiring the showing of picture identification before being allowed to vote. The Center for American Progress and other liberal groups believe that these new rules are a conservative and Republican effort to deter millions of voters, particularly those of low income, minorities, or college students, those most likely to vote Democratic. A report by the Center points out as evidence that a full 25 percent of blacks don't now have a form of government ID compared to 11 percent of all other races. The Center's report concludes that nothing less than "[t]he right to vote is under attack all across our country."

Conservatives and Republicans bristle at these charges. They argue instead that the purpose of the new rules is to cut back on fraud and ensure fair voting. Responding to the report, a senior fellow for the conservative Heritage Foundation pointedly said: "This is clearly a campaign by the left to demonize Republicans, to play the race card and to use this as an issue to make believe that Republicans are suppressing minority voters, which is clearly not the case."

The impact on future elections of these measures is unclear, with many now being litigated for various reasons in courts around the country. Back in 2008, the U.S. Supreme Court upheld the basic constitutionality of the Indiana photo ID requirement, saying few would be burdened and that the state had a valid interest in preventing voting fraud. Dissenting Justice David Souter disagreed, arguing the law is unconstitutional because the actual existence of voter fraud was unproven, while "the law imposes an unreasonable and irrelevant burden on voters who are poor and old." If the Brennan Center for Justice at New York University is correct, one thing seems clear. These laws may be chasing a problem that doesn't exist, raising the question of their real purpose. The NYU group concludes that these measures simply are unnecessary because there is no "credible evidence" that voter fraud is a very serious problem.[37]

The Electoral College: Your Vote May Not Matter

In 2000, for the fourth time in American history the person chosen to be president by the Electoral College came in second in the popular vote. But this isn't the only inequity caused by that antiquated institution.

In 2012, the campaign for president was limited to nine battleground or "swing" states, where the great bulk of the campaign events happened, campaign money including for TV advertising was spent, and most serious voter mobilization took place. If you lived in one of them, you were at ground zero and, for example, inundated with TV ads: Ohio (219,414 ads), Florida (197,603), Virginia (163,740), Iowa (132, 911), and Colorado (114, 876). Ohio was the bull's eye. Not only did each campaign run its most ads there, of Obama's 599 campaign field offices across the nation, 131 offices were in Ohio, a state that former Massachusetts Governor Mitt Romney visited *fifty-one* times, leading all candidate state campaign visits.

The logic of the game of winning presidential elections hadn't changed from before. If you lived and voted in Texas, Mississippi, California, Illinois, or any of the other states thought "safe" for either Mitt Romney or Barack Obama you were recruited to donate money, and maybe even to volunteer to help work on (or go to and work in) a true battleground or borderline battleground state. Otherwise you and your state were pretty much ignored. Why this emphasis on battleground states? Because the president is chosen not by the popular vote but by winning a majority of electoral votes in the Electoral College (see Chapter 8). In all states but two (Nebraska and Maine), all the electoral votes go to the winner of a plurality (one more than anyone else—not necessarily a majority) of the popular vote in that state. Why campaign at all in a state you've already "won" or "lost"?

In the election of 2012, the consequences for democracy of taking for granted the citizens in the forty-one non-battleground states and D.C. were clear. Voters in those states voted at a rate 7.4 percent *lower* than voters in "swing" states.[38]

Pop Quiz

Why Does America Look Like This On Election Day?

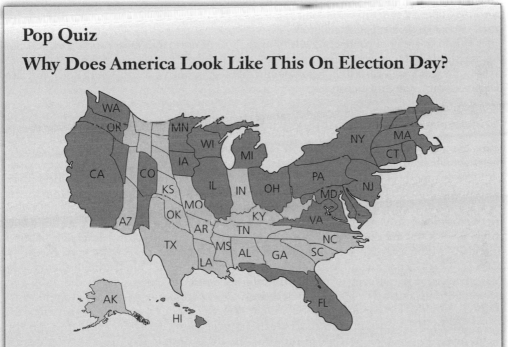

ANSWER: If the United States were drawn according to the number of Electoral Votes each state gets it would look something like this. That's because each state gets a number of electors equal to the two senators each has plus the total number of members of the House of Representatives it gets based on its population.

Questions for Thought: Why are geographically large states such as Wyoming, Montana, Idaho, and the Dakotas so small on this cartogram that it can't even fit their initials? If the map were drawn according to population alone, these states would appear *even* smaller. Why? Does that mean that—judged by the principle of "one person one vote"—these states are overrepresented or underrepresented in the Electoral College?

Source: Map courtesy of: Mark Newman, Department of Physics and Center for the Study of Complex Systems, University of Michigan, http://www-personal.umich.edu/~mejn/election/2012/.

Winner-Take-All Elections: Your Wasted Vote

In America, with few exceptions elections are contests to represent or administer geographic districts in which the person who wins a plurality of the vote wins all of the political power. Consider the consequences of such a **winner-take-all** plurality system. When any of us go to vote, whether for president, Congress, or City Council, we often see an array of political parties on the ballot. If we are dissatisfied with the two major-party candidates, many of us nevertheless will still vote for one of them. We fear that if we choose a minor-party candidate, even one we really like, we'll be doing more damage than simply wasting our vote; we'll actually be helping the major-party candidate we dislike most to win. This psychology is called choosing "the lesser of the two evils." It is a potent dynamic in winner-take-all plurality electoral systems like our own, making it extremely difficult for small parties to gain support and grow.

While this way of conducting elections may seem normal to most Americans, it is not the practice in many other countries. Under "New Reform," we describe a variety of ways to combat the lesser-of-two-evils psychology and thereby broaden our real voter choice and also our interest in voting participation.

Noncompetitive Elections: Why Bother Voting?

When Americans vote for the House of Representatives, or members of state legislatures, they generally vote in districts whose geographic lines are carefully designed by state legislators. In drawing these lines, legislators seek to maximize support for their own political party, or to protect incumbents of both parties if compromises are needed. Although House seats must be redistricted at least every ten years in line with the U.S. Census, the process of redistricting of House seats has produced, in effect, an "incumbent protection program" in which very few elections are competitive. "Orphaned" citizens—those stuck as permanent political minorities within rigged legislative districts—have few incentives to organize or to vote.

The results are striking. In 2004, 98 percent of all U.S. House incumbents won reelection, and 95 percent of them won by noncompetitive margins. In the 2006 and 2008 elections, during which power decisively *moved* from one party (the Republicans) to the other (the Democrats), the incumbent reelection rates were still 94 percent each year. And in 2010 with an even more decisive ejection of the Democrats from power, incumbents *still* won 85 percent of the time. In 2012, despite Congress getting dismal approval ratings from citizens, the rate actually went back *up* to 90 percent: 391 members of Congress sought reelection; 351 were successful. Elections for the Senate were a similar story: twenty-three members sought reelection; twenty-one are now back in Washington. In fact, at least as far back as 1964 House incumbents have been reelected a minimum 85 percent of the time, with the rate hitting 98 percent in five of the last fourteen congressional elections.[39]

Is Reform Worth It?

Many of these obstacles to voting and to fuller equality have a long history in the United States. Would changing them make a difference? We do know that in other countries with different rules, levels of participation are indeed higher, sometimes *much* higher in general, and also higher among the less affluent and less educated. As our discussions above of political agenda and mobilization patterns show, more is involved in the problem of nonvoting than the rules of the game. Still, rules and laws do matter. The "New Reform" box summarizes some of the major changes proposed by groups and advocates interested in solving the problem of nonvoting and its socioeconomic bias.

New Reform

New Reform New Reform New Reform New Reform

Making Votes Count

Here are some provocative reforms designed to make our elections more participatory and therefore more democratic. Which do you think we should consider? Which—if any—are you ready to support right now?

Increasing Voter Registration and Turnout

- *Automatic voter registration.* In most countries, governments are responsible for compiling lists of eligible voters. Why not do that here? North Dakota abolished voter registration more than sixty years ago. Why not at least allow citizens to register at the same time they go to vote, as they can right now in ten states and Washington D.C. —with California soon to follow?

- *Enfranchise people who have served their time.* The United States may imprison a higher percentage of its population than any country in the world. If they've done their time, why not let them vote?

- *Vote on "Democracy Days" rather than a workday.* Why not establish "Democracy Days"—two days of balloting scheduled for a Sunday and Monday in November? Or hold elections on weekends? Or at least make the Tuesday of Election Day into a real Democracy Day—a national holiday comparable to the Fourth of July?

- *Abolish the Electoral College and directly elect the president.* Each state gets a number of electors equal to its number of senators and representatives. States with large and small populations alike,

each get two electors for their two senators—that's plain undemocratic. Having the Electoral College "elect" the president can also lead to undemocratic results, as it did in 2000, by choosing the loser in the popular vote. Direct election of the president would avoid these problems (see Chapter 8, "Flunking the Electoral College")

Enriching Democratic Choice

- *Direct election of the president with a runoff.* In France, presidential elections often consist of two rounds (held on a nonworking Sunday). If no one gets a *majority* on the first round, then a second round is held between the top two vote getters. The French can vote their passion in the first round and then be pragmatic in the second. In 2012, *73 percent* of the French voted in the *second* round. Why not use a system like this here?

- *Establish **proportional representation** for the House of Representatives.* If states were to choose representatives in proportion to the percentage of the overall votes the parties received, small parties would have a chance to compete and voter interest and choice would be broadened. It would also eliminate all the problems caused by the gerrymandering of geographic districts. Why not at least discuss ideas like this one?

- *Instant runoff voting.* Increase voter choice by having voters rank-order candidates according to their preferences. If no one wins on the first ballot, the candidate with the least votes is eliminated and her or his voters' second preferences are counted toward the next tally, and so on, until someone gets a majority. Some local and foreign governments are already using this procedure.

Sources: Lani Guinier, "What We Must Overcome," *American Prospect* (March 12–26, 2001); Burt Neuborne, "Reclaiming Democracy," *American Prospect* (March 12–26, 2001); Stephen Hill and Rob Richie, "America: In Search of Electoral Standards," (December 21, 2004), www.tompaine.com; "Where Instant Runoff Is Used," Fair Vote (May 2012), www.fairvote.org.

Grassroots Politics Matters

Institutional obstacles to fuller participation are quite real. Still, voter turnout has sometimes been much higher, even with the kinds of legal and institutional constraints we have discussed—and sometimes with far greater barriers in full operation. Here are some examples of types of grassroots politics in action.

The Populist Movement

In the 1880s and 1890s, the farmers of the Great Plains and rural South were economically poor and relatively uneducated. Yet over time, they formed "farmer's alliances" to purchase and market their farm produce and to pool their resources to gain cheaper credit than distant banks provided. The alliances were originally nonpolitical and nonpartisan, and they provided a framework for otherwise isolated farm families to meet, socialize, talk, and have a good time. But the alliances eventually evolved into Populism, one of the strongest—if somewhat short-lived—political and social movements in U.S. history.

Throughout the late nineteenth century, the Populist Party and its allies mobilized farmers and rural people, helping boost participation in local elections to historic highs. At their height in 1892, they ran James B. Weaver for president, garnering electoral votes from six states, and four years later joined the Democrats in nominating William Jennings Bryan, in a losing effort against Republican William McKinley.

The Civil Rights Movement

When African Americans and their allies organized themselves in the 1940s and 1950s against the system of white domination, Jim Crow laws had been in force since the turn of the twentieth century. Aided by a strong community of churches and by white and black students and supporters from the North, southern blacks took on the system of racial apartheid through boycotts, sit-ins, marches, and prayer vigils.

People who had previously thought that politics was not for them joined in. One of them, Fannie Lou Hamer, had worked as a servant for a white plantation owner in Mississippi all her adult life. But after she talked to a civil rights organizer and attended some meetings, she decided to try and register to vote. After three attempts and a beating, she passed the highly biased literacy test administered by a hostile white county official. When she got back to the plantation, she told her boss what she had done. He fired her. Hamer went on to become a full-time political organizer and a leader of the Mississippi Freedom Democratic Party. In 1964, her party challenged the "regular" lily-white Democratic Party of Mississippi, prompting a civil rights revolution in the national Democratic Party's rules.

[MAKING A DIFFERENCE]

Mobilizing Latinos to Vote

Latinos and Asians are the fastest-growing segments of the U.S. population. Latinos now comprise nearly 17 percent of the total population, and accounted for more than half of U.S. population growth since 2000.[40] However, only 7 percent of all voters were Latinos in the decisive 2010 congressional elections. One reason they are so underrepresented is that many Latinos are either too young to vote or are not citizens. Still, even among Latinos who are eligible to vote, turnout lags seriously behind that of white and African American voters.[41]

For many years now there have been concentrated efforts in cities such as Los Angeles and its working class suburbs to build strong community organizations to mobilize voters. Back in the 1970s and 1980s, for example, activist Willie Velásquez began the Southwest Voter Registration Project (SWVRP). A former leader of the United Farm Workers union, Velásquez cajoled and prodded his fellow Mexican Americans both to vote and to run for office. "The revolution started when we got Mexican-American candidates saying, 'Vote for me and I'll pave your streets,'" Velásquez once said.

Velásquez's example spurred even more ambitious efforts by a new generation of Latino activists in the 1990s and early 2000s, especially voter registration and turnout drives of some 1 million voters. Latino voter participation jumped for yet another reason. Building on their strength in the Latino communities, the trade unions of Los Angeles launched important organizing drives. Between 1998 and 2000, the Latino vote in L.A. County alone grew by more than 100,000—a 50 percent increase in two years. Reversing historic patterns, Latinos in Los Angeles voted in higher proportions than non-Latinos.

Over the years since then, the Latino vote has become clearly recognized as indispensable to winning many elections, including the presidency in 2012. Unfortunately, in spite of progress achieved by people like Willie Velásquez, that power continues to stem from the growing size of the Latino population rather than its rate of voter participation. To truly tap this enormous potential, the nation needs many more people like Willie Velásquez.[42]

Willie Velásquez, the founder of SWVRP, died back in 1988. But some measure of his achievements came when President Clinton posthumously awarded him the Presidential Medal of Freedom, the nation's highest civilian honor.

Sources: "California Latino Voter Survey," Tomás Rivera Institute of Public Policy, January 2000, Claremont, CA; Matt Barretto and Nathan Woods, "Voting Patterns and the Dramatic Growth of the Latino Electorate in Los Angeles County, 1994–1998," Tomás Rivera Policy Institute, 2000; Antonio Olivo, "Voting Project Uses Carnivals," *Los Angeles Times* (December 18, 2000), B3; Harold Meyerson, "A Tale of Two Cities," *American Prospect* (June 7, 2004); David Leal, Matt Barreto, Jongho Lee, and Rodolfo O. de la Garza, "The Latino Vote in the 2004 Election," *PS* (January 2005); Roberto Suro, Richard Fry, and Jeffrey Passel, "Hispanics and the 2004 Election," Pew Hispanic Center, *www.pewhispanic.org*; Paul Taylor, "Hispanics and the 2008 Election, A Swing Vote?", *Pew Hispanic Center*, www.pewhispanic.org; Mark Hugo Lopez, Seth Motel, and Eileen Patten, "A Record 24 Million Latinos Are Eligible to Vote, but Turnout Rate Has Lagged That of Whites, Blacks," *Pew Research Hispanic Center* (October 1, 2012), http://www.pewhispanic.org/2012/10/01.

Fannie Lou Hamer's experience was not very different from that of thousands of others in the South who were the foot soldiers in this movement. Under pressure from them, Congress passed and President Johnson signed the Civil Rights Act of 1964, and the Voting Rights Act of 1965. Yet it is important to note that even before these laws, people like Hamer had won something else equally essential for democratic change—they had gained the sense that popular democracy was possible and that exercising the right to vote had personal meaning.[43] Together, the development of the civil rights movement, passage of the Voting Rights Act, *and* active *mobilization* of African Americans, sparked a dramatic increase in black voting turnout in the 1960s. When the movement and political mobilization tapered off in the 1970s, so did voter turnout.[44] Since then it has waxed and waned in response to mobilization efforts and candidate appeal. African American turnout peaked in 2008 and 2012 when African Americans made up 13 percent of all voters, roughly equal to their proportion of the population as a whole, and up 2 percent from 2004. And as we've seen, in 2012, for the first time, African American turnout was actually slightly higher than whites', symbolizing both the historic legacy of the Civil Rights Movement, and the continuing importance of voter mobilization for achieving a degree of equality in American politics.

The Labor Movement

All things being equal, people with less education and engaged in low-wage work tend to vote less than others. However, when such workers are organized through active unions that represent their interests, voting participation can rise. In 1998 and 2000, the AFL-CIO launched aggressive campaigns to register new voters in "union households"—families where there is at least one union member. More than 500,000 union members were registered and the proportion of voters who were members of union households nearly doubled, from a low of 13 percent in the 1980s to 26 percent of the vote in 2000.

The long-term trends for unions, however, are not good. By 2012, union membership comprised *only* just over 11 percent of all wage and salary workers (and *just* 6.6 percent of nongovernment workers), down from its highpoint of about 35 percent in 1954.[45] There are many reasons for this. They include low wage pressure from states hostile to organized labor and from developing nations abroad, from a slow-growth economy, especially after the fiscal crisis, and from a more hostile political environment toward unions at least since the 1980s. In Wisconsin in 2011–2012 labor's problems were dramatized, first by the passage of a law weakening the collective bargaining rights of public sector unions, and then by a major national union effort that failed to unseat through a "recall" election Republican Governor Scott Walker, who sponsored and signed the legislation. In addition, voters from union households as a proportion of the population has been declining steadily since 2000, from 26 percent to just 18 percent in 2012.

Not all is gloomy, however, for unions. In 2008, they won the biggest prize they sought, the election of Barack Obama. Obama, in turn, then crafted the 2009 "bailout" of the auto industry, strongly desired by the United Auto Workers Union, a plan vehemently opposed by Mitt Romney. In 2012, unions spent over fifty million dollars more on the election than they had four years earlier and mobilized thousands of volunteers to get out the vote, thereby helping reelect the president. Ironically, the same Supreme Court's 2010 ruling, *Citizens United v. the Federal Election Commission* (see Chapter 7), that weakened campaign finance laws by giving corporations (and unions) the right to spend unlimited money, had a "silver lining" for unions. While it deepened their fundraising disadvantage in comparison to business, it freed them from the restriction of only being legally allowed to mobilize union members. This led the AFL-CIO, the main federation of labor unions, to pledge that by Election Day it would double the number of staff and volunteers it deployed: It promised to have 400,000 canvassers out knocking on doors, knowing they could now knock on every door, not just those of union members.

On Election Day 2012, that new freedom paid off. According to Mike Podhorzer, political director of the AFL-CIO, labor was instrumental in winning a bigger share of white non-unionized blue-collar workers for Obama than he otherwise would have had. Some labor leaders also believe Obama would have lost critically important swing states without labor's support, especially Ohio, Wisconsin, and Nevada, states with large union memberships. "We did deliver those states," argued AFL-CIO president Richard Trumka. In spite of its weakened position in the economy, the labor movement showed it is still a potent political force. [46]

The Tea Party

Grassroots activists had already been at work. However, when on February 19, 2009, CNBC TV market commentator Rick Santelli took to the airwaves from the floor of the Chicago Mercantile Exchange and called for the formation of a Chicago Tea Party, it struck a chord with many conservatives throughout the country. Santelli's famous "rant" was aimed at President Obama's mortgage relief plan, which he claimed would subsidize "losers' mortgages." For many conservatives, however, it encapsulated their broader economic outrage as they had "already seen billions of dollars flow toward sagging financial firms." Aided by social media such as Facebook and Meetup, Tea Party chapters sprang up and mobilized around the country.

The time was right. The country was in economic crisis. Republicans had just been routed at the polls in 2008 and Democrat Barack Obama was president. According to one study, the Tea Party movement "provided conservative activists with a new identity" at a time that conservative demoralization was a real danger.

Antigovernment in orientation, Tea party supporters were incensed by President Obama's financial and auto bailouts (both begun under President Bush), economic stimulus plan, and national health insurance law, and many distrusted him as a person, including questioning his birthplace and religion. They were also opposed to "excessive" taxation, federal budget deficits, environmental regulation, social programs they feel improperly help the poor at their expense, "lax" immigration policies, and "big-government" in general that they believe threatens not just American values but the American Constitution. Many were also socially conservative on issues like abortion and gay rights, and more religious and Christian fundamentalist than the average citizen. Demographically they tended to be male, married, and white, and older, wealthier, and better educated than the general public.

What is called the Tea Party is not itself an organization. There are hundreds of local "Tea Party" groups, as well as several major national organizations such as Tea Party Express, Tea Party Patriots, Tea Party Nation, and the National Tea Party Federation. Nor is its ideology of "economic liberty" new in America, nor its populism. As with past populist movements, the Tea Party reaction ignited during bad economic times. Unlike the economic populists of the late 19th century, however, Tea Partiers focused their animus only on the government, which earlier populists also were suspicious of, but which they also saw as a potentially democratic counterweight to large-scale private economic power and corporate abuse. And unlike earlier grassroots populists, the Tea Party movement received indispensable elite support from billionaires, such as Rupert Murdoch through Fox News, and David and Charles Koch who gave major financial support and training; as well as from media stars like Glenn Beck and Rush Limbaugh; and from political heavyweights like former House Majority Leader Dick Armey and Sarah Palin.

On tax day, April 15, 2009, 250,000 Tea Party supporters rallied around the country, many proclaiming Taxed Enough Already! That summer many Democratic members of Congress were shocked when movement members appeared at town hall meetings to protest health care reform. In January 2010, Tea Party–backed candidate Scott Brown amazingly won the Senate seat in Massachusetts opened up by the death of liberal lion Ted

Kennedy. Throughout the year it fought against and defeated some Republican incumbents, pushed the Republican Party further to the right, and helped energize the conservative base. By November, the Tea Party was a major force in American politics. Ultimately, it helped create the climate that allowed Republicans to sweep back into power in the House of Representatives, including electing some newcomers with strong Tea Party credentials, such as Senators Rand Paul in Kentucky and Marco Rubio in Florida. There were setbacks too. In Nevada, a weak Tea Party–supported candidate helped Democratic Senate Majority Leader Harry Reid survive low approval ratings and win reelection.

By 2011 support had ebbed. In October a *Time* magazine poll said that the Occupy Wall Street movement had become twice as popular. Many in the Republican Party had also become more concerned, fearing the Tea Party limited their flexibility and appeal, and they tired of internecine warfare. Mitt Romney, Republican establishment personified, won the Republican nomination in 2012, and at his convention not one of the fifty-one speakers, including Tea Party favorites, mentioned the Tea Party by name. In the election itself, only four of sixteen Tea Party–backed Senate candidates won. Worst of all, President Obama was reelected, ending Tea Party hope that his program would soon be rolled back. Some analysts believe that with Obama's reelection, remaining Tea Party supporters are dispirited and have lost a unifying focus and are splitting into more minor or even hopeless causes. Indeed, in early January 2013, the conservative pollster *Rasmussen Reports* published a poll showing that just 8 percent of Americans said they were Tea Party "members"—down from 24 percent in April 2010.

In light of losses in the 2012 elections, will the Republican Party establishment try to marginalize the Tea Party, as its post-election task force report implied it should? Whatever its future, however, there is no denying that over the last several years the Tea Party movement has had a major impact on American politics.[47]

Occupy Wall Street

When Occupy Wall Street burst on the American political scene, like the Tea Party, it changed political discourse in America.

It began on September 17, 2011, when protesters encamped in privately owned Zucotti Park near Wall Street in Manhattan's financial district. Inspired by the Arab Spring and anti-globalization protests, the call had been posted two months before on the website of the Canadian anticonsumerist magazine *Adbusters*: "flood into lower Manhattan, set up tents, kitchens, peaceful barricades and occupy Wall Street." New York activists responded. A Facebook page invited people to an open participatory "general assembly." The Occupy movement was on.

"We are the 99 percent" became the rallying cry. It powerfully reminded people, as one analyst put it, that much of the "economic gains during the neoliberal era had been disproportionately taken by the wealthiest one percent of American households."

On September 24, 2011, with the encampment continuing, protestors peacefully began to march uptown to Union Square when "efforts [by police] to maintain crowd control suddenly escalated."[48] At least eighty arrests were made. Several people were pepper-sprayed, with footage going viral on YouTube. The national media started paying more attention. Then on October 1, 2011, more than 700 demonstrators were arrested trying to march across the Brooklyn Bridge. Within weeks of the encampment, Occupy protests appeared in Los Angeles, San Francisco, Chicago, Boston, and other cities, on campuses, in Europe, Asia, and elsewhere in the Americas. On October 10, 2011, 400 were arrested in Oakland. Again in Oakland, on November 2, 2011, occupiers with union support tried to organize a general strike, and then marched to the busy Oakland port, temporarily closing it down. More arrests. In New York, Oakland, and elsewhere police overreaction, with charges of abuse and brutality, became an issue itself and also caught the media's attention.

The movement's main focus was on growing economic and social inequality, corporate greed, and the corruption of politics by money. Other issues were also raised, including health care, minimum wage, student loans, debt, globalization, and the environment. Local issues emerged as well. Tactically, the movement emphasized direct action, such as the encampments, marches, and blockades, rather than running or supporting candidates, or lobbying for specific reforms. Political leaders, nevertheless, paid attention. President Obama expressed some sympathy, and several unions helped out. Former Republican House Speaker Newt Gingrich, saw things differently, however, calling the "concept of the 99 and the one," "un-American" and class warfare.

The movement was funded by small contributions, but it also received help from liberals in business such as the founders of Ben & Jerry's Ice cream. *Adbusters* even received $20,000 from a former Wall Street heavyweight, ironically, who also gave money to Mitt Romney. The protestors themselves tended to be liberals who disapproved of Obama's job performance. The average age was thirty-three, most were white, most had attended at least some college, and were without full time jobs. About one quarter was still in school. A majority were men. Thirty percent were blacks, Latinos, and Asians. While the main discussion and decision-making occurred in face-to-face meetings via "general assemblies," social media played an essential role, especially Facebook, but also Twitter, YouTube, Meetup, Livestream, and individual websites.

After midnight on November 15, 2011, police moved in and cleared out Zucotti Park. Police and law enforcement cleared out encampments in other places around the country. Without the encampments as the visible symbol of the protest, the movement faced a strategic crisis: how to remain relevant? Other tactics were tried, including "sleep-ins," protests at the major political party conventions, attempting to reoccupy Zucotti Park, and blocking off the stock exchange on the one-year anniversary. Recently, some have helped provide relief to Hurricane Sandy victims in New York, and others still are raising money to buy up and then forgive people's debt.

Occupy Wall Street has mostly faded from the news. Some believe it lost its "narrative" because—by design—it had no organizational structure, identifiable leadership, or political strategy. One commentator said it produced "no tangible results" because it "has been as much about self-expression and experiments in creating a new networked community as it has about public policy." Andrew Ross Sorkin, writing in the *New York Times*, even called it a "fad" with little effect. Some compared it negatively to the Tea Party, which had clear policy goals and an effective electoral strategy.

Former New York Governor Elliot Spitzer provides a better perspective. "Give credit where credit is due," he said. "For an essentially—and indeed, intentionally—disorganized group of folks to have that enormous impact, redefining and rebalancing our political discourse, is quite an accomplishment." Coming at a time when politics and imagination had been dominated by Tea Party discourse, Occupy Wall Street somehow put inequality squarely back on the American agenda. And unlike the Tea Party, it carried its message to the world too. Whether or not Occupy itself has a future, those were very special things to do.[49]

Netroots Activists

"Netroots" is the bringing together of grassroots politics with the Internet. The progressive netroots movement has been expanding its power since being kicked off by Moveon.org in the late 1990s. Since then the movement has grown enormously in size and technical sophistication. Using innovative technologies, activists have become very effective at producing or locating political commentary or information, narrative and visual, and directing its flows, raising money, and communicating with participants.

New Reform

New Reform New Reform New Reform New Reform New Reform

The Twenty-Eighth Amendment to the Constitution: A Proposal

Read the Amendment and Take the Quiz

The DEMOCRACY Amendment:

SECTION 1: This Constitution of the United States establishes a democracy in which political equality is a fundamental right of all human beings who are citizens, in choosing, influencing, and holding accountable their governments.

SECTION 2: The right to vote, and the equal opportunity to be elected to, or influence election to, public office, and to influence the adoption of the laws, or other public policy, and to register to vote and to vote, and to do so in fair and competitive elections, are fundamental rights that shall not be denied because of economic disadvantage or other unfair or arbitrary discrimination.

SECTION 3: The president and the vice president shall together be directly elected, with all citizens of the United States having a right to vote, by a majority of the votes cast; if a majority shall not be attained by any candidates, the two candidates for president and vice president with the most votes shall be presented to the voters for another election, two weeks hence. Any dispute shall be resolved by the House of Representatives, with each member casting one vote.

SECTION 4: The federal and state governments shall have the power to enforce this article, by limiting contributions and expenditures used in elections, or to influence public officials, by reasonably defining and enforcing "fair and competitive elections," and by other appropriate means.

The Democracy Amendment Quiz:

1. Why does this amendment include the words *democracy* and *political equality*? Aren't they already in the Constitution? What purpose does it serve to put them there?

2. What Constitutional rights does this amendment either reinforce or create? How might you use such rights in court to protect your ability to fairly participate in American democracy? Why are the words "human beings" included?

3. Which of the specific obstacles to fair and equal participation that we have identified in this chapter does this amendment help overcome? Which does it miss?

4. In your view, would this amendment create a problem for freedom of speech?

5. Overall, do you favor or oppose this amendment? What about specific parts of it? Do you support or oppose some parts more strongly than others?

The progressive netroots movement consists of groups that publish news and commentary, and activist blogs like the Daily Kos, Moveon.org, Huffington Post, firedoglake.com, crooksandliars.com, and many others. They have mobilized millions of people to engage in a variety of politically motivated activities, such as fundraising, mobilizing voter registration and turnout, sending letters and e-mails to Congress, organizing volunteer "meet-ups," and attending rallies. The liberal fundraising site Act Blue alone claimed that since 2004 it had raised and funneled over $240 million to Democrats.[50] The political right has its own net-roots movement activists and blogger sites. Red State Morning Briefing, Hot Air, the Drudge Report, and Breitbart are just some examples.

Sometimes the competition between the two sides can take a comic twist. In 2011 the conservative netroots project RightOnline put its annual conference at the same time and place as that of the liberal Netroots Nation. It even held its meeting at the main hotel at which the liberals were staying. Not everyone was amused.[51]

Whatever their political persuasion, netroots activists make use of sophisticated web tools, such as social network online communities like Facebook and other forms of communication through devices such as YouTube, Twitter, RSS (Rich Site Summary) feeds, and "wikis," collaborative websites of a type made famous by the nonpolitical Wikipedia.[52] The most controversial application of web technology was when Julian Assange's WikiLeaks released to the public massive numbers of secret U.S. State Department cables in 2010–2011. (See chapter 9).[53]

Social networking and other netroots techniques have already played especially impor-tant roles in countries with less freedom than ours: in Iran in 2009, in Egypt and Tunisia during the ongoing "Arab Spring," and even in China today.

Some questions remain regarding netroots as a primary medium for political partici-pation, including whether all the time spent online is time well spent, and whether the cost and know-how needed for the technology put it out of the reach of too many. After studying various online participatory activities, several political scientists bluntly conclude that the "hope" that the Internet "might disrupt long-standing patterns of participatory inequality" is largely "unfounded."[54]

Despite these questions, there is no doubt that netroots activism has accomplished a lot, and has further potential. It offers platforms for issues and causes that might not otherwise have them, and it engages the young more than they otherwise would be, perhaps lessening participatory inequality across the generations.

Mobilizing Nonvoters: Would It Make a Difference?

Nonvoters tell pollsters that voting is an important right and a civic duty that they may and should undertake sometime in the future. What difference would it make if these nonvoters came to the polls in large numbers?

Some argue that the Democratic Party would gain if such citizens became voters because its strongest supporters are among the working class and racial and ethnic minorities— the groups in U.S. society whose turnout is below the median.[55] Others question whether the policy preferences of voters and nonvoters are sufficiently different to influence election out-comes, were nonvoters to go to the polls.[56] Still other analysts argue that, in any case, the corporate financial and other elite backing of both major parties makes each of them uninter-ested in fully mobilizing all those who currently don't vote.

Mobilizing nonvoters, however, does have the potential to widen the democratic debate to include concerns not often voiced. Once this debate is more fully engaged, how would it then shape and reshape the opinion of the electorate in general and nonvoters in particular?

Yet which comes first? Must nonvoters become voters and force new issues on the agenda? Or must the agenda first be changed so that nonvoters become interested in electoral politics? Nonvoters are not likely to show up at the polls by appeals to duty and civic virtue alone. Nor will easing registration and other voting requirements or reforms of the electoral structure by themselves solve the problem. More is needed. At the end of an exhaustive study of participation, two scholars concluded that "participation in electoral politics rises when political parties contact, when competitive election campaigns stimulate, when social movements inspire."[57]

This much is clear: To the extent America's limited electorate is expanded, so is the likelihood that we will have a fuller and richer democratic debate. That is one reason why the high rates of nonvoting in America—and the class skewing of the electorate—are not just blemishes. They are fundamental problems preventing America from reaching its democratic promise.

In future chapters, we explore at greater length the dilemmas and opportunities that popular democracy faces in a world of parties, media, interest groups, and movements. Next, we turn in Chapter 7 to election campaigns themselves.

Reader's Guide

Critical Thinking Questions

1. What do you think of when you think of *political* equality, and how important an idea is it to you?
2. What types of political participation are legitimate in a democracy, and which one do you think is most important?
3. Do you agree with the elite democratic or popular democratic view of the causes and consequences of nonvoting? What's your argument?
4. What is the cycle of bias with regard to voter participation? Are there ways you would like to help break this cycle to get more people to the polls?
5. What would be the consequences for future politics if nonvoters were mobilized and voted in large numbers? Would you like to see this happen? Why?

Key Word Definition

political equality   An equal legal right and equal opportunity to participate in politics. An equal chance in politics for individuals and groups to develop or support ideas, values, and interests and have them considered, and to develop or support policies and have them implemented.

civil society   The public space between the formal realm of government and the private realm of the family in which people form voluntary ties to each other.

new working class   Those who make wages and labor in subordinate positions in the service industries that have grown rapidly in the past four decades.

mail order politics   The modern tendency for some to participate in politics through monetary contributions to Washington lobbying groups.

political efficacy   The extent to which persons believe that their participation in politics makes a difference for what government and political leaders do.

structural inequality   A nexus of laws, institutions, and practices that enforces systematic advantages for some over others. In U.S. electoral politics, this nexus prevents high voter turnout and the mobilization of many new voters.

personal voter registration   The practice, introduced in the Progressive era of the early twentieth century, whereby individual citizens are given the responsibility to register to vote. In most countries, the government itself assumes the responsibility of registering citizens.

Jim Crow laws   A series of measures, instituted by southern state governments around the turn of the twentieth century, enforcing strict racial segregation as well as exclusion of African Americans from political participation by means of literacy tests, poll taxes, and "whites only" party primary contests. "Jim Crow" was struck down by a series of federal civil rights acts in the 1960s.

Voting Rights Act of 1965   The law that removed the barriers that southern officials had placed in the way of African Americans who sought to register to vote, and legislated federal supervision of the voting process where voting rights had been violated.

winner-take-all   An electoral system based on geographic districts, each of which only chooses one representative. Whoever wins the most votes in that district becomes the sole legislator—wins all the power—in that district. It is often contrasted with proportional representation.

proportional representation   An electoral system in which legislators are elected at large and in which parties receive electoral representation in proportion to the percentage of total votes they receive.

7

Campaigns: Organized Money versus Organized People

EXHIBIT: THE PRESIDENTIAL CAMPAIGN

ELITE DEMOCRACY: CAMPAIGN RULES

RULES OF THE CASH GAME

WHAT THE MONEY BUYS: THE SCIENCE OF MASS PERSUASION

POLITICAL MARKETING VERSUS GRASSROOTS CAMPAIGNS:
  IS THERE A DIFFERENCE?

CONCLUSION: CAMPAIGNS AND ELITE VERSUS POPULAR
  DEMOCRACY

In democratic lore, elections are the times when opposing candidates and parties engage in campaigns to win public support for their programs and thereby gain the legitimacy to govern. When these contests are open, fair, and competitive—when the issues are clearly debated and the candidates forthrightly tell us what they believe and what they will do—American democracy shines its brightest. Both popular and elite democrats share this hope for America. However, they profoundly disagree on the role elections should play in democracy and on how well American elections are today playing their part.

In the elite democratic view, the purpose of elections is simply to allow the public to select the most skillful leaders from among qualified American elites. As Joseph A. Schumpeter famously put it: "democracy does not mean and cannot mean that the people actually rule...Democracy means only that the people have the opportunity of accepting or refusing the men who are to rule them."[1] Once leaders are selected, the people should then step aside and let them do their job. In Schumpeter's classic elite democratic view, democracy is a *method* of selecting leaders from among elites through elections.

Popular democrats disagree. They believe that all people have the right and potentially the ability to fully participate. Many are held back, however, by inequalities in participatory resources, including access to media, expertise, quality education, organizational support, and the money and time needed for full participation. Many also become discouraged from participating by a system that doesn't address their needs.

Which view in this debate best understands American campaigns and elections?

•   •   •

It all begins months—if not years—before the first candidacy is announced. Deeply entrenched features of campaigns and elections are already at work, too often narrowing the range of issues discussed—and the field of candidates "taken seriously"—to those favored by campaign contributors, professional marketers, elite interests, and key groups. To understand how the democratic debate is limited in these ways, let's look at the "rules" of the game for that most important of American elections—the race for the presidency.

Exhibit: The Presidential Campaign

The first and perhaps most important feature of the race for the White House is that we have **candidate-centered campaigns.** This fact permeates our political system, but it is especially pronounced here. It means that candidates as individual personalities are extremely important each step of the way. Table 7.1 lists the key steps in some detail. Let's briefly discuss what's involved.

Table 7.1   The Road to the White House: Essential Steps

Two Years Before the Election: Exploration and Organization

Goal: Become a *viable* candidate.

1. Establish a narrative about why *you* should be president. Who are *you,* and why should people vote for you? Form a target electorate among your party's active voters based on your history and appeal.

2. Visit key early delegate states like New Hampshire and Iowa. Visit key politicians elsewhere. Put together a contributors' list and raise money. Campaign for your party's candidates in the off-year elections.

3. Establish media contacts. Draw attention by appearing before key interest groups. Become credible by appearing on shows like *Meet the Press.* Become visible by doing TV with Jon Stewart, Stephen Colbert, David Letterman, and Jay Leno. Do as many of these as you can.

One Year Before the Election: The Invisible Primary

Goals: Build a competent campaign team, achieve **name recognition**, and raise enough money to hire a campaign staff, do early advertising, and meet the requirements for the federal campaign subsidy.

1. Establish an "exploratory" campaign committee and register as an official campaign organization with the Federal Election Commission.

2. Fundraise in at least twenty states, with a minimum goal of $5,000 in each, to qualify for federal matching funds during the primaries. Or opt out of federal help and raise *lots* of your own money.

3. Get mentioned by elite news reporters as an up-and-coming presidential candidate with fresh, new ideas and broad appeal.

4. Assemble a campaign team that includes high-tech, Internet and data-analysis consultants, political managers, pollsters, direct-mail specialists, lawyers, and experts in press relations, media, speechwriting, and issue development.

(Continues)

Table 7.1   The Road to the White House: Essential Steps   *(Continued)*

5. Plan strategy according to the primary and caucus calendar and build organizations in targeted states.

6. Announce candidacy.

Primary Season and Convention: January–September, Election Year

Goal: Assemble a majority of delegates to your party's national convention in the summer.

1. Win or take a close second in Iowa caucuses and New Hampshire primary in January. Keep raising money. Win at least one really big state in other "frontloaded" primaries, and pick up a few small states.

2. Win decisively on "Super Tuesday" or at least some key states, forcing some competitors to drop out. Get them to endorse you.

3. Win later primaries by decisive margins, forcing more contenders to drop out and support you. Become the "presumptive" nominee.

4. Turn your attention to your most likely opponent from the other party in the fall. Plan a media campaign to define both your opponent and yourself. Decide what the battleground states are. Choose a vice presidential candidate.

5. Plan and hold a well-organized national party convention that you control. Use it to launch your fall campaign. In your acceptance speech, unite your party while also telling the nation why it should choose you.

General Election: Convention to Election Day in November

Goal: Amass 270 electoral votes and win the presidency.

1. As a major-party candidate, collect public matching funds or raise lots of your own money (as Obama and Romney did), and plan to spend it. Help your party raise money so it can "independently" help you win.

2. Campaign in the battleground states and saturate them with media ads. In those states focus on both winning over undecided voters and in mobilizing your likely supporters to be sure they vote and help.

3. Use supporters in all the non-battleground states efficiently to help fundraise and mobilize battleground voters. If you didn't accept matching funds—fundraise, fundraise, fundraise!

4. Stick with your script about why you should be president, unless focus groups and polling say it is failing. Adjust and persist.

5. Win the presidency, and put your transition team in place.

First, it's a long race. Presidential bids start up to three years before the election year and culminate in the more than fifty separate primaries and caucuses that potential candidates may face to win a major party's nomination. Incumbent presidents have it much easier than challengers because their public images are already formed, and they usually don't have strong opponents within their own party.[2] Challengers face daunting obstacles, especially a filtering process mediated by the **gatekeepers** of American politics: elites in the media, politics, and fundraising who have enormous influence in determining whether or not a candidate is taken seriously as a presidential contender.[3]

Then there is the so-called **invisible primary**, involving endless phone calls and dinners with potential donors to establish a fundraising base. Passing the test of the invisible primary means developing a campaign theme that appeals to donors; it also involves finding campaign professionals whose reputation shows others that the candidate means business. Once candidates believe they're passing this test, they will usually officially announce their candidacy, campaign organization, and purpose for running. Many potential candidates, however, fail this test.

Whoever successfully emerges goes on to compete in the primaries and caucuses. They pick and choose which contests to enter by developing a strategy that gives them the best chance of winning the nomination. Sometime in the spring, a leading candidate in each party emerges from the pack as the inevitable party nominee. Once a candidate feels the nomination is sewn up, he or she then must *both* solidify support with the party base, and *also* appeal to a general election audience more centrist than the party primary voters and caucus goers. The candidate also begins to choose a running mate, with both political and prudential considerations in mind. And the candidate begins to look past the summer conventions and the official party nomination to position herself or himself favorably with respect to the opponent she or he will face in the fall. The nomination of the presidential and vice presidential candidates is formally designated when the party conventions meet late in the summer. The two sets of party nominees then square off in the general election, which takes place in November.

There is no better way to illustrate the dynamic interplay of candidate, political parties, political interests, campaign money, strategies, and voters than by looking directly at what happened in the last election.

Example: President Obama's Reelection

That Barack Obama should have been a president running for reelection in 2012 at all seems very improbable, and speaks well of *contemporary* American democracy. The son of a Kenyan father, raised by his Caucasian mother and grandparents, he was one of only five African Americans to have ever served in the Senate. With only two years on the job, he ran against and defeated in a very close contest, former first lady and New York's powerhouse two-term senator, Hillary Rodham Clinton for the 2008 Democratic Party nomination. Obama then picked the well-known thirty-five year veteran of the Senate, Joe Biden, to be his vice presidential running mate, balancing out his own inexperience.

His opponent was Arizona Republican Senator John McCain. A former POW in North Vietnam, he had successfully cultivated media and other gatekeepers, particularly with the idea that he was "maverick," someone who could think independently of the party line. McCain won the Republican nomination, defeating Mitt Romney among others. He then stunned the nation, choosing the virtually unknown governor of Alaska, Sarah Palin, to be his running mate, the first woman to be on a Republican national ticket. The Palin pick would soon prove very controversial, as she gained a loyal and energetic conservative following, but seemed out of her depth on important issues.

Obama was operating on a very favorable playing field, given the Great Recession and the deep unpopularity of Republican President George Bush and his economic and foreign policies. Obama was a disciplined and charismatic candidate and passed the ultimate test of "looking presidential," according to media gatekeepers. His campaign was superbly organized and run, and much better financed than McCain's. On Election Day, Obama beat McCain 2 to 1 in the Electoral College, and received the largest popular vote percentage for a Democrat since Lyndon Johnson's 1964 landslide. Voter turnout was the highest since 1968, and the Democrats increased their majorities in the Senate to nine seats and in the House to seventy-nine seats.

By November of 2010, however, the Grand Old Party (GOP) stormed back into power in the House of Representatives and cut the Democratic majority in the Senate to just three seats. Obama himself said he'd received a "shellacking."

The 2012 Election

Reelection seemed decidedly uphill for Obama when he announced his candidacy in April 2011.[4] Unemployment was at 9 percent and economic growth was an anemic 1.8 percent. No president since the Great Depression of the 1930s had been reelected with an unemployment rate above 7.2 percent. One political science model based largely on economic data of this kind predicted Romney easily winning. Applied to the last eight elections, the model had been right every single time.[5]

The Republican Nominating Contest A former governor of Massachusetts, and failed candidate for the Republican nomination in 2008, Mitt Romney was well known to Republicans. He was a fabulously successful businessman, who made millions as managing director of Bain Capital, a private equity and leveraged buyout firm. He was also known for his role helping save the 2002 Winter Olympics. His father, George, a governor of Michigan and chairman of American Motors Corp., had unsuccessfully sought the nomination a generation before.

Romney wasn't trusted by conservatives, however, having signed into law a health care plan that was a model for the president's own law, and having been pro-choice when he ran for governor of liberal Massachusetts. His move to the right began in earnest after the 2004 election, when he began contemplating the presidency. While running for governor in 2002, he had proclaimed, "my views are progressive." By February 2012 he was telling a skeptical Conservative Political Action Conference that he had been a "severely conservative" governor of Massachusetts.[6] With Obama looking vulnerable, multiple candidates sought the Republican Party nod, with Romney the strongest in a weak field. Early on a writer for conservative Fox News asked: Who will be the "anti-Romney?" Other "frontrunners," in fact, rose and fell. The Republican nomination contest was quite negative, and Romney made some gaffes that reinforced his image as an out-of-touch multimillionaire. In Iowa: "Corporations are people, my friend." In New Hampshire: "I like being able to fire people who provide services to me." In Detroit (to show loyalty to its cars): "[my wife] Ann drives a couple of Cadillacs."

By the last Republican debate in Mesa, Arizona, in February, only Romney, former House Speaker Newt Gingrich, libertarian Texas congressman Ron Paul, and socially conservative ex-Pennsylvania senator Rick Santorum were left. After winning six Super Tuesday primaries on March 6, Romney's nomination became inevitable. He had been battered "black and blue" in the primaries, especially by charges by fellow *Republican*s that he was a "corporate raider" and "vulture capitalist." Finally, he could now "focus entirely on President Obama."[7]

The General Election Because of the candidate-centered nature of American politics, the ability to define how the public sees your opponent can be decisive. In May, well before the nominating conventions, Obama's campaign put out TV ads depicting Romney as the "corporate raider" Gingrich's supporters had said he was. Just before the Republican Convention, it had Bill Clinton in an ad warning that economic ideas like Romney's were "what got us in trouble in the first place."[8]

One of the most important decisions a successful candidate makes is to choose a running mate. Two weeks before the Republican Convention, Romney chose Wisconsin Representative

President Obama and Governor Romney in their second debate, at Hofstra University in Hempstead, NY, October 16, 2012.

Paul Ryan, the young chair of the House Budget Committee. Popular with conservatives, Ryan was well known as the author of a budget plan that, in addition to cutting spending, would have changed Medicare into a voucher program. Rather than reaching out to the middle, the Ryan choice showed Romney still felt he needed to solidify his conservative base.

The Republican National Convention convened on August 27 in Tampa, Florida. Ann Romney effectively showed her husband's caring side, telling the TV audience: "This is the man America needs." Paul Ryan's acceptance speech, however, created a firestorm of criticism for distorting events and facts. Then actor Clint Eastwood caused a stir, debating an empty chair in which Obama was "sitting," implying at one point that the president was cursing out Romney. Romney's acceptance speech was competently written and given. Obama had promised hope in 2008, he said, but delivered "disappointment and division." Romney would restore and unite America.[9]

The main Republican convention theme, "We Built It," was itself based on something Obama had said a couple of weeks before: "If you've got a business, you didn't build that—somebody else made that happen." The convention and the Romney campaign seized upon this comment as evidence that Obama believed all success comes from government rather than initiative and hard work. In reality, Obama simply was stating the truism that even successful people depend on others, such as teachers. Obama had gone on to say: "When we succeed, we succeed because of our individual initiative, but also because we do things together." Polls later showed this line of attack to be ineffective.[10]

The Democrats kicked off their national convention on September 4 in Charlotte, North Carolina. Michelle Obama reminded viewers—the contrast with Romney's privilege was obvious—that her husband was one of them: "Barack knows the American dream," she said, "because he's lived it." The political highlight was Bill Clinton, who laid out a clear Democratic narrative. The Republican argument was pretty simple, Clinton said: "'We left him [Obama] a total mess, he hasn't finished cleaning it up yet, so fire him and put us back in.'" Instead, Clinton boomed, "I like the argument for President Obama's reelection a lot better." After Biden made the case for Obama, the president made his own case for a second term. His 2008 message of "hope" had been "tested," he acknowledged, but he was "as hopeful as ever." To show growth, he said, "times have changed—and so have I." "The path we offer may be harder," he argued, "but it leads to a better place." He asked for more time.[11]

Analyzing the impact of the conventions, Nate Silver of *The New York Times* concluded that where the Republican Convention gave Romney a small fleeting bounce, the Democratic Convention put Obama in the position of front-runner again.[12]

The fall campaign was on, and, judged by media buys, it was the most negative presidential campaign in history.[13] Negative campaigns are enabled by the candidate-centric nature of American politics, where the individual, and not just the party program, is a very inviting target. However, decisions to go negative are largely tactical. The key question is, will the attacks be effective? The Obama campaign needed to discredit Romney the expert businessman as a viable alternative to Obama for rescuing the troubled economy. It judged that his privileged background, corporate record, and personality left him vulnerable. Obama's campaign's attacks, therefore, were "designed to portray Romney as too flawed personally to be a viable political alternative." On the other hand, the Romney camp was wary of seeming to personally attack the president. Many Americans personally liked Obama. Personal attacks could backfire, especially with independents. Still, "woven throughout [Romney's] campaign" was the familiar suggestion ever since the 2008 campaign, that Obama was somehow un-American.[14]

In spite of the negativity, very important policy differences emerged. Romney criticized Obama for overspending, deficit explosion, and overregulation, all engendered by a big government philosophy. Obama accused Romney of being indifferent to the middle class and less well off; he defended his policies, and proposed more government "investment"—another stimulus—to create jobs. The differences were sharp on taxes, especially the expiring "Bush tax cuts" on income. Romney wanted to renew them for everyone, while Obama wanted to renew them only for individuals making less than $250,000 per year. On health, Romney pledged to repeal "Obamacare," the president's signature health care law. He proposed major changes to Medicare (government health insurance for seniors), emphasizing giving recipients a fixed amount of "premium support" to buy insurance; for Medicaid (government health insurance for people with low income and few resources, and some disabled people), he would substitute block grants to the states for the present way the federal government pays its portion of the program. Obama argued Romney's proposals would curtail services to the elderly and to the poor. Romney sharply attacked Obama for overregulation of business, hampering freedom and efficiency, and said he would repeal the 2010 Dodd-Frank law Obama signed that regulates Wall Street. Obama argued that Romney wanted to protect the "fat cats," and that deregulation would invite another financial crisis.

On immigration, Romney had for some time taken a hard line. He supported a border fence with Mexico, and opposed the DREAM Act that would have created a path to citizenship for kids brought into the country illegally. During a GOP debate, he said his policies would encourage immigrants without documents to "self-deport" because, without papers, they wouldn't be able to find jobs. Obama supported the DREAM Act and comprehensive immigration reform and had already issued an order allowing many undocumented young immigrants to stay in the country. On social issues, Romney opposed gay marriage and abortion rights, while Obama, reversing himself on gay marriage, supported both.

Romney supported vigorous oil drilling and the Keystone XL pipeline, and he downplayed the importance of climate change. He accused Obama of losing fossil fuel–based jobs. Obama supported controlling fossil fuel emissions, but didn't seriously make climate change a real issue. There were a few major differences on foreign and defense policy. Perhaps the most significant policy difference was that Obama pledged to trim military spending, while Romney wanted to increase it. Romney also tried the familiar Republican tactic of attacking Democrats as weak on national security. He criticized Obama, for example, for not supporting Israel enough regarding Iran's nuclear program, and for the attack in Libya, that left the U.S. ambassador and three other Americans dead. He also pledged to be tougher with China, for example, on currency manipulation. With a war-weary nation, Romney didn't make a serious attempt to criticize Obama on Afghanistan or Iraq.[15]

Two events defined the campaign. In September, a videotape of a private Romney fundraiser was made public, in which Romney had claimed that the 47 percent of Americans who pay no income taxes formed an unshakable Obama constituency. "I'll never convince them they should take personal responsibility and care for their lives," Romney lamented. His remarks were a PR nightmare, reinforcing his plutocrat image. Moreover, they were incorrect. While 47 percent of Americans pay no *income* taxes, many are working, paying all sorts of other taxes, and others are retired, in the military, or disabled. Many are Republicans and undoubtedly voted for him. They certainly weren't freeloaders, as Romney implied.[16]

Then came the first debate on October 3 in Denver Colorado. It was an unmitigated disaster for Obama. The president performed poorly, while Romney very effectively reintroduced himself to the public as a reasonable alternative. Then Obama got lucky, slowing the bleeding. Unemployment dropped below 8 percent, for the first time in 43 months, weakening one of Romney's favorite lines of attack. Nevertheless, the debate had a *huge* impact, making the race very close. In two subsequent debates, Obama rebounded, reassuring nervous supporters. He used the second debate in particular to shore up support among women with a vigorous defense of federal funding for Planned Parenthood, which Romney wanted to end, and by accusing Romney of wanting to end mandated health insurance coverage for contraception, which had become controversial on religious grounds.[17]

Throughout October the president slowly gained strength in the polls. Then Hurricane Sandy hit, giving the president an opportunity to demonstrate successful leadership and perhaps the importance of so-called "big government," to Romney's disadvantage.[18]

American presidential elections are decided in the Electoral College (see Chapter 8). This one would be settled in nine battleground or swing states: Ohio, Florida, Virginia, Colorado, Iowa, Nevada, New Hampshire, North Carolina, and Wisconsin. Virtually all $900 million in TV ad money was spent in these states plus Michigan. The most hotly contested states were Ohio, Florida, and Virginia, which the candidates visited the most, and on which they spent more than half of the ad money.[19] For most Americans, there was hardly a campaign at all.

Obama was reelected with 332 electoral votes, to 206 for Governor Romney, and had almost 5 million more popular votes. He became the first president since Ronald Reagan to twice be elected with more than 50 percent of the popular vote, and the first Democrat to do it since Franklin Roosevelt in the 1940s. The only battleground state he lost was North Carolina. Ohio was perhaps the biggest prize. With one in eight workers in jobs related to the auto industry, Obama had sown the seeds for a (tight) victory there with the auto bailout right at the beginning of his first term.

Shock and Awe When Fox News called Ohio for Obama on election eve, former Bush adviser and Fox contributor Karl Rove insisted that it should wait until more votes were counted. Rove wasn't alone in disbelief. Many conservative analysts and pundits had been predicting a Romney win. Fox News had itself helped create an echo chamber of conservative misjudgment. Most comical was Dick Morris, ironically a former Clinton adviser, who just before the election predicted a Romney "landslide."[20]

Romney himself was "shell-shocked" at the results. Campaign crowds had been large and enthusiastic, polls had shown greater Republican enthusiasm, and his own internal polls showed him ahead both nationally and in key battleground states. He expected the undecided vote to break for him. His analysis was wrong.[21]

The Democrats also added two seats to their majority in the Senate, a notable achievement because more Democratic seats were up for grabs than Republican. In the House, the Democrats only added eight seats, leaving Republicans in the majority. Across the nation, Democratic House candidates had actually gained 1.4 million votes more than the Republicans. However, the GOP's sweeping win in the 2010 election not only gave them control of the House but also kept or put them in charge of many state houses. That meant that after the 2010 census they were in a position to redraw many congressional district lines to their advantage—a process called gerrymandering (see Chapter 8)—which they did, helping protect their 2010 House victories.[22]

Why Obama Won

There are many theories as to why Obama won. Nate Silver, the most accurate forecaster of this election, suggests that rather than one cause, the president's slow and steady rise in the polls after the debacle of the first debate indicates a number of factors were in play.

Here are some to consider from different analysts. Obama had the superior campaign both strategically and organizationally. He "focused like a laser on the states he needed to win." Some think his campaign's tactical decision to spend early to negatively define Romney was decisive. Obama's team used its resources more efficiently than Romney's, for example, buying TV ads earlier in the campaign when they were cheaper, thereby spending less but running more ads. Obama's campaign spent twice as much on cable, allowing it to customize its ads better by group and by region, and twice as much on online ads, too. By contrast, according to conservative operative Richard Viguerie, the Republicans "were stuck in a 20th century air war campaign strategy." In general, the

Obama campaign had a broad superiority in social media, e-mail, and other digital or online platforms.[23]

Ultimate campaign mastery is gauged on Election Day. In order to efficiently marshal resources, campaigns need to know exactly who their likely voters are and, throughout the day, to make sure they've voted. Obama's digital platform Narwhal continuously updated voter and volunteer information and phone-bank availability, greatly enhancing the efficiency and effectiveness of his get-out-the-vote operation. Meanwhile, "Romney's much-hyped get-out-the-vote digital tool, Orca, famously crashed." According to one conservative analyst, Obama's get-out-the-vote operation was "arguably better than anyone has ever done it before." Confessed one of Romney's digital specialists, "They were playing chess while we were playing checkers."[24]

Perhaps of greater importance, instead of allowing the election to be a referendum on the incumbent, Obama's campaign turned it into a choice between two people. Obama had the edge. The public generally related to him better than to Romney. He was the better campaigner, had the White House as a stage, and the old master Bill Clinton covering his back. Finally, Romney's personal story made him a flawed messenger on the economy. Regardless of how personally successful he was, it was hard to explain to average voters just how he made his own money (and why he would only release two years of tax returns) and easy to characterize his wealth as coming at the expense of people like them. Perhaps fearing anti-Mormon prejudice, he was also reticent about his years of devoted service through his religion, keeping private a side of his life that might have softened his business CEO public persona.[25]

Some think Romney's real problem was that the Republican Party was simply too strident, alienating key constituencies and pushing its candidates too far to the right. For example, although the Tea Party's influence (see Chapter 6) had ebbed somewhat since 2010, its views still had very significant drawing power among many Republicans. And there was still the specter of George W. Bush, blamed by many voters for the economic distress and the Iraq War—neutralizing traditional Republican advantages in foreign policy. To cap it off it was Obama, the Democrat, who had given the order to kill Osama bin Laden. Vice President Biden could say at a rally, and repeat at the Democratic Convention: "Osama bin Laden is dead, and General Motors is alive."[26]

Changing demographics clearly favored the president. Back in 1980, when Republican Ronald Reagan handily defeated Democrat Jimmy Carter, ushering in modern conservatism, 88 percent of all voters were white, and only 2 percent were Hispanic. By the 2012 election, the share of white voters had decreased to 72 percent of the electorate, while Hispanics had grown to 10 percent and given 71 percent of their votes to Obama. Asian Americans, a far smaller but also growing demographic group, gave Obama 73 percent. Many thought African Americans and voters under thirty lacked the enthusiasm they'd had in 2008. In fact, African Americans maintained the 13 percent share of the electorate they had in that election, with 93 percent choosing Obama. Although Obama's support among this group was down slightly from 2008, for the first time overall voter turnout among blacks exceeded that of whites (see Chapter 6). While Romney cut into Obama's 2008 margin among voters under 30, they slightly increased their share of the electorate, still giving six in ten votes to the president. And as hard as the Romney campaign tried to bridge the gender gap, Obama captured 55 percent of women voters. While overall voter turnout was down from 2008, the share of all voters either increased among Obama's key groups, as in the case of Latinos and youth, or stayed the same, as with African Americans and women.[27]

There was concern among Democrats that Republicans might eke out a close win by making voting more difficult, thereby "suppressing" the votes of minorities. In some states, Republicans had enacted new voter identification laws (see Chapter 6), shortened

Election Night

periods for early voting, ended voting on the Sunday before Election Day, obstructed voter registration drives, and required voters to provide proof of citizenship. It's hard to know whether these tactics succeeded, or whether they caused a rallying around Obama. If the goal was to keep minority voters away in very large numbers, they failed.[28]

Romney said because he could never win over the "47 percent," he'd pitch his message to others. On Election Day, enough people accepted Bill Clinton's narrative instead: Obama had inherited "a total mess" from people just like Romney. He needed more time. Ironically, 47 percent sided with Romney.

Elite Democracy: Campaign Rules

What lessons can we learn from the 2012 election? Three rules stand out. First, elections are candidate focused, although especially during times of incumbent difficulties and serious national problems, issues and party labels matter. Second, candidates must position themselves in a very specific way to be taken seriously by elite opinion makers and funders and to win over enough of the public to win. Finally, while money doesn't buy happiness— or elections—having it and using it as effectively as possible is essential.

Elite Campaign Rule 1: It's All About the Candidate

During the course of the electoral campaign, voters learn more about the personalities, families, quirks, gaffes, misdeeds, strategies, and tactics of the candidates than anything else. Moreover, the individual candidates are the ones engaged in a personal struggle to build a campaign organization, raise money, hire strategists, craft a message, contain their temper, and strike a theme. The news media often emphasizes the purely personal, whether through issues of moral character or personal style. The result is that rather than the great clash of issues between the platforms of great political parties, we often end up with an effort by one candidate's campaign team to discredit the opponent. It also means that personal style, personality, and life story can trump governing skill, judgment, and even political platform. Finally, the media often treat campaigns as if they are horse races (see Chapter 9), in which the candidates are the horses racing for money, media attention—and votes.

Candidate-centered campaigns have become even more pronounced in American politics because of party dealignment (see Chapter 8) and the various ways modern campaign technology enables focus on personal narratives. Although many voters are partisans and vote straight party tickets, the deciding margin often consists of **undecided and swing voters.** To influence them, candidates must achieve high name recognition and craft consistently favorable images that impress those voters.[29]

Given the volatility of a candidate-centered world, incumbents seek security by engaging in the "**permanent campaign.**" Members of Congress, for example, never stop "running" for reelection. They use all means at their disposal to make it difficult for challengers to beat them and to dissuade potentially formidable opponents from even trying. They do this by getting federal money for their districts, catering to elite financial backers, using their official committee positions as platforms for publicity, championing popular sides on "hot button issues"—and constantly raising campaign money.[30]

Candidate-centered—and "permanent"—campaigns can undermine popular democracy by drawing attention to personalities and away from fundamental issues, such as economic inequality. Candidate-centered campaigns can have another pernicious effect. Feeling that issues that matter are not being addressed, citizens may be drawn into efforts to demonize political opponents—or they may simply stay home. When a candidate loses because of real or contrived personal flaws rather than rejected ideas, his or her program and its supporters go down too, demoralizing many citizens.[31]

Elite Campaign Rule 2: Position Yourself Very Carefully

Candidate-centered campaigns favor those with certain kinds of elite credentials or those who can develop them quickly by passing key media and money tests and being declared by opinion leaders to be a "viable candidate." While personality is important it, is even more important to be considered a "responsible" member of the political community, neither too left nor too right, nor too unorthodox in personality or approach.

Candidates first carefully position themselves within their party. For the politically ambitious in the United States, that means within one of the two major parties. This amounts to calculating where your natural base of support lies and figuring out who else is available for you to reach out to, whether interest groups, other leaders, or fat cats. If you win your party's nomination, you must next position yourself in relation to your opponent from the other party in the general election. As you make these calculations, you are not just thinking about voters, but about which positions the donors, editorial boards, talking heads, bloggers, and radio talk show hosts take seriously, and which they shun or demean. If you want to be taken seriously, voters are only one of your constituencies.

Elite Campaign Rule 3: Raise Money, and Lots of It

The biggest hurdle for all candidates is raising enough money to run a viable campaign. In federal elections—races for the House, Senate, and presidency—the amounts spent have risen dramatically in virtually every election since the 1970s, when detailed records began to be required.

How much money is spent on elections? Over $6.3 billion was spent by campaigns, parties, and independent committees on all federal elections in 2012. That was more than double than the amount spent in 2000, which in turn was double the figure for 1992. "Every presidential election is the most expensive ever. Elections don't get cheaper, " remarked Ellen Weintraub, Chairwoman of the Federal Election Commission (FEC).[32]

Such escalating costs create a fundraising treadmill. Judging from 2012's results, today the average successful senator has to raise about $4,800 *each* day of a six-year term, whereas victorious House members have a quota of about $2,300 daily for two years. The average price tag for a Senate seat in 2012? A cool $10.5 million.[33] These daily figures are only a part of the story because they detail only those monies controlled directly by the candidates. More cash is dispensed by the national political parties and their committees, by the **independent issue advocacy** groups named after their tax-code status, the 527s and 501(c)s, by PACs, and since 2010 by a whole new entity called Super PACs (more on all of these later). Who benefits, and who is hurt by the money game?

D.C. on $4,800 a Day: Who Money Favors. Theoretically, anyone who fits the constitutional qualifications can run for Congress. In reality, money is the premier advantage in modern campaigns. Here are four laws of modern campaign finance.

Law 1. Incumbent members of Congress nearly always receive more money than their challengers. Partly for this reason, incumbents almost *always* get reelected.

Law 2. Challengers are able to defeat incumbents only when (a) they raise something close to the totals raised by the incumbent, or (b) the incumbent is very unlucky, openly corrupt, or does or says stupid things, or (c) there is a "wave" election sweeping out many incumbents of one party by newcomers in the other, as happened most recently in 2010.

Law 3. The most unpredictable, competitive, and expensive races are the open-seat contests where incumbents have retired.

Law 4. Raising lots of money is not just important to win elections. It also *sets the stage* for winning by scaring off formidable opponents, allowing a well-financed candidate to run against weaker and more poorly financed adversaries.

The strength of Laws #1 and #2 should be clear. Incumbents almost always win, and they almost always have far more money than their challengers. In 2008, if a challenger did not raise $1 million or more for a race for the House of Representatives, then the odds against winning were about 300 to 1.[34] In the historic 2010 congressional "wave" election, when Republicans took back firm control of the House of Representatives, reelection rates were lower, but incumbents in the House and Senate were still reelected about 85 percent of the time, raising a little under three times the amount of their challengers. In 2012, incumbents in the House again enjoyed a three to one financial advantage, although the figure in the Senate dropped to a little better than 1 ½ to 1. Still, nine out of ten in each body were reelected. (see Table 7.2)

Both Laws 3 and 4 also seem in good shape. There were fifty-six seats without incumbents in 2012. In almost one-third of them, party control of the seat switched.[35] As to Law 4, it is not always easy to identify potential candidates who are scared off by incumbent war chests. However, even incumbents in safe seats often raise large sums of money to scare off strong challengers. In 2000, five-term Michigan Republican congressman David Camp raised more than $1 million for his reelection bid, in spite of having won with 91 percent of the vote two years earlier. Not surprisingly, he faced a weak challenger and outspent his unknown opponent 200 to 1, easily beating him.[36] Table 7.2 details incumbent reelection rates in recent elections.

Table 7.2   Incumbent Reelection Rates, 2000–2012

		House	Senate
	Reelection Rates in General Elections (percent)		
2000	Bush wins; Republicans retain control of Congress	98	79
2002	Republicans retain congressional control	96	86
2004	Republicans make further gains in Congress	98	96
2006	Democrats retake Congress	91	79
2008	Obama wins; Democrats expand congressional majority	94	83
2010	Republicans win House decisively	85	84
2012	Obama wins; Republicans keep House	90	91

Sources: "Reelection Rates Over the Years," "Money Wins Presidency and 9 of 10 Congressional Races in Priciest U.S. Election Ever," OpenSecrets.org, Center for Responsive Politics, www.opensecrets.org; BGOV Barometer, Bloomberg.

Rules of the Cash Game

There's a profound irony to the permanent campaign and the money game it engenders. Tons of money flows, yet there is a complex web of laws, rules, and court decisions that seek to define the proper role of money in a democracy. The most important contemporary laws were passed by Congress in two waves, in 1974 and in 2002, with each later significantly weakened by Supreme Court decisions.

Campaign Finance Reform and the Supreme Court

The First Reform Wave: The FECA of 1974. The first set of laws was the result of revulsion at President Richard Nixon's 1972 campaign's shady fundraising activities and the Watergate scandal that followed. The 1974 **Federal Election Campaign Act (FECA)** was passed in the hope of preventing, or at least revealing, such practices.[37]

The act requires public disclosure of the names of campaign donors exceeding $200 in contributions, and it limits the size of donations to national party organizations and the official campaign organizations of federal candidates. (See Table 7.3.) It also provides public funding for presidential candidates (but not for congressional candidates) in exchange for voluntary agreement to limits on the amount of money they raise and spend. The FECA also bans direct contributions from corporations, unions, and foreigners to candidates. But it allows the formation of **political action committees (PACs)** through which corporations, unions, or other organizations can solicit contributions from their executive and administrative personnel, stockholders or members, and their families, and donate in amounts regulated by law to candidates, parties, and other PACs. The law also establishes a regulatory body—the **Federal Election Commission (FEC)**—made up equally of Democrats and Republicans to monitor the FECA's implementation.

The Supreme Court Derails Reform I: *Buckley v. Valeo*. The law's ability to stem the domineering role of money in elections was immediately stymied by the 1976 Supreme Court ruling in the case *Buckley v. Valeo*. In its decision, the Court struck down as unconstitutional the part of FECA that restricted campaign *expenditures* as interfering with the "unfettered interchange of ideas" and therefore free speech as protected by the First Amendment. The limits on *contributions* were upheld as a valid government effort to stop corruption. As a consequence of *Buckley*, Congress and state legislatures may only limit the money chase through laws, should they decide to pass them, in which candidates choose to *voluntarily* accept spending limits in exchange for public funding. Because *Buckley* struck down the expenditure limits, it became imperative for campaigns to raise as much money as possible so as to not be outspent.

The Second Reform Wave: The Bipartisan Campaign Reform Act (BCRA) of 2002.
Politicians and political interests soon found a way around *contribution* limits as well. Under federal election law, the amount of money political parties can spend in coordination with campaigns is regulated.[38] However, FEC opinions and rulings from 1977–1995 allowed political parties to raise money *without* contribution limits for "party building" activities, including get-out-the-vote and voter registration drives, and "legislative advocacy" media ads—but not for the "express advocacy" of the election or defeat of a candidate. Because this money was largely unregulated it was called **soft money**. On the other hand, **hard money** refers to donations *regulated* by the FEC that has contribution limits (see Table 7.3). In reality, "issue advocacy" ads were developed that served the same purpose as candidate advocacy ads put out by candidates. The national parties also cleverly channeled soft dollars to state parties, which then spent the money to help federal candidates in the states. In 1996, the Supreme Court also allowed political parties to spend unlimited amounts of soft money to support their candidates as long as these were "**independent expenditures**," separate from the candidate's campaign. The overall result was that the spirit of the law was evaded, and huge sums of soft money, without contribution limits, were raised and spent to elect candidates.[39]

The rise of soft money—from a trickle in the 1980s to a flood of about half a billion dollars in the election of 2000—soared to amounts that nearly matched regulated, hard money. It sparked a reform movement, spearheaded in Congress by Republican senator John McCain and Democratic senator Russell Feingold. The McCain-Feingold law—the **Bipartisan Campaign Reform Act (BCRA)**—passed Congress in 2002. The most significant provision of the law is that it prohibits national parties from raising or spending soft money. However, sponsors of the bill also agreed to *double* the maximum hard money contributions—from $1,000 to $2,000—that could be given directly to candidates.[40] Table 7.3 shows today's limits.

The Supreme Court Derails Reform II: *Citizens United v. the FEC.*
Then, in 2010, came another blockbuster Supreme Court ruling, *Citizens United v. the Federal Election Commission*. In BCRA—in addition to the soft money ban—Congress had also tried to limit the use of so-called "issue ads," produced and aired by independent groups with unregulated money for what in reality were clearly campaign-oriented electioneering purposes. Back in 1947, the Taft-Hartley Act had already barred the use of corporate or union treasuries to advocate for or against candidates. In *Citizens United*, a "bitterly divided" Supreme Court struck down the BCRA prohibition on "electioneering" ads and ended the Taft-Hartley restrictions. By a 5–4 vote it found such bans on corporate or group political advocacy in violation of the First Amendment's protection of free speech. It thus freed corporations, unions, and other associations to spend unlimited sums of unregulated money as long as they did so in a way that was not coordinated with candidates' campaigns. The case, however, didn't upend long-standing laws that stop corporations and unions from directly contributing money to political campaigns. Nor did it affect the part of BCRA that banned soft money contributions to political parties.[41]

The *Citizens United* decision caused a storm of controversy and inspired a number of constitutional amendments (see New Reform box). One particularly heated argument concerned whether corporations had First Amendment rights just like persons. And by allowing unregulated, independent spending on direct political advocacy for or against

Table 7.3   The Federal Election Campaign Act: Disclosure and Contribution Limits

Disclosure: Candidate committees, party committees, and PACs must file periodic reports disclosing money they raise and spend. Candidates must identify PACs and party committees that give them contributions, and individuals who give more than $200 in an election cycle. They must also disclose expenditures exceeding $200 per election cycle to any individual or vendor.

Contribution Limits: The FECA also places limits on contributions by individuals and groups to candidates, party committees, and PACs. The chart below shows how the limits apply to some participants in federal elections. It also shows the specific contribution limits for 2011–2012 and for 2013–2014.

Major Contribution Limits, 2011–2012 and 2013–2014

	To Each Candidate or Candidate Committee per Election[1]	To National Party Committee per Calendar Year	To State, District, and Local Party Committee per Calendar Year	To Any Other Political Committee per Calendar Year	Special Aggregate Limits
Individual may give	2011–2012: $2,500[a] 2013–2014: $2,600[a]	2011–2012: $30,800[a] 2013–2014: $32,400[a]	2011–2014: $10,000 (combined limit)	2011–2014: $5,000	Overall biennial limit: 2011–2012: $117,000[a] *as follows:* $46,200[a] to all candidates *plus* $70,800[a] to all PACS and parties[b] 2013–2014: $123,200[a] *as follows:* $48,600[a] to all candidates *plus* $74,600[a] to all PACs and parties[b]
National party committee may give	$5,000	No limit	No limit	$5,000	To Senate candidate per campaign: 2011–2012: $43,100[a] 2013–2014: $45,400[a]
State, district, and local party committee may give	$5,000 (combined limit)	No limit	No limit	$5,000	No limit
PAC (multicandidate)[c] may give	$5,000	$15,000	$5,000 (combined limit)	$5,000	No limit

1. Primary and general elections are counted as separate elections.

[a] These contribution limits are indexed for inflation.

[b] No more than $46,200 in 2011–12, or $48,600 in 2013–14, of this amount may be contributed to state and local party committees and PACs.

[c] Multicandidate committees (the most important type of PAC) are those with more than fifty contributors who have been registered for at least six months and (with the exception of state party committees) have made contributions to five or more federal candidates.

Source: Adapted from the Federal Election Commission, http://www.fec.gov/pages/brochures/fecfeca.shtml#Disclosure.

candidates, the decision unleashed a torrent of money in the 2010 and especially the 2012 elections—in the form of Super PACs.

Big Money Finds a Way: 527s, 501s, and the Super PACs

Even after BCRA was passed, soft money without contribution limits continued to flow. Because of that law, however, it moved in new directions.

Soft Money's Back Doors: The 527's and 501(c)'s. In the 2004 election, the most important direction for soft money was to so-called "527" organizations. Named after a section in the tax code, the term "527s" refers to political committees that are only allowed to advocate on issues, not for or against candidates. Nor are they allowed to coordinate with candidates' campaigns. A 527 is an attractive destination for money because there is no upper limit on contributions, and 527s can receive money from anyone, including corporations and unions. In reality, 527s find a way to produce ads that "portray federal candidates in such a way that there is little doubt as to the message."[42] The classic example occurred in 2004. "Swift Boat Veterans for Truth" was a 527 funded by wealthy supporters of President Bush's reelection. It put out false but effective ads discrediting Democratic candidate and decorated war veteran John Kerry's Vietnam War service (and subsequent antiwar activity), thereby undermining a central appeal of his candidacy.

Soft money has also evaded BCRA through so-called 501(c)s, named for another section of the tax code governing tax exempt organizations, including, among others, those serving educational, charitable, or social welfare purposes. Some of these are allowed to use a significant portion of their resources to advocate for or against candidates, something 527s are technically not allowed to do. And unlike 527s, candidates, parties, PACs, and Super PACs, they do *not* have to publicly disclose the identities of their donors. In July 2012, an effort to require disclosure of contributions to these operations was again killed in the Senate by a Republican filibuster. In the 2008 election, the 527s and 501(c)s expended more than $400 million in soft money, each spending about half that amount. In 2012, expenditures by 501(c)s rose to about $311 million, with conservative groups spending 85 percent of that total. Meanwhile, spending by 527s slipped to half their 2008 level, in part because of the advent of a new and even "better" way to inject big money into politics—the Super PAC.[43]

Soft Money's New Front Door: The Super PACs. The *Citizens United* decision fundamentally changed the nature of soft money. In its wake, a new breed of fundraising animal was spawned: the Super PAC.

Super PACs can raise money from individuals, corporations, unions, or other associations. Like normal PACs, donors who give more than $200 are publicly disclosed, but unlike them, Super PACs can accept contributions of any size. Like 501(c)s and 527s, they cannot donate to political campaigns and must theoretically operate independently of candidate committees. Unlike 527s and some 501(c)s —this is critically important—they can *directly* advocate for the election or defeat of political candidates.

Super PAC spending exploded, reaching $950 million in the 2012 elections. Former staffers of Mitt Romney established the largest of the Super PACs, called Restore Our Future, spending about $142 million. It played an essential role in helping Romney win the Republican nomination by hammering Romney's Republican challengers, Newt Gingrich and Rick Santorum. Seventy-five percent of *all* the money spent by all the Super PACs in 2012 was put into negative advertising, including 90 percent of money spent by Restore Our Future. Priorities USA Action, the main pro-Obama Super PAC, spent all of its $65 million to attack Mitt Romney.[44]

From 2008 to 2012, as we've seen, spending by 527s declined while spending by 501(c)s increased. And in 2012 spending by Super PACs took off like a rocket. Money had moved to more desirable destinations: the Super PACs where advocacy for and against candidates is permitted, and the 501(c)s where donors needn't be disclosed.

While BCRA stopped the flow of soft money to the political parties, major soft money had found another way to influence elections. Right after BCRA became law, Senator Mitch McConnell gave it its first challenge in the Supreme Court. After hearing the court rule against him in 2003, McConnell said: "This law will not remove one dime from politics." Helped by a very different court ruling in *Citizens United*, his prophecy came true.[45]

New Reform
New Reform New Reform New Reform New Reform New Reform New Reform

....

**Amend the Constitution:
Overturn *Buckley v. Valeo*
and *Citizens United v. FEC***

Two constitutional amendments have been introduced into the House of Representatives by Massachusetts representative Jim McGovern. One would effectively overturn *Buckley*, freeing Congress and state legislatures to regulate campaign *spending*, as well as contributions. The other would overturn *Citizens United*, making it crystal clear that constitutional rights apply only to living, breathing people and *not* to corporations.

According to John Bonifaz, the executive director of Free Speech for People: "These two constitutional amendment bills reflect the growing calls across America that Congress must act to reclaim our democracy...A national movement supporting these amendments is on the rise."[46]

Following is the body of each amendment.[47] Which would overturn *Buckley* and which would overturn *Citizens United*?* The answer is at the end of this text box.

Proposing an amendment to the Constitution of the United States

113th CONGRESS

**IN THE
HOUSE OF REPRESENTATIVES**
January 22, 2013

House Joint Resolution 20

Article—

Section 1. To advance the fundamental principle of political equality for all, Congress shall have power to regulate the raising and spending of money and in-kind equivalents with respect to Federal elections, including through setting limits on—

(1) the amount of contributions to candidates for nomination for election to, or for election to, Federal office; and

(2) the amount of expenditures that may be made by, in support of, or in opposition to such candidates.

Section 2. To advance the fundamental principle of political equality for all, a State shall have power to regulate the raising and spending of money and in-kind equivalents with respect to State elections, including through setting limits on—

(1) the amount of contributions to candidates for nomination for election to, or for election to, State office; and

(2) the amount of expenditures that may be made by, in support of, or in opposition to such candidates.

Section 3. Congress shall have power to implement and enforce this article by appropriate legislation.

House Joint Resolution 21

Article—

Section 1. We the people who ordain and establish this Constitution intend the rights protected by this Constitution to be the rights of natural persons.

Section 2. The words people, person, or citizen as used in this Constitution do not include corporations, limited liability companies or other corporate entities established by the laws of any State, the United States, or any foreign state, and such corporate entities are subject to such regulation as the people, through their elected State and Federal representatives, deem reasonable and are otherwise consistent with the powers of Congress and the States under this Constitution.

Section 3. Nothing contained herein shall be construed to limit the people's rights of freedom of speech, freedom of the press, free exercise of religion, freedom of association and all such other rights of the people, which rights are unalienable.

*Answer to question from top of the text box: House Joint Resolution 20 would overturn *Buckley.* House Joint Resolution 21 would overturn *Citizens United.*

Not Super?—They Still PAC a Punch

Long before Super PACs first appeared on the scene, when people used the word "PAC," they were referring to an older-style political action committee that goes back to the 1940s. Although federal law bars corporations or unions from contributing to candidates or parties, as we have seen, it allows them to establish associated PACs. These PACs are regulated by the FEC, and, unlike Super PACs, have contribution limits (see Table 7.3). Before the advent of soft money, PACs were one of the chief concerns of campaign finance reformers because many PACs represent companies, industries, or groups that have business before government (see Table 7.4 for PAC giving by economic sector).

Despite all the talk about Super PACs, according to an FEC estimate, these traditional PACs spent $1.2 billion for the 2012 elections, $250 million *more* than Super PAC spending. Northrop Grumman Corporation is a case in point. In 2010, it was the fourth largest arms-producing company in the world and second in U.S. defense contracts, bringing in almost $11 billion. For the 2012 elections its PAC doled out $2.4 million in political contributions.[48]

Who Gives: Taking Care of Business

Affluent individuals dominate soft money contributions. This is hardly surprising because there are no contribution limits. In 2012, the top 1 percent of donors gave two-thirds of all the money the Super PACs received. And within this select group, the top five gave $173 million, almost one-fifth of the total. At the summit, Las Vegas moguls Sheldon and Miriam Adelson contributed a stunning $93 million to support conservative candidacies.

Powerful businesses and industry organizations dominate PAC giving. In 2012, 68 percent of all PAC donations were from trade association and business PACs. Of more than 3,500 PACs, business and trade associations far outnumber and outspend those of any other category. Although labor unions claim seven of the top twenty PACs, overall they are relatively few in number, contributing only 14 percent of total PAC donations. Table 7.4 shows PAC spending by sector.[49]

Table 7.4 PAC Contributions To Federal Candidates in 2012				
Industry	Amount (millions of dollars)	Given to Democrats (%)	Given to Republicans (%)	Number of PACs
Agribusiness	24.2	32	68	273
Communications/electronics	25.8	44	56	183
Construction	14.7	28	72	126
Defense	15.3	41	59	49
Energy and natural resources	33.7	25	75	273
Finance, insurance, real estate	70.5	37	63	452
Health	56.1	43	57	370
Ideological and single issue	64.8	45	55	835
Labor	59.7	90	9	202
Lawyers and lobbyists	15.1	57	43	173
Transportation	22.8	33	67	169
Misc. business	41.9	34	66	389
Other	1.8	49	51	29
Total	446.4	$202.3 million	$243.5 million	3,523

Source: Table compiled from categories and data in "PACs," 2012, Center for Responsive Politics, www.opensecrets.org (accessed, March 20, 2013).

With all the talk about Super PACs since *Citizens United*, and about soft money and PACs before it, we often lose sight of the fact that regulated *hard* money remains the most important source of money in politics. In spite of contribution limits it is also extremely dependent on a relatively small number of well-off Americans. Table 7.3 shows current limits for giving to candidates, PACs, parties, and in the aggregate—the maximum combined total—for one election. For the 2014 elections, one individual will be able to give an aggregate of $123,200 in *hard* money to a combination of candidates, parties, and PACs.

Has this system of regulated hard money facilitated greater participation in the democratic debate? According to the Center for Responsive Politics, "a tiny fraction of Americans" give money to candidates, parties or PACs—13 percent in 2004 and 2008. Within this pool, large contributions dominate. Of all the hard money given in the 2012 election, nearly two-thirds, or $2.7 billion, was donated by people who gave more than $200, the figure at which donors must be disclosed to the FEC. Of this amount, *three-quarters* was given by people who gave $2,500 or more—only one-tenth of 1 percent of adults. Nearly *half* was given by people who gave $10,000 or more.[50]

Bundling and Maxing Out When the serious financial players agree to give their own maximum contribution to candidates, they are just getting started. They then also give to a variety of national and state party committees and PACs.[51] If they're really serious, they also give "**bundled contributions**." An individual puts together—"bundles"—her or his own maximum individual contribution with those of others, such as business partners, associates, and employees, and friends and relatives, and gives them as a group to a candidate's campaign committee—and possibly party committees and PACs. Such bundled contributions can come from particular industries, interest groups, businesses, or other groupings, and they can add up to hundreds of thousands of dollars or more.

A key goal of campaigns, parties, and PACs is to ensure that individual contributors "max out"—that is, give the maximum allowed by law. To ensure maxing out, and to efficiently raise money and direct it to where it will do the most good, a campaign can set up a separate victory fund. In the 2012 presidential election, the "Obama Victory Fund" and "Romney Victory" each encouraged affluent contributors to give $75,800—the maximum total that one person is allowed by law to give to one candidate's campaign and to various party committees (see Table 7.3). The fund then ships the money to the campaign and to select party committees, such as state committees in battleground states. If you maxed out for either Obama or Romney, you gave them $23,000 *more* than the yearly American median household income.[52]

To Give Is Better When You (Then) Receive Leaders and executives in the finance, banking, health care, military, agribusiness, and a host of other sectors often urge their executives and employees to participate in bundling for political campaigns. It enables them to try to influence elections, gain access to people with political power, and allows them to speak with a united voice. This can be very useful for an industry or company that has business with the government—or is being regulated by it.

Financially backing a winner, of course, brings other perks. President Obama in his first term appointed Cynthia Stroum, a Seattle venture capitalist, ambassador to Luxembourg. According to one account, she handled that job so poorly that some of her employees requested transfers—to Iraq and Afghanistan. Nicole Avant became ambassador to the Bahamas; Charles Rivkin got the attractive posting to France and Monaco. What did Stroum, Avant, and Rivkin have in common? Each bundled at least $800,000 for candidate Obama.

Some perks begin long before Election Day. The more you give, the more entrée you gain to the campaign and its stars, including the candidate and spouse. Bundling $500,000 made you one of the "Romney Stars"; for Obama, $500,000 qualified you for the National Finance Committee. A major Romney fundraising highlight was a three-day retreat in the mountains of Utah, including barbecue with the candidate, tea with his wife, and meetings with many luminaries. Donors were especially eager for "face time" with insiders in a Romney White House. "That's the price of admission right there," one donor said to another, "your six minutes with [Karl] Rove." For its part, Obama's campaign was equally hard at work with fundraisers, while also using the powers of incumbency. The president invited "major contributors to state dinners, put them on his Job Council and... allowed them into the White House for meetings with advisors."[53]

Who Gets: The Political Impact of Receiving

Once inclined to hedge its bets by funding the powerful in both parties, donations from corporate, financial, and banking elites moved to favor the GOP after the sweeping Republican congressional victories in 1994. With the Democrats retaking Congress in 2006 and strengthening their majorities in 2008, corporate giving again became more bipartisan. Following Republican victories in the 2010 congressional elections, and with many corporate executives chagrined at Democratic efforts to more closely regulate Wall Street and raise income taxes marginally on the wealthy, corporate giving swung back to the Republicans. In 2008, Democrats received a little more than half of contributions of over $200 from people affiliated with businesses. For 2012, the proportion dropped to 41 percent.[54]

Looking within the various economic sectors gives us a better idea of where the money comes from. People working in finance, insurance, and real estate gave well over $600 million, strongly favoring Republicans. People in health, energy and natural resources, construction, agribusiness, transportation, and defense gave almost $700 million, also very strongly backing Republicans. However, the Democrats did very well with the $600 million given by people affiliated with these groups: labor, communications and electronics, lawyers, and lobbyists. Regardless of which party receives the most, the purpose of the donations is the same: to promote interests and to gain influence with whoever has power.[55]

[MAKING A DIFFERENCE]

Fair Elections Now

Common Cause, along with many other nonpartisan organizations, is making a difference by supporting the Fair Elections Now Act. This is why.

It's no surprise that special interests and wealthy donors have enormous influence in Washington. Wall Street spent over a billion dollars on campaigns and lobbying in Washington and kept Congress and regulators at bay—until it was too late to prevent the 2008 market meltdown that nearly destroyed our economy.

The American people strongly support Fair Elections as a way to change pay-to-play Washington politics: In a 2012 survey of voters in fifty-four "battleground" House districts, more than half supported a citizen-funded Fair Elections system.

In a citizen-funded Fair Elections system, candidates would be able to run for Congress on a blend of small donations and public funds.

The Fair Elections Now Act would:

- Reduce the influence of big donors over federal elections, the main driver of pay-to-play politics in Washington;
- Enhance the power of small donors; and
- Offer a voluntary campaign finance system that both incumbents and challengers will find attractive.

It's time to get federal officials out of the money chase and let them do the job we elected them to do: tackle tough problems and represent their communities. In the 112th Congress, the bipartisan Fair Elections Now Act was introduced by Senator Dick Durbin (D-IL) in the Senate (S. 750) and Rep. John Larson (D-CT) in the House (H.R. 1404). The bill is expected to be reintroduced in the 113th Congress during 2013.

Policy Snapshot: Fair Elections

The Fair Elections Now Act would fund congressional campaigns with small contributions from individuals and limited public funds.

Candidates would qualify by raising a certain number of contributions of $100 or less from individuals in their home state. They would then receive a grant of Fair Elections funds for the primary and general election, and they could continue raising unlimited small contributions. Each additional $1 raised would be matched by $4 from a new Fair Elections Fund, ensuring that candidates who use the system could compete even against well-financed opponents.

States including Arizona, Connecticut, Maine, and North Carolina have used similar citizen-funded election systems for at least some of their elections with great success. The Fair Elections Now Act would build on those successes and carry them to Congress.

Source: Excerpted and adapted from "Fair Elections Now," *Common Cause*, www.commoncause.org (accessed February 8, 2013).

A Broken System: The Class Basis of Money in Politics

Those opposed to regulating money in politics argue that because—in their view—campaign spending is equivalent to free speech, restricting spending stifles our liberty. Does the present system of unrestricted spending really contribute to the freedom of political choice of the average citizen?

The One Percent (of the One Percent). Several studies on campaign financing and its consequences suggest a variety of ways in which our present system of financing campaigns undermines the democratic character of the political choices that elections offer. According to a study of the 2010 congressional elections, a little less than one in ten thousand Americans (.01 percent) gave almost *one-quarter* of all the money received by candidates, parties, PACs, and independent expenditure groups. The study found that more than 80 percent of party committee money came from those elites. It concludes: "*The One Percent of the One Percent* effectively play the role of political gatekeepers. Prospective candidates need to be able to tap into these networks if they want to be taken seriously."[56]

Who are these gatekeepers? They are not average Americans: "Overwhelmingly, they are corporate executives, investors, lobbyists, and lawyers."[57] Another analysis points out that the "one percent"—those with a median net worth of $7.5 million—are far more politically active in every way than average citizens. In a study of Chicago elites, one-fifth said they had bundled campaign contributions, something very few Americans do. Their priorities were also different from average citizens. For them, budget cuts, for example, to programs like Social Security were a preferred solution to economic problems rather than revenue increases or a combination of increased taxes with more modest cuts. Overall, they tended to think the common good is best achieved by "getting government out of the way" of the free market and of philanthropy. What happens when there are significant policy differences between Americans of different income levels? Yet another report concludes: "policy outcomes strongly reflect the preferences of the most affluent but bear virtually no relationship to the preferences of poor or middle-income Americans."[58] Perhaps this shouldn't be surprising because very affluent but unrepresentative "gatekeepers" have enormous influence on our elections, including on our recent contests for the presidency.

The Obama and Romney Cash Machines In 2008 and 2012, the Obama campaign portrayed its fundraising as propelled by small donors. If true, that might alleviate the undemocratic effect of money in politics and the influence it has later on policy. But was it true? The answer is yes—and mostly no.

The Obama campaign did have a strategy to seek out small donors and repeatedly go back to them for more money. Moreover, the campaign knew that small donors often become enthusiastic grassroots volunteers.[59] However, while Obama had a higher proportion of small donors (those giving $200 or less) than his opponents in both of his campaigns, it is a "myth" to think they dominated his finances in either election. In 2012, while only 12 percent of Romney's money came from small donors, only 28 percent of Obama's money did so as well. Over *70 percent* of it came from larger contributions: 34 percent from those who gave $201 to $999; 39 percent from those who gave $1,000 plus.[60]

In 2008, Barack Obama became the first candidate in history not to participate in the system of the public financing of presidential candidates in the general election because he knew he could raise far more money on his own. In 2012, for the first time, *both* major party candidates rejected public funding with its obligatory spending limits, leaving the system moribund. Why didn't they take the money? They would each have received $91.2 million for the entire general election campaign—$20 million less than Obama raised in the last *two and a half weeks* of the campaign.

Overall, when you add together the money taken in by the candidate's committee, the joint victory funds, and the national political parties for the presidential election, the Obama camp is estimated to have taken in about $1.1 billion, while Romney's campaign took in about $1 billion. When we include the kinds of independent outside spending organizations we discussed earlier in the chapter, the party conventions, and all the other candidates, total spending on the election comes to over $2.6 billion, with Romney's "red team" out-spending Obama's "blue team" by about $130 million. Regardless of who receives the money, the more important point is this: in order for these kinds of sums to be raised, multiple layers of elite financial gatekeepers had to give the green light.[61]

Campaign Spending and the Democratic Debate

In spite of the breathtaking sums raised for 2012, in the way that matters most 2012 was just like any other election year. Well before the campaign begins, the ability to raise money from wealthy contributors helps determine who can seriously run for office on what kind of platform. Money doesn't just buy access and possibly favors after the election. It shapes who gets into the game and with what message—right from the very start. That kind of corruption of democracy is far more profound than the buying of favors. It occurs without breaking a single law.

There are practical alternatives to this money-driven system. The Making a Difference box on "fair elections" shows one direction we can take to build for ourselves a more democratic system of campaigns and elections.

What the Money Buys: The Science of Mass Persuasion

Expensive privately funded campaigns create serious problems regarding inequalities of political influence. But what is all the money spent on?

Political Consultants

One big expense is comprised of the professional experts themselves. Back in the old days, party bosses made money too, but they dealt in votes and jobs and favors, district by district, in direct contact with voters through complex party organizations. The modern political consulting business began roughly five decades ago. Back then, consultants were from the worlds of advertising, public relations, and communication. Now, political consulting is its own profession. Its currency is high technology applied to politics.[62]

What do consultants offer? According to Dennis Johnson in *No Place for Amateurs*, because "[s]o much can go wrong...[c]ampaign professionals are needed to bring order out of chaos, maintain message and strategy discipline, and keep the campaign focused." As campaigns get more technologically sophisticated, experts are needed in a variety of complex fields. The rise of political consultants also parallels the growth of the permanent and personal campaign.[63]

PAUL J. RICHARDS/AFP/Getty Images

For sale?

Polling

Polling serves as the basis for all other campaign activities. Just about every reputable congressional campaign conducts a **benchmark survey**, which probes the name recognition, job ratings, and potential strengths and weaknesses of candidates in the race. **Tracking surveys** record voter reaction to the campaign's ads and themes. Pollsters also manage **focus and dial groups**, allowing candidates to "test-market" specific appeals and statements. Dial groups can actually evaluate reactions to each word in a candidate's speech.

Media Advertising

Most studies indicate that few voters change position by watching TV ads alone. But effective ads are essential in a modern campaign. They can reinforce existing positive impressions, or they can "go negative," defining opponents in the public mind before they have a chance to do so themselves. Although people say they don't like negative ads, they can be very effective, especially when the subject is not strongly defined in voters' minds or has vulnerabilities that can easily be exaggerated or caricatured. The overall cost of ads has risen because there are more of them, and rates, as well as media profits, have soared. Spending is also up because there are far more media outlets than the traditional broadcast stations, such as cable and online advertising. Nevertheless, TV ads are usually the greatest portion of expenses for any national or statewide campaign.

The importance and expense of campaign media specialists have grown apace. Media "buys" are a much more complex science than before. Ads must change with the tracking polls, reach different demographic groups, aim at the specific audiences for various media, and, in presidential races, precisely target interests and viewpoints within battleground states. In presidential campaigns, each team may produce hundreds of separate commercials.[64]

Advertising is essential to establish a candidate's identity, to negatively define an opponent, and to set the campaign's agenda. In this ad produced for national cable TV comedy channels (an example of targeting ads to media markets), the Obama campaign mocks Mitt Romney's claim that he'd do better than Obama in managing the economy. It takes off on comments Romney made in the first presidential debate: "I like PBS, I like Big Bird," he said. But he pledged: "I'm gonna stop the subsidy to PBS."

"Big Bird" from October 9, 2012 (approx. 30 seconds):

OBAMA (VOICEOVER) (VISUAL OF OBAMA): I'm Barack Obama, and I approve this message.

[MUSIC] MALE ANNOUNCER (VISUAL OF THESE MEN): Bernie Madoff. Ken Lay. Dennis Kozlowski. Criminals. Gluttons of greed. And the evil genius who towered over them? One man has the guts to speak his name.

ROMNEY (CLIP OF ROMNEY FROM THE PRESIDENTIAL DEBATE): Big Bird.

ROMNEY (CLIP OF ROMNEY SPEAKING IN IOWA): Big Bird.

ROMNEY (CLIP OF ROMNEY SPEAKING IN ILLINOIS): Big Bird.

BIG BIRD (VISUAL OF BIG BIRD): It's me. Big Bird.

MALE ANNOUNCER: BIG. YELLOW. A menace to our economy. Mitt Romney knows it's not Wall Street you have to worry about; it's Sesame Street.

ROMNEY (CLIP OF ROMNEY FROM THE PRESIDENTIAL DEBATE): I'm going to stop the subsidy to PBS.

MALE ANNOUNCER (VISUAL OF BIG BIRD): Mitt Romney. Taking on our enemies, no matter where they nest.[65]

Fundraising, Internet, Direct Mail—and More Fundraising

Consultants, polls, and especially ads are all expensive. Ironically, to afford them, campaigns must hire very expensive fundraising specialists. In congressional races, maintaining contacts with PACs and with the national and state parties that dispense money requires trained experts. So too, of course, does organizing all of the kinds of big donor events and tactics like "bundling" discussed earlier in the chapter. Today, fundraisers who deal with ordinary citizens use a variety of digital means to raise money, including websites, e-mail, social media, and, most recently, mobile devices, using applications such as Square. They also use more traditional methods, such as direct mail and toll-free numbers.

Despite the continued use of traditional methods, nowadays presidential fundraising has clearly entered a new era, a digital one. Fundraising on the Internet took off in 2004. By 2012, the Obama campaign was able to take in $690 million electronically. Most of it—over half a billion dollars—was generated through digital platforms, whether e-mail, social media, mobile devices, or its website. The rest was solicited in other ways, such as high-end events, and simply logged through the website.

Consultants in electronic fundraising and direct mail gather information from a diversity of sources such as friendly political organizations, magazine subscription lists, the professions, interest groups, consumer databases, and tailor the text of computer-generated "letters" to the concerns of the recipients. Like polling and advertising, whether digital or snail mail, these "communications" are strictly one way. Approval or disapproval is measured solely in terms of net money gained.[66]

Press and Media Relations

Today's press relations techniques are much more complex than in the past. For years now, a candidate's "events" and entire campaigns have been heavily scripted. This is especially true in presidential elections, where consultants are needed to make it appear that the candidate is accessible, but at the same time to shield the candidate from unscripted moments, lest he or she wander "off message" or make mistakes.

Media specialists also reinforce *and* defend the overall narrative of a campaign by disseminating stories and information that appear to support it. They also provide "information" to reinforce, if not help create, negative images of their opponent. In 1992, the Clinton campaign set up its famous "War Room," which choreographed "rapid responses" to attacks on him by George H. W. Bush, sending them to every news outlet in the country.[67] Techniques pioneered by the 1992 Clinton campaign have been refined to a science, with the media-targeted e-mail wars of 2008, and the more broadly targeted Twitter wars of 2012 as examples.

Digital Mass Persuasion

In today's political world, campaigns also need to hire experts, consultants, and vendors in what might be called the new science of individualized mass persuasion.[68] What's called microtargeting is used to find links between consumer preferences and political proclivities. Rather than blanketing media markets, neighborhoods, or phone lists with the same message, the goal is to customize message to what's important to different voters, partly by coordinating marketing databases and political databases. This technique was pioneered by the Bush campaigns in 2000 and 2004. "We did what Visa did...predict how people will vote—not based on where they live, but how they live," said Ken Mehlman, Bush's reelection chair.[69] By 2008, the Obama campaign had used microtargeting even more effectively than Bush had.

In 2012, the Obama campaign also made a major commitment to predictive analytics and persuasion modeling. These techniques supplement basic knowledge about who is more—or less—likely to vote for a candidate with predictions about the kinds of specific appeals and contacts by a campaign that are more—or less—likely to persuade an individual voter to support that candidate; follow-up campaign action (or inaction) with the person is then based on these predictions. Predictive models were also used to recruit volunteers, and to improve the frequency and timing of fundraising, yielding more contributions. According to Obama's chief data scientist, analytics gives campaigns "the agility and speed" to best use huge amounts of online, constantly changing data.[70]

Mining and Integrating Data Information for campaign operations is gained through what's called "data mining." This involves locating data in a wide variety of sources, including: voter records, consumer databases, political activity databases, and websites and social networks, including Facebook, Twitter, LinkedIn, and Groupon. Twitter and especially Facebook are becoming especially important sources of consumer data and political affiliations. The databases of the national political parties, however, remain extremely important.

Data is most effectively used when it is available to all the units of a campaign. A main innovation of the 2012 Obama campaign was its ultra modern digital platform Project Narwhal. It was designed to integrate volumes of information collected by different campaign units, such as about potential voters, volunteers, and funders, including both online and offline profiles of individuals, and make the integrated data available to all parts of the campaign.[71]

Social Media

Mastering social media has also become a staple in modern campaigns. Today it is used in many facets of campaigning, from developing networks of volunteers, to fundraising, to mobilizing voters, to communicating with campaign networks and the media. Recognizing the importance of social media, the Romney campaign tripled the number of Facebook friends that Obama had in 2008. Meanwhile, the Obama campaign increased its total more than *eight* fold. The Obama campaign illustrated one particularly adept use of social media, when it endeavored to deploy its Facebook "friends" as "online ambassadors" to "personally" contact and persuade their own Facebook friends to get involved with the campaign and, of course, to vote.

•   •   •

On Election Day, 2012, Robert L. Mitchell, writing for *Computerworld*, suggested that Obama's campaign was "the world's first top-to-bottom, data-driven campaign." It was an experiment, he said. The vote tally wouldn't only choose a president. It would be a referendum on the campaign's analytic model itself. "If Obama wins," according to Mitchell, "it will forever change the rules of the campaign game."[72]

Political Marketing versus Grassroots Campaigns: Is There a Difference?

Alexander Gage, the man who pioneered microtargeting for President Bush, suggested that the information was now available to both parties. The real question was "what do you do with it?"[73] From a popular democratic point of view, there is a far more important question than technological proficiency. Does the modern high-tech campaign advance or retard *authentic* voter participation? Does it turn voters into spectators and judges, or real participants and activists?

Can campaigns be run differently, where voters and not experts are powerful from the start? Such efforts might be called **grassroots campaigns**. These value volunteer efforts, small monetary donations, and people-based organizations; downplay the role of advertising and money; and make the candidates responsive to voters for direction, support, and advice. They make organized people just as important as organized money.

The late Minnesota senator Paul Wellstone showed how grassroots campaigns could actually beat the odds. Back in 1990, Wellstone was a well-known activist but a political science professor with not a lot of money. In his first race, he took on an incumbent Republican senator who had accumulated over seven times more campaign money than Wellstone had. Wellstone rented an old school bus to use as a mobile campaign headquarters and traveled the state, attacking his opponent for taking big business donations, and promising to be an independent fighter for average wage earners.[74] He won, and proved to be as independent as promised, becoming one of the leading liberal and progressive voices in the United States Senate for almost twelve years. Tragically, he and his wife and daughter were killed in a plane crash in 2002.

There are dozens of examples of successful grassroots campaigns. The fact remains, however, that without fundamental campaign finance reform, the money-driven campaign is here to stay. Are there signs, however, within recent presidential campaigns that a more participatory politics can be achieved? From 2004 through 2012, we have seen campaigns that were highly professional, enormously expensive, and *also* that featured the activity of a higher number of committed volunteers than any campaigns in recent history. The two Obama campaigns are particularly interesting because they expertly designed and managed innovative Internet techniques to create "grassroots" political and social networking sites that increased participation.[75] Perhaps his campaigns, even more than others, displayed the full-force of a lurking contradiction. Successful modern campaigns are highly orchestrated, hierarchically organized, and require enormous sums of money. But many in the public may really want something more.

Conclusion: Campaigns and Elite versus Popular Democracy

In order to sustain and make meaningful the hopeful signs of grassroots activism, whether in recent presidential campaigns, or in the variety of social movements active in America, the basic rules of the campaign game will need to be changed. Ultimately, the modern money driven campaign benefits elite democracy by favoring funders and experts over grassroots activism and the power of ordinary people to shape the political agenda. It is understandable why political candidates find the power of expensive modern campaigns compelling. But there is a cost to American democracy.

Citizens have three choices. They can withdraw from their already limited role in politics. They can passively accept the inevitability of elite dominance. Or they can choose to fight to reshape the game. The quests for campaign reform, for grassroots campaigns, whether traditional or modern, and for new ways of bringing politicians into dialogue with voters are healthy signs that the democratic debate may be reviving. Such a revival, however, will not happen if left to the goodwill of elites. It requires citizens to bring it about for themselves.[76]

Reader's Guide

Critical Thinking Questions

1. President Obama achieved a strong victory in 2012. Were the voters giving him a mandate for a program of action? If so, what is that program?

2. Would you prefer campaigns to be less money driven and professionally organized from the top and more grassroots in nature? If they were, would you participate in them? In what ways would you like to participate?

3. How does the emphasis on marketing and positioning political candidates affect the kind of issues that get debated in a campaign? In the 2012 presidential election, what issues would you have liked to see addressed that weren't?

4. How does the need to raise such large sums of money to pay for professionally run campaigns affect the political program of a candidate? Are there issues that you think are left out because of the influence of large campaign contributors?

5. How does the way we fund campaigns affect the goal of political equality in America? In an ideal world, what system of campaign financing would exist? How close can we come to this ideal in the real world of American politics?

Key Word D. Guildon

candidate-centered campaigns   candidate success is based more on personality, distinctive record, and campaign organization than on political party and its program.

gatekeepers   Prominent media pundits and reporters or powerful funders or other elites who can make or break candidacies early on by giving or withholding credibility or financial support.

invisible primary   The preelection-year competition for money, support, and media attention among potential presidential candidates.

name recognition   The extent to which a candidate's—or potential candidate's—name is known by voters.

undecided and swing voters   Voters who tend to lack firm party loyalties and whose allegiances can shift, depending on election strategies and tactics.

permanent campaign   The process by which incumbent officeholders are constantly gearing their official actions toward their reelection prospects.

independent issue advocacy   Expenditures of money raised with unregulated contributions that may not advocate election or defeat of candidates for federal office, and must not be coordinated with formal organizations of candidates and political parties.

Federal Election Campaign Act (FECA)   A series of federal laws regulating the size of campaign donations to federal candidates for office, administered by the FEC.

political action committee (PAC)   An organization, registered with the FEC, that funnels voluntary hard money contributions from individuals in corporations, trade associations, labor unions, and other groups into political campaigns.

Federal Election Commission (FEC)   The regulatory body that enforces the FECA and the Bipartisan Campaign Reform Act of 2002.

soft money   Money raised for the purpose of affecting federal elections but that is not subject to limits and prohibitions of federal campaign finance law.

hard money   In federal elections, the regulated contributions by individuals and PACs to specific candidates, party committees or other PACs. These contributions are subject to contribution limits and may be used to advocate for or against a candidate.

independent expenditures   Campaign expenditures by Super PACS, PACS, parties, corporations, unions, individuals, 527s, and 501(c)s that occur independently of the formal organizations of candidates and political parties. Independent expenditures cannot be coordinated with parties and candidate organizations.

Bipartisan Campaign Reform Act (BCRA)   Also known as the McCain-Feingold Law, it banned "soft money" contributions to political parties. It also raised very significantly individual contribution limits to candidate and national party committees, and the aggregate biennial limit, and indexed these for inflation.

bundled contributions   A practice most often employed by business and trade association groups, to gather together legal individual contributions and deliver them in a "bundle" to parties and candidates in order to maximize the group's influence.

benchmark survey   A poll conducted by professional campaign consultants that investigates a potential candidate's name recognition and reputation among voters; one of the preliminary steps for all potential candidates in large electoral districts and states.

tracking survey   Polls conducted on a frequent, sometimes daily basis that gauge voter changes in opinion and mood. Tracking surveys are most used by campaigns to measure the influence of campaign themes and propaganda on voters.

focus and dial group   A selected sample of voters intensively interviewed by campaign consultants to gain knowledge about reactions to particular candidates and their campaign messages and themes.

grassroots campaign   A run for office that emphasizes volunteer efforts, person-to-person contact, and voter organization rather than paid advertising, extensive polling, and other costly activities managed by a central staff.

U.S. Parties: Who Has a Voice?

The People's Party rally began with a long procession from town to the grove. Each Alliance and People's Party club member carried an appropriate banner. For two days, over a thousand people heard speeches, listened to band music, and sang songs. Nearly everybody, men, women, and children, wore the same kind of badge. "Equal rights to all, special privileges to none" was the favorite.

Dateline: Kansas, 1892

As chairman, president and chief executive of Safeway Inc., the world's eleventh largest grocery chain, Steven Burd…filled ten tables with Safeway suppliers, including rice farmers, strawberry growers, and a cheese manufacturer, plus representatives of Breyers ice cream, Sunkist produce, and Del Monte canned goods, who paid $2,000 to hear Bush talk. Each donor wrote a four-digit "solicitor tracking code" assigned to Burd on the check so that the Safeway CEO will receive credit from Bush campaign officials.… The possible rewards, depending on how much money he can bring in, include cocktails with campaign architect Karl Rove, dinner with Commerce Secretary Donald L. Evans, and photo opportunities and sessions with the president.[1]

Dateline: California, 2003

More than a century apart, these two campaign reports show that American party politics and electioneering are about the business of gaining loyal supporters and staging often spectacular events. Yet these accounts also signify enormous changes that have transformed our political parties and the meaning of elections.

Return for a moment to 1892. Kansas farmers rallied under the banner of a political party, the "people's party," or Populists. However, the purpose of their massive, open-air rally was not only support for a political candidate but also a community festival. A thousand farmers, most probably with little schooling, put up with two days of political speech making. The

175

Green Party presidential candidate Jill Stein and her running mate Cheri Honkala being arrested trying to be included in the second presidential debate at Hofstra University on Long Island, New York, on October 16, 2012. Third party candidates were barred from participating in the presidential debates.

banners they brought testified to the larger Populist goals: economic equality and an end to Wall Street misdeeds. Blending a community festival with serious political discussion, the party politics of the nineteenth century was a collective effort.

For these Populists, or even for their Democratic and Republican counterparts in 1892, the fundraising events of 2004 might be a shock. Safeway's Mr. Burd, as well as the company's suppliers, were less committed to a crusade than to their own very specific economic self-interest. Many of the donors were not even Republicans but rather representatives of interest groups who gave to both parties.

Much has changed about what political parties mean to people and what the parties actually do. One hundred years ago they were seen as important vehicles of grassroots participation. Today's parties still stage rallies, but most of what they do to win votes involves raising and spending enormous amounts of money—more than ever before. They must pay for the marketing, consultants, polls, ads, and get-out-the-vote drives they run. They also increasingly recruit, train, and finance candidates. In the process, they themselves become dominated by fundraisers, consultants, pollsters, and marketers.

In Chapter 7, we saw how candidates and parties raise money for the campaigns. Here the central question is: Does our party system today help to expand democracy by increasing the quantity, quality, and equality of participation and voting in U.S. elections? Or in its present form, does it serve to limit all three?

Why Political Parties Are Important

Whatever other disagreements they have, most political scientists believe political parties are essential to modern democracy. Without doubt, other political endeavors are also very important, such as social movements, interest groups, and public interest campaigns. It is only the political party, however, that brings individual citizens, groups, and movements together around the practices of election campaigns and of voting itself, the most egalitarian of all political acts. That is why political parties are so special.

As individuals, ordinary people don't have much money; can't lobby much, if at all; and have few personal connections. But parties can transform a relatively meaningless single vote into a representative collective voice and help level the playing field. They also can provide a public, democratic space where people can converse, debate, and finally come to some agreement on an array of different concerns.

Parties naturally want to win elections and therefore build *coalitions* among religions, regions, classes, races, ethnicities, and other differences relevant to public opinion and public policy. As political scientists put it, political parties **aggregate interests**, that is, bring together diverse group interests into a concrete political program. Effective political party coalitions slowly alter the narrow claims of groups and individuals, turning them into a broader vision of the public interest through compromise and discussion. This *party philosophy* becomes an enduring identity that holds together different kinds of voters over time.

In theory, strong parties can project to the electorate distinctive identities and choices, take responsibility for them, and thereby promote accountability. They also can *recruit* and *nominate* candidates and provide the resources to help them campaign for public office. This potentially both makes politics as a career available across socioeconomic barriers *and* means that candidates remain accountable to the party and its platform. Rather than insulate officeholders from the public, long an aim of elite democrats, strong parties can maintain discipline over elected officials, helping assure correspondence between what they do and the *party platforms* on which they asked voters for support.[2]

Why American Parties Are Unique

Scholars of American politics have coined the term **responsible parties** to summarize the potentially democratic virtues of strong parties in a democratic society. Yet, for most of American political history, our parties haven't performed the functions of "responsible parties" all that well.

Have the Democratic and Republican parties endeavored to organize all potential voters, or have they excluded some? Do they really provide the electorate with a space to debate the policies and philosophies that reflect both the commonalities and the wide differences of the citizenry? Or do they distort and muddle the real issues when it comes to campaigns, and then govern as they please when in power? Overall, do American parties work to retard or increase further political participation?

Our two major parties have complex histories. In many ways, our parties are unique. To assess their achievements as institutional agents of democracy, let's take a close look at the key elements of the American party system.[3]

Age and the Weight of Tradition

Americans often think of their nation as young. Yet, born in the 1790s and energized by Andrew Jackson in the 1820s, the Democratic Party is considered by many to be the oldest political party in the world. The Republican Party is younger but it can still trace its origins to the 1850s and the battles to limit slavery's expansion. Both parties were competing before the modern corporation existed and before the United States was a great world power. The fact that our two major parties are old might be a sign of their ability to adjust. But it might also be a sign of their ability to exclude—or co-opt—competition and innovation. Their longevity is an achievement, but it also makes them quite unwieldy instruments of rapid electoral change.[4]

Samuel Huntington has commented that "our parties resemble a massive geological formation composed of different strata, each representing a constituency or group added to the party in one political era, and then subordinated to new strata produced in subsequent political eras." Change can sometimes come quite slowly, despite important changes in culture and in the economy.[5]

Political Parties as Local Organizations

Both national parties have historically been loose coalitions of state and local groups, with little in common but their desire to nominate a winning presidential candidate. Take as an example the contradictory social groups within each party in 1920. In rural northern areas such as in New York State, the GOP was a party of small-town, native-born Protestant farmers and shopkeepers, while in the cities it was the party of big business and urban professionals, and, in the South, the descendants of African American slaves and a few dissenting whites. The 1920 Democrats contained both Irish and Italian Catholic immigrants in cities like New York and Boston *and* Protestant plantation owners and businessmen of the South. The 1920 Democratic Convention featured bitter debates about whether to support or condemn the Ku Klux Klan, which targeted Catholics as one of its victims.[6]

Today, reflecting their nineteenth-century beginnings and American federalism itself, parties are still organized to control powerful state and local offices. Only fairly recently have the parties organized as more truly national institutions with distinctive agendas and identities.

Ideological Fuzziness

Both the local and preindustrial origins and the complex social diversity of American parties present a big contrast to their distant European cousins. Generally, Western European parties were born out of the class tensions accompanying the Industrial Revolution. They developed national identities around strong political ideologies and comprehensive party platforms. The first European "mass" parties were critical of industrial capitalism and tried to advance democracy by campaigning for mass suffrage, which had already been achieved by white males in the United States before the Civil War. Clearer about whom they wanted to organize than were Democrats or Republicans, Europe's mass parties thrived on activism and voter mobilization, forming party "sections" and "branches" in factories and city neighborhoods. More often than not, the upper and middle-class parties that formed to compete with labor, socialist, and social democratic parties developed similarly strong national identities.[7]

America's two largest and oldest parties have never been primarily organized around the issue of social and economic inequalities. Although it may be hard to believe it after recent elections, the range of ideological disagreement between the parties has been relatively limited in historical and comparative terms, although it certainly has grown in the last few decades. "Democrats" and "Republicans" are broad party names that offend few people. In contrast with some European Labor parties, neither party has been critical of corporate capitalism as an economic *system* or supported national economic planning, or wealth redistribution. However, at various times in their histories, some leaders within each party—although largely within the Democratic Party over the last eighty years—have been critical of some corporate *behavior* and supported using government to ease economic distress or address economic problems. Both also strongly have supported a dominant international role for the United States. However, there has been an anti-interventionist wing among liberals in the Democratic Party for some time, and very recently among a few conservative Republicans as well, reminiscent of the "isolationist" wing in that party before Word War II. While we always have had "minor" or "third" parties, including a Socialist Party once able to win 6 percent of the national vote, our dominant parties often, though not always, have blurred social differences and ideological distinctions, even when deeper conflicts existed in U.S. society.[8]

Indicative of the fact that American parties were historically decentralized, both parties, until relatively recently, maintained only a skeletal national staff and headquarters. In 1972, when Nixon's "plumbers" burglarized the Watergate headquarters of the "biggest and oldest" political party in the world—the Democrats—they found an office that was far smaller than the Safeway supermarket downstairs and the luxury co-op apartments and hotel rooms above.

Why Only Two Parties?

Democrats and Republicans have dominated elections for nearly 160 years. This **dominant two-party system** is a rarity in the world. What accounts for it?

Some say that despite important disagreements, most Americans don't have truly fundamental political differences, which makes it hard for smaller, more ideological parties to get off the ground. Yet the two-party system can also make it *appear* that important differences don't exist, in part by using its long occupation in power to create legal and structural obstacles to competitors in the marketplace of ideas and action. As a result, potential political issues and the conflicts they address may exist, in fact, but remain submerged, losing out to the set of political arguments favored by the two parties. The costs to choice, representation, and participation can be enormous.[9]

The largest structural instrument sustaining the party duopoly is taken for granted by most Americans and by both parties. The **single-member district (winner-take-all) electoral system** (see also Chapter 6) makes it very unlikely that small parties can win any representation, rendering them perpetually invisible. In systems using **proportional representation**, on the other hand, third-party supporters win legislative seats in proportion to the share of votes they receive in an election.[10]

Getting a third party on the ballot is no picnic either. For the most part, new political parties and candidates have to spend most of their scarce resources just fulfilling the peculiar rules of each state, including spending much of their time in petition drives to get on the ballot, while established parties usually have permanent ballot positions. Third parties often occupy poor ballot positions as well, making it hard for voters to find them on the ballot at all. Historically, third parties have gained visibility and strength when they were able to put major-party candidates also on their third-party line—a practice called "fusion"—instead of running their own candidates. In two-thirds of the states, however, "fusion" is illegal. In 1997, the Supreme Court found such state prohibitions constitutional.[11]

The **Electoral College system** also discourages third-party candidates from running for president and discourages voters from supporting them. Why? In all but two states, whoever gets a plurality of the vote in a state wins *all* of its electors. The reality is that unless a party has extremely strong roots in one state or several states with strongly felt similar concerns, that party will come away from a presidential election with no electoral votes, even after making a strong popular vote showing. The last times non-major parties were able to win electoral votes were in the 1940s and 1960s when pro-segregationist parties won some states in the South.

In 2000, the well-known consumer advocate Ralph Nader, running as the Green Party candidate, ran at close to 10 percent in some polls. He wound up with 2.7 percent of the total. Many potential Nader voters—and Democrats—decided that to vote for him would be to help Republican George W. Bush. The psychology of "the lesser of the two evils" sent them back to Democrat Al Gore. Gore's extremely narrow loss to Bush (by 537 votes in Florida, costing Gore the presidency) further underscored for many the "danger" of voting for a third party. Many Democrats were livid about Nader's role, blaming him for costing Gore the election. Thus, this election and its legacy helped sustain the lesser of two evils psychology and the two-party duopoly of presidential contests.[12] (See New Reform: Flunking Out of the Electoral College.)

There are other obstacles to third parties as well. The system of public financing for presidential elections doesn't award general election money to minor parties until they win 5 percent of the vote. Without money, however, it's difficult to be noticed. Which comes first, the chicken or the egg? Similarly, the presidential debate commission, not surprisingly headed by a Democrat and a Republican, discriminates by excluding minor parties from presidential debates unless they meet a 15 percent threshold in five national polls. Ross Perot, who in 1992 had the second largest popular vote total of any minor party candidate in the 20th century, was not allowed to participate in the 1996 presidential debates. The presidential debate system is "an instrument of the two political parties to ensure that the presidency is passed back and forth between them," said 2000 Reform Party candidate and former Nixon speechwriter Pat Buchanan. "It's a monopoly."[13]

Then there is **gerrymandering**, the drawing of congressional and state and local legislative district lines in such a way as to maximize the number of seats a political party will win and to protect incumbents. It is a very widespread practice and extremely partisan, as well as a major reason incumbent reelection rates have been as high as 98 percent in the House of Representatives in recent years. While gerrymandering is designed to stifle *two*-party competition, it also helps reinforce a political geography in which third parties have no place.[14]

Third Parties and Popular Democracy

Despite all these obstacles, third parties have played important roles in U.S. history and continue to do so today. Third parties have often served to shake up the dominant two-party system by trying to bring new issues and even new voters into politics.

On the political right, third parties interested in preserving states' rights and racial segregation won presidential electors in 1948, 1960, and 1968, reflecting a "white backlash" against the growing civil rights proposals of the national Democratic Party. Before that, on the political left, there were farmer-labor parties like the Populists in the 1890s, the Progressives in 1924 (both of which won electors), and the Socialist Party, which won many local offices in the early twentieth century, and whose presidential candidate won over 900,000 votes in 1920—while in jail for "sedition." The abolition of child labor, the progressive income tax, the direct election of U.S. senators, and women's suffrage were all reforms first pressed by these parties.

In recent years, two new parties have emerged, among others, to contest what they see as the undemocratic, elite character of the Republicans and Democrats. In 1995 the Reform Party was formed. Initially a vehicle for billionaire Ross Perot, the Reform Party was a strong opponent of federal budget deficits, corporate-sponsored international trade agreements, and corruption by the money and lobbying of Washington politics. Perot received 19 percent of the presidential vote as an independent 1992, and 8 percent as the Reform Party candidate in 1996, winning exactly *zero* electoral votes each time. The party lost significant momentum in 2000, winning only four-tenths of one percent of the vote, and today is insignificant.

The Green Party is a loose national confederation of state organizations dedicated to progressive environmental and economic policies. The Green Party is an important force in a number of European countries, and in the United States it holds a number of local elective offices. After playing an important role in the 2000 election, it only received three-tenths of 1 percent of the vote in 2012. Its vote total was probably hurt by the fact the election was

Why American Parties Are Unique

The 2012 Campaign You Never Saw: The Silenced Third Parties

Did you know that in the 2012 presidential election there were—according to one survey—as many as *19* political parties *besides* the Republicans and Democrats on the ballot in at least one state? If you didn't you're not alone. In fact, there were a total of 415 candidates for president registered with the Federal Election Commission besides Barack Obama and Mitt Romney.

Because in the United States each state writes its own rules for ballot access—even for federal elections—the number of parties on *your* ballot on November 6, 2012 depended on the state you were in. If you voted in Colorado, besides the main parties, there were 14 additional candidates on the ballot for president, in Florida 10, in Tennessee 5, in Oklahoma 0. How many choices did you have in your state? How many of them had you heard of?

Many of the parties that made it to the ballot, and their candidates, had well-formed programs. Some had sufficient grassroots support to get on the ballot in many states, and some of them were even led by prominent politicians who bolted from one of the main parties.

For example, Gary Johnson was a former Republican governor of New Mexico. In 2012, he headed the Libertarian Party ticket, which had enough support to get on the ballots in 48 states. Libertarians support a less powerful state in general, including much less economic regulation, and a completely "free" market, personal freedom, strong civil liberties, and a non-interventionist foreign policy. One of Johnson's prominent themes was to: "bring the troops home!" Doctor and activist Jill Stein, nominee of the Green party, also had a serious message. She wanted to "end corporate rule" and ran on a platform of economic justice, stopping climate change, civil liberties and ending military intervention. She was on the ballot in 38 states. Former Salt Lake City, Utah, Mayor Rocky Anderson headed up the progressive Justice Party, on the ballot in 16 states, and former Virginia Member of Congress Virgil Goode headed up the conservative Constitution Party, on the ballot in 27 states. The messages of these parties were all different—and that's the point!

There is one thing all these parties and candidates had in common, however. They were all excluded from the major presidential debates, public funding for the general election, and serious coverage in the media, keeping the two party duopoly secure. Actually, the Libertarian Party has already made history. Back in its first campaign in 1972, its female vice presidential candidate became the first woman to receive an electoral vote for president or vice president. The vote was courtesy of a "faithless elector" who had been chosen to support the Nixon-Agnew ticket but voted for the Libertarians instead.[15]

To understand just how strong the two party duopoly is in American politics, consider this:

The last time in American history that a new or third party became one of the two major parties was in 1856. That party's name? The Republican Party. Its candidate, John C. Fremont, came in second that year. Four years later, its candidate was Abraham Lincoln. Perhaps that should tell us something about how—today—we should treat third parties.

very partisan and perceived to be very close, and because Obama is very popular, despite grumblings, among liberals. The Libertarian Party did the best of the small parties in 2012, winning 1 percent of the vote. This was an improvement over recent years, but slightly less than its peak percentage in 1980.

Despite many loyal activists, many minor parties of the left, the middle, and the right have suffered the same fate as the Reform Party, the Greens, the Libertarians, and plain independents. The problem with assessing the reach of third parties is that, because they are never on a level playing field with the two major parties, it is impossible to know how

New Reform
Flunking Out of the Electoral College

How the Electoral College Works

Each state gets one electoral vote for each of its two senators and for each member it has in the House of Representatives (the District of Columbia gets three electoral votes). The states decide how the electoral votes are to be allocated. All but two states allocate *all* the electoral votes to the popular-vote winner of that state. Maine and Nebraska give two electoral votes to the statewide winner and one to the candidate who wins each congressional district.

The electors are partisans who are pledged to vote for their party's candidate. (On rare occasions, a "faithless elector" has voted for someone else, but it has never made a difference.) After the election, the electors meet in their state capitals, cast their votes, and then in early January Congress certifies the result. The candidate with 270 electoral votes—a majority—wins the presidency.

Why the Electoral College Is Undemocratic

The Electoral College is undemocratic in at least four ways. First, because every state gets two senators regardless of its population, and therefore two electors, small states are overrepresented in the Electoral College. The result is, for example, that each voter in Wyoming carries *three* times the weight in the Electoral College of a voter in California.[16] Second, the "unit rule," by which whoever wins a plurality of the popular vote wins all the electoral votes, means it makes no sense for candidates to campaign where they have little chance of winning—or losing. The result is that during general elections presidential campaigns ignore millions of voters in noncompetitive states, which in 2012 included nearly forty states.[17] Third, also because of the "unit rule," the Electoral College reinforces the two-party duopoly because in order to get any electoral votes a party's candidate must "carry" a state—win the most votes in it—a very hard thing for a third party to do. Finally, and most notoriously, as happened in 2000 and three other times in American history, a candidate who loses the national popular vote can still win a majority of the Electoral College and become president.

Historical Power Base

So what keeps the Electoral College going? Historically, it was the power of the southern slave states—although slaves couldn't vote, they counted as three-fifths of a person for the allocation of representatives (and therefore electors). After Reconstruction, freed slaves were counted as full persons for purposes of allocating representatives (and electors) but were still prevented from voting by **Jim Crow laws**, intimidation, and terrorism. Popular election of the president both during and after slavery, therefore, would have weakened the white South's influence in the selection of the president. In 1969–1970, the country came close to getting rid of the Electoral College, only to be blocked, in part, by a filibuster led by South Carolina's Strom Thurmond in the Senate. Today, the value of the Electoral College to states with small populations, many in the Mountain West and Great Plains (and supportive of the GOP), may still preclude achieving the supermajorities needed to amend the constitution.

Solutions

Still, since the 2000 debacle, the call for the College's abolition has grown. One alternative is to keep the Electoral College as is, but allocate electors in proportion to the percentage of the vote that a candidate gets in a state. Through one recent and very creative idea, states are being asked to join an interstate compact. Once states constituting a majority in the Electoral College join in, by law the compact will kick in. All states who have joined will then be required to send electors to the Electoral College who support the winner of the national popular vote, regardless of who wins the popular vote in those states. California, Hawaii, Illinois, Maryland, New Jersey, Vermont, Washington, Massachusetts, and the District of Columbia with a total of 132 electoral votes—almost half of the 270 needed for the compact to go into effect—have signed up so far.

Sources: George Edwards, *Why the Electoral College Is Bad for America* (New Haven, CT: Yale University Press, 2004); Alexander Keyssar, "The Electoral College Flunks," *New York Review of Books* (March 24, 2005); Jack Rakove, *The Unfinished Election of 2000* (New York: Basic Books, 2001); National Popular Vote, www.nationalpopularvote.com.

much latent support they might have. We do know that since about 2006 polls show that more Americans agree than disagree with the view that "with respect to representing the American people" the major parties "do such a poor job that a third major party is needed." Yet, ironically, any third-party challenge to the rules of the game that so favor the major parties is precluded by the fact that third parties lack powerful elected officials in part because of the present rules.[18]

Agents of Change—Sometimes

The vast democratic potential of political parties has often been compromised by their unique history in the United States. Often, they've acted as elite democratic devices, holding onto their power by supporting laws and practices that serve to depress participation and representation by large numbers of people. The "localism" of American parties means they have often ignored or even suppressed conflicts and debates about national and international issues in favor of defending the power structures in the areas where they've been dominant. The old age of American parties often makes them resistant to social changes.

To some elite democrats, the two-party system may be preferable to a multiparty one because it brings stability. Giovanni Sartori, a prominent scholar of political parties, has praised them precisely for their ability to "control society."[19] But as popular democrats point out, there is a price: limited democratic participation.

However, it would be a mistake to dismiss the two major parties simply as instruments of elite democrats. At crucial moments, they've been indispensable agents responding to—and sometimes even promoting—massive political change. The democratic debate within and about our political parties has been most heated before and immediately after what scholars call **critical**, or **realigning**, **elections**. Table 8.1 lists these important electoral moments. In the past 220 plus years, these events have been rare but incredibly important. Walter Dean Burnham, the foremost student of realigning elections, has called them "America's surrogate for revolution."[20]

Realigning periods are usually prompted by a crisis that the existing party alignments cannot contain. Andrew Jackson's 1828 victory established the modern Democratic Party, and Abraham Lincoln's 1860 win brought the first national victory to the new Republican Party.

Table 8.1	Realigning Elections and Their Consequences		
Election	*Party System*	*Big Issues*	*Partisan Consequences*
1800 (Jefferson)	*First:* Democratic-Republicans over Federalists	"Privilege"; agrarian vs. urban interests; power of national government	Repudiation of Federalist Party
1828 (Jackson)	*Second:* Democrats over Whigs	Democracy of common man; state vs. federal power	First mass-party system; introduction of patronage; Democratic predominance
1860 (Lincoln)	*Third:* Republicans over Democrats	Slavery; states' rights; North vs. South	Republicans as party of Union; growth of urban machines; the Solid Democratic South
1896 (McKinley)	*Fourth:* Republicans over Democrats and Populists	National depression; industrialized North vs. agrarian South and West; monopolies vs. "the People"	Republicans as party of modern business prosperity; decline of party competition; Jim Crow in South
1932 (Roosevelt)	*Fifth:* Democrats over Republicans	Depression; social rights; government responsibility for economy	Democrats as party of equality and prosperity; mobilization in North; Solid South persists
1968 (Nixon)	*Sixth:* Partisan dealignment; GOP ascendancy	Law and order; economic decline; economic deregulation; American strength as world power; "moral values," wedge issues; war on terrorism	Party decomposition at grassroots; breakup of Democratic South; Reagan coalition; increasing polarization of parties in closely divided electorate
2008 (Obama)?	*Seventh?:* Democratic ascendance?	New economic insecurity; health insurance and safety net; re-regulation of capital; careful deployment of American power abroad; new internationalism	Democratic inroads in formerly "Red" states; breakup of Reagan coalition; further polarization; demographic changes favoring Democrats

In other periods, such as 1896 and 1932, the by-then-old parties kept their names but managed to succeed by altering their philosophies and appealing to new parts of the electorate with changed platforms and appeals. Critical elections can shake up the electorate's existing political allegiances, as the parties respond to new social movements and to groups seeking redress. In a critical election, new voters come to the polls. After such events, new dominant **party regimes** are built, in which a majority party enacts big policy and institutional changes, while the opposition succumbs or retreats to the states and locales where it remains strong.

The two "realigning elections" with the most profound impact on today's politics are arguably still the 1896 and 1932 contests.

The System of 1896

Held in the aftermath of a severe economic depression, the 1896 election featured two contrasting visions of the nation's past and future. The first, crystallized in the Populist and Democratic presidential candidacy of the Nebraskan William Jennings Bryan, recalled the anti-federalist and popular democratic vision of the early republic. Bryan, and most especially his followers, claimed that the growing power of banks, trusts, and corporations was strangling a democracy of small farmers, merchants, and laborers. The Republican nominee, William McKinley, ran the first modern big-money campaign. Estimates vary, but Ohio businessman and Republican National Committee Chairman Mark Hanna raised between $3.4 million and $7 million for the effort. This allowed McKinley to outspend his rival, Bryan, by up to twelve to one in a crusade promising corporate-led prosperity.

The 1896 contest split the nation's regions, with the West and South siding with Bryan and his Populist/Democratic coalition, and the densely populated Northeast and Midwest backing the GOP. Here, McKinley's campaign money helped win the election by a relatively narrow margin of 4 percent. With an 80 percent turnout, the 1896 election was a dramatic and polarizing struggle about American political identity.

The result was the **system of 1896**, thirty-six years of mostly continuous Republican national dominance of both Congress and the White House. For present politics, the system of 1896 had profound and ironic effects. Soon after this election that mobilized and stimulated the electorate, the leaders of the victorious GOP and defeated Democrats went on to suppress political participation and debate in the regions they each controlled.

In their midwestern and northeastern strongholds, the GOP and their allies effectively disenfranchised some industrial workers and immigrants whose loyalty to the GOP was either tenuous or nonexistent. They did so by imposing difficult voter registration laws and literacy tests, which were particularly hard on immigrants and the poor. In the South, the system of 1896 was much more brutal. Here, the potential voters to be controlled were poor, black, or both—the people who had supplied support for the Populist Party in the 1890s. The region's factory owners and big landowners moved successfully to take over the Democratic Party. While race had long been a useful instrument to divide the poor in the South, the new elites instituted segregation through Jim Crow laws. In elections, white elites instituted all-white primaries, poll taxes, literacy tests, and outright violence and terrorism against those who protested.

The legacy of the system of 1896 was thoroughly undemocratic. There were dramatic declines in voter turnout, accompanied by one-party rule throughout the South and in many Northern states. A huge class and race gap developed between ordinary citizens and the southern Democratic Party, and between industrial workers and the affluent Republicans in the northern and midwestern states. The most important states became one-party kingdoms. By 1924, only 30 percent of the working-class voters of industrial Pittsburgh, Chicago, and Philadelphia went to the polls. In Democratic-dominated Virginia, less than one-quarter of the overall citizenry—and less than 2 percent of the African American citizenry—voted.

Overall voting turnout had averaged over 78 percent in the second half of the nineteenth century. In the early twentieth century it steadily declined, reaching its nadir of 49 percent in 1924. With a demobilized electorate, the GOP held onto power at the national level, while the Democrats exerted iron control of their southern bastions and a few northeastern cities. Overall, the effect of the system of 1896 was to produce a party system friendly to corporate power in the North and white-owned plantations in the South.[21]

1932: Rise of the New Deal Democrats

Relying as it did on pro-business prosperity and profound social inequality, the system of 1896 was shaken by the collapse of the business system in 1929, the year the Great Depression began. Under Republican Herbert Hoover, by 1933 one-quarter of the American workforce was unemployed, life savings disappeared as banks failed, and the entire financial system was on the brink of total collapse. Under these pressures, a new voter realignment occurred—at least in the industrialized North and West. In the elections of 1932 and 1936, the revived Democrats and Franklin Roosevelt swept into power, winning large majorities in Congress and taking over the White House. With their developing philosophy of active government dedicated to promote prosperity and some degree of economic justice, the Democrats forged a new dominant party by drawing in new voters, especially in the North.

The **New Deal Democratic coalition** was based on the new electoral mobilization of northern industrial workers, small farmers, working-class Catholics, and the unemployed in a reformed Democratic Party. Senators and House members from highly industrialized states and depressed rural areas provided the impetus for reforms that made the federal government responsible for the national economy and for providing a minimal standard of living for all. New Deal legislation created government jobs, allowed the growth of the union movement, and established a minimum wage and the Social Security system. The Democrats and Franklin Roosevelt posed as a party opposed to the "economic royalists" who hoarded the country's wealth. By the 1940 election, the U.S. electorate and the two parties were more divided by social class than probably at any time before or since. Low-income voters in the North generally backed the Democrats, and they voted in large numbers. Middle- and upper-class voters moved to support the now-minority Republicans.

By emphasizing economic justice as the central issue of U.S. politics, the realigned New Deal party system fed off renewed voter participation. Yet voter turnout in national elections during the New Deal never nearly reached the high levels of the 1896 election. The grand limitation of the New Deal system was racism. In the solidly Democratic South, the 1896 system largely persisted, and blacks and many poor whites remained disenfranchised. Some southern Democrats arose to challenge the old elites of the Democratic Party and made direct appeals to tenant farmers and industrial workers. Yet even these "reform" southern Democrats—Louisiana's Huey Long is the most famous—at their most radical never challenged Jim Crow. Despite his liberalism, President Roosevelt really didn't challenge Jim Crow either, because his party depended on the "Solid South" to maintain its majorities in Congress and keep the White House. Still, the southern Democrats, along with the Republicans in Congress, were a conservative drag on the pro-labor and pro-farmer policies of northern New Dealers.[22]

The New Deal at Retirement Age

Like all party regimes, the New Deal Democrats endured, and we live partly in their shadow even today. After World War II, the coalitions forged in the 1930s created what some called a "normal" politics of Democratic majorities in Congress and—Republican Dwight Eisenhower excepted—Democratic presidents from Harry Truman through John Kennedy and Lyndon Johnson. Government was now responsible for the economy and for maintaining some level of economic and social support when the capitalist markets didn't provide it. Important New Deal programs and policies—Social Security, disability and unemployment insurance, and the GI Bill—became largely uncontroversial, as Republicans didn't challenge their essentials. By the 1950s, the New Deal Democratic Party rested on its laurels, seeking to maintain its majorities rather than engage in new efforts at mobilization. Nevertheless, because it was the dominant, governing party and because of its reform traditions, it still became the vortex for all the big new issues and contending groups that were spawned in the 1960s. Since the 1960s, four central divides in American society have broken the dominance of the New Deal Democrats.

The Democrats and Race. After some foot-dragging, Democratic presidents Kennedy and Johnson and the Congress responded to the moral force and political power of the civil rights movement with a series of federal civil rights acts dismantling the legal framework of southern segregation and black disenfranchisement. President Johnson and liberal members of Congress launched the War on Poverty and the Great Society programs, establishing new commitments to end poverty, to provide new assistance for affordable housing, decent schools, and income guarantees, and to make Medicaid available for the poor and Medicare available for seniors.

Confronting racist political structures in both the South and North provided the Democrats with moral authority and African American votes. But it also imposed severe electoral costs. It moved what had been the "Solid South"—theretofore the most dependable piece of the New Deal coalition—into the Republican camp. It also angered many northern urban whites upset by efforts to integrate schools and neighborhoods, who had been important New Deal coalition members. Some came to believe that the Democrats were willing to help "minorities" but were now ignoring people like them. And some of these people would defect from the party and later be referred to as "Reagan Democrats."[23]

Vietnam, Liberals, and "Communism." In the postwar period, Democrats and Republicans alike pursued a bipartisan foreign policy based on "containing" communism. This policy led to the Vietnam War, which, arguably, began under President Dwight Eisenhower, a Republican, then was expanded under Kennedy, a Democrat, and then turned into a major conflagration under Johnson, also a Democrat. The war eventually spawned a huge antiwar movement, shattering the bipartisan foreign policy consensus and deeply dividing the Democratic Party. Antiwar sentiment crystallized electorally in the candidacies of Senators Eugene McCarthy and Robert Kennedy as they sought the 1968 Democratic nomination. When President Lyndon Johnson decided not to seek reelection because of deep controversy over the war, party establishment support for the war shifted to his vice president, Hubert Humphrey, who won the nomination. Tensions peaked at the party's 1968 Chicago convention, where convention delegates, journalists, and demonstrators were beaten in the streets by a police force headed by Mayor Richard J. Daley, himself a prominent old-style New Deal Democrat. The war split the nation and sunk the fractious Democrats led by Humphrey. Republican Richard Nixon was narrowly elected in 1968 and then reelected in a landslide against Democratic peace candidate George McGovern in 1972.[24]

Culture Wars. In addition to the anti-war and civil rights crusades, movements among other ethnic and racial minorities, feminists, environmentalists, civil libertarians, gays and lesbians, and the young also emerged in the 1960s and 1970s (see Chapter 11) with their members questioning the conventions of American life and challenging military, corporate, political, and educational elites. Many of these citizens were part of, or at least sometimes overlapped with, the so-called "counterculture" that was experimenting with alternative lifestyles, new music, and sometimes drugs. Being a diverse coalition of "outsiders," the Democrats were far more open to these various cultural currents than were the Republicans.

Yet each battle over "liberation" produced a backlash from many traditional Democrats, who perceived the new movements as a threat to their beliefs and to their authority. The culture wars were thus born. The Democrats' ability to retain the support of northern working-class whites was threatened, even as the party was attacked as too conservative by many in the environmental, feminist, civil rights and "black power," and antiwar communities.[25]

Economic Stagnation and the New Economy. The New Deal party system's greatest strength was its ability to provide economic growth and distribute some of the resources to middle- and lower-income voters by means of federal programs and tax policies. Chapter 4 details how the transformation of the corporate economy since the 1960s made this accommodation more difficult. The economic stagnation that began in the early 1970s hit the Democrats hard by the end of the decade in the area in which they had the strongest public support—their ability to manage the economy—and eroded their support among middle- and working-class voters. Elected in 1976, Democratic President Jimmy Carter moved the party's economic policies to the right in the face of business demands for less government spending, regulation, and taxation. In the effort to fight inflation, Carter's (and the Federal Reserve's) policies increased unemployment without, in the short run, taming inflation, and saw the beginning of a downward pressure on working- and middle-class wages. No longer would the Democrats be so clearly identified as the party of the "working person."[26] Prosperity during the Clinton years in the 1990s, however, did help restore some of the Democratic credentials with regard to managing the economy, and the Great Recession, beginning in late 2007 under George W. Bush, seriously tarnished the Republicans again.

The Next Political Era?

After Richard Nixon's victories in 1968 and 1972, there was substantial scholarly and partisan debate over whether his presidency was the harbinger of a new Republican era. Unlike 1896 and 1932, the electoral realignment had occurred gradually, some believed, with Ronald Reagan's and George H. W. Bush's presidential victories, then the "Republican Revolution" of 1994 that took control of Congress, and finally the 2004 reelection victory of George W. Bush and continuing GOP gains in Congress and the states. Despite the absence of a single critical election, from this perspective the new Republican era was built on the GOP's ability to "change the subject" from the New Deal era's emphasis on economic equality and social justice. The new agenda would be one of patriotism, national security, a greater role for religion in public life, and support for what some call "traditional" or "moral values" and strong opposition to crime, welfare, abortion, gay marriage, and permissiveness in general. The aggressive new GOP at first succeeded in harnessing a backlash against the supposed excesses of the 1960s but also gradually became a party designed to "roll back" the programs of the Great Society and New Deal.[27]

Other analysts argued that although the GOP had occupied the White House and had achieved majorities in Congress, its successes were sporadic, held up by only razor-thin electoral margins and sustained by gerrymandering, campaign money, and effective mobilization of its base of support. From this perspective, the GOP continually overstated its mandate from the voters, and it may have won by being more politically competent and deft than because of deeper changes in the public.

The most obvious argument against the existence of a new Republican era was Bill Clinton's ability to win the presidency. Clinton did so in 1992 and 1996 by effectively holding together much of the New Deal base of his party while garnering support from socially tolerant professionals and by taking positions that neutralized issues that had hurt liberals in the past, such as welfare, the death penalty, and "big government."[28] The idea of a lasting Republican era, of course, has now decisively been laid to rest by the sweeping Democratic victories in 2006 and especially 2008, and after a serious setback in 2010, another very strong Democratic victory in 2012. However, even before these political shifts, the idea of the Republican era was challenged in a deeper way.

It has been suggested that beginning around 1968, we entered a period of **electoral dealignment**: a period in which ticket splitting and the number of self-identified independents increased, and intensity of attachment to political party decreased along with voter turnout. Dealignment suggests a political crisis of sorts in both parties and in our party system as a whole, as the parties fail to provide consistent and coherent alternatives for public consideration.

Unlike past periods of realignment and strong party regimes, since the sixties there have been characteristics of dealignment, such as disillusionment and indifference among many citizens, in part, because the debates between the parties haven't adequately addressed the needs of many in today's economy. Instead, to gain power party leaders have often shifted the debate to emotional symbols and resentments. For example, Republicans have frequently appealed to working-class and middle-class voters on the basis of symbolic "wedge issues"—highly charged issues used to create divisions within the opposition—such as welfare, the flag, prayer in public schools, the death penalty, and opposition to gay marriage. Democrats may have made themselves susceptible to such wedge issues in ways that prevented them from helping sharpen the democratic debate and mitigate dealigning tendencies. In order to appeal to independents, according to Thomas Frank, Democrats dropped "the class language that once distinguished them sharply from Republicans.…[leaving] themselves vulnerable to cultural wedge issues like guns and abortion."[29]

Of course, issues such as these are not merely symbolic. Sometimes they do tap into real and important cultural, moral, or political differences between citizens. However, they often are used to divert debate from critically important economic and social needs. That's

Note: Eric Holder is President Obama's Attorney General.

what President Reagan did, according to Christopher Lasch, using "values" issues to deflect attention from his real goals, which were economic: "Reagan made himself the champion of traditional values, but there is no evidence he regarded their restoration as a high priority. What he really cared about was the revival of the unregulated capitalism of the twenties: the repeal of the New Deal."[30]

Parties that articulate clear and consistent positions on the most important economic and social questions are critical for a vibrant and healthy party system to exist, and necessary for a full democratic debate to occur. They allow the country to assess how best to address the nation's most important needs in changing times. Periods of drift and dealignment, however, make these goals harder to attain.

What kind of period are we in now? We still see features of dealignment, for example, present in the very large number of independents (see Figure 8.1). However, for some years now we also have witnessed greater partisan differences and sharp polarization between the political parties and between some citizens (see also Chapter 5). The Partisan Snapshot box shows that the gap between Republican and Democratic views on many key issues has grown sharply more polarized since 1987. Parties with clearer differences and internally more coherent ideologies are characteristic of stronger party systems. Over the last three presidential

FIGURE 8.1 | **Trend in Party Identification, 1939–2012**

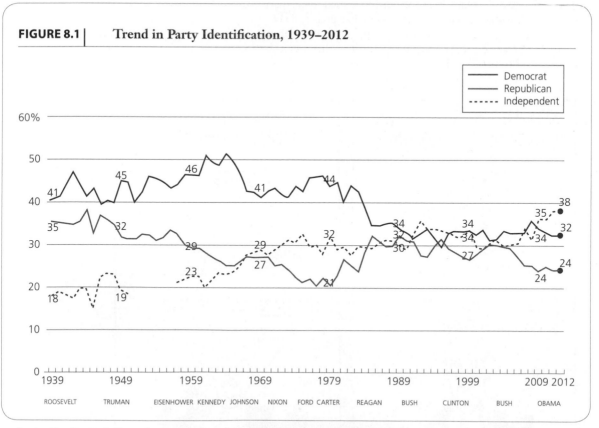

Source: Pew Research Center for the People and the Press, http://www.people-press.org.

Note: For this graph with an interactive feature that allows you to choose the year of comparison go to: http://people-press.org/2012/06/01/trend.

Partisan Snapshot: Increasing Polarization on Ideology

Question: How do those who identify with the two main parties describe their views and how have they changed over time?

Republicans

Percentage who think of themselves as:	2000	2012
Conservative	60	68
Moderate	29	24
Liberal	7	5

Democrats

Percentage who think of themselves as:	2000	2012
Conservative	24	20
Moderate	41	38
Liberal	28	38

Answer: Republicans are much more conservative than Democrats are liberal. However, Republicans have become more conservative, and Democrats have become more liberal. Independents haven't changed much during this time period.

Question: Where has partisanship grown the most over time?

Answer: Look at the tables below...

Statement, Response, and Growing Partisan Gap between Republicans and Democrats (as percent of those agreeing)

The Government: When something is run by the government, it is usually inefficient and wasteful.

Year	Democrats	Republicans	Independents	Rep/Dem Gap
1987	59	65	65	6
2012	41	77	63	36

Bipartisanship: I like political leaders who are willing to make compromises in order to get the job done.

Year	Democrats	Republicans	Independents	Rep/Dem Gap
1987	77	66	70	11
2012	90	68	83	22

The Poor: It is the responsibility of the government to take care of people who can't take care of themselves.

Year	Democrats	Republicans	Independents	Rep/Dem Gap
1987	79	62	70	17
2012	75	40	59	35

Social Welfare: The government should help more needy people even if it means going deeper into debt.

Year	Democrats	Republicans	Independents	Rep/Dem Gap
1987	64	39	50	25
2012	65	20	39	45

Environment: There needs to be stricter laws and regulations to protect the environment.

Year	Democrats	Republicans	Independents	Rep/Dem Gap
1992	93	86	91	7
2012	93	47	75	46

Family Values: I have old-fashioned values about family and marriage.

Year	Democrats	Republicans	Independents	Rep/Dem Gap
1987	86	92	86	6
2012	60	88	72	28

Regulation: Government regulation of business usually does more harm than good.

Year	Democrats	Republicans	Independents	Rep/Dem Gap
1987	50	61	55	11
2012	41	76	58	35

Labor: Labor unions are necessary to protect the working person.

Year	Democrats	Republicans	Independents	Rep/Dem Gap
1987	76	58	64	18
2012	82	43	61	39

National Security: The best way to ensure peace is through military strength.

Year	Democrats	Republicans	Independents	Rep/Dem Gap
1987	50	67	50	17
2012	44	73	52	29

Immigration: We should restrict and control people coming to live in our country more than we do now.

Year	Democrats	Republicans	Independents	Rep/Dem Gap
1992	74	78	75	4
2012	58	84	69	26

Source: Trends in American Values: 1987–2012, "Partisan Polarization Surges in Bush, Obama Years," The Pew Research Center (June 4, 2012), www.people-press.org.

election cycles, we have also seen voter turnout at its highest point since 1968, accompanied by high levels of activism and interest, all potential signs of realignment.

The decisive 2008 election raised the question of whether Obama's big win had ushered in a new party era led by Democrats. Then, in 2010, the Republicans quickly and decisively swept the Democrats out of power in the House of Representatives. After the Democrats' strong 2012 win, some are starting again to speculate. They especially point to the growing populations of Hispanics, Asians, highly educated women, unmarried women, and the young, all of whom voted very strongly for Obama. Perhaps it would be prudent to agree with conservative *New York Times* columnist Ross Douthat that all we can really say right now is that "The age of Reagan is officially over, and the Obama majority is the only majority we have." Still, not all transformational party periods are signaled by blowouts like the 1932 election that propelled Roosevelt's New Deal. They will be generated by relatively close elections that create grounding coalitions that grow and endure. Although McKinley's win over Bryan was by a modest 4 percent, it nevertheless ushered in "the system of 1896." That's about the same margin of victory Obama won by in 2012. Time will tell whether the Republicans can and will adjust, and whether the Obama coalition can itself persevere.[31]

Two Nations or Three? Democrats, Republicans...and Others

In the accompanying maps, table, and figure, snapshots of the parties and their strength in the electorate are presented. Map 8.1 displays "red" (Republican) and "blue" (Democratic) America in terms of how states voted for the major-party presidential candidates in 2012. Map 8.2 does the same for 2004, the last Republican presidential victory. Figure 8.1 tells an

MAP 8.1 | 2012: The Present Winning Democratic Electoral College Coalition

Democratic Republican

Total 2012 Electoral Votes Obama: 332 | Romney 206

MAP 8.2 | **2004: The Last Winning Republican Electoral College Coalition**

■ Democratic   ■ Republican   **Total 2004 Electoral Votes** Bush: 286 | Kerry: 251

important story about **party identification** and how it has changed over time, and Table 8.2 shows a breakdown of social groups and how they voted for president in 2012.

Taken together, these graphics tell several important tales. The Democrats once had a mammoth lead in party identification, as high as 26 percent in 1964. That lead had mostly evaporated by the late 1980s, although the Democrats have recently rebounded somewhat. Although exit polls in 2012 showed more people thought of themselves as Democrats (38 percent) than Republicans (32 percent) or Independents (29 percent), some surveys examining party identification (see Figure 8.1), show Independents catching up with—and even surpassing—Democrats. When the two parties were matched up in ratings of favorability surveyed after the election, 51 percent had a favorable view of the Democrats, while only 43 percent viewed the Republicans that way. However, in 2008 post-election surveys, the Democrats did even better and Republicans much worse.[32]

The other stories can be told in terms of shifts and continuities in how the parties divide on the basis of geography, religious affiliation, race, gender and marital status, and social class.

Geography. Map 8.1 shows that Republicans have a solid hold on the interior West and the Great Plains. Democratic strength is very solid in the Northeast, Pacific West, and, to a certain extent, the mid-Atlantic states and upper Midwest. It is growing in the Southwest. The map also shows just how much the South had become a reliable part of the Republican coalition. The defection among southern whites from the Democrats, especially since the 1960s, in fact, had provided the best case for the argument that a new Republican era had begun. Over time, the South moved from the most solidly Democratic to the most Republican region in the country. Starting in the 1970s, the GOP captured a solid majority of the South and Mountain West's congressional delegation of House and Senate members.

Table 8.2 How Americans Voted: A Portrait of the 2012 Party Presidential Vote

Democratic Party Candidate—Barack Obama: 51.1% or 65,899,660 votes
Republican Party Candidate—Mitt Romney: 47.2% or 60,932,152 votes

Obama		Romney		Obama		Romney
Women 55%	but	Men 52%	but	Blacks 93% Asians 73% Latinos 71%	but	Whites 59%
18–29 years 60% 30–44 years 52%	but	45–64 years 51% 65+ years 56%	but	High school grad 51% Some college 49%* Post-grad study 55%	but	College grad only 51%
Under $30K 63% $30–$50K 57%	but	$50K+ 53% $100K+ 54%	but	Big cities 69% Mid-size cities 58%	but	Small cities 56% Suburbs 50%*
Unmarried 62%	but	Married 56%	but	Gay, lesbian, bisexual? Yes 76% No 49% (tie)	but	Gay, lesbian, bisexual? No 49% (tie)
Attend religious services occasionally 55% Never 62%	but	Attend religious services weekly 59%	but	Catholic 50%* Jewish 69% Other Christian 50%*	but	Protestant 62% White Evangelical/Born Again 78% Mormon 78%
Work full time for pay 49% (tie) No 53%	but	Work full time for pay 49% (tie)	but	Think of self as Democrat 92%	but	Think of self as Republican 93%

Sources: The information in this table is taken from polls conducted as people left the voting booth by Edison Research for the National Election Pool, a consortium of major media outlets. The data here was compiled from "President Exit Polls," 2012, *The New York Times* (www.nytimes.com) and "2012 Fox News Exit Polls," Fox News (www.foxnews.com). The popular vote totals are the actual votes tallied by the Federal Election Commission, http://www.fec.gov/pubrec/fe2012/2012presgeresults.pdf.

*If a percentage given is 49% or 50% for one of the candidates without a tie being indicated that means that the other candidate received fewer votes.

However, in the 2008 presidential contest, the Democrats held onto their bases on the coasts and the upper Midwest and extended the electoral map beyond them in crucial ways. They picked off Indiana, winning it for the first time in forty-four years. They made key gains in the southwest (and also in Montana and the Dakotas, although losing there) and made very significant inroads in the South. For the first time since the Johnson landslide of 1964, a Democratic presidential candidate carried Virginia—and then did so again in 2012. Although in 2012 the Democrats narrowly lost North Carolina, four years earlier they carried it for the first time since southerner Jimmy Carter ran in 1976. Growing Democratic strength in states like New Mexico may also prefigure greater competitiveness in states with large and growing Hispanic populations, perhaps at some point including the biggest southern prize, and second biggest national prize of all—Texas. Changing demographics of some of these states were important to these victories, as were changes of heart in 2008 prompted by a deeply unpopular Republican administration weakened by economic crisis. Both in 2008 and 2012, the notion of which states are crucial swing states was extended well beyond the expected battlegrounds of

Florida (2000) and Ohio (2004) and deep into traditional red territory, to the disadvantage of the Republican candidates of those years, John McCain and then Mitt Romney.

While maps filled with red and blue help us see where the Electoral College votes are going, they are also misleading. Most of the nation's populous counties are neither solidly red nor blue but a mixed blend of both. Repeating age-old patterns, in most states big cities remain strongly Democratic. Suburbs, where a majority of Americans live, are generally split between the two parties, and rural areas and small towns are strongly, although not always overwhelmingly, Republican. At the congressional and state and local levels many states are far more competitive than the red-blue electoral maps lead us to believe.[33]

Religious Affiliation and Church Attendance. In addition to region, religious affiliation and its intensity play important roles in the shifting fortunes of our political parties. In the 1950s and 1960s, Catholics and especially Jewish voters were heavy New Deal Democratic supporters, and white evangelical Christians split their party allegiances fairly evenly. Weekly churchgoers were just as likely to be Democrats as Republicans. Since the 1990s, however, that has changed. Basically, the more frequently one attends a Christian church, the more one tends to vote Republican. Meanwhile, although Jews continue to be strong Democrats, party identification among Catholics has become more evenly divided. Although Bush narrowly defeated a Catholic candidate, John Kerry, among this group in 2004, Obama handily beat John McCain among Catholics in 2008, and edged out Mitt Romney in 2012. White evangelical Protestants, however, gave Romney four out of every five of their votes.

Today, strength of religious affiliation seems to matter in party choices. For those voters who attend church "weekly," six in ten voted in 2012 for Mitt Romney. The Democrats are drawing strong support, however, from Americans less committed to religious institutions, with Obama winning six in ten of those who "never" attend, and also 55 percent of the vote among those who attend "occasionally."

Race and Ethnicity. Racial divisions have been central in American society and continue to be a big divide in partisan politics. Since the Democratic landslide in 1964, the Democrats have never again won a plurality of the white vote in any presidential election. In 2008, McCain defeated Obama by 12 percent among whites, even though Obama that year won the third highest percentage of white votes of any Democratic candidate since 1964. He did worse in 2012, however, losing the white vote to Romney by 20 percent.

Today America's racial and ethnic makeup is much more diverse than it was in the past, and even though newly naturalized citizens vote in lower proportion than native-born whites, the percentage of people of color in the electorate is steadily growing. Although whites of European original heritage still constitute 72 percent of voters, that's down from 88 percent in 1980. As Table 8.2 reveals, Democrats maintain a huge nine to one advantage among African American voters, and among a growing Latino and Asian American electorate in 2012 they rolled up sizeable majorities of about seven to three.

Gender and Marital Status. Besides southerners, there's been no group since the 1970s that has moved to the GOP more than men, especially white, affluent men from all areas of the country. On the other side, women, especially low-income and unmarried women, have moved to the Democrats. In 2004, it was more of a one-sided gender gap, with Kerry edging Bush by only 3 percent among women, whereas Bush won by 11 points among men. In 2008, the one-sidedness was reversed, with Obama beating McCain by 13 percent among women, and even edging him by a single point among men. But Romney beat Obama by 7 percent among men in 2012, while Obama still comfortably won 11 percent more of the female vote. The gender gap is exacerbated when marital status is considered: The gap between unmarried women (mostly Democratic) and married men (mostly GOP) was about 30 percent in 2012.[34]

Social Class and Education. Social class matters in how people vote, but it matters less than it does in other Western democracies—or than it did during the New Deal—and far less than one might expect given growing economic inequalities since the 1980s. Historically, the wealthier a person was, the more likely that person was to vote Republican. For example, as recently as the 2004 presidential election, the wealthiest Americans, those with family incomes at $200,000 or above, voted nearly two to one Republican. The poorest Americans, those with family incomes of $15,000 or below, who vote proportionally much less often, gave about the same advantage to the Democrat that year. The Democrats now do better than they did with these wealthier voters, remarkably winning them by six points in 2008, then losing them by a slightly larger margin than that in 2012, while still doing much better than in 2004. If we look at broader categories in 2012, we see that the Democrats garnered about 60 percent of the vote of those with family incomes below $50,000, while the Republicans won about 53 percent of voters above that income (see Table 8.2).

Some have suggested that although lower income earners as a whole vote Democratic, *white* working class voters have trended Republican for years. Since the Democratic Party has traditionally thought of itself as the party of the working person, this has been the basis for a lot of criticism and intraparty soul-searching, going back to concerns about its candidates losing the "hardhats" of the late 1960s, and then the so-called "Reagan Democrats" of the 1980s. Actually, Democrats have lost the overall white vote in all presidential elections except one since the 1940s. However, as Figure 8.2 shows, those losses are *not* because of defections by low income white voters. They gave Democratic presidential candidates an average of 51% of their vote from 1976–2004—the most recent elections covered in the graphic. In fact if anything, lower income whites have trended a little more Democratic over time since the low point of 1972.

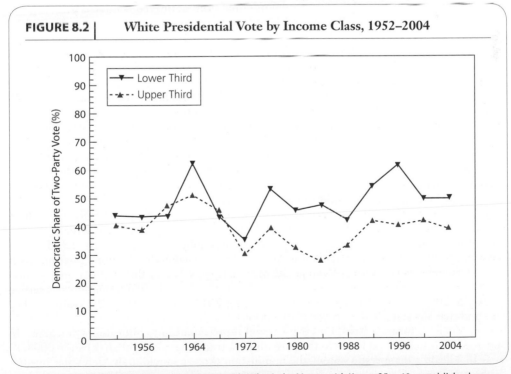

FIGURE 8.2 | **White Presidential Vote by Income Class, 1952–2004**

Source: Larry M. Bartels, "What's the Matter with *What's the Matter with Kansas?*," p. 40 unpublished paper (September, 2005) www.princeton.edu/~bartels/kansas.pdf.

If we look at education, going back to about 1988, we find Democrats with a clear advantage among those with less than a high school education (although this group is only about 3 percent of voters now) and a growing advantage among those with a postgraduate education. The in-between categories were more or less evenly split, although college grads slightly preferred the Republicans. If we bring race into the educational equation, among whites without a four-year college degree we find that support for Democrats has trended slightly downward since the 1950s while support among college graduates has trended upwards. However, Democrats have been on the losing end of the white vote at both levels.[35]

Parties from the Top Down

Earlier in this chapter, we said that American parties were highly localized and not very well organized nationally compared to major parties in other wealthy democracies. Today, however, that may no longer be true—especially for the kind of new Republican Party that has gradually emerged from the 1960s until the present, and the Democratic Party that has been strongly developing more recently. Before we get to this issue, however, let's discuss the basics of what both parties do.

Figure 8.3 shows the pyramid of party organization. The pyramid captures what seems to be a democratic flow of influence from ordinary voters through local and state committees to the top of the national party. Later we'll see how the formal structure may disguise some important issues about just how the parties really operate and compete with each other.

What are the formal mechanisms for nominating candidates for president? Since the sixties, the process has been transformed. In most states, voters—rather than party officials or officeholders—choose delegates to the national nominating conventions (although in both parties, some delegate slots are reserved for officeholders). In about four-fifths of the states, voters make their selections through **party primaries**. Primaries come in two varieties, depending on each state and its laws. Closed primaries limit the voting electorate in a party to those who register to vote as members of that party. Depending on the state, open primaries allow either all voters, or all independents, to vote along with party members in choosing a party's candidate. Some states, most famously Iowa, choose delegates through *caucuses*, in which all voters registered in a party are asked to meet in their electoral district to choose a smaller number of delegates to a state convention, which in turn chooses the state's national convention delegates.

There is one other very important factor—the party rules—and each party is different. Democrats *require* that delegates be equally divided between men and women (Republicans encourage that idea) and have an affirmative action policy to assure fair representation of historically discriminated-against minorities.

Democratic Party rules also call for assigning most delegates proportionally to the share of primary votes or caucus delegates a candidate wins in a state, with a 15 percent threshold before a candidate receives any delegates. The Republicans had previously left delegate selection to the states, which generally opted for winner-take-all selection. That means if you get the most votes in a state, you get *all* of its delegates. Under this formula, and because many states chose to hold their primaries quite early, the Republican nomination was settled quickly in 2008. Republicans changed their rules for 2012 to try to extend the contest. They required that any state, with a couple of exceptions, that held its primary before April 1 would have to devise a formula based on proportional representation to allocate its delegates. In fact, the 2012 nomination battle in the party did last somewhat longer than it had in 2008.

In a healthy democratic system, the nomination process should draw high voter turnout by the grass roots. Generally, however, primaries have very low turnouts. This is in part due to **frontloading**, whereby states schedule their primary elections and caucuses to occur as early

FIGURE 8.3 | Pyramid of American Party Organization

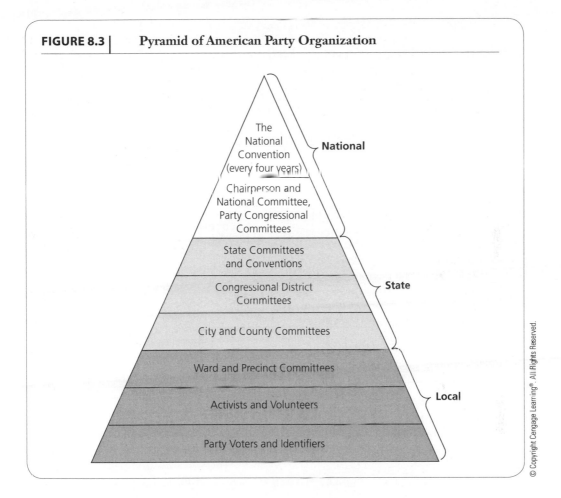

as is feasible so as to remain relevant to the nominating process, and to enable the party to unite quickly around a candidate. Once a likely nominee emerges, however, turnout drops. Although in 2008 primaries and caucuses had relatively strong voter participation, in the three prior presidential contests it was disappointing, and participation declined in the Republican Party in 2012 (the Democrats had no real contest) although there was a hotly contested race.

Primaries and caucuses elect delegates to the **national party conventions**, which in turn decide on a party platform and nominate the presidential and vice-presidential candidates. For most Americans, the party conventions have been the only occasions where the national parties, with all their factions and personalities, display themselves in public. In the olden days, conventions were often rancorous, with dramatic disputes over the most important issues of the day and bare-knuckle battles between presidential contenders. Most of all, the spectacle was covered gavel to gavel by the three major networks.

In the new era, the delegates decide little, the platform is composed in advance, and the event is scripted by party operatives to showcase the new presidential and vice-presidential nominees. The conventions do provide an important opportunity for making new contacts and for networks to form. Yet the delegates, supposedly elected to represent the views of voters, are there less to discuss than to ratify choices and cheer for the nominee. Worse, not only have conventions become stage-managed, but also they are often vehicles for big donors,

Who Were Those Masked Men?

Shortly before Christmas in 2011, the New Hampshire Institute of Politics held *The Lesser-Known Candidate Forum* at St. Anselm College in Manchester, New Hampshire, featuring nine Republicans and seven Democrats (all men). All candidates on New Hampshire's presidential primary ballot not invited to the main party debates were invited here.

One Democrat, John Wolfe, said he was "in the race because there's a progressive void that's left by President Obama," who, according to Wolfe, sides with Wall Street because that's where he gets his funding from. Jeff Lawman, a Republican, said he was a "fiscal conservative, social moderate, environmental progressive" and was running a "zero-dollar grassroots campaign." Democrat John Haywood urged adopting the British national health care model because it "is incredibly more efficient."

There was a little theater too, as perennial Democratic candidate Vermin Supreme, running on a satirical platform of ponies for all Americans and zombie preparedness, sprinkled glitter dust on well-known anti-abortion activist and fellow Democrat Randall Terry.

Many of the candidates, however, raised very important questions about government, health care, the economy, constitutional government, the environment, and war and peace.

Even more than the minor party candidates, these Republican and Democratic candidates were far less than a blip on the political radar screen of the election. Who knew that *anyone* tried to challenge Obama for the Democratic nomination? About the debate itself, moderator Pat Griffin concluded, "If you want tight sound bites and rules, spin rooms and handlers, tune into one of the cable or network debates. You can be sure Wolf Blitzer would never allow 'pixie dust' in a CNN debate! Rock on Vermin!"[36]

Note: You can watch the debate at http://www.c-spanvideo.org/program/303284-1.

corporations, and economic sectors to influence the parties and their officeholders. Whether because of their predictable, scripted quality, or media greed, beginning in 1996, the networks stopped broadcasting their daily proceedings live. In 2012, on average, they covered each convention one hour each evening.[37]

GOP Revolution

While it is very important to know the formal mechanisms of party structure and program, it's also important to understand the context in which they operate. In response to New Deal and Great Society liberalism, the 1970s conservative movement gave birth to foundations, which in turn created conservative **think tanks**, most notably the Heritage Foundation, the American Enterprise Institute, and the Cato Foundation. Their objectives were to change both elite and popular opinion on a wide range of issues from foreign policy to Social Security. More than 500 conservative foundations and think tanks now dot the landscape.[38]

The conservative movement, led by its corporate business supporters, over time also created a very significant media sounding board that includes FOX News and political talk radio and is reinforced by the enormous scope of the Christian Broadcasting Network (CBN).

Think tanks, foundation money, corporate lobbyists, pundits, interest group operatives, pollsters, and professional campaign consultants have all been effectively linked to officeholders, party candidates, and party operatives through informal coordinating groups in Washington. The purposes are diverse: to generate consistent "talking points" for Republicans in the public eye, to direct money into the party, and to recruit, train, and get media exposure for new candidates, to name a few. Republicans went so far in the "K Street Project," which began in 1995, as to try to ensure that lobbying firms in Washington employed exclusively Republican operatives, something Republicans could attempt when they controlled both branches of Congress.[39]

Given these developments and strategies, the formal Republican National Committee (RNC) and the Republican congressional campaign committees were revived as the apex of a dense and vast network of fundraising, media, research, intellectual, consulting, training, and campaigning operations. Unlike the past model of decentralized parties, the modern GOP exerted new power over who gets to run and who doesn't, and on its own elected officials, by its control of expertise, technology, and purse strings from the center. In 2004, the Bush/Cheney campaign and the RNC put these diverse operations to work in what, to that date, might well have been the most disciplined and nationally directed party organization in U.S. history. However, the poor Republican showing in 2008 and 2012 cast some doubt on the party's post-Bush capacity to maintain such a high level of organizational prowess.

The Democrats Respond

By all accounts, one of the causes and results of the Democrats' decline since the 1970s had been their relative inability to match the money, influence, expertise, or coordination of the Republican innovations. After their loss of the White House in 1980, however, the Democrats at the center stressed professionalization as well. They built a national headquarters and a media operation, and they gathered enough money in the Democratic National Committee (DNC) to remain competitive. However, they lacked the extent of foundation, think tank, and media power of the Republican power structure. Out of power in Congress since 1995 and out of the White House in 2001, they also lacked the ability to compete effectively with Republicans in extracting money from and implanting operatives in the large lobbying firms, trade associations, and industry interests that had centered around the GOP. Most of all, the Democrats were far from unified after their defeats and lacked the disciplined message machine of the GOP.

In 2004, this Democratic disadvantage began to change. Like the Republicans, Democrats and their supporters built effective structures outside of the party through 527 and 501(c) organizations (see Chapter 7). MSNBC very soon became a very liberal and pro-Democratic cable television station, with the ambition of battling the stronger pro-Republican Fox News for supremacy.

Howard Dean, who took over as as chair of the DNC from 2005–2008, also worked to improve the party's organizational ability. By 2008, "for the first time in decades," political scientist Daniel Galvin observed, the Democratic nominee for president found "a much more reliable party organization with which to work." The excellent organizational ability of the Obama campaign and its capacity to recruit volunteers also helped the party-building effort. Galvin concluded, "change may finally be afoot in the Democratic Party."[40]

Indeed it was. By 2008, the Democrats had two fully national databases up and running. The Obama campaign was not only superior to McCain's, it was even better than Bush's excellent effort four years earlier. His campaign's salesmanship was so effective, for example, that it was selected *"marketer of the year"* by *Advertising Age*, decisively beating competitors

Apple, Zappos, Nike, Coors, and Republican John McCain. As we saw in Chapter 7, in 2012 the Obama campaign perfected its merger of modern techniques with campaign strategy, very effectively using social media, refining microtargeting, employing predictive analytics, and making excellent use of its ultra-modern digital platform Narwhal to record and integrate information and aid the effort to get out the vote. Sasha Issenberg writes, "when it comes to the use of voter data and analytics, the two sides appear to be as unmatched as they have ever been on a specific electioneering tactic in the modern campaign era."[41]

There is no doubt that in 2012 the Obama and Democratic campaign effort was superior to that mounted by Romney and the Republicans, thoroughly reversing—in case 2008 left any question—the Republican edge from 2004. The main issue is to what degree the Obama campaign organization will share and fully integrate its resources and expertise with the Democratic Party organization. Some Democrats were already worried that the Obama campaign, Obama for America, "took resources away from the Democratic National Committee's party-building mission." Indeed, instead of integrating itself into the party, Obama for America recently transformed itself into an independent advocacy effort called Organizing for Action, a nonprofit that can raise unlimited amounts of money and effectively counter similar GOP efforts like Karl Rove's Crossroads GPS. This new organization will endeavor to keep people involved, advocating for the president's program in Congress. However some Democrats "aren't pleased that Obama didn't fold his powerful grassroots operation back into the DNC," while worrying, as Howard Dean does, that it will be "all about Obama" and will leave the Democratic Party unprepared when the president leaves the scene.[42]

There is no question that the 2012 election has already had an effect on the future national infrastructure and support networks of each party. The Republicans will undoubtedly redouble efforts to counter recent Democratic success. From a popular democratic perspective, however, we should ask: will each party make future party building and adjacent independent efforts more responsive—or less responsive—to the concerns of the ordinary party supporter?

Conclusion: Strong Parties and the Democratic Debate

What do the developments we have described portend? Some argue that demographic shifts—such as increases especially in the Latino, but also the Asian population; in highly educated women; in unmarried women; in the number of professionals; and higher voting participation among the young—favor the Democrats into the future. Whether these shifts can be transformed into a party realignment is harder to see.

For the sake of an invigorated party system with a full and rich democratic debate, the Republican Party would do well to leave behind the strategy of using wedge issues—especially (but not only) those involving race, ethnicity, and sexual identity—to win elections. Although effective for forty-five years, the strategy doesn't seem to be working so well now. Moreover, even when it worked, it weakened the democratic debate by too often winning the authority to govern on a set of symbolic and cultural issues, while using the power thereby won at the ballot box to largely concentrate on unrelated economic policies. Finally, it does a disservice to core Republican beliefs: whether of limited government, low taxes, large outlays for national security, protection of the private market against state regulation, or defense of "traditional values." From a popular democratic point of view, it diverts attention from the debate that Americans deserve to have over the Republican agenda.

The revitalized Democrats, too, must improve the role they play in the democratic debate, especially if they are poised to win more than their share of future national elections. To do so, they need to renew, under contemporary conditions, their commitments to social justice, and to economic fairness, equality, and security in a way that can engage all voters, including the majority of whites who haven't voted Democratic in fifty years. Much will depend on how the revitalized Democrats use the power they have, and whether, through their governing actions, they can solidify their support, while reaching out to the vulnerable who didn't support them, and to those who didn't vote at all. For the Democrats, according to Robert Reich, "It is crucial to build a political movement that will endure beyond a particular electoral contest."[43]

If the Republicans and Democrats take prescriptions such as those we offer here to heart, they could have a truly substantive debate for quite some time. Each party must now consider how it will handle the years ahead. The future of the party system—and the quality of the democratic debate between the parties—will be determined by what each party decides to do.

Reader's Guide ★ ★ ★

Critical Thinking Questions

1. As you review the 2008 election, would you consider it to be a watershed election, in which the political party system went through fundamental change? Or do you think of it as just another election with few permanent effects?

2. What kind of contact have you had with a political party over the last few years? Were you contacted by the party, or did you contact it? What was the purpose of the contact?

3. Do you think America is well served by the current two-party system? Do you think we would be better off with more parties? What kinds of parties would you like to see?

4. What do you think of the current system of the way we elect our officials using winner-take-all elections? Would American democracy be better served with some form of proportional representation?

5. Who has a voice in the current two-party system? Can enough people get their views heard? What would be the best way to further democratize our political party system?

Key Word Definition

aggregate interests   When a political party brings together different groups and diverse interests into a coalition supporting its overall party program or philosophy.

responsible parties   A scholarly ideal in which parties fulfill their democratic character by forming consistent and meaningful ideologies and programs that become well known to the voters and in which the winning party is held accountable by voters for implementation of programs and their consequences.

dominant two-party system   The idea that Democrats and Republicans together control the electoral machinery and legal frameworks that promote their near monopoly on most political offices. While third parties are not prohibited in the United States, the two-party system tends to perpetuate itself through single-member electoral districts, the Electoral College, and control of ballot access.

single-member district (winner-take-all) electoral system   The principle and practice of electing only one representative for a given electoral district. Typically, the winner receives a plurality of the votes cast. Ubiquitous in the United States, single-member districts contrast with other forms of representation such as multimember districts in which representation is shared in a given electoral district based on the proportion of votes received.

proportional representation   An electoral system in which legislators are elected at large and in which parties receive electoral representation in proportion to the percentage of total votes they receive.

Electoral College system   The body of electors, whose composition is determined by the results of the general election in each state, that chooses the president and vice president of the United States. Winning candidates must garner a majority of the 538 electoral votes in the Electoral College.

gerrymandering   The practice of drawing electoral districts to favor one outcome over another, named after eighteenth-century Massachusetts politician Elbridge Gerry. In recent years, gerrymandering has been used in most states to ensure the reelection of incumbents of both parties.

Jim Crow laws   A series of measures, instituted by Southern state governments around the turn of the twentieth century, enforcing strict racial segregation as well as exclusion of African Americans from political participation by means of literacy tests, poll taxes, and "whites only" party primary contests. "Jim Crow" was struck down by a series of federal civil rights acts in the 1960s.

critical (realigning) election   An election that ushers in and shapes an ensuing electoral era; it features increased voter turnout and a reshuffling of the social groups that support each party, resulting in the domination of one party in succeeding elections.

party regime   The long-term domination by one party of most of the political agenda and offices, following a critical or realigning election.

system of 1896   The electoral era initiated by Republican William McKinley's defeat of Democrat/Populist William Jennings Bryan in 1896. The system featured Democratic control of southern state governments, Republican control of the big states and the national government, as well as low voter turnout and the initiation of restrictions on voter registration based on race.

New Deal Democratic coalition   The Democrats' alliance of the Solid South, organized labor, Catholics, and urban ethnic groups stemming from Franklin Roosevelt's policies of the 1930s.

electoral dealignment   The weakening of the party system caused by growing popular indifference to the parties themselves.

party identification   A person's psychological identification with or tie to a particular political party.

party primary   An election in which voters decide which of a party's candidates will be nominated to run for office in the general election. Closed primaries permit only those registered in a particular party to participate. Open primaries leave the balloting open to nonparty registrants.

frontloading   The decisions made by state governments to move their presidential primaries to dates earlier in the election year in order to increase their influence on presidential candidates.

national party convention   Meetings held every four years to determine a political party's national platform and presidential and vice-presidential candidates. Generally, convention delegates are selected through primaries and caucuses held in every state during election years.

think tank   A nonprofit institution, funded primarily by foundations and corporate grants, that conducts public policy research.

The Media: Who Sets the Political Agenda?

Many of you may not have strong opinions about the fine points of public policy, and it may be difficult to get worked up over the abstractions of political theory. Yet, with the media, things are different. Their direct effect on us is undeniable. Love them or hate them, the media play a large role in shaping what we know.

We begin with a critically important, although puzzling, example of the political influence of the media. In 2004, the United States witnessed one of the most important elections in modern times. Turnout soared, activism exploded, presidential debates were held, and billions of dollars were spent by the candidates and their allies. The American print and broadcast media produced thousands of accounts of the dramatic campaign. One of the biggest issues was the Iraq War.

In a nationwide survey conducted just before the election, University of Maryland researchers discovered that nearly three-quarters of the supporters of President George W. Bush believed that weapons of mass destruction had been found in Iraq. A nearly similar percentage reported the view that Saddam Hussein's regime had supplied support to Osama bin Laden's Al Qaeda. Two-thirds believed that the president had supported the Kyoto treaty on global warming, the International Criminal Court, and the international treaty banning land mines. Big majorities of President Bush's voters believed that people around the world supported the Iraq War, including most Muslims in the Middle East.[1]

If this survey is right—and no one has really contested its findings—there is a problem here for democracy *and* for the media. The view of reality shared by most of President Bush's supporters was simply factually wrong on each and every point. How do we account for this?

Were people voting to reelect the president regardless of what should have been widely known facts? In the same survey, people said, for example, that if weapons of mass destruction hadn't been found, it might make a difference in their opinions. So facts mattered to them. Were they just tuning out, then? No. Other surveys reported that Bush supporters showed at least as much interest in the news as did those of his Democratic opponent, Senator John

Kerry. The pollsters had their own explanation. They thought that people believe what they want to believe: Because people liked Bush, they adjusted their beliefs about the facts into a frame that allowed them to continue to like him.

We suggest another interpretation. The perceptual screens that people employ and their need to identify with political symbols and images *do* matter. However, the quality of information and analysis, and the diversity of perspectives, available to the public matter just as much. Indeed, it is in helping provide these resources that the media play their central role in the democratic debate. Trying to understand where the media fall short in this role—and what we can do to improve their performance—is the subject of this chapter.

The Democratic Debate and the Mass Media

In the abstract, elite and popular democrats alike support the mass media's freedom, independence, and essential role in democratic life. The concept of a vast public arena in which ideas and diverse information are freely exchanged appeals to all. Yet here the consensus ends; elite and popular democrats differ about who and what control today's media marketplace, who should control it, and to what effect. They agree that something is wrong but can't agree on what or why. Indeed, there is profound conflict about the main features of our media system.

For elite democrats, the existing mass-media system embodies the virtues of a free marketplace. Media producers enter the market, invest capital in media products, compete with others, and sell their products to consumers. When they are successful, profits are made, and consumers are satisfied. Because consumers fulfill their wants by preferring some privately owned media companies and products over others, the whole media system is considered to be fair and free. For elite democrats, therefore, the public interest is served when private producers compete for the consumer's attention. To preserve this freedom, they believe that meddling by government or others in the rights of the private producers must be minimized. In this sense, they view the news media marketplace just like they would view any other market.

To be sure, elite democrats can be critics of the mass media. Some are concerned when the mass media defy established authority, or tweak dominant cultural values, or spread indecency. Ironically, such criticisms are often couched in terms of the media's "elitism." Some people who have few problems with corporations owning the media do have serious concerns about some of the people the owners employ, who are often accused of looking down on mainstream values, or trying to make a cheap buck, or being willing to satisfy the darker cravings of human nature. Strangely, these critiques are rarely linked to questions about whether the profit-driven and commercialized character of the media system itself leads to questionable choices about programming and personnel.

In our own times, the major support for the elite democrats' idea that only a commercial media can maximize our freedom is usually associated with what is called the media revolution. Innovative telecommunications, said to be a product of healthy market competition, have greatly expanded people's access to all kinds of information, facts, opinions, and images. The media revolution features greater choice, increased interaction, and healthy competition. The possibility of greater public knowledge and enriched debate is claimed to be a result. With close to 2,000 cable and satellite channels, still as many as 1,400 daily newspapers, some 20,700 magazines, countless websites and postings, and a new generation of bloggers, the face of media and the sources and definition of the news media have been transformed.[2]

Thus, to its boosters, the media have never been more democratic: No longer are passive consumers limited to a few national TV programs and stodgy newspapers. Communication is faster and cheaper; eighty-five percent of the public go online every week, and a growing majority turn to the Internet for news and information, as well as for shopping and entertainment.[3] Isn't this enough of a marketplace? In fact, why call this view of the media "elite" democratic at all?

Popular democrats are also interested in a marketplace of ideas and believe that the technological revolution presents some profound possibilities for democracy. Yet, they doubt that profit-driven and commercialized media are alone able to provide the diversity of ideas and perspectives and the information of high quality that can prepare citizens to make free and fully informed choices. This is especially important regarding the news media. While there are thousands of print, broadcast, and Internet outlets, nearly all of them have a commercial purpose. They must fulfill this purpose not only by selling products and thereby shaping consumer needs, but also by making themselves attractive and marketable to the kind of consumer demographics that will impress advertisers and therefore their own stockholders.

Popular democrats are also very concerned by media concentration. The sheer number of outlets and sites may be impressive, but ownership is more concentrated than at any time in U.S. history. Across the news media spectrum—from newspapers to the Internet—about twenty corporations control the vast bulk of what Americans *actually* read, see, and hear on the radio, television, in newspapers, and online. Concentrated private power in the media industry contradicts the image of a marketplace of small producers in which all can participate. Far from being apolitical, these media companies are completely intertwined with major corporations that have many other interests at home and abroad. For example, companies like Disney or Comcast and General Electric own not only ABC and NBC respectively but also own interests in nuclear weapons and theme parks, as well as publishing companies and sports teams.[4]

For popular democrats, a commercial media dominated by a few giants hardly promotes the political independence said to be the chief virtue of a free market. Like other industries, media corporations employ an army of lobbyists and deliver ample campaign contributions to politicians. They seek favorable tax breaks, subsidies, and the kind of regulations that restrict rather than enlarge the marketplace of ideas. They also must renew the licenses that allow them to dominate the "public airwaves." In short, rather than being independent actors, the news media are intertwined with political elites and codependent with the powers that be. They have few reasons to offend the powerful, and every reason to concentrate on those stories that please advertisers and attract consumers. It is entirely possible, therefore, to watch a hundred channels and still encounter a filtered reality that somehow doesn't get around to airing political basics. There is sometimes more the illusion of choice rather than its reality.

Has the growth in media power fulfilled the hopes of those, like Jefferson, who assumed that it would be an instrument of democratic rule? Or do the media too often impede active democratic citizenship, as they seek to protect—and to promote—their bottom line?

Media Power and U.S. History

Two fundamental historical developments help to answer these questions. First, commercial media have grown in American life but have done so by crowding out other ways of getting information and sharing and debating ideas about politics and the nation. While the family, the school, the local community, the tavern, the church, and the political party used to be the chief sources and arenas for political knowledge and conversation, most of what Americans know and think today about politics comes from TV, radio, magazines, newspapers, and established sources on the World Wide Web. Second, media power and influence have followed the same tendencies rampant in the global political economy, which are outlined in Chapter 4. Over time, the character of "private ownership" of the media has changed. It has passed from local newspapers with individual owners, sometimes undoubtedly with their own interests, to global corporations with direct economic interests in influencing public policy and politics on a broad scale. How did the present situation come about? Do these trends make any difference for our marketplace of ideas?

Newspapers

Today we'd think it odd if *USA Today* or the *Los Angeles Times* mixed its detailed weather reports and sports coverage with political philosophy essays on current topics. Yet New York City's *Independent Journal* printed the entire text of the *Federalist* in 1787 and 1788, the famous set of papers that argued for ratification of the Constitution. That newspaper's role was hardly novel: From the Revolution to the Civil War, U.S. newspapers served as the premier vehicle of political communication. Making money was a secondary concern to the broader role of newspapers as instruments of partisan debates and attacks. In sharp contrast to today, newspapers were locally owned—they represented the democratic debate in towns, villages, and small cities of the early republic.[5] After the Civil War, the strictly partisan press began to be challenged by a new generation of owners. These press barons wanted to make money and achieve personal political influence, and they therefore sought the highest possible circulation in the big cities. While politics was hardly ignored, the definition of news was expanded, and it became a commodity to be manufactured, bought, and sold. William Randolph Hearst and Joseph Pulitzer helped to pioneer **yellow journalism** (named for the Yellow Kid, a cartoon character), which attracted readers with sensationalized accounts of crimes and scandals. The Sulzberger family took a contrary approach with the *New York Times*. The *Times* promoted the new doctrine of journalistic objectivity and professionalism, but its commercial aim was to sell papers to a growing middle class of urban professionals.[6]

During the twentieth century, titans like Hearst, Pulitzer, and Sulzberger were generally replaced by the cool and impersonal calculation of the corporate boardroom. With increasing momentum after World War II, formerly independent dailies in cities and towns were merged or eliminated. Today, newspaper "chains"—among them Gannett, The McClatchy Company, Scripps, the New York Times Company, and the Hearst Corporation itself—have absorbed most of the nation's dailies. The result has been a diminishing role for hard-hitting, independently owned local newspapers and the effective end of competition among newspapers in most metropolitan areas.

Newspaper readership has declined since the 1980s, and efforts to expand it by including new sections on lifestyle issues such as cooking, entertainment, and fashion trends have not reversed the trend. Over the last twenty years, paid weekday newspaper circulation has dropped over thirty percent to a low of fewer than forty-two million customers today. Ten years ago, four in ten Americans between the ages of eighteen and thirty-four read a daily newspaper regularly. Today, fewer than one in four do so. In spite of these trends and contrary to what some think, newspapers have managed to remain somewhat profitable—although profits are way down from the heyday of the late 1990s. Profitability, however, is largely achieved by managing—that is—cutting costs, which may mean undermining coverage by standardizing the news, cutting the news gathering workforce, and giving short shrift to many important, especially local, stories. While newspaper websites increase readership, there is no guarantee they can generate sufficient advertising to bring in the revenues needed to maintain current levels of operation. The Internet itself poses a variety of threats to newspapers—from competing news sources to formats devoid of news—that can draw away potential readers. Along with readers go advertisers' dollars. In 2010, for the first time more money went into advertising on the Web than into newspaper ads, a direct result of the long term drop-off in print readership.[7]

Radio and Television

Newspaper ownership consolidated partly because of the competition from radio in the 1930s, network television in the 1950s, and now cable and satellite TV and the Internet. In radio's early days in the 1920s, stations were often owned by not-for-profit organizations, and the ownership was local. But the passage of the Federal Communications Act in 1934 promoted corporate ownership and the end of not-for-profit dominance on the radio. The Radio Corporation of America (RCA) quickly became the industry leader. Its new network featured little political news, concentrating instead on entertainment programming ranging from music to soap operas and comedies. World War II changed that, with the new CBS Radio Network and its reporter in war-torn London, Edward R. Murrow, leading the way.

Born from RCA, NBC, along with CBS and ABC, dominated early television, the revolutionary new medium of the 1950s. And yet, much like radio in its early days, TV in its childhood was not particularly news oriented. As a result, the news divisions of the major networks were relatively free of the profit imperative. Instead, they were supposed to provide prestige to the network's image. Although underfunded, they sometimes produced outstanding and even risky independent and professional news and documentaries.[8]

The real growth and expansion of TV news as the most watched and thus most profitable form of news coverage occurred only in the 1960s. Technological advances expanded the popular appeal of the evening television news. Handheld cameras, and then satellite transmission and videotape, meant that TV journalism could move out of studios and newsreels and go where the live action was at home or abroad. Television news anchors like Walter Cronkite and David Brinkley became trusted celebrities, while the networks discovered that their news divisions could make a profit by drawing large audiences.[9]

The 1960s provided plenty of lively political events to cover. The televised presidential debates between Richard Nixon and John Kennedy in 1960 began the trend. After that, television became the premier medium of influence for politicians, and the coverage of presidential campaigns became the most important source of images and impressions. In turn, politicians began to treat television as the most valuable means of communication with voters.

"Take us to Jon Stewart."

For good or ill, for roughly thirty years the network news did create a national audience and something like a public conversation around common issues like the civil rights movement, the Vietnam War, Watergate, and Iran-Contra. Today, that centrality has withered. These days, the audience for television news is much more fragmented into niche markets and infotainment formats like those of *20/20* and the *Today* show. The nightly network evening news programs still remain the largest single sources of national news, with an average of 22.5 million viewers each night. Yet that number is down significantly from its high point of nearly half the adult population. The network news audience today has an average age of over sixty-two years old, and less than one-fifth of young adults watch network news regularly. The decline in network news may have been prompted by declining network budgets for news and documentary but also by the rise of "new news" formats and "niche marketing" to specialized audiences.[10]

Cable television news, pioneered by CNN, first challenged the networks. By the late 1990s and the turn of the new century, the Fox News Channel, MSNBC, and even C-SPAN featured "all news all the time" formats, gaining specialized audiences.

Cable television also picked up on debate shows that had been on broadcast TV, such as William F. Buckley's *Firing Line* and *The McLaughlin Report*, and took them to a new level of explicit partisanship with *The O'Reilly Factor*, *The Ed Show*, *Hannity*, and *The Rachel Maddow Show*—to name just a few. Relatively cheap to make, their "stars" are *very* well paid. Some of these shows are often short on hard information or news and very successful at creating the illusion that winning debating points is the same thing as getting at the truth. They are part of the rise of what some call the "punditocracy." Once rebellious challenges to network news, however, these cable outlets also have a graying audience. To take one example, Fox cable news is still the most watched cable news network. However, it has been losing viewers, and its average viewer's age at sixty-five is a little older even than that of the networks.

In any case, news for some time has not been the exclusive purview of journalists or even pundits alone. Old stand-by shows like Oprah Winfrey's, Jay Leno's, and David Letterman's, and in more recent years Jon Stewart's *The Daily Show* and then Stephen Colbert's *The Colbert Report*, mix parody, entertainment, and political commentary outside of news formats. For many young people, they are the major source of "news" coverage.[11] Even more profound changes, however, have been in the works for some time.

The Internet and Its Platforms

If novel formats for news were transforming the old media, something dramatically new also entered the scene. By 2012, almost half of U.S. adults were getting news from the Internet at least three times a week. Today, virtually every advocacy and research group has its own website. The young and the comparatively affluent are particularly likely to consult the Web for news, but the new medium is making steady inroads among other groups as well. Meanwhile, media companies have invested millions in websites that serve as promotion vehicles for their TV, newspaper, and film offerings. They are also utilizing the capacity of digital television and broadband communication to bring together cable television, telephone, and Internet services in one hookup.[12]

The growth of online news sources accompanies a widespread redefinition of what "news" is. The Web may have millions of sites, but most individual Americans don't (and couldn't possibly) consult more than a tiny fraction of them. Service providers and search engines lead users to "preferred" links, often headlines, sports, and weather that come from the major media corporations. The most popular news sites are about weather, the stock markets, and sports. For most, but hardly all, Internet users, political news appears as a headline, followed by a brief story if one clicks on the "link." Easy access to digital news also makes it increasingly likely that people, and especially younger people, will "graze" the news—check in on it from time to time—rather than get it at set times. Not surprisingly, those who get

Table 9.1 Changing Trends in News Consumption, 1993–2012

	1993	1996	2000	2004	2006	2008	2010	2012
Regularly watch...	%	%	%	%	%	%	%	%
Local TV news	77	65	56	59	54	52	50	48
Nightly network news	60	42	30	34	28	29	28	29***
Network morning news	–	–	20	22	23	22	20	22***
Network TV magazines	52	36	31	22	NA	NA	NA	NA
Cable TV News	–	–	–	38	34	39	39	34
Fox News Channel	–	–	17	25	23	23	23	21
CNN	35	26	21	22	22	24	18	16
MSNBC	–	–	11	11	11	15	11	11
CNBC	–	–	13	10	11	12	8	NA
C-SPAN	11	6	4	5	4	5	4	NA
Listened/read yesterday...								
Radio	47*	44	43	40	36	35	34	33
Newspaper	58*	50	47	42	40	34	31	29
Online news three or more days per week	–	2**	23	29	31	37	46	46

*From 1994
**From 1995
***From 2011
Source: Pew Research Center for the People and the Press, April–May 2004. Reprinted by permission.
Updated, September 2012, www.people-press.org.

their news from digital news platforms are more likely to graze the news than those who get it from the more traditional sources of newspapers or TV. Thus, far from enriching the news mix, the Web may actually encourage shortened attention spans and a redefinition of news away from politics and public policies. (See Table 9.1.)

For all the promise of the Internet, it presents another problem to consider. It may create an exaggerated sense of citizen empowerment and accomplishment. The popular social news and entertainment website Reddit, for example, claims to be "the front page of the Internet," while Digg, the site Reddit copied and surpassed in popularity, still says it is "what the Internet is talking about right now." Digg's goal was to be "a place for people to discover and share content from anywhere on the web," free of editors, with the goal of changing "the way people consume information online." Yet according to David Carr, while Google, sites like Reddit and Digg, and various RSS feeds may put data at our fingertips, "they never made a phone call, never asked hard questions of public officials, never got an innocent man out of jail....The smartest Web robot in the world is going to come back dumb if there is nothing out there to crawl across."

Yet this entirely appropriate emphasis on who actually does the hard work of digging up news and information may overlook the positive effects on news dissemination of relatively new technologies, such as smartphones and tablets, and of the phenomenon of social media itself.

For some time, more than three-quarters of American adults have owned computers. By 2012, forty-five percent owned smartphones, and another twenty-five percent owned tablets—a proportion that doubled just over the previous year. Consequently, while more than half of Americans still get their news via desktop or laptop computers, today nearly one-quarter use combinations of computers, smartphones, and tablets. More Americans are becoming, in other words, "multiplatform digital news consumers." There is potential good news here. News consumption may be becoming more of "an additive experience" across multiple devices. Mobile users also consume news somewhat differently, by spending a lot more time employing news apps, viewing more pages, and going back to them more often than those on computers, and tablet users may actually read longer, more in-depth articles as well. According to one comprehensive study by the Pew Center's Project for Excellence in Journalism, data such as these suggest "that the move toward mobile holds some promising options for news producers, including increasing the amount of overall news being consumed." It warns that "[t]o capitalize on that potential" the news industry "will need to do a better job" than it did with desktops of understanding audience behavior and adapting to it. What the report doesn't mention, however, is that even if the industry successfully adapts, the quality of news consumption will only be as good as the quality of the news produced. New technology changes none of that.

In a 2011 report, Pew pointed to another striking digital development that is much discussed these days. It concluded: "If searching for news was the most important development of the last decade, sharing news may be among the most important of the next." Here, social media play an important role through their various platforms, such as Facebook for networking, YouTube for content sharing, Blogger for blogging, Twitter or Tumblr for microblogging, and Wikipedia for collaborative research. With 133 million "active users" in America (and something like 500 million worldwide), Facebook is currently able to dominate the nexus between news and social media, with Twitter also playing an increasingly important role. Yet, are those who are real consumers of news really relying on Facebook for that news? To answer this question, Pew did another study in 2012. Although the new report "confirms that Facebook and Twitter are now pathways to news," it questions the size of their role because the numbers who use these sites for getting *news* "is still relatively small"; news consumers "have not given up other methods of getting news, such as going directly to websites, using apps or through search." Pew concludes: "social media are additional paths to news, not replacements for more traditional ones."[13]

There is no question that the Internet revolution and the technologies it has made possible are having an enormous impact on how we learn, what we know, and ultimately what we do in politics. Look at the important informational and mobilizing role of social media in the "Arab Spring" of 2011, the inventive ways Chinese bloggers criticize their government, or the way American politicians use a variety of platforms to disseminate propaganda—and the way Americans use them to hold their politicians accountable and express their own points of view.

Yet, while the Internet revolution can help us research and share information, it remains no substitute for digging it up in the first place, or for having the drive and ability to make "unholy secrets knowable."[14] While it can facilitate our ability to express our views, or learn the views of others, it can't do the hard work of refining our viewpoints and really engaging with others, rather than socializing through politics with those with whom we already agree. There is no doubt that the Internet is increasingly important as a part of today's marketplace of ideas. But even at its best—even if it were thoroughly democratic—it would still provide the marketplace, not the ideas. Whether with pen, or iPad, typewriter, laptop, or quill—they are still up to us.

Diverse Marketplace or Vast Wasteland?

In theory, the media revolution has made a broader range of news sources available to more people than at any other time in human history. Some even talk of a **virtual democracy**, an era marked by instant communication between people and between citizens and powerful institutions. There are reasons to be cautious regarding such claims.

Although media consumers can choose between hundreds of profit-making commercial outlets, few have political content, and many appeal to specialized tastes. The same is true of the virtually unlimited number of Internet sites that, even when they are political or news-oriented, often tend to produce niches for people with similar views and interests. This can contribute to fragmentation, and perhaps even erosion, of the capacity for common political discourse. The network news's dominance, whatever its problems, at least provided a common political vocabulary and set of reference points for most Americans. Produced by professional journalists partly shielded from the commercial interests of parent companies, the network news contained some recognized standards of reporting. The mass media today may be a marketplace, but to what degree are they a free market of important ideas?[15]

The average American still interacts with some form of media more than eight hours each day, and eight in ten Americans hear some news every day via radio, TV, newspapers, or cyberspace. Taken together, the news media remain extraordinarily powerful. The important question is how people understand what they read, see, and hear in the news media sources they use. Back in the 1940s, researchers found that most people balanced what they learned through the news media with other influences from civil society: friends, coworkers, family members, and local members of interest groups and political parties. In the 1970s, scholars found that the media did little to change political opinions, as people tuned out news stories they didn't care about or disagreed with and remained quite skeptical about what they saw and heard.[16]

Today, it may be comforting to believe that what the news media convey is balanced by and interpreted in the context of a rich civil society, thereby sometimes generating healthy popular skepticism. However, with the decline of trade unions, many public associations, and even the political parties, the mass media assume an increasingly important power as the commanding—even only—source of political information and talk. The modern news media are **agenda setters**. While the mass media may not tell us exactly what to think, they do tell us what to think about. They select the stories and choose the narratives, and those they omit become invisible. Because the media have such a large influence in setting the political agenda, we must ask: Which institutions and people define the agendas of the news media? Whose voice is reflected, and what kind of politics is bypassed or distorted?[17]

Corporate Ownership and Control

Competition in the private marketplace is supposed to promote free speech and the public interest. Yet the most dramatic changes in American news media history are the increasing **concentration of ownership** in the media business, and the giant size and diverse activities of the new corporate owners, for whom news production is part of vast private entertainment empires.

In a free market, there is supposed to be easy entry for new producers of goods as well as extensive competition. But the markets in media are hardly free and open to new voices because they often are oligopolies in which a few firms dominate.

The trend toward concentration became a revolution over the last thirty years. In the 1980s, General Electric absorbed NBC, formed NBC Universal after the merger with Vivendi in 2004, and sold a majority stake to Comcast in 2011. In the 1990s, ABC and its parent company, CapCities, were gobbled up by Disney, Inc. Time-Warner, the biggest media corporation on the planet, first bought Ted Turner's CNN and then sold itself to the world's largest Internet provider, America Online (in what turned out to be an ill-fated alliance that ended in 2009 at a cost of some $100 billion in shareholder value). Rupert Murdoch's News Corporation, which purchased the *Wall Street Journal* in 2007 (as well as Dow Jones & Co.), Japan's Sony, and German-based Bertelsmann round out the list of media giants.[18]

These companies have consolidated holdings that span industries such as traditional television, cable television, satellite transmission, radio, newspapers, magazines, movies, book publishing, and music. Their news divisions are linked, through parent corporations, to industries like coal and gold mining, international nuclear power and armaments, chemicals and their disposal, medical services and research, worldwide finance and investment banks, theme parks, and housing developments. Mark Crispin Miller calls this new order of things the **national entertainment state**. Figure 9.1 provides a list of the partial holdings of just one of these megacorporations, News Corporation.

Figure 9.1 doesn't reflect the struggle for corporate mergers and consolidation in the telecommunications industry, where competition today seems to be headed toward new concentration tomorrow. The same giant corporations are fighting it out for the rights to control

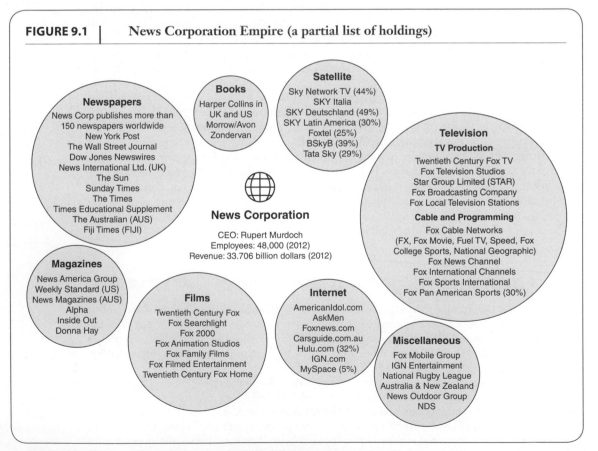

FIGURE 9.1 | **News Corporation Empire (a partial list of holdings)**

Newspapers
News Corp publishes more than 150 newspapers worldwide
New York Post
The Wall Street Journal
Dow Jones Newswires
News International Ltd. (UK)
The Sun
Sunday Times
The Times
Times Educational Supplement
The Australian (AUS)
Fiji Times (FIJI)

Books
Harper Collins in UK and US
Morrow/Avon
Zondervan

Satellite
Sky Network TV (44%)
SKY Italia
SKY Deutschland (49%)
SKY Latin America (30%)
Foxtel (25%)
BSkyB (39%)
Tata Sky (29%)

Television
TV Production
Twentieth Century Fox TV
Fox Television Studios
Star Group Limited (STAR)
Fox Broadcasting Company
Fox Local Television Stations

Cable and Programming
Fox Cable Networks
(FX, Fox Movie, Fuel TV, Speed, Fox College Sports, National Geographic)
Fox News Channel
Fox International Channels
Fox Sports International
Fox Pan American Sports (30%)

News Corporation
CEO: Rupert Murdoch
Employees: 48,000 (2012)
Revenue: 33.706 billion dollars (2012)

Magazines
News America Group
Weekly Standard (US)
News Magazines (AUS)
Alpha
Inside Out
Donna Hay

Films
Twentieth Century Fox
Fox Searchlight
Fox 2000
Fox Animation Studios
Fox Family Films
Fox Filmed Entertainment
Twentieth Century Fox Home

Internet
AmericanIdol.com
AskMen
Foxnews.com
Carsguide.com.au
Hulu.com (32%)
IGN.com
MySpace (5%)

Miscellaneous
Fox Mobile Group
IGN Entertainment
National Rugby League
Australia & New Zealand
News Outdoor Group
NDS

Source: *Columbia Journalism Review*, www.cjr.org; www.newscorp.com.

broadband and other technologies that will promote the consolidation of the cable, television, Internet, and other industries. If events unfold as predicted, a new media system will emerge where a few corporations will produce the programming, news, and films and distribute their products through digital television, the Internet, and entertainment "multiplexes" that they own.

Disney is a good example of such **vertical integration**, where firms control both the development of media content and its distribution through dozens of marketing conduits. With $42.28 billion in sales (2012), here's a company that can produce a film at Walt Disney Films, market it on the Disney channel or on its ABC network, sell it as a paperback through Hyperion books, advertise it on its 277 radio stations, sell toys based on the movies' characters through its chain of Disney stores, and after the movie goes to DVD, the company can rerun it for ad money on ABC Family or Lifetime.[19]

Concentration of ownership in the Big Six of American media companies (Comcast, Disney, News Corporation, Time Warner, Viacom, and CBS) has sent shock waves through other media industries. "Second tier" companies such as Clear Channel, the New York Times Company, and Gannett tend to be the major players in a single media industry. Gannett, Inc., publisher of *USA Today*, expanded its holdings to become the largest publisher of suburban newspapers. In radio, Clear Channel, known for organizing pro–Iraq War demonstrations, competes with Viacom's Infinity network. Together, both now do more business and reach more audiences than the rest of the radio industry combined.[20]

Corporate Censorship?

What are the effects of megacorporate ownership on the news media? Stories critical of the global economy's treatment of labor and the environment were never dominant in American media. How will they fare today when editors and producers know that their livelihoods depend on companies with widespread investments in everything from nuclear waste disposal to disposable diapers? One cautionary tale occurred after Disney's purchase of ABC. Back before the Disney buyout, ABC's *Prime Time Live* ran several stories on the Disney Corporation, tracing the often negative effects of its theme parks on surrounding communities. After the merger, observers noted that ABC news programs tended to highlight Disney movies and products; its *World News with Peter Jennings* even buried a story dealing with pedophilia and sexual harassment at Orlando's Disney World.

More frequent than outright censorship of stories is media silence on newsworthy topics critical of a parent media corporation or of business more generally. Since 1976, journalism professors and media watchers have been compiling a list of major developments ignored by the mainstream media. Leading Project Censored's uncovered list were: the association of oil companies with domestic terrorism abroad, the rising tide of workplace injuries, the profiteering of drug companies in the United States and abroad, and the growth of wealth and income inequality. Censored, or ignored, were the media mergers themselves and the ambitious legislative agenda of the National Association of Broadcasters (NAB), the industry's major trade association.[21]

Also disappointing is coverage of organized labor. Fifty years ago, virtually every major newspaper and most networks had a full-time reporter assigned to American labor. Today, although there are well over a thousand business reporters on staff at the U.S. major dailies, fewer than ten full-time reporters cover the labor movement for the mainstream mass media.

Coverage of economic struggles over the shape of the world economy can also be biased. The commercial media's coverage of the 1999 and 2000 demonstrations in Seattle and Washington, D.C., against the policies of the International Monetary Fund (IMF) and World Trade Organization (WTO), is a case in point. One study found that demonstrators were generally stereotyped as "lawless anarchists," even though all but tiny minorities of partici-pants at both demonstrations were peaceful and few arrests led to formal charges. The same study found that both TV and newspaper coverage scorned or ignored protesters' claims, while police, IMF, and WTO public relations spokespeople were given more than three-quarters of the quotations and citations. To what degree does this unbalanced coverage relate to the fact that the media giants that produce international programming and news have a material stake in relaxing trade rules, enforcing copyright protection, and other measures opposed by the protestors?[22]

Commercialism and the News

In the past, when media companies were smaller and less driven by the effort to *maximize* profits, there were some social barriers that balanced the pursuit of profits with the search for quality and even prestige. Today's megacorporations, however, are more impersonal organiza-tions capable of enhancing their image even as they are single-mindedly concerned with the bottom line. The prime motive of such corporations is to attract the widest and richest pos-sible audience, and then market it to advertisers, which provide the bulk of media companies' revenues and profits.

The power of advertisers need not be direct to have effects. The richer the audi-ence base for news, the more likely its members are to be able to buy products adver-tised through the mass media, and the more companies can charge for advertising. But the search for people with **upscale demographics** may bias both the definition and content of news covered and presented. One example of bias is the proliferation of pro-grams and newspaper space about business and the stock market. Rarer are stories that appeal to or are about the lives of the working poor, such as what it is like to live on the minimum wage.[23]

The drive for profits has also led news organizations to cut costs by reducing the number of reporters and news bureaus, using outsourced reporters, and creating "syn-ergy" by using the same reporters in their diverse print, TV, and radio operations. In the last twenty or more years, the number of broadcast reporters in Washington has been halved, and foreign bureau stations have been cut back even more as news divisions of the megacorporations cut costs by using fewer journalists to cover the various TV, radio, and Internet venues. As David Carr puts it, "Serious reporting used to be baked into the business, but under pressure from the public markets or their private equity owners, newsrooms have been cutting foreign bureaus, Washington reporters and investigative capacity." The result is that news is often reported from single sources, and much foreign news is left unreported or is covered only by the wire services, themselves reduced to the corporate-owned Reuters and the Associated Press. By 2005, for example, *CBS News*, once the flagship and standard of professional TV journalism, had only one reporter assigned to cover all of Asia. Carr's conclusion is pointed: "Under this model the newsroom is no longer the core purpose of media, it's just overhead."[24]

Here at home, harried journalists complain that they lack the time and resources to con-centrate on important stories and, as a result, are more apt to rely on official sources and the packages handed to them by public relations spokespeople. Nationally, reporters increasingly rely on reporting official sources because it is more economical to do so. Too often, stories that are cheap to cover and incur no political risk take precedence: Accidents, natural disas-ters, and dramatic crimes fit the bill on the local news.[25]

Many observers have also noted an erosion of the wall separating the business opera-tion of a media corporation from the newsroom. The most blatant example is to use the news to promote the direct commercial interests of the parent corporation. Some assert that NBC news programming was used to do just that by reporting about both the 2008 Beijing

Olympic Games and the 2012 London Olympic Games as if they were "news" stories of monumental importance. Deploying a force of 450 people, including 25 reporters and its star anchor Brian Williams to London, NBC gave updates on the Olympics on Williams's "Nightly News," and also generated soft stories about it on its morning "Today Show," for weeks leading up to the event. Meanwhile, ABC News had an "on air team" of only five, ESPN—the sports network—sent just two reporters to London, and CBS and Fox News sent none, relying instead on their London bureaus. According to NBC network executive David Verdi, the Olympics are "a huge story" of great interest to its audience. Why didn't the other networks view it in quite the same way? NBC's parent company had paid a fee of $2.2 billion to become the "official" American broadcaster for the 2010 winter and 2012 summer games. Much of the coverage was driven, some critics contend, "not by newsworthiness, but by corporate synergy, in which the news division generates stories to heighten interest in NBC's prime-time Olympic telecasts." "Call me old school," media critic Paul Farhi writes, "but in the journalism textbooks, it says the news division is supposed to make up its own mind about what to cover without being too mindful of what the bosses in corporate are pushing."[26]

Some examples are less subtle. The *Des Moines Register* once offered its reporters' services to the newspaper's biggest advertisers to develop special sections in which their products and companies were mentioned. Dozens of "business correspondents" happily plugged "hot" stocks before the stock market's 2001 decline because they were being paid by advertisers on their "business news" programs. Celebrity journalists can also make big money, as PBS's Charlie Rose did when he appeared as the master of ceremonies for the annual Coca-Cola Company shareholders meeting.[27]

Economic pressures toward commercialization of the news have intensified, especially after the sharp economic downturn in 2008. On January 5, 2009, for the first time, *The New York Times* printed a 2 ½ inch display advertisement horizontally across the bottom of its front page. Other newspapers had already been printing display ads on their front pages, including *The Wall Street Journal*, *USA Today*, and the *Los Angeles Times*, and the *Washington Post* would begin doing so the following year. According to the *New York Times* reporter covering the story, this was a change regarded by people he called "traditionalists as a commercial incursion into the most important news space in the paper." Ironically, the ad was bought by CBS.[28]

Is the Internet an Alternative?

The Internet is the vanguard of the media revolution. It has allowed people all over the world to reach a wide audience without having extensive financial resources. Yet, the World Wide Web has also become more and more a multi-stop shopping mall, where the big companies compete to provide the ads, the promotions, the programming, and the brand names to dominate the search engines and the service-providing business. As Douglas Rushkoff, once an idealistic young booster of the Internet suggests, it has slowly but surely been "surrendered to commercial use."[29]

Today, most people receive their Internet hookups through broadband communication, which are linked to telephones and cable TV transmissions. Companies like Time Warner Cable, AT&T, Verizon, and Comcast are trying to position themselves to control which sites can and can't be transmitted through broadband by charging for transmission rights and speed and discriminating in favor of their own services and content. This threatens the principle of "net neutrality," the very openness that gives the Internet its democratic promise. It has provoked a reaction from activists who oppose the multimillion-dollar lobbying campaign aimed at Congress and the Federal Communications Commission being waged by corporate telecom giants.[30] In 2006 a net neutrality bill was rejected by Congress. New bills with bipartisan support were again introduced in 2008 and 2009, again without success.

The Web Captivates World Wide.

In fact, when in December of 2010 the Federal Communications Commission (FCC) itself adopted net neutrality rules, preventing network providers from picking and choosing which traffic to route through their networks, House Republicans came back the next year with their own bill to reject those rules. Senate Democrats refused to go along, however, and had the bill come to his desk, President Obama said he would have vetoed it.

According to then Congressman, now Senator, Ed Markey, the Democrat from Massachusetts who had sponsored the net-neutrality legislation in the House: "At its core, the debate over Internet freedom is a battle about innovation and voices." The goal, he contends, is not one of regulation. Instead, it is to enshrine in law the "principles which have guided the Internet's development and expansion" and make them "guide stars for U.S. broadband policy."[31]

Struggles regarding Internet freedom are now also playing out in countries throughout the globe—and on the world stage in what one writer for the *Economist* called "a digital version of the cold war." There are now international efforts at regulation, according to Internet Society, that include data censorship, and control of domain registration, IP address, and other aspects of online life. In fact, in December 2012 in Dubai, at the World Conference on International Telecommunications, representatives from 193 nations to the United Nation's International Telecommunications Union (ITU) gathered to consider changes to the quarter century old International Telecommunications Regulations treaty. According to Elise Ackerman, writing in *Forbes*, some of the proposals to regulate "endorsed by authoritarian countries would have increased censorship, potentially restricted the free flow of information and undermined the voluntary framework that forms the basis of today's Internet". The United States led the opposition, with Russia and China on the other side. The United States said its goal was to defend an "open Internet." And its opposition was effective. Although the updated treaty was ultimately signed by a majority of the countries, it will have little effect. The refusal to sign was too widespread and the opposed countries too powerful. Moreover, the ITU doesn't have the power to compel nations. The failures of negotiations and the meeting itself, according to Ackerman, show just how much the ITU is "woefully out of step with the most technologically advanced sectors of the global society."

How should we evaluate the U.S. role? According to *The Economist* magazine, we should first "welcome" "America's willingness to stand up for the internet." However we also should recognize that "no other country benefits as much from the status quo in the online world." The United States houses much of the Internet infrastructure, is a conduit for most of the world's Internet traffic, "is in a unique position to eavesdrop, should it be so inclined" (prophetic words, in light of revelations in 2013 by former National Security Agency contractor Edward Snowden), and its companies reap most of the online profit. In other words, by defending the Internet as it is now, the United States also defended its interests." And the enormous U.S. diplomatic delegation to the meeting did, in fact, include representatives of the U.S. Defense Department, Facebook, and Google. Nevertheless, opposition to national government efforts to exert greater control over the Internet remains extremely important: as protestors from Beijing to Moscow well know.[32]

Government Influence on the Media

The new media corporations justify their power in the name of a free marketplace and technological efficiency. Ironically, though, corporate power in the marketplace is made possible by very friendly government policies. But there is a price: The media sometimes have abetted rather than checked abusive practices of government.

Disinformation and Intimidation

Private ownership of the mass media doesn't guarantee independence. From the Spanish-American War through the World Wars, Vietnam, conflicts in Central America, and the Persian Gulf wars, the mass media have often cooperated with government officials and policies. During World War II, for example, no major daily even expressed doubt about the incarceration without due process of law of 110,000 ethnic Japanese, many of whom were U.S. citizens.

During the Cold War, the CIA organized "disinformation" campaigns to plant fabricated stories in the media that discredited domestic critics and foreign opponents of government policy. In the 1980s, for example, CIA director William Casey successfully disseminated false information about the supposed connections between Nicaragua's Sandinistas and the drug trade.[33]

Selective use of information, silencing dissenting government experts, and outright disinformation reached heights during the prelude to the Iraq War. The heart of President Bush's case for war rested on the idea that Saddam Hussein's Iraq was hiding weapons of mass destruction, including the potential for a nuclear arsenal and substantial stores of biological and chemical weapons. On CNN, National Security Advisor Condoleezza Rice famously warned: "We don't want the smoking gun to be a mushroom cloud."[34]

For the most part, the American media bought into these claims, including the elite media of the *New York Times*, the *Washington Post*, CNN, and other outlets. As it has turned out, however, none of these claims were true. Not everyone went along. Knight Ridder (now McClatchy) newspapers was one of the few media outlets that reported dissent from within the government. According to its Washington bureau chief, John Wolcott, "we began hearing from sources in the military, the intelligence community, and the foreign service of doubts about the arguments the administration was making." These sources were not only better informed than their superiors, he claims, "they were deeply troubled by what they regarded as the adminis-tration's deliberate manipulation of intelligence...if you relied exclusively on traditional news sources—assistant secretaries and above—you would not have heard things we heard."[35]

Was the false case for the Iraq war a product of conscious deception or unconscious misinformation? Whatever the answer to that question, the media's record during the run-up to the Iraq War demonstrates that, although privately owned, they are not always sufficiently independent of government influence.

Sometimes, however, media independence is threatened through no fault of their own. In 2005, *New York Times* reporter Judith Miller was jailed by a federal judge for refusing to tell a federal prosecutor the name of a confidential source. Miller had investigated the White House "outing"—revealing the identity of—CIA agent Valerie Plame, whose husband, diplomat Joseph Wilson, had helped discredit the Bush administration claims about Iraq's nuclear weapons pro-gram. The prosecutor wanted to know whom Miller had spoken to, even though Miller had never written an article about the story. She refused to tell him for good reason. If reporters were to reveal the names of confidential sources it would become very difficult for them get informa-tion from people who, by giving it, would put themselves at risk. This would particularly affect the willingness of those inside government to "blow the whistle" about government wrongdoing and weaken the press's ability to provide the public with vitally needed information.[36] Unfortu-nately, trying to intimidate reporters into revealing their sources has a long history.

Government Secrecy: Media Independence in the Internet Age?

Sometimes, however, the media rejects disinformation and intimidation and exerts indepen-dence even in the highly sensitive area of national security. The most famous case of this occurred during the Vietnam War. Military analysts Daniel Ellsberg and Anthony Russo pho-tocopied what became known as "The Pentagon Papers," a classified government history of U.S. involvement in the war that included revealing, damning, and embarrassing information about government policy. Ellsberg then gave most of the study to the *New York Times*, which began publishing excerpts. The Nixon Administration immediately tried to suppress publica-tion. The U.S. Supreme Court, however, rejected its effort. (See Chapter 16.) It then tried to retaliate against Ellsberg personally, trying to steal his psychiatrist's records, an event that would become part of the Watergate scandal that would force Nixon to resign.

Fast-forward now to the age of the Internet. Throughout 2010, the Internet online organization WikiLeaks clandestinely obtained hundreds of thousands of U.S. secret gov-ernment documents and put them on its website, sharing some first with selected media. WikiLeaks had been started in Australia in 2006 by Julian Assange under the theory, as Assange put it, "that transparent government tends to produce just government." The released documents covered the Afghanistan and Iraq wars, and also 250,000 State Depart-ment diplomatic cables. Although much of the material was routine, some of it included undisclosed revelations about torture, killings, human rights abuses, civilian casualties, and embarrassing and revealing details of diplomacy. Major media outlets such as the *New York Times* and others in Europe published some of the cables. The episode, known as "Cablegate," stirred up enormous controversy. The U.S. government claimed the revelations compro-mised national security and endangered the lives of American personnel and those of allies. Attorney General Eric Holder began an investigation into Assange to see if he should be indicted on espionage charges, and Army PFC Bradley Manning, who admitted to giving WikiLeaks the material, is being court-martialed, with a possible life sentence.

Some called Assange a hero for "subverting the secrecy regime that is used to spawn all sorts of evils." Others predicted that the overall result would not be fewer secrets but much more secrecy, as government finds better ways both to protect its secrets and to track down and catch leakers. Some feared Congress would rewrite espionage laws to make them more effective against not just the leaker, but against the media itself.[37]

The sheer volume of material downloaded, copied, and given to WikiLeaks—inconceivable in Ellsberg's day of photocopying and paper—was astounding. Does the WikiLeaks episode mean that the new era of the Internet and computers makes possible ever-greater penetration into government secrets and their dissemination? Although Assange wound up cooperating with some major news outlets, especially regarding releasing the cables, neither he nor the leaker was dependent on major news institutions to get the material out.

There is no doubt that WikiLeaks created an additional avenue of independence from government—and from the mainstream media too. Indeed, its very action raised the question of whether the media had been effective in holding government accountable, thereby putting pressure on it to be more independent.

How are we best to understand the *overall* role institutions like WikiLeaks play in fostering a more independent media? Using the Pentagon Paper story as an analogy, Naomi Wolfe suggests that, in terms of legal responsibility, WikiLeaks was akin to the *New York Times*, the publisher, rather than Daniel Ellsberg, the source of the leaks. However, in terms of the overall job of media, there are differences. Originally, Julian Assange just wanted to release unfiltered information to the public, regarding it as the most transparent way to proceed. After encountering too much public indifference to reams of undigested information, and other problems, including strong criticism for publishing material that may have put people's lives at risk, he began collaborating with major newspapers. In other words, WikiLeaks was neither philosophically inclined, nor had the capacity to sift, evaluate, digest, and put the volumes of material into context. It was a conduit of information—but that's only part of journalism.

WikiLeaks showed there is a new and very independent way to provide an easily available platform independent both of government and major media institutions. However, real independence also requires more. It needs people to find the information, analyze it, put it into context—in other words it needs good journalists to discover and tell those stories we need to hear. Still, something is changing with the Internet revolution. As journalist Charlie Beckett at the London School of Economics puts it: "Now people like WikiLeaks are creating much greater diversity in journalism, some of which is dangerous, some of which is incompetent, but lots of which is incredibly informative and, this is an important point, it's incredibly popular." Or, as Abbe D. Lowell, a lawyer very familiar with the legal issues raised by WikiLeaks, suggests: "The WikiLeaks events tee up the question of defining "media" in the new, Internet era like no previous case."[38]

The Revolving Door

Sometimes government influences media independence in ways that take more subtle forms than disinformation, intimidation, or trying to stop the media from increasing government transparency. One example is the **revolving door**.

Quite often, independent journalists are picked to be government officials, and government officials find new and distinguished careers as reporters "covering" the institutions they recently left. In either case, the wall of separation between media and political authority may be weakened, and the incentive for reporters to file objective stories is greatly lessened.

"Celebrity" journalists are particularly prone to be beneficiaries of the revolving door. George Will soared to journalistic fame through ABC and a widely syndicated column, but in 1980 he coached Ronald Reagan for his debate with Jimmy Carter. Employed by ABC at the time, Will later praised Reagan's debate performance in front of the TV cameras. (After his dual role of coach and commentator was revealed, Will apologized.) Both liberal George Stephanopoulos and conservative William Kristol parlayed government service into lucrative contracts with major networks, as did Karl Rove, architect of George W. Bush's two presidential and two gubernatorial campaigns.

The media's independence might be most compromised when it comes to the choice of "experts" on national news programs. Experts chosen are often fellow insiders, former government officials, academics associated with insider Washington think tanks, or officials themselves. *Chicago Tribune* columnist Clarence Page has labeled this phenomenon the **Rolodex syndrome**. When a dramatic story appears, the news media all seem to call on a similar guest list of former government officials recast as journalists or neutral experts. In 2005, two prominent pundits were even found to be on the payroll of a public relations firm hired by the Bush administration.[39]

Government Regulation of Broadcasting: Who Owns the Airwaves?

The people of the United States are the official owners of the airwaves. Licenses for all TV and radio stations are granted in return for a promise to serve the public interest as trustees. Since 1934, the power to regulate and license has been vested in the Federal Communications Commission (FCC), a body whose members are appointed by the president and approved by Congress.

Through the FCC, government thus possesses an enormous power to shape (or retard) public access to the airwaves. Historically, labor, consumer, and other citizens groups have pressed government for a media system where public access and even publicly owned, noncommercial broadcasting were promoted. Indeed, the statute establishing the FCC commands it to prevent monopolies, promote competition, and ensure that a wide diversity of news and views is disseminated. But the 1934 act provided few concrete provisions that defined public access or control and said nothing at all about public broadcasting.

Since the 1930s, periods in which popular democratic movements have been strong are also periods where the mass media's commercialism has given way to increased public access and diversity in both ownership and programming. In the late 1960s, media activists carved out limited public space for what soon became National Public Radio (NPR) and the Public Broadcasting Service (PBS), partly funded through tax dollars. Both were meant to be free of overt commercial influence.

From the 1940s through the early 1980s, the FCC did impose some obligations and rules on private broadcasters using the public airwaves. Stations were required to reserve part of their programming for public affairs. If stations aired advertisements for one political candidate, they were required to give the same opportunity to others. (Communists were excluded.) The Fairness Doctrine required broadcasters to provide reasonable time to contrasting views on controversial topics. Monopolies in local markets were prohibited, as no single corporation could own local newspapers, television stations, and radio stations.

Yet over time and with increasing frequency since the Reagan presidency in the 1980s, most of the regulations and laws that promoted public access to the airwaves were gutted by Congress or the FCC or ruled unconstitutional by the federal courts. Through its powerful lobbying arm, the National Association of Broadcasters (NAB), the media industry led a very successful charge against regulation. In the 1980s, the FCC's staff and budget were cut, making it difficult for the regulators to monitor television and radio companies. License renewals for TV and radio stations every eight years no longer required hearings and could be done by mail. The Fairness Doctrine was eliminated, and the obligation to broadcast public affairs programming was ended.

As we've seen, one important barrier to corporate monopoly was FCC restrictions on ownership; companies could not own newspapers, TV stations, and radio stations in the same media market. In the mid-1990s, the development of new broadcast technologies combined with increased competition among corporate media and telecommunications giants. These developments led to new pressure on the government to "update" broadcasting regulations. The result was that the **Telecommunications Act of 1996** passed with substantial bipartisan support in the Senate and House. The ostensible goal of the bill's supporters was to stimulate competition and innovation in the new "Information Age" by breaking down the existing walls that prevented one industry from entering the market of another.

In fact, instead of increased competition, the act has promoted massive concentration. The new law also gutted remaining restrictions that once prevented telephone, cable, television, and radio companies from competing in one another's markets. It also allowed them to combine in ever-larger megacorporations that control communications in entire markets. Perhaps the most disturbing aspect of the bill has been the FCC's interpretation of it. In 2009, the United States moved to use of a "digital spectrum," a new technology that allows hundreds of new TV channels to transmit over the airwaves. Although in theory the public owns the digital spectrum just as it owns the other airwaves, by late 1997 the government was already giving it away (with a then market value of $70 billion) to the corporate mega-giants that already controlled the TV airwaves. Corporations like Rupert Murdoch's News Corporation and the Disney Corporation may use the new airwaves and cyberspace to make as much money as they want, without any obligation to broadcast news or public service programming, or even provide debating time to political candidates. The scale of corporate welfare offended even conservatives such as columnist William Safire, who branded the giveaway a "rip-off on a scale vaster than dreamed of by yesteryear's robber barons."[40]

In 2003, media industries came back for more. By late 2002, Federal Communication Commission Chair Michael Powell and his colleagues proposed a closed-door process that would dismantle the last federal media ownership limits on local media markets. Powell opined: "Monopoly is not illegal by itself in the United States. The public interest works with letting the market work its magic." Supported by the corporate media's lobbying arm and by all of the country's major media owners, Powell's proposed new "rules" would have allowed one company to own TV stations, radio stations, and newspapers in one "media market" or community, thereby becoming dominant. For the first time in four decades, however, a broad-based coalition formed, overturning the FCC's decision. The Making a Difference feature box details how this new media movement finally drew the line against even more media oligopolies.[41]

Making (and Creating) the News

We've traced the story of increasing corporate concentration in ownership and control of the media. It's a little more difficult to understand, however, the ways in which average journalists are affected by corporate ownership as they go about their day-to-day job of "reporting the news."

Media Bias: Which Way Does It Go?

Perhaps journalists are independent, professional, and willful enough to ignore or defy the companies that own the institutions at which they work. Indeed, conservatives often argue that working journalists are biased toward liberals and prone to grind ideological axes against big corporations and traditional family values. Ironically, the attacks became more vehement as frankly conservative media outlets and personalities—from talk radio, best embodied by Rush Limbaugh with the highest rated talk radio show; multimedia stars, such as TV and radio personality and media entrepreneur Glenn Beck; and cable TV news's top rated Fox

[MAKING A DIFFERENCE]

The Media Reform Movement

Could a movement of determined citizens overturn a powerful majority on the arcane Federal Communications Commission? The odds seemed impossibly long, yet that is just what a growing movement for media reform did in 2003.

The opposition started small. The Media Access Project and Center for Digital Democracy had worked for years to strengthen media access rules. They pushed for open hearings on FCC chairman Michael Powell's proposal to further weaken rules on media consolidation. They were joined by a courageous FCC commissioner, Michael Copps, who said that he'd hold public meetings throughout the country even if Powell didn't attend. The organizers were astounded by the turnout at Copps's hearings, numbers propelled in part by anger at poor press coverage of the Iraq War.

The FCC was deluged with more than 750,000 e-mails opposing Powell's proposals, and so was Congress. Groups like Common Cause, which had never been active in media policy issues before, were joined by organizations of journalists like the Newspaper Guild and the National Association of Black Journalists. Media reformers made alliances with evangelical Christian groups, and even got the National Rifle Association on board. Republican senators like John McCain and Trent Lott joined the battle, and so did almost all the Democrats in both houses of Congress. Public opinion polls revealed that the public was overwhelmingly against the FCC proposal.

Under increasing political pressure, Chairman Powell, in concert with the National Association of Broadcasters, nevertheless held firm. In June 2003, he forced a favorable three-to-two vote in the FCC. The deregulation measures were poised to go into effect. Although the House of Representatives was deluged with opposition letters and e-mails, its Republican leadership delayed a vote on the plan. The Senate, however, voted down the new (de)regulatory policy, and in June 2004, a federal court rejected the FCC's new regulation. It ordered the commission to come up with a reason to justify why further media concentration would be in the public interest.

If 2003 was a special year that catalyzed the media reform movement, according to media activist Josh Stearns, 2008 was a year of "movement building that proved ... media reform is here to stay." In December 2007, the FCC again tried to gut the cross-ownership ban between newspapers and broadcast media. More than one-quarter million people wrote to their senators, and in a near unanimous vote on May 15, 2008, the Senate again vetoed the FCC ownership rule changes. According to Stearns, 2008 didn't just show that media reformers can have an impact; "more importantly, we proved we can maintain the pressure." And they did. In 2011, the movement mobilized again, this time to stop the AT&T merger with T-Mobile, to save funding for public broadcasting, and defeat another attempt by the FCC in court to gut media ownership limits.

Sources: Robert McChesney, *The Problem of the Media: U.S. Communication Politics in the Twenty-first Century* (New York: Monthly Review Press, 2004); Neil Hickey, "Media Monopoly: Behind the Mergers Q & A," *Columbia Journalism Review* (May–June 2003); "About the FCC June 2 Vote," Free Press, www.freepress.net/rules; Robert Siegel, "Federal Appeals Court Tosses Out FCC Regulations," National Public Radio, *All Things Considered,* June 24, 2004; Josh Stearns, "Top Five Media Ownership Moments of 2008," (December 31, 2008), www.stopbigmedia.com; "2011, A Year of Media Reform Victories," Free Press, freepress.net.

News—have grown in numbers and influence. Meanwhile, supposedly liberal outlets like NPR and PBS have become more dependent on corporations "underwriting" their funding. Such charges, however, don't sufficiently take into consideration the conservative effects of ownership that we've outlined above, and they assume that journalists are not just "liberal" but are in complete control of what they cover and how they cover it. Nonetheless, it is still important to ask: Are journalists more "liberal"?

Surveys of journalists indicate that they are more likely than the public at large to vote for Democrats for president, and to be generally more liberal than the average citizen in their political views. In its most recent survey on the political ideology of journalists, the Pew Center for the People and the Press found that about one third of national journalists called themselves "liberal," while a majority identified as "moderate." Local journalists were somewhat less liberal and more moderate in ideology than national journalists, but each group was more liberal than the general public, and relatively few in either group identified as "conservative." Internet journalists as a group were somewhat more liberal than those in traditional media. The 36 percent of people in the general public who identify themselves as conservative was double that of local journalists and three times that of national and Internet journalists.

There may be a little more to this story, however. There is some evidence that journalists may be more "liberal" about hot-button social questions, such as abortion, gay marriage, and the death penalty, than on important structural issues such as taxation, Social Security, corporate regulation, and trade policies. Most journalists identify themselves as centrists, and their views actually are fairly similar to other professionals with similar educational and class backgrounds. "Providing analyses of complex problems" and "getting news to the public quickly" rank more highly as professional values than being an "adversary of business." Even the self-proclaimed "liberals" among journalists define themselves as "not bound by doctrines or committed to a point of view in advance."[42]

The salaries of celebrity journalists like Anderson Cooper, Diane Sawyer, Brian Williams, or Bill O'Reilly and those who write for the most prestigious publications notwithstanding, most reporters' salaries average less than those of teachers and college professors. African Americans, Latinos, Asian Americans, and especially women have made employment gains in journalism over the last thirty years. However, progress has been uneven, with setbacks. Both women and minorities remain substantially below their proportion of the population or their share of the markets their media outlets serve. And increases in minority employment have been much slower than minority population growth.

Most journalists, much like those in some other important professions, are white males with graduate degrees. Often, as James Fallows demonstrated in his study about journalists and their coverage of "free trade" disputes, the Washington "press displays...an instinctive sympathy with the interests of the educated elite. The press chose the college-boy side of the argument—apparently without realizing that it was choosing sides." While journalists may be more liberal on some social issues, then, none of these other characteristics support the idea that journalists are biased against the most important established political and economic interests and institutions, much less given to ultra-liberal critiques of them.[43]

Professional Standards

But even if a thoroughgoing liberalism did predominate among journalists, the new work routines imposed by the companies that employ them combine with traditional professional standards to create a far different bias. For the average journalist, reporting the news consists of the nondramatic daily business of gathering facts, making phone calls, attending meetings and press conferences, and meeting deadlines. For news editors who supervise reporters, producing the news is about assigning reporters to particular stories, ensuring that reporters' stories live up to professional standards, and making decisions about which stories will appear, where, and when.

For journalists, professional standards are supposed to produce a firewall between the business interests of media corporations and what journalists actually do. Reporters are taught to be *objective*, in that they remove from their stories their own ideological point of view and let the facts speak for themselves and the chips fall where they may. As they seek *balance*, they report the diverse views of different spokespersons when a dispute arises, trying to help create that wide "marketplace of ideas" that is supposed to be the major justification for media competition and press freedom in the first place.

Most media professionals are sincere in their attempts to uphold these standards of objectivity and balance. Still, the structure of modern news organizations, the context they operate within, and the routine of how stories actually are defined and pursued make it difficult to do so. Objectivity and balance are difficult to maintain when powerful public and private institutions have an advantage over ordinary citizens in influencing what journalists see as important news stories and in defining the limits of "respectable" debate. And objectivity and balance work within rules and constraints that define them in particular ways.

The Problem of Source Bias

Issues, facts, and events become news only when editors and reporters decide to cover them. Thus, the "beats" chosen by news organizations for their reporters to cover, and which sources are consulted, often determine what is considered news.

The vast majority of American political reporting comes from Washington, D.C., the White House, Congress, the Justice Department, the Pentagon, and other governmental agencies, which are the major "beats" of political reporters. These institutions as well as major interest groups are not only the primary objects of political reporting but are the important sources for most political news as well. There is certainly no lack of government and corporate press relations personnel to "inform" and influence the press. In Washington alone, an army of 13,000 federal employees generates publicity for several thousand correspondents; the Pentagon alone spends several billion dollars annually on public relations.

Despite enormous resources and large news bureaus, even the more prestigious media fall victim to **source bias**. It is understandable that the doings in Washington make news. But Washington reporters mostly report what they hear from their sources there. Day after day, reporters travel between the press briefings of private and public organizations that have the wherewithal to establish themselves as legitimate sources and newsmakers, and which spend millions on creating favorable public images for the people and institutions they represent. In the last four and one half decades, corporate sponsors and political conservatives have been particularly successful in funding important think tanks, precisely because they serve as prime "sources" and experts for journalists.[44]

Journalists come to rely on the staff of these governmental and private organizations to provide them access to the interviews, background information, and inside scoops necessary to get the job done. As a consequence, too often the issues covered and the sides of a debate—often both sides—are defined by positions taken in this Washington world. The result, Robert Entman has claimed, is that "the news largely consists of information supplied by sources who support democracy in the abstract, but must in specific encounters with the press subordinate that ideal to the protection of their own political interests."[45]

To the extent "balance" is achieved it is within these confines, with outsider views or dissident voices too often excluded. For example, what is said by the presidential press secretary must be reported, even if it is false. For "balance" or a response, yet another governmental official, probably from the opposing political party, is quoted. If the "legitimate" opposition doesn't oppose, as most Democrats didn't during the prelude to the Iraq War, then the issue is dropped. Outside of this "debate" are those groups, often at the grassroots, without extensive clout, and who can't afford to employ the media experts, lawyers, and lobbyists that government, corporations, and well-funded interest and advocacy groups can.

The invasion of Iraq provides some classic cases of source bias. *New York Times* reporter Judith Miller learned the hard way. She filed a page-one story about an Iraqi scientist who purported to know where a stash of weapons of mass destruction (WMDs) was buried. The source, supplied by the Pentagon's favorite Iraqi in exile, Ahmad Chalabi, was never named by Miller, but the story was used as evidence by the Bush administration that their claims about hidden WMDs were about to be vindicated. As it turned out, Miller and the *Times* had been misled. The story was false. Miller was hardly alone. In Iraq War reportage, source bias was a very serious problem, and its consequences were severe, building public support for the war based on false information.

In this variety of ways, media source bias rather than overt censorship helps replicate a "reality" and set of debates as they are construed by important institutional players. Professor Lance Bennett comments: "Cooperation between reporters and officials is so routine that officials rarely have to employ intimidation tactics." [46]

McNews

The concentration on similar sources does not mean that all news is reported in exactly the same way. Television news specializes in the dramatic and the immediate, and it is more likely to cover onetime events and the activities of famous people and celebrities. In contrast, the print media tend to report on institutions, issues, and policies more extensively and in most cases provide stories with more information and factual support than does television. With the exception of National Public Radio and a few other sources, like the Pacifica Radio Network, radio news consists of short bulletins and little depth. Internet news tends to come as headlines, and the major sites link the user to transcribed TV or newspaper stories or to more extensive databases. In recent years, bloggers and nonestablished sources like Internet columnists have entered the media picture, pressuring media organizations with stories that they'd have otherwise been unlikely to cover.

Yet despite these important contrasts between outlets, the similarities between "news products" are remarkable. Modern news organizations draw from other media sources, which tends to "standardize" how the media as a whole defines and reports news. Many newspapers, and networks, for example, rely on the wire services of the Associated Press. Moreover, news happening outside the reach of the national news bureaus stationed in such cities as Washington, D.C., New York, Los Angeles, Chicago, Atlanta, or Houston is likely to get less attention. And the New York Times Company and other media giants supply articles that are often picked up by smaller newspapers.

The corporate pressure to cut costs might be the chief culprit for such standardized "McNews." To save money, local news stations—now more than ever owned by media conglomerates—often depend on their parent networks to lead them to important national stories. It is also cheaper for TV crews to cover planned "events" organized by institutions and organizations with the resources to do so, because such events are predictable and can be prepared for. This puts other sources of news at a competitive disadvantage. And new stations often find it cheaper and more profitable to cover sensational crimes, feature stories, weather, and sports. "Investigative journalism is just too expensive," explained one student of the subject.[47] Finally, to gain increased ratings, networks have even turned to "infotainment"—mixing news with entertainment.

Although print and TV reporters do compete for stories, they also cooperate in a phenomenon known as **pack journalism**. Most of the time, reporters who are covering everything from political campaigns to presidential trips travel together, receive the same press kits, attend the same press conferences, and face the same requirements to file a story by the deadline. In these interactions, they acquire a collective sense of what the "story" is.

The result is a remarkably similar "spin" on a story and a strong consensus, forged by what the pack sees and hears, shaped in turn by the nature of the "beat" itself and the PR talent of the organizations or people being covered. Reporting on the 2000 presidential race, the *Washington Post*'s Dana Milbank told how the pack would assemble at the site of each presidential debate, sit in the same room, and watch the event together, interviewing the same "spinmeisters" of each candidate after the "show" was over. The pack can also miss important stories, as it did the Watergate scandal of the 1970s and Iran-Contra scandal in the 1980s.

Journalists thereby create common **media frames**, or ideas about what should be emphasized and what should be de-emphasized in their depictions. In 2004, the press "pack" came to a consensus that Democratic primary candidate Howard Dean was mistake prone and possibly unstable. They interpreted his famous "scream" in a speech following a primary loss—from Dean's perspective an effort to buck up his supporters and trying to be heard in a noisy room—through that frame. The media frame prevailed, helping derail his candidacy.[48]

Producing McNews, however, doesn't mean that all news media say the same thing. Much like fast-food chains, McNews can feature a seemingly broad fare even though it is all assembled with the same factory-like techniques. What changes are the performances and the formats, as important and substantive news yields to entertaining and "cost-effective" news designed to garner an audience.

Fox News has helped pioneer how to make "news" entertaining and emotionally appealing, so as to attract a significant cable TV audience.[49] One very particularly worrisome example occurred during the run-up to the Iraq War, and during the war itself. Fox would accompany its *news* coverage with the "headline" "The War on Terror," both on TV and on its website. Whether the Iraq War had anything to do with combating terrorism, however, was itself a critical issue under *debate* as to whether the war was worth fighting in the first place.

Companies usually justify McNews by saying that news, like any other product, is simply a response to what media consumers want. If that were true, would it mean that news is merely a consumer preference unrelated to real events? But is it true? Might people be watching McNews because it is the dominant choice available? Media surveys rarely ask people what they really want or need to learn, confining their questions to choices about things like news anchor clothing styles or studio decorations. More expensive, perhaps riskier, alternative ways of defining and reporting the news are not options sufficiently considered.[50]

Off to the Races: Journalists, Politicians, and Campaigns

Political campaigns are perhaps the most important moments when a full democratic debate could be possible. Instead, source bias, the commercial impulse, and pack journalism are embodied in a unique and unenlightening campaign media form, **horse race journalism**.

The term captures the penchant of campaign media to cover the personalities, strategies, tactics, and drama of the presidential race. Media frames are created that allow journalists to judge the ups and downs of the race in terms of who is ahead, who is behind, and why each candidate's performance and the strategies and tactics of campaign consultants are or are not effective. The voters appear in polls, which in turn feed the media frame about how well or poorly the candidates are performing. The historical contexts in which particular elections occur, substantive issue differences between candidates, and the reasons why political and economic interests might support with their money one party and candidate or the other too often give ground to the drama of the race. Not enough is said about how the electoral outcome might affect ordinary voters and the world, but quite a bit is said about how candidates have committed gaffes, or possessed momentum, or appeared "presidential"—or not.

Horse race journalism has come to predominate campaign news. Reflecting on past media election coverage from the vantage point of the 2008 campaign, CNN/US President Jon Klein remarked: "I think the impulse [to cover the horse race] has been baked into political journalism for the last 40 years."[51]

Partisans often believe the media are biased against their candidate. But horse race journalism creates a much more potent form of bias away from substance and toward framing and then judging the character and performance of the candidate. In 2012, horse race journalism was actually lower than the election before—that is until the first debate on October 3. After the debate, which the media and public agreed had been won by Governor Romney over President Obama, news reports of the campaign as a horse race returned nearly to 2008 levels. What measurements did analysts use to proclaim Romney the winner? The media frame used often emphasized comparisons of temperament and of facial expressions more than facts. Opining about the state of the horse race rather than discussing issues that require substantive knowledge gives pundits and journalists much to talk about while also sounding competent.

Perhaps this is why, from 1968 to the present, the sound bites of presidential candidates have been reduced from one minute, on average, to about eight seconds, while journalists have increased their talking time sixfold. In the average two-minute campaign story, candidates speak for twenty seconds, while journalists take up more than half the time putting the story in context or in making commentary.[52]

What might be some other effects of horse race journalism's predominance within U.S. politics? It relies on scoops and insider information, and it is very subject to source bias. In its focus on who can win, it excludes alternative voices and frames third-party candidates as "spoilers." It reinforces the idea that politics is just a game, thereby devaluing the purpose democratic debate and competition.[53] And in its hunger for dramatic narratives of personality and character, it often displaces issues that really do affect daily life.

Some argue that campaign journalism is the way it is because that's what the "consumers," that is the voters, want. Yet both public opinion polls and TV ratings indicate that the media rendition of politics as a game turns off many citizens. Indeed, coverage often misses what voters are concerned about. What needs to be done?

New Reform
What Would Media Democracy Look Like?

Here are some of the ideas, mostly gleaned from the advocates for media reform at Free Press:

- *Let noncommercial TV and radio flourish.* Digital TV and low-power FM create plenty of room on the spectrum for thousands of small stations owned by community groups or towns to flourish. Why not let them try? Thanks to the pressure of community radio activists, in 2010 Congress passed the Local Community Radio Act and President Obama signed it into law. Let's make sure this act is fully enforced.

- *Revive and democratize public broadcasting.* PBS and NPR lack the resources and power to compete with megacorporations and have become dependent on them for grants and gifts. Build up these entities with a voluntary check-off of up to $100 on tax returns, and link them to community radio and television stations.

- *Make Internet access available to everyone.* In 2008, candidate Barack Obama pledged to expand "broadband lines across America." As president, he has delivered on some of his reforms but the country is still far off from "true broadband in every community in America." It's time to enact a national broadband policy to provide universal, affordable broadband access to all Americans.

- *Guarantee Net Neutrality.* Congress and the FCC need to strongly protect "Net Neutrality," the principle that prevents phone and cable companies from discriminating against websites and services that they don't own.

- *Remember public interest regulation?* Now is the time to insist on regulations that promote the public interest over private interests. At the very least, let's promote more commercial free broadcasting.

- *Free airtime for candidates.* All candidates should have the opportunity to speak directly to the public. Give candidates both of major *and* minor parties free airtime. This will both make campaigns fairer and less expensive, while weakening the Supreme Court's argument that limitations on campaign spending weaken free speech.

- *The Internet: Make it a freeway, not a toll road.* Why should companies have the right to charge for Internet access if it can be provided by cities and communities, as Philadelphia and others have tried to do? Why not build a network of free, noncommercial Internet providers that privilege the work and sites of a wide range of community groups, from religious congregations to environmentalists?

- *Innovate! Innovate!* Invest in Internet TV and other new potentialities. With some tech savvy and a very modest investment, individuals and groups could create their own news shows with relative ease.

- *Break up the media oligopolies.* Why allow six gargantuan companies to dominate what we see and hear? In America's past, antitrust laws provided the means to prevent concentrated private power. Let's start using those laws again when it comes to the media industry and create some real competition.

Does all this sound like pie in the sky? Although the status quo is sustained by the government, citizens have the power to change what government does. For democratic media activists, the time is now.

Sources: FreePress, "Media Reform Action Guide," 2012, freepress.net; Robert McChesney, *Rich Media, Poor Democracy* (New York: The New Press, 2001), final chapter; Elaine Kamarck and Joseph Nye Jr., *www.democracy.com* (Hollis, NH: Hollis, 1999); authors' correspondence with Michael Parrott.

Conclusion: Democratizing the Mass Media

The media play an essential role in shaping the political agenda in America. They presume to do so without bias. Yet, the features of corporate-run media and the commercial pressures besetting the newsroom today bolster elite, rather than popular, democracy. If popular democracy is to develop and thrive in the United States, then the decisions now made about who owns and operates the media must be subject to a wider democratic debate. In the "New Reform" box, we describe some of the proposals of the growing media reform movement.

There is hope. Despite all the powers of commercial media, large numbers of Americans, and especially young people, have tuned out the mainstream media and created an explosion of alternatives potentially capable of breaking stories and pioneering new trends. Jon Stewart's *The Daily Show* and its offshoot *The Colbert Report* reach millions of viewers with their sharp and humorous barbs skewering the mainstream media. Interestingly, Stewart's audience was found to be not only young but more knowledgeable about campaign issues than those who followed them in newspapers and on cable television. In journalism itself, rebellion is also alive, fueled by awareness that traditions of investigative journalism are in danger from the profit-making demands of big media.

The developing blogosphere also presents the possibility of "new news." Since 2000, bloggers have been exposing many of the distortions of mainstream news media, as well as providing new energies to political campaigns. Blogging also has its limitations: One election study found that most popular blogs were even more partisan renditions of the "horse race" that dominates mainstream news. Then there is the problem of the "Daily Me," in which people look for only the news they want and filter out alternatives. Only time will tell if the new Internet forms will foster fragmentation or help create a more democratic public space.[54]

All is not lost. The media can and sometimes do reflect and enrich the democratic debate. For popular democrats, prompting the media to live up to their full democratic potential remains a central task.

Reader's Guide

Critical Thinking Questions

1. Are you satisfied with the kind of news you get from broadcast and cable TV and from radio? What about from the Internet? Are there any gaps that you feel should be filled?

2. As you watch the media present news and commentary, can you spot any ways in which the media's commercial interests seem to interfere with their responsibility to cover the news?

3. What feeling do you get from mainstream network and cable media as to what the main issues and debates are? What about from the Internet sources that you frequent? Are there other issues or other ways of framing debates that you think important that are not being presented now to enough people?

4. Try to envision what a democratic media would look like. How would it affect the kind of television, radio, and Internet news and commentary that we now experience? What kinds of stories do you think would appear that we now don't often see, hear, or read? What kinds of people would be featured in these stories?

5. Is media reform possible? What reforms do you think are the most important? Which do you think most practical? Putting the two together, what package of reforms should we focus on over the next five years?

Key Word Definition

yellow journalism   A form of reporting pioneered in the late nineteenth century by the Hearst and Pulitzer newspaper chains, emphasizing entertaining and often lurid scandals as news.

virtual democracy   The idea that the information superhighway created by the Internet and the World Wide Web will facilitate new debates and discussions between citizens and officeholders.

agenda setters   The media and their ability to determine what issues are considered legitimate, or even worthy of discussion, within the political arena.

concentration of ownership   The tendency toward bigger and more coordinated ownership of capital, assets, and information technology. In the mass media, concentration has resulted in the emergence of media corporations who own across diverse enterprises, from cable television to book and movie production.

national entertainment state   Term used to describe the increasing concentration of ownership and control of new and old media by a few media conglomerates.

vertical integration   For corporate media organizations, the tendency toward single corporate ownership of a chain of production, distribution, and marketing arrangements across diverse media. The idea is to create a synergy that promotes the sale of diverse media products, from theme parks to films, books, and TV and radio stations, across a wide spectrum.

upscale demographics   The tendency of advertisers and media outlets to appeal to high-income, big-spending consumers.

revolving door   The phenomenon whereby people working in Congress or in an executive branch agency become lobbyists or journalists once they leave government service, using their experience and knowledge for the benefit of their clients.

Rolodex syndrome   The journalistic practice of relying on the same, very limited sources for quotes and information. The practice tends to exclude voices from outside the elite circles of think tank and leadership opinion.

Telecommunications Act of 1996   Sweeping federal legislation that abolished many of the Federal Communications Commission's previous restrictions on radio and television ownership by individuals and corporations. The Telecommunications Act ostensibly promotes competition between different parts of the telecommunications and media industries, but has instead prompted new corporate mergers and concentration.

source bias   The tendency of modern journalists to seek a limited range of opinions and views from certain groups and institutions as they report the news.

pack journalism   The development by a group of reporters of similar views after receiving the same information and insights from the same sources.

media frames   The ways in which the news media establish routine ways of defining and reporting on a news story. Frames create a uniformity in modes of determining what is, and what isn't, important in a news story. In electoral campaigns, such frames often mean a concentration on strategy, tactics, and candidate personality.

horse race journalism   The tendency of the media to report election campaigns in terms of who is winning and losing rather than in terms of what issues are at stake.

Courtesy of Shutterstock

Interest Group Politics: Popular Pressure or Elite Bias?

THE CHANGING NATURE OF INTEREST GROUP POLITICS

THE CLASS BIAS OF THE INTEREST GROUP SYSTEM

TRADITIONAL LOBBYING: THE INSIDER STRATEGY

THE RISE OF PUBLIC INTEREST GROUPS

THE NEW LOBBYING: ELITE COUNTERMOBILIZATION

CONCLUSION: WHAT CAN BE DONE?

Interest group politics can be defined as any attempt by an organized group to influence the policies of government through normal extra-electoral channels, such as lobbying, letter writing, testifying before legislative committees, or advertising. Interest groups focus on changing the policies of government, whereas the first goal of political parties is to change the personnel who run government. In recent years, however, the distinction between interest group politics and electoral politics has blurred, as interest groups have used campaign contributions to achieve extraordinary power over legislation. In addition, in what has become known as the **revolving door**, former members of Congress and the executive branch go to work as lobbyists, using their political connections to land jobs as highly paid lobbyists. According to the Center for Responsible Politics, 296 former members of Congress are now registered as federal lobbyists.[1] Consider the case of Billy Tauzin.

Billy "the Swamp Fox" Tauzin was first elected to the House of Representatives as a Democrat from Louisiana in 1980. A founder of the House Blue Dog Caucus,* a group of conservative Democrats, Tauzin switched to the Republican Party in 1995 and soon became chairman of the powerful Energy and Commerce Committee. For thirty years he was a leader of the annual Mardi Gras celebration in Washington, where thousands of partygoers would take over a giant Hilton Hotel for a three-day party hosted by the Louisiana congressional delegation and paid for by corporate sponsors and lobbyists. In 2003, Tauzin paid more than $1 million for a 1,500-acre Texas ranch, inviting a dozen corporate executives and lobbyists with issues before his committee to cover his mortgage by paying dues as members of a new "hunting club."

The same year Tauzin bought his Texas ranch he was a primary author and supporter of the Medicare Prescription Drug Benefit program. Signed into law by President Bush in December 2003, the legislation greatly expanded coverage of prescription drugs for seniors enrolled in Medicare. Costing more than $500 billion over ten years, the program has been highly profitable for the pharmaceutical industry. One of the provisions supported by Tauzin prohibits the federal government from negotiating lower prices with drug companies.

* The name Blue Dog originated when one representative said conservative Democrats had been "choked blue" by left-wing Democrats.

A few months after Tauzin's success with the Medicare Prescription Drug Benefit program, he left Congress to go to work as the CEO of the Pharmaceutical Research and Manufacturers America (PhRMA) for a reported $2 million a year.

The question raised by the career of Billy Tauzin is whether he did favors for the pharmaceutical industry while in Congress knowing he could subsequently "cash out" his favors for a lucrative job as a lobbyist. In 2010, Tauzin set a record for ex-members of Congress, making just over $11.5 million as head of PhRMA. Shortly after he negotiated PhRMA's support for the Obama administration's health care reform act, Tauzin resigned his position and joined a prominent lobbying firm.

The Billy Tauzin story is instructive because, according to all accounts, everything Tauzin did in the way of influence peddling was perfectly legal. Many Americans think that lobbyists carry around bags of cash that they use to buy the votes of politicians. Certainly, corruption exists but it's not the main way wealth corrupts political decision making. The process by which wealthy interests manipulate the interest group system is more subtle, and more pervasive, than the conventional image of politicians cutting deals in smoke-filled rooms suggests.

As disturbing as it often is, interest group politics is necessary in a democracy. Indeed, the right of groups to organize and "petition the government for a redress of grievances" (in the words of the Constitution) is the lifeblood of democracy. But elite and popular democrats view interest group politics very differently. Interest group politics nicely suits the elite democratic conception of democracy and human nature—that most people are not interested in politics for its own sake but rather view politics as a way of protecting their own private interests. Since most citizens have neither the time nor the inclination to participate directly in politics, the interest group system allows people's wants and desires to be represented by political specialists called lobbyists. According to pluralism (which we examine later), a variant of elite democratic theory, the interest group system in the United States is open and accessible. Not every group has equal access, but every group can make itself heard at some point in the system.

Popular democrats are more critical of interest group politics than are elite democrats. By relying on representatives and hired experts, they say, interest group politics asks too little of ordinary citizens, who are given few opportunities for meaningful participation. With decisions made behind closed doors, where industry experts and technocrats dominate the discussions, interest group politics narrows the scope of conflict and excludes the masses of ordinary citizens. In short, interest group politics is easily manipulated by elites—technical experts and political insiders who know how to play the Washington "inside-the-Beltway" game.

Popular democrats see two major flaws in the argument that the interest group system is free and equal. First, narrow business interests led by small numbers of powerful corporations are, by their nature, easier to organize politically than millions of spread-out consumers and workers. The rise of public interest groups in the 1960s, including consumer, environmental, and women's groups, temporarily leveled the playing field, but elite interests successfully co-opted many of the techniques of public interest groups, once again, tilting the playing field in their favor.

The second major flaw is that it takes resources to organize interest groups, and wealthy interests are able to drown out the voices of the disadvantaged. Money buys access to people, like Billy Tauzin, with strong connections to powerful decision makers. It also buys the services of sophisticated public relations professionals. Over time, the gap between interests relying on people and interests relying on money has widened as public relations technologies have become more sophisticated. In fact, if you have enough money, you can now buy a grassroots movement—or at least the appearance of one.

The Changing Nature of Interest Group Politics

Interest groups play a more powerful role in U.S. politics than in most other Western democracies. The main reason is that American political institutions stimulate interest group politics. As we know from Chapter 2, fearing tyranny of the majority in a democratic government, the Federalists wrote a Constitution that fragmented policy-making authority, including the separation of powers into three branches, the bicameral Congress (with decision making further fragmented into committees and subcommittees), the authority of the courts to intervene in administrative decisions, and the division of power among federal, state, and local governments. In this way, the Constitution created a government that provides many access points for interest groups. In addition, interest groups in the United States are able to intervene on the administrative side of government, influencing the implementation of a law after it is passed. Critics of the interest group system charge that in striving to protect the country against tyranny by majorities, the founders may have created a system that allows too much interest group penetration, making it prone to tyranny by privileged minorities.

It may surprise the reader to learn that the three richest counties in the nation are suburban counties surrounding Washington, D.C.[2] They are not rich because people who work for the federal government are rich. They are rich because those who try to influence the federal government or work for companies that do business with the federal government make a lot of money. In 1975, federal civil servants were making about 10 percent less than private-sector workers doing similar work. By 1990, public employees made 40 percent less. (The method for calculating the difference was changed somewhat.) The gap has undoubtedly grown since then. By 2005, congressional staffers or administrative officials could double or triple their salaries by moving to a lobbying firm where starting salaries were $300,000 a year.[3] You can make a decent living working for the federal government, but you will never get rich. You *can* get rich working to influence the federal government.

Interest group politics is big business in Washington. Legally, in order to work the halls of Congress as a lobbyist, one must register under the Lobbying Disclosure Act of 1995. The Center for Responsive Politics estimates that there were 12,633 registered lobbyists operating in Washington, D.C., in 2011, up from 10,689 in 1998. This vastly underestimates the number of lobbyists. In order to register as a lobbyist you have to meet face-to-face with lawmakers or federal officials. Mitt Romney accused Newt Gingrich of being a highly paid lobbyist in the 2012 Republican presidential primary. There is no doubt that the former Speaker of the House of Representatives was paid millions of dollars by corporate interests, such as the pharmaceutical industry, to influence legislation, including the 2003 Medicare drug plan. Gingrich admitted that he hired legal experts in lobbying to make sure that his own activities did not come under the legal definition of a lobbyist.[4] There many others like Gingrich who are not registered as lobbyists but who are hired to influence federal legislation.

The amount of money spent on lobbying the federal government soared from $1.44 billion in 1998 to $3.3 billion in 2011 (Figure 10.1). The largest lobbying firm, Patton Boggs, received an astounding $452 million in fees during this time. But these figures greatly underestimate the size of the lobbying industry because they include only professional paid lobbyists who directly contact public officials. Besides trying to influence legislation, interest

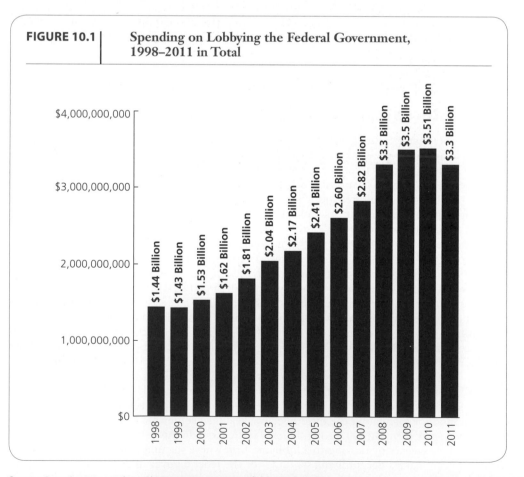

FIGURE 10.1 | **Spending on Lobbying the Federal Government, 1998–2011 in Total**

Source: OpenSecrets.org: http://www.opensecrets.org/lobby/index.php.

groups also try to influence the implementation of laws through decisions by executive agencies and the courts. When the lawyers, lobbyists, public relations specialists, and trade association and corporate representatives who make a living by keeping track of and attempting to change federal regulations are included, according to political scientist James Thurber, the number of people employed lobbying the federal government rises to 261,000.[5]

The Washington interest group community is large and diverse. It includes powerful business associations, such as the American Bankers Association, and narrow trade associations representing specific industries, such as the American Beekeepers Association. It includes organizations with millions of members, such as the AFL-CIO coalition of unions, and organizations with only one member, in particular, the Washington offices of national corporations, such as IBM and GM. It includes public associations, such as the National Governors Association and the National League of Cities. It also includes lobbyists hired by foreign governments to represent their interests in Washington, a feature of our interest group system that has increasingly come under attack. Two of the best represented foreign governments are Israel and Japan. Figure 10.2 lists top spenders on lobbying. With the exception of the AMA, which represents doctors, and AARP (formerly American Association of Retired Persons), all of the top spenders are private corporations.

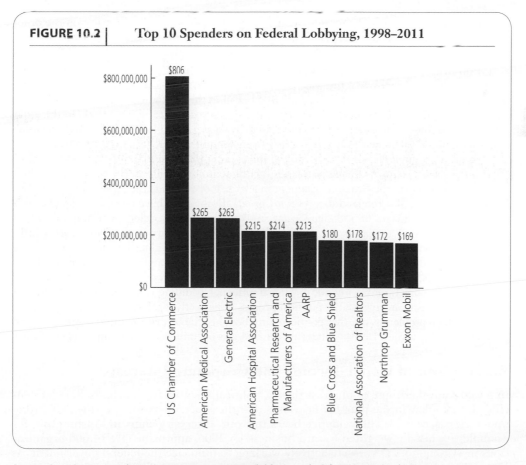

FIGURE 10.2 | Top 10 Spenders on Federal Lobbying, 1998–2011

Source: OpenSecrets.org: http://www.opensecrets.org/lobby/top.php?showYear=a&indexType=s.

The Class Bias of the Interest Group System

If the U.S. interest group system represented the many diverse interests of the citizenry, then it would be one of the most democratic features of our political system. In fact, this argument is the cornerstone of a variant of elite democratic theory called **pluralism**.[6] Pluralist theory views the interest group system as a kind of political marketplace with the following characteristics:

1. *Free competition.* Most people do not participate directly in decision making but, like consumers in the economy, are represented in the system by political entrepreneurs who compete for their support. Competition ensures that all major interests will be heard.

2. *Dispersed power.* Money is an important source of power, but other resources are equally important, including motivation, leadership, organizational skills, knowledge, and expertise. Elites who are influential in one issue arena tend not to be active in others. Power is widely dispersed.

3. *Bargaining.* Success in the interest group system requires bargaining and compromise with other interests, discouraging rigid moralistic or ideological politics that threaten democratic stability.

4. *Balance.* Mobilization on one side of an issue produces countermobilization on the other side; public policies thus reflect a balance of competing interests that represent the interests of all major groups in society.

Pluralism has an element of truth to it. Since the 1960s the interest group system has become more representative of the wide array of interests in American society. Reflecting what Jeffrey Berry calls the "advocacy explosion" that began in the 1960s,[7] the number of politically active organizations more than doubled between 1981 and 2006, reaching 35,000 in the latter year.[8] Many of these new groups represented issues, such as gay and lesbian rights and Christian evangelical moral values, which had previously been absent from the interest group system.

Interest groups are often referred to as lobbies, as in the "gun lobby" or the "steel lobby." (The term *lobbyist* stems from the mid-seventeenth century, when citizens would plead their cases with members of the British Parliament in a large lobby outside the House of Commons.) Interest groups are also referred to as *pressure groups*. Both terms have taken on negative connotations, evoking images of potbellied, cigar-smoking influence peddlers prowling the halls of Congress in search of legislators to buy off with bags of money. Laws on the books outlaw bribery or corruption; you cannot exchange your vote for anything of value. This is known as a *quid pro quo*. Bribery does occur and the media loves to play up such examples. Unlike in many Third World countries, however, the direct buying of votes is relatively rare in the United States. As one prominent book on lobbying put it, "illegal influence peddling is not the norm."[9] The fact is, wealthy interests can corrupt the political process in perfectly legal ways.

The main problem is not that politicians are bought off, but that the interest group system is so heavily tilted toward wealthy elites that the interests of common people can barely be heard.

Bias in Favor of Upper-Income and Corporate Interests

In a well-known critique of pluralist theory, political scientist E. E. Schattschneider concluded, "The flaw in the pluralist heaven is that the heavenly chorus sings with a strong upper-class accent."[10] The evidence bears this out. Interest groups in Washington, for example, are heavily weighted toward business. In 2006, approximately 14,000 organizations in Washington, D.C., were actively working to influence the federal government. As Figure 10.3 shows, over half of them represented corporations and other business interests.

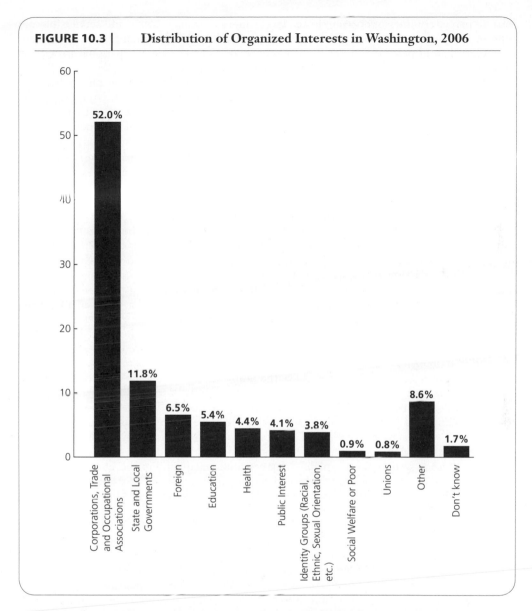

FIGURE 10.3 | Distribution of Organized Interests in Washington, 2006

Source: Kay Lehman Schlozman, Sidney Verba, Henry E. Brady, Philip Edward Jones, Traci Burch, "Who Sings in the Heavenly Chorus?: The Shape of the Organized Interest System," paper prepared for delivery at the Annual Meeting of the American Political Science Association, Boston, MA, August 28–31, 2008.

Since 1981, 2,486 more business-related associations have become active in Washington politics; less than 1 percent represent unions.

If we look at organizations that represent people where they work, it becomes clear that the interest group system is highly skewed toward high-income professionals. Even though only 10 percent of the workforce is in executive, managerial, and administrative positions, 74 percent of the workforce associations in Washington represent these highly paid positions.

The 80 percent of the workforce in lower-level white-collar, blue-collar, and service jobs are represented by only 9 percent of the economic associations.[11] Other than unions, which represent less than 12 percent of American workers, there is not a single occupational association in the interest group system to defend the interests of workers in low-skill jobs.[12]

We can also examine how well citizens are able to defend their government benefits. Corporate welfare, such as tax breaks, is well defended by powerful corporate interest groups. Agricultural interests have been able to successfully defend crop subsidies. But there is not a single association in the interest group system to represent the interests of poor people receiving means-tested benefits, such as food stamps or Temporary Assistance for Needy Families.[13] Head Start, a program to help low-income children get ready for school, has no association to defend it. By contrast, the elderly are well represented in the interest group system by the largest membership organization in the nation, AARP (formerly known as the American Association of Retired Persons). Because of the power of the elderly as an interest group, Social Security is known as the "Third Rail" of American politics—touch it and you die.

The new public interest associations that began springing up in the 1960s have tended to focus more on quality-of-life issues rather than on bread-and-butter economic issues. As people become more affluent and educated, they become more concerned with what are called "postmaterial" concerns that address issues of culture and lifestyle (gay marriage, abortion), quality-of-life issues (environment, consumer safety), and social justice issues (civil rights for minorities and the handicapped). At the same time that liberal groups have moved away from addressing economic inequality, conservative groups have done the same. Exceptions to the decline of national membership associations are the evangelical churches, which have been organized into a national network by the Christian Coalition. They have been extraordinarily effective at mobilizing citizens to oppose abortion and gay marriage. As important as all these postmaterial issues are, however, they have the unfortunate effect of pushing the economic concerns of the poor and working class off the national agenda.[14]

What this means is that poor people are not well represented in the interest group system. For example, 22 percent of those who receive Medicare, a program benefiting all elderly who worked, were members of a political association, but only 4 percent of those on Medicaid, health care for the poor, were members of a political association.[15] The class bias of the interest group system helps explain rising economic inequality in the United States (see Chapter 4) and why programs for those who need help the most, such as welfare, have been cut back at the same time that spending on Social Security and veterans' benefits has soared (see Chapter 17).

Figure 10.2 shows the top ten spenders on federal lobbying activities. Note that almost all of them are business interests. Ordinary workers and poor people are nowhere to be found. Fully 72 percent of expenditures on lobbying come from organizations that represent business.[16] Those in the top 20 percent of the income range vote at a rate 1.8 times that of those in the bottom 20 percent, but they contribute 76 *times* the amount of money to political campaigns and interest groups than those in the bottom 20 percent do.[17] Money does not normally buy a legislator's vote, but it does buy a legislator's time—so donors can make the case for their preferred policies. One study estimated that you can purchase a legislator's time for about $10,000 an hour.[18] Money also buys access to the president. Among those who gave $30,000 or less to President Obama and the Democratic Party, only about 20 percent visited the White House. About 75 percent of those who gave more than $100,000 visited or had meetings at the White House.[19]

An award-winning study of lobbying concluded, surprisingly, that money spent on lobbying often fails to succeed. But they also conclude that since the status quo often represents the interests of the wealthy, just by preventing change, they win. And issues representing the needs of "the poor and the economic security of working-class Americans" are generally nowhere to be found in the agenda of the interest group system.[20] One of the reasons money dominates the interest group system is the development of new technologies by public relations professionals.

Reliance on Professionals and New Technologies

Interest groups have shifted from relying on members to relying on campaign technologies and public relations experts. The technologies that interest groups use to influence the political process have become more sophisticated and more expensive. These technologies include computerized direct-mail solicitations, sophisticated polling and focus groups, advertising campaigns, faxes, e-mails, websites, blogs, and computerized telephone messages. In what is called "warm transfer," individuals dial an 800 number and their call is automatically transferred to the Washington office of their senator or representative.

We examine some of these technologies in greater detail below. However, what they all have in common is that they require money—not just to buy the technology but to hire experts to run it. As a result of interest groups' dependence on expensive technologies, money has increasingly replaced time as the primary contribution most people make. Money is used not just to lobby but to frame issues, generate a nationwide campaign, and even manufacture grassroots support.[21]

Rich people and poor people have roughly equal amounts of time to contribute to political organizations. But if interest groups are more concerned about raising money than about recruiting volunteers, they will obviously seek out the wealthy. Instead of citizens mobilizing from below to influence the political system, targeted portions of the public are singled out for what Steven Schier calls "activation" by political groups.[22] Advances in technology have enabled interest groups to recruit narrow slices of the population ("niche marketing"). Activation is class biased. A national study asked people whether they had received requests to participate in politics (in an electoral campaign, protest, or lobbying of government officials). As Figure 10.4 shows, only 24 percent of those in the bottom 20 percent of the income range

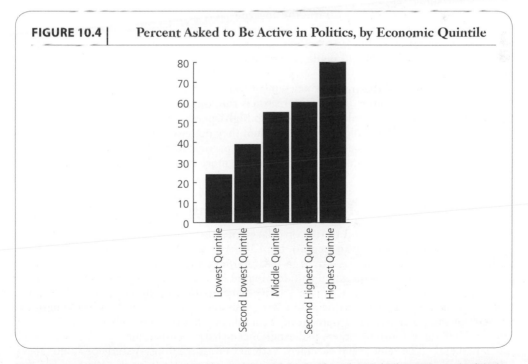

FIGURE 10.4 | Percent Asked to Be Active in Politics, by Economic Quintile

Source: Kay Lehman Schlozman, Sidney Verba, and Henry E. Brady, *The Unheavenly Chorus: Unequal Political Voice and the Broken Promise of American Democracy* (Princeton, NJ: Princeton University Press, 2012), 456. Based on Citizen Participation Survey (1990).

were invited to participate, whereas 80 of those in the top 20 percent were asked to participate. Recruiters target higher income citizens because they are more likely to participate and
they have more money to contribute. One of the reasons poor people do not participate in
politics is because they are not asked.

Does the Internet Help Level the Playing Field?

Politics is being changed profoundly by the Internet. E-mail, websites, Facebook, Twitter,
and blogging have reduced the cost of communicating political information. Barack Obama's
2008 campaign for the presidency demonstrated the power of the Internet. He raised over
half a billion dollars online, with 6 million of the 6.5 million contributions being for $100
or less.[23] The Internet has enabled people at the grassroots to communicate rapidly to stage
demonstrations (think of the demonstrations that touched off democratic revolutions in the
Middle East) and to organize lobbying campaigns. Because the Internet makes it so easy to
share information and to participate in politics, many believe that it can reduce the class bias
in civic engagement.

There is no doubt that the Internet has enhanced democracy in important ways. For
example, one of the sources we rely upon heavily in this textbook is the website of the
Center for Responsible Politics (www.opensecrets.org). This website enables anyone with
a computer and access to the Internet to follow the money trail in politics—who makes
and who receives political contributions. You can see how much corporations contribute
to lobbying campaigns and you can search by zip code to see how much your neighbors
are contributing to politics. The Internet has also helped to overcome the "age gap" in
politics, the underrepresentation of young people in the interest group system. Because
young people are more likely to use the Internet and to be familiar with such tools as
Facebook and Twitter, the new technology has helped them to close the gap with their
elders in political participation. A 2008 national survey found that 8 percent of those
between the ages of 25 and 40 made contributions online, while only 3 percent of those
over the age of 71 did so.[24]

Overall, however, the Internet has tended to reinforce the class bias in political participation and representation. Part of the reason is the "digital divide," the well-documented
fact that fewer poor households have access to high-speed Internet at home than middle-
income and wealthy households. Moreover, when they do have access to the Internet, those
with lower incomes and less education tend not to participate politically online.[25] Political
recruiters are still going to seek out those who have more time, skills, and money to participate in politics.

Decline in National Membership Organizations

National interest groups used to rely on a large membership base to exert power. Organizations such as the American Legion, the Elks, and the PTA were federations of local
associations that sent representatives to national meetings to elect national leadership.
Although often racially segregated and dominated by men, these organizations recruited
members across class lines and enjoyed active participation at the grass roots. Since the
1960s, national membership associations have declined. A study of twenty-three national
associations that had at least 1 percent of the adult population as members in 1955 found
that by 1995 three-fourths of them had experienced sharp membership losses, some as high
as 70 percent.[26] The same trend is evident with newer associations. A study of 3,000 "social
welfare" and "public affairs" organizations formed from the 1960s to the 1980s found that
nearly half claimed no members at all in 1998.[27] The number of Americans who don't
belong to any political organization or don't participate in any political activity other than

voting has increased significantly.[28] Interest groups now cater not to those who want to participate but to those who can write hefty checks.[29] Instead of membership organizations, we now have more "checkbook organizations," or what Theda Skocpol calls "advocates without members."[30]

Traditional Lobbying: The Insider Strategy

In discussing interest group politics, it is important to distinguish between an insider strategy and an outsider strategy. The **insider strategy** is what we normally think of as interest group politics: face-to-face meetings in which the lobbyist tries to persuade the decision maker that the interest group's position makes sense.[31] The insider strategy depends on intimate knowledge of how the game is played in Washington and access to what used to be called the "old boy" network. The **outsider strategy**, by contrast, relies on mobilizing forces outside Washington to pressure decision makers. The insider and outsider strategies are often coordinated with each other, but traditional interest group politics is usually associated with the insider strategy. (We examine the rise of the outsider strategy later in the chapter.)

The insider strategy takes place largely behind closed doors and is most effective when applied to issues sufficiently narrow in scope not to have caught the public's attention. Speaking about lobbying regarding the 1986 Tax Reform Act, Representative Pete Stark, Democrat of California, observed that "the fewer the number of taxpayers affected, and the more dull and arcane the subject matter, the longer the line of lobbyists."[32] The effectiveness of the insider strategy stems from the fact that legislation has become so complex that neither legislators nor their staffs are able to keep up with all the relevant information. As we show in Chapter 12, most of the work of Congress now takes place in committees and subcommittees, but even the specialized staffs attached to these committees cannot keep up with the staggering growth of information that pertains to policy making. Lobbyists perform an important function in a modern democracy: They provide decision makers with detailed information on the effects of different policies.

The insider lobbying strategy applies to the executive branch as well as Congress. Many political decisions still need to be made *after* a bill is passed. Congress usually formulates broad policies that leave many decisions to the discretion of executive branch employees. For example, the Environmental Protection Agency (EPA) has the power to set standards for pollutants. When agencies formulate policies, they usually do so by issuing draft regulations in the *Federal Register*, a publication of all administrative regulations issued by the federal government. Interest groups try to influence the regulations before they are issued in final form.

Whether dealing with Congress or the executive branch, a successful lobbyist must develop relationships of trust with key decision makers. Lobbyists who lie or misrepresent the facts will soon be ostracized. Lobbyists are not completely objective, however; they specialize in information that favors their client's cause. Members of Congress are especially interested in how a bill will affect their home districts. In opposing Clinton's 1994 proposal for national health insurance, which would have required businesses to provide health insurance for their employees, lobbyists provided information to members of Congress on the number of businesses in their districts that would have been affected—implying that many businesses would have been harmed by the requirement.

From morning phone calls to afternoon golf dates to evening cocktail parties, lobbyists spend most of their time cultivating personal contacts and seeking out the latest information. Access is the key. A survey of interest groups found that 98 percent contacted government officials directly to express their views, and 95 percent engaged in informal contacts with officials—at conventions, over lunch, and so forth.[33] Skilled lobbyists make decision makers dependent on them. Policy makers begin to call on the lobbyists, who become sources of hard-to-obtain information for overworked political staffs and government officials. As one legislative aide observed,

> My boss demands a speech and a statement for the *Congressional Record* for every bill we introduce or co-sponsor—and we have a lot of bills. I just can't do it all myself. The better lobbyists, when they have a proposal they are pushing, bring it to me along with a couple of speeches, a *Record* insert, and a fact sheet.[34]

A troubling aspect of lobbying is the so-called revolving door. Overall, about 50 percent of Washington lobbyists have prior government experience. When they leave government service, they get jobs with lobbying firms or interest groups, usually at much higher pay, exploiting their access and knowledge to the benefit of their clients. James Watt, former Secretary of the Interior under Ronald Reagan, reportedly received $250,000 from a client for a single phone call to a high-level official in the Department of Housing and Urban Development (HUD). According to one study, 43 percent of representatives and senators who left Congress between 1998 and 2004 became lobbyists.[35] In the case of Billy Tauzin we saw how valuable former congressmen can be to wealthy special interests. Essentially, money buys access to the trusted connections between congressmen and their former colleagues. Outlawing bribes is easy. Outlawing cozy relationships is not.

The Rise of Public Interest Groups

Notwithstanding their limits today, the rise of public interest groups beginning in the 1960s was a victory for popular democracy—in part because these groups reaffirmed the popular democratic view of human nature. Usually, narrow economic interests tend to dominate the interest group system, not just because they have greater resources, but because they find it easier to overcome what political scientists call the **collective action problem**.[36] Assume that each member of a group will benefit from a desired government action and that to provide that common benefit an interest group needs to be formed to pressure the government. The collective action problem is that *everyone* in the group will benefit regardless of his or her contribution to the collective action (and one individual's contribution rarely makes a difference in the outcome). Thus most people will be "free riders," enjoying the benefits of the collective good without contributing to its provision. When most participants try to become free riders, the group never gets off the ground.

Collective action is less of a problem for corporations, however, when a small number of companies dominate an industry. With fewer members in the interest group, each member recognizes that his or her contribution is necessary for success. Analysis of the problem of collective action helps explain why producer groups dominated by a handful of corporations are more successful in organizing interest groups and obtaining favorable policies than consumer groups, which face the daunting challenge of mobilizing millions of dispersed consumers.

In the 1960s and early 1970s, defying the collective action problem a distinct species of organized interest, the public interest group, flowered. A **public interest group** can be defined as any group seeking government action that will not principally benefit the members of the group. Special-interest groups seek benefits for their members; for example, a steel producers' lobby seeks limits on imported steel to shut out foreign competition. A public interest group, on the other hand, seeks policies that, at least in the minds of its members, will benefit society as a whole. The League of Women Voters, which seeks a better-informed electorate, is a classic example of a public interest group. Environmental groups that advocate for cleaner air, as well as religious groups such as the Christian Coalition, are public interest groups because everybody will presumably benefit, not just the members of the group.

Public interest groups would appear to have a difficult time overcoming the collective action problem because their benefits are so widespread. The rise of public interest groups confirms the popular democratic view of human nature—that people will join groups not only to benefit from them materially, but also because they believe in the purposes of the group, whether it be safer cars, cleaner air, or fewer abortions. Environmental groups, such as the Sierra Club (1.4 million members) and the Environmental Defense Fund (700,000 members), have successfully attracted members even though the benefits of the collective action are widely distributed. (We should note that nearly all public interest groups also provide their members with specific benefits for joining—all the way from bumper stickers to magazine subscriptions.) People are also attracted to citizens' groups by the companionship that arises from participating with like-minded people in a political cause.

Public interest groups have been a positive development for popular democracy. They have brought new issues into the interest system that were previously absent, such as the rights of gays, lesbians, and transsexuals, the legalization of marijuana, and prayer in public places. But public interest groups are still a small portion of all interest groups, representing only 4.6 percent of all organizations in the interest group system.[37] Representing "identity" or "postmaterialist" issues, public interest groups do not represent the interests of the poor who have very little voice in the system. In addition, the tendency of many public interest groups to be dominated by professionals and to have few members or grassroots chapters cripples their ability to serve as vehicles of popular democracy.

Cultivating the Outsider Strategy

The public interest groups that burst on the scene in the 1960s cultivated an outsider strategy in which they appealed to citizens outside Washington to put pressure on Congress and the executive branch to address their issues. Instead of trying to persuade individual politicians and officials behind closed doors (the insider strategy), they took their issues to the public, dramatizing the effects of inaction and skillfully using the media to communicate their message to the American people. By carefully documenting the facts and exposing problems, often through emotional congressional hearings and published exposés, public interest groups swayed public opinion. Politicians were forced to act.

One of the most successful practitioners of the outsider strategy was Ralph Nader. Nader's highly visible and controversial runs for the presidency in 2000, 2004, and 2008 have tended to overshadow his extraordinary success in opening up the interest group system to new issues and interests.

After graduating from Harvard Law School, Nader became obsessed with the issue of automobile safety. Moving to Washington, D.C., in 1964 he served as a consultant to the U.S. Labor Department, where he wrote a dry 234-page report with 99 pages of footnotes criticizing Detroit automakers on safety issues. Like most government reports, Nader's probably would have gathered dust on a shelf if not for other developments. First, in 1965 Nader published *Unsafe at Any Speed*,[38] an emotional indictment of the auto industry that replaced the dry technical language of the report with vivid accounts of the mayhem caused by unsafe auto design. When General Motors was caught spying on Nader in order to discredit him, he became an instant celebrity. Nader sued GM for violation of privacy and after a four-year legal battle settled out of court for $425,000. He used the profits from the lawsuit, book royalties, and speaking fees to start up *public interest research groups* (PIRGs) in states around the country. In 2008, PIRGs were active in forty-seven states and the District of Columbia and on about ninety college campuses. Supported by student fees, they lobby and conduct research on behalf of students and consumers.

The safety features that we take for granted today—seat belts and shoulder harnesses, head rests, collapsible steering columns, padded dashboards—grew out of the great automobile safety debate in the 1960s that Nader triggered. The government-mandated and "voluntary" safety devices that were introduced beginning in the 1960s have saved tens of thousands of lives. Even though Americans drove many more miles each year, automobile-related deaths declined steadily in the 1970s and 1980s, beginning to rise again only in 1993.

Nader and his public interest groups are credited with helping to enact key consumer laws, including the Wholesome Meat Act of 1967, the Natural Gas Pipeline Safety Act of 1968, and the Comprehensive Occupational Safety and Health Act of 1970. Nader's vision of citizen action, however, has a flaw. The consumer issues that Nader has concentrated on benefit the middle class more than the working class and the poor. As we noted earlier, many public interest groups with offices in Washington have become staff dominated, surviving on grants from wealthy patrons and direct-mail contributions. Groups in which the staff communicates with members only through direct-mail fundraising techniques are more consistent with elite democracy than popular democracy.

The New Lobbying: Elite Countermobilization

Public interest groups opened up the elite-dominated interest group system in Washington to a surge in popular democratic participation. Although the outsider strategy employed by citizens' groups helped to democratize the pressure group system, elites soon learned how to use the outsider strategy themselves to reassert their power. In August 1971, Lewis Powell Jr., who would be appointed to the Supreme Court by Richard Nixon a few months later, wrote a confidential memo to the U.S. Chamber of Commerce.[39] Titled "Attack on the Free Enterprise System," the Powell memorandum depicted American corporations as politically "impotent," the victims of a "massive assault." As a director on eleven corporate boards, Powell was especially sensitive to attacks on business. Charging that Ralph Nader and his allies were out to destroy the free-enterprise system itself, Powell asserted that "there should be no reluctance to penalize those who oppose [the system]." What is remarkable about Powell's memo is that it lays out a broad strategy focused on four areas—universities, the media, the political establishment, and the courts—that would actually be implemented over the ensuing decades by big business pretty much as Powell recommended.

Business counterattacked along a broad front—all the way from traditional lobbying to litigation centers, think tanks, and increasingly sophisticated public relations. One of the major outgrowths of the Powell memo was the formation of the Business Roundtable in 1972, an organization made up exclusively of CEOs from the top 200 corporations in the country. The Business Roundtable was able to impose a remarkable degree of "class solidarity" among its members that enabled it to defeat a 1977 attempt by unions to repeal the right-to-work provisions of the Taft-Hartley Act. Inspired by the Powell memorandum, Joseph Coors gave a quarter of a million dollars to found a right-wing think tank known today as the Heritage Foundation.

As business organized, the corporate presence in Washington, D.C., grew. Business interests now dominate lobbying organizations in Washington. Following the economic meltdown of 2008, Congress held hearings to regulate Wall Street so that the American taxpayers would not be put on the hook again to bail them out to the tune of hundreds of billions of dollars. In the battle over reforming derivatives, highly speculative investments with little transparency, corporate opponents of reform outspent pro-reform advocates by more than 11-to-1.[40] Eventually, Congress passed the Dodd-Frank Act to regulate Wall Street but, under pressure from bank lobbyists, Republicans in Congress refused to appoint a director to the Consumer Financial Protection Bureau. President Obama eventually made a recess appointment, bypassing Congress, in order to get the agency up and running.

It would be wrong to characterize the countermobilization by corporate elites as just a power grab. In classic elite democratic fashion, they argue that elites should filter the emotional demands of the people. Too much democracy, they say, overloads the system with too many demands.[41] The masses are being manipulated into supporting government regulations by emotional appeals from liberal activists who would benefit from the new jobs in the expanded regulatory state. In the long run, elite democrats argue, regulatory burdens will stifle growth, hurting all Americans' living standards.

Corporate elites have portrayed their views not as private interests but as a new version of the public interest: Freeing business from regulatory and tax burdens will, in the long run, benefit all Americans; "a rising tide lifts all boats." Faced with a stagnating economy, ordinary citizens have been receptive to the message that excessive regulations and high taxes are choking off economic growth.[42] The financial meltdown of 2008, made possible by the lack of strong government regulations, temporarily swung the pendulum in the direction of greater regulation of corporations. Riding the backlash against the government bailout of Wall Street firms that were deemed "too big to fail," however, corporate interests have been remarkably successful at shifting the blame from Wall Street to Washington.[43]

Direct Marketing

One effective method that money can buy is **direct marketing**, the targeted solicitation of individuals for political support, by phone or more often by mail. The advantage of direct marketing is that, much more than with radio or television, the political appeal can be adapted to specialized audiences. Pioneered by public interest groups, which often rely on individual membership dues for funding, direct marketing has been greatly enhanced over the years by high-speed computers that maintain huge mailing lists broken down into segments for specialized appeals.

Direct-mail marketing begins by contacting a large mailing list. This is an expensive task, and usually only 1 or 2 percent reply to the appeal. Respondents make up the "house list," which can be successfully solicited again and again for support, typically with a 10 to 20 percent response rate. Mailing lists are traded and sold between organizations. One enterprising researcher enrolled her four-month-old son in six organizations to trace direct-mail fundraising. Over the next year and a half, the infant received eighteen pounds of mail—185 solicitations from the original six organizations and 63 from thirty-two other organizations that bought or rented mailing lists.[44]

Direct-mail solicitations are cleverly designed so that they will not be thrown in the wastebasket unopened. A licked stamp looks more personal than metered mail. They are often addressed directly to the individual ("Dear Mr. Malone"), are marked "urgent," and contain emotional appeals that evoke an exaggerated threat. A letter from Common Cause talked about "the threat posed by the torrents of special interest campaign cash," which it calls "Alarming. Outrageous. Downright Dangerous." A solicitation from the Christian Right begins "Just When You Thought Your Children Were Safe from Homosexual Advances, Congress Introduces House Resolution #427: The 'Gay Bill of Rights.'"[45]

Computers break down mailing lists into niches and specialized appeals. By a simple command, a computer can be ordered to produce letters for all those on the mailing list who live, for example, in the districts of representatives who serve on the House Banking, Finance, and Urban Affairs Committee. Lobbyists increasingly see direct mail as a way to supplement their insider strategy with an outsider strategy that carefully orchestrates grassroots pressure on Congress. Direct mail campaigns are not available to all interest groups; they cost a great deal of money.

Astroturf Lobbying

The new style of lobbying developed by the public interest movement in the 1960s and 1970s tilted the playing field of interest group politics. Previously, lobbying was dominated by **iron triangles**—literally three-pointed relationships between executive branch agencies, committees in Congress, and interest groups. A good example is the strong relationship defense contractors have formed with subcommittees in Congress and top officials in the Defense Department. Iron triangles still exist, but in many areas political scientists believe they have been replaced by looser, more open and decentralized **issue networks**.[46] Complex new regulatory laws helped to make congressional hearings more important, with expert witnesses amassing mountains of information on each issue. In general, many issues have been taken out from behind closed doors in Congress to be decided in more public forums, with public opinion (the outsider strategy) playing a more important role.

It would seem reasonable to conclude that the opening up of the interest group system to broader participation—what political scientists call "expanding the scope of conflict"—would make it more open to popular democratic input. However, this has not been the case. First, the greater emphasis on information in the policy-making process gives an advantage to those who control information. Elected representatives, even presidents, are forced to defer to the issue networks as democratic control passes from elected leaders to unelected experts. Few citizens possess the expertise or the free time to track complex regulations on new drugs or the latest scientific knowledge on carcinogens. Corporations do.

More important, corporate elites have devised their own outsider strategy to counter the outsider strategy of the public interest groups. Politicians want to know what the public thinks about an idea before they vote for it. If they think there is a significant grassroots movement that opposes a proposed law, they will vote against it. Corporations now have the ability to create fake grassroots movements—to use the appearance of popular democracy to achieve the objectives of elite democracy. Corporate mergers have spawned a new generation of public relations firms in Washington, D.C., that can, for the right amount of money, generate a grassroots movement for either side on just about any issue. Lloyd Bentsen, a longtime Democratic senator from Texas, coined the term "**Astroturf lobbying**" to describe artificial grassroots campaigns created by public relations firms.[47] By 1995, Astroturf lobbying was an $800-million-a-year industry, according to *Campaigns and Elections* magazine.[48] What's more, Astroturf lobbyists do not even have to register as lobbyists because they do not fit the legal definition of a lobbyist. Astroturf lobbying is unregulated and highly secretive.

A good example of the new breed of Astroturf lobbyists is Bonner & Associates, a public relations firm located near the Capitol in Washington that bills itself on its website as offering "Strategic Grassroots/Grasstops support to help you win." Founder Jack "Bombs Away" Bonner emphasizes that corporate grassroots politics was borrowed from the public interest groups that perfected the technique of using factual accusations to generate emotional public responses. "Politics turns on emotion," Bonner says. "That's why industry has lost in the past and that's why we win. We bring emotion to the table."[49] Bonner takes pride in being able to find ordinary citizens who have no financial interest in the policy but are willing to support his corporate clients' positions; "white hat" citizens, he calls them. The offices of Bonner & Associates have a boiler room with hundreds of phone lines and a sophisticated computer system. Young people sit in little booths every day, dialing around the country in search of "white hat" citizens who are willing to endorse corporate political objectives. To oppose a law that would have required Detroit automakers to build more fuel-efficient cars, Bonner enlisted seniors and people with disabilities who had concerns about getting in and out of smaller cars. They also got police officers, who feared their police cruisers would be replaced by Toyotas, to speak out against the proposal. The bill was defeated.

The key to Astroturf lobbying is deception—the politicians must never know who is really behind the "grassroots" campaign. Bonner, for example, has its callers ask whether the person would be willing to sign a letter of support and then fax it back to them. Bonner then scans the signature onto a computer and puts it on a petition, deceiving lawmakers into thinking that people went door-to-door gathering signatures. So-called "stealth campaigns" utilize a series of front organizations to mask the true source of the lobbying.[50] For example, Bonner used the letterhead of Consumer Alliance, a Michigan nonprofit that opposes laws to lower the cost of prescription drugs to low income consumers, to solicit signatures. In fact, the entire effort was funded by the Pharmaceutical Research and Manufacturers of America.

In a large country like the United States, the increasing sophistication of the mass media and direct marketing has given an advantage to interests with large amounts of money. American politics is approaching "democracy for hire." Researchers found that only 9 percent of corporate interest representatives in Washington expressed a need for more. On the other hand, 58 percent of unions and citizens' groups said they needed more money.[51] A chemical company can deduct the cost of flying its executives to Washington to testify against the Clean Air Act; ordinary citizens must pay their own way.

Think Tanks: Shaping the Agenda

Control over information and ideas is crucial in policy making. One of the best examples is Charles Murray's 1984 book *Losing Ground,* which played a key role in building momentum for welfare reform by arguing that welfare, far from curing poverty, was actually a *cause* of poverty. Welfare rewarded people for not working or marrying, Murray argued, helping to entrench a culture of poverty in urban ghettos. His recommended solution was to scrap "the entire federal welfare and income-support structure."[52] Murray's book had tremendous influence on the 1996 welfare reform (see Chapter 17) because it enabled conservatives to frame cutting welfare spending and limiting recipients to no more than three years of benefits in a row as compassionate, not punitive. Murray successfully framed welfare as more like a dangerous drug than a helping hand to single mothers and their children.

The influence of Murray's thinking was due not just to the persuasiveness of his arguments. Indeed, the evidence suggests that Murray greatly exaggerated the negative effects of welfare.[53] Besides funding Murray for two years to write the book, the Manhattan Institute, a conservative think tank, hired a public relations specialist who sent out more than 700 free copies and even flew in influential politicians, academics, and journalists, putting them up at an expensive New York hotel so that they could attend a seminar on Murray's book. Most think tank projects are not as influential as Murray's book, but by continuously seeding the ground with ideas and research, think tanks can play a crucial role in setting the policy agenda and framing the policy alternatives. Increasingly, **think tanks**—private, not-for-profit research and advocacy organizations—play the role of evaluating programs and generating new policy ideas. According to one scholar, there are 1,736 think tanks in the United States.[54] (See Table 10.1 for a list of influential think tanks.)

To maintain their tax-exempt status, think tanks must remain nonpartisan; they cannot support political parties or candidates running for office. Increasingly, however, think tanks have taken on an ideological and partisan edge. A study of media hits by think tanks in 2008 showed that think tanks on the right of the political spectrum get more media attention but the gap has narrowed (Table 10.1).

Table 10.1   Influential Washington Think Tanks

	Approximate Annual Budget (in millions of $)	Political Orientation	Media Hits (2008)
1. Brookings Institution	102.0 (FY 2011)	Centrist	2,166
2. American Enterprise Institute	32.1 (2011)	Conservative	985
3. Heritage Foundation	60.7 (2011)	Conservative	922
4. Cato Institute	20.4 (2011)	Conservative/ Libertarian	591
5. Economic Policy Institute	7.8 (2009)	Progressive	356
6. Urban Institute	77.5 (2008)	Center-Left	527
7. Center on Budget and Policy Priorities	27.7 (2010)	Progressive	319
8. Center for Economic and Policy Research	1.7 (2010)	Progressive	315

Percentage of Media Citations by Ideology

Conservative or Center-Right	31%
Centrist	48%
Progressive or Center-Left	21%

Source: Nexis database on major newspapers, radio, and TV transcripts; Michale Dolny, "Right Ebbs, Left Gains as Media 'Experts': Think Tank Balance Still Skews Right," Fairness and Accuracy in Reporting; http://www.fair.org/index.php?page=3857&printer_friendly=1 (accessed May 27, 2012).

New Reform

New Reform New Reform New Reform New Reform New Reform Reform

Wealthy elites and corporations dominate the interest group system in Washington. It often seems like this is inevitable. Is there anything we can do about it? In fact, there are many things we can do. The government cannot suppress or support particular interest groups, but it can help to level the playing field. Here are some ideas.

1. *Tighten campaign finance laws:* The Center for Responsive Politics estimates that an astounding $5.8 billion was spent on the 2012 elections. Because of the blurring of the distinction between interest group politics and partisan politics, the most important reform to interest group politics would be to regulate campaign contributions. The 2010 *Citizens United* Supreme Court decision equated the spending of money on elections with free speech. Corporations can spend unlimited amounts of money on a campaign so long as they act independently of the candidate. So-called "Super PACs" have proliferated, engaging vicious attack ads. Rightfully so, many members of Congress are worried that if they cross wealthy corporate interests they will be

subject to crippling attack ads. We need to overturn *Citizens United* and regulate money in elections. Every other advanced industrial democracy in the world uses some form of public funding of elections.[55] Until we better regulate the flood of money in elections, the wealthy will continue to buy privileged access.

2. *Require more disclosure of lobbying activities:* An effective way to level the playing field is to inform the public about efforts to influence the government. The Honest Leadership and Open Government Act of 2007 made important progress in forcing lobbyists to disclose their activities. It requires, for example, quarterly reports and the creation of a publicly searchable electronic database. The Center for Responsive Politics sponsors a website, opensecrets.org, which is a goldmine of information on lobbyists. One problem is that these disclosure requirements can miss so-called grassroots lobbying, the phalanx of public relations specialists, pollsters, and ad companies that wealthy clients hire to shape public opinion, and ultimately influence Congress. If the citizens knew that it was the drug industry that was sponsoring Citizens for Better Medicare, they would be much more skeptical about their ads against the government negotiating lower drug prices for seniors.

3. *Improve media oversight:* One of the greatest protections against special political privileges is exposure by the media. It is the duty of journalists to inform the public about who is behind so-called grassroots groups. This will be less likely if the media are controlled by a few giant corporations and there is little competition. (We discuss the importance of the media for popular democracy in Chapter 9.)

4. *Encourage genuine debate:* The problem is not that wealthy corporations are involved in lobbying; clearly, corporations have a valid viewpoint that deserves to be heard in the political system. The problem is the way well-heeled interest groups make their cases, using stealth campaigns and relying on ten-second sound bites, with misleading claims hitting "hot button" issues. According to two experts on interest group politics, "Electronic smear campaigns have become a key by-product of new communications technologies and typically are filled with misleading, erroneous, or outright malicious claims."[56] It is difficult for the government to directly regulate these activities, though some states have experimented with "truth in communications" codes or even the banning of false or deceptive ads. Their experiences deserve watching. Codes of ethics in the consulting industry can help. On the positive side, the sponsorship of "deliberative polls" would show that public opinion looks very different when citizens are given a chance to gain information and discuss issues with other citizens— instead of being forced to make snap judgments about fixed alternatives to an anonymous phone call. Some have even called for Deliberation Day, a national holiday in which citizens would be paid to participate in all-day small-group discussions of national issues.[57]

In short, the government could do many things to level the playing field of interest group politics. But the one essential ingredient that no government laws can create is a vigilant citizenry. Get involved in the issues you care about and expose the efforts of elites to pull political strings behind the scenes.

Why have conservative think tanks been more influential than liberal think tanks? First, they are better funded. But how the funding is used is more important than how much there is. In fact, large foundations that are often considered liberal, such as the Rockefeller and Ford foundations, have much more money than the conservative foundations, like the Lynde and Harry Bradley, Sarah Scaife, and John M. Olin foundations. But the liberal foundations tend to fund direct-service projects, such as providing affordable housing or clean water, rather than ideologically driven policy analysis. The liberal think tanks tend to be less political and more scholarly. The Urban Institute, one of the oldest and biggest, supports government programs for cities and the poor but views itself primarily as a scientific evaluator of public policies; its research agenda is driven by government contracts, not by a political vision. The Economic Policy Institute, which receives most of its funding from unions, has a clear political agenda, but it is tiny compared to the large number of pro-corporate think tanks.

With a permanent staff of about 250 generating hundreds of publications every year, the Heritage Foundation has been one of the most powerful think tanks in Washington. Devoting more than one-third of its budget to marketing, Heritage has been especially successful at gaining media attention for its publications. Most of its publications are designed to meet the "briefcase test"—short enough to be read in the time it takes for a taxi to travel from Washington's National Airport to a congressional hearing on Capitol Hill (about twenty minutes).[58] Senior scholars at Heritage are available to produce a paper on a policy issue for a sympathetic member of Congress in a matter of hours.

Conservative think tanks and foundations are also making efforts to shape political debates on college campuses, which they maintain have long been dominated by leftist ideas. The Liberation News Service (LNS) provides editorial services for left-wing college papers, but it is not nearly as well funded or organized. Accuracy in Academia (AIA) is an explicit attempt to counter the alleged left-wing bias in American universities. Started by Reed Irvine, also founder of a similar group called Accuracy in Media, AIA recruits students to monitor college classes and report professors who fail to include the conservative point of view or who have "Marxist leanings." The results are published in AIA's monthly newspaper, *Campus Report*, which is distributed online and is free to about 1,500 colleges and high schools. The effects of these efforts are uncertain, but they demonstrate a capacity by conservative think tanks and foundations to reach out beyond Washington.

At their best, think tanks provide objective research that challenges the status quo and devise innovative solutions to longstanding problems. Unfortunately, most think tanks are closely tied to elite corporate interests. This is not surprising because wealthy individuals and corporations provide most of the funding for think tanks. Think tanks that are closely tied to one interest in society will not be able to think out of the box. Increasingly, think tanks have become wrapped up in the polarized partisan atmosphere in Washington. We need new thinking about public policy that is responsive to the problems of ordinary Americans and involves them directly in solving those problems.

Charles Barsotti / The New Yorker Collection / Cartoonbank.com

"What are you complaining about? It's a level playing field."

Conclusion: What Can Be Done?

At the present time, interest group politics faces a dilemma: Democracy requires that we protect the rights of all groups to organize and "petition the government for a redress of grievances" (in the words of the Constitution), but this freedom of association has led to an interest group system today that is highly unequal, even undemocratic. In particular, developments in communications technology have enabled interest groups with large sums of money to manipulate public opinion with stealth campaigns and clever sound bites. In what political scientists call "feedback effects," moneyed interests have used their political power to enhance their economic position, setting in motion a vicious circle of widening economic and political inequalities that threaten the very core of our democracy.

The situation cries out for governmental action to level the playing field. As we noted earlier, government can take action, such as campaign finance reform, to level the playing field. However, these efforts can only go so far, and any attempt by the government to restrict or subsidize interest groups would be abhorrent. Who would pick which groups to stifle or aid? As James Madison said in *Federalist No. 10*, "Liberty is to faction [selfish interest groups] what air is to fire." Thus, it would be foolish to suppress factions, Madison concluded, because to do so would destroy the very atmosphere that breathes life into the democratic process. The cure would be worse than the disease.

It may be tempting for popular democratic groups to fight fire with fire, hiring their own slick consultants to manipulate public opinion. But it won't work; elites will always have more money and slicker consultants. Ultimately, the only way to counter the Astroturf lobbying of moneyed interests is for ordinary citizens to form powerful grass roots organizations. The reason why the interest group system became more accessible to ordinary citizens in the 1960s and 1970s is because people were mobilized into mass organizations that went door-to-door and took to the streets to publicize their causes. Landmark laws like the civil rights laws and the Clean Air Act passed because elites felt threatened. Sensing that the alternative was radical change, they became more open to sensible reforms. In the next chapter we turn to protest politics, the ultimate outsider strategy that, under the right circumstances, can give popular democrats a weapon that money cannot buy.

Reader's Guide

Critical Thinking Questions

1. Do you or your friends belong to any interest groups? Are they effective? Why or why not?

2. Do you think former government officials should be forbidden to lobby their agency for a certain amount of time after leaving government service? Why or why not?

3. Collect examples of direct-marketing appeals sent to your household. Do they appeal to fears or exaggerate the facts? Do you think the end justifies the means, or do direct-marketing appeals go too far?

4. Do most citizens decide issues on the basis of rational judgment or on the basis of emotion? Give examples of rational appeals and emotional appeals by interest groups. Which do you think is more effective?

Key Word Definition

interest group politics   Any attempt by an organization to influence the policies of government through normal extra-electoral channels, such as lobbying, writing letters, testifying before legislative committees, or advertising.

revolving door   The widespread practice of former elected or government officials becoming lobbyists for interests they formerly dealt with in their official capacity.

pluralism   The elite democratic theory that views the interest group system as a political marketplace in which power is dispersed among many interest groups competing for influence through a process of bargaining and compromising.

insider strategy   The use by an interest group of face-to-face, one-on-one persuasion to convince decision makers in Washington that the interest group's position makes sense.

outsider strategy   The mobilization by an interest group of forces outside Washington to put pressure on decision makers to act in ways favorable to the interest group.

Federal Register   The daily government publication of all national administrative regulations.

collective action problem   The difficulty in getting individuals to act collectively to obtain a common good when everyone in a group will benefit regardless of whether she or he contributes to the collective action.

public interest group   Any association seeking government action, the achievement of which will not principally benefit the members of the association.

direct marketing   The direct solicitation of individuals for political support, by phone or more frequently by mail.

iron triangle   An alliance between a congressional committee, an interest group, and an executive agency that serves each one's interest, often at the expense of the general public.

issue network   Loose networks of experts and advocates that are active in particular issue areas.

Astroturf lobbying   A lobbying campaign that appears to be a spontaneous expression of citizens at the grassroots but in fact is purchased through consultants and public relations firms.

think tank   A nonprofit institution, funded primarily by foundations and corporate grants, that conducts public policy research.

11

Mass Movement Politics: The Great Equalizer?

PROTEST POLITICS: GOALS AND TACTICS

MASS MOVEMENTS IN AMERICAN HISTORY

MASS MOVEMENTS: THE NECESSARY INGREDIENTS

PROTEST TACTICS: WALKING A FINE LINE

THE ELITE RESPONSE TO MASS MOVEMENTS

THE DEMOCRATIC DEBATE OVER PROTEST POLITICS

CONCLUSION: THE FUTURE OF PROTEST POLITICS

Protest politics can be defined as political actions, such as boycotts and demonstrations, designed to broaden conflicts and activate third parties to pressure the bargaining situation in ways favorable to the protesters.[1] Because protest politics operates outside of ordinary political institutions, it is sometimes called "extraordinary politics."[2] When protest politics mobilizes large numbers of previously passive bystanders to become active participants, it reaches the stature of a **mass movement**. The Occupy Wall Street protests that began in the fall of 2011 show that protest politics can change the agenda of American politics. They also show how protest politics has become a global phenomenon and how protestors have learned to use the Internet and social media to coordinate their actions and make their voices heard. Finally, Occupy Wall Street demonstrates that protests can erupt like wildfire but they can also burn out quickly. Occupy Wall Street rose up in 2011, but by the fall of 2012 it had faded from view.[3]

The Occupy Wall Street movement traces its roots back to the Arab Spring, a series of demonstrations that started in Tunisia and spread quickly to Egypt, Libya, Yemen, and other Arab countries. The demonstrators used Facebook and other social media to spread the word and coordinate action behind the backs of the government. The Internet is difficult for any government to control, short of shutting the whole system down—which is what the Egyptian government under Hosni Mubarak did on the evening of January 27, 2011. Suddenly, Egypt, a nation of 80 million people, with 23 million Internet users, disappeared from the Internet. Under pressure from businesses and others harmed by being cut off from the worldwide web, the Egyptian government restored Internet service five days later.

The sight of young demonstrators risking their lives to bring down brutal authoritarian regimes inspired citizens in other countries to plan their own protests. In mid-2011, the Canadian group that publishes *Adbusters*, a free magazine that mocks consumerism, issued a call on its website for a "Tahrir moment" (the square in Cairo where the Egyptian revolution began) in America—with people peacefully occupying Wall Street to protest economic inequality and corporate privilege. One of the founders of *Adbusters* registered the web address OccupyWallStreet. org. The idea went viral—but there was still no coherent plan on *how* to occupy Wall Street.

Zhang Baoping/ZUMAPRESS/Newscom

Fueled by protests against budget cuts in New York City, people began meeting to plan the occupation of Wall Street. Influenced by two activists who had participated in 2010 protests in Athens, Greece, the protestors began meeting as a general assembly, or GA, a radical form of participatory democracy in which all decisions are made by consensus. GAs include equitable processes such as a "progressive stack" in which people form lines to speak, with those from marginalized groups, such as women and minorities, deliberately moved to the front of the line by stack keepers. Instant feedback arises spontaneously from the assembly, with participants who agree with what is being said wagging the fingers of both hands up in the air and those who don't agree waving their fingers down. The protestors decided that D-Day for "Occupy Wall Street" would be September 17, 2011. A key moment occurred when the protestors adopted the phrase "We are the 99%." Originating out of a Tumblr blog page, the phrase refers to the fact that most of the wealth is concentrated in the top 1 percent. (We document the concentration of wealth in Chapter 4.)

When the day arrived, about 2,000 people marched toward Chase Manhattan Plaza on Wall Street but found it barricaded by police. By consensus, the protestors decided to occupy Zuccotti Park, a small slice of land just north of Wall Street. Because the land was privately owned, the police could not evict the protestors without a specific request from the owners. The protestors immediately began building a permanent camp, with tents, kitchens, and eventually a library with 5,000 volumes. Every evening protestors attended a GA to decide what to do next. Inspired by the symbol of protestors occupying ground in the shadow of Wall Street, by October 9, 2011, Occupy protests had taken place in 82 countries, including 600 communities in the United States. On November 14, 2011, however, authorities launched a coordinated assault on encampments around the globe. In the middle of the night, more than one thousand police forcibly cleared out Zuccotti Park. The arrests of thousands of people around the world provided the movement with free publicity. Footage of campus police at the University of California, Davis casually pepper spraying peaceful protestors went viral—fueling more protests.

Although the Occupy Wall Street movement has lacked specific demands and has had little direct impact on elections, there is no doubt that it profoundly changed the political conversation in the United States. In a remarkably short time, the political agenda shifted from a focus

on the budget deficit to a focus on economic injustice and inequality. According to *Politico*, mentions of "economic inequality" in print publications, online news stories, and broadcast transcripts increased by more than 500 percent from the beginning to the end of October 2011.[4] Many believe that Occupy helped push the banks to agree to a stronger settlement to help homeowners unfairly foreclosed on and gave President Obama the political space to talk about the rich paying more in taxes in his January 2012 State of the Union address and successful presidential campaign.

Mass movement politics with its direct participatory methods is very different from electoral politics and representative democracy. But the two kinds of politics interact in powerful ways. Throughout American history mass movements have planted the seeds that grew into significant reforms. To be effective, protest movements must raise specific demands and fight for them in the arena of representative democracy and electoral politics. Usually, the demands raised by mass movements are initially viewed as too radical, as outside the mainstream. But often, decades later, they are passed into law. The progressive income tax, eight-hour day, old-age insurance, and voting rights for women and African Americans all began as radical demands by protestors. Far from being examples of the "co-optation" or selling out of mass movement, concrete reforms are an essential component of successful mass movements.[5]

The Tea Party movement is an example of a mass movement that is the opposite of Occupy Wall Street—not just politically (right-wing instead of left-wing) but also in its willingness to push for specific laws and get directly involved in partisan electoral politics. The Tea Party movement shows the danger that mass movements will be co-opted by politicians is real. Clearly, the Tea Party has been successful at moving the Republican Party to the right and played a key role in the Republican takeover of the House of Representatives in 2010. However, Tea Party candidates were widely rejected by the voters in 2012 and may have cost the Republicans control of the U.S. Senate.

When a mass movement becomes too closely identified with one political party or with wealthy contributors, grassroots activists lose control. Successful mass movements stay focused on issues, not parties or patrons. Not all mass movements are popular democratic. Paradoxically, the participatory processes of protest politics can be used to limit democracy. Later in this chapter we discuss why the Tea Party, despite being named after the event that helped launch the American Revolution, is not a popular democratic movement. Although the Tea Party is fueled by grassroots activism and populist anger, its hostility to immigrants, unions, and government regulation of markets will ultimately shrink the space for popular democratic participation.

The spread of protests is a sign that people feel that the normal operations of representative democracy are failing. Indeed, it is impossible to understand American politics today without understanding protest politics. Throughout American history, mass movements have enabled outsiders—the poor, minorities, the disabled—to make themselves heard and influence policy. For this reason, the right of people to protest, even to the point of making life uncomfortable for ordinary Americans, should be given special protection by the government. But violent protest should not be tolerated. Protestors should never be given so much leeway that they can blackmail the public into supporting their demands.

In this chapter, after examining the goals and tactics that distinguish protest politics from electoral and interest group politics, we explore the dilemmas that leaders of mass movements face in keeping protests alive—using the civil rights movement as a model of a successful mass movement. After analyzing the ways that elites respond to mass movements, we examine how mass movements fit in the democratic debate. Finally, we evaluate modern mass movements, including Occupy Wall Street and the Tea Party. Protest tactics can be misused and abused, but when the institutions of representative democracy are failing, they provide a way to level the playing field of politics, helping to fulfill the participatory promise of American democracy.

Protest Politics: Goals and Tactics

Like interest groups, mass movements are a form of extra-electoral politics; they try to influence the government outside of elections. Interest group politics and mass politics often blend into each other. Interest groups sometimes organize demonstrations, and it is common for mass movements to lobby Congress. Over time, mass movements often spawn interest groups that become part of the pressure group system in Washington. Nevertheless, interest group politics and protest politics are distinct phenomena with different approaches on two dimensions: (1) goals, and (2) the means or tactics used to achieve those goals.

In the pages ahead, we illustrate the lessons of protest politics by focusing on the very beginning of the American civil rights movement in the Montgomery, Alabama, bus boycott in 1955–1956. Reaching its zenith in the mid-1960s, the civil rights movement was probably the most successful mass movement in American history. Led by a charismatic black preacher by the name of Martin Luther King Jr., the civil rights movement began modestly in 1955 with the goal of desegregating the Montgomery bus system. The movement reached its zenith with the passage of the 1964 Civil Rights Act, which prohibited segregation in public accommodations and discrimination in hiring, and the 1965 Voting Rights Act, which revolutionized politics across the nation, and especially in the South, by guaranteeing blacks the right to vote.

Mass Movement Goals: Beyond Material Benefits

In contrast to interest groups, which usually focus on specific economic goals, such as lower taxes or more governmental benefits, mass movements seek broad moral and ideological goals

Table 11.1 Mass Movements in American History

Movement	Primary Period of Activism	Major Goal(s)
Abolitionist	Three decades before Civil War (1830–1860)	Abolition of slavery
Nativist	1850s and 1890s–1920s	Restriction of immigration
Populist	1880s and 1890s	Democratic control over railroads, banks, and nation's money supply
Labor	Reached peaks in the 1880s, 1890s, and 1930s	Enhance power of workers to achieve decent wages and benefits, protect jobs, and guarantee safe working environments
Women's suffrage	Late nineteenth and early twentieth centuries	Voting rights for women
Temperance	Late nineteenth and early twentieth centuries	Prohibition of alcohol
Nuclear disarmament	Late 1950s and early 1960s Late 1970s and early 1980s	End of nuclear testing Banning the bomb
Civil rights	1950s and 1960s	Equal rights for black Americans
Anti–Vietnam War	Late 1960s and early 1970s	United States out of Vietnam
Student	1960s and 1970s	Student rights and democratic governance of universities
Neighborhood organizing	1960s–present	Community control
Women's liberation or feminist	1970s–present	Equality for women in all aspects of life
Antinuclear	1970s and 1980s	Reducing the use of nuclear power
Environmental	1970s–present	Stop environmental destruction
Pro-life	1970s–present	Outlawing abortion, stem cell research, euthanasia
Native American rights	1970s–present	Tribal autonomy
Gay rights	1970s–present	Equal rights for homosexuals
Antiglobalization	1990s–present	Controls on multinational corporations
Anti–Iraq War	2002–2010	United States out of Iraq or UN takeover
Tea Party	2009–present	Lower taxes, less government
Occupy Wall Street	2010–present	Greater economic equality

that affect the whole society, such as the "right to life" of the anti-abortion movement or the equal treatment of the civil rights movement. As a result, mass movement goals are not easily subject to bargaining and compromise. The abolitionist movement, for example, refused to compromise on its goal of abolishing slavery. For mass movements, it is not a matter of more or less, but right or wrong. Table 11.1 lists the most important mass movements in American history together with their main goals.

The civil rights movement shows how groups can make the transition from interest groups to mass movements. In the mid-1950s, Montgomery, Alabama, like most southern cities, had laws requiring segregation of nearly all public facilities, including public transportation.[6] Blacks were required to sit in the backs of buses. They could not pass through the white section at the front of a bus, which meant that after a black had bought a ticket, he or she had to get off and reenter through the back door. The ordinance in Montgomery had a special twist: Bus drivers, all of whom were white, were empowered to enforce a floating line between the races. As more whites got on, bus drivers would order a whole row of blacks to stand up and move to the back of the bus to make room. A number of black women could thus be forced to stand to make room for one white man.

On December 1, 1955, Rosa Parks, a dignified, middle-aged African-American woman, boarded a bus in downtown Montgomery. The thirty-six seats on the bus were soon filled with twenty-two blacks and fourteen whites. Seeing a white man standing in the front of the bus, the driver turned around and told the four blacks sitting in the row just behind the whites to get up and move to the back. Rosa Parks refused. The driver threatened to arrest her, but Parks again refused to move. Summoned to the scene, police officers arrested Parks, took her to the police station, booked her, fingerprinted her, and put her in jail.

Word of Parks's arrest spread quickly through the black community, which immediately organized a highly successful boycott of the bus company. Initially, however, the goals of the movement were very modest, resembling more the goals of an interest group than a militant mass movement. The boycott had three demands: (1) courteous treatment on the buses; (2) seating on a first-come, first-served basis; and (3) the hiring of black drivers for black bus routes. The protesters were not calling for an end to segregation but simply for reforms that would make it more humane.

The white establishment in Montgomery refused to compromise. Instead, they tried to suppress the movement by harassing the boycotters and throwing the leaders in jail on trumped-up charges. The refusal of whites to compromise on these issues, King later wrote, caused a shift in people's thinking:

> The experience taught me a lesson. . . . even when we asked for justice within the segregation laws, the "powers that be" were not willing to grant it. Justice and equality, I saw, would never come while segregation remained, because the basic purpose of segregation was to perpetuate injustice and inequality.[7]

At that moment, the goals of the Montgomery boycott shifted from better treatment for blacks within segregation to an end to segregation, or equal rights for all—a goal that could not be compromised. At that point, Montgomery's blacks made the transition from an interest group to a mass movement that could appeal to all Americans on the basis of human dignity, equality, and fairness.

Mass Movement Tactics: Protest as a Political Resource

Mass movements are differentiated from interest groups not only by their goals but also by the political means they use to achieve their goals. Mass movements have a broad array of *protest tactics* to choose from, including petitions, demonstrations, boycotts, strikes, **civil disobedience**, confrontations and disruptions, riots, and even violent revolution (see Figure 11.1). Unlike interest groups, mass movements do not target their efforts directly at decision makers; protests are a form of political theater designed to educate and mobilize broader publics, who in turn put pressure on decision makers. Mass movements attempt to broaden the scope of conflict in the hope that battles that are lost in the narrow hallways of Congress can be won in the streets or in the broad arena of public opinion. Therefore, mass movement politics has more participatory potential than interest group politics. By relying on mass mobilization and the moral appeal of

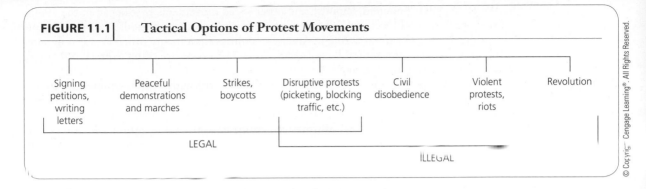

FIGURE 11.1 | **Tactical Options of Protest Movements**

Signing petitions, writing letters — Peaceful demonstrations and marches — Strikes, boycotts — Disruptive protests (picketing, blocking traffic, etc.) — Civil disobedience — Violent protests, riots — Revolution

LEGAL

ILLEGAL

their cause, people with little money or political clout can use protest tactics to gain power in the political system.

Mass movement tactics vary all the way from the legal to the clearly illegal, with a large gray area in the middle. Protesters often agonize about whether to cross over the line into illegal tactics. In choosing tactics, protesters must go far enough to dramatize their cause but not so far as to alienate potential supporters—a phenomenon known as *political backlash*. Most tactics used by mass movements are legal and protected by the First Amendment guarantees of freedom of speech, press, and "the right of the people peaceably to assemble, and to petition the Government for a redress of grievances" (U.S. Constitution). When legal protests are ignored, protesters become frustrated and sometimes resort to illegal methods, including violence, to dramatize their cause.

In many ways, protest movements are evidence of the failure of our democratic institutions to respond to deeply felt needs and issues.[8] Even if a democracy guaranteed majority rule, it would still need ways for minorities to make themselves heard. For example, blacks in Montgomery could not use electoral politics to achieve their objectives. Representing only 37 percent of the city's population, African Americans lacked the votes to control city government through elections. More important, they were prevented from registering to vote by legal obstacles and outright intimidation. In 1952, only about one in five eligible blacks in the South was registered to vote.[9] Interest group politics was also not a viable option, because whites in Montgomery were unwilling to bargain or compromise; for them, segregation was an all-or-nothing matter.

Following normal political channels, therefore, Montgomery blacks had no chance of success. However, the boycott was a weapon they could use: By withdrawing their fares from the bus company, they could inflict fiscal pain. But it is unlikely that the boycott alone would have brought significant change. The only chance the blacks had was to appeal to a broader audience to put pressure on the entrenched white elite in Montgomery to alter the system of racial segregation. As King said in his speech calling for the boycott, the only weapon they had was the "weapon of protest."

Mass Movements in American History

American politics has been shaken repeatedly by mass movements. About once in a generation, waves of democratic participation, with strong leveling tendencies, sweep the country: the original revolutionary thrust of the 1770s; the Jacksonian era of the 1830s; the culmination of the antislavery movement in the 1850s; the Populist movement of the 1890s; the economic reform movements, including the labor movement, that rose out of the Great Depression of the 1930s; the environmental, feminist, and other social movements that began in the 1960s; and the Tea Party and Occupy Wall Street protests in the current period. Mass movements have probably played a greater role in American politics than in any other Western democracy. Issues that are represented by political parties in Europe are often expressed through protest movements in the United States.

Some mass movements in the United States, such as the nativist (anti-immigrant) movement and one of its offshoots, the Ku Klux Klan, have had antidemocratic goals of excluding certain groups from full citizenship. Today, protest movements against new rights for gays, immigrants, and minorities (e.g., affirmative action) have the same antidemocratic potential. Most mass movements, however, have been popular democratic in character, striving to include previously excluded groups (e.g., blacks, Hispanics, women, workers, students, gays, Native Americans, and the disabled) in the full benefits of democratic citizenship. In appealing to the American people, popular democratic mass movements have called on two deeply held sets of beliefs—one rooted in politics and the other in religion—that counter Americans' well-known individualism.

First, Americans share a set of core political beliefs in liberty, equality, democracy, and the rule of law. These beliefs are embodied in sacred political texts, including the Declaration of Independence ("all men are created equal"), the Constitution's Bill of Rights (freedom of speech and press), and Lincoln's Gettysburg Address ("government of the people, by the people, and for the people"). The language of rights has been a powerful tool in the hands of the disadvantaged. As Martin Luther King Jr. put it, our creed, expressed in the Declaration of Independence, manages "to forever challenge us; to forever give us a sense of urgency; to forever stand in the midst of the 'isness' of our terrible injustices; to remind us of the 'oughtness' of our noble capacity for justice and love and brotherhood."[10] Being able to tap into a wellspring of egalitarian political beliefs, popular democrats have historically had an ideological advantage over elite democrats.

Popular democratic mass movements have also been nurtured by American religious traditions stressing that everyone is equal in the eyes of God, that even the least of us should be treated with dignity and respect, and that morality is a force in the world. King's frequent use of the language of the Old Testament, comparing the liberation struggles of blacks to the struggles of the tribes of Israel to escape from exile in Egypt, is a brilliant example of the political relevance of religion in American politics. The abolitionist and temperance movements were also firmly rooted in religious traditions, as is the modern pro-life, anti-abortion movement, which has adopted many of the direct-action tactics of the civil rights movement.

Mass Movements: The Necessary Ingredients

Protest is a political resource that can be used by disadvantaged groups lacking traditional sources of political power, such as money or connections, to influence the system. However, protest cannot be used by any disadvantaged group at any time to level the playing field of democratic politics. All the necessary ingredients must be in place before a protest movement can come together and succeed. About half of the eligible voters don't even get to the polls for a presidential election every four years. Protest movements require much deeper levels of commitment than voting, as exemplified by the willingness of blacks in Montgomery to walk to work for thirteen months instead of taking the bus.

Protest movements engage the whole personalities of participants, transcending ordinary politics. And even when participants are engaged, remarkable leadership is necessary for movements to stay alive and achieve their goals. For protest movements even to get off the ground, five ingredients are necessary.

1. *Rising expectations.* History has shown that people will endure oppressive conditions for a long time without rebelling. People do not rebel when conditions are at their worst but when conditions have begun to improve and people begin to perceive a gap between the way things are and the way they could be. According to one theory, it is not deprivation itself that drives people to rebel but the feeling that one's group is being deprived of resources and opportunities available to other groups in the society. This is known as the theory of **relative deprivation**.[11]

   In the case of the civil rights movement, blacks had suffered under Jim Crow segregation laws since the nineteenth century, but resistance had been limited. One event that raised black expectations was World War II. Many African-American men died fighting fascism. Those who returned were less willing to accept second-class citizenship, especially after President Truman integrated the armed forces. Urbanization of blacks following the mechanization of southern agriculture also brought many African Americans into contact with new ideas and new opportunities that raised expectations. Most important, the 1954 Supreme Court decision in *Brown v. Board of Topeka* put the power and prestige of the Supreme Court behind the cause of integration. Black people felt they were not alone. As King proclaimed in his speech the night the black community decided to begin the boycott, "If we are wrong, the Supreme Court of this nation is wrong."

2. *Social resources.* Isolated individuals cannot build social movements. Social movements require networks that can spread the word and involve people in the movement.[12] Social movements need what Sara Evans and Harry Boyte call "free spaces"—organizations located between private families and large public organizations, where people can learn self-respect, cooperation, group identity, and the leadership skills necessary for democratic participation.[13] Black churches provided spaces for the civil rights movement that were free from white domination, where blacks could express their true feelings and develop confidence in their abilities. Most of the leadership of the civil rights movement came out of the black churches, where traditions of commitment to the congregation and skills in sermonizing nurtured effective leaders. The national organizations of black Baptist churches formed networks that helped the Southern Christian Leadership Conference (SCLC) spread the Montgomery model throughout the South.

   All protest movements in American history have been nurtured in free spaces. Building on earlier farmers' organizations like the Grange, the Populist movement of the late nineteenth century built a vast network of Farmers' Alliances that within a few years involved 2 million families. The purpose of the local alliances was to cooperatively market crops and purchase supplies, but they also created free spaces where people could learn the skills of democracy.[14]

   The feminist movement grew out of the free spaces created by the civil rights movement in the South and the anti–Vietnam War movement, which was organized mainly on college campuses. Ironically, it was discrimination in these supposedly egalitarian movements that drove women to form their own movement. In the civil rights movement, women, who performed much of the crucial behind-the-scenes work, developed confidence in their abilities and learned the skills of political organizing. At the same time, they were excluded from decision making and public leadership roles. When women in the Student Nonviolent Coordinating Committee (SNCC, known as "snick"), the radical student wing of the civil rights movement, raised the issue of sex roles, one of the leaders, Stokely Carmichael, is reported to have said that "the only position for women in SNCC is prone."[15] Such remarks caused many black women to examine gender, along with race, as a cause of discrimination.

3. *An appealing moral cause.* Mass movements in the United States fail unless they can appeal to fundamental American values. For example, animal rights activists have a moral cause, but they have been unable to make the transition to a mass movement because most Americans do not believe that animals deserve the same rights as human beings. The civil rights movement, on the other hand, had an appealing moral cause because the demand for equal rights resonated with all Americans. By wrapping itself in Christian values and the rhetoric of equal rights, the movement was nearly impossible to criticize as un-American. Later, when parts of the civil rights movement shifted from the rhetoric of equal rights to the rhetoric of black nationalism and black power, appealing more to African and Muslim traditions, white majority support for the movement swiftly eroded.

4. *Consciousness raising.* When the necessary ingredients are present for a mass movement, a sudden change of political consciousness occurs and people look at political facts differently. Soon after Rosa Parks was arrested, the leaders of Montgomery's black community called for a meeting to discuss what to do. They asked Martin Luther King Jr. to address the crowd. King had barely twenty minutes to prepare his speech. That night the Holt Street Baptist Church was jammed. Loudspeakers amplified the speeches to the crowd that spread over several acres outside. King began slowly, carefully describing the circumstances of the boycott, including the arrest of Rosa Parks, and praising her integrity and "Christian commitment." Then King paused and intoned in his resonant voice, "And you know, my friends, there comes a time when people get tired of being trampled over by the iron feet of oppression." As if releasing years of frustration, the crowd broke instantly into a flood of yeses, cheers, and applause.

Supported by civil rights leaders, Memphis sanitation workers marched for union recognition in 1968.

Getting to the heart of the matter—the justice of their cause—King continued: "If we are wrong, the Supreme Court of this nation is wrong. If we are wrong—God Almighty is wrong! And we are determined here in Montgomery," King went on quoting the words of an Old Testament prophet, "to work and fight until justice runs down like water, and righteousness like a mighty stream!" The crowd erupted in a release of pent-up emotion.

King's rhetoric seemed to lift the crowd onto a higher level of unity and resolve. Reflecting on the moment at the Holt Street Baptist Church after King's electrifying speech, when Montgomery's black community voted to continue the boycott, Ralph Abernathy described just such a change in consciousness: "The fear that had shackled us across the years—all left suddenly when we were in that church together."[16]

One of the most remarkable changes in consciousness occurred in the so-called "velvet revolutions" that swept across Eastern Europe in 1989. Before then, democratic social movements were violently repressed by Soviet troops and the secret police. In 1989, encouraged by Mikhail Gorbachev's reform leadership of the Soviet Union, the people of Eastern Europe became bolder in their opposition to Soviet domination. Once they realized that the troops would not fire on peaceful demonstrators, people began to mobilize in massive demonstrations. When the fear disappeared and citizens were able to gather together to feel their collective power, people suddenly realized they had the power to overturn communism and institute democratic regimes. Overnight, the Berlin Wall tumbled and communist regimes across Eastern Europe fell to democratic mass movements. That same year, however, a similar democratic social movement in Beijing's Tiananmen Square was brutally suppressed by Chinese troops.

5. *Transformational leadership.* The leaders of parties and interest groups are usually **transactional leaders**, who broker mutually beneficial exchanges between their followers and elites, such as votes for patronage jobs or campaign contributions for tax breaks. Mass movements, however, require **transforming leaders**, who engage the full personalities of followers, teaching them to go beyond self-interest and express their commitments in direct political action.[17] Martin Luther King Jr. was such a leader who challenged his followers to live up to their highest moral beliefs. Only twenty-six years old, King was articulate and intelligent, having just received a doctorate from Boston University. But according to some participants, he was chosen because, having lived in Montgomery for only a few months, he was completely independent—the white establishment had not yet "put their hand" on him.

Elizabeth Cady Stanton, the early leader of the women's suffrage movement, was also a transforming leader. In 1848, Stanton adapted the language of the Declaration of Independence to the cause of women's rights by writing the Declaration of Sentiments, a kind of bill of rights for women. By word and by example, Stanton encouraged women to step out of their assigned sphere of family and home and become actors in the public sphere of democratic politics. For more than fifty years she lectured, petitioned, organized, and wrote to encourage women to find their public voices.[18]

Protest Tactics: Walking a Fine Line

Although protest tactics can be a powerful political resource, if not properly handled they can explode like dynamite in the faces of those they are designed to help. By its very nature, protest politics is confrontational and tension producing; protesters deliberately provoke those in power to get a reaction from them. Protest leaders face a tactical dilemma: They must push confrontation far enough to satisfy the needs of the protesters for direct action and dramatize the issues to a broader public. If they push too far, however, they can alienate potential supporters or even create a backlash that strengthens their opponents.

Conflict has two benefits for protest movements: First, it mobilizes the protesters themselves; second, it captures the attention of bystanders who are moved to support the cause of the protesters. Saul Alinsky was a master practitioner and theoretician of protest politics. In the 1930s, he organized the Back of the Yards district of Chicago, an area made famous by Upton Sinclair's exposé of the meat-packing industry in his muckraking novel *The Jungle*. Alinsky understood the necessity of conflict if disadvantaged people were to gain power. "A PEOPLE'S ORGANIZATION is a conflict group," Alinsky wrote.[19] A good fight against a common enemy unifies an organization, heightens morale, and mobilizes energies.

Conflict also has the effect, especially if the protesters are viewed as underdogs, of drawing the broader public into the fray, putting pressure on the elites to negotiate. Protest is a form of political jujitsu; a movement with few political resources can use the strength of its opponent to its own advantage. In Montgomery, the indictment of eighty-nine African Americans, including twenty-five ministers, on trumped-up charges of conspiring to boycott brought national attention to the cause. The protesters celebrated the arrests because they knew the media would paint the white establishment as the aggressors and themselves as the underdogs. Later, SCLC orchestrated Project C—for "confrontation"—in Birmingham, Alabama. "Bull" Connor, Birmingham's commissioner of public safety, played his assigned role perfectly, using powerful fire hoses and vicious police dogs against defenseless children. As the media sent out pictures of police brutality, sympathy for the civil rights movement soared.

Protest tactics can backfire, however, if they go too far. A majority of Americans were opposed to the Vietnam War, but when they saw protesters burning the American flag and destroying property, most people sympathized with the government, not the protesters. Similarly, violence against abortion clinics and doctors did not help the pro-life, anti-abortion cause.

One method for coping with this tactical dilemma of how hard to push confrontation is civil disobedience, which can be defined as the deliberate violation of the law to dramatize a cause by activists who are willing to accept the punishment of the law. Civil disobedience is not an attempt to evade the law. An act of civil disobedience, such as being arrested while blocking the shipment of arms during the Vietnam War, is done completely in the open, without any violence, and with a sense of moral seriousness. Civil disobedience provides a middle ground between peaceful demonstrations (which are often ignored) and violent confrontations (which can cause a backlash).

The American tradition of civil disobedience can be traced back to Henry David Thoreau (1817–1862). Passionately opposed to slavery and to the Mexican War, which he saw as a fight for the slave masters, Thoreau refused to pay his poll taxes. As a result, he was thrown in prison. In 1849 Thoreau wrote a powerful essay, later titled "Civil Disobedience," in which he maintained that unjust laws should not be obeyed: "The only obligation which I have a right to assume is to do at any time what I think right."[20] Thoreau acted as an individual; he was not part of a mass movement. However, his writings inspired many leaders to incorporate civil disobedience into their movements.

Mohandas K. Gandhi (1869–1948) read Thoreau and incorporated his ideas about civil disobedience into his successful movement to free India from British rule. Gandhi believed that a careful campaign of civil disobedience could mobilize *satyagraha* (pronounced sa-TYA-gra-ha), or "truth force," to persuade opponents of the justice of a cause. Gandhi stressed that movements of civil disobedience must be willing to negotiate at all times, as long as basic principles are not sacrificed.

As a college student, Martin Luther King Jr. read Thoreau, and later he adapted the ideas of Gandhi to American conditions. King did not begin the Montgomery campaign with a planned strategy of nonviolent resistance. Drawn to nonviolence by his religious training, King reflected on the experiences of the civil rights movement and gradually developed a sophisticated philosophy of nonviolent resistance. King was able to adapt to new conditions and learn from the experiences of others. Dissatisfied with the slow progress being made under the leadership of King and the other ministers in SCLC, college students formed SNCC to push a more aggressive grassroots approach to the struggle. King later praised the student sit-ins at lunch counters across the South for having sought nonviolent confrontations with the segregation laws. His "Letter from Birmingham Jail," originally written in the margins of a newspaper and on scraps of toilet paper, has become a classic defense of nonviolent protest that is read the world over.

Mass movement leaders like King, often find it difficult to balance the needs of protesters, who demand more and more radical action to express their moral outrage, with the need to appeal for outside support, which usually requires moderation and patience. In the civil rights movement, young blacks became frustrated watching their brothers and sisters being beaten by racist police. In the mid-1960s, the civil rights movement split, with more radical blacks joining the "black power" movement under the leadership of the Black Panther Party for Self-Defense and the Black Muslims, led by the charismatic Malcolm X. The movement never recovered from the split. The issue of integration versus separatism, or black nationalism, divides the African American community to this day.

The Elite Response to Mass Movements

Notwithstanding repeated elite democratic warnings that mass movements threaten political order, elites have many resources for controlling mass movements. However, it takes as much leadership skill to deflate a mass movement as it does to build one. Political elites have two basic strategies: repression (forcibly attacking the movement) or co-optation (giving in to some of the demands). Political elites face a strategic dilemma that is similar to that faced by mass movements: If they give in too readily, they risk encouraging more militancy and more demands; on the other hand, if they refuse to give in at all and attack the protesters with force, they risk creating public sympathy for the protesters. Essentially, political elites engage in a complex game of chess with mass movements and their leaders.

The accessibility of American political institutions to interest groups has enabled the demands of mass movements to be incorporated into the system. In this way, mass movements are converted into interest groups. Meeting limited demands of protesters deflates the moral indignation of the movement and splits reformers from the radicals. If the white leadership in Montgomery had given in to the initial demands of the boycott to humanize the system of segregation on the buses, the effect would have been to deflate, or at the very least divide, the movement. By refusing to give an inch, the white leadership in Montgomery made a fatal tactical error. Their intransigence fueled the movement and caused the protesters to shift their goal from reforming segregation to ending it altogether.

Skillfully devised reforms, on the other hand, not only can divide the movement but also can draw parts of the leadership into the system to administer the new reforms. A good example is President Lyndon Johnson's War on Poverty, which was partly a response to the civil rights movement and the urban riots of the 1960s. The War on Poverty gave activists jobs in federal antipoverty programs, deflecting their energies away from organizing. Derisively called "poverty pimps," militant leaders were co-opted by federal money.[21] To a certain extent, democracies are supposed to operate this way—making concessions in the face of popular pressure. As we discussed in the previous chapter, mass movements

267

generated the pressure that enabled public interest groups to pass reform legislation in the 1960s and 1970s, including new laws on environmental protection, minority rights, and worker safety. Interest group politics, then, is a safety valve that can deflate mass movements.

In choosing a strategy of concessions or co-optation, those defending the status quo have an advantage: Time is on their side; mass movements cannot maintain a fever pitch of activism for long. Delay is one of the best weapons in the hands of elites. When a problem is brought to public awareness by a mass movement, those in power commonly appoint a commission to find a solution. This strategy gives the impression that something is being done without commitment to specific actions. By the time the commission's report comes out, the movement will have lost its momentum. Even if the report recommends new policies, there is no guarantee that they will be enacted. A good example is President Johnson's appointment of the Kerner Commission in 1967 to study the causes of the urban riots. The Kerner Commission recommended significant reforms, but few were ever enacted.[22]

Another tactic used by elites is *tokenism*, responding with insignificant reforms or symbolic gestures to create the impression that serious action is being taken to solve the problem. These symbolic gestures quiet the protesters, but few tangible benefits are delivered. Political scientist Murray Edelman called this "symbolic reassurance."[23] Appointing members of the aggrieved group—minorities, women, or gays, for example—to commissions or highly visible governmental posts is often used to create the impression of change. The leaders of student movements demanding radical changes in college curricula in the 1960s were often appointed to committees to study the problems and come up with solutions. The opportunity to serve on committees with professors and top administrators was flattering, but the effect was often to separate student leaders from the movement and ensnare them in a long process of negotiation. The key to the success of co-optation is calming the confrontational atmosphere that feeds mass movements long enough for protesters to lose interest. Once stalled, mass movements are difficult to restart.

When mass movements reach a certain momentum, the tactic of concessions loses its effectiveness and elites often turn to repression.[24] Just as protesters feel justified in using confrontation and sometimes even violence to promote their causes, elites sometimes feel justified in using repression when mass movements threaten their power or violate the law. The United States has a proud tradition of upholding the civil rights of dissenters, but as Chapter 16 shows, when elites have felt threatened by mass movements they often have resorted to repression. American labor history is especially violent. Governments frequently intervened on the side of owners. In 1877, 60,000 National Guardsmen were mobilized across ten states to defeat the first national railroad strike. In the Pullman strike of 1894, President Grover Cleveland, at the request of the railroads, called in federal troops, who, along with municipal police, put down the strike by railroad workers at a cost of thirty-four deaths and millions of dollars of property damage. Fearing further protests Congress rushed through a law, signed by President Cleveland, establishing Labor Day as a national holiday.

The Democratic Debate over Protest Politics

As the name suggests, mass movements involve large numbers of ordinary citizens in direct political actions. The protest tactics used by mass movements are disruptive and confrontational. Therefore, it is not surprising that mass movements and their protest tactics have been the subjects of heated controversy between elite and popular democrats.

The Elite Democratic Criticism of Mass Movements

From the time of Shay's Rebellion, before the Constitution was written, to the violent demonstrations against globalization, elite democrats have always been suspicious of mass movements. Their attitude is reflected in Alexander Hamilton's statement: "The People! The People is a great beast!"[25] The direct involvement of the masses in political action is dangerous, according to elite democrats, because mass movements can quickly degenerate into lawless mobs that threaten stable democracy. It is safer for political passions to be filtered through representative institutions, where elites can deliberate on the long-term interest of the country as a whole.[26]

Elite democrats maintain that the goals of mass movements in American history have often been utopian and impractical. Critics of those who protested Bush's invasion of Iraq charge that the protesters were naive; they didn't understand that the UN is powerless and the United States must engage in preemptive war to kill the terrorists before they kill us. The Populist movement at the turn of the nineteenth century was attacked as an emotional reaction to progress and industrialization, an ill-fated attempt to hold on to a doomed agrarian way of life. (The contemporary environmental movement has been attacked on similar grounds.) According to elite democrats, mass movements lack concrete programs for reform that can benefit the people; instead, they seek moral or ideological goals that are impractical and threaten to overwhelm democratic institutions. Lacking practical reforms, mass movements traffic in moral absolutes.[27]

Elite democrats criticize not only the goals of mass movements but also their tactics. In stable democracies, participation is channeled through electoral politics and interest group bargaining. Protest politics brings masses of people into direct participation through confrontational tactics that threaten to divide society into warring camps, elite democrats warn, and undermine the norms of tolerance and civility essential to a healthy democracy. Mass movements are not expressions of people's natural desire to participate in politics. Instead, people are enticed into mass movements by demagogues who manipulate emotions, whipping up resentment against the wealthy and the privileged.

Elite democrats charge that protest tactics are basically used to blackmail society. The protesters threaten chaos if their demands are not met. In the 1960s, elite democrats charge, protest tactics began to be used by any group that wanted to "shake more benefits from the government money tree." In a biting essay satirizing the 1960s, titled "Mau-Mauing the Flak Catchers," Tom Wolfe described how protest tactics had gotten out of hand:

> Going downtown to mau-mau the bureaucrats got to be routine practice in San Francisco. . . . They sat back and waited for you to come rolling in with your certified angry militants, your guaranteed frustrated ghetto youth, looking like a bunch of wild men. Then you had your test confrontation. If you were outrageous enough, if you could shake up the bureaucrats so bad that their eyes froze into iceballs and their mouths twisted up into smiles of sheer physical panic, into shit-eating grins, so to speak—then they knew you were the real goods. They knew you were the right studs to give the poverty grants and community organizing jobs to.[28]

Social movements sometimes encourage minorities—from blacks to women, from Native Americans to gays, from students to the disabled—to demand their "rights" with little concern for the general welfare of society.

The Popular Democratic Defense of Mass Movements

The attitude of popular democrats toward mass movements is reflected in a statement by Thomas Jefferson. Remarking on Shay's Rebellion, which Federalists viewed as a sign of impending anarchy, Jefferson wrote to James Madison: "I hold it that a little rebellion now and then is a good thing, and as necessary in the political world as storms in the physical."[29] After all, popular democrats note, the country was born in protest. The Boston Tea Party was an illegal destruction of property intended to dramatize the colonists' opposition to British rule, in particular, "taxation without representation."

Although popular democrats acknowledge excesses in social protest movements, they argue that, overall, direct participation by citizens in protests has strengthened American democracy rather than weakened it. Whenever long-suppressed issues are finally addressed by a political system, conflict is bound to result. Conflict is inevitable in a democracy—and healthy. The main threat to democracy comes not from a "democratic distemper"—ordinary people demanding their rights—but from an "elite distemper": elites, fearful of losing their powers and privileges, reacting to protesters with repression and violence.[30]

Ironically, the civil rights movement, which was committed to nonviolence and democratic rights, had its civil liberties repeatedly violated by the government in an attempt to discredit it, and especially its charismatic leader, Martin Luther King Jr. The Federal Bureau of Investigation (FBI) secretly planted newspaper articles alleging that the movement was manipulated by communists. Convincing evidence for this charge has never been made public. Under the direction of FBI chief J. Edgar Hoover, the FBI treated King as an enemy, employing a campaign of character assassination using wiretaps of King's phone conversations. The FBI fed information on King's sex life and the plans of the civil rights movement to the Kennedy administration, helping it to resist pressures for racial change.[31] The FBI sent King a tape of his extramarital encounters, threatening to make them public if he did not commit suicide.[32]

Perhaps the most serious charge against protest movements is that they don't accomplish anything; they simply stir people up and create conflict. Popular democrats maintain that protest movements have not been mere expressions of emotion; they have been the driving force behind reforms that made this country more egalitarian and democratic, including abolishing slavery, winning the vote for women and blacks, and regulating corporations. Pursuing normal channels of electoral and interest group politics, many groups find it difficult even to get their issues onto the agenda for discussion. Protest movements have succeeded in putting previously ignored issues, like equal rights for African Americans, onto the political agenda.

Measuring the effectiveness of protest movements is difficult because their effects are often hidden and indirect. As we noted in the previous chapter, new issues represented by public interest groups never would have made it onto the agenda of interest group politics without the threat of mass protests to goad the system into action. Protest movements have "ripple effects" that extend beyond the initial splash to affect the entire society. These ripple effects include changes in culture and the way we perceive issues.

In the controversy over protest politics, we often lose sight of the wide range of reforms enacted by mass movements. A few of their accomplishments follow.

1. *The civil rights movement.* The civil rights movement began the long process of integrating African Americans into the democratic process. Largely as a result of changes in voting laws, the number of African American elected officials in the United States increased from 1,469 in 1970 to 9,430 in 2002 (see Figure 11.2). Barack Obama would never have been elected president of the United States in 2008 (and 2012) without the civil rights movement. Critics often point out that U.S. race relations are still highly problematic. However, consider what race relations would be like if African Americans were still being denied basic civil rights like the right to vote.

2. *The environmental movement.* As a result of the environmental movement, large construction projects must now issue environmental impact statements (EISs), giving the public a chance to comment. Substantial progress has also been made in cleaning up the nation's polluted waters, with aquatic life returning to many bodies of water, and in communities across the nation, recycling programs are saving energy and reducing the volume of solid waste.

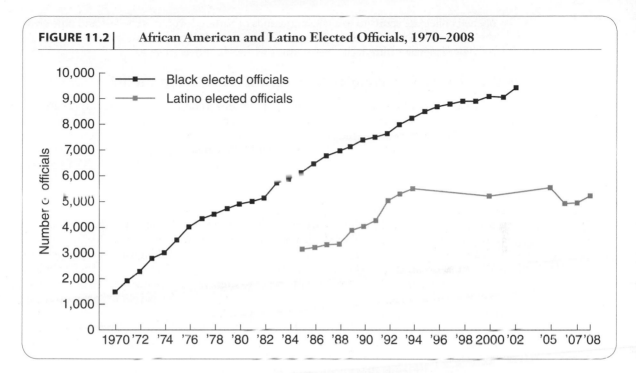

FIGURE 11.2 | African American and Latino Elected Officials, 1970–2008

Note: Official government data on African American elected officials have not been collected since 2002.

Source: U.S. Bureau of the Census, *Statistical Abstract of the United States: 2012* (Washington, D.C.: U.S. Government Printing Office, 2012); http://www.census.gov/compendia/statab/2012/tables/12s0421.pdf.

3. *The neighborhood organizing movement.* Sometimes lying down in front of bulldozers, neighborhood protestors stopped highway engineers and urban renewal planners from ramming their projects through low-income and minority neighborhoods and forcing residents out of their homes. Many cities in the country have now decentralized policy-making authority to neighborhood governments, expanding the scope of democratic participation.[33]

4. *The antinuclear movement.* The antinuclear movement succeeded in pushing the regulatory agencies to fully consider the dangers of nuclear power plants. As a result, few new nuclear power plants are constructed in the United States anymore. The chances of a Chernobyl-type disaster are low, and alternatives to nuclear energy, including solar energy and conservation, are being pursued more vigorously.

5. *The gay rights movement.* As a result of years of protests, many state and local governments have passed laws protecting the rights of gays and lesbians, freeing them from employment discrimination and giving them the right to adopt children. Gay couples have acquired many of the rights of heterosexuals in civil unions, and as of January 2013, nine states and the District of Columbia have recognized gay marriage.

6. *The feminist movement.* Probably the most influential of all, the feminist movement transformed American society, opening opportunities for women that were previously unthinkable. As a result, there are now many more women doctors and lawyers, as well as mail carriers, construction workers, professional basketball players, and movie directors. Women's wages have steadily gained relative to men. Title IX of the 1972 Higher Education Act

opened collegiate sports to women. Thousands of battered-women's shelters and rape crisis shelters have opened in communities across the country. The feminist movement even altered our language, introducing new terms such as *Ms.* and *chairperson*.

Is the Tea Party a Popular Democratic Mass Movement?

The Tea Party has all the signs of a genuine popular democratic mass movement: A national face-to-face network of grassroots activists using direct action to dramatize their cause, the Tea Party aims to "take back" the country from government elites and return it to founding principles rooted in the American Revolution and U.S. Constitution. While the processes of civic engagement that marked the rise of the Tea Party followed the classic lines of popular democratic mass movements, over time the movement has been partially co-opted by the right-wing of the Republican Party and super-wealthy patrons. More troubling, some goals of the movement, if achieved, would undermine popular democracy. Despite outward appearances, the Tea Party is very different from the democratic mass movements that have struggled over the years to make American democracy more egalitarian and inclusive.[34]

The Tea Party can trace its roots to a "rant" delivered by CNBC business reporter, Rick Santelli, on February 19, 2009 from the floor of the Chicago Board of Trade. Angry about a federal bailout program that would provide relief to homeowners facing foreclosure, Santelli charged that such a program would use funds from hardworking taxpayers to "promot[e] bad behavior" and "subsidize the losers' mortgages." Raising his arms Santelli shouted: "How many of you want to pay for your neighbor's mortgage that has an extra bathroom and can't pay their bills?" Connecting his grievances to Benjamin Franklin and Thomas Jefferson, Santelli called for a Chicago Tea Party to protest the injustices.

Coming one month after Obama took office, the Tea Party symbolism was immediately seized upon as rhetorical gold by conservative forces who were alarmed by what the Democratic Party could do with its newly won control of the presidency and Congress. Overnight,

272

websites were calling for Tea Party protests, and eight days later activists coordinated protests in forty cities across the country. Grassroots Tea Party groups began forming around the nation. Right-wing television and radio broadcasts played a key role in providing publicity to the movement, but it was not long before mainstream media were portraying it as a major new development in American politics. The "Don't Tread On Me" flag of the early American Revolution became a favorite patriotic symbol at rallies that featured handmade signs mocking Obama and individuals dressed up as patriots from the time of the American Revolution.

What is most impressive about the Tea Party is the way that activists began almost immediately to organize themselves into local groups to educate and activate citizens to their cause. By the spring of 2011, about 800 active local Tea Party groups had sprung up across the nation.[35] Local groups set their own agendas, created websites, invited in national speakers, and formed committees to delve deeper into the issues. In the best tradition of popular democracy, they began to teach each other about how to influence the political process and hold politicians accountable.

Tea Party activists represent a slice of the American public who feel threatened by social and political change. They are more likely to be men than women and tend to be older, whiter, and more economically comfortable than average. They are also overwhelmingly Republican and right-wing. Motivated by a fear that hard work is no longer being rewarded in America, Tea Party advocates believe that government is redistributing rewards to the undeserving. They are not against all government programs. They generally feel that hardworking, older Americans deserve the government benefits they receive from Social Security and Medicare. Young people, on the other hand, are viewed as having lost the work ethic and prone to think they are entitled to government programs paid for by others. Young people are viewed as part of a general societal decline characterized by bad behavior and loose morals. Tea Partiers tend to be anti-immigrant and, even though they shun overt racism, Tea Party activists tend to view minorities, like young people, as prone to government dependency and moral decline. Underlying nearly all Tea Party positions is the belief that big government is eroding the freedom and sturdy self-reliance that once characterized American society.

The Tea Party is not a single organization that speaks with one voice. It is a loose collection of conservative activists with diverse and, in some cases, contradictory beliefs. One of the key tensions is between social conservatives, who want more government intervention to enforce moral behavior (such as banning abortion) and libertarians, who want the government to get out of people's lives. The movement has been generally successful at managing these tensions—primarily because Tea Party adherents are united against a common enemy. What unites Tea Partiers is a fear that they are losing control of the country they love. The election of Barack Hussein Obama, the first African American president, crystallized the fear that America is changing into a diverse society, increasingly dominated by strangers who do not share patriotic American values.[36] It is no accident that the Tea Party emerged one month after Obama took office.

The Tea Party began as a spontaneous grassroots movement, not controlled by the Republican Party or wealthy elites. Over time, however, politicians and wealthy elites have used the Tea Party grassroots network to promote their own careers and policy agendas. Americans for Prosperity (AFP), for example, a Washington-headquartered right-wing organization that has received millions of dollars from the petrochemical billionaire Koch brothers, was able with the help of the Tea Party to expand its contact lists from about 270,000 in 2008 to 1.5 million in 2011. Tea Party activists have never formally endorsed the AFP agenda but the AFP has employed the network to further its agenda. The way elite interests have been able to leverage Tea Party networks to their own advantage raises questions about the grassroots character of the movement. As two political scientists put it: "What kind of mass rebellion is funded by corporate billionaires, like the Koch brothers, led by over-the-hill former GOP kingpins like Dick Armey, and ceaselessly promoted by millionaire media celebrities like Glenn Beck and Sean Hannity?"[37]

One of the weaknesses of the Tea Party is that it does not have democratic processes for holding national leaders accountable. Unlike many national movements, there is no federated structure in which local chapters elect representatives to state organizations, which in turn send representatives to run the national organization. Like most mass movement activists, Tea Partiers are suspicious of formal rules and representative structures. As a loose collection of local organizations, however, the Tea Party is vulnerable to self-appointed national leaders who may not represent the people at the grassroots. Michele Bachmann, Republican Representative from Minnesota, became a national spokesperson for the movement by appointing herself chair of the House "Tea Party Caucus." Given her failure in the Republican presidential primaries, however, it is unlikely that the masses of Tea Party activists would have chosen her.

The most troubling aspect of the Tea Party is not its decision making processes; all mass movements grapple with the tension of how to remain true to their grassroots and still influence elections and policy making. From the viewpoint of popular democracy, the problem with the Tea Party is that many of its goals would shrink the space for democratic decision making. Paradoxically, the Tea Party is a populist, grassroots movement with fundamentally undemocratic goals. Fundamentally, it promotes intolerance toward people who are different from white, middle-class Americans. Tea Partiers are hostile to immigrants and Muslims and would restrict their rights. The Tea Party is also on record as opposing the rights of unions. In Chapter 4, we noted that unions are one of the few checks against corporate power.

The core ideology of the Tea Party is "market populism," the idea that free markets represent the epitome of freedom and democracy. Clearly, the market does represent an important sphere of freedom, which is epitomized by millions of small businesses and wide consumer choice in many markets. Protecting business and consumers from undue government interference is essential in our democracy. But as we saw in Chapter 4 on political economy, big corporations have achieved unchecked power in many areas of the economy. The Tea Party program of radical deregulation would result in more abuse of power by private actors, like the predatory mortgages that banks pushed, leading to the financial meltdown of 2008 that the American public is still paying for. Unregulated corporations would be able to use their expanded profits to further corrupt the political process. Finally, Tea Party proposals to further cut taxes on the wealthy and slash spending on the poor will increase economic inequality—perhaps the greatest threat to popular democracy in the present period.

Conclusion: The Future of Protest Politics

Some argue that protest today has become almost a routine part of American politics and that protesters are more concerned with venting their anger than with achieving democratic reforms. Instead of enhancing politics, protest has become a substitute for politics.[38] We disagree.

Protest politics provides three important benefits for American democracy. First, on those rare occasions when the proper ingredients come together, mass movements can level the playing field of American politics, offering a way for minorities and the politically disenfranchised to acquire influence. Second, protest movements provide a way to overcome the inertia created by the elaborate system of checks and balances established by the Constitution, enabling political outsiders, especially those with broad political or moral concerns, to get their issues on the agenda. Finally, participation in protest activity creates better citizens. Research shows that compared to nonprotesters, activists who participated in the social movements of the 1960s later participated more in politics, exhibited greater degrees of tolerance, and retained a passionate commitment to their ideals (even those who acquired fortunes).[39]

Notwithstanding the many benefits of protest politics, however, lines must be drawn around it. There is some truth to the elite democratic critique that giving protesters complete freedom to disrupt people's lives and to engage in civil disobedience without punishment would enable minorities to dictate terms to society. Violent protesters who injure other people should be swiftly punished. On the other hand, to outlaw nonviolent boycotts, strikes, pickets, and marches and to severely punish civil disobedience would stifle protest politics altogether. Recognizing this, the courts have given special protection to political speech designed to influence public opinion. We believe that if society errs in any direction, it should err in the direction of tolerating more protest activity.

Beyond the courts, the best protection from the destructive effects of protest politics should come from the protesters themselves. Protests should never be carried out simply to vent emotions or shake people up; the purpose should be to enter into negotiations with the powers that be to institute significant reforms. As a well-known book on black political advancement in California cities, *Protest Is Not Enough*, argued, the goal of protests should be to reform the basic institutions of democratic governance so that they can respond to the deeply felt issues of every group in the population. Until that time, however, protest politics will be necessary to keep the participatory promise of American democracy alive.

Reader's Guide ★ ★ ★

Critical Thinking Questions

1. Think of a political reform or goal you support. How far would you be willing to go with protest tactics to achieve that goal: writing a letter to your congressional representative, attending a demonstration, being arrested by joining in an act of civil disobedience?

2. Why are students today less inclined to participate in protest politics than students in the 1960s?

3. Where should the government draw the line on protest politics? For example, should abortion protesters have the right to block access to an abortion clinic or should protesters be able to shout down a speaker on a college campus who denies the reality of the Holocaust? If not, what punishments should the government mete out for these activities?

Key Word Definition

protest politics   Political actions designed to broaden conflicts and activate outside parties to pressure the bargaining process in ways favorable to the protesters.

mass movement   The participation of large numbers of previously passive bystanders in a political protest action.

civil disobedience   The deliberate violation of the law by persons willing to accept the law's punishment in order to dramatize a cause.

relative deprivation   The theory that people mobilize politically not when they are worst off, but when they perceive that they are deprived unjustly, relative to other groups in the population.

transactional leader   A party or interest group leader whose leadership is based on brokering beneficial exchanges with followers, such as patronage jobs for votes.

transforming leader   A mass movement leader who engages the full personalities of followers, helping them to go beyond self-interest and participate in direct political action.

satyagraha   "Truth force," or the belief of the Indian pacifist Mohandas K. Gandhi that a carefully orchestrated civil disobedience plan can persuade one's opponents of the justice of one's cause.

12

Congress: A Vehicle for Popular Democracy?

THE INDIVIDUALISTIC CONGRESS

REVOLUTION IN CONGRESS

THE PARTISAN CONGRESS

CONGRESS AND THE EXECUTIVE

CONCLUSION

Congress has often been called "the people's branch" of the federal government. It is the only one of the three branches directly elected by the people, and its members are more accessible to ordinary citizens than are the executive or the judiciary. Yet the people are not very happy with "their" branch these days. Recent polls show Congress hitting record lows in public approval. In a December 2011 Gallup Poll, only 11% of Americans approved of Congress's performance, while 86 percent disapproved.[1] In an era in which Republicans and Democrats agree on very little, their partisans share scorn for Congress.

As the most representative branch of American national government, Congress might be expected to speak for the concerns, grievances, and interests of popular democracy. Yet as we saw in previous chapters, the active and assertive citizenry that might bring out Congress's popular democratic potential is undermined by many contemporary developments. With a mass media dominated by corporate interests and official sources, with parties weak at the grassroots level, and with "democracy for hire" by wealthy interest groups while a majority of eligible voters fail to turn out for congressional elections, the forces to which Congress responds are as likely to represent elite democracy as popular democracy.

The democratic character of Congress has, in fact, always been a matter for controversy. The Federalists designed the House to be more democratic and the Senate more elitist but hoped that representatives in both houses would be superior men who would filter out the people's passions and promote their true welfare. The Anti-federalists worried that legislators of this elite stripe would become arrogant and corrupt and argued for representatives who would closely resemble ordinary people. Some of the Federalists' and Anti-federalists' hopes have been realized—and some of their fears as well. Present-day Congress is a volatile mixture of elite and popular democracy.

Elite democracy, as the Federalists hoped, is reflected in a membership of well-educated political professionals whose lengthy careers produce expertise in the various fields of public policy. Elite democracy, as the Anti-federalists warned, is reflected in a membership whose continuance in office is financed by economic elites and rewarded with aristocratic "perks" of high office. Yet Congress still remains open to the pressure of popular democracy. With members of the House facing reelection every two years and senators facing the voters every six years (as a result of the Seventeenth Amendment, adopted in 1913), representatives need to stay in close touch with their constituents if they hope to enjoy a career in Congress.

The Individualistic Congress

Congress has some permanent elements, based in the Constitution, and some near-permanent features, such as the committee system, that go back to the nineteenth century. But much of the landscape of Congress, as unchanging as it may appear to frustrated reformers, is periodically reshaped by socioeconomic, political, and institutional tides.

Above all, Congress is susceptible to partisan forces. For four decades prior to 1995, the Democratic Party had majorities in the House and the Senate. Under Democratic rule, scholars studying the institution perceived an *individualistic Congress*. But a dramatic uprising by Republicans took over the national legislature in 1995, and under Republican rule the institution was best characterized as a *partisan Congress*. Although the Democrats regained congressional majorities in both houses of Congress between 2007 and 2011, with the Republicans recapturing the House majority in the 2010 elections, partisanship remains the dominant feature of legislative politics today.

To gain an understanding of the profound transformations that Congress has undergone in recent years, it is important to begin by looking at how Congress worked before the Republican revolution of 1995. Four factors, in *descending order of importance*, appeared to be important in the era of the individualistic Congress:

1. Individual members and their districts
2. Committees
3. Parties
4. Leadership

As we will see, the Republican revolutionaries of 1995 attempted nothing less than a reversal of this order.

Individual Members and Their Districts

Most political scientists' explanations of congressional behavior before 1995 placed the individual members first in importance. Individual members were extensively involved in a permanent quest for reelection that oriented them toward the interests of their own districts or states. Their voting behavior and non-legislative activities were designed to secure individual success by pleasing the electorate back home.[2] The decentralized structures of Congress also encouraged individualism, with members promoting their favorite policy ideas in entrepreneurial fashion. (We use the past tense to describe activities before 1995, but some of the features of Congress discussed in this section persist.)

Getting Elected. At the heart of congressional individualism was the electoral process. In earlier eras of American politics, the parties played a major role in recruiting congressional candidates, financing their campaigns, and mobilizing voters on their behalf. But in an era of party decline, the typical congressional candidate was self-selected. Successful candidates usually shared certain characteristics: First, they were experienced public officials, having gained visibility and stature in such offices as mayors, district attorneys, or state legislators. Second, they were ambitious—running for Congress requires an ego strong enough to overcome attacks and insults and to compensate for loss of privacy, family time, and more lucrative career opportunities. Third, they were willing to work hard—a congressional race required physical and emotional energy.

Even individuals possessing all of these qualifications faced one daunting barrier: **incumbents** were almost always reelected in House elections, and in Senate elections challengers had only a slightly better chance. Unless there was an open seat (the incumbent has retired or died), the odds against the aspiring candidate winning a congressional race would scare off all but the boldest political gamblers. In the House, incumbents regularly won over 90 percent of the contests. Sometimes, incumbent reelection rates ran as high as 98 percent. Senate incumbents were often nearly as successful. The aspiring candidate had a greater chance to win at a moment of political turmoil, when incumbents were more vulnerable.[3]

Why did incumbents do so well and challengers so poorly? Many factors favored the incumbent, especially money. With years in office to stockpile campaign funds, the incumbent generally had an enormous head start in fundraising. Special interests and business political action committees (PACs) seeking access to legislators (and assuming that those in office were good bets to be reelected) contributed primarily to incumbents. As a result, the typical incumbent had a huge advantage over the typical challenger in campaign funds.

Since even fundraising advantages could not guarantee reelection, members of Congress voted themselves further resources to keep their offices. Through the **franking privilege,** they sent mass mailings to constituents without having to pay postage. For example, newsletters publicized their accomplishments and often asked constituents to express their views on major national issues, portraying incumbents skilled in the ways of Washington yet open to the sentiments of the folks back home. Through generous travel allowances, members returned to their districts often, attending group meetings, mingling at ceremonial events, and making their faces as familiar as possible. Benefiting from the growth of personal staff, members could assign staffers in their district offices to help constituents facing problems with federal agencies, a practice known as **casework**. Casework earned the gratitude of individual voters and enhanced the incumbents' reputations among their family and friends.

All of these advantages made it more likely that on Election Day the voters would recall the names of incumbents while not knowing the people challenging them. Such advantages in fact tended to scare off the kind of politically experienced challengers who might give incumbents a difficult race.

Why was incumbency somewhat less powerful in the Senate than in the House? As a more prestigious institution (and with only two positions per state), the Senate draws more prominent individuals into challenges to incumbents. Such individuals have a better chance of raising the funds to conduct a serious campaign. Statewide constituencies reduce incumbents' opportunities to mingle with them while necessitating more reliance on mass media, through which well-financed challengers can hope to match incumbents in name recognition. Finally, senators' positions on controversial national issues are more visible to their constituents, leading to greater vulnerability should the incumbent have taken unpopular stands.

The Individualistic Legislator. Legislators who held their positions through their own extensive efforts could not be dictated to by party leaders or presidents. Individualistic motives and practices prevailed in legislative behavior prior to 1995. For example, in deciding how to cast their votes on legislation, members thought first about their own constituents: could they explain controversial votes to the folks back home? If signals from constituents were weak or divided, members felt free to vote their own policy preferences.[4]

Reforms adopted by House Democrats in the early 1970s also fostered congressional individualism (although this was not the goal of the reforms). With power more widely dispersed under these reforms, even junior legislators became *policy entrepreneurs*, pushing their own individual policy preferences rather than uniting behind a common party program. Skilled at winning reelection, and savvy about capturing media attention, a new generation in Congress competed to see whose ideas could win majority support. Entrepreneurship was even more rampant in the Senate, where a fluid structure encouraged legislators to go their own ways.[5]

Compared to the Congress of the 1950s and 1960s, where a small corps of conservative chairs ruled in hierarchical fashion, the individualistic Congress of the 1970s to early 1990s appeared more egalitarian and open to new ideas. Yet there was a price to be paid for this individualism: behavior that served the rational self-interest of the members was often harmful to Congress as an institution and to the collective welfare of the American people. A decentralized Congress, fragmented along individual lines, frequently frustrated the popular democratic desire to see majority will at the polls translated into majority rule in the legislature.[6]

Congressional Committees

Second in importance to individual members and their districts in Congress before 1995 was the **committee system**—the system whereby most of the work of Congress is done by smaller groups. There are several kinds of committees in the House and the Senate. *Standing committees*, the most important, are permanent bodies that perform the bulk of the work. They gather information through investigations and hearings, draft legislation (this is called the *markup*), and report it to their parent chambers for a potential vote. The majority of bills proposed by individual members of Congress never get past the standing committee that considers them; these committees thus have great negative power. *Conference committees* meet to reconcile differences when the House and Senate pass alternative versions of the same law. Composed of the members from each chamber of Congress who have been the central actors on the bill in question, they produce the final language of the law. Congress also creates *select committees* for short-term investigations and contains a few *joint committees*, with members from both houses, for the purpose of gathering information.

Because much of an individual member's legislative life is spent in committee work, obtaining an assignment to a standing committee is a matter of great importance. Party committees in each house attempt to place members in accordance with their wishes. In the Senate, with its smaller numbers, every member is assured a spot on one of the most prestigious committees. In the House, however, there is often intense competition for places on the Appropriations, Ways and Means, and Budget committees. Some legislators are less concerned about winning a spot on one of these powerful committees than on joining a committee that deals with a subject crucial to their constituents. For example, representatives and senators from farm states gravitate toward the agriculture committees.

Once a member has joined a committee, the usual pattern is to remain there, developing expertise and, even more important, **seniority**. Before the Republican revolution of 1995, seniority was crucial to gaining a leadership position. Under the congressional seniority system, the member from the majority party who had the most years of continuous service on a committee became its chair. Reforms initiated by the House Democrats in the early 1970s allowed for occasional breaches in the seniority system to make committee chairs more responsive to the majority of the party, yet seniority still determined committee leadership in all but a handful of cases.

Although the committee system had long been central to the organization and functioning of Congress, its character changed somewhat in the two decades before the Republican revolution of 1995. One important trend affecting the system was the growth in committee staff. As the regular workload of committees increased—and as committee leaders sought to gain media attention by initiating new and innovative legislation—large numbers of staff aides were hired. Legislators turned over so much of their work to their staffs that one congressional scholar, Michael Malbin, dubbed these staffs our "unelected representatives."[7]

A second trend affecting committees involved subcommittees—smaller and more specialized units of the parent committee. Although greater reliance on subcommittees, like greater reliance on staff, reflected Congress's expanded workload, the real impetus to the rise of subcommittees came during a wave of congressional reform in the early 1970s. The Democrats in the House strengthened subcommittees at the expense of committees for two reasons: to diminish the power of committee chairs and to allow newer representatives to claim a piece of the legislative "pie." When important legislative provisions were drafted and discussed in subcommittees, it was often the case that only a handful of legislators played any active part.[8]

Through division of labor and specialization, the system of committees and subcommittees provided Congress with *expertise*. Faced with myriad subjects to consider, members of Congress looked for guidance to the experts on its committees and subcommittees, particularly their chairs. Committee expertise was critical in legislative-executive relations as well; without it, Congress would not stand much of a chance in conflicts with policy experts working for the president. The expertise found among longtime members of committees is important evidence for the elite democratic claim that elites bring greater expertise to the art of governance.

Although the committee system divided the congressional workload and fostered expertise, it also created some of Congress's most enduring problems. One is a classic problem of elite democracy: greater expertise is fostered, but this expertise is self-serving. Legislators often join a particular committee because they wish to serve interest groups that are important in their home districts or states. These legislators form alliances with the major interest groups and executive agencies with which their committees interact.

In the **iron triangles** that result, interest groups testify before the committee in favor of existing and potential programs that benefit them. Committee members support such programs in the bills they draft—and gain political support and campaign contributions from the interest groups. The agencies, with their missions and budgets supported by interest group and committee, implement the programs in a way that pleases the interest group and the committee (see Figure 12.1). In recent years, many iron triangles have become less rigid, with outside policy experts, public interest groups, and the press having more input. Some scholars believe that looser *issue networks* with shifting participants are now more common than the

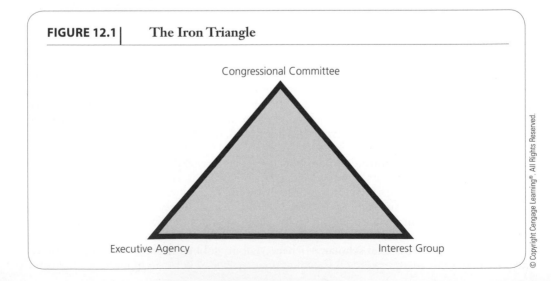

FIGURE 12.1 | **The Iron Triangle**

Congressional Committee

Executive Agency

Interest Group

FIGURE 12.2 | **How a Bill Becomes a Law**

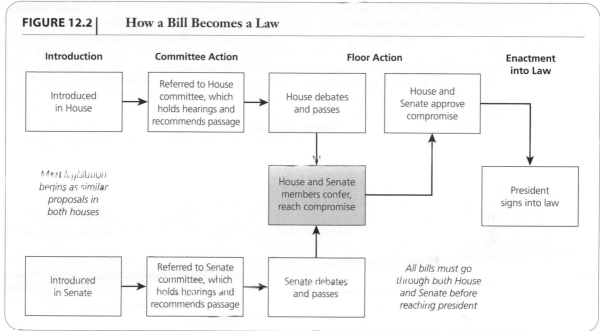

old triangular alliances. Yet the narrowly focused expertise that shapes the work of congressional committees and subcommittees remains for the most part the expertise of those whose interests are at stake.

The committee system also tended, like congressional individualism, to make collective action difficult. The more expert and powerful committee chairs were, the more they tended to push their own agendas, even if these agendas conflicted with the objectives of their party and its leaders. Moreover, Congress had few mechanisms to relate or compare the bills produced by its various committees, resulting in inconsistent legislation. (For an overview of how a bill becomes a law, see Figure 12.2.)

Parties in Congress

Third in importance in shaping congressional action before the revolution were the political parties. Independents are occasionally elected to Congress (an independent socialist, Senator Bernard Sanders of Vermont, sits in the 113th Congress), but almost all members belong to one of the two major parties. Party is the vehicle through which the House and Senate are organized. Seats on committees and committee leadership are determined on the basis of party. Party gatherings—called *caucuses* by the House Democrats, and *conferences* by the House Republicans and both parties in the Senate—choose leaders to run their institutions and sometimes set broad policy directions as well.

Traditionally, congressional parties were weak, at least when compared to the strong, disciplined parties found in most parliamentary democracies around the world. If legislators gained and retained their offices through their own efforts rather than through their parties, they were going to place the task of pleasing their constituents ahead of the task of cooperating with fellow partisans. Party weakness also stemmed from the ideological diversity characteristic of America's major parties. A Republican Party divided between moderates, pragmatic conservatives, and far-right conservatives, and a Democratic Party split between northern liberals and southern conservatives, had a hard time finding common party ground.

Beginning in the 1980s, however, the parties in Congress grew more cohesive and unified. Measures of party unity in voting (which indicate how frequently members of the same party vote together) showed increases in both parties and both chambers. The most dramatic change came in the partisan behavior of southern Democrats, who had often voted with Republicans in the past. In 1972, the party unity score for southern Democrats in the House was 44 percent; by 1992, this score had risen to 79 percent.[9]

Why did partisan unity increase if parties had traditionally been weak and were then on the decline among the electorate? Several factors came together to spark a resurgence of parties in Congress. Among the Democrats, a key factor was the shrinking ideological difference between northern and southern members. After passage of the Voting Rights Act of 1965, southern Democrats gained large numbers of African American supporters at the same time that they were losing many white conservatives to the Republicans; as their electoral base came to resemble that of northern Democrats, so did their voting behavior. Among the Republicans, the electoral successes of Ronald Reagan made the party more conservative; ideological diversity within the party diminished.

The two legislative parties represented distinct coalitions of ideology and interests, and to understand Congress before the revolution of 1995, it is important to understand the ideology and interests represented by the majority party, the Democrats. Reflecting their heritage as the party of Franklin Roosevelt's New Deal and Lyndon Johnson's Great Society, as well as their electoral strongholds in the urban centers of the Northeast and Midwest, the Democratic Party that controlled Congress before the revolution was a party of government activism. It retained a predominantly liberal character, even as the electorate became more ideologically conservative during the Reagan era.[10] Yet its liberal policy priorities in such areas as education, the environment, and Medicare retained substantial majority support.

As a coalition of interests, congressional Democrats were remarkably diverse. Despite their liberal ideology, they did not pose much of a threat to the most powerful and wealthy forces in American politics. In crafting programs for the economy as a whole, Democratic leaders of such committees as Appropriations and Ways and Means were mindful of "the privileged position of business" (see Chapter 4) and generally supported corporate priorities.[11] In crafting programs for more specific sectors of the economy, Democratic chairs and members of the other committees were influenced by the flow of contributions from business and trade association PACs that aided their reelection. Yet the forces that kept the congressional Democrats a party representative of elite democracy were balanced by more popular democratic forces. Minority groups, women's groups, environmentalists, labor unions, senior citizens, and government employees looked primarily to congressional Democrats for representation of their interests and concerns. Further, most minority and female members of Congress were Democrats. Although these groups were often disappointed in the majority party's performance, they did not doubt that they would be worse off should the Republicans become the new congressional majority. (The role that women play in Congress is the subject of the "Making a Difference" box in this chapter.)

Given the diversity of its coalition, the Democratic majority in Congress was often divided. It was easier for it to unite in opposition to a Republican president than in support for a Democratic one. The Democrats' lack of cohesion was both the cause and the effect of the individualism and committee decentralization that had characterized Congress before the revolution. Often ineffective in taking action to address the nation's problems, yet complacent after many decades in control of Congress, the majority Democrats made a fat target for public discontent in the 1990s.

[MAKING A DIFFERENCE]

Women in Congress

Although Congress is supposed to be the "people's branch," in the past it has resembled a men's club that excludes one-half of the people. That women become U.S. representatives and senators in growing numbers is a major goal of popular democrats. Female representatives can provide "substantive representation" for women's interests: they can bring women's distinct experiences and concerns to the legislature and promote measures that foster equality between the sexes. They can also function as symbolic representatives, offering American women role models for political careers and assuring them of the democratic legitimacy of the political process.

Congress did not have any female members until 1917, when Jeannette Rankin of Montana entered the House. The numbers of women in Congress have grown slowly since then. "The Year of the Woman"—1992—produced dramatic gains, as the number of women in the House leaped from twenty-eight to forty-seven and the number of women in the Senate tripled from two to six. In the 113th Congress (2013–2014), there are twenty female senators and seventy-eight female representatives. Research on women's membership in the legislatures of twenty-five democracies around the globe shows that even with recent improvements, the United States still ranks in the bottom half.

Discrimination against female candidates appears, according to research by political scientists, to be a thing of the past. Voters no longer prefer male to female candidates; there may even be a small bias in favor of women as more caring and honest. The parties are eager to put forward female candidates. And women seem to do as well as men in raising money for congressional races. A factor that has curtailed gains for women has not been discrimination but rather incumbency advantages: with so few male incumbents susceptible to defeat, opportunities for women to replace them have been scarce.

The influence of women in Congress has been limited by more than just the small number of members in the female contingent. On the average, women enter Congress at a later age (because of child rearing) and have shorter careers than men; few gain the seniority that many male legislators achieve. Another factor affecting the influence of women in Congress has been diversity among female representatives. Before the Republican revolution of 1995, most Republican women joined with Democratic women in a Congressional Caucus for Women's Issues. But Newt Gingrich's revolution brought to Congress a new kind of female representative, whose conservative ideology made antifeminism a cardinal principle. In 1995, six of the seven freshman Republican women refused to join the caucus.

Despite limited numbers and ideological divisions, women have made a difference in shaping the agenda of Congress. Recognizing their responsibilities as spokespersons for women in general, Democratic and moderate Republican female legislators have taken the lead in promoting women's rights and fighting for policies of special importance to children and families. They have placed on the legislative agenda such issues as pay equity, child care, women's health, and domestic violence. Women are more likely to sponsor bills on these subjects than men with similar ideological positions.

The hardest realm for congressional women to reach has been legislative leadership. Until 2001, no woman had ever held a top leadership position in either party or chamber. That year, Democrat Nancy Pelosi of California became the first woman to break through the "marble ceiling" when she was chosen by her colleagues as House minority whip. In 2003, she moved up to the post of House minority leader, and four years later she became the first female Speaker of the House. Pelosi remained Speaker until Republicans returned as the majority party in 2011; at that time she reverted to the role of minority leader.

Most Republicans and some Democrats predicted that Pelosi was too much of a "San Francisco liberal," too far to the left of the congressional mainstream to be a successful legislative leader. Yet she has proven the critics wrong. As the top Democrat in the House, Pelosi has demonstrated a blend of leadership skills. In the words of political scientists Ronald Peters and Cindy Simon Rosenthal: "Pelosi often exhibits a leadership style consistent with findings…that women tend toward more collaborative styles than do men. She also presents herself as a tough-minded and hard-nosed politician." Under Pelosi's leadership, House Democrats have achieved the highest level of party unity in voting in over four decades.

Sources: Barbara C. Burrell, *A Woman's Place Is in the House: Campaigning for Congress in the Feminist Era* (Ann Arbor: University of Michigan Press, 1994); Sue Thomas, *How Women Legislate* (New York: Oxford University Press, 1994); Michele L. Swers, *The Difference Women Make: The Policy Impact of Women in Congress* (Chicago: University of Chicago Press, 2002); Cindy Simon Rosenthal, ed., *Women Transforming Congress* (Norman: University of Oklahoma Press, 2002); and Ronald M. Peters, Jr. and Cindy Simon Rosenthal, *Speaker Nancy Pelosi and the New American Politics* (New York: Oxford University Press, 2010).

AP Photo/J. Scott Applewhite

Nancy Pelosi, the first female Speaker of the House of Representatives

Congressional Leadership

Fourth—and least powerful—among the factors shaping behavior in the individualistic Congress was leadership. Among the top leadership positions in Congress, only one—**Speaker of the House of Representatives**—is specifically mentioned in the U.S. Constitution. The Speaker of the House is the most visible and prestigious congressional leader (and stands second, after the vice president, in the line of presidential succession). Technically chosen by the whole House but in practice selected by a vote of the majority party in that chamber, the Speaker exercises a combination of procedural, policy, and partisan leadership.

The Speaker is the top figure in a complex leadership structure in the House. Beneath the Speaker, on the majority-party side, is the **majority leader**, While the Speaker officially presides over the House (junior members actually perform this routine function most of the time), the majority leader is responsible for managing party operations on the floor. Along with the Speaker, the majority leader shapes the legislative schedule, confers with members of the party, consults with the president (when he or she is from the same party), and promotes a party perspective through the national media. Underneath the majority leader are whips, who assist the party's top leaders by gathering information and "counting noses" on forthcoming votes, and by encouraging partisan loyalty through persuasion and personal attention. The minority party has a similar leadership structure. The **minority leader** runs party operations on the floor of the House and is also assisted by an elaborate whip system.

There is no equivalent figure to the Speaker in the Senate. Constitutionally, the vice president presides over the Senate, and when he or she is absent, the presiding officer is the *president pro tempore*—usually the most senior senator from the majority party. The most important leaders in the Senate are the majority and minority leaders, assisted by their whips. These Senate leaders perform many of the same functions as their House counterparts.

Before the revolution, congressional leaders were more notable for their weakness than for their strength. Because members won their seats on their own, their "bosses" were their constituents and not their party leaders. Further, congressional leaders did not have a large number of favors to bestow on legislators who provided them support or punishments to exact on legislators who frustrated their objectives. Unable to issue orders, congressional leaders had to be talented at persuasion. Coalition builders rather than commanders, they might occasionally twist arms to achieve results but relied mostly on the arts of negotiation, conciliation, and compromise.

Beginning in the 1970s, congressional reformers began to strengthen the hand of the leadership in the hope of fostering more effective collective action. In the House, the Speaker was given several new powers. For example, the Speaker was now able to name the majority members of the Rules Committee, whose decisions determine how much time is devoted to floor debate of a bill and what kinds of amendments can be offered on the floor. Under an *open rule*, any germane, or relevant, amendment can be offered. Under a *closed rule*, no amendments can be introduced. Through their domination of the Rules Committee, Speakers could now restrict amendments offered either by the minority party or dissidents from the majority party when priority party legislation faced floor action.[12]

Senate leaders faced a more difficult challenge in pushing party priorities. The Senate, less than one-quarter the size of the House, offers greater freedom of action to individual members. Unlike the House, amendments to most Senate bills do not have to be germane to their subjects. The ability of individual senators to attach *riders* (unrelated provisions) to bills allows them to play strategic games on the floor. For example, a senator who favors a measure that has been bottled up in committee can attach it as an amendment to an unrelated bill; a senator opposed to a bill may load it with amendments to draw a presidential veto.

The minority party in the Senate also has weapons to defeat the majority-party leadership that are absent in the House. Senators are unrestricted in the time they can talk about a bill. Senate debate can go on as long as senators insist. The practice of trying to talk a bill to death is known as the **filibuster**. Filibusters were most commonly employed by southern opponents of civil rights legislation in the 1950s and 1960s. But in recent decades, filibusters have been often used by the minority party to block many different kinds of legislation. The Senate does have a procedure, known as **cloture**, whereby debate can be terminated by a vote of three-fifths of the membership. Yet such a large majority usually is hard to obtain.

Revolution in Congress

Public anger toward Congress rose sharply during the half decade before the 1994 elections. Congress was widely blamed for its failure to address the nation's problems, especially the enormous budget deficits. Citizens were irate about the sizable pay raises that members voted themselves and by the practice of widespread check bouncing by members using the House bank.

In 1994, public anger was focused entirely on the Democrats, and their majorities in the House and Senate were swept away by an electoral tidal wave. The GOP takeover culminated a decade of partisan strategizing and guerrilla actions by the new Republican leader, Newt Gingrich. Having seized majority control, Gingrich and his followers aspired to a revolution in the House—and through this a conservative transformation of American society. But revolution in the House required a reversal in the order of importance for the factors shaping congressional action: The last (leadership) had to become first, and the first (individualism) had to become last.

Leadership and Partisanship

Speaker Newt Gingrich was at the center of the revolution in Congress in 1995. He became the most powerful Speaker since the early years of the twentieth century.[13] At the start of the 104th Congress, Gingrich took control of the House largely into his own hands. He chose all of the committee chairs, in several cases bypassing senior members in favor of his own loyalists. He also controlled committee assignments and cemented his hold over newly elected Republicans by giving many of them slots on the most prestigious House committees. Republican rules changes reinforced Gingrich's personal assertions of prerogative. Committee chairs were subjected to a three-term limit on tenure, further reducing their independence. Subcommittees were subjected to their parent committees in a reversal of what the Democrats had done two decades earlier, adding to the centralization of power.

Gingrich's success as a revolutionary leader of the House depended on an unusual experiment in party government. Under the Democrats, individualism and committee autonomy tended to be stronger than party loyalty and unity; the Republicans promised a new era of congressional government in which the party would take precedence over the committee and the individual. It was a testament not only to the skills of Gingrich and the other Republican House leaders but to the ideological and electoral appeal of a strong, disciplined party that House Republicans did indeed reach unprecedented levels of party unity during the revolution of 1995. In 1995, House Republicans achieved a party unity score of 91 percent![14]

The Republicans had a greater opportunity to try party government than the Democrats because they were a more ideologically cohesive party. Republican moderates in Congress were a dwindling band, drawn mostly from the Northeast; conservatives dominated the party's legislative ranks everywhere else. Republican campaigners in 1994 had capitalized on middle-class and working-class anger at President Clinton and the congressional Democrats. But the core of their party's active constituency was religious conservatives and economic elites.

Revolution in the House required a new type of legislator. If the individualistic pursuit of reelection defined most members during the era of Democratic dominance, the collective pursuit of a partisan and ideological agenda was supposed to define Republicans bent on revolution. The party unity scores achieved in 1995 suggested that members *were* acting differently, *were* voting their party and ideology more than their districts.

Reflecting the anti-politician mood in the country, several of the new Republican members of the House proudly proclaimed that they had no prior political experience. They were coming to Congress, they announced, not to join the corrupt "Washington system" but to purge it.[15] The Senate too had its share of new anti-politicians.

Although the revolution led by Newt Gingrich transformed the House, it fell far short of transforming the nation. Gingrich and his followers had made two fundamental errors. First, they had read too much into the election results: a revolution in national policy needed greater public backing than the 20 percent of the eligible electorate who had voted Republican in 1994. Second, in disregard of the constitutional system of checks and balances, they had tried to dominate the government from the House of Representatives; the Senate and especially the president thwarted the fulfillment of the Speaker's agenda.

As President Clinton blocked much of the conservative agenda and handily won reelection, Republicans in Congress were frustrated. Their majorities began to shrink, and Gingrich's erratic style of leadership increasingly alienated his own followers. On the heels of a clumsy attempt to remove Clinton from office through impeachment, it was the Republican speaker and not the president who resigned his position.

The Partisan Congress

Although he fell from power as dramatically as he had risen, Newt Gingrich left a lasting imprint on Congress. His vision of a cohesive legislative majority united behind a conservative policy agenda was carried on by new Republican leaders different in character but equally aggressive and ambitious. Especially after the White House came under Republican control in 2001, congressional Republican leaders revived their hopes for a conservative transformation of American politics. The Republican House and the Republican Senate became even more partisan than before. When the Democrats regained power in 2007 after Republican failures, their new congressional majority took several pages from the Republican playbook and operated a partisan Congress of its own.

The Partisan Congress under Republican Leadership

From 1999 to 2006, House Republicans were headed by a pair of leaders: Speaker Dennis Hastert and Majority Leader Tom DeLay. As political scientist Ross Baker observed, Speaker Hastert was "a very, very tough partisan who [hid] behind a kind of cuddly teddy-bear exterior."[16] DeLay was the more hard-charging and influential of the two leaders, wielding power in the House with a relentless focus on winning at all costs. Known as "the Hammer," DeLay built a large and efficient operation to ensure that rank-and-file Republicans toed the revolutionary line. He put the fear into Washington lobbying firms: Unless they dropped their bipartisan practices and began hiring only Republicans, he warned, they would be frozen out by the House leadership.[17]

Some analysts believe that the Hastert-DeLay team centralized power in the House even more effectively than Gingrich did. Picking the leadership of committees, tightly managing the agenda and schedule, and manipulating the rules to shut the minority Democrats out from any significant say on legislation, the House Republican leadership went a long way toward building a disciplined majority that has been rare in modern congressional history. Despite the narrow Republican advantage in seats, conservative legislation was advanced through the House with consistent success, with the small number of moderate Republicans muscled into line when their votes appeared crucial.[18]

Dominance by the leadership over congressional committees and their chairs was a keynote of the partisan Congress under the Republicans. The seniority system, a basis for committee independence when Democrats were in the majority, was effectively dead in the Republican House. To become a chair, the important credentials instead were conservative ideology, the ability to raise money to help fellow Republicans get elected and maintain the party's majority status, and, above all, loyalty to the leadership.[19]

In the Senate, Republican leadership resembled the House model more than in Gingrich's day. Bill Frist, a Tennessee heart surgeon who was a close ally of President Bush, was a soft-spoken majority leader, but underneath his courtly demeanor was a determined partisan and fervent ideologue.[20] Like previous Republican majority leaders, however, Frist could not wield power on behalf of a conservative agenda in quite the fashion of Hastert and DeLay, due to the greater independence of individual senators, the prospect of defection by a small but critical bloc of Republican moderates, and the capacity of the minority Democrats to block Republican legislation through the filibuster.

Republican control of Congress came to an end in the elections of 2006. Having loyally backed President George W. Bush, congressional Republicans suffered when Bush and his war in Iraq became increasingly unpopular. The party's losses were also due to corruption scandals in the House. The Republicans, who had taken power in 1995 by claiming to save the public from a power-hungry and self-serving congressional majority, now appeared in the eyes of many voters to have become the very thing they had once denounced.

The Partisan Congress under Democratic Leadership

As the Democrats took over majority control of the House and Senate in 2007, they brought in stronger party leadership than they had featured during the individualistic Congress. Speaker Nancy Pelosi and Senate Majority Leader Harry Reid were aggressive partisan figures who, learning from the Republican example, took control of the congressional agenda. Like Republican leaders in the partisan Congress, Pelosi and Reid often supplanted committee chairs both in originating important bills and in negotiating the final details in a new law.[21] They sought, with some success, to mold the formerly divided Democrats into a unified legislative majority.

However, the Democrats did not take centralization of power quite as far as the Republicans did under Gingrich or DeLay. Whereas Republican leaders picked their own loyalists to chair committees, under the Democrats the old seniority system was restored for the most part. As a result, Democratic committee chairs were older legislators from the party's safest districts or states. Ironically, the same seniority system that once made Democratic committee chairs disproportionately conservative southerners now made these chairs disproportionately northern liberals. Democratic committee chairs were much more diverse than their Republican predecessors: All twenty chairs in the last House under Republican control were white males, but when the Democrats took over there were four African Americans, two Hispanics, and three women.[22]

The shift from Republican to Democratic control of a partisan Congress also changed the composition of the interest groups who enjoyed a favorable hearing on Capitol Hill. Under Republican rule, evangelical Christians and business interests, such as the oil and drug industries, had ready access to the congressional leadership. Under Democratic rule, they were replaced by labor unions, environmental organizations, and activist groups opposed to the war in Iraq.[23]

Although the Democrats savored their rise to majority status, they met with frequent frustrations during the last two years of Bush's presidency. Republicans, now in the minority, charged that the new Democratic majority was forcing them to the sidelines, denying them significant input into the legislative process. On the other hand, Democrats charged that the Republican strategy was to employ every procedural trick in the book to block Democrats from passing their agenda. Democratic successes in the House were often undercut by Republican filibusters in the Senate, and even when the Democrats could get over the Senate hurdle, they faced vetoes from President Bush. The top item on the Democrats' congressional agenda—putting an end to the war in Iraq—was stymied by this combination of Senate filibusters and presidential vetoes.[24]

Democrats scored sizeable gains for the second time in a row in the 2008 congressional elections. In his first two years in office, President Barack Obama was favored with the largest House and Senate majorities in a generation. Yet congressional Republicans took partisan polarization to new heights, resisting nearly everything on the Democrats' agenda. Democratic bills could gain support from only a handful of Republicans, if that. On the most controversial legislative item of all, health care reform, not a single Republican in either the House or the Senate voted *yes*. And even when the Democrats could get a bill through the House, it often died in the Senate because of a Republican filibuster.[25] With few exceptions, Senate Republicans attempted to block the passage of anything Obama proposed, breaking past records for the number of filibusters in a single session.

In the face of this wall of Republican opposition, Democrats were more unified than they had been when the ... Congress before 1995. Without that unity, President Obama's health care and financial regulation reforms could not have been passed. Nonetheless, Democrats remained more ideologically diverse than Republicans, so their party leaders in Congress had more problems maintaining support from moderate members. Thus, defections from a small number of moderates doomed the Democrats' energy bill in the Senate. Even when moderate Democrats voted with their party on health care and financial-regulation reforms, party leaders had to water down these reforms in order to hold on to moderates' votes.

More Partisan Than Ever: The Republican Comeback in Congress

It seemed during the congressional session of 2009–10 that partisan polarization could not possibly get worse—but it did, in 2011–12. Amid the deepest economic crisis since the Great Depression, with angry conservatives mobilized by the Tea Party movement and demor-

---

Table 12.1 Members of 112th Congress (2011–2012)

	House	Senate
Party	242 Republicans 193 Democrats	51 Democrats 47 Republicans 2 Independents
Average age (years)	56.7	62.2
Top previous occupations	Business, Public Service, Law	Law, Public Service, Business
Average time in Congress (years)	9.8	11.4
Gender	364 male 71 female	83 male 17 female
Ethnicity		
African American	42	0
Hispanic	29	2
Asian or Pacific Islander	9	2
American Indian	1	0

Source: Jennifer E. Manning, "Membership of the 112th Congress: A Profile," Congressional Research Service, March 2011.

alized liberals wondering what had happened to the "hope and change" that Obama had promised in 2008, the Republicans made a stunning comeback. They won huge victories in the congressional elections of 2010, taking back majority control in the House and shrinking the Democrats' margin of control in the Senate.

The new Republican majority in the House contained 87 newcomers, many of them candidates of the fervently conservative and anti-Obama Tea Party movement. Much like the Republican revolutionaries of 1995, the Tea Party freshmen of 2011 prided themselves on their self-described identity as anti-politicians. These House freshmen were fired up by the vision of challenging what they perceived as Washington's wicked ways. At the top of their agenda was the goal of slashing federal spending.[26]

The new Republican speaker of the House, John Boehner, was a more experienced and pragmatic legislator than the highly ideological newcomers in his party's caucus, but he tried to handle these newcomers gently rather than adopting the strong-arm tactics of a Gingrich or DeLay. The newcomers welcomed Boehner's openness to their concerns, but they periodically rebelled against his leadership when he tried to strike compromises with the Obama administration. After a string of embarrassing retreats when his caucus would not follow his lead, Boehner came under fire as a weaker Republican leader than Gingrich or DeLay had been.[27]

By pushing the federal government on several occasions to the brink of a shutdown or default on the national debt, Tea Party Republicans in the House found some success in their drive to cut spending. Reductions in the federal budget were larger than either Republican congressional leaders or the Obama White House had anticipated at the beginning of 2011. Nonetheless, the victories of the new hard-core conservatives fell far short of their militant goals, so, by the end of their first year in Congress, many freshmen voiced frustration over how little they had actually changed Washington's ways.[28] Meanwhile, the confrontational tactics of the Tea Party Republicans further deepened partisan polarization in Congress. Increasingly stalemated between Republicans in the House and Democrats in the Senate, widely condemned as a dysfunctional legislative body, Congress sunk to the new low in public approval that we noted at the beginning of this chapter.

At the beginning of the 2012 campaign season, congressional Republicans had high hopes of gaining majority control of the Senate while retaining their majority in the House. With far more Democratic than Republican seats at risk in 2012, it would only have taken a net Republican gain of four to shift party control of the Senate. But the congressional results in 2012 turned out to look very different than two years earlier. Surprising almost all forecasters, the Democrats gained two seats in the Senate, expanding their margin to 55–45, while chipping away at the Republican majority in the House with a pickup of eight seats.

Evaluating the Partisan Congress

Although partisanship is now the most decisive factor in shaping congressional behavior, it is not the only factor. Members of Congress still pay considerable attention to the interests of their constituents, just as they did in the era of the individualistic Congress. Sometimes, members pursue personal interests even when they clash with their party's program. For example, Republicans who generally favor reducing federal spending may favor increasing public spending in areas like cancer research or mental-health treatment because of their own experience with how these maladies affected their loved ones.[29]

Where partisanship is most decisive is in determining the legislative agenda—what gets debated and voted on the floor in the House or Senate. Majority party leaders in each chamber use control over the agenda to ensure that only the bills favored by a majority in their party have a chance to prevail on the floor. Political scientist Sean Theriault has shown that partisan polarization is most extensive on procedural votes, such as motions to restrict amendments or motions to recommit a bill to the committee from which it originated.[30]

Through these procedural mechanisms, the legislative goals of the party in the minority are effectively blocked. In the Senate, the minority party's leader can also use a procedure—the filibuster—to make it much harder for the majority party to bring its bill to a vote requiring only a simple majority.

The partisan Congress has been evaluated in a negative light both by the American public and by most scholars who study legislative politics. So it is worth remembering that its predecessor, the individualistic Congress, was also widely criticized, especially for self-serving behavior by incumbents who, in pursuit of reelection, placed the interests of their districts or states above the common good. In defense of congressional partisanship, it can be argued that it has produced majorities who work as a team to advance legislative agendas on national issues. Moreover, as the two parties have become more ideologically cohesive, they offer clearer choices to the public than was the case when casework and pork-barrel politics claimed local voters' allegiances.

Nevertheless, the costs of current congressional partisanship are high, especially when measured against democratic ideals. When partisan majorities ram through their agenda without room for minority input or time for genuine debate, Congress fails to achieve the thoughtful deliberation that is supposed to be its distinctive virtue. As political scientist Barbara Sinclair observes, "Current arrangements in the House of Representatives promote decisiveness more than deliberation or inclusiveness. . . . The current process excludes the minority party and the interests and segments of society it represents."[31]

A Congress polarized between two parties, both of which have shed most of their moderate members and gravitated toward the ideological ends of the spectrum, is also an institution torn by ill feelings that make compromise, or even cooperation, difficult. The individualistic Congress was a friendlier place, as incumbents of both parties practiced a live-and-let-live ethic. The partisan Congress has been described instead as a "fight club." As journalist Juliet Eilperin writes, "It is hard to exaggerate how much House Republicans and Democrats dislike each other these days. . . . They speak about their opponents as if they hail from a distant land with strange customs, all of which are twisted."[32]

Congress and the Executive

The Constitution places Congress first among the three branches of the federal government, devoting Article I to the selection, organization, and powers of the legislature. During the nineteenth century, except for brief periods under strong presidents, Congress was the pre-eminent branch. But the twentieth century witnessed the rise of "presidential government," with the executive seizing the lead and Congress following.

Although the overall balance of power has shifted from Capitol Hill to the White House, the dynamic of power between the two branches never remains static. From the New Deal of Franklin Roosevelt to the Great Society of Lyndon Johnson, Congress acquiesced in the rise of a strong presidency, particularly in foreign and defense policy. But the Vietnam War prodded Congress to challenge the presidency on international affairs and war making. The sweeping power plays of President Nixon compelled Congress to reassert itself in budget making and domestic policy as well. During the periods of "divided government" that have been occurred since 1981, warfare between the two branches has been common on almost every major issue.

Budgetary Politics

One of the primary elements in the rise of presidential government during the middle decades of the twentieth century was presidential capture of a preponderant share of the power of the purse. A legislature dominated by scattered committee power could not produce a coherent budget; a unitary executive, aided by a Bureau of the Budget (renamed the Office of Management and Budget in 1970), could. Congress found itself reduced to snipping budgets framed by the executive. Two developments in the early 1970s, however, propelled Congress to recapture some budgetary power. First, a fragmented congressional budgetary process generated excessive spending. Second (and probably more important), President Nixon usurped Congress's budgetary authority so aggressively that he forced legislators to develop new defensive weapons.

The vehicle Congress chose to reassert its budget-making authority was the **Budget and Impoundment Control Act of 1974**. This act established new budget committees in the House and Senate. It also created a Congressional Budget Office (CBO), a staff of budgetary and economic experts that provided members with information and analysis comparable to those supplied to the president by the Office of Management and Budget. With the assistance of the CBO, Congress hoped to subject the budget to a more coherent review and establish its own priorities against those of the president.

The new budget process did increase congressional power, but it also intensified conflict between Congress and the executive. It was the presidency of Ronald Reagan that turned the budget into the annual battlefield of national politics. In 1981, Reagan dominated Congress, achieving massive tax cuts and increases in defense spending. However, he did not persuade Congress to cut domestic spending as deeply as he wished. The result was mounting federal deficits that loomed over almost all congressional deliberations.[33]

Congress and the executive made little headway in getting deficits under control throughout the 1980s. However, two bipartisan compromises, under the first President Bush in 1990 and under President Clinton in 1997, restored budgetary discipline. Helped by a booming economy as well, federal deficits finally gave way to surpluses during the closing years of the Clinton presidency. Yet the new era of budget surpluses, projected at the beginning of George W. Bush's administration in 2001 to last throughout the first decade of the new century, instead ended almost immediately, with the president's tax cuts and two wars abroad hurling the budget back into large-scale deficits.

The onset of the Great Recession in 2008 further worsened the budgetary situation. Deficits normally grow during recessions as tax revenues decrease and government spending to relieve distress rises. Faced with the worst economic crisis to hit the United States since the Great Depression, the Obama administration combated the downturn with a mix of new spending and tax cutting that further exploded the deficit. By 2011, Republicans and Democrats were agreed that strong measures were needed to bring deficits under control. Yet their polarized positions—President Obama and congressional Democrats wanted higher taxes on the rich while congressional Republicans wanted all the budgetary reduction to come from spending cuts—made compromise difficult and progress limited.

President Obama and Senate Minority Leader McConnell discuss the budget

Foreign Policy

Foreign policy has been the preferred field of action for most presidents over the last century. Presidents have substantial authority and resources in this policy arena. Preference, authority, and resources have sometimes led presidents and their supporters to claim foreign policy as almost exclusively the prerogative of the executive. Yet the Constitution bestows authority and entrusts responsibility to Congress as well as the executive in shaping the relationship of the United States to the rest of the world. Through its appropriations authority, Congress funds American activities abroad. It has the sole power to declare war and is responsible for raising and maintaining military forces. The power "to regulate commerce with foreign nations" draws it into matters of international trade. Moreover, the Senate has the responsibility to deliberate on treaties with other countries.

Despite these constitutional powers, Congress largely accepted presidential dominance over foreign policy from World War II to the Vietnam War, the era of the "Cold War consensus." It was the disaster of Vietnam—a presidential war—that shook Congress out of its compliant stance. Starting in the early 1970s, Congress began to reassert its role in foreign policy issues: war making, covert actions by the CIA, arms sales to foreign nations, and trade strategy. When it has engaged in battles with the White House, the presidency still usually has the upper hand. Yet Congress has won some notable victories—for example, instituting economic sanctions, over a veto by President Reagan, against the apartheid government of South Africa in 1986.

Perhaps because it is closer to the people than is the executive branch, Congress has been more likely in recent decades to reflect the popular democratic tradition of skepticism toward the engagement of the United States in military actions abroad. It is almost always the president who advocates military action; Congress often goes along but sometimes puts up resistance. Such resistance is occasionally effective, particularly when a large and cohesive congressional majority opposes a president of the other party. "Facing vocal opposition from legislators and the media, and anticipating congressional reprisals at the first sign of failure," write political scientists William Howell and Jon Pevehouse, "presidents may decide to take passes on especially risky military ventures."[34] The inability of Congress to question President Bush's false premises for the war in Iraq, on the other hand, suggests that legislative checks on presidential war powers will seldom be very strong.[35]

Many analysts are unhappy when Congress asserts itself on issues of national security and foreign policy. They believe that if the United States is to follow a coherent and prudent global policy, Congress should not interfere very often with the president's decisions. Congress, they allege, moves too slowly, acts too indecisively, deliberates in too much ignorance, is swayed too much by ideological obsessions, and is too preoccupied with reelection pressures to handle the dilemmas of diplomacy and war. But its inadequacies in foreign policy, congressional scholar Eileen Burgin observes, are exaggerated. Congress can act swiftly if necessary, employing expedited procedures; besides, most foreign policy matters require careful consideration. Although most of its members are inexpert on matters of foreign policy, its Foreign Affairs and Armed Services committees boast many impressive students of international affairs. If Congress approaches global events with one eye on the reactions of constituents, the same is often true of the president.[36] And Congress has no monopoly on ideological obsessions in foreign policy, as the presidencies of Ronald Reagan and George W. Bush have demonstrated.

The real question about congressional involvement in foreign affairs is not whether it interferes too much with the presidency but whether it defers too often to presidential initiatives.[37] Congress is not always prudent about international affairs. In recent years, its involvement has at times been distorted by ideological rigidity. But the congressional voice is welcome in foreign policy because the alternative is a presidential monologue. When presidents have dominated foreign policy, they have been inclined to secret deliberations, covert actions, and manipulative rhetoric. Congressional participation in foreign policy opens this arena, generating debate, increasing options, and allowing public input. Elite democrats admire a president who is the sole master of foreign policy. Popular democrats turn to Congress to ensure the public's voice in foreign affairs.

Congressional Oversight of the Executive Branch

The most extensive relationship between Congress and the executive involves legislative oversight of the bureaucracy. **Oversight** is the review by congressional committees of the operations of executive branch agencies. In one sense, oversight is simply a logical process—Congress must review what the bureaucracy does to see if laws are being properly implemented. In another sense, oversight is a highly political process—Congress's chief means for contesting the president over guidance of the federal bureaucracy.

Oversight can take many forms. The most visible is the congressional hearing. In an oversight hearing, top agency administrators appear before a congressional committee to report on their implementation of programs and to answer questions. Members of Congress not only elicit useful information but also signal the administrators as to who controls their statutory authority and budget. Informal methods of oversight are even more common, and usually less conflictive. Committees may request written reports from agencies, or committee staffers may engage in extensive communications with their agency counterparts.

Hypocritical oversight of Obama's stimulus program

Oversight hearings can be turned into partisan instruments whose primary objective is to embarrass the president and his administration. Congressional Democrats employed committee hearings to probe the alleged misdeeds of Republican presidents from Nixon through the elder Bush. When Republicans gained control of Congress in 1995, they began to pay the Democrats back with even more frequent hearings. At almost any point during the last six years of the Clinton administration, there was usually at least one congressional committee investigating the White House, whether it was about the Whitewater scandal, the alleged misuse of Federal Bureau of Investigation (FBI) files, campaign finance shenanigans, or a host of other activities.[38]

Vigorous in their oversight of the Clinton presidency, Republican committee chairs became more relaxed once the White House was in the hands of their own party. The Bush administration's failures, such as the blunders that undermined the reconstruction of Iraq after American conquest of the country, produced little oversight activity in either the House or the Senate. Only when Democrats regained the majority position on congressional committees in 2007 did the Bush administration have to cope with serious oversight of its actions.

The majority of oversight hearings are not dramatic or partisan. Nevertheless, some critics still object to extensive oversight on the grounds that by this technique Congress is interfering excessively with the executive branch and trying to "micromanage" its operations. This complaint has been justified in some instances.

Yet an increase in congressional oversight is, on balance, a welcome development, at least from the standpoint of popular democracy. To be sure, some oversight is technical and dull; some is narrowly self-serving advocacy. And, on occasion, oversight is little more than partisan theatrics to humiliate the executive. But oversight is one of the chief means that Congress possesses to hold the presidency and the civil service accountable. Vigorous oversight activities prevent the bureaucracy from becoming a closed world of inaccessible experts. Many oversight hearings have alerted the public to matters that otherwise would have been known only to a small circle of elites.

Conclusion

From the standpoint of popular democracy, Congress has critical roles to play in budgeting, foreign policy, and oversight. But how well can Congress perform these and other roles? How well can it give expression to the strengths of popular democracy? Examining the transformation from the individualistic to the partisan Congress, the story we tell in this chapter, gives us some clues into the potential for Congress to represent the public's ideas and interests.

There are elements of genuine popular democracy in the partisan Congress, whether under Republican or Democratic control. The decline of individualism and localism, and the dramatic new emphasis on party responsibility, are important if Congress is to take collective action and address the nation's problems. Even the centralization of power in the hands of the leadership, often disturbing in the authoritarian methods it has spawned, has at least produced a coherent agenda that the public can understand and debate.

But the partisan Congress has so far fallen short of popular democratic standards in important respects. Contesting for power in a narrowly divided legislature, party leaders have sought electoral advantage by steamrolling their opponents if they are in the majority or obstructing their opponents if they are in the minority. Amid the intensity of partisan warfare, mutual hostility precludes thoughtful deliberation and debate. The interest groups and lobbyists who cluster around the majority obtain special benefits through transactions that are concealed from the public.

The polarized and often nasty party conflict that has characterized Congress since the 1995 revolution feeds public disenchantment with legislative politics in the nation's capital. But present partisan excesses should not obscure the continuing importance of Congress's democratic revitalization. A strong and effective Congress is indispensable for popular democracy in America.

Elite democrats argue that in a complex, dangerous, and technological world, Congress, with its inefficient methods of decision making, has become outdated. They point out that in most other political systems, legislative powers have receded and strong executives have become dominant. Popular democrats respond that unless legislative power balances executive power, democracy is in trouble. Only a vital Congress can ensure that government will be sensitive to the concerns of ordinary citizens and forge genuine compromises among their diverse viewpoints. Above all, whereas the executive branch makes decisions behind closed doors, in the halls of Congress citizens can hear public arguments about the public good.

Reader's Guide ★ ★ ★

Critical Thinking Questions

1. Should members of Congress mainly follow the wishes of voters in their districts/states? Or should they base their votes mainly on their own understanding of the national good?

2. How and why did the individualistic Congress give way to the partisan Congress?

3. Is it desirable that congressional parties are now more centralized and unified? What are the advantages and disadvantages?

4. Which reforms might reduce the level of mutual hostility that observers see in today's partisan Congress? How might these reforms improve public perceptions of Congress's performance?

Key Word Definition

incumbent   The person who currently holds an office.

franking privilege   The benefit enjoyed by members of Congress of free postage to send mass mailings to their constituents.

casework   The help given individual constituents by congressional staffs.

committee system   The division of the legislative workload among several congressional bodies assigned specific issues.

seniority   The congressional norm that dictates that the member from the majority party who has the most years of continuous service on a committee becomes its chair.

iron triangle   An alliance between a congressional committee, an interest group, and an executive agency that serves each one's interest, often at the expense of the general public.

Speaker of the House of Representatives   The presiding officer of the House of Representatives, who is chosen by the majority party in the House and is second, after the vice president, in the line of presidential succession.

majority leader   The head of the majority party in the House of Representatives or Senate.

minority leader   The head of the minority party in the House of Representatives or Senate.

filibuster   The Senate tradition whereby a senator can try to delay or defeat a vote on legislation by talking the bill to death.

cloture   A Senate procedure for terminating debate and ending a filibuster, which requires a three-fifths vote of the membership.

Budget and Impoundment Control Act of 1974   A law that reasserted congressional authority in budget making by creating new budget committees and the Congressional Budget Office.

oversight   Congressional attempts to exercise control over the activities of executive branch agencies through a variety of techniques, including hearings and investigations.

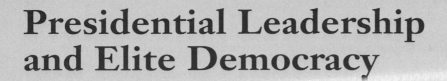

Presidential Leadership and Elite Democracy

Contemporary presidents present themselves to the American people as champions of popular democracy. Aided by a large public relations machine in the White House, they dramatize their status as the sole elected representative of a national majority and their commitment to battle for the public good against selfish special interests. But should we take presidential claims to the title of popular democrat at face value? This chapter suggests that there are circumstances in which popular democracy can indeed be furthered by a leader in the White House. But it also proposes that we be wary of prevailing presidential imagery: most of the time, as we shall see, the presidency is closer to elite democracy than to popular democracy.

In the original debate over presidential power, the most brilliant advocate of strong presidential leadership was an arch elite democrat, Alexander Hamilton. Hamilton believed that the American Revolution had gone too far in placing government directly in the hands of the people and in making legislators immediately answerable to the people. A strong executive of uncommon talent and experience was needed to guide public affairs. As Hamilton put it, "Energy in the executive is a leading character in the definition of good government."[1] Only an energetic executive, Hamilton argued, could overcome the tendency of the political system to stalemate and provide creative political direction. Conditions of crisis would make executive leadership even more imperative: "Decision, activity, secrecy, and dispatch will generally characterize the proceedings of one man in a much more eminent degree than the proceedings of any greater number."[2]

To the original popular democrats, the Anti-federalists, the new presidency evoked painful memories of royal governors and British kings. They suspected that Hamilton's lofty executive office would be a breeding ground for elitism. Patrick Henry lamented that "there is to be a great and mighty President, with very extensive powers: the powers of a King.

He is to be supported in extravagant magnificence."[3] Another Anti-federalist, George Mason, called upon citizens to look to their own commitment "to their laws, to their freedom, and to their country" rather than depending for their salvation upon a single leader of great power.[4] Anti-federalists placed their political hopes in the people's energies and not the executive's.

Positions in the democratic debate over the executive seemed to be reversed in the twentieth century. First with Theodore Roosevelt and Woodrow Wilson, and even more decisively with Franklin D. Roosevelt, the presidency came to be associated with popular democracy. After FDR's New Deal, which was a genuine outpouring of popular democratic energies, most journalists, political scientists, and historians came to believe that presidents were the principal agents of democratic change in the American political system. Advocates of economic reform, social justice, and racial equality began to rest their hopes on White House leadership.

These hopes were frequently disappointed: presidents after FDR rarely seemed to bring about as much democratic change as they promised when they ran for office. And while the bond between the presidency and popular democracy was celebrated, presidents were expanding their powers in ways that threatened democratic values. With the Vietnam War, Nixon's Watergate scandal, Reagan's Iran-Contra affair, the campaign finance scandals of the Clinton presidency, and the assaults on civil liberties by the administration of George W. Bush, the undemocratic potential of executive power was underscored. Anti-federalist warnings, forgotten in the twentieth-century celebration of presidential power, became relevant once more.

This chapter assesses the part that presidents play in the democratic debate. We consider presidents as individual leaders who seek to enact their agendas and make their marks upon history. But we give equal weight to the forces that constrain and condition their leadership: Congress, the bureaucracy, economic elites, the media, and the public. It is the balance of these forces, rather than personality, we suggest, that determines whether the president sides with popular or elite democracy.

The Personalized Presidency

When Americans think or talk about a president, his or her personality is usually the focus of their attention. The man or woman in the White House makes a more engaging subject than the institutional apparatus or policy agenda of his or her administration. Media coverage reinforces this personalization of the presidency. After observing a president's portrayal in the media, citizens are more apt to know trivial details—Ronald Reagan liked jellybeans; Bill Clinton had a cat named Socks; George W. Bush was a fervent cyclist; Barack Obama loves to play basketball—than to know the name of the president's chief of staff or the substance of the administration's trade policy.

Media coverage of the president also prompts most Americans to assume that how well a president does in office depends almost entirely on his or her strengths and weaknesses. In this light, Ronald Reagan's presidency was viewed through the disparity between his strong communication skills and his weak grasp of his own policies. The elder George Bush was portrayed as an experienced administrator who lacked a vision of where he wanted to lead the nation. Bill Clinton was depicted as a puzzling combination of political talent and moral delinquency. George W. Bush was presented as an incurious leader who nonetheless charted a bold and risky course abroad. Barack Obama is often described as able to excite vast crowds yet remain personally aloof. Political skill, intellect, and character thus seem to matter more than anything else in determining each president's record of successes and failures.

Several political scientists have attempted to provide a more systematic understanding of the contribution of the person to the presidency. For example, James David Barber's famous work on presidential personality places presidents into different categories depending

White House Photo/Alamy

on whether they are active or passive in doing their job and whether they are positive or negative in viewing their office as a source of personal satisfactions. The most desirable type of president, Barber argues, is the active-positive president, who pours considerable energy into the job, has fun in doing so, and possesses sufficient self-esteem to be flexible and adaptable when inevitable roadblocks stand in the way of major presidential goals. In Barber's analysis, active-positive presidents include Franklin D. Roosevelt, Harry Truman, John F. Kennedy, Gerald Ford, Jimmy Carter, and the elder George Bush. The least desirable type of president, according to Barber, is the active-negative president, whose energetic performance is driven by grim self-doubt and who tends to rigidify behind a failing policy at great cost to the nation's welfare. Barber's active-negative presidents are Woodrow Wilson, Herbert Hoover, Lyndon Johnson, and Richard Nixon.[5]

[MAKING A DIFFERENCE]

President Barack Obama

Of the forty-three presidents of the United States, Barack Obama is surely the most unusual. Prior to Obama, the presidency had been characterized by the least diversity of any American political institution. The national origins of the first forty-two presidents were limited to the British Isles and Western Europe. With a father from Kenya, Obama broke the presidential mold. As the first African American to occupy the White House, he represents a dramatic change that few Americans expected to occur until long into the future.

For those who believe that the success or failure of a president depends on personal qualities, Obama brought to the presidency an impressive combination of talents. His intelligence is widely recognized: he was the editor of the Harvard Law Review and is the author of two insightful (and bestselling) books. His political savvy is evident in his extraordinary political ascent: In only his first term in the U.S. Senate, he plotted and executed a brilliant presidential campaign, upsetting an acclaimed frontrunner, Hillary Clinton, for the Democratic nomination and then outdueling an acknowledged hero, John McCain, in the general election. Obama is one of the most gifted rhetoricians in modern American history. His speeches during his run for the presidency captivated millions of followers.

Yet the success or failure of a president depends on historical circumstances as well as personal abilities. Aided by substantial Democratic majorities in the House and Senate when he took office, President Obama scored major victories with an economic stimulus, health care reform, and financial regulatory reform. Yet he faced unyielding opposition from congressional Republicans; as a result, some of his major legislative initiatives failed when a handful of congressional Democrats did not back him, and even his victories in Congress were riddled with compromises. Overshadowing all else was the deepest economic crisis since the Great Depression; stubbornly high unemployment rates and collapsing values in housing deflated the hopeful mood after Obama's electoral victory and diminished his standing in the polls. With Democrats discouraged and Republicans angered by Obama's first two years in the White House, the president's opponents scored huge gains in the elections of 2010.

Although circumstances might be blamed for a significant part of Obama's frustrations, his own failings also played a role. Perhaps his greatest error was to believe that he could overcome partisan polarization in Washington while simultaneously advancing a traditional Democratic agenda. Obama's gestures toward bipartisanship were repeatedly rebuffed by the Republicans, even as they depressed Democrats who chided the president for his naïve belief that he could bring together ideological foes. Only late in Obama's third year in office did he seem to abandon his hopes for unity and adopt a combative partisan stance in support of a populist economic program.

No president since Franklin D. Roosevelt had won reelection with an unemployment rate as high as that facing President Obama in 2012, so most experts predicted that he would face an uphill battle to keep his office. But Obama won a surprisingly strong victory in both the Electoral College and the popular vote. He was aided by the weakness of his Republican opponent, Mitt Romney, whose association with the rich, frequent verbal gaffes, and vague policy proposals failed to attract many voters beyond the Republican base. Obama and his advisers ran a skillful campaign and convinced a majority of Americans that he deserved more time to bring about an economic recovery. Backing the president was a coalition of women, racial minorities, youth, and highly-educated professionals that signaled a changed landscape in American politics. As Obama began his second term in 2013, his political position was stronger than it had been the previous two years, when Tea Party Republicans had forced him to play defense.

Sources: Theda Skocpol and Lawrence R. Jacobs, eds., *Reaching for a New Deal: Ambitious Governance, Economic Meltdown, and Polarized Politics in Obama's First Two Years* (New York: Russell Sage Foundation, 2011); Bert A. Rockman, Andrew Rudalevige, and Colin Campbell, eds., *The Obama Presidency: Appraisals and Prospects* (Washington, D.C.: CQ Press, 2012); Stephen Skowronek, *Presidential Leadership in Political Time: Reprise and Reappraisal*, 2nd ed. (Lawrence: University Press of Kansas, 2011).

But how much can a focus on the personalized presidency really explain? Can Barber's categories, which lump together such diverse presidents as Harry Truman, John F. Kennedy, and George H. W. Bush, tell us much about why their presidencies turned out so differently? Character, skill, and intelligence matter in the White House, to be sure, but when we focus on them to the near exclusion of all else, we fail to understand the presidency very well. Overshadowed by a preoccupation with the personalized presidency are the varying political and historical circumstances in which presidents have to operate. Unfortunately, the presidency as an institution tends to be obscured when we concentrate primarily on the person who is president.

The Presidency as an Institution

In our concern for presidential leadership, we focus on the individual who occupies the White House. Yet the presidency—as distinct from the president—is an institution, and we need to understand its institutional features. The institution of the presidency has expanded dramatically over the last century. Although this expansion has been justified in popular democratic terms—the presidency has had to grow to fulfill public expectations of executive leadership—the consequences have sometimes been unfortunate for popular democracy. Surrounded by a sizable staff and bureaucracy of their own, presidents can become isolated from the people who put them into office. And this staff and bureaucracy can be used to carry out actions that run counter to what Congress has legislated and what the public wants.

White House Staff

The part of the institutional presidency that most directly surrounds the individual president is the **White House staff** (known officially as the White House Office). The White House staff comprises the president's personal aides and advisers along with their numerous assistants, and it has undergone dramatic growth over the last seventy years. Before Franklin D. Roosevelt, presidents had only a handful of personal aides. Abraham Lincoln had to cope with the Civil War with the help of only two personal secretaries. When a telephone was first installed in the White House, Grover Cleveland answered it himself. As late as World War I, Woodrow Wilson typed many of his own speeches.

During the Great Depression of the 1930s, as new responsibilities flooded the White House, Franklin Roosevelt recognized, in the words of the Brownlow Committee that he appointed, that "the president needs help." It was Roosevelt who initiated the dramatic expansion of the White House staff. But later presidents would oversee a staff far larger than Roosevelt had imagined. At its height, FDR's staff numbered around fifty. By Richard Nixon's second term, the staff had grown to more than 500 people. Nixon's successors, responding to charges that the presidential staff had become dangerously bloated, cut it back a bit.[6]

The White House staff has not only expanded since the 1930s; it has also taken on important new functions. Before Franklin Roosevelt, presidents tended to turn for advice to cabinet members. Although presidents still consider their cabinet selections important, since the 1930s they have downgraded most cabinet heads, relying instead on their staff for assistance in decision making and even in managing federal policies. Staff members have done more than serve as the president's extra eyes, ears, and hands. Some have become key decision makers and top advisers, such as Karl Rove during the presidency of George W. Bush and Rahm Emanuel in the first two years of the Obama presidency.

The organization and work patterns of the White House staff are shaped, at least in part, by the personality of the president. Bill Clinton's staff was largely youthful, and his White House was notorious for meandering meetings that reflected the president's own lack of discipline. By contrast, the White House of George W. Bush was designed, according to a report by *New York Times* correspondent Richard Berke, "to function with the crisp efficiency of a blue chip corporation."[7] In the Bush White House, meetings started and ended on time, briefing memos were restricted to no more than two pages, and staff members had to observe a formal dress code in the Oval Office (ties and jackets for men, business attire for women). This corporate-style White House allowed Bush to spend fewer hours on the job than did his predecessor.[8]

Why have recent presidents turned to White House staff rather than cabinet members for advice? To understand this phenomenon, we must consider the differences between cabinet members and White House staffers.

A president may have had little personal contact with most members of the cabinet before assuming office. The cabinet is selected with several criteria in mind: public prestige, managerial ability, interest group or geographic representativeness (for example, the secretary of the treasury is usually drawn from the business or financial communities). Potential cabinet heads must pass Senate scrutiny and receive senatorial confirmation. Further, cabinet secretaries can be summoned to appear before congressional committees, where they may be pressed to reveal information that the president would rather keep confidential.

In contrast, top staffers usually don't come to their jobs from power positions. Rather, many are individuals personally attached to the president—men or women who have worked for the president in the past and whose loyalty is of long standing. White House staffers don't need Senate confirmation. Unlike cabinet heads, they cannot ordinarily be questioned by Congress because of claims of separation of powers and executive privilege.

Considering the differences between cabinet and staff presents clues about why presidents prefer to work with staff. A president has greater flexibility with staff: he or she can hire anyone, move staff members from task to task, and replace ineffective staff members with less public notice than when dismissing a cabinet member. A president can also assume greater loyalty from staff. Cabinet members must answer to many forces besides the president who appointed them: congressional committees that control the budget and statutory authority for their departments, the interest groups that are important clienteles for their departments, and the civil servants who work in their departments. But White House staffers answer only to the president.[9]

Offering a president greater flexibility and loyalty than the cabinet, a large and powerful White House staff seems to increase the president's reach and power. But growth of this kind of White House staff has been a mixed blessing for presidents. Like presidents themselves, staffers can become isolated from the world outside the White House. David Gergen, who served as a high-level aide to presidents Nixon, Ford, Reagan, and Clinton, observes that "even in the best of times, the White House can be closed off to reality; in the worst of times, it is a bunker."[10]

Isolated from the public, dependent on the president for their jobs, and highly loyal, White House staffers do not necessarily make the best advisers. Desiring to curry favor with a president, staff members have sometimes presented their bosses with distorted pictures of the reality outside the White House. Rather than enhancing presidential power, they have produced a peculiar form of presidential blindness, akin to the monarchical mentality against which Patrick Henry had warned.[11]

Executive Office of the President

The White House Office is part of the **Executive Office of the President (EOP)**, established under Franklin Roosevelt in 1939. The other most important components of the EOP are the Office of Management and Budget (OMB), Council of Economic Advisers (CEA), and National Security Council (NSC). Whereas the White House staff was designed to provide the president with personal and political assistance, the other EOP units were intended to provide institutional—that is, objective and expert—advice to the president as a policy maker (see Figure 13.1).

The largest and most important institutional unit in the EOP is the **Office of Management and Budget (OMB)**. OMB prepares the annual presidential budget. It scrutinizes legislative proposals originating in the agencies of the executive branch to ensure that

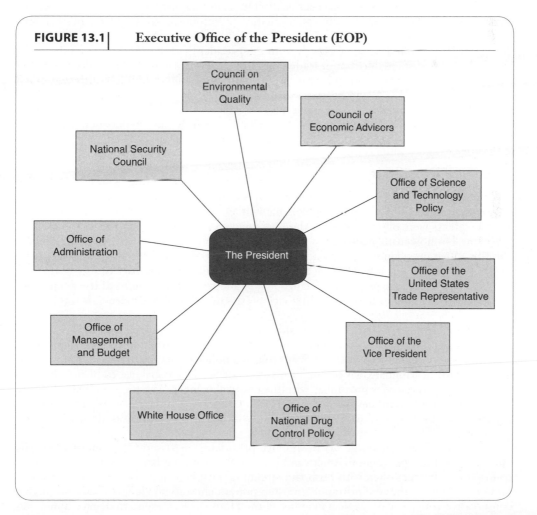

FIGURE 13.1 | Executive Office of the President (EOP)

- Council on Environmental Quality
- Council of Economic Advisors
- Office of Science and Technology Policy
- National Security Council
- Office of the United States Trade Representative
- Office of Administration
- The President
- Office of the Vice President
- Office of Management and Budget
- Office of National Drug Control Policy
- White House Office

Source: White House, 2013.

they accord with the program of the president. It recommends signing or vetoing legislation. In addition, it oversees the management methods of the entire executive establishment.

The **Council of Economic Advisers (CEA)** was established in 1946 to provide regular assistance from professional economists. The CEA has a chair and two other members, along with their staffs. It analyzes economic conditions, projects economic trends, and drafts the president's annual economic report.

The **National Security Council (NSC)** was established in 1947 to coordinate the military and diplomatic aspects of foreign policy in an age of American global involvement. Officially, it brings together the top national security decision makers. More important than formal meetings of the NSC, however, is the work of its staff, headed by the president's assistant for national security. (See Chapter 18 for a more detailed discussion of the NSC.)

Although the original purpose of the EOP was to provide a president with expert institutional advice to balance the more personal and partisan advice of the White House staff, the distinction has diminished in recent years. The White House has made the institutional components of the EOP more political, more directly responsive to the president's personal views and political needs.[12]

This extension of personal power, from the president's Oval Office outward, has been justified as an indispensable tool of leadership. But the enhancement of presidential power has not always meant the enhancement of presidential wisdom. A highly politicized OMB under Budget Director David Stockman manipulated the budgetary math to conceal how Reagan's 1981 tax cut would generate a massive deficit. A highly politicized NSC helped Reagan stumble into the disaster of the Iran-Contra affair. Some scholars believe that the EOP might serve the presidency better if it were not so intensely politicized.

The Vice President

An important new political and institutional support for presidents in recent years has been the expanded role of the vice president and his staff. For most of the history of the presidency, vice presidents were obscure figures. Abraham Lincoln is generally regarded as the greatest president, but how many people know the name of his first vice president? (It was Hannibal Hamlin.) Vice presidents were usually chosen because they enhanced the prospects that a party's presidential ticket would win; after the election, they had almost nothing to do with the presidency. The vice presidency seemed dreary and frustrating to most of its occupants—in the words of Franklin Roosevelt's first vice president, John Nance Garner, it was "hardly worth a pitcher of spit."[13]

As the burdens placed on the presidency multiplied, however, contemporary chief executives realized that vice presidents and their staffs could provide valuable assistance. The first vice president to play a significant role as a policy and political adviser to the president was Walter Mondale, who brought his years of Senate experience to bear in helping Jimmy Carter, an outsider unfamiliar with the political habits of Washington, D.C. Al Gore played an even more influential role during Bill Clinton's two terms. Until tensions arising from Gore's own bid for the presidency drove them apart, Gore was almost a partner to Clinton.

Richard Cheney, George W. Bush's vice president, surpassed Gore and become the most powerful vice president in American history. Cheney was perhaps the president's closest counselor, conferring often with Bush and attending most high-level meetings in the White House. And he was the administration's most important emissary to Congress; his own highly conservative voting record while a member of the House of Representatives gave him a special stature among Republicans on Capitol Hill. Cheney's most controversial role was as the Bush administration's chief advocate for going to war against Iraq. He made the case for war even more hyperbolically than did President Bush and continued throughout the course of the administration to portray it in glowing terms, while fiercely denouncing war opponents. Critics blamed Cheney for much of what went wrong in the Bush presidency, dubbing the gruff and grim vice president "Darth Vader."

Joseph Biden, Barack Obama's vice president, brings considerable Washington experience—more than three decades in the United States Senate—to his position. Like Cheney, Biden has aided a president with less Capitol Hill experience

than his own in the crucial area of congressional relations. But his principal role has been as a top adviser and trouble-shooter for Obama in international relations. While avoiding Cheney's much-criticized accumulation of power, Biden has maintained a major voice in the Obama administration's decision-making process. Journalist James Traub has dubbed Biden "the second most powerful vice president in history."[14]

Cabinet

Beyond the White House staff, the EOP, and the office of the vice president lies the cabinet and the vast expanse of the executive branch. The **president's cabinet** is composed of the appointed heads of the fifteen principal executive agencies, plus a few others, such as the U.S. ambassador to the United Nations. Americans use the term *cabinet* in two ways. In the first, the cabinet is simply the collection of individuals appointed by the president to head the principal executive agencies. In the second, the cabinet is a collegial body, meeting together with the president to supply its collective advice.

Most presidents talk of using the cabinet as a collective forum. Meetings of the cabinet make excellent TV and photo opportunities, showing off the president surrounded by prestigious and weighty advisers. In actuality, cabinet meetings are routine affairs, useful for little more than symbolism. Not surprisingly, most cabinet members come to meetings to pursue the interests of their own departments. Presidents learn not to expect much from a cabinet meeting and instead solicit advice from individuals directly engaged in policy matters.

Therefore, the cabinet is more accurately described as a collection of individual department heads. In this collection, not all heads are equal. As presidency scholar Thomas E. Cronin has shown, presidents turn most often to their *inner cabinet*, composed of the secretaries of state, defense, and treasury, along with the attorney general.[15] These cabinet secretaries handle the subjects most important to the president. Controversial nominees for inner cabinet posts can provoke intense political conflict, as was evident in the confirmation battle over George W. Bush's first attorney general, John Ashcroft, a Christian conservative.

The *outer cabinet* contains the remainder of the departments, such as agriculture, education, and transportation. The business of these departments is not ordinarily central to a president's program. Members of the outer cabinet often find that the prestige of their title is not matched by their proximity to the president. For example, when President Nixon's secretary of the interior, Walter Hickel, unhappily resigned in 1970, he observed that he had seen the president in private only twice in fifteen months.[16]

In recent administrations, presidents have been expected by constituency groups and the media alike to have women and minorities in their cabinets. Until President Clinton appointed Janet Reno as attorney general in his first term, women and minorities had only held positions in the outer cabinet. Since Reno's appointment, women and minorities have been moving more frequently into the inner cabinet. Clinton appointed Madeleine Albright as secretary of state during his second term. In his first term, the younger Bush appointed Colin Powell, an African American, as secretary of state. At the beginning of his second term, Condoleezza Rice, an African-American woman, served as secretary of state, and Alberto Gonzales, a Hispanic, served as attorney general.[17] Barack Obama's first-term inner cabinet included Hillary Clinton as secretary of state and Eric Holder, an African American, as attorney general.

Managing the Bureaucracy

If presidents are to control the vast federal bureaucracy, they need the assistance of a strong cabinet. But cabinet members are subject to tugs besides the directives of the White House—pressures from Congress, from interest groups, from the staffs of their own agencies. Presidents and their White House staffers have complained about members of the outer cabinet "going native" (that is, taking on the perspectives of the departments they were appointed to head) or building personal empires.

Whatever help they receive from their cabinet appointees, presidents find the management of the federal bureaucracy arduous. Prescribed by the Constitution, it is a task that requires a president to "take Care that the Laws be faithfully executed." In traditional management theory, the executive branch should be a pyramid, with the president on top and bureaucrats underneath carrying out orders. But the modern administrative state diverges from this theory.

A number of factors limit a president's control over the bureaucracy. The vast size of the modern administrative state is itself a limitation, because no president, even with the help of a large White House staff, can keep track of more than a fraction of what is taking place in the bureaucracy. The historical shift from patronage to civil service has also limited presidential control. Civil servants, unlike White House staffers, do not depend on the president for their jobs and are likely to be less concerned about the success of the president than about the mission, budget, and growth of their own agencies. (The perspective of civil servants may seem narrow compared to that of the White House, but civil servants often have more experience and knowledge in their fields than do White House staff.) In addition, Congress has considerable influence over executive agencies through its budgetary and statutory authority.

The capacity of executive agencies to resist directives has frustrated presidents. As President Truman prepared to hand over his office to the newly elected General Eisenhower, he predicted: "He will sit here and he'll say, 'Do this! Do that!' And nothing will happen. Poor Ike—it won't be a bit like the Army!"[18] Frustration with managing the bureaucracy has led presidents to try to shift functions from that bureaucracy into the White House itself. More recently, it has led to determined campaigns to make the bureaucracy serve the president's agenda.

In seeking control over the bureaucracy, an important tool is the **executive order**. An executive order is a presidential directive to subordinates in the executive branch that carries

Guest Op-Ed

Stephen Skowronek
Yale University

PRESIDENTS AS AGENTS OF POLITICAL CHANGE

In anticipation of the departure of George W. Bush, the candidates in the 2008 presidential race competed on the promise of political change: "change you can believe in," "the experience to change things," "the change you deserve." So what really makes a president an effective agent of political change? Is it the ability to move public opinion on behalf of a policy proposal? Is it insider knowledge of how to work the system to achieve results? Is it political sensitivity to the issues of the day and mastery of the alternatives available? Is it strong majorities in Congress?

All this stuff is important, but it is seldom enough. In fact, a focus on these factors misconstrues the nature of the problem. They tell us what it takes for presidents to get things done, as if getting things done is synonymous with effective political change. This supposition is faulty on several counts. All presidents get things done, and all presidents change things; yet few are able to stay abreast of the changes they set in motion, and those who do more are not necessarily more effective in this regard than those who do less. By the standard indicators, Lyndon Johnson had it all: public support, overwhelming congressional majorities, consummate skill, and advice from the best and the brightest. And by the measure of getting things done, he would rank as the most effective political leader of the twentieth century. But Johnson self-destructed in office. He lost control over the changes his actions instigated, and he withdrew from his reelection bid in the face of the mounting discontent.

Getting things done has never been as much of a problem for presidents as securing the legitimacy of the changes they effect. Presidents who lend authoritative meaning to political change bind friends and foes alike; those who fail to do so find that the changes they instigate foment political controversy among their allies and mobilize their opponents.

Presidents are effective as agents of political change only when their actions redefine the terms and conditions of legitimate national government.

This is a tall order indeed. Most presidents fail to control the meaning of their actions. Good intentions often run up against intractable circumstances, and in the course of events, even apparent successes can be redefined by one's foes as failures.

More sobering still is the historical observation that those who have mastered this test have all come to power in the same rare circumstances. The most effective agents of political change in American presidential history—Thomas Jefferson, Andrew Jackson, Abraham Lincoln, Franklin Roosevelt, and Ronald Reagan—rose to office as leaders of insurgent movements. They stood against the commitments of ideology and interest of a long-dominant party at a time when those commitments were vulnerable to forthright repudiation for their manifest failures and moral bankruptcy. It would appear that nothing is so effective for presidents in controlling the meaning of the changes they set in motion as the rare opening to repudiate and denounce a collapsing status quo and to offer up their leadership as the nation's only alternative to national ruin.

On reflection, it may not be that surprising that presidents are most effective as agents of political change when they stand opposed to a regime that has, in the course of events, lost all authority. But this simple fact has grim implications for the many who come to power affiliated with established commitments or those whose opposition is constrained by the residual political resilience of those commitments. These presidents will find it very difficult to control the meaning of their actions. They will surely change things, but on the crucial test of changing things authoritatively, in a way that will last, they are likely to fall short.

the force of law. Executive orders not only set rules for bureaucrats; they also are binding on individuals and organizations in the private and nonprofit sectors if these receive federal funds. Through executive orders, presidents have promulgated major policy changes without needing legislation. President Truman desegregated the armed forces through an executive order. President Johnson instituted the controversial policy of affirmative action for federal contractors with an executive order. President Reagan subjected federal regulations to cost-benefit analysis through an executive order. However, executive orders do not always have the staying power of legislation, for what one president can order another can reverse. President Reagan ordered a ban on federal funding of international agencies that offer abortion counseling, President Clinton directed that the ban be lifted, the second President Bush reinstated it, and President Obama eliminated it for the second time.[19]

One area where the administration of George W. Bush used this form of power to alter the bureaucracy was in the relationship between religious institutions and social services. Although achieving little in promoting a "faith-based initiative" through legislation, the Bush White House advanced religion's role in welfare policy through administrative action. By executive order, Bush established a new White House Office of Faith-Based and Community Initiatives. Smaller offices also were created in existing cabinet departments, such as Education, Health and Human Services, and Housing and Urban Development, to facilitate greater financial support to religious institutions providing social services. Reversing a rule established by President Johnson prohibiting organizations receiving federal grants from discrimination on the basis of race, creed, color, or national origin, President Bush announced a new rule whereby religious organizations contracting with the federal government to supply social services may consider religious beliefs in their hiring decisions. In accordance with his own profession of faith, and in service to the Christian conservatives that are a major element of the Republican Party coalition, Bush thus turned the federal bureaucracy into an ally and financial supporter of religious institutions.[20]

The Presidency and the Congress

The relationship between the president and Congress is seldom smooth. Conflict is more common than cooperation—as the framers of the Constitution intended. In *The Federalist Papers*, James Madison set down the theory of checks and balances: "Ambition must be made to counteract ambition."[21] The clash of presidential and congressional ambitions is constitutional theory in action.

This clash is often presented by journalists or political scientists as a competition between the national viewpoint of the presidency and the local viewpoint of members of Congress—a portrayal that makes the president the unique champion of popular democracy at the national level. But the idea that the presidency is almost always bound to be a better servant of the public interest than Congress is not well founded. Sometimes, presidents do take a national standpoint, while Congress responds with parochial objections. Generally, however, it is more accurate to say that even though presidents speak for a broader coalition of interests than *individual* members of Congress, Congress *as a whole* may speak for an equally broad, or broader, coalition.

Before accepting the claim that Congress is locally oriented and the president alone speaks for the public interest at the national level, we should remember that neither branch has a monopoly on the representation of public ends. Some public ends have been represented better by the White House at one time, and by the majority in Congress at another. Social welfare and civil rights legislation drew greater support from Presidents Kennedy and Johnson than from Congress between 1961 and 1969, but from 1969 to 1977 the same kind of legislation had more backing in Congress than in the administrations of Presidents Nixon and Ford. In this case, insisting that what the presidency favors is more in the national interest than what Congress favors would require us to believe that social welfare and civil rights programs ceased to be in the national interest the moment the White House changed hands.

The image of presidents as champions of popular democracy at the national level draws upon periods in which presidents achieved dramatic legislative breakthroughs: Franklin Roosevelt in 1933–1935, Lyndon Johnson in 1965, Ronald Reagan in 1981. But these were moments when presidents enjoyed electoral mandates and congressional backing—that is, when they could legitimately claim to represent a majoritarian popular democratic coalition. Absent these relatively rare political conditions, president and Congress reflect differing coalitions, and it is often hard to tell which institution has the better claim to represent popular democratic goals.

Congressional Roadblocks

Why does Congress so often oppose the president? Perhaps the most important source of conflict is electoral. Chosen in districts or states, members of Congress have a different constituency than the president. To keep their jobs, they must satisfy voters who are not necessarily backers of the president. Moreover, members of Congress build their own campaign organizations and raise their own campaign funds. With different constituencies and independent political bases, they must chart their own courses.

Analyses that use the personalized presidency approach suggest that a president's ability to overcome congressional roadblocks hinges mainly on personal skill in legislative matters. But paying attention to historical context suggests that presidents come into office with widely varying opportunities for major legislative achievements. Although skill is never irrelevant, variation in such factors as the public mood or the size of the election victory opens the window for legislative triumphs for some presidents, while leaving others facing almost inevitable frustrations at the hands of Congress.[22]

Divided government—in which one party controls the White House and the other party controls one or both houses of Congress—has a significant impact on a president's prospects for obtaining passage of legislation. In recent years, the institutional context of divided control between polarized parties has made it even harder for presidents in Congress than in the past. As a consequence of divided government, neither the elder George Bush nor Bill Clinton (after his first two years) attempted to push as many large-scale initiatives through Congress as their predecessors had.[23] Barack Obama also had to scale back his legislative ambitions after Republicans captured the majority in the House in the 2010 elections.

On the other hand, polarization in the context of unified government may work to a president's advantage. Although his partisan majorities in the House and Senate were small, the discipline and cohesiveness of congressional Republicans amid conditions of partisan warfare were indispensable for George W. Bush's legislative victories in the areas of taxes and Medicare. Barack Obama would never have achieved health care reform in 2010 without strong Democratic majorities in Congress.

In the face of roadblocks from Congress, presidents are hardly helpless. Which factors are most important in determining their success with Congress? Political scientist George C. Edwards has argued that a president's success in securing passage of legislation depends on the partisan composition of Congress and the president's standing with the American public. Examining the years 1953 to 1996, Edwards found that the level of support for a president's program from members of his own party was usually more than thirty percentage points greater than the level of support from members of the other party.[24] A president enjoying a sizeable partisan majority in Congress (such as Obama in 2009–10) thus can hope for a successful legislative record, whereas a president facing a majority from the other party has dubious legislative prospects. Compare, for example, the legislative situations confronting the two Bushes when each took office. Although George W. Bush had only a narrow Republican majority in the House and a fifty-fifty split in the Senate in 2001, he was still in a far more advantageous position than his father, who faced Democratic majorities of ten in the Senate and eighty-five in the House in 1989.

Even unified government does not guarantee legislative success, however, as Bill Clinton painfully learned during his first two years in office. A president's standing with the public is another important factor with Congress. Presidents whose popularity is sinking cannot count on as much party loyalty as can more popular executives. To be successful with Congress, a president usually needs both a favorable partisan majority in the legislature and a favorable standing in the public opinion polls.

Presidential Resources

The president does have some resources that improve the prospects that he or she gets congressional approval. The White House legislative program sets the congressional agenda. By establishing a strong, well-timed agenda, a president can shape the terms in which subsequent congressional debate is conducted. Working for that agenda on the president's behalf is the legislative liaison staff, a portion of the White House staff that spends its time on Capitol Hill. Members of the liaison staff keep the president informed of the political maneuvering for important bills and provide favors to members of Congress in the hopes that they will later return these favors to the White House with their votes.

The favors that the White House can offer are valuable but limited. To win a few swing voters in a tight legislative contest, presidents can promise federal judgeships or positions as U.S. attorneys. Federal grants or contracts can be steered to the district or state of a crucial legislator. Minor provisions of a bill can be altered to favor interest groups.

A resource that the White House possesses in somewhat greater abundance is the mystique of the presidency. To be photographed with the president or called to meet with the president at the White House can boost a representative's standing with constituents. Apart from political gain, few members of Congress are immune to the mystique of presidential authority. Ronald Reagan thus bestowed presidential cufflinks on numerous members of Congress and invited legislators to use the presidential box at the Kennedy Center in Washington. George W. Bush cultivated the goodwill of legislators by bestowing chummy nicknames on them.

If all else fails, a president retains the constitutional weapon of the **veto**. When Congress presents the president with a bill, ten days (Sundays excepted) are given to sign it into law, veto (disapprove) it and return it with a message explaining objections, or do nothing, in which case it becomes law without a signature. Should the president exercise the second option, a two-thirds vote in each legislative branch is necessary to override the veto. If Congress adjourns during the ten-day period and the president does not sign the bill, it is blocked with a *pocket veto*.

Overrides of presidential vetoes are infrequent. The elder Bush had only one veto overridden during his presidency, and only two vetoes were overridden in Clinton's two terms. The veto is a particularly important weapon for an administration in which the opposition party controls Congress and is pursuing its own legislative agenda. Thus, Clinton used vetoes—and threats of vetoes—to stop the Republican revolution of 1995 in its tracks. By contrast, enjoying the advantage of Republican dominance in Congress, the younger Bush did not veto a single bill during his first term. Once Democrats took charge of Congress in 2007–2008, however, Bush frequently used his veto pen. Vetoes and veto threats are not only handy for obstructing the legislation favored by the other party. Employed in a strategic fashion, they can compel the congressional majority to modify legislation so that it will be closer to the preferences of the White House.

Vetoes are not the only weapon that presidents possess to block legislative provisions that they oppose after Congress has enacted them. **Signing statements**, issued when bills are signed into law, are employed by presidents to say that certain provisions in the bill are of questionable constitutionality and might not be enforced by the executive branch. President George W. Bush was not the first or last to issue signing statements, but he made unprecedented use of this weapon to put his own stamp on legislation. Bush opposed the Detainee Treatment Act of 2005, which contained a provision banning the use of torture by the U.S. government, but when Congress passed the bill by veto-proof majorities, he announced that he would not be bound by the prohibition on torture if he decided that it infringed upon his authority as commander in chief. Critics of signing statements argue that through this practice presidents can wield a secondary veto—and that unlike the constitutional form, this one can't be overridden by Congress.[25]

That presidents cannot regularly dominate Congress has been frustrating to those who assume that the executive is the only champion of popular democracy in national politics. But neither wisdom nor democratic purpose is always on the president's side. Congressional checks on the president fulfill the original constitutional concern to avert a dangerous concentration of power.

The Presidency and Economic Power

Congress is not the only powerful and independent institution with which a president must come to terms. Numerous centers of private power possess resources presidents want, as well as resources to constrain them. Clashes between the White House and Capitol Hill are familiar dramas in American politics. Less visible are the connections between the presidency and the reigning powers of the political economy.

Before the New Deal, presidents seldom tried to affect overall economic conditions. But once the Great Depression revealed the disastrous consequences of an uncontrolled economy, Franklin Roosevelt asserted presidential responsibility. His role became a legal responsibility of every president after him, thanks to the **Employment Act of 1946**. It gave the federal government—and especially the president—the duty "to foster and promote free competitive enterprise, to avoid economic fluctuations or to diminish the effects thereof, and to maintain employment, production, and purchasing power." The act also established the Council of Economic Advisers to assist the president and required an annual economic report to Congress.

What can presidents do to promote a healthy economy? Two major policy tools are available to the president as an economic manager: fiscal policy and monetary policy. Fiscal policy involves federal taxation and spending to affect economic conditions. For example, the president can propose a tax cut; such a cut will, predictably, increase economic activity. Monetary policy involves the money supply and the level of interest rates. For example, the president can, with the cooperation of the Federal Reserve, slow down inflationary pressures in the economy through higher interest rates that make borrowing money more expensive.

These actions require the president to obtain the agreement of other powerful actors and institutions. A president can propose changes in federal taxation or spending, but Congress has the final authority over them. Presidents can suggest monetary policy, but the Federal Reserve Board has the ultimate say.[26]

Presidential power over the economy also is limited by the structural power of the corporate sector, which, as we saw in Chapter 4, plays a decisive role in determining the level of private investment in America. This investment is critical to the health of the economy. Although investment decisions are made largely on economic grounds, spokespersons for big business like to attribute lagging investment to the lack of "business confidence" in a president with whom they differ. No president wants to be viewed as undermining business confidence.

Some presidents have smooth sailing with the corporate sector. Republican presidents are more likely to have personal roots in the corporate world: Ronald Reagan had been a spokesperson for General Electric, while both Bushes (and Vice President Dick Cheney) had been executives in the oil industry. Regardless of their résumés, Presidents Eisenhower, Nixon, Ford, Reagan, and the two Bushes ran administrations whose personnel and policies pleased the corporate sector. Reagan's tax cuts and deregulation of business redistributed income from working people to owners of corporate assets. The pro-business policies of George W. Bush had the same economic effect.

Other presidents, most often Democrats, have had a rockier relationship. Elected in the face of corporate opposition, Presidents Kennedy, Carter, and Clinton struggled against charges that they were undermining business confidence and jeopardizing the health of the American economy. Clinton played up to Wall Street with his initial deficit-reduction program in 1993 and allied himself with corporate lobbyists on several occasions to push free-trade legislation through Congress. Despite his efforts, most business executives continued to favor his Republican opponents. Clinton did not get much credit from the business community for the good things he had done for it.[27]

President Obama has been the latest Democrat to feel the wrath of business leaders. His financial regulatory reform and proposal for higher taxes on the wealthy led corporate and banking CEOs to label him as an "anti-business" president. These business leaders blamed low levels of investment and job creation not on sluggish consumer demand in the Great Recession but on the unfriendly signals coming from the White House. Obama tried to assuage corporate antipathy by appointing William Daley, a former business executive, as White House Chief of Staff, but the complaints from the business community kept on coming.[28]

Whether Republicans or Democrats occupy the White House, the power of the corporate and financial sectors has a major influence on presidential action. The business community does not have to have one of its own in the White House to benefit from presidential policy making. Its weapon of business confidence generally deters presidents—even ones elected primarily by the votes of ordinary working people—from pursuing a popular democratic economic agenda.

The Presidency and National Security

Presidential freedom of action is more extensive in foreign and military policy. Presidents enjoy greater leeway here to protect the national interest, promote democracy around the globe, or act as peacemakers. Yet if presidential dominance in foreign affairs is supposed to serve popular democratic goals, its recent history smacks more of elite democratic methods. Since World War II, presidents have made war on their own initiative, concealed some of their actions in the deepest secrecy, and employed the agencies under their control to repress opponents. What historian Arthur Schlesinger Jr. has labeled the "imperial presidency" of the Cold War era resembles the dangerous monarch that the Anti-federalists predicted.[29]

Presidents are not free of opposition in conducting foreign and military policy. Nonetheless, they have exceptional resources when they engage in international relations—resources that cannot be matched by any other national institution.

The Constitution is an important source of these resources. It entrusts the president with making treaties and appointing American ambassadors, although it requires the concurrence of two-thirds of the Senate for the first and a majority of the Senate for the second. The president also receives ambassadors from other governments, and although this power may appear merely ceremonial, it has been interpreted as giving the president a unilateral power of U.S. recognition.

The Supreme Court has upheld a paramount role for the president in the conduct of American foreign policy. In *United States v. Curtiss-Wright Corporation* (1936), the Court gave presidents wide latitude. Writing for the majority, Justice Sutherland proclaimed "the very delicate, plenary, and exclusive power of the president as the sole organ of the federal government in international relations—a power which does not require as a basis for its exercise an act of Congress."[30]

If the Constitution and the Supreme Court have bolstered the president's position in international affairs, so have the institutional resources of the executive branch. The president receives information from American diplomatic and military personnel stationed around the globe, besides secret information from the Central Intelligence Agency (CIA) and the military intelligence services. When foreign policy controversies arise, presidents claim to be the most knowledgeable actors on the scene.

Presidential Dominance in War Making

Believing that placing the decision to go to war in the hands of a single individual was dangerous, the drafters of the Constitution entrusted that decision to the assembled representatives of the people. The president was to be the commander in chief of the armed forces once Congress determined the need for armed hostilities. Historically, however, it proved hard to keep presidents in this secondary role. Without any congressional declaration of war, presidents began to use American forces to repulse attacks on American property abroad, to suppress domestic turmoil, or to fight small-scale wars. (see Table 13.1)

The capacity of a president to employ American armed forces became controversial during the Vietnam War. Presidents Johnson and Nixon were determined to carry out their Vietnam policies against rising antiwar protests from American citizens and within Congress. Once the legal authority for their war making was questioned, they asserted that the commander-in-chief clause in the Constitution gave them vast military powers. When Nixon extended the war into neighboring Cambodia in 1970, he justified his action on the grounds that, as commander in chief, he had the right to take any action necessary to protect American troops. With even less justification, he ordered the continued bombing of Cambodia in 1973, even after all American ground forces had been withdrawn. Nixon became precisely what both the framers of the Constitution and their Anti-federalist critics feared: the eighteenth-century British monarch who involved the nation in war on the basis of personal whim.

Congressional Attempts to Rein in the Executive

Congress attempted to reassert its constitutional role in war making by passing—over Nixon's veto—the **War Powers Resolution of 1973**. According to this resolution, the president must, if circumstances permit, consult with Congress before sending American forces into a situation where armed conflict is anticipated. The president must also provide Congress

Table 13.1 Presidential Engagement in Military Conflicts Since World War II	
President	*Military Conflicts*
Harry S. Truman	Korean War
Dwight D. Eisenhower	None
John F. Kennedy	Vietnam War
Lyndon B. Johnson	Vietnam War
	Dominican Republic conflict
Richard M. Nixon	Vietnam War
Gerald R. Ford	Vietnam War
	Mayaguez incident
Jimmy Carter	None
Ronald Reagan	Civil war in Nicaragua
	Air strikes against Libya
George H. W. Bush	Invasion of Panama
	First Persian Gulf War
	Somali conflict
Bill Clinton	Somali conflict
	Air strikes against Serb forces in Bosnia
	Air strikes against Serb forces in Kosovo
George W. Bush	War in Afghanistan
	Iraq war
Barack Obama	War in Afghanistan
	Air strikes against Libya

Source: Compiled by the authors.

with a written report within forty-eight hours of dispatching American forces into combat. After sixty days, the president must withdraw these forces from combat unless Congress has declared war or otherwise authorized continued engagement. An additional thirty days is granted to remove them from combat if the president claims that this period is needed for a safe withdrawal.

Presidents since Nixon have complained that the War Powers Resolution ties their hands and harms American national security. The resolution actually has had little effect. Dramatic military actions since 1973 have not been hampered by the War Powers Resolution. Because the president has enjoyed a near monopoly on information in these situations and the public has supported presidential actions, Congress has been reluctant to insist on the requirements it established in 1973.

The end of the Cold War made only a minor difference in control over war making. President Clinton was just as insistent as Cold War executives of his right to deploy American troops abroad without needing legal authority from Congress. In March 1999, Clinton, in concert with the United States' NATO allies, began air strikes against Yugoslavia to force the dictator Slobodan Milosevic to call an end to the killing of ethnic Albanians in the Yugoslav province of Kosovo. Legislation authorizing the president to conduct the air war against Yugoslavia passed the Senate, but—on a tie vote—the House failed to pass the measure. The president ignored this rebuff from the House and waged war anyway. Clinton, wrote political scientist David Gray Adler, claimed in the Kosovo crisis "an unlimited, unreviewable, unilateral presidential war power."[31]

The shock of the terrorist attacks of September 11, 2001, restored presidential war-making capacity to a level not seen since the war in Vietnam. Unlike President Clinton, President Bush had little difficulty with Congress in taking the nation into wars in Afghanistan and Iraq. Moreover, he asserted sweeping new authority as commander in chief to label captured forces as "enemy combatants" and imprison them at the Guantanamo Bay naval base for an indefinite duration. Once the war in Iraq went badly, and the public was shocked by ugly pictures of American troops humiliating Iraqi detainees at Abu Ghraib prison, Bush faced mounting opposition in Congress and the courts. Despite a loss of public support and a shift to Democratic control of Congress, however, he was still able to control American military strategy to the end of his presidency.

As a senator, Barack Obama was a vocal critic of President Bush's war-making claims. As president, however, Obama has made similar claims for unilateral presidential authority over the dispatch of U.S. forces into armed conflicts. When the U.S. assumed an important role in the aerial campaign to topple the regime of Libyan dictator Muammar Qaddafi in 2011, Obama ignored the War Powers Resolution on the grounds that American military actions fell short of full-scale combat.[32] Charging that the president's actions with respect to Libya violated the U.S. Constitution, law professor Bruce Ackerman wrote that "Barack Obama's administration is breaking new ground in its construction of an imperial presidency."[33]

Presidential Secrecy

Inadequate though it may be, the War Powers Resolution at least serves as a statement that we recognize the potential for abuse in the presidential power to make war. There is similar potential in the **presidential power of secrecy**. Once the United States became involved in a worldwide Cold War against communism, revolution, and nationalism, new powers of secrecy were assumed by the White House. As we shall see in more detail in Chapter 18, the CIA, created in 1947, became a weapon of presidential policy making in foreign affairs. Through the CIA, presidents could intervene covertly in the politics of other nations, bribing politicians, financing pro-American parties, or encouraging military coups against governments that the president regarded as unfavorable to U.S. interests. Some evidence even suggests that the CIA offered presidents means to assassinate foreign leaders.[34]

When presidents' dominant foreign policy roles have been challenged, some have resorted to repressive tactics. The Nixon administration undertook a notorious secret campaign to destroy its critics. Journalists had their phones wiretapped. A secret White House unit, known as the Plumbers, engaged in illegal break-ins to gather damaging material on foes of Nixon's Vietnam policy. The White House compiled a large list of these critics—the Enemies List—and sought to use the auditing mechanisms of the Internal Revenue Service to harass them. Fundamental American liberties became insignificant when they stood in the way of presidential power.[35]

The George W. Bush administration secretly went after critics of the war in Iraq. When former ambassador Joseph Wilson disclosed in the *New York Times* that administration "facts" about Iraq's search for nuclear weapons materials were a fabrication, Bush's top advisers leaked information to the press to discredit Wilson by revealing that his wife, Valerie Plame, was a CIA agent. Advisers to Bush falsely denied their involvement in the leak about Plame; one of them, "Scooter" Libby, the top aide to Vice President Cheney, was convicted of perjury and obstruction of justice for his part in the affair.

Secret action is enticing. It offers a president the opportunity to advance foreign policy goals through methods that would raise ethical and constitutional questions if pursued openly. It allows a policy to persist even when it lacks support from majorities in Congress and the American people. Moreover, it is rationalized by the elite democratic argument that presidents have a superior vantage point and greater expertise than Congress and the public in international affairs. But secret action denies the people presidential accountability and undermines the democratic debate.

The President and the Public

Rooted in the assumptions of elite democracy, the framers of the Constitution did not want a president to get too close to the American people. They placed the immediate choice of the chief executive in the hands of electors, who were supposed to be the most distinguished political elite in each state. The framers expected that the dignity of the president's office and the long duration of the president's term would provide insulation from mass passion or popular demand for economic change.[36] Modern presidents, in contrast, claim a close bond with the American people. The voice that originates from the White House purports to be the voice of popular democracy. Cultivating public support has become a central activity of the presidency.

Present-day presidents campaign hard for public support because they believe it boosts their political influence. Congress, they presume, will react more favorably to a popular than an unpopular president; bureaucrats and interest group leaders similarly will be impressed by high presidential poll ratings. To gain public support, presidents are increasingly, in the words of political scientist Samuel Kernell, "going public." A growing percentage of presidential time is spent on the road, selling White House policies. Kernell suggests that "public speaking, political travel, and appearances before special constituencies outside Washington constitute the repertoire of modern leadership."[37]

Ironically, as presidents fly around the country to promote their democratic bond with the public, their vehicle, Air Force One, is the epitome of power and luxury. Air Force One has become as widely recognized a symbol of the president's uniquely elevated stature as the regal carriage of the British monarchy.[38] Patrick Henry would not have been surprised!

A president's effectiveness in "going public" depends in part on his or her communication skills. Most modern presidents have not been especially talented at presenting their personalities and programs to the public. Yet even with skilled communicators in the White House, the impact of presidential rhetoric is often exaggerated. Ronald Reagan, labeled "The Great Communicator" by the media, was unable to win support for his anti-Communist policy in Central America. Bill Clinton and Barack Obama fought losing public-relations battles on behalf of their health care plans.[39]

Why is the president's "bully pulpit" overrated? Many citizens are simply inattentive to presidential messages. Because those messages typically have a partisan spin, some citizens may reject the president's case because they identify with the opposing party.[40] Further, presidents do not have the field of public communications all to themselves; opponents of their policies in Congress or interest groups can contest the president through the media.[41] So even when presidents set out to sway public opinion to their side on a priority program, any gains they can make through "going public" are likely to be small and may not last long enough to make a difference with Congress.

Public evaluations of a president, as measured by opinion polls, are most affected by events that impact the lives of ordinary citizens. The greatest blows to presidential popularity have come from failed wars (Truman in Korea, Johnson in Vietnam, and the second Bush in Iraq) and weak economies (Ford, Carter, both Bushes, and Obama). Scandals slashed the public's approval scores for Nixon (Watergate) and Reagan (Iran-Contra), but not for Clinton (the Lewinsky affair). Suffering from both a failed war and a weak economy, George W. Bush set the record for public disapproval of a president in 2008.

The President and the Media

The media play a major role in a modern president's relationship with the American people. If we listened only to presidents and their White House staffs, we might conclude that the media function as an impediment to presidential communication with the public. A large corps of journalists is stationed at the White House to report on a president's every word and deed; when the president travels, the press corps follows. Presidential blunders or White House staff conflicts are often highlighted by the media, while the president's policy proposals are closely scrutinized by reporters and editorial columnists for hidden political motives. Some presidents' political standing has been badly damaged by negative media coverage.

However, White House complaints about the media tell only one side of the story. The media—especially television—provide a means through which a modern president can cultivate support. The White House devotes more staff resources to communicating through the media than to any other function. An estimated 350 staffers were directly or indirectly involved in communications activities at the beginning of George W. Bush's second term.[42] At the core of this White House publicity machine are the Press Office and the Office of Communications. If these units are skilled at public relations, the media provide opportunities for dramatic presidential appearances, colorful photo opportunities, and engrossing human interest stories about the "first family." If the president has an attractive personality and is a skilled public speaker, the media can amplify his or her charm, wit, or eloquence in a manner that presidents living before the age of television might well have envied.[43]

Among recent administrations, Ronald Reagan's achieved the greatest mastery over the media. In contrast to Reagan, Bill Clinton had a rocky relationship with journalists from the start. But developments in relations between the White House and the media transcend personalities. The most important changes have been technological, especially the decline of the three major television networks and the emergence of multiple cable channels. As political scientist Jeffrey Cohen documents, presidents in office since the rise of cable television receive a smaller volume of news coverage than previously, reporting on their actions is more negative in tone, and the audience for their speeches has shrunk.[44]

The constraints on presidential communication in an age of 24/7 news coverage will be unfortunate if a president wants to educate the American people about important problems and policies. But they may also reduce the capacity of the White House to manipulate the public through the media. From the standpoint of popular democracy, the diminishing ability of a president to dominate the media is welcome. A vital democratic debate is not monopolized by the occupant of the White House.[45]

The Presidency and Democratic Movements

Presidents try to sway public opinion through the media. Can members of the public directly sway the president? What impact can popular democratic movements have on presidential policies?

Democratic movements can help to hold presidents in check when they engage in dubious uses of power. Popular protests have compelled some presidents to alter their courses of action. For example, President Nixon ignored public unhappiness about the war in Vietnam when he expanded the battlefield to the neighboring nation of Cambodia in 1970. In response, college campuses around the nation erupted in protest, and a huge throng of demonstrators descended on Washington, D.C., to let the president know of their outrage.[46] Shortly thereafter, the president withdrew American forces from Cambodia.

Some of the finest presidential moments have come when the chief executive responded to citizens and moved the nation closer to fulfillment of its democratic values. When Abraham Lincoln responded to mounting abolitionist pressures by emancipating slaves, when Franklin Roosevelt supported mobilized labor for collective bargaining rights, when Lyndon Johnson endorsed the civil rights movement by voicing its slogan, "We shall overcome," the presidency became an instrument of popular democratic leadership. These presidents were moved in the direction of popular democracy by the force of popular pressures, which compelled them to rethink their previous political calculations. But their popular democratic leadership was not simply a matter of gaining new support or attracting new voters. Mass movements educated these presidents, giving them a deeper understanding of democratic responsibilities.[47]

Barack Obama is the first president actually to have a background in mass-movement politics. However, once his cautious approach as president fell short of the high hopes that his presidential campaign had encouraged, he began to feel the heat from mass-movement pressure. Criticism from gay and lesbian organizations prodded Obama to end the "Don't Ask, Don't Tell" policy that maintained discrimination in the military. The dramatic "Occupy" encampments that sprang up in numerous American cities in 2011 helped push Obama into a more populist stance against the wealthy "one percent." These and other movements demonstrated democratic possibilities that the president otherwise might not have considered.

Conclusion: The Elite Democratic Presidency

The history of occasional presidential collaboration with mass movements is encouraging to supporters of popular democracy. Nonetheless, popular democrats must be aware that the pressures toward elite democracy will operate on every president, including those like Obama who share popular democratic values.

What is required for a president genuinely to support popular democratic goals? If presidents are concerned about promoting popular democracy, then they need to respect the capacities and intelligence of the people they claim to lead. Rather than attempting to manipulate public opinion, they should engage in a dialogue with citizens. Rather than aiming only to boost their own power, they should recognize their responsibility to empower ordinary citizens.

Presidents have not played the part of popular democratic leader very often in the past. More frequently, the presidency has been an instrument of elite democracy. Surrounded by a huge staff and living like monarchs, presidents tend to be cut off from ordinary Americans. Elitist attitudes and secrecy further distance the president, while making accountability difficult. Connections to and pressures from organized private interests, especially from the corporate and financial sectors, contradict the presidential claim to represent popular democracy. Presidents may cloak themselves in the symbols of popular democracy, but the usual presidential drama, featuring larger-than-life chief executives and passive citizens, is a far cry from the authentic American tradition of popular democracy.

Reader's Guide

Critical Thinking Questions

1. What are the most desirable personal qualities that a president should possess? Could these individual qualities overcome unfavorable circumstances facing the president?

2. Why have recent presidents become so dependent on their White House staffs? How might a president reduce this dependence?

3. Under what conditions can presidents achieve a high level of success with their legislative agendas?

4. Why has the power to make war shifted from Congress to the president? Is this shift necessary? Is it desirable?

5. Do presidents generally try to *educate* the public with their speeches on important issues, or do they try to *manipulate* public opinion for their own benefit?

Key Word Definition

White House staff   The president's personal aides and advisers along with their numerous assistants.

Executive Office of the President (EOP)   The complex of support agencies designed to assist the chief executive, including the White House staff, the Office of Management and Budget, the Council of Economic Advisers, and the National Security Council.

Office of Management and Budget (OMB)   The agency responsible for preparing the annual presidential budget and for scrutinizing legislative proposals originating in the agencies of the executive branch to ensure that these proposals are in accord with the president's legislative program.

Council of Economic Advisers (CEA)   A body of professional economists who provide the president with regular assistance.

National Security Council (NSC)   A governmental body created in 1947 to advise the president and coordinate foreign and defense policy.

president's cabinet   The executive body composed of the appointed heads of the fifteen major executive departments, plus any others designated by the chief executive.

executive order   A presidential directive to subordinates in the executive branch that carries the force of law and may alter public policies.

veto   The constitutional power of the president to reject legislation passed by Congress, subject to a two-thirds override by both houses.

signing statement   A written pronouncement from the president issued when a bill is signed into law, expressing the president's intent about how the new law will be implemented.

Employment Act of 1946   A law giving the federal government responsibility to promote free enterprise, avoid economic fluctuations, and maintain jobs, production, and purchasing power.

War Powers Resolution of 1973   An attempt by Congress to reassert its constitutional authority in the area of war making.

presidential power of secrecy   The ability of the chief executive to make foreign policy and national security decisions that are not subject to public scrutiny.

Bureaucracy: Myth and Reality

THE DEMOCRATIC DEBATE OVER BUREAUCRACY:
  A SHORT HISTORY

THE MODERN ADMINISTRATIVE STATE IN AMERICA

BUREAUCRATS AS POLICY MAKERS

THE POLITICAL ENVIRONMENT OF BUREAUCRACY

BUREAUCRACY AND THE POLITICAL ECONOMY

HOW WELL DOES THE GOVERNMENT WORK?

CONCLUSION: BEYOND MONSTER BUREAUCRACY

Thousands of protestors poured into Wisconsin's state capitol in February 2011, chanting "come out, come out." The target of their wrath, the newly elected Republican governor, Scott Walker, ignored the protestors and stayed in his office. Emboldened by his recent victory, part of the Republicans' national tide of electoral successes in 2010, Walker was proposing major changes in Wisconsin law affecting public employees and their unions.[1]

Like other governors facing huge budget deficits amid the "Great Recession," Walker looked for savings by cutting back on the wages, health benefits, and pension plans of public employees. What made him stand out—and evoke so much anger—was his further proposal to restrict sharply the capacity of public-employee unions to bargain on behalf of their members. To his opponents, this move was not necessitated by Wisconsin's budget problems, but rather represented a strategy to cripple unions in the state, which typically mounted strong electoral opposition to Republicans such as Walker.[2]

After a chaotic political battle, Walker prevailed and his restrictions on public-employee unions became law. However, polls indicated that his initiative was not popular. The governor thought he was aiming at an easy target: bureaucrats. But the protests succeeded in putting more appealing faces on public employees—the faces of teachers, police, firefighters, and many others who worked for Wisconsin's state and local governments. Walker's opponents forced the governor into a recall election, but he survived it by a comfortable margin.

Allies of Walker in neighboring states also experienced a backlash from a public that was more sympathetic to public employees than anticipated. Ohio's Republican governor, John Kasich, steered a bill similar to Walker's through his state's legislature. But in Ohio the voters were able to have their say on the issue in a November 2011 referendum. The result: a landslide majority of 62 percent to repeal Kasich's legislation.[3]

Walker and Kasich engaged in one of America's favorite political sports: bureaucracy-bashing. **Bureaucracy** comprises the units of the executive branch organized in a hierarchical fashion, governed through formal rules, and distinguished by specialized functions.

This chapter primarily concentrates on bureaucracy at the national level. Although all federal bureaus have hierarchy, rule-bound behavior, and specialization, they vary considerably in how they are organized, who staffs them, and what work they do. The employee of the Social Security Administration in Washington processing checks for Social Security recipients and the forest ranger checking on wildlife in the remote reaches of a national park are both bureaucrats. Bureaucracy is not the drab monolith that bureaucracy bashers condemn.

Humongous HMO.

Bureaucracy is indeed a problem for a democratic political order, but it is also a necessity. It is a problem because bureaucratic hierarchy, expertise, and insulation from direct accountability can produce government operations that ignore the concerns of ordinary citizens. It is a necessity because in modern society the government programs that a democratic majority wants require skilled public administration.

The Democratic Debate over Bureaucracy: A Short History

Bureaucracy has been one of the principal battlegrounds between elite democrats and popular democrats, both of whom have approached the issue with mixed emotions. Elite democrats have usually been the ones building up bureaucratic capacity in the federal government, but sometimes they have feared that what they have built might be transformed into an instrument of popular democratic control. (This fear is central to the contemporary elite reaction against bureaucracy.) Popular democrats have usually resisted the growth of bureaucracy, but sometimes they have needed it to turn popular democratic objectives into reality.

The Beginnings of American Administration

The Constitution says little about how the president, as chief executive, will delegate the enforcement of the laws. When the first administration was formed under George Washington, there was not much of a bureaucracy. Befitting the aristocratic perspective of the Federalists, administrators were recruited from the class of "gentlemen," and it was assumed that their personal character and reputation would ensure their good conduct without the need for impersonal rules and institutional checks.

The first major challenge to the rule of gentleman administrators came from Jacksonian Democracy. Speaking the language of popular democracy, President Jackson proclaimed that "the duties of all public officers are, or at least admit of being made so plain and simple that men of intelligence may readily qualify themselves for their performance."[4] Although Jackson stated that ordinary citizens should fill most federal posts, in practice he removed only about 10 percent of the civil servants who had labored under his predecessors and replaced them mostly with well-connected lawyers. However, Jackson's presidency was notable for relying less on trust in the personal character of administrators and more on formal rules and procedures to supervise their behavior. In this regard, political scientist Matthew Crenson writes, "the chief administrative legacy of the Jacksonians was bureaucracy."[5]

The Spoils System and Civil Service Reform

Jackson's successors followed his rhetoric more than his practice, turning out large numbers of officeholders and replacing them with supporters. Under this **spoils system**, the victor in each presidential election considered federal employment mostly as an opportunity for political patronage. In one sense, the nineteenth-century spoils system was democratic: It allowed ordinary people, through their work in a political party, to obtain government positions previously reserved for elites. But the periodic shuffling of civil servants made for inefficient administration, and the ties of civil servants to party machines opened the door to corruption.

The system's defects sparked a reform movement after the Civil War that advocated a different basis for selecting national administrators. Reformers demanded that federal employment be based not on party service but on competitive examinations and other measures of competence. Their cause was given a boost when a disappointed office seeker, crazed by his failure to get a patronage position, assassinated President James A. Garfield in 1881. With public attention now fixed on the evils of the spoils system, Congress passed the Pendleton Act in 1883, establishing a civil service commission to administer a merit system for federal employment. Civil service reform, although an important step toward a more efficient federal bureaucracy, was also a victory for elite democrats: Reformers were mainly from the upper class and expected that their class would regain its once-dominant role in administration through examinations that favored the highly educated.

As industrialization transformed American life in the closing decades of the nineteenth century, the problem of regulating giant business corporations gave a further impetus to builders of bureaucracy. Allied with upper-class civil service reformers seeking to expand the administrative capacities of the federal government was a new class of professionals, especially lawyers and social scientists. These state builders were largely elite democrats whose goal was a more rational, expert-dominated administrative order insulated from the partisan strife of popular politics.[6]

It was in the first decades of the twentieth century—the Progressive era—that the bureaucratic state in America first assumed its modern form. The Progressives hoped to combine popular democracy and elite democracy. They sponsored reforms, such as the initiative, referendum, and recall (which allow citizens to vote on legislation and to remove elected officials), that aimed to take power away from party bosses and return it directly to the people. They also proposed to staff an expanded administrative order with scientifically trained and politically neutral experts. As political scientist James Morone has written, "At the heart of the Progressive agenda lay a political paradox: government would simultaneously be returned to the people and placed beyond them, in the hands of the experts."[7]

The New Deal and Bureaucracy

The Great Depression led to an expansion of the federal bureaucracy beyond even the hopes of the Progressive reformers, and the New Deal changed the attitudes of popular democrats toward bureaucracy. Just as with the case of federalism (see Chapter 3), the need to achieve control over the corporations compelled popular democrats to accept a more powerful and bureaucratic federal government. Yet elite democrats still retained considerable influence within this government. The hastily built administrative apparatus of Franklin Roosevelt contained both popular democratic and elite democratic elements.

Harry Hopkins, the administrator of federal programs to aid the unemployed, was an example of New Deal success in reconciling popular democracy and bureaucracy. Putting a public works program for the unemployed into operation with remarkable speed, Hopkins proclaimed that "the only thing that counts is action—and we are going to surround [the program] with as few regulations as possible." Determined to avoid bureaucratic red tape, Hopkins was equally determined to avoid the bureaucrat's reliance on a formal hierarchy of superiors and subordinates.[8]

Unfortunately, much of the bureaucratic machinery created by the New Deal did not reflect Hopkins's popular democratic approach. To cope with the emergency conditions of the Depression, the New Deal tied many of the new administrative agencies to the industrial and agricultural interests with which they dealt. When the Depression passed, the tight bonds between private interests and public agencies remained. The bureaucratic state became, to a disturbing degree, a special-interest state in which administrative expertise was placed in the service of economic elites.

The next major expansion of American bureaucracy came during the 1960s and early 1970s, with new administrative units established to carry out popular democratic goals such as environmental protection, consumer safety, and the elimination of poverty. Yet while the bureaucracy was becoming a more complicated mixture of elite and popular democratic elements, its image was becoming more simplistic and negative. Bureaucracy—with a capital *B*—became a bogeyman for critics of every political persuasion. Conservatives saw a swollen and monstrous Bureaucracy as the chief threat to individual freedom. Liberals and radicals saw an arrogant and stifling Bureaucracy as the chief barrier to social change. It was the conservatives, with the election of Ronald Reagan in 1980, who had the chance to act on their ideological hostility to bureaucracy.

From Ronald Reagan to Barack Obama: Attack or Reinvent Bureaucracy?

President Reagan entered office as an avowed enemy of bureaucracy. During his eight years as chief executive he presided over an unprecedented assault on federal administration. Because Congress blunted many of his attacks, Reagan was not able to enact drastic cuts in the federal bureaucracy. But he did manage to heap scorn on bureaucracy and to broadcast negative stereotypes of it to the public. Big government, the president told Americans, best served the public by "shriveling up and going away."[9]

President Clinton and Vice President Al Gore tackled the topic of bureaucratic reform through a program they labeled as "Reinventing Government." Even though they hoped, like Reagan, to reduce the size of the bureaucracy, their principal goal was different: They wanted the federal government to work better, not to shrivel up and go away.

George W. Bush did not enter the presidency with the overt antibureaucratic agenda of Ronald Reagan. Yet Bush was just as determined as Reagan to assert control over federal agencies and to bring them into line with conservative objectives. Political scientist Paul Light observes that under Bush, White House control over the bureaucracy was "more coordinated and centralized than it has ever been."[10] Coming into office after the pitfalls in weakening government capacity had been made plain during Bush's administration, Barack Obama began to reverse the trend begun by Reagan.[11] Liberals frequently complained that Obama was too compromising in the face of criticism from foes of the federal bureaucracy. Conservatives saw it differently, painting Obama as an unabashed champion of bureaucratic government. The most important accomplishment of the Obama administration in this area, Wall Street reform, will be discussed later.

The Modern Administrative State in America

The present-day federal government is largely an **administrative state**. It is involved in regulating or supporting almost every imaginable form of social activity by means of a large, complex, and diverse bureaucracy.

The Civil Service

Approximately 2.8 million Americans work as civil servants in the federal bureaucracy. Contrary to the image of a centralized bureaucratic machine, the vast majority of federal employees work outside Washington, D.C. Most deliver services where the people are—whether as Social Security branch workers, air traffic controllers, or civilian employees at military installations. Although the federal bureaucracy draws the most attention from critics, it is actually smaller in terms of personnel than state and local governments (see Figure 14.1).

A majority of federal bureaucrats hold their positions in accordance with the General Schedule, a merit-based personnel system in which there are eighteen pay grades. Competitive examinations and formal education are the two principal determinants of merit in the General Schedule. At the highest level of the bureaucracy are the president's political appointees. Their merits are not necessarily the same as those of career civil servants. Certainly, managerial competence is valued for political appointees, but so are loyalty to the president and agreement with his or her political program.

Types of Federal Agencies

The administrative state in America is made up of a bewildering variety of bureaucracies. Federal agencies differ from one another on many scores: form of organization, type of leadership, breadth or narrowness of function, political dependence on or independence from the president, financial dependence on or independence from Congress.

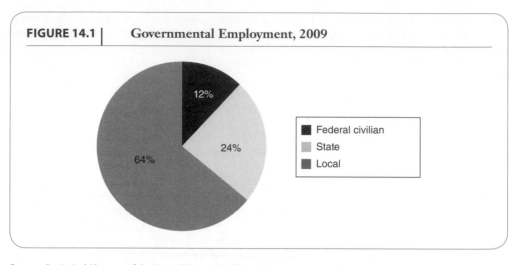

FIGURE 14.1 | Governmental Employment, 2009

Source: *Statistical Abstract of the United States 2012* (http://www.census.gov).

Cabinet departments are the bureaucratic agencies most familiar to Americans. When the federal government was formed, its first agencies were the departments of State, Treasury, and War (along with the individual position of attorney general). Today, there are fifteen cabinet departments, each headed by a secretary appointed by the president: State, Treasury, Defense, Interior, Agriculture, Justice, Commerce, Labor, Health and Human Services, Housing and Urban Development, Transportation, Energy, Education, Veterans Affairs, and Homeland Security. Each is responsible for a broad area of governmental operations whose administration is divided up among specialized bureaus within the department.

Independent agencies stand outside the cabinet departments and generally handle narrower areas of government operation. Examples are the Environmental Protection Agency (EPA), the National Aeronautics and Space Administration (NASA), and the Central Intelligence Agency (CIA). Like cabinet departments, most independent agencies are headed by a single individual appointed by the president.

Independent regulatory commissions are designed to regulate various sectors of the economy. Examples are the Nuclear Regulatory Commission, which regulates the nuclear power industry, and the Securities and Exchange Commission (SEC), which regulates the stock market. By creating multimember commissions drawn from both parties and by giving the commissioners long terms and exemption from presidential removal, Congress has tried to distance these agencies from political pressures and make them neutral and expert regulators. In practice, however, the independent regulatory commissions have not been able to separate administration from politics.

Public corporations are government agencies that engage in business activities. The most familiar of these is the Postal Service (until 1971, the Post Office was a cabinet department). Others are the Tennessee Valley Authority (TVA), which generates and sells electric power; Amtrak, which operates passenger railroads; and the Corporation for Public Broadcasting, which sponsors public television and radio. Public corporations have been created largely to carry out economic activities deemed unprofitable by private businesses.

Federal foundations or endowments allow the government to sponsor scientific and cultural activities that might otherwise languish for lack of funds. The National Science Foundation (NSF) is a major donor to scientific research in the United States. The National

Institutes of Health (NIH) funds research on dangerous diseases, such as acquired immune deficiency syndrome (AIDS). The National Endowment for the Humanities (NEH) and the National Endowment for the Arts (NEA) support the creative projects of scholars, writers, and artists.

Myth and Reality in the Administrative State

To its many detractors, the federal bureaucracy is a bastion of elite privilege and irresponsibility. The expertise and power wielded by bureaucrats lend some credence to these criticisms. But myths about bureaucracy exaggerate its elitist character; in reality, the federal bureaucracy is a complex mix of elite and popular democratic features.

Probably the most powerful of the myths about the modern administrative state concerns the identity of the typical bureaucrat. The faceless bureaucrat of myth is inefficient and lazy on one hand, aggressive and hyperactive in meddling in people's lives on the other. But in truth bureaucrats are ordinary people. Compared to presidents, members of Congress, or judges, bureaucrats as a group are more representative of the American population.

Adding together the figures for federal, state, and local personnel, approximately one in seven American workers are employed by government. Many of these workers—e.g., school teachers, police, and firefighters—are not commonly thought of as bureaucrats, but they do fit the definition of bureaucracy. Political scientist Michael Lipsky calls such public employees *street-level bureaucrats*. A street-level bureaucrat deals directly with members of the public; moreover, instead of rigidly following a rule book, he or she exercises substantial discretion as to how to apply the rules under varying circumstances.[12] Some of you reading this book will become street-level bureaucrats.

Even if bureaucrats do resemble other Americans, proponents of the bureaucratic myth contend that the rigid rules of bureaucracy attract people with authoritarian personalities, and that the tedious nature of bureaucratic work frustrates and irritates civil servants. In this view, bureaucrats, however average their backgrounds may be, are afflicted with a "bureaucratic mentality." Yet there is little evidence that such a mentality is common. Several studies demonstrate that on the average, bureaucrats are as open-minded and flexible as employees in the private sector and approach civil service jobs with strong levels of motivation and pride.[13]

But if bureaucrats are ordinary people with regular personalities and a positive attitude toward their work, why do most citizens have a negative attitude toward bureaucracy? Actually, this view has more to do with bureaucracy in the abstract. It reflects constant bureaucracy bashing by politicians and the media. When questioned about contact with civil servants, a large majority report satisfactory experiences.[14]

The myth of bureaucracy rests not only on stereotypes of the individual bureaucrat but also on stereotypes of the organizations that make up the federal bureaucracy. According to these stereotypes, federal agencies are gigantic, aggressively growing larger all the time, and immensely powerful. In reality, federal agencies come in many sizes and shapes, from the massive Department of Defense, with approximately 775,000 civilian employees, to the Department of Education, which has fewer than 5,000 employees (see Table 14.1).

The mythical bureaucratic agency is power hungry, eagerly grasping for ever-larger functions, programs, and budgets. But real bureaucratic agencies are hesitant about growth if it threatens their identity. Most agencies have a **mission**, a central task to which its members are committed. They welcome more authority and money in pursuit of this mission. But they are not eager to take on divergent missions even when these would bring growth to the agency.[15]

The mythical bureaucratic agency is monopolistic and tries to keep others inside and outside of government from playing a part in implementing public policies. Increasingly, however, national policies are carried out by complex organizational networks. Federal

Table 14.1	Size of U.S. Government Cabinet Departments: Civilian Personnel, 2010
Department	**Personnel**
Agriculture	106,867
Commerce	56,856
Defense	772,601
Education	4,452
Energy	16,145
Health and Human Services	69,839
Homeland Security	183,455
Housing and Urban Development	9,585
Interior	70,231
Justice	117,916
Labor	17,592
State	39,016
Transportation	57,972
Treasury	110,099
Veterans Affairs	304,665

Source: *Statistical Abstract of the United States 2012* (http://www.census.gov).

agencies are a central participant in these networks, but bureaucracies at other levels of government, nonprofit organizations, and private-sector companies may also play significant roles.[16]

In criticizing the prevalent myth about bureaucracy, we do not claim that all is well with the American administrative state. We are pointing out that the myth focuses attention on bureaucracy simply to turn it into a scapegoat. Bureaucracy is a convenient scapegoat for elected politicians who divert attention from their inability to carry through on the promises they make to voters. It is a convenient scapegoat for citizens who resent the taxes they pay and the social ills that never seem to get cured by federal spending.

Bureaucrats as Policy Makers

Understanding bureaucracy in a realistic way requires, above all, recognition that bureaucracy is a *political* institution. The scholars who founded the study of public administration in the United States (one of them a future president, Woodrow Wilson) sought to distinguish administration from politics. Bureaucracies existed, they claimed, only to provide the technical means for carrying out ends that political (that is, elected) officials had decided.[17] Today, few believe in the politics-administration dichotomy. Administrators operate in an intensely political environment, and they must make key political decisions themselves. They are policy makers, not just technicians.

Administrators are politically influential because they possess **expertise**. Bureaucrats tend to know more than anyone else about their particular areas of responsibility. Expertise may come through a combination of specialization and experience. Compare the career civil servant, who has spent many years dealing with a single policy area, to the elected official, who must tackle many different policy areas with a shorter base of experience. An even more formidable ground of expertise is professional training. "A variety of highly trained elites," writes political scientist Francis Rourke, "practice their trade in public organizations—physicists, economists, engineers."[18] The arguments of these elites carry special weight because they are presumed to draw from professional knowledge. Elected officials are the bosses of civil servants but often defer to their expertise.[19]

Administrators are also politically influential because they exercise considerable **discretion**. Handed broad and vague policy guidelines by elected officials, administrators give policy substance through numerous, more concrete decisions. For example, Congress directs the Occupational Safety and Health Administration (OSHA) to protect employees from cancer-causing chemicals in the workplace. It is up to OSHA to set allowable exposure levels for various carcinogens. In determining these levels, OSHA administrators make decisions about which companies and unions are likely to disagree; inevitably, the decisions will be political and not just technical.

A worker from the Environmental Protection Agency cleans up toxic material after Hurricane Katrina.

Expertise and discretion make administrators influential in policy making. They employ that influence indirectly and directly. Administrators exercise *indirect influence* over policy in their capacity as advisers to elected officials. When a president, for example, faces a major policy decision, he or she turns to the pertinent bureaucratic agency for data, analysis, and recommendations. The agency cannot determine what the president will decide, but it may be able to shape how he or she thinks about the decision. An agency is likely to tell the president to achieve a desired end by giving it, rather than another agency, the resources and the responsibility to do the job.

Administrators exercise *direct influence* through the **rule-making authority** that Congress delegates to the bureaucracy. When agencies give specificity to vague congressional mandates by issuing rules, these rules carry the force of law. Each year, the bureaucracy issues a far larger number of rules than Congress passes laws. Before a new rule can be put into effect, however, interested citizens and groups must receive advance notice and be permitted to comment on it.

A common complaint about bureaucrats is that the rules they issue in abundance tie up government in reams of **red tape**. This term refers to restrictions on individuals, organizations, and even the administrators themselves that delay action without serving any useful purpose. Some bureaucratic rules do add to red tape. But what looks to disgruntled citizens like red tape may simply be the requirement that government agencies treat individuals alike, without favoritism. Moreover, government agencies require more rules than private businesses because they are accountable to elected officials for honest performance.[20]

Rule making by administrators is considered *quasi-legislative*. The bureaucracy also possesses *quasi-judicial* authority in the form of **administrative adjudication**. Whereas rules govern a large number of parties and cover future behavior, adjudications affect only the individual parties in a case and cover past behavior. Adjudication is the province of administrative law judges. Cases in administrative law must follow the rules of due process, but the requirements of due process are not as strict as in the regular courts; thus, there is no right to a jury trial in administrative law.

American citizens most often come into contact with federal authority through rules issued by administrators and decisions handed down by administrative law judges. Indeed, bureaucrats make many of the policy decisions that affect our lives. As Cindy Skrzycki observes, they "shape decisions that influence the quality of the air you breathe, how safe your car is, which immigrants will enter and stay in this country, how airports will be protected from terrorism, what you can expect from your employer in terms of working conditions and pension, and how safe that hamburger is that you just put in your mouth."[21]

The Political Environment of Bureaucracy

Bureaucracy is a political institution not only because administrators possess political influence but also because they operate in a highly political environment. A formal, hierarchical, technically focused bureaucracy could wait passively for elected officials to order it into action. But real bureaucratic agencies exist in an environment where policies reflect political, rather than technical, values; where resources are scarce; and where rivals seek to encroach on cherished turf.

Seeking Political Support

Some administrative agencies, such as the Federal Maritime Commission, function largely out of sight of the general public. However, other agencies are highly visible to the public and take steps to ensure favorable citizens' impressions—the more favorable the public is, the better the agency is likely to be treated by Congress and the president. Agencies can inform the public about their work while casting that work in a positive light through free booklets, public service ads on television, and Washington headquarters tours. They can attempt to wrap their activities in the mantle of mysterious expertise and glamorous risk taking—these have been favorite tactics of both the armed forces and NASA.

The public is too inattentive, and its backing too fickle, to provide most agencies with all the political support they need. "Hence," Francis Rourke observes,

> It is essential to every agency's power position to have the support of attentive groups whose attachment is grounded on an enduring tie. The groups an agency provides tangible benefits to are the most natural basis of such political support, and it is with these interest groups that agencies ordinarily establish the firmest alliances.[22]

The immediate masters of bureaucratic agencies are Congress and the president, so their political support is indispensable. Congress determines the statutory authority of an agency and holds the purse strings for its annual appropriation. The leadership of an agency must therefore take care to cultivate good will on Capitol Hill. Political support is often derived from the key legislative and appropriations committees by respectful, even deferential treatment and by more tangible promises of benefits for members' districts.[23]

The good will of the president is also a goal of bureaucratic chiefs, who do not want the White House staff or the Office of Management and Budget (OMB) frowning on their legislative and budget requests. Yet presidents often complain that bureaucrats are insufficiently loyal and thus take steps to bring the bureaucracy under tighter White House control.

The more successful an agency is in gaining political support from the public, interest groups, Congress, and the president, the greater **autonomy** it will enjoy in the sense of freedom from control by external forces. Autonomy allows a bureaucracy to pursue its mission unhindered. Although this can be desirable, too much autonomy may also prove dangerous.

Probably the extreme case of an autonomous federal agency was the Federal Bureau of Investigation (FBI) under J. Edgar Hoover. By cultivating public support through highly publicized captures of criminals and by courting presidents with inside information on their political rivals, Hoover won extraordinary autonomy for his FBI. This autonomy led to autocratic uses of power. During the early years of the Cold War, Hoover was a fanatical anti-Communist who employed the FBI to destroy the careers and lives of numerous individuals suspected of "subversive" activities. When the civil rights movement rose to its zenith in the 1960s, he developed a personal loathing for Martin Luther King Jr. and set out to destroy him. Under Hoover, the FBI became a nightmare bureaucracy.[24]

Constraints on Bureaucracy

Fortunately, the kind of autonomy that Hoover achieved at the FBI is rare. Agencies struggle to mobilize political support not only to increase their autonomy but also to fend off threats to already established autonomy. The political environment that most agencies face is filled with potentially constraining forces: other agencies, Congress, the president, the courts, interest groups, and the public. These checks and constraints are double edged: They prevent most agencies from becoming arbitrary and oppressive, but they also make it harder for bureaucrats to design and carry out coherent programs.[25]

An agency seeking to carry out its core mission may be threatened by another agency promoting *its* core mission. A classic illustration of such conflict between agencies, which scholars call **bureaucratic politics**, is the feud between the Air Force and the Navy over bombing. Since the end of World War II, there has been a belief among Navy officers that the Air Force seeks to control all aviation and a conflicting belief among Air Force officers that the Navy, with its aircraft carriers, tries to encroach on the Air Force specialty of strategic bombing. The services have competed to promote their core missions. During the Vietnam War, former National Security Council (NSC) official Morton Halperin writes, this competition "probably led each service to exaggerate the effectiveness of its bombing to outshine the other."[26]

In the competitive world of bureaucracy, agencies look for allies on Capitol Hill and in the White House. But friends in high places can sometimes turn into bosses, interested less in supporting the agency's agenda than in advancing their own. Both Congress and the president have in recent years intensified their own competition to shape bureaucratic behavior. This struggle between Congress and the presidency over the bureaucracy is an ongoing one rooted in the Constitution itself.[27]

A third competitor has entered the picture in recent decades: the federal courts. For most of American history, judges did not intervene in the actions of bureaucrats, believing that administrative discretion was not subject to the same judicial scrutiny as legislation. But since the New Deal, the federal courts have been more willing to take up cases of agency decision making. The courts have enabled citizens to bring suits against agencies and have required agencies to justify their discretionary actions. Judges have even ordered federal agencies to change how they implement policy. Administrators now must worry not only about how a congressional committee or a White House staff member may respond to their behavior but also about how a district court judge may question its legality.

Bureaucracy and the Political Economy

How much bureaucracy do Americans need? The initial answer of a popular democrat would be, "Far less." Many citizens complain that the administrative state stifles individual freedom with excessive forms, rules, and personnel. Yet the most influential advocates of bureaucratic downsizing have not been ordinary citizens but members of the business community, and their unhappiness with bureaucracy has less to do with freedom than with profits. In the face of business assaults on bureaucracy since the 1970s, popular democrats have found themselves in the unexpected position of having to defend it.

Popular democrats historically opposed the bureaucratization of American politics and remain worried about the reign of unaccountable elites in the administrative state. Nevertheless, they have also had to acknowledge that their past victories in extending protections to ordinary people against the abuses of private power can be preserved only with the help of administrative agencies. Hence, the historical roles of elite democrats and popular democrats have largely been reversed: Elite democrats largely built the administrative state but now want to shrink it, while popular democrats defend an administrative state they once feared.

The contemporary debate over bureaucracy has focused primarily on those agencies that regulate the economy. **Regulation** is "a process or activity in which government requires or proscribes certain activities or behavior on the part of individuals and institutions—and does so through a continuing administrative process, generally through specially designated regulatory agencies."[28] Understanding the contemporary struggle over regulation means distinguishing two different types. **Economic regulation** is usually conducted by an independent regulatory commission, covers a specific industry, and focuses on matters of prices, quality of services, and ability to enter or leave the industry. **Social regulation** is usually conducted by a single-headed agency answerable to the president, covers all industries, and focuses on such matters as environmental protection, safety, health, and nondiscrimination. It is the latter type that has generated the most controversy.

Economic Regulation

Economic regulation has the longer history in American politics. As industrialization strained the capacities of a weak national state, Congress created independent regulatory commissions to bring the changing economy under some measure of control. The prototype of the new regulatory agency was the Interstate Commerce Commission (ICC), formed in 1887 to regulate the railroad industry. Industrial abuses paved the way for the development of economic regulation, which has often been portrayed as a victory for popular democracy over economic elites. However, revisionist historians have shown that industrialists themselves sometimes pushed for federal regulation, hoping to limit competition or to avert public ownership.[29]

Although most economic regulation has not been very burdensome to business, there has been a movement in recent years, promoted by economists and backed by business elites, to scale down the role of the government in the economy. Advocates of such **deregulation** argue that market forces will promote the interests of producers and consumers alike far more efficiently than the intrusive hand of government. Deregulation began during the presidencies of Gerald Ford and Jimmy Carter, and accelerated during the presidency of Ronald Reagan, with the most notable changes in the fields of transportation, communications, and banking. Existing regulatory controls were relaxed, and private economic forces were trusted to serve the public interest by engaging in market competition.

Deregulation has worked well for some industries, but its effects on the financial industry have at times been disastrous. When Congress and the president removed federal controls from savings and loan companies (S&Ls) in the early 1980s, their management went wild. Poorly conceived real estate loans, financial gimmicks that bilked small investors, and outright looting by operators sent many S&Ls into bankruptcy. Thanks to government insurance of customer deposits up to $100,000, the federal government and ultimately the taxpayers had to pick up the tab of $132 billion.

Undaunted by the failure of the free market to promote the public good in the case of S&Ls, champions of deregulation proceeded further in limiting federal oversight of banking, and this time the consequences were even worse. In the "subprime mortgage crisis" that struck in 2008, individuals with low incomes and/or poor credit histories were enticed by unregulated lenders offering low initial interest rates on adjustable-rate mortgages. Once these rates soared a few years into the life of the mortgages, many families were unable to make the higher monthly payments, and their homes were foreclosed. Meanwhile, the high-interest, risky mortgages had been turned into securities by Wall Street banks and purchased by international investors; once borrowers stopped paying, huge losses on these securities rippled through the global economy. A deregulated financial-services sector was suddenly in crisis, and its ill health spread to the entire American economy.[30]

Attempting to prevent future abuses on Wall Street and to avert another financial meltdown, President Obama and the congressional Democratic majority overcame opposition from legions of banking lobbyists and passed a financial reform bill, the Dodd-Frank Wall Street Reform and Consumer Protection Act, in 2010. Representing the most sweeping regulatory reform of the U.S. financial system since the New Deal, "Dodd-Frank," as it came to be known, established new federal oversight of esoteric financial devices that had profited banking insiders while mystifying and exploiting ordinary investors. The legislation also placed limits on the speculative practices that had led to the crash of some of America's largest investment banking houses. Most controversial, Dodd-Frank set up a new Consumer Financial Protection Bureau (CFPB) to safeguard ordinary consumers seeking bank loans, credit cards, or mortgages from predatory practices by the financial-services and real-estate industries.[31]

[MAKING A DIFFERENCE]

Elizabeth Warren and the Protection of Consumers

"It is impossible to buy a toaster that has a one-in-five chance of bursting into flames and burning down your house. But it is possible to refinance an existing house with a mortgage that has the same one-in-five chance of putting the family out on the street—and the mortgage won't even carry a disclosure of that fact to the homeowner." These are the opening sentences of "Unsafe at Any Rate," an article written by Elizabeth Warren that appeared in 2007. Like many authors, Warren was dramatizing a problem in order to recommend a novel solution—in this case, a new federal commission to protect consumers from manipulative practices by financial-services companies. Unlike most authors, Warren's article made a huge difference: within three years, her idea was a centerpiece of the Obama administration's financial-reform program.

Because Elizabeth Warren was a law professor at Harvard, opponents of her proposal tried to discredit it as the work of an East Coast elitist. Warren's background is hard to square with the elitist label. She was born and grew up in Oklahoma City. Her father was a janitor and her mother worked in the catalogue-order department at Sears. As a champion high-school debater, she won a scholarship to George Washington University at the age of 16. She married young and taught school, and she did not receive her law degree until she was 27. In short, Warren is a classic example of a self-made American.

Warren's article was written to defend ordinary Americans against exploitation by economic elites. Her target was banks, credit-card companies, mortgage brokers, payday lenders, and other financial-services companies that "built tricks and traps into some credit products so that they could ensnare families in a cycle of high-cost debt." No longer subject to effective regulations, as they had been in the New Deal era, providers of financial services offered long, technical descriptions of their products that few ordinary people could understand and steered unwary consumers into debts that many could not afford. As Warren wrote in her article: "For families who get tangled up with truly dangerous financial products, the result can be wiped-out savings, lost homes, higher costs for car insurance, denial of jobs, troubled marriages, bleak retirements, and broken lives."

To find a remedy for these abuses, Warren cited as a model the Consumer Product Safety Commission, which develops safety standards, orders the recall of defective goods, and bans products that pose severe risks to users. The work of the Consumer Product Safety Commission had substantially reduced injuries and deaths from such physical goods as cigarette lighters and cribs, and it was time, Warren wrote, to extend similar regulatory authority over credit instruments. What was needed, she suggested, was a Financial Product Safety Commission. This commission would gather data, set new guidelines for easier-to-understand descriptions of credit offerings, and block the marketing of exploitative financial products before they could mislead the public.

From Warren's perspective, the commission she was proposing would restore balance in government between economic elites and middle-class citizens. In recent decades, she argued, government policies had favored corporations and banks, while neglecting to protect ordinary consumers. As she put it in an interview: "when they start to make decisions about who's going to be helped and who's not going to be helped, there needs to be at least one person in the room who asks the question: how will this affect America's families? Not just how it will affect America's banks, not just how it will affect America's businesses, but how it will affect America's families."

Professor Warren assisted the Obama administration in creating precisely the kind of regulatory agency she had proposed—although it was given a different name, the Consumer Financial Protection Bureau, than the one she had suggested. By now, her work in protecting consumers had made her highly unpopular among financial elites. Liberal supporters called upon the Obama administration to appoint Warren as the first director of the bureau; however, anticipating that Senate Republicans allied to the financial-services industry would block her appointment through a filibuster, the president made her a White House aide instead. In this capacity, she established the bureau's structure, hired its initial staff of 500, and began to turn her original idea into an administrative reality.

Disappointing Warren's admirers, President Obama avoided a tough political fight the following year and passed her over in selecting the bureau's first director. But Warren soon found a new arena for championing the cause of consumer financial protection. She challenged Massachusetts's Republican senator, Scott Brown, in the 2012 elections. Defeating Brown by a solid margin, Warren entered the United States Senate in January, 2013.

Sources: Elizabeth Warren, "Unsafe at Any Rate," *Democracy: A Journal of Ideas*, Summer 2007; Amy Goodman, radio interview with Elizabeth Warren, *Democracy Now*, September 7, 2010; Suzanna Andrews, "The Woman Who Knew Too Much," *Vanity Fair*, November 2011.

Social Regulation

Debates over economic regulation versus deregulation center on which approach has a more beneficial effect on people's pocketbooks. Debates over social regulation versus deregulation tend to pit the physical, moral, and aesthetic well-being of the American people against considerations of economics. Whereas economic regulation goes back to the late nineteenth century, social regulation has largely been a product of the 1960s and 1970s. Examples of social regulation include consumer safety, worker safety and health, antidiscrimination protection, environmental protection, and wildlife protection.

When contemporary foes of bureaucracy rail against "overregulation," it is often social regulation that they have in mind. Social regulation draws so much fire from the business community in part because it touches almost all businesses, unlike the more narrowly targeted approach in economic regulation. Social regulation also imposes costs on businesses that cut into profits.

The origins of social regulation hold another clue to business hostility. The social regulation measures of the 1960s and 1970s were supported by Congress and the president in response to the civil rights movement, the environmental movement, and the consumer safety movement. Social regulation has been a potent political vehicle for popular democrats in their struggle against economic elites.

A major assault on social regulation was launched during the presidency of Ronald Reagan. Overregulation, the Reagan administration charged, was imposing such massive costs on American businesses as to prevent them from investing in productive new technologies, a crippling practice in an era where they faced mounting international competition. To cut back on social regulation, the Reagan administration adopted a variety of tactics. Budgets for the social regulatory agencies were slashed, and political appointees were selected who were known to be hostile to the missions of the agencies they were to head.

New social regulation now had to clear the hurdle of a mode of analysis with a built-in bias against such regulation. The Reagan administration claimed that it was using

cost-benefit analysis as a neutral tool, determining if the dollar benefits of proposed regulation were greater than the dollar costs. The problem was that no clear dollar value could be placed on such intangible benefits as the worth of a human life or the beauty of a natural setting, whereas the costs incurred by an industry were readily quantifiable. Consequently, many new regulations were bound to fail the test of cost-benefit analysis.

The success of the Reagan administration's attack on social regulation was somewhat limited by the counter-mobilization of its defenders. The attack was next resumed by George W. Bush. During his presidency, Joel Brinkley wrote in the *New York Times*, "Health rules, environmental regulations, energy initiatives, worker-safety standards and product-safety disclosure policies have been modified in ways that often please business and industry leaders while dismaying interest groups representing consumers, workers, drivers, medical patients, the elderly, and many others."[32]

As Barack Obama revived both social regulation and economic regulation (though more cautiously than his liberal supporters desired) amid the persisting economic crisis that began shortly before he took office, champions of deregulation mounted a strong attack on his policies. Republicans routinely claimed that Obama's new regulations "killed jobs," preventing the economy from regaining strength. But in the view of most economists there is not much evidence that the new regulations are an obstacle to renewed economic growth. As *The Washington Post* reported, "Data from the Bureau of Labor Statistics show that very few layoffs are caused principally by tougher rules. Whenever a firm lays off workers, the bureau asks executives the biggest reason for the job cuts. In 2010, 0.3 percent of the people who lost

Popeye and the FDA.

their jobs in layoffs were let go because of 'government regulations/intervention.' By comparison, 25 percent were laid off because of a drop in business demand."[33]

In the end, the issue of how much government regulation Americans need is a matter of what citizens want from government. Certainly, bureaucratic agencies can be too big, inefficient, or wasteful. And agency accountability remains a pressing issue. But much of the present-day administrative state is necessary to protect the public and provide it with the services it desires.

How Well Does the Government Work?

Since bureaucracy does the work of government, evaluating bureaucracy comes down in the end to an important question: how well does government work? Especially with respect to the federal government, standard answers to this question follow from individuals' ideology: conservatives believe that the federal government is incompetent and wasteful, comparing poorly to the efficient operations of private companies, whereas liberals believe that the federal government, while not without its share of problems, does essential work to expand opportunity for ordinary citizens and to limit the abuses of business elites.

Public opinion on this subject largely coincides with the conservative view. Trust in the federal government has declined over the past several decades and has hit new lows amid current economic difficulties. Asked in a September 2011, CNN poll whether the government in Washington, D.C., can be trusted to serve the public's welfare most of the time, only 15 percent answered *yes*. In a Gallup Poll conducted the same month, survey respondents estimated that "the federal government wastes 51 cents of every dollar it spends."[34]

Well-publicized bureaucratic failures and commonplace bureaucratic irritants fuel public skepticism. Periodic outbreaks of *E. coli* or salmonella underscore the inadequacies of federal food inspection. Near-misses between jetliners dramatize the weak points in federal air-traffic control. Intrusive screenings at airports set passengers' nerves on edge. Exposures of FBI and CIA misdeeds reveal unlawful behavior by America's national law-enforcement and security agencies.

Experts in the field of public administration acknowledge that all is not well with the federal bureaucracy. Political scientist Paul Light writes: "The federal service is losing its energy to faithfully execute the laws, especially if vigor and expedition are defined as full exertion on the public's behalf, jobs that allow employees to make a difference, adequate provision of support, rewards, and discipline, and the respect of the public served."[35] The notion that the federal government provides especially meaningful and satisfying work, a part of the idealistic glow that we associate with the eras of Franklin Roosevelt and John F. Kennedy, is no longer widely held. Light conducted surveys in which college seniors were asked to compare the attractiveness of careers in business, nonprofit organizations, and the federal workforce. The federal government came in last.[36]

However, before we conclude that critics of bureaucracy have all of the evidence on their side, we need to inquire as to why public trust in the federal government has plummeted and why the performance of federal workers has suffered. A first point that suggests caution in making sweeping judgments brings us back to the complexity of the federal government that we depicted earlier. Waste or failure in some federal agencies receives far more attention in the media than dedicated and effective performance by many other agencies.

A second point in a balanced evaluation of how well government works is the difficulties under which many federal agencies labor. Federal agencies are tasked to solve some of the most intractable problems of the nation, such as stopping illegal immigration or lifting people out of poverty. Their missions are more extensive and complicated than the simpler objective of businesses to produce and sell products. Yet even as public expectations of federal problem-solving remain high, the resources provided to the federal workforce, as well as the size of that workforce, have been shrinking. Even the technology with which federal agencies are supplied tends to lag behind the up-to-date equipment of the corporate sector.[37]

Political leaders who scapegoat bureaucracy are a third contributing factor to the current difficulties of the federal service. Citizens who only hear harsh comments from elected officials about federal workers are likely to echo these negative judgments in opinion surveys. Bureaucracy-bashing by leaders lowers the morale of the individuals who currently work in federal agencies and increases the difficulty of recruiting talented young people to join the federal service.

Fourth, some of the most notorious cases of governmental incompetence or abuse have occurred during Republican administrations that have been ideologically committed to a negative view of government. No president made as great a contribution to mistrust of government as Richard Nixon with his Watergate scandal. More recently, President George W. Bush made the U.S. government appear incompetent abroad with the Iraq fiasco and at home with the Hurricane Katrina fiasco. Ironically, conservative critics of "big government" get to prove their own case when they are the ones in charge of the administrative state.

While aiming to withdraw the federal bureaucracy from some areas in which it operates today (e.g., by eliminating such cabinet agencies as the Department of Energy and the Department of Education), critics of "big government" acknowledge the legitimacy of many public purposes. Yet they insist that these public purposes often don't need to be accomplished by bureaucratic agencies. Instead, some purposes can be better served by replacing programs run by government with vouchers that allow individuals to decide what kind of education, housing, or health care they wish to purchase. And where private companies can perform tasks more cheaply than government agencies, government should contract out these functions—an idea known as **privatization**.[38]

Privatization has been advocated for many public services, including schools, prisons, fire departments, and social services. But the experience with privatization so far at the state and local levels often has not produced the promised gains in efficiency. And it has revealed difficulties with privatization that have been overlooked by those who believe that competitive markets are the solution to every problem.[39]

Once core functions of government are contracted out to private firms, the performance of those functions can be distorted by the pursuit of profits. An example is the rise of corporate-run prisons, which are used by a number of states. Analysts have noted that in the drive to lower costs and increase profits, prisons run by private firms cut back on counseling and vocational training, reduce staff and have to rely as a result on manacles and isolation cells when inmates are unruly, and keep prisoners incarcerated for longer periods than public prisons. Some of these firms have even lobbied for longer sentences for criminal offenses, which would ensure higher revenues per inmate.[40]

The terrorist attacks of September 11, 2001, brought home to Americans that some public functions are too important to be left to the profit-seeking of the market. Prior to September 11, airport screening of passengers and baggage had been the responsibility of the airlines. The slack security on September 11 drew attention to the poor quality of screening by the private firms hired by the airlines. Concerned primarily with maximizing profits, these firms had paid low wages and assembled an inexperienced workforce that included illegal immigrants and ex-convicts. Despite opposition from President Bush, Congress created a new Transportation Security Administration, and screening of passengers and baggage became the responsibility of public employees.[41]

New Reform

New Reform New Reform New Reform New Reform New Reform

Transparency

What do the following have in common?

- A requirement that food companies list the amounts of sugar, salt, fats, and other nutritional information on the labels of their products

- A requirement that automobile manufacturers provide prospective buyers of SUVs with data on their models' rollover rates

- A requirement that industries post data on chemical hazards at workplaces so that their employees can learn about the risks to which they might be exposed

All of the above are examples of *transparency* policies. These policies seek to achieve public purposes through legal mandates that businesses, nonprofit organizations, or government agencies disclose to the public previously concealed information about the riskiness or the quality of goods and services. If members of the public properly use this information to reward providers of goods and services with favorable records and to shun providers of products or services that are riskier or poorer in quality, then the latter will be compelled to improve what they provide or face a sharp decline in business.

Although transparency policies at the national, state, and local levels have multiplied in recent years, they have been adopted in a haphazard fashion, with little attention to critical issues of effectiveness. The objective of the Transparency Policy Project, located at Harvard's Kennedy School of Government, is to develop designs to make transparency a more consistently effective tool of public policy.

A huge volume of information, say the scholars associated with the Transparency Policy Project, is not necessarily what the public needs. It is essential that the information disclosed be user-friendly—neither too technical nor too complex for ordinary citizens to comprehend. The information must also be in a form that members of the public can readily include in their customary decision-making processes. Finally, the information should prompt members of the public toward taking the actions that legislators wish to promote—for example, eating a healthier diet, purchasing safer vehicles, or avoiding hazardous substances at work.

The Internet is a powerful aid for transparency policies. Not only do new information technologies make transparent information more quickly and easily accessible to individual users, but they also allow individuals to collaborate with others, pooling their experiences and knowledge. Existing groups, such as environmental or community organizations, also are assisted in their relations with powerful interests which have been required to reveal facts about their activities that they would have preferred to remain secret.

Transparency policy is not a substitute for government action. Legislators must design disclosure policies that carry sanctions, typically fines, to discourage noncompliance. Civil servants must monitor those entities that are subject to disclosure policies to ensure that they are making public the information that the law requires. What makes transparency policy especially appealing for popular democrats, however, is that government action is complemented by citizen action.

Whether as consumers, workers, or voters, ordinary citizens and citizen groups are the ones who ultimately determine the effectiveness of transparency policies. As Archon Fung, Mary Graham, and David Weil of the Transparency Project explain: "The provision of information doesn't automatically enable people to make more informed choices. That requires an alert and engaged public that understands the dynamics of transparency and is ready to participate energetically in using new information and in shaping more effective policies."

Sources: Archon Fung, Mary Graham, and David Weil, *Full Disclosure: The Perils and Promise of Transparency* (New York: Cambridge University Press, 2007); The Transparency Policy Project, Kennedy School of Government, Harvard University, www.transparencypolicy.net.

Conclusion: Beyond Monster Bureaucracy

In contemporary American political discourse, Bureaucracy—with a capital *B*—is a monster. This Bureaucracy is composed of massive organizations staffed by authoritarian drones. It smothers individual freedom under a blanket of unnecessary rules. And it grows more powerful all the time, not in the interest of the American people but in the service of its own voracious appetites.

Monster Bureaucracy is a mythical creature—a hobbyhorse for irate citizens and a scapegoat for calculating politicians. When we look at real American bureaucracies, we see their diversity: They come in different organizational forms and sizes, and they pursue an enormous variety of missions. The people who staff them are not a perverse bureaucratic breed but rather a cross-section of the American people. And the interests that bureaucrats promote range from the narrowest and most selfish to the loftiest and most communal. Some agencies are entangled with economic elites in cozy, mutually rewarding alliances. Others try to put into practice the most important legislative victories that popular democrats have won against these elites.

Monster Bureaucracy has to be hit with a club. Real bureaucracies may need reform. But how we approach reform depends on where we stand in the democratic debate. If we follow the newest school of elite democracy, which claims the inherent superiority of private markets to public agencies, we should make efficiency our standard and let business do much of what government is accustomed to doing. If we follow the popular democratic tradition, with its commitments to citizen action and civic virtue, we should open up the world of bureaucracy wherever possible to the grievances, viewpoints, and democratic hopes of ordinary people.

Reader's Guide

Critical Thinking Questions

1. How should we conceive of federal bureaucrats as a group—as inefficient time servers or as dedicated public servants?

2. Why do unelected bureaucrats exercise so much influence over public policies?

3. Is government regulation mostly bureaucratic interference in the free market or administrative protection of the public against abuses by powerful private actors?

4. Will privatization—contracting government functions out to private companies—provide the public with the services it wants at lower cost, or will it leave the public vulnerable to exploitation by companies concerned only for making a profit?

Key Word Definition

bureaucracy   Units of the executive branch, organized in a hierarchical fashion, governed through formal rules, and distinguished by their specialized functions.

spoils system   The awarding of political jobs to political supporters and friends.

administrative state   A national government involved in regulating or supporting almost every form of social activity by means of a large, complex, and diverse bureaucracy.

cabinet departments   The fifteen major divisions of the executive branch, each responsible for a broad area of governmental operations.

independent agency   An executive branch organization that stands outside of and generally handles more narrow areas of governmental operation than the cabinet departments.

independent regulatory commission   A governmental body that controls a sector of the economy and is directed by commissioners who are appointed by the president, have long terms, and are exempt from presidential removal so that the agency is distanced from political pressures.

public corporation   A government agency that engages in business activities.

federal foundation or endowment   Organization that enables the federal government to sponsor scientific and cultural activities.

mission   The central task to which the members of a government agency are committed.

expertise   The specialized knowledge of administrators about their particular areas of responsibility.

discretion   The latitude that administrators have in carrying out their agency's mission.

rule-making authority   The power of an executive agency to issue regulations that carry the force of law.

red tape   Unnecessary bureaucratic rules that delay or obstruct action.

administrative adjudication   The quasi judicial powers delegated to executive agencies to try individuals or organizations that have violated legally binding agency rules.

autonomy   Greater freedom on the part of executive agencies from control by external forces.

bureaucratic politics   The conflict that arises when an agency seeking to carry out its core mission is threatened by another agency promoting its own core mission.

regulation   A process by which the government imposes restrictions on the conduct of private citizens and organizations.

economic regulation   Control by an independent regulatory commission of a specific industry that focuses on prices, quality of services, and the ability to enter or leave the industry.

social regulation   Executive agency rules that cover all industries and focus on such matters as environmental protection, safety, health, and nondiscrimination.

deregulation   The reduction or elimination of government control of the conduct or activities of private citizens and organizations.

cost-benefit analysis   A method of determining if the dollar benefits of proposed government regulation are greater than the dollar costs.

privatization   The turning over of governmental functions to the private sector when it can perform functions more cheaply than government agencies.

15

The Judiciary and the Democratic Debate

JUDICIAL POWER AND THE DEMOCRATIC DEBATE

THE SUPREME COURT IN HISTORY

JUDICIAL SELECTION

THE FEDERAL COURT SYSTEM

THE SUPREME COURT: PROCESS

THE SUPREME COURT: POLITICS

THE SUPREME COURT AND THE POLITICAL SYSTEM

CONCLUSION: LAW, POLITICS, AND THE DEMOCRATIC DEBATE

Traditionally, justices of the U.S. Supreme Court sit stone-faced as they listen to the president deliver the State of the Union address, signaling their distance from the realm of political controversy. Yet, when President Barack Obama criticized the Court's recent decision to allow unlimited campaign spending by corporations in his 2010 address, Justice Samuel Alito, unable to hide his displeasure at the president's remarks, was caught on camera shaking his head and mouthing the words "not true." Alito appeared to be offended that the president was injecting politics into a matter of law.[1] However, it is one of the central themes of this chapter that law and politics actually can't be separated and that the Supreme Court is a political as well as a legal institution.

The nine justices of the Supreme Court are a unique elite. Appointed rather than elected, for tenures that run on "good behavior" until retirement or death, the justices have carved out for themselves the formidable role of serving as final arbiters of the Constitution. Their authority is strengthened by powerful symbolism, as they hand down decisions wearing their black robes in their marble temple, and is protected by the cloak of expertise, as they pronounce their judgments in the esoteric language of the law. In all these ways, the judiciary is the least democratic branch of the federal government.

Yet the Court's relationship to elite democracy and popular democracy is not this simple. The Supreme Court may be (and has been in its history) a pillar of elite democracy, upholding the interests of the powerful and privileged in the name of authority, expertise, or private property. But the Court also may be (and has been in its history) a champion of the fundamental rules of democratic politics in the face of intolerant and repressive majorities. And the Court may be (and has been in its history) the last hope for the weakest citizens—racial minorities, the poor, persons accused of crimes. Elitist in form and character, the Supreme Court is nonetheless a vital participant in the democratic debate.

Judicial Power and the Democratic Debate

What is the place of an unelected judiciary in a democratic republic? Answers to this question begin with a recognition of the Supreme Court's fundamental power: **judicial review**. This is the power of the Court to invalidate the actions of legislatures and executives on the grounds that these actions conflict with the Constitution. This power was first asserted by the Supreme Court in the landmark case of *Marbury v. Madison* (1803). Although the *power* of judicial review remained controversial for much of the nineteenth century, today few question it. But questions do arise about the proper *extent* of judicial review. How far should the Court go in overturning the actions of the other federal branches or the state governments? In setting these actions against the language of the Constitution, how should the Court interpret the Constitution? Can the Court, despite its elite composition and procedures, advance the goals of popular democracy?

The Judiciary and Democracy

There are several ways in which the Supreme Court is *not* a democratic institution. First, members of the judiciary are not elected; they are nominated by the president and confirmed by the Senate. Second, federal judges serve during good behavior—that is, until they retire, die, or are impeached by the House and convicted by the Senate. No justice of the Supreme Court has ever been removed through impeachment and conviction. Consequently, members of the Court are held accountable only indirectly—by Congress through its power over jurisdiction, by presidents through their appointment power, and by members of the public through their decisions on complying with judicial rulings.

Third, justices wield their power of judicial review by striking down actions taken by elected officials at the federal or state level. The exercise of judicial review is thus *countermajoritarian*, meaning that majority rule has to give way if the Court believes that the actions of the majority conflict with the Constitution.

Fourth, the federal judiciary historically has been even less representative demographically than Congress and the executive branch. Almost all justices have been white, male, and affluent. (Women and minorities have finally won some representation on the federal bench in the past four decades.) Equally important, they have all been lawyers. One of the most powerful branches of the national government is the exclusive domain of the legal profession.[2] There is, it seems, a potent democratic case to be made against a strong and active judiciary.

Yet judicial power in America has sometimes played an essential part in preserving democratic values and rules. Nowhere is this role more apparent than in the areas of individual and minority rights. Majority rule can be used to impose unwelcome beliefs on individuals and to prohibit the expression of unconventional views. Majorities can repress and exploit minorities, whether of race, creed, or color. A democracy with unrestrained majority rule would eventually undermine the very conditions of personal and political freedom that gave it life. It would be like a sports league in which the team that won the first game was able to set the rules for all succeeding games. Therefore, the democratic case for a countermajoritarian judiciary is that it stands as a guardian for the abiding values and conditions that democracy requires.[3]

The Court serves democracy not only when it protects individual and minority rights from infringement by majorities but also when it publicly explains its actions. The Court's impact on public thinking may be limited by its legal language, yet no other branch of government offers such extensive and reasoned accounts of its decisions or elaborates on so many

fundamental democratic principles. For example, it was the Supreme Court that explained to Americans why segregated schools denied African Americans the equal protection of the laws and why coerced confessions denied criminal defendants the right to a fair trial.

Conflicting Views of the Judiciary

Questions about the role of the judiciary in American democracy are not merely of academic interest. A politically important debate has been waged in recent decades about the courts and democracy. What initially generated this debate was the liberal activism of the Warren Court (discussed later in this chapter and in Chapter 16).

Unhappy with many of the Warren Court's landmark rulings, conservatives have developed a philosophy that condemns "judicial activism." Antonin Scalia, the intellectual leader of the conservatives on the current Supreme Court, denounces the liberals' idea of a "Living Constitution," which regards our fundamental law as a flexible instrument that should change with the times. To Scalia, this misguided doctrine permits justices to turn the Constitution's meaning into whatever they prefer at the moment rather than what the framers of the document originally set down in a text designed to endure. The proper method of interpretation, according to Scalia, is "textualism": Justices following this approach read the text of the Constitution in light of its "original meaning" and do not try to smuggle new meanings into its unchanging language.[4]

Liberal justices have countered the conservative attack with their own philosophy on the essential role of the courts in advancing American democracy. Justice Stephen Breyer scoffs at Scalia's "textualism," arguing that under the cloak of fidelity to the founders it is actually a vehicle for the values and preferences of modern conservatives. To Breyer, justices on the high court inevitably bring values to bear on the task of applying the Constitution to

New Reform

New Reform New Reform New Reform New Reform New Reform

Populist Constitutional Law

Most observers were surprised when the U.S. Supreme Court agreed to hear George W. Bush's lawsuit seeking to block the Florida recount that might make Al Gore the winner of the 2000 presidential election. When a five-to-four majority on the high court halted the recount and handed the White House to Bush, critics were quick to denounce the political motives that seemed to lie behind its decision. Yet there was never any doubt that the Court's verdict on the election would be accepted by all parties. Once the Supreme Court interprets the language of the Constitution, its meaning is fixed—at least until the Court speaks again on the same subject.

Must we be so deferential to the Supreme Court when it comes to constitutional interpretation? Law professor Mark Tushnet, a prominent figure among the progressive skeptics we have described, says no. In *Taking the Constitution Away from the Courts*, he calls for a new approach to interpreting the Constitution. When questions arise about detailed provisions in the Constitution, Tushnet says, the courts are the proper bodies to ascertain constitutional meanings. But when questions arise about fundamental constitutional guarantees of liberty and equality, the courts should not have a monopoly over debate. Disagreements about the application of these guarantees, Tushnet writes, "are best conducted by the people in the ordinary venues for political discussion," assisted by their elected representatives.

This perspective sounds novel, but it is actually rooted in the popular democratic tradition. Larry Kramer,

another law professor, writes: "Both in its origins and for most of our history, American constitutionalism assigned ordinary citizens a central and pivotal role in implementing their Constitution." Popular democratic leaders such as Thomas Jefferson, Andrew Jackson, and Abraham Lincoln all insisted that the other branches of government and the people had as much right as the courts to interpret the Constitution.

"Populist constitutional law," as Tushnet calls it, does not guarantee any particular outcome. Its basis is the commitment to take democracy seriously, and its assumption is that the American people are capable of making good use of democracy. A number of practical difficulties can be imagined in "taking the Constitution away from the courts," and Tushnet believes that it will require a constitutional amendment to achieve greater public control over constitutional interpretation.

The value in Tushnet's ideas may lie less in their prospects for adoption than in the challenge they pose to public complacency. As he writes, "Neither the people nor their representatives have to take the Constitution seriously because they know—or believe—that the courts will. Political calculations might change if people knew that they were responsible for the Constitution."

Sources: Mark Tushnet, *Taking the Constitution Away from the Courts* (Princeton, NJ: Princeton University Press, 1999); Larry D. Kramer, *The People Themselves: Popular Constitutionalism and Judicial Review* (New York: Oxford University Press, 2004).

contemporary controversies. He suggests that the Court should be guided by a commitment to the democratic ideal of a self-governing people; such a commitment, he insists, serves the higher objectives of the founders and keeps the Court squarely in the mainstream of the American legal tradition.[5]

Standing off to the side of this debate, and critical of both arguments, are the "progressive legal skeptics." These authors (many of them law professors) agree that "textualism" is a false facade for contemporary conservative objectives but doubt that the liberal activist alternative can achieve the democratic advances that it claims. To these skeptics, the democratic achievements of the Warren Court were an exception for an institution that has supported the privileged through most of its history. As the bastion of a profession whose members were socialized in law schools to assume lucrative careers serving economic and political elites, the Court has a bias toward the status quo. Those who want to remedy inequities in the American political system, say these skeptics, should devote their time and resources to political movements for change rather than getting bogged down in the slow-moving processes of the courts.[6]

The Supreme Court in History

For an institution that derives authority from its role as sacred guardian of a timeless text, the Supreme Court has been profoundly shaped by its history. However, the Court's relationship to history is double edged. On one hand, the Court treats history with reverence, claiming to follow past decisions as **precedents** and applying them to new circumstances. On the other hand, the Court has engaged in some dramatic historical shifts. For most of its history, the Supreme Court was a pillar of elite democracy, a champion of national authority and private property against the popular democratic forces struggling for greater equality. Beginning in the 1930s, however, the Court largely abandoned its stance as the protector of economic elites, adopting instead a new focus on civil liberties and civil rights. The 1990s witnessed another shift: the expression (by a narrow majority) of a conservative jurisprudence that favors federalism over national action.

John Marshall and Judicial Power

The Supreme Court did not become a major force in the American political system immediately on ratification of the Constitution. Article III of the Constitution, establishing the judicial branch, was brief and vague, leaving the role of the Court an open question. During its first decade under the Constitution, the Court was relatively weak. Nonetheless, popular democrats feared its potential as a home for a judicial aristocracy.

As Thomas Jefferson began his presidency, John Marshall took over as chief justice of the Supreme Court. Appointed by President Adams in the waning days of his administration, Marshall, a Federalist, was gifted with great intellectual force, rhetorical grace, and political shrewdness. And he had a vision for the Court: to establish it coequally with the other branches and turn it into a sponsor of national authority and economic development. Marshall dominated the Supreme Court for thirty-four years, serving from 1801 until his death in 1835. The Marshall Court, more than the words of Article III, established the judicial branch as the powerful force that later generations of Americans came to regard as an integral part of the constitutional design.

Marshall's agenda for the Court depended on establishing the power of judicial review. But he wanted to avoid a head-on collision with the Jeffersonian majority that controlled the executive and legislative branches. In a stroke of judicial genius, he found the perfect vehicle for judicial review in the case of ***Marbury v. Madison*** (1803). William Marbury had been appointed by President Adams to a position as justice of the peace for the District of Columbia, but the papers for his commission had not been delivered by the time Jefferson supplanted Adams in the White House. Jefferson's secretary of state, James Madison, refused to hand over the papers. Marbury asked the Supreme Court to order Madison, through a *writ of mandamus* (a court order directing an official to do something), to give him his commission.

Marshall's opinion in *Marbury v. Madison* held that the secretary of state had wrongfully withheld the commission. But the Supreme Court, he went on, could do nothing to rectify this injustice because the authority to issue *writs of mandamus*, mandated by the Judiciary Act of 1789, was unconstitutional—it expanded the original jurisdiction of the Court beyond what was specified in Article III. In bold rhetorical strokes, Marshall crafted the doctrine of judicial review. It was evident, he argued, that "a law repugnant to the constitution is void" and that "it is emphatically the province and duty of the judicial department to say what the law is."[7] Notice how shrewdly Marshall bolstered the power of the Supreme Court. He avoided a confrontation with the Jefferson administration by ruling that the Supreme Court was powerless to reverse the action toward Marbury. But he advanced the Supreme Court's power in the long term by making it, and not the other branches, the final arbiter of constitutionality.

Once Marshall had established the Court's power of judicial review, he moved gradually to further his vision of a powerful national government promoting capitalist economic development. Striking down Maryland's attempt to tax the Bank of the United States in ***McCulloch v. Maryland*** (1819), he emphasized the constitutional supremacy of the federal government over the states (see Chapter 3). And then in ***Gibbons v. Ogden*** (1824), the Marshall Court ruled that the Interstate Commerce Clause, under which Gibbons held a federal coasting license for his steamboat line, was superior to the steamboat monopoly granted to Ogden by the state of New York. As the *Gibbons* case indicates, Marshall was able to advance his goal of economic development in conjunction with his goal of national authority. He read the Constitution, legal historian Robert McCloskey writes, "so as to provide maximum protection to property rights and maximum support for the idea of nationalism."[8]

The Taney Court

When John Marshall died, and President Andrew Jackson, a frequent foe of the chief justice, appointed Roger Taney to the position, supporters of the Marshall Court feared radical reversals in constitutional law. But Marshall had set the Court on a course that was not easily altered, and historians now find more continuity than change between the Marshall and the Taney Courts.

Taney's most notorious decision came in ***Dred Scott v. Sandford*** (1857). The *Dred Scott* decision is universally regarded as the worst in the history of the Supreme Court. In a remarkable miscalculation, Taney thought that the Court could solve with one decision the brewing crisis between North and South over slavery. His solution took the southern side on every burning question of the day: Slaves were held to be a form of property protected by the Constitution, and Congress was told it had no power to forbid or abolish slavery in the western territories. Taney went even further, almost taunting northern champions of the antislavery cause with his vicious racist remark that blacks were regarded by the founders "as beings of an inferior order" who "had no rights which the white man was bound to respect."[9] Taney's ruling and rhetoric incensed the North and increased sectional tensions, helping to lead to a civil war that would obliterate his fateful misuse of judicial power.

From the Civil War to the Roosevelt Revolution

The Civil War confirmed on the battlefield what John Marshall had claimed on the bench: the supremacy of the federal government over the states. After the Civil War, the Supreme Court became preoccupied with Marshall's other major concern: the rights of property. For seventy years, the Court played a critical, activist role in the development of corporate capitalism in America. The Court reread the Constitution, turning the eighteenth-century founders into proponents of the free-market capitalism worshiped by business elites of the late nineteenth century. Legal expertise and judicial authority were weapons that elite democrats fired repeatedly—and successfully—to shoot down the cause of popular democracy.

The industrial capitalist order that was growing rapidly in the years after the Civil War imposed heavy costs on workers, farmers, and owners of small businesses. Popular democratic forces, such as the agrarian Granger movement and the Populist movement, gained power in some states and passed legislation to protect ordinary people against capitalist exploitation, especially by the railroads. As the popular democratic forces mobilized, legal historian Michael Benedict writes, "the justices became convinced that the Court must serve as the bulwark of property rights against threatened radical legislation."[10] The Court set up a roadblock against state efforts to regulate the railroads in *Wabash, St. Louis & Pacific Railway Co. v. Illinois* (1886), ruling that states had no power to regulate rail rates for shipments that crossed their borders.

The Court stretched the doctrine of laissez-faire (that is, government should not interfere in the free market) the furthest in redefining the meaning of "due process of law." It was a violation of due process, the Court ruled, when a state interfered with the contractual freedom of employers and employees to make whatever "bargains" they wished. In *Lochner v. New York* (1905), the Court used this argument to invalidate a New York law setting maximum hours for bakery workers. "Freedom of contract" was the watchword of the Court, and popular democratic legislation to protect working people from oppressive conditions was declared unconstitutional.

After World War I, the majority of the Court further hardened its laissez-faire dogma. It was this majority that fought the bitterest battle in the history of the Court—against Franklin Roosevelt and the New Deal. Once Roosevelt and his Democratic majority in Congress passed far-reaching measures to revive an economy mired in the worst depression in its history, the question of power over the economy was joined by the Court. It invalidated the two linchpins of the New Deal: the National Industrial Recovery Act and the Agricultural Adjustment Act. The 1936 election gave Roosevelt the largest mandate in presidential history, but the Supreme Court now seemed an impassable barrier to his efforts to improve the economy and reform it in popular democratic fashion.

Early in 1937, Roosevelt unveiled a program to smash through this barrier. He claimed (in deceptive fashion) that he was acting only to enhance the efficiency of a Court dominated by elderly judges. His proposal was that the president be given the authority to add an additional justice each time a sitting justice over the age of seventy refused to retire. (The size of the Supreme Court is not set by the Constitution.) Popular though Roosevelt was, his **court-packing plan** was a political fiasco. Public opinion sided with the Court, and Roosevelt suffered a major defeat in Congress.

Nonetheless, Roosevelt won the larger battle with the Court in the end. While the debate raged over the court-packing plan, the Court narrowly approved two key New Deal measures—the National Labor Relations Act and the Social Security Act—during the spring of 1937. And in the next few years, deaths and resignations of the conservatives who had stymied the president permitted him to name a New Deal majority to the Court. Roosevelt's appointees ended seventy years of laissez-faire doctrine. In one of the most important shifts in the history of the Supreme Court—a "Roosevelt revolution"—they took the Court largely out of the business of economic policy.

The Modern Court

For several decades after the Roosevelt revolution, the Court's role largely centered on civil liberties and civil rights (see Chapter 16). However, it was only with the emergence of the Warren Court (1953–1969) that it blazed a straightforward path in support of individual liberties and the rights of racial minorities. The Warren Court's liberal activism on behalf of the rights of dissenters, criminal defendants, and African Americans won it many vocal enemies, including successful presidential candidate Richard Nixon in 1968.

Nixon had the opportunity to name four new justices, among them Warren Burger as replacement for the retiring Earl Warren. (For membership changes on the Supreme Court since 1960, see Figure 15.1.) Yet the Burger Court (1969–1986) did not carry out the conservative counterrevolution that Nixon had advocated. Holdovers from the Warren Court and Nixon appointees who proved more moderate than expected made the Burger Court a transitional body, cutting back on some of the Warren Court landmarks, especially in matters of criminal procedure, but also announcing a fundamental new right in the area of abortion.

It was in the era of the Rehnquist Court (1986–2005) that a new conservative jurisprudence, shaped by the appointees of Presidents Reagan and the elder Bush, crystallized. Often by five-to-four votes, a conservative majority, led by Chief Justice William Rehnquist, partially shifted the Court's focus from questions of rights back to older questions of authority. During this period, conservatives continued to complain about liberal "judicial activism," yet the Rehnquist Court was, in the judgment of political scientist Thomas Keck, "the most activist Supreme Court in history."[11]

For the first time since the Roosevelt revolution, the ability of the federal government to exercise broad regulatory authority was challenged by the Court. In *United States v. Lopez* (1995), a federal law making it a crime to carry a gun within 1,000 feet of a school was struck down, with the conservative majority arguing that the law was unrelated to interstate commerce and intruded on the police powers of the states. In *Printz v. United States* (1997), a portion of the Brady gun control law was invalidated because it required local law enforcement

Justices of the U.S. Supreme Court: Standing (from left): Sonia Sotomayor, Stephen Breyer, Samuel Alito, Elena Kagan. Seated (from left): Clarence Thomas, Antonin Scalia, John Roberts (chief), Anthony Kennedy, Ruth Bader Ginsburg.

Steve Petteway, Collection of the Supreme Court of the United States

FIGURE 15.1| **Membership of the Supreme Court, 1960s–2012**

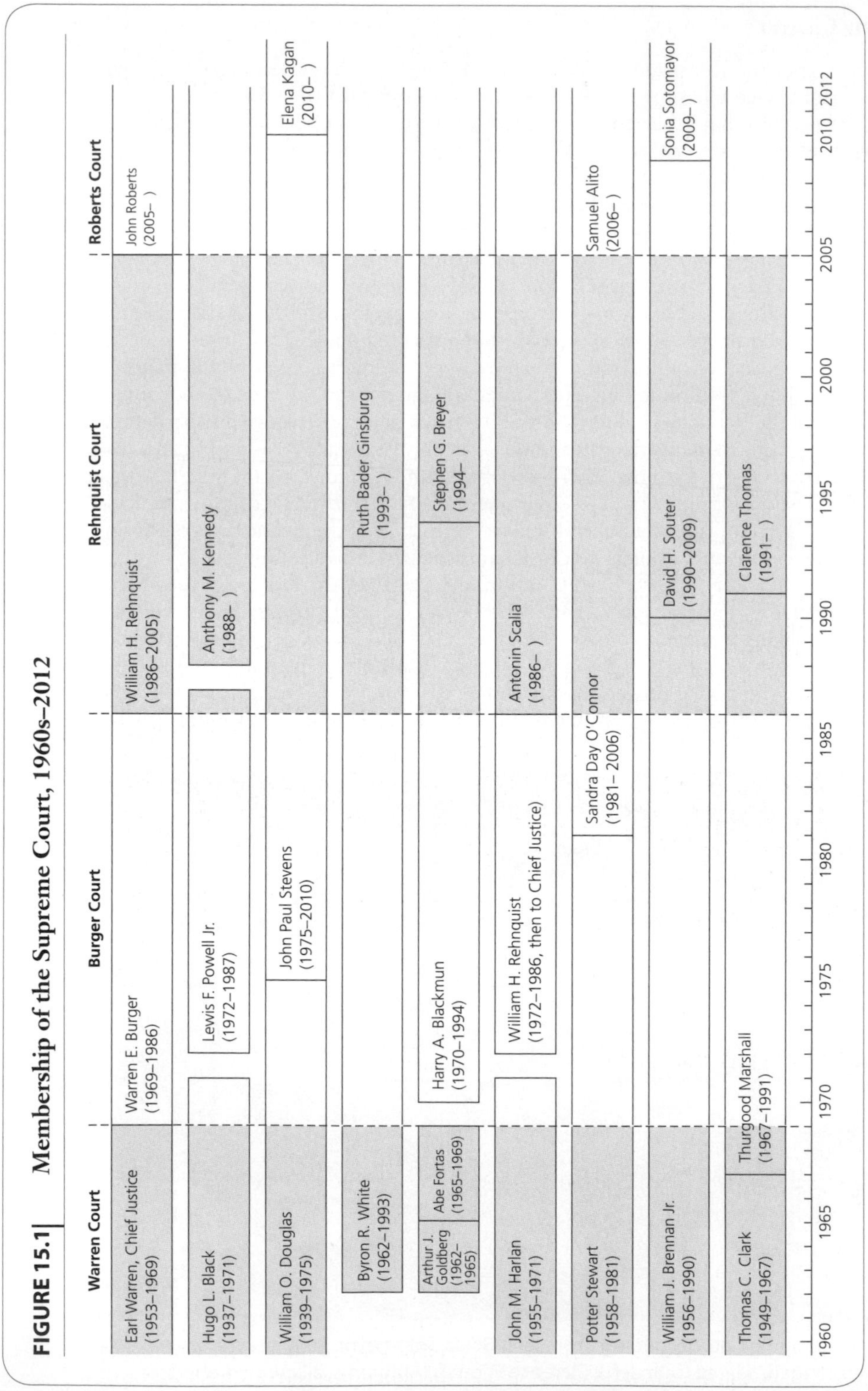

Source: From WASBY. Supreme Court in the Federal Judicial System, 4E. © 1993 Wadsworth, a part of Cengage Learning, Inc. Reproduced by permission. www.cengage.com/permissions. Updated by the authors.

officers to run background checks on prospective handgun purchasers, with the same conservative majority stating that Washington cannot command state officials to administer a federal regulatory program. The states' rights philosophy of the Rehnquist Court majority carried profound implications for both federal regulations and civil rights.[12]

Although Rehnquist and his four allies on the Court made states' rights the central theme of their judicial philosophy, they abandoned states' rights when the presidency of the United States was at stake. In *Bush v. Gore,* decided in December 2000 by the same five-to-four lineup as the federalism cases cited above, the Court's conservative majority overturned the order of the Florida Supreme Court to proceed with a statewide hand recount that would determine who gained Florida's twenty-five electoral votes and thus the presidency. Effectively awarding the White House to Republican George W. Bush, the majority argued that hand recounts, by being subject to varying standards in different counties, violated the constitutional guarantee of equal protection of the laws. Five justices, all appointed by Republican presidents, thus put another Republican into the White House, where he could be assumed to make future nominations to the Court that would solidify and expand its conservative majority.

What the majority in *Bush v. Gore* anticipated came to pass early in George W. Bush's second term. When Chief Justice Rehnquist died, the president replaced him with John Roberts, and shortly afterwards Samuel Alito took over the seat of the retiring Sandra Day O'Connor. The second Bush appointment had the larger impact on the Court's ideological balance, as the reliably conservative Alito replaced the moderate O'Connor. The new Roberts Court quickly shifted the law further to the right, issuing decisions that gratified conservatives in such areas as abortion, school integration, and prisoners' rights.[13]

The Roberts Court became an antagonist to the Obama administration with its landmark decision on campaign finance, *Citizens United v. Federal Election Commission,* announced in January 2010. Overturning numerous precedents, the five conservative justices ruled that federal law could not prohibit corporations or unions from spending unlimited funds during campaigns so long as the money did not go directly to candidates. Corporate spending, the Court's majority proclaimed, was free speech and thus protected under the First Amendment. It was the *Citizens United* decision that President Obama criticized in his 2010 State of the Union address for allowing powerful special interests to enhance their influence in elections through massive amounts of campaign cash.

President Obama's landmark health care reform faced numerous legal challenges as soon as it was enacted into law in 2010, and some observers predicted that the five-to-four conservative majority on the Roberts Court would strike it down. But the Chief Justice surprised almost everyone by breaking with his four fellow conservatives and upholding Obama's Patient Protection and Affordable Care Act. In *National Federation of Independent Business v. Sebelius,* announced in June 2012, Roberts wrote that the controversial provision in the new law that mandates a monetary penalty if individuals do not obtain health insurance falls under Congress's taxing power and is thereby constitutional.

Judicial Selection ★ ★ ★

Article II, Section 2 of the Constitution states that the president "shall nominate, and by and with the advice and consent of the Senate, shall appoint . . . judges of the supreme court." The same clause applies to judges in the lower federal courts, which were created by acts of Congress. These few words did not specify the processes by which a president would pick judicial nominees and the Senate consider them or what advice and consent comprised. Should the Senate defer to the president's judgment, rejecting a nominee only when that individual was found lacking in judicial competence or personal integrity? Or should the

Senate's judgment be equal to the president's, allowing the Senate to reject a nominee of unquestioned competence and character on political or ideological grounds? With so little settled by the language of the Constitution, judicial selection has become, for presidents and senators alike, an intensely political affair.

Lower Federal Court Nominations

The politics of judicial selection operates differently for the lower federal courts than for the Supreme Court. Judges of the district courts serve only in a district within one state, and the senators from that state are normally involved in their selection. According to the tradition of **senatorial courtesy**, if the senior senator from the president's party objects to a district court nominee for his or her state, the Senate as a whole will withhold consent. As a consequence, presidents consult senators on district court nominations and may turn the choice over to them in exchange for future political support on other matters. Senatorial courtesy was weakened under President Reagan and his Republican successors. Individual senators have always had less power—and presidents have had more leeway—in appointing judges to the U.S. courts of appeals, whose jurisdiction extends over several states.

Although presidents have to share power over lower federal court nominations, they have much to gain by taking a strong interest in judicial selection at this level. Since the Supreme Court hears only a small number of cases, the vast majority of federal court decisions are rendered by the district courts and courts of appeals. Since retirement rates are higher on the lower courts than on the Supreme Court, and since Congress periodically creates new judicial positions to keep up with the expanding workload of a litigious society, a president sometimes can exercise more influence through lower court nominations than through Supreme Court nominations. For example, during Ronald Reagan's eight years as president, he appointed approximately half of all lower court judges (372 out of 736), giving the lower federal courts a more conservative slant.[14]

However, growing partisan polarization in the Senate since the Reagan years (see Chapter 12) has affected a president's ability to reshape the lower courts. Many of President Clinton's nominees were bottled up by Republicans in the Judiciary Committee. Democrats mounted filibusters against several nominees of President Bush on the grounds that they were too ideologically extreme. Under President Obama, lower court nominations have been stalled or blocked even more frequently. *New York Times* court-watcher Linda Greenhouse writes that Senate floor action on Obama nominees "has been proceeding at a slow crawl."[15]

Starting with Jimmy Carter, presidents have been evaluated by the diversity as well as the ideology of their judicial nominees. Democratic presidents have appointed a higher percentage of women and minorities to the lower federal courts than have Republicans. Barack Obama has far surpassed his predecessors from both parties in this area, drastically departing from the historical norm of white male nominees to the federal bench. During his first two years in the White House, more than 70 percent of his nominees that won Senate confirmation were women, minorities, or both.[16]

Supreme Court Nominations

Most presidents have less of an opportunity in the course of a four-year term to reshape the Supreme Court than to reshape the lower federal courts. George W. Bush did not have a single opportunity to nominate a Supreme Court justice until 2005, his fifth year in office. Nonetheless, any presidential nomination to the Supreme Court today is likely to initiate a high-stakes political drama, for every new member may make a major difference in determining what the Constitution and the laws mean. Some of the Court's landmark decisions, including the one that made George W. Bush president, have come in five-to-four votes; a replacement of only one justice would have produced a different outcome. And some new appointees influence the Court with more than just their votes. They may prove to be a catalyst for the formation of a firm voting bloc, as was the case with the liberal Justice William Brennan. Or they may bring to the Court a forceful ideological perspective, as is the case with conservative Justice Antonin Scalia.[17]

The appointment process for a new justice of the Supreme Court begins when an existing justice retires or dies. In deliberating over a replacement, contemporary presidents tend to rely heavily on the Justice Department and legal counselors on the White House staff for advice on prospective nominees. Viewing Supreme Court decisions as critical to the constituencies they represent, many interest groups are involved in the politics of judicial selection as well. Thus, several of the nominees of Presidents Reagan and the elder Bush were vigorously opposed by civil rights and women's groups, which feared that these nominees would roll back the equal rights advances of recent decades.

The drama of Supreme Court nominations reaches its apex in the hearing room of the Senate Judiciary Committee. In this televised forum, senators are able to question nominees directly about their legal experience and judicial philosophy. Although questions about controversial issues currently before the Court, such as abortion, are supposed to be off limits, senators usually find means to probe these matters. Some recent nominees, such as Robert Bork (who was rejected by the Senate), have entertained these questions. Others, such as Samuel Alito, perhaps learning from Bork's experience, have fended them off with bland generalities.

In announcing the nomination of a new justice, the president is likely to highlight the legal expertise of the nominee. Less will be said about the real criterion that governs most selections: politics. As David O'Brien observes, "The presidential impulse to pack the Court with politically compatible justices is irresistible."[18]

Presidential nominations are influenced by important political forces in the nation. In the past, geographic considerations were significant, as presidents tried to ensure that each region of the country was represented on the Court. Geographic considerations have faded in the face of issues of gender and race. Thus, when Thurgood Marshall, the first African American justice in the history of the Supreme Court, retired in 1991, the elder President Bush found an African American conservative, Clarence Thomas, to replace him. An even more important political factor is ideology. Presidents' impacts on public policy depend not only on the legislation they sponsor or the executive actions they take but also on the decisions of the Court that reflect the ideological difference that their nominees have made.

Do justices, with the independence of lifetime tenure, continue to stick to the ideological path that the presidents who appointed them anticipated at the time of nomination? Legal scholar Laurence Tribe says yes. Tribe debunks what he calls "the myth of the surprised president." Presidents who have set out deliberately to alter the ideological direction of the Court, he shows, have generally succeeded in their strategies.[19] Nevertheless, a few counterexamples suggest that presidents don't always predict the future correctly. For instance, President George H. W. Bush's first appointee, David H. Souter, surprised everyone by becoming one of the Court's more liberal members.

Given the political basis of Supreme Court nominations, presidents are sometimes unsuccessful with them in the Senate. About 20 percent of nominees have failed to win confirmation, with rejection rates running particularly high in the mid-nineteenth century and the past forty-five years (both periods of intense partisan conflict). The odds for presidents' success drop when they are in their final year in office or when the opposition party has a majority in the Senate.[20]

Recent experience indicates that presidents have an easier time when their Supreme Court nominees lack a hard ideological edge. Robert Bork, an outspoken conservative jurist nominated by President Reagan, was rejected by a substantial margin in the Senate, while the equally conservative Clarence Thomas, nominated by Reagan's successor, narrowly avoided the same fate. Since the Thomas nomination, presidents have selected less controversial figures, and the nomination process has proceeded more smoothly.

Neither of President Obama's appointments to the Supreme Court in 2009–2010, Sonia Sotomayor and Elena Kagan, faced strong ideological opposition, especially because they were taking the places of retiring justices whose views were similar to theirs. More noteworthy than their judicial views are their race and gender. Sotomayor is the first Latina to sit on the Supreme Court. Once Kagan joined her, a third of the Court's membership was, for the first time in history, female.[21]

The Federal Court System

Presidential appointees to the judicial branch serve in a three-tiered federal court system: district courts, courts of appeals, and Supreme Court. (In addition, there are a number of specialized federal courts, such as bankruptcy and tax courts.) The Constitution specified only "one Supreme Court," leaving it to Congress to create "inferior courts" as it deemed necessary. Since the creation of the courts of appeals in 1891, the basic structure of the federal court system has been set. Figure 15.2 outlines the current structure of the federal court system.

U.S. District Courts

On the bottom level of the three-tiered federal court system are the U.S. district courts. The district courts are courts of **original jurisdiction**, meaning the courts where almost all federal cases begin. And they are the trial courts for the federal system, resolving both criminal

FIGURE 15.2 | **Basic Structure of the Federal Court System**

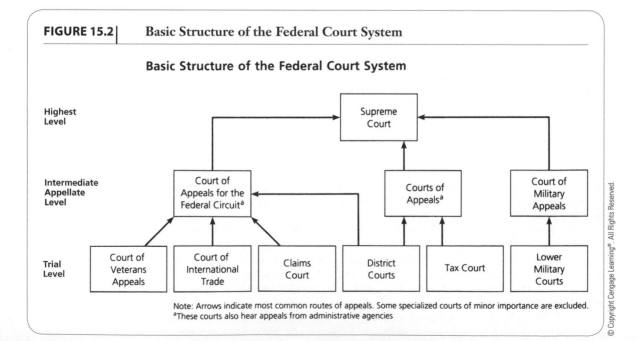

Note: Arrows indicate most common routes of appeals. Some specialized courts of minor importance are excluded.
[a]These courts also hear appeals from administrative agencies

and civil cases, sometimes with judge and jury and sometimes with judge only. There are currently ninety-four U.S. district courts; each state has at least one, and the larger states have as many as four.

The caseload of the district courts is large and rapidly expanding. In the great majority of these cases, the district courts have the final say: Decisions are not appealed, are settled before any higher court rulings occur, or are affirmed by the courts of appeals.

U.S. Courts of Appeals

The U.S. courts of appeals, the middle tier of the federal court system, hear appeals of decisions rendered by the district courts, specialized courts, and federal regulatory agencies. As **appellate courts**, the courts of appeals bear some resemblance to the Supreme Court and have sometimes been called "mini-Supreme Courts." Yet there are some major differences in the appellate role of the two. Whereas the Supreme Court can choose the cases it hears, courts of appeals must hear every case brought to them. Whereas the Supreme Court is interested in large questions of constitutional and statutory interpretation rather than the fate of the particular parties in a case, courts of appeals seek to correct errors in lower court decisions to ensure that justice is done to the individuals involved. Because the Supreme Court is too busy to consider many types of federal cases, however, the courts of appeals do effectively decide policy in a number of areas of law.

There are twelve courts of appeals with general appellate jurisdiction— one in the District of Columbia and eleven numbered circuits that cover several contiguous states plus associated territories. The circuits vary in size from six to twenty-eight judges.

Courts of appeals hearings do not retry cases. New factual evidence is not introduced, and no witnesses appear. Lawyers for the two sides in a case make oral arguments and present written briefs to the judges. Ordinarily, a three-judge panel will hear a case (and decisions are sometimes made by two-to-one vote). In especially important cases, a court of appeals may sit *en banc*, with all of its members participating. What makes the courts of appeals so significant a force in the federal court system is that few of their decisions are ever overturned.

U.S. Supreme Court

The highest tier of the federal court system is the Supreme Court of the United States. Not only does it take cases that originate in the lower federal courts; it also hears cases that originate in state courts if these cases raise constitutional issues (see Figure 15.3). That the Supreme Court is "the highest court in the land" invests it with great authority. As Justice Robert Jackson once wryly observed of the Court, "We are not final because we are infallible, we are infallible only because we are final."[22]

The Supreme Court has both original jurisdiction and appellate jurisdiction. The Constitution limits original jurisdiction to "all cases affecting ambassadors, other public ministers and counsels, and those in which a State shall be party." Few cases arise that qualify under these terms. Almost all of what the Supreme Court does falls under its second constitutional role as an appellate court.

Supreme Court decisions are powerful not only because they are the final judicial rulings in a case but also because they establish precedents that bind the lower federal courts and the state courts. Once the Supreme Court has spoken, judges at lower levels are supposed to bring their decisions into line with its interpretation of the Constitution and the laws. But guidance to lower courts is imperfect when the language of Supreme Court decisions is vague or when new circumstances arise that differ from those of the case used to establish a precedent. Consequently, decision making in a complex area such as criminal procedure or affirmative action may shuttle back and forth for years between the lower courts and the Supreme Court.

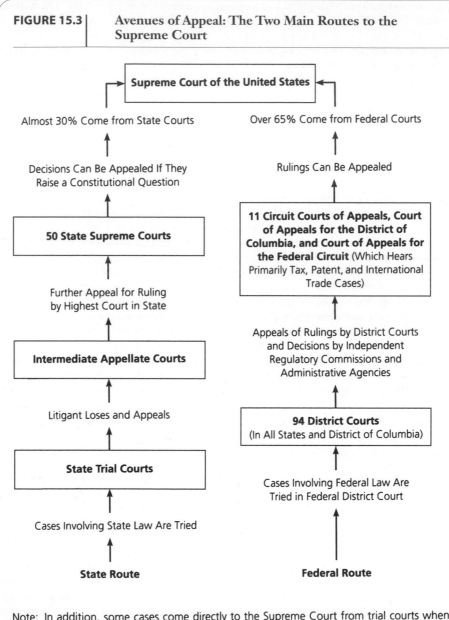

FIGURE 15.3 | Avenues of Appeal: The Two Main Routes to the Supreme Court

Supreme Court of the United States

Almost 30% Come from State Courts

Over 65% Come from Federal Courts

Decisions Can Be Appealed If They Raise a Constitutional Question

Rulings Can Be Appealed

50 State Supreme Courts

11 Circuit Courts of Appeals, Court of Appeals for the District of Columbia, and Court of Appeals for the Federal Circuit (Which Hears Primarily Tax, Patent, and International Trade Cases)

Further Appeal for Ruling by Highest Court in State

Intermediate Appellate Courts

Appeals of Rulings by District Courts and Decisions by Independent Regulatory Commissions and Administrative Agencies

Litigant Loses and Appeals

94 District Courts (In All States and District of Columbia)

State Trial Courts

Cases Involving Federal Law Are Tried in Federal District Court

Cases Involving State Law Are Tried

State Route

Federal Route

Note: In addition, some cases come directly to the Supreme Court from trial courts when they involve reapportionment or civil rights disputes. Appeals from the Court of Military Appeals also go directly to the Supreme Court. A few cases come on "original jurisdiction" and involve disputes between state governments.

The Supreme Court: Process

Unlike the legislative and executive branches, the Court is an institution in which the logic and rules of the law matter a great deal. But so, too, do the personalities and political values of the human beings who pronounce the law.

Choosing Cases

Each session of the Supreme Court begins on the first Monday in October and concludes in late June or early July of the following year. At present, approximately 10,000 cases are filed per year; of these, the Supreme Court will grant a review and produce a written opinion in fewer than one hundred cases! Disgruntled parties in lawsuits often swear that they will appeal the verdict "all the way to the Supreme Court." Obviously, the chance that the Supreme Court will hear their appeal is minuscule.

In all but a handful of areas, the Court is free to choose the cases it wishes to hear. Today, about 99 percent of the Court's cases arrive through a **writ of *certiorari***. The losing party in a lower court proceeding petitions the Supreme Court for this writ; should the Court choose to "grant cert" (shorthand for *certiorari*), it orders the lower court to send the records of the case.

The mountain of cert petitions that arrives at the Supreme Court by the beginning of its fall term has to be sifted through to find the few worthy of the Court's full attention. Because the number of petitions has risen, justices have turned over the work of screening them to their law clerks, recent graduates of the nation's elite law schools. Armed with memos from clerks, the justices meet to decide which cases to hear. According to the informal **rule of four**, at least four justices must agree that a case deserves consideration.

Since almost all cases reach the Court through writs of certiorari, the justices have considerable latitude in setting their own agenda. In each year's session, they can accept cases that allow them to grapple with a constitutional or statutory issue that they deem ripe for determination and reject cases if they wish to sidestep some other controversial issue. Even when the Court agrees to take a case, it may choose to decide it without full consideration, a process known as *summary disposition*. After denying the vast majority of petitions for certiorari, and handling some of the remainder through summary dispositions, the Supreme Court turns its attention to the few cases that have made it through its filters.

Deciding Cases

When a case is granted full treatment, attorneys for the two sides are given several months to prepare briefs—written statements that argue their respective legal positions to the justices. Additional briefs may be filed by individuals or groups that are not parties in a lawsuit but have an interest in the issues it raises; these are known as *amicus curiae* (friend of the court) briefs. Having read these briefs, the justices allow attorneys for the contending litigants to appear in **oral argument**. In most instances, each side has only half an hour to present its strongest arguments to the Court. Oral argument often proves to be a battle for the attorney—but less with opposing counsel than with the justices themselves. Lawyers are not allowed to read from prepared texts, and some justices have a habit of asking barbed questions during oral arguments.

The justices meet in conference twice a week to discuss the cases they have just heard in oral argument. Ordinarily, formal votes are not taken in these meetings since the positions of the justices have been made clear in their comments. After all nine justices have spoken, one is selected to write a majority opinion for the Court. If the chief justice is in the majority, he or she assigns the opinion. If the chief justice is in the minority, the senior justice on the majority side makes the assignment. The voting alignment at this stage is tentative. Justices may still switch their votes—which makes the next stage, the writing of opinions, all the more crucial.

The crucial test of a majority opinion is not whether it sparkles in style but whether it wins the necessary votes. The justice assigned to write the opinion for the Court must hold on to the votes that constituted the initial majority and, if he or she is persuasive enough, perhaps pick up additional votes. The risk is that an opinion may lose votes along the way.

The majority opinion announces the position of the Court. Justices who do not want to add their names to this opinion have two options. If they agree with the result announced in the majority opinion but not with the reasoning that justifies this result (or if they simply want to make additional points not found in the majority opinion), they can write a **concurring opinion** that sets out their alternative course of argument. If they disagree with the result, they can write a **dissenting opinion** that challenges the majority's view of what the law should be. Other justices may then sign these concurrences or dissents. In recent years, heated ideological differences and a growing preference for individual expression over institutional loyalty have led to a marked increase in concurrences and dissents.

Once all opinions have been drafted, the justices make their final decisions about whether they will "join" the majority opinion, concurring opinions, or dissents. The Court is now ready for a public announcement of its holding in a case.

The Supreme Court: Politics

Throughout the process of decision, from screening cases to announcing opinions, the procedures and precedents of the law are central to the work of the Supreme Court. But the process is political as well as legal. Three political factors influence the Court in this regard: the leadership of the chief justice, the strategic action of other justices, and the central role of ideology in shaping judicial results.

The Chief Justice and Leadership

The chief justice has certain special prerogatives during the decision process, such as speaking first in conference and assigning opinions for the Court when in the majority. In addition, the chief justice has unique administrative responsibilities, both over the Court's own building and personnel and over the federal judicial system as a whole. Nevertheless, chief justices are only "first among equals"; when it comes to votes, they have only one. Whether a chief justice is a leader depends on intellectual talent, interpersonal skills, and ability to manage the business of the Court.

Replacing William Rehnquist (whom he had once served as a law clerk) after his death in 2005, John Roberts has been the kind of chief justice that the president who selected him anticipated. Low-key and convivial, Roberts describes himself as a consensus builder on the court. However, Roberts's conservative ideology, which has contributed to a rightward trend since he and Samuel Alito were appointed by President Bush, works against consensus on such a divided court. Hence, dissents from the Court's liberal bloc have remained as frequent and as sharply worded as they were in the Rehnquist Court.[23]

Strategic Action

The chief justice is not the only member of the Court who can exercise leadership. Any of the other eight justices can use *strategic action* to win a majority for a legal doctrine they favor. Justices who engage in strategic action calculate the mix of tactics that will likely win over enough votes to their preferred position. Such tactics may include (1) persuasion on the merits—intellectual arguments to change minds, (2) ingratiation—using personal warmth to woo potential supporters, (3) sanctions—threats to write a stinging concurrence or dissent, and (4) bargaining—negotiation over the argument and language of a decision.[24]

That the Supreme Court is the most elite domain in American politics hardly frees it from internal conflict. Indeed, the Court's elite nature may exacerbate conflict. Protected by lifetime tenure, justices may bring strongly held opinions and large egos to "battles on the bench." However, these battles are ordinarily kept from getting out of hand by prudent calculations (you may need your current adversary's vote in a future case) and considerations of authority (too much visible conflict undermines the legitimacy of the Court).[25]

Ideology

Although the leadership abilities of a chief justice or the strategic action of other justices may significantly affect the work of the Court, the most powerful political factor is ideology. In deciding how to cast votes and frame opinions, justices are profoundly influenced by their own convictions about society. Changes in the doctrines announced by the Supreme Court stem less from developments internal to the law than from the arrival of new justices with differing ideological perspectives.[26]

The most common ideological distinction among justices is that between liberals and conservatives. Liberal justices tend to favor individual rights (for example, of political dissenters and criminal defendants) when they clash with governmental authority, to support measures toward greater equality for such previously excluded groups as African Americans

"IT IS NOT OFTEN IN THE LAW THAT SO FEW HAVE SO QUICKLY CHANGED SO MUCH."
—JUSTICE STEPHEN BREYER

Justice Breyer describes the power of the Court's conservative majority.

359

and women, and to validate government regulation of the economy. Conservative justices are more inclined to cherish the peace of the existing social order and the authority of the officials (executives, bureaucrats, police, prosecutors) who maintain it, and to look with greater favor at the rights of property owners. Some justices fall midway between these ideological poles; in a closely divided Court, these "centrists" may hold the balance of power.[27]

Students of the Supreme Court look not only at the ideology of individual justices but also at the formation of **ideological blocs**. An ideological bloc is a group of two or more justices who vote the same way with a high degree of regularity. Thus, we can speak of liberal blocs, conservative blocs, or moderate blocs, such as the bloc of four conservatives who frustrated Roosevelt's New Deal or the bloc of five liberals who spearheaded the expansion of civil liberties in the later years of the Warren Court. Members of an ideological bloc may directly coordinate their actions or may simply vote the same way out of shared beliefs, even in the absence of close personal relations.

The Supreme Court and the Political System

Ideology is the single most potent force shaping the decisions of the Supreme Court. But other factors enter in, among them, concern for how decisions will be received by other political actors. A Supreme Court decision must take into account multiple audiences: the lower courts that must apply the decision to other cases, the government officials who must enforce the decision, and the segment of the public that must abide by the decision. Lacking the power of the purse (financial power) and the power of the sword (executive power, including the use of force if necessary), the Supreme Court is dependent for its power on the reaction to its decisions. As political scientist Stephen Wasby remarks, "The Supreme Court may make law, or the law may be what the Supreme Court says it is, but *only after all others have had their say.*"[28]

When Supreme Court decisions require federal action, the response of the president is most important. Historically, presidents who have come into office committed to large-scale transformations in American life have fought epic contests with court majorities whose roots lay in a previous political era. Jefferson, Jackson, Lincoln, and Franklin Roosevelt all claimed that the head of the executive branch has just as much of a right to interpret constitutional powers as does the Supreme Court.[29]

Most presidents have backed up the Court, regarding the enforcement of its decisions as a requirement of their oath of office. Occasionally, though, they drag their feet on implementation or repudiate a particular decision altogether. President George H. W. Bush sharply criticized the Supreme Court's decision in *Texas v. Johnson* (1989), which upheld the right of a protester to burn an American flag as a form of symbolic speech protected under the First Amendment. He proposed a constitutional amendment to ban flag burning but failed to steer the amendment through Congress.

Congress has power to chastise or discipline the Supreme Court since the legislative branch determines the appellate jurisdiction and even the size of the highest court. During the nineteenth century, Congress sometimes altered the size of the Court. Since Roosevelt's court-packing fiasco, however, it has been politically imprudent to propose adding or subtracting members, and the figure of nine justices has seemingly become sacred. Supreme Court decisions based on the Constitution can be overturned only through the difficult process of constitutional amendment, so the ability of members of Congress to reverse specific decisions is far greater when the Court has been engaged in statutory interpretation. Thus, the Civil Rights Act of 1991, placing the burden of proof on employers in job discrimination lawsuits, overturned a dozen recent Supreme Court holdings.

[MAKING A DIFFERENCE]

Justice William J. Brennan Jr.

In a 1990 survey conducted by the *National Law Journal,* only 3 percent of Americans recognized the name William Brennan Jr. Yet few public figures in the last half of the twentieth century had as great an impact on the lives of Americans as this remarkable associate justice of the U.S. Supreme Court.

The son of Irish immigrants, Brennan grew up in Newark, New Jersey. From his father, a coal heaver who rose to become a labor union official and local political leader, he inherited a commitment to activism on behalf of society's have-nots. Brennan maintained this commitment even as he, in turn, ascended into the higher ranks of the judicial elite. Appointed to the U.S. Supreme Court by President Eisenhower in 1956 (an appointment that Eisenhower later regretted), Brennan served until 1990. He died in 1997.

During his thirty-four years on the Court, Brennan was a leading force for judicial activism. No other justice of modern times matched his record for penning landmark decisions. In area after area—reapportionment, the law of libel, obscenity, school prayer, the rights of criminal defendants, equal rights for minorities and women—Brennan crafted decisions that reshaped the rules by which Americans live.

Brennan's influence stemmed as much from his skills at strategic action as from his popular democratic convictions. Unlike his fellow giants of liberal jurisprudence, Hugo Black and William O. Douglas, who were combative and uncompromising, Brennan was adept at building coalitions and molding consensuses. In *New York Times v. Sullivan* (1964), the most conservative members of the Court wanted to retain the existing standard of libel law, by which a newspaper could be sued for an erroneous statement injuring the reputation of a public official, while the most liberal members insisted that the right of free speech barred any judgments for libel in such cases. Brennan found a middle ground: To win a libel suit, a plaintiff must show that falsehoods printed about her or him are intentional and motivated by "actual malice." Patiently rewriting his opinion to satisfy colleagues on both sides— it took eight drafts!—Brennan revolutionized libel law and expanded the freedom of the press.

The height of Brennan's influence came during the Warren Court revolution. But he continued to use his intellectual and political talents to shape the law even during the years in which the Burger and Rehnquist Courts sought a counterrevolution. Brennan mounted a powerful defense of the essential achievements of the Warren Court and frequently frustrated conservative ambitions. He was even able to extend Warren Court departures in several areas. Adept as always behind the scenes, he played a major role in shaping the Court's support for abortion rights in *Roe v. Wade* (1973). And he wrote new landmark decisions on women's rights (*Craig v. Boren,* 1976) and symbolic speech (*Texas v. Johnson,* 1989).

Yet the conservative trend on the Court pushed Brennan frequently into the role of dissenter, particularly on the issue of the death penalty. Here, the usually affable and pragmatic Brennan was passionately unyielding. To him, the core of the Constitution and the Bill of Rights was a commitment to human dignity. "The fatal constitutional infirmity of capital punishment," he wrote, "is that it treats members of the human race as nonhumans, as objects to be toyed with and discarded." Unlike famous Supreme Court dissenters of the past, Brennan did not relish this role; he preferred being the strategic actor who could find the common ground upon which a majority could be built. Yet his stance on the death penalty expressed his commitment to justice for the most unpopular and powerless of Americans.

Sources: Kim Isaac Eisler, *A Justice for All: William J. Brennan, Jr., and the Decisions That Transformed America* (New York: Simon & Schuster, 1993); Charles G. Curtis Jr. and Shirley S. Abrahamson, "William Joseph Brennan, Jr.," in *The Oxford Companion to the Supreme Court of the United States,* ed. Kermit L. Hall et al. (New York: Oxford University Press, 1992), 86–89; Owen Fiss, "A Life Lived Twice," *The Yale Law Journal* 100 (March 1991): 1117–29.

Even though the justices don't face the public in elections, they know that compliance with their decisions depends ultimately on public opinion. General public support for the Supreme Court is higher than for Congress or the presidency. On the other hand, public knowledge about the Court is lower. Surveys indicate that a majority cannot name even one sitting justice. The public is more aware of controversial Court rulings than of the Court as an institution.[30]

Respect for law and the Supreme Court inclines most Americans to abide by judicial decisions, even those they disagree with. When the Court treads in the most sensitive areas, however, it may face major problems of evasion or resistance. Its ruling in *Engel v. Vitale* (1962) forbade prayer in the public schools as a violation of the First Amendment, yet decades later some public schools still conduct various forms of religious observance.

Conclusion: Law, Politics, and the Democratic Debate

In our examination of the federal judicial system, and especially in our treatment of the Supreme Court, law and politics are separate yet intertwined. The judicial branch is fundamentally different from the other branches in that it is a legal order. Its business is resolving lawsuits or criminal cases. It follows legal procedures and rules for determining how cases are brought to and then handled by the high court, and gives considerable weight to past decisions as precedents on the grounds that law should be, as much as possible, settled and known. The impressive symbolic power of the Supreme Court—the black robes, the marble temple, and the confidential deliberations—rests on the mystique of the rule of law as something that transcends politics.

Yet politics shapes appointments to the Supreme Court, as presidents try to pick justices who will carry out the chief executives' political and ideological agendas. Politics is found within the internal processes of the Court, as chief justices attempt to exercise leadership and other justices engage in strategic action. Political values influence the Court, with ideology the paramount factor in determining how different justices will vote on cases. Political sensitivity to other institutions and to public opinion characterizes a judicial branch aware of its dependence on others to carry out its decisions. Finally, the Court is political because its decisions set national policy on some of the issues that matter most to Americans.

It is because the judiciary is political, and indeed so important a policy maker, that there has been an intense democratic debate in recent years over its proper role in American life. Popular democrats of the past generally mistrusted the Court as a nondemocratic defender of elite privileges. Their arguments have been taken over by modern conservatives, whose very different policy agenda also requires a Court that practices self-restraint and does not interfere much with other institutions. In contrast, liberal jurists want popular democrats to reexamine their attitude toward the judiciary, arguing that only an activist Court that adapts and modernizes the Constitution can bring out its true democratic character. Progressive skeptics question both the conservatives' fear of the Court and the liberals' hope for it. In their thinking, the Court can be of only modest value in the struggle for popular democracy. Citizens who seek popular democratic reform must rely on their own political activities rather than looking for salvation from the judicial elite.

Reader's Guide ★ ★ ★

Critical Thinking Questions

1. Should the U.S. Supreme Court use the "textualist" method and search for the original meaning of the Constitution, or should it be guided by the idea of a "Living Constitution" and adapt old words to new times?

2. In deciding whether to confirm a presidential nominee to the federal courts, should senators consider only personal integrity and legal credentials, or is it legitimate for them to weigh the ideology of the nominee as well?

3. Is it inevitable that political factors play such a large role in the decisions of the Supreme Court?

4. Looking at the Supreme Court in history and today, is it more often an agent for democratic change or a supporter of the status quo?

Key Word Definition

judicial review   The power of the courts to invalidate legislative or executive actions because they conflict with the Constitution.

precedent   A previous decision by a court that is treated as a rule for future cases.

Marbury v. Madison   The 1803 case in which the Supreme Court established that it had the right to exercise judicial review even though that power was not stated in the Constitution.

McCulloch v. Maryland   The 1819 case in which Justice Marshall emphasized the constitutional supremacy of the federal government in striking down Maryland's attempt to tax the Bank of the United States.

Gibbons v. Ogden   The 1824 case in which the Supreme Court broadly defined the congressional power to "regulate commerce among the states," thereby establishing the supremacy of the federal government over the states in matters involving interstate commerce.

Dred Scott v. Sandford   The infamous 1857 case in which the Supreme Court decided that blacks were not citizens and that slaves were property protected by the Constitution.

court-packing plan   A failed attempt by President Franklin Roosevelt in 1937 to change the direction of the Supreme Court, by giving the president the power to name one new justice to the Court for each current justice over the age of seventy.

Bush v. Gore   A five-four Supreme Court decision in December 2000, which halted Florida's hand recount of ballots, ensuring that George W. Bush would become president.

senatorial courtesy   The Senate's withholding of consent to the nomination of a district court judge if the senior senator of the president's party from the nominee's state objects to that nomination.

original jurisdiction   The power of a court to hear a case at its inception.

appellate court   A court that possesses the power to review the decisions of lower courts.

writ of *certiorari*   An order from the Supreme Court granting an appeal from a ruling of a lower court.

rule of four   An informal Supreme Court standard whereby if any four justices vote that a case deserves consideration, the Court will grant certiorari.

oral argument   The spoken presentation of each side of a case to the justices of the Supreme Court.

concurring opinion   A written statement by a Supreme Court justice about why he or she agrees with the decision reached in a case by the majority of the Court but not with the majority reasoning.

dissenting opinion   A written statement by a Supreme Court justice about why he or she disagrees with the decision reached in a case by the majority of the Court.

ideological bloc   A group of two or more Supreme Court justices who vote the same way with a high degree of regularity on the basis of a shared legal philosophy.

16

Civil Liberties and Civil Rights

Some of the most stirring words in the history of American democracy have been penned by judges in support of the civil liberties and civil rights of unpopular individuals and groups. "If there is any fixed star in our constitutional constellation," wrote Supreme Court Justice Robert Jackson, upholding the right of young Jehovah's Witnesses not to salute the American flag in school, "it is that no official, high or petty, can prescribe what shall be orthodox in politics, nationalism, religion, or other matters of opinion or force citizens to confess by word or act their faith therein."[1] "If there is a bedrock principle underlying the First Amendment," wrote Justice William Brennan, upholding the right of a citizen to express political dissent by burning an American flag, "it is that Government may not prohibit the expression of any idea simply because society finds the idea itself offensive or disagreeable."[2] Against the grim background of intolerance and repression that has characterized most political systems around the globe, such affirmations of fundamental liberties and rights stand as one of the proudest accomplishments of democracy in the United States.

However, civil liberties and rights have been a focus of bitter conflict, not a subject of comfortable consensus, throughout American history. What strong supporters of civil liberties consider basic freedoms have appeared to other Americans as threats to order, morality, or community. The right of persons accused of crimes to the protection of due process of law strikes many Americans as favoritism toward criminals at the expense of their victims. The right of authors, photographers, or filmmakers to portray sexual activity with minimal restrictions strikes many as the protection of filth that corrupts society. The right of revolutionaries to call for the overthrow of our constitutional order strikes many as a denial of society's right of self-defense against its worst enemies. Struggles over civil liberties and civil rights often pit unpopular minorities or individuals against the popular majority and its elected representatives.

Civil liberties refer to the freedoms that individuals enjoy and that governments cannot invade. **Civil rights** refer to the powers and privileges that belong to us by virtue of our status as citizens. Freedom of speech and the free exercise of religion are liberties that need protection *from* government; voting and nondiscriminatory treatment in education and employment are rights that need protection *by* government. Such familiar civil liberties and civil rights are in fact a recent accomplishment. Despite the grand words of the Bill of Rights and despite the historic breakthrough of the Civil War amendments, for most of American history free speech was repressed, individual privacy invaded, and African Americans and women treated as second-class citizens. The flowering of civil liberties and civil rights has taken a long time and required a fierce struggle. And some of the advances that have been made remain precarious. Civil liberties and civil rights continue to be a central arena in the democratic debate.

The ultimate voice in this debate has been that of the courts. Many social, political, and intellectual forces have battled over the definition of American liberties and rights. Since these liberties and rights are rooted in the Constitution, however, it has largely been the province of the federal judiciary to have the decisive say on their meaning and scope. Consequently, our focus in this chapter is mainly, though not exclusively, on Supreme Court cases.

Civil Liberties and Civil Rights: Foes and Friends

It has often been argued on the basis of survey evidence that elite democrats are supportive of civil liberties and civil rights, whereas the ordinary citizens in whom popular democrats trust are intolerant and repressive. Unfortunately, elite support for civil liberties and civil rights is less impressive in practice than in theory. The major attacks on civil liberties in recent times were spearheaded by elites: Senator Joseph McCarthy, Director of the FBI J. Edgar Hoover, Attorney General John Ashcroft, President Richard Nixon. When it comes to opposition to civil liberties and civil rights, blame must be shared by elite democrats and popular democrats alike.

Where are the friends of civil liberties and civil rights to be found? Focusing on court cases, as this chapter does, may give the impression that it has been justices of the Supreme Court, such as Oliver Wendell Holmes Jr., Hugo Black, and William O. Douglas, who have single-handedly advanced liberties and rights out of the depths of their own conscience and democratic faith. This is not the case: Ordinary citizens and democratic social movements have also played a key part in the struggle. Advances in this area have been produced by collaboration between elites and popular democratic forces. The credit for progress in civil liberties and civil rights, like the blame for hostility to them, must be shared by elite democrats and popular democrats.

The American Civil Liberties Union (ACLU), formed to defend free speech against government repression of dissenters during World War I, has taken the Bill of Rights as its cause ever since. The ACLU has fought for civil liberties and civil rights in many different areas, arguing more cases before the Supreme Court than any other organization save the federal government. The ACLU prides itself on upholding the liberties of the most unpopular groups. Its clients have included not only Communists but also Nazis and Ku Klux Klan members.[3]

Civil Liberties and Civil Rights: Historical Bases

Americans regard civil liberties and civil rights as their birthright. After all, the great charter of our freedom, the Bill of Rights, is almost as old as the nation itself. Yet the ringing words of the Bill of Rights took on a powerful meaning *in practice* only through a long struggle waged mainly by popular democratic forces. We concentrate on three critical moments in this struggle: (1) the establishment of the Bill of Rights, (2) the Civil War amendments to the Constitution, and (3) the constitutional revolution of the 1930s.

The Bill of Rights

The Constitution drafted at Philadelphia in 1787 gave only limited recognition to civil liberties and civil rights. Provisions were incorporated to guarantee individuals the right of *habeas corpus* (persons placed under arrest must be promptly brought before a judge), except under dangerous circumstances of insurrection or invasion, and to prohibit the federal government from passing *bills of attainder* (laws that inflict punishment on individuals without trials) or *ex post facto laws* (laws that make an act committed in the past a punishable offense). But the Constitution left out most of the fundamental rights that had been incorporated in the bills of rights of the revolutionary state constitutions. The Federalist argument was that the Constitution was the charter of a limited government, so written restrictions on nonexistent powers to invade the people's liberty were unnecessary.

Anti-federalists were not persuaded by this argument. Recognizing the potential for an enormous concentration of power in the federal government, they insisted that the Constitution be amended to guarantee explicitly the basic liberties and rights of the people. Heeding this protest, the first Congress, sparked by the leadership of James Madison, drafted and passed ten amendments to the Constitution, collectively known as the Bill of Rights.[4] However, this monumental victory for the popular democrats of the founding era was restricted to white males. The Bill of Rights did not address the issue of equality for racial minorities or women.

Civil liberties in America in the decades after passage of the Bill of Rights were much more precarious than its words would suggest. The impact of the Bill of Rights was limited by two factors. First, the meaning of its words would be determined only as specific cases reached the Supreme Court—whose members would not necessarily be civil libertarians. Second, the Supreme Court ruled, in the case of *Barron v. Baltimore* (1833), that the Bill of Rights applied only to the federal government and did not impose any restraints on state governments. Because political activity in nineteenth-century America was mostly at the state and local levels, the Bill of Rights lacked much practical impact in this era.

The Civil War Amendments

Civil liberties and civil rights in America had a second founding: the three constitutional amendments passed during the Civil War and Reconstruction era. The Thirteenth Amendment abolished the institution of slavery. The Fourteenth Amendment protected the freed slaves against discrimination or repression by their former masters. Its key provision stated that "no state shall make or enforce any law which shall abridge the privileges or immunities of citizens of the United States; nor shall any state deprive any person of life, liberty, or property, without due process of law; nor deny to any person within its jurisdiction the equal protection of the laws." The Fifteenth Amendment extended the right of suffrage to the freed slaves—but only if they were male.

The **Civil War amendments**, an accomplishment of popular democratic struggle by abolitionists, radical Republicans, and African Americans, extended the Bill of Rights in two respects. First, to the emphasis of the first ten amendments on liberty, they added a new emphasis on equality. At least one previously excluded group—African Americans—was now promised equality under the Constitution. Second, they aimed to prohibit invasions of rights by state governments rather than by the federal government. Contrary to the decision in *Barron*, the Civil War amendments seemed to safeguard liberty against infringement by government at any level.

But the promises of the Civil War amendments were not kept for several generations. As the passions of the Civil War cooled and as the northern industrial elite made its peace with the southern agricultural elite, the protection of the former slaves ceased to be of importance to persons in positions of power. The Supreme Court validated this change, ruling—in a painful historical irony—that the Fourteenth Amendment protected corporations, but not African Americans, from hostile state actions. Nevertheless, the Civil War amendments remained part of the text of the Constitution, available for a later generation that would reclaim their words and redeem their promises. Indeed, the modern flowering of liberties and rights has been based in large part on the just-quoted words of the Fourteenth Amendment.

The Constitutional Revolution of the 1930s

For most of its history, the Supreme Court was more concerned with questions of property rights than with issues of civil liberties and civil rights. Yet when the Court backed down from further confrontation with President Franklin Roosevelt in 1937, and when Roosevelt had the subsequent opportunity to name a majority of justices, the Court was poised for a profound historical shift. The constitutional revolution of the 1930s, an expression of the popular democratic spirit of the New Deal, made civil liberties and civil rights for the first time the principal business of the Supreme Court.

This constitutional revolution was clearly enunciated in the case of *United States v. Carolene Products Co.* (1938). Writing for the Court, Justice Harlan Fiske Stone upheld congressional authority over commerce in this seemingly routine lawsuit. But Stone added a footnote to his opinion that pointed out how differently the Court might view governmental authority if civil liberties or civil rights, rather than commerce, were at issue.

Stone's **footnote 4** set out three conditions under which the Court would not grant government actions the "presumption of constitutionality." First, government actions would be questioned by the Court if they fell within the prohibitions of the Bill of Rights or the Fourteenth Amendment. Second, they would be questioned if they restricted "those political processes which can ordinarily be expected to bring about repeal of undesirable legislation" (for example, free elections). Third, they would be questioned if they were directed at "particular religions, or national or racial minorities."[5] With footnote 4, Stone signaled that the Court would now have as its priority the safeguarding of the Bill of Rights, of political freedoms, and of the rights of religious or racial minorities subjected to discriminatory treatment by an intolerant majority.

Footnote 4 articulated what scholars call the "double standard" of the modern Supreme Court. Legislation aimed at regulating the economy is subject only to "ordinary scrutiny" by the Court; the Court presumes that such legislation is constitutional so long as the government can show that the law has a "reasonable" basis. In contrast, legislation that might impinge on civil liberties and civil rights must meet the test of **strict scrutiny**, meaning the Court will strike down the law unless the government demonstrates that a "compelling interest" necessitates such a law. This double standard has been justified on three grounds: that the freedoms protected by strict scrutiny are the basis of all other freedoms, that civil liberties

A CLOSER LOOK

Civil Liberties in Times of War

Throughout American history, civil liberties have been restricted during times of war or warlike crises. In 1798, only seven years after ratification of the Bill of Rights, the Federalists passed the Alien and Sedition Acts to silence Jeffersonian critics of the "quasi-war" with France. During the Civil War, President Abraham Lincoln suspended the writ of habeas corpus and his generals tried civilians under martial law. Using another Sedition Act passed during World War I, President Woodrow Wilson deported or jailed radical critics of his war policies. Soon after the attack at Pearl Harbor brought the United States into World War II, Japanese Americans were forced to leave their homes on the West Coast and relocate to internment camps for the duration of the conflict. The anti-Communist crusades led by Senator Joseph McCarthy and his allies during the early years of the Cold War damaged the lives of numerous individuals accused of "un-American" activities.

After the wars have ended and the crises have passed, many Americans have had second thoughts, coming to regard these past actions as excessive in boosting the power of government at the expense of basic rights. The same issue has been raised again by the war on terror that the Bush administration proclaimed in response to the attacks of September 11, 2001.

Six weeks after September 11, Congress passed and President Bush signed the USA Patriot Act, which armed federal authorities with stronger tools of surveillance, detention, and punishment against those involved in terrorist activities. Among its more controversial provisions are: (1) expanding the powers of the federal government to inquire into such private activities as obtaining reading matter from libraries and bookstores or surfing the Internet; (2) permitting the government to detain noncitizens on the basis of suspicion, holding them without trials or immigration hearings for many months while keeping their names secret; and (3) allowing federal officials to wiretap conversations between individuals detained in relation to suspected terrorist activities and their lawyers. In addition to the Patriot Act, President Bush claimed inherent authority as commander in chief to detain those he labeled "enemy combatants" for an indefinite duration and to bring them before military tribunals for trial and punishment without review by civilian courts. Pursuant to presidential orders, hundreds of alleged Al Qaeda fighters seized in Afghanistan and Pakistan were transported to the U.S. naval base at Guantanamo Bay in Cuba; some of them remained incarcerated a decade later.

Do the Patriot Act and the executive orders of President Bush resemble earlier wartime excesses that Americans have later regretted, or are they more carefully tailored measures that are invaluable to the U.S. government as it combats an insidious new enemy? The Patriot Act and the president's orders as commander in chief were touted by the Bush administration as effective weapons in the war on terror. Viet Dinh, principal drafter of the Patriot Act while he served in the Department of Justice, insisted that the act's provisions were more carefully limited and less intrusive to liberty than the critics comprehended. Fundamentally, Dinh wrote, liberty requires order as a precondition;

without the security that the Patriot Act was designed to enhance, fearful Americans could have lost some of their most precious freedoms.

To critics, however, the gains to homeland security from the policies of the Bush administration have been small, while the costs to American liberties have been large. Bush policies on homeland security drew fire from an unusual coalition, uniting liberals concerned about a danger to civil liberties with conservatives concerned about an ominous expansion of the federal government. Both kinds of critics saw the Patriot Act and Bush's executive orders as tilting the balance between authority and liberty too far toward presidential power. In the view of law professor Stephen Schulhofer, "The domestic security policies of this administration encroach on three principles that are fundamental to the preservation of freedom: accountability, checks and balances, and narrow tailoring of government's power to intrude into the lives of citizens. In each case, the administration has overlooked or dismissed alternative approaches that would strengthen the nation's security at least as effectively without weakening fundamental freedoms."

The Patriot Act has withstood legal challenges, but Bush's policies on "enemy combatants" have not been as successful in the courts. In 2004, the U.S. Supreme Court rejected Bush's claim that the commander in chief's authority over wartime situations cannot be reviewed by anyone else, ruling that those seized and held as alleged terrorists by the military, whether citizens or noncitizens, must be allowed to challenge their status in civilian courts. In a six-to-three decision, the Court ordered the administration to provide the detainees at Guantanamo Bay with access to lawyers and review by the judicial branch. As Justice Sandra Day O'Connor observed, the Court's message was that "a state of war is not a blank check for the president when it comes to the rights of the nation's citizens."

Under pressure from the Bush administration, which had been frustrated by the Supreme Court, Congress passed the Military Commission Act of 2006, legitimating the president's system of military tribunals and stripping prisoners at Guantanamo of the right of habeas corpus. Once again, however, the Court insisted on the preservation of constitutional rights. In a 2008 decision, a five-to-four majority overturned Congress's decision and upheld habeas corpus for the detainees. In the words of Justice Anthony Kennedy, "The laws and the Constitution are designed to survive, and remain in force, in extraordinary times."

As a presidential candidate, Barack Obama argued that Bush's post-9/11 policies too often invaded the civil liberties at the heart of American democracy. Once in office, Obama broke with his predecessor's approach by issuing an executive order forbidding torture of suspected terrorists and a second ordering closure of the Guantanamo prison. Yet the second order was never implemented, and before long Obama found himself reinstating Bush's policies on indefinite detentions and military tribunals. Moreover, Obama signed a renewal of the Patriot Act in 2011. Civil libertarians have become nearly as critical of Obama as they had earlier been of Bush.

Sources: Viet Dinh, "Defending Liberty against the Tyranny of Terror," in *Debating Democracy: A Reader in American Politics*, 6th ed., ed. Bruce Miroff, Raymond Seidelman, and Todd Swanstrom (Boston: Houghton Mifflin, 2009); Stephen Schulhofer, "No Checks, No Balances: Discarding Bedrock Constitutional Principles," in *The War on Our Freedoms: Civil Liberties in an Age of Terrorism*, ed. Richard C. Leone and Greg Anrig Jr. (New York: Public Affairs, 2003); Geoffrey R. Stone, *Perilous Times: Free Speech in Wartime from the Sedition Act of 1798 to the War on Terrorism* (New York: W. W. Norton, 2004); *Hamdi v. Rumsfeld* (2004); *Boumediene v. Bush* (2008).

and civil rights are explicitly guaranteed by the Bill of Rights and the Civil War amendments, and that courts are ill equipped to determine economic policy but well equipped to handle the definition of fundamental liberties and rights.[6]

Footnote 4 did not make clear whether the Court intended to apply strict scrutiny to actions by state governments as well as actions by the federal government. Earlier, in 1925, the Court had announced in the case of *Gitlow v. New York* that free speech was part of the liberty protected from state interference by the Due Process Clause of the Fourteenth Amendment. **Incorporation**—the requirement that the clauses in the Bill of Rights apply to the states as well as to the federal government—has been followed selectively since the *Gitlow* decision. By the end of the 1960s, however, the Warren Court had serially incorporated almost all of the provisions of the Bill of Rights. Today, the combination of the Bill of Rights and the Fourteenth Amendment protects civil liberties and civil rights from both the federal and state governments.

The First Amendment

The words of the First Amendment, though few in number, establish the foundation of constitutional liberty in the United States: "Congress shall make no law respecting an establishment of religion, or prohibiting the free exercise thereof; or abridging the freedom of speech, or of the press; or the right of the people peaceably to assemble, and to petition the government for a redress of grievances."

This promise of liberty was more easily set down on paper than fulfilled in practice. For much of American history, the First Amendment was a frail barrier to repression. Consider the guarantee of freedom of speech. Less than a decade after the adoption of the Bill of Rights, the ruling Federalists passed a sedition act and dispatched several of their Jeffersonian opponents to jail for criticizing the administration in power. Later, when socialists and anarchists denounced the new capitalist elite, their meetings were frequently broken up and their publications suppressed. The free speech of which we are so proud is a very recent phenomenon.[7]

Free Speech

The original proponents of a constitutional guarantee of free expression were most concerned with protecting *political speech*, such as criticism of the government or its officials. The prohibition on government interference was thus set down in absolute terms: "Congress shall make *no law* . . ." (emphasis added). But no Supreme Court majority has ever regarded the First Amendment as conferring an absolute protection for speech. The Court has had to grapple repeatedly with where to draw the boundary line dividing free speech from unprotected, and therefore punishable, speech.

The Supreme Court was first moved to draw such a boundary line in *Schenck v. United States* (1919), a case involving prosecutions of dissenters during World War I. In announcing the Court's decision, Justice Oliver Wendell Holmes Jr. explained, in words that became famous, that speech was subject to the **clear and present danger test**:

> The most stringent protection of free speech would not protect a man in falsely shouting fire in a theater and causing a panic.... The question in every case is whether the words used are used in such circumstances and are of such a nature as to create a clear and present danger that they will bring about the substantive evils that Congress has a right to prevent.[8]

Fear of political radicalism lay at the heart of the repression of free speech during World War I and its aftermath. This same fear fostered a new repressive climate after World War II, as Americans became obsessed with an external threat from the Soviet Union and an internal threat from domestic Communists. Fueling anti-Communist hysteria during the early years of the Cold War were demagogic politicians, preeminent among them Senator Joseph McCarthy of Wisconsin. The senator gave his name to the phenomenon of **McCarthyism** by his tactics: waving phony lists of supposed Communists in the government before the press, hauling individuals before his congressional committee and tarring their reputation for no other end than publicity, labeling any who opposed him conspirators against American freedom.

Influenced by the sour climate of McCarthyism, the Supreme Court at first went along with the effort of the executive branch to send the leaders of the American Communist Party to prison. It was only after McCarthy and his methods came into disrepute that the Court backed away from a repressive stance. It ruled in *Yates v. United States* (1957) that abstract advocacy of Communist Party doctrine about revolution was protected speech.

During the 1960s, many Americans began to engage in vocal political protests, especially against the war in Vietnam. It was at the end of this turbulent decade that the Warren Court, in *Brandenburg v. Ohio* (1969), finally gave a broad interpretation to the right of free speech. Clarence Brandenburg, a Ku Klux Klan leader, was convicted under an Ohio law for advocating racial conflict at a televised Klan rally. Overturning Brandenburg's conviction, the Court stated that government could punish an individual for advocating an illegal act only if "such advocacy is directed to inciting or producing imminent lawless action, and is likely to incite or produce such action."[9] Under such a test, only a few utterances—such as a speech that called for a riot and actually helped begin it—were still punishable. Political speech in the United States was at last given broad protection—nearly 180 years after the adoption of the Bill of Rights!

Just how broad that protection is can be seen in the case of *Snyder v. Phelps*, decided in 2011. The Westboro Baptist Church of Topeka, Kansas, pickets the funerals of service members killed in combat to protest America's tolerance for homosexuality. Church members hold up signs outside the cemetery grounds with such messages as "Thank God for Dead Soldiers." The father of a Marine killed in Iraq sued the church for the emotional pain it had inflicted on his family. But the Supreme Court, with only one dissenter, ruled that no matter how hurtful were the messages from the church at a moment of family grief, they concerned matters of public significance and were entitled to constitutional protection.

In recent decades, the Court has brought **symbolic speech**—political expression that communicates with visual symbols instead of words—under the protection of the First Amendment. Several high school and junior high school students in Des Moines, Iowa, were suspended after they wore black armbands to school as a way of protesting the war in Vietnam. Voiding the suspensions, the Court stated in *Tinker v. Des Moines Independent Community School District* (1969) that wearing an armband as a silent form of protest was "akin to pure speech."[10] More controversial than the *Tinker* decision was the Court's defense of symbolic speech in *Texas v. Johnson* (1989). Johnson had burned an American flag outside the 1984 Republican convention in Dallas, Texas, to protest President Reagan's policies. Five justices—an unusual coalition of liberals Brennan, Marshall, and Blackmun and conservatives Scalia and Kennedy—voted to overturn Johnson's conviction on the grounds that the Texas statute against flag burning violated the First Amendment by punishing the communication of a political message.

Unprotected Speech

Not all speech has been granted broad protection by the Supreme Court. Some kinds of expression are considered by the Court to be **unprotected speech**—speech unworthy of full First Amendment protection either because its social value is insignificant or because it verges on conduct that is harmful to others. For example, *libel*—written communication that exposes the person written about to public shame, contempt, or ridicule—is subject to lawsuits for monetary damages. However, the Court ruled in *New York Times Co. v. Sullivan* (1964) that for a public official to win a judgment against a writer, the official must prove not only that the charge in question was false but also that it had been made with malice.

Drawing the line between protected and unprotected speech has been hardest for the Supreme Court in the area of **obscenity**. Probably no other term has been as difficult for the Court to define. The Court first entered the thicket of sexual expression in *Roth v. United States* (1957). In this case, Justice Brennan, declaring obscenity to be unprotected by the First Amendment, defined it as sexual material that appealed to "prurient interest"—that is, excited lust. Confronted by a book, magazine, or film about sex, the Court would decide "whether to the average person, applying contemporary community standards, the dominant theme of the material taken as a whole appeals to the prurient interest." Attempting to protect the free expression of ideas, even about sex, Brennan added that a work should be judged obscene only when it was "utterly without redeeming social importance."[11]

As sexually explicit material became a booming market for enterprising pornographers, the conservative justices appointed by Richard Nixon tried to tighten the definition of obscenity in *Miller v. California* (1973). Chief Justice Burger's opinion made two significant changes in obscenity doctrine. First, a sexually explicit work could no longer simply claim minimal social importance (for example, by including a brief scene on some social or political theme); now the work had to possess "serious literary, artistic, political, or scientific value."[12] Second, prurient interest could be measured by local, rather than national, standards, which permitted a bookseller in a small town, for instance, to be prosecuted for selling a work that could be legally sold in a more cosmopolitan city. But the *Miller* decision did little to stem the tide of pornography.

Speech that would be protected if uttered by adults may be punishable when it comes from students in a school, as the colorful case of *Morse v. Frederick* (2007) demonstrates. When the Winter Olympics torch passed through Juneau, Alaska, in 2002, Joseph Frederick, a high school senior, stood on the sidewalk across the street from school premises and, aiming to attract television cameras, held up a sign that read "BONG HITS 4 JESUS." School principal Deborah Morse suspended Frederick, whose appeal on free speech grounds went all the way to the Supreme Court. Writing for the majority, Chief Justice Roberts rejected the appeal, stating that "school speech" can be restricted by authorities, especially when they have a compelling reason such as deterring drug use.

Freedom of the Press

If the right of free speech promotes an open debate about political matters, the right of a free press provides democratic citizens with the information and analysis they need to enter intelligently into that debate. In authoritarian political systems, the government openly owns or covertly controls the press. In a democracy, the government is expected to keep its hands off the press.

The landmark case defining freedom of the press was *Near v. Minnesota* (1931). Minneapolis officials obtained a court injunction to close down J. M. Near's *Saturday Press* under a Minnesota law that allowed the banning of scandal sheets. The Supreme Court struck down the Minnesota law as a violation of freedom of the press because the law imposed **prior restraint**. A publisher like Near could be sued for libel, but he could not be blocked from printing whatever he chose in the first place. The Court recognized that prior restraint, by allowing government officials to determine what information could be kept from publication, would effectively destroy freedom of the press.

Prior restraint was also at issue in a case involving the *New York Times*; this time the issue was government secrecy and deception during the Vietnam War. When a disillusioned Defense Department official, Daniel Ellsberg, leaked a copy of a classified department study of the war's history, known as the Pentagon Papers, to the *New York Times*, the Nixon administration obtained a lower court order temporarily halting the paper's publication of excerpts from the study. The Supreme Court's decision in *New York Times Co. v. United States* (1971) voided the order and permitted publication of the Pentagon Papers. Of the six justices in the majority, however, three suggested that they might have allowed prior restraint in these circumstances if the administration had made a convincing case of potential harm to national security.

Even though broadcast media (radio and television) enjoy much the same freedom as print media (newspapers and magazines), they are subject to certain constraints because they enjoy the government-sanctioned use of limited frequencies. In *F.C.C. v. Pacifica Foundation* (1978), the Supreme Court upheld a ban on further radio broadcasts of a monologue by comic George Carlin about Americans' obsession with "seven dirty words"—which Carlin used freely as part of his routine.[13] The issue here was not obscenity—Carlin's monologue did not excite lust and had artistic value—but the harm done to children who might hear the seven offensive words.

Is the Internet to be treated like print or like broadcast media? In the most important decision so far about the Internet, *Reno v. American Civil Liberties Union* (1997), the Supreme Court struck down the Communications Decency Act of 1996, which criminalized the transmission of "indecent" materials that minors might view, as an infringement of the First Amendment. The Court announced that the Internet, like print media, deserves the highest level of constitutional protection. Congress took another crack at the issue of "indecent" materials with the Child Online Protection Act (1998), but it too failed to pass strict scrutiny by the federal courts.

Separation of Church and State

The opening words of the First Amendment bar Congress from passing any law "respecting an establishment of religion." At the time the Bill of Rights was adopted, these words were aimed mainly at preventing the federal government from bestowing on any religious denomination the special privileges enjoyed by the official Anglican Church in England. But in modern times, the Supreme Court has given a far broader meaning to the **Establishment Clause**, reading it as requiring an almost complete separation of church and state. Religion and government are kept apart—even though America is one of the most religious nations in the world. Public opinion surveys, notes scholar Garry Wills, show that "eight Americans in ten say they believe they will be called before God on Judgment Day to answer for their sins" and that the same percentage "believe God still works miracles."[14] This religious majority sometimes has difficulty understanding why the Supreme Court believes that government is not supposed to be in the business of supporting God.

School prayer cases illustrate how the Supreme Court, flying in the face of majority sentiments, has insisted that government stay out of religion. The Court has struck down the daily reading of a nondenominational prayer in New York public schools (*Engel v. Vitale* [1962]), Bible reading in Pennsylvania public schools (*Abington School District v. Schempp* [1963]), and even a moment of silence for meditation or prayer in Alabama public schools (*Wallace v. Jaffree* [1985]). School prayer, the Court has reasoned, represents a government endorsement of religion that inflicts psychological injury on students (and their parents) who are not religious believers. The Establishment Clause of the First Amendment mandates government neutrality toward religion.

The Establishment Clause has also been central to the issue of government financial aid to religious schools. However, the Supreme Court's decisions in this area have not been as unpopular as in the area of school prayer because Protestants and Jews do not favor aid that would go mostly to Catholic schools. Beginning in the 1940s, a long series of cases established the principle that government could not financially support religious schools, even in the name of secular educational purposes, although it could provide direct aid to their students (for example, bus transportation). Chief Justice Burger summed up the Court's approach in *Lemon v. Kurtzman* (1971)—a ruling invalidating state payments for the teaching of secular subjects in parochial schools. According to the **Lemon test**, government aid to religious schools would be constitutional only if (1) it had a secular purpose, (2) its effect was neither to advance nor to inhibit religion, and (3) it did not entangle government and religious institutions in each other's affairs. More recently, the Rehnquist Court's conservative majority eased up on these criteria.

A new arena of controversy in church-state relations opened up in 2001, when Alabama's Chief Justice, Roy Moore, had a two-and-a-half-ton monument to the Ten Commandments placed in his state's supreme-court building. Two years later, the monument was removed from public view upon order of a U.S. District Court judge. Like the school prayer decisions, the removal of the Ten Commandments from a courthouse as a violation of the First Amendment was unpopular; a Gallup Poll reported that 77 percent of Americans disagreed with the district court judge's order. Public opinion did not sway the Supreme Court on this issue: In June 2005, the Court ordered two Kentucky courthouses to remove framed copies of the commandments from their walls.

Free Exercise of Religion

The Establishment Clause in the First Amendment is followed by the **Free Exercise Clause**—the right to believe in whatever religion one chooses. The Free Exercise Clause is a legacy of America's colonial past, as many of the original white settlers had fled religious oppression and persecution in England and other parts of Europe. It is also a practical necessity in a nation where the diversity of religious faiths is staggering.

The landmark free exercise case is *West Virginia State Board of Education v. Barnette* (1943). At stake was the right of schoolchildren to refuse to salute an American flag because their religious faith—Jehovah's Witnesses—forbade it. Three years earlier, in *Minersville School District v. Gobitis*, the Court had approved of expelling Witness children from school for refusal to salute the flag. But that decision led to brutal physical assaults on the Witnesses in many towns and also became an embarrassment as the United States entered a war against Nazi tyranny in the name of democratic freedom. With the powerful words of Justice Jackson (quoted at the beginning of this chapter), the Court changed its mind and gave a firm endorsement to the free exercise of religion even when it offended the most cherished sentiments of the majority.

Although the Free Exercise Clause protects any form of religious belief, the matter of religious conduct is more complicated. What happens when a religious order prescribes practices for its adherents that violate local, state, or federal laws having nothing to do with religion? The Court first struggled with this dilemma in *Reynolds v. United States* (1879), when it approved the outlawing of polygamy (where a man takes several wives), a key practice of the Mormon faith at that time. However, the position of the Court was more supportive of religious conduct in *Church of Lukumi Babalu Aye v. City of Hialeah* (1993). When the Florida city passed an ordinance to stop the practitioners of Santería, an Afro-Cuban religion, from engaging in animal sacrifice as a ritual, the Court overturned it as a blatant attempt to restrict the free exercise of religion.

Corbis

The Second Amendment

The most ambiguous language in the Bill of Rights is found in the Second Amendment: "A well-regulated militia, being necessary to the security of a free state, the right of the people to keep and bear arms, shall not be infringed." In recent decades, constitutional law experts have debated the meaning of the amendment's two major clauses. Does the reference to "a well-regulated militia" imply that the amendment derives from the Antifederalist fear of an all-powerful central government and protects only the collective right of citizens organized in state militias to possess firearms? Or does the reference to "the right of the people to keep and bear arms" imply that individual citizens have the right to own guns?

Not until 2008, in the case of *District of Columbia v. Heller*, did the Supreme Court make a pronouncement on this issue. A five-to-four majority, composed of the Court's conservative members, struck down a strict ban by the nation's capital of the possession of handguns in the home for self-defense. Writing for the majority, Justice Scalia argued that the Second Amendment's opening words merely announce a purpose but don't restrict the meaning of the later phrase to a right related to militia service; rather, the amendment protects the right of individuals to own guns for private uses. However, Scalia's opinion was limited to the possession of arms in the home. He suggested that most existing public regulations on firearms—for example, requiring licenses, prohibiting concealed weapons, or forbidding guns in such places as government buildings and schools—are permissible under the Second Amendment.

The *Heller* decision only pertained to federal law, which governs the District of Columbia. In 2010, the Court incorporated the *Heller* doctrine in *McDonald v. Chicago*, ruling that the Second Amendment limits local and state governments in the same ways that it limits the federal government.

"And I say, if pies were outlawed, only outlaws would have pies!"

A satire on a common argument against gun control.

The Rights of Persons Accused of Crimes

The constitutional bases for the rights of persons accused of crimes are the Fourth, Fifth, Sixth, and Eighth Amendments, applied to the states through incorporation in the Fourteenth Amendment. The Fourth Amendment protects individuals from "unreasonable searches and seizures" in their "persons, houses, papers, and effects." The Fifth Amendment prohibits double jeopardy in criminal cases, protects individuals from self-incrimination, guarantees "due process of law," and provides that private property can only be taken for the use of the public with proper compensation. The Sixth Amendment requires that a person accused of a crime must have a "speedy and public trial by an impartial jury," ensures the right of the accused "to be confronted with the witnesses against him," and guarantees the right of the accused to the services of a lawyer in mounting a defense against the charges. The Eight Amendment prohibits "cruel and unusual punishments."

Application of these amendments to the criminal justice system at the state and local levels, where the vast majority of criminal proceedings takes place, is a recent phenomenon. The Warren Court of the 1960s set down most of the landmark precedents in the area of criminal procedure. The Burger (1969–1986), Rehnquist (1986–2005), and Roberts (2005–) Courts, appointed by "law-and-order" presidents and responsive to the public outcry about crime, have carved out numerous exceptions to these precedents.

Criminal Procedure: The Warren Court

Clarence Earl Gideon, a penniless drifter with a criminal record, was convicted for the felony offense of breaking and entering a poolroom and sentenced in a Florida court to five years in prison. Unable to afford an attorney, Gideon had to defend himself after the judge refused to appoint professional counsel for him. The Supreme Court accepted Gideon's petition (appointing a prominent lawyer to argue his case before it) and ruled in *Gideon v. Wainwright* (1963) that the Sixth Amendment right of counsel is so essential to a fair trial that the state must pay for a lawyer for indigent defendants charged with a felony. Gideon won the chance for a second trial, at which he was acquitted after his court-appointed counsel convincingly demonstrated that the prosecution's star witness, who had fingered Gideon for the break-in, was probably the culprit.[15]

Cleveland police officers forced their way into the home of Dolree Mapp without a search warrant in the belief that she was hiding a man wanted for a recent bombing as well as possessing illegal gambling paraphernalia. Their search of the house turned up neither a fugitive nor gambling materials—but they did discover sexual books and pictures. On the basis of this evidence, Mapp was sent to jail for possession of obscene literature. In *Mapp v. Ohio* (1961), the Warren Court reversed her conviction, holding that material seized in an illegal search could not be introduced as evidence in a state court, a doctrine known as the **exclusionary rule**. This rule, based on the Fourth Amendment, had been applied since 1914 to defendants in federal prosecutions. But its extension from the tax evaders and other white-collar defendants typically tried in federal courts to the wider range of defendants tried in state courts, including violent criminals, made the *Mapp* decision controversial.

Ernesto Miranda was arrested by Phoenix police on suspicion of rape and kidnapping. At first, Miranda maintained his innocence, but after two hours of police interrogation he signed a written confession to the crime. At no point had the police advised Miranda that he had a right to have an attorney present during the interrogation. In *Miranda v. Arizona* (1966), the Warren Court ruled the confession to be inadmissible as evidence at trial, a violation of Miranda's Fifth Amendment right not to incriminate himself. The Court's majority, in this five-to-four decision, argued that police custody and interrogation tended to create such an intimidating atmosphere that individuals felt pressured to incriminate themselves in the absence of a lawyer's counsel. With the confession thrown out, Arizona retried Miranda for the same crime and convicted him on the basis of other evidence.

The effect of the decision was that police had to change their behavior and provide suspects with what came to be known as the **Miranda warnings**. Criminal suspects must be advised that (1) they have the right to remain silent, (2) anything they say can be used against them, (3) they have the right to speak to an attorney before police questioning and to have him or her present during interrogation, and (4) if they cannot afford to hire an attorney, one will be provided at state expense before any questioning can take place.

The *Mapp* decision, and even more the *Miranda* decision, fueled widespread attacks on the Warren Court for handicapping law enforcement at a time of rampant crime, although these decisions actually did not free many criminals. Presidential candidate Richard Nixon seized on crime as a campaign issue in 1968, lambasting the Warren Court for coddling criminals and promising that his administration would appoint only law-and-order judges. Nixon's success with the issue encouraged other candidates, especially his Republican successors in the White House. Supreme Court justices appointed by Nixon, Reagan, and both

Bushes have thus been less likely than were justices of the Warren Court era to emphasize the constitutional rights of criminal suspects or defendants and more likely to emphasize the practical needs of police and prosecutors.

Criminal Procedure: The Burger, Rehnquist, and Roberts Courts

Of the three landmark Warren Court decisions on criminal justice just described, only the *Gideon* decision was received without controversy. No one seemed to doubt the proposition that there could not be a fair trial where the state was represented by a professionally trained prosecutor and the defendant had to represent himself or herself.

In the more controversial areas of the exclusionary rule and the *Miranda* warnings, however, the Burger, Rehnquist, and Roberts Courts have trimmed back Warren Court precedents—without explicitly disavowing them. Thus, in *United States v. Calandra* (1974), Justice Lewis Powell's majority opinion argued that illegally obtained evidence, although still barred from trials because of the exclusionary rule, could be admitted before grand juries considering whether to indict suspects and thus bring them to trial. In *Pennsylvania Board of Probation v. Scott* (1998), Justice Clarence Thomas wrote that illegally seized evidence could be used in parole revocation hearings because parolees were more likely than other citizens to commit crimes. In *Hudson v. Michigan* (2006), Justice Antonin Scalia declared that police armed with a search warrant no longer need to knock and announce their presence before entering a residence and seizing evidence. And in *Kentucky v. King* (2011), Justice Samuel Alito upheld the actions of Lexington, Kentucky, police officers in breaking down a door because they heard sounds indicating that suspects in a drug bust were destroying evidence.

The Burger and Rehnquist Courts made it easier for police to obtain confessions by loosening up the requirements for *Miranda* warnings. For example, in emergency situations such as a threat to the safety of the arresting officer, the warnings are not required (*New York v. Quarles* [1984]). However, the Miranda decision survived a frontal challenge in *Dickerson v. United States* (2000). Although a longtime critic of the *Miranda* warnings, Chief Justice Rehnquist, writing the majority opinion in the *Dickerson* case, stated that the warnings were a constitutional rule rather than merely a set of procedural guidelines that Congress was free to change.

The criminal procedure decisions of the Burger, Rehnquist, and Roberts Courts have been more congenial to public opinion than those of the Warren Court. However, critics of these decisions say that constitutional rights should not be decided by a popularity test. They argue that the Bill of Rights does not prevent us from putting criminal offenders behind bars, but it does require that we do so in a fair manner. This philosophy is expressed by Justice Brennan: "The interest of…[the government] is not that it shall win a case, but that justice shall be done."[16]

The Right of Privacy

The controversy surrounding constitutional rights spelled out in the Bill of Rights has been extended to the issue of whether other rights can be legitimately derived from the text of the Constitution even if they are not spelled out there. A **right of privacy** is at the center of this debate. Civil libertarians have long contended for this right. In a 1928 dissent, Justice Louis Brandeis wrote that "the makers of our Constitution conferred, as against the government, the right to be let alone—the most comprehensive of rights and the right most valued by civilized men."[17] But what words in the Bill of Rights established the right to be let alone—the right of privacy?

The Supreme Court finally answered this question in 1965 in *Griswold v. Connecticut*, invalidating a Connecticut law that made it a crime for any person to use a drug or device for birth control. Writing for the majority, Justice William O. Douglas argued that the enumerated guarantees of constitutional rights in the First, Third, Fourth, Fifth, and Ninth Amendments had "penumbras" (shadows) that extended beyond their specific words. These penumbras suggested the existence of "zones of privacy" that the government could not invade.[18] Few outside the Court paid attention to a decision striking down an antiquated law that even the dissenters in the case considered to be "silly." However, the right of privacy generated a fierce controversy when it was extended from a couple's freedom to choose contraception and avoid pregnancy to a woman's freedom to choose an abortion and terminate an unwanted pregnancy.

The abortion issue was brought before the Supreme Court by two young lawyers, Sarah Weddington and Linda Coffee, who were inspired by the new feminist movement that had emerged in the 1960s. Their client in **Roe v. Wade** (1973) was Norma McCorvey, a twenty-one-year-old woman who had carried an unwanted pregnancy to term because Texas, like most other states at that time, forbade abortions except to save the life of the mother. (McCorvey's identity was protected from publicity by the pseudonym "Jane Roe.") By a seven-to-two vote, the Court struck down anti-abortion statutes in Texas and all other states on the grounds that they violated a woman's right of privacy, located in the Due Process Clause of the Fourteenth Amendment.

Authored by Justice Harry Blackmun, the decision for the Court divided pregnancy into three trimesters. During the first trimester, a state cannot interfere with a woman's right to choose an abortion in consultation with her doctor. During the second trimester, when abortions pose more of a medical risk, states can regulate them to safeguard maternal health. Only during the final trimester, when a fetus may be capable of surviving outside the womb, can a state impose severe restrictions or prohibitions on abortion. To the dissenters in the case, Justices Byron White and William Rehnquist, the Court was imposing on the states a "right" that had been neither enumerated in the Bill of Rights nor envisioned by the drafters of the Fourteenth Amendment.

Hailing the decision on abortion as a great victory for women's rights, the women's movement shifted its attention to other issues. But as supporters of *Roe* grew complacent, opponents of the decision mobilized to fight its results through a "right-to-life" movement. The religious fervor of this movement was captured for political purposes by the conservatives of the New Right, whose candidate and hero was Ronald Reagan. Once in the White House, Reagan made abortion a litmus test for his nominees to the federal judiciary. By the end of his two terms, he had named three new justices to the Supreme Court, and *Roe* was at risk of reversal.[19]

Awakening to the peril to *Roe*, the "pro-choice" forces mobilized their supporters. Right-to-life forces girded for battle as well. The Supreme Court's decision in *Webster v. Reproductive Health Services* (1989) favored the right-to-life side, upholding restrictions that the state of Missouri had placed on abortion, but it stopped short of overturning *Roe* itself. One member of the majority, Sandra Day O'Connor, the only woman on the Supreme Court at that time, was not willing to go that far.

Allied with the right-to-life movement, the first President Bush replaced two retiring supporters of the original *Roe* decision, Justices William Brennan and Thurgood Marshall, with David Souter and Clarence Thomas. The stage seemed set for the demise of *Roe* when the Court heard the case of *Planned Parenthood of Southeastern Pennsylvania v. Casey* (1992). But in a surprise twist to the historical drama of abortion rights, *Roe* survived. Most of Pennsylvania's restrictions were sustained by the Court, imposing further obstacles to women seeking an abortion. Yet even though four justices wanted to overturn *Roe*, restoring to the states the power to prohibit abortions, the critical fifth vote was still lacking. Justice O'Connor was now joined by Justice Anthony Kennedy (a Reagan appointee) and Justice Souter in a moderate conservative bloc willing to uphold restrictions on abortion but not willing to disclaim the constitutional right of a woman to choose an abortion. In an unusual joint opinion, the three argued that *Roe* was an important precedent deserving of respect and that overturning it would diminish both the legitimacy of the Supreme Court and the public's belief in the rule of law.

For right-to-life supporters, legal disappointment in the *Casey* decision was followed by political disappointment as the first pro-choice president in twelve years, Bill Clinton, was elected in 1992. Clinton appointed two pro-choice justices, Ruth Bader Ginsburg and Stephen Breyer, and for the time being *Roe* was safe from challenge.

Once George W. Bush placed conservatives John Roberts and Samuel Alito on the high court during his second term, however, the status of abortion rights again became an open question. In 2000, a five-to-four Court had struck down a Nebraska law that prohibited partial-birth abortions. But in 2007, in the case of *Gonzales v. Carhart*, a different five-to-four majority upheld a similar ban on partial-birth abortions passed by Congress. What explained the shift in the Court's doctrine on this type of abortion was the replacement of the retiring Justice O'Connor by Justice Alito.

Civil Rights ★ ★ ★

Although this chapter highlights legal and legislative victories in the struggle for civil rights, primary credit for progress in the struggle belongs to the civil rights movement. The decades-long struggle by African Americans and their allies for civil rights not only prodded the white majority to act but also inspired similar movements for equality among Hispanic Americans, Native Americans, Americans with disabilities, women, and gays and lesbians. These groups' victories, such as the Americans with Disabilities Act of 1990, have redeemed a basic promise of popular democracy: respect for the dignity of every citizen.

Fighting Segregation: From *Plessy* to *Brown*

Despite the constitutional amendments drafted during the Civil War and Reconstruction to protect blacks, they soon found themselves in a position of economic, political, and legal subordination. The commitment of the Fourteenth Amendment to equal protection of the laws for former slaves was mocked by a series of Supreme Court decisions refusing to enforce the amendment in the face of the southern states' new system of "Jim Crow" segregation. The last of these decisions, *Plessy v. Ferguson* (1896), established a legal justification for racial segregation that African Americans would have to combat for more than half a century.

The Supreme Court had to consider in the *Plessy* case whether a Louisiana law requiring railroads to provide **separate but equal** facilities for whites and blacks violated the equal protection of the laws. All but one of the justices found the practice legal, arguing that separation of the races did not imply that either race was unequal. If there was a stigma of black inferiority in segregation, the majority said, it was only because blacks viewed it that way. Repudiating this reasoning, the lone dissenter in the case, Justice John Marshall Harlan, offered a powerful and prophetic alternative: "The Constitution is color-blind, and neither knows nor tolerates classes among citizens."[20]

A little more than a decade later, in 1909, the **National Association for the Advancement of Colored People (NAACP)** was founded to take up the battle against racial segregation and discrimination. In the 1930s, its legal arm developed a careful, long-term strategy: Rather than a head-on assault on Jim Crow, which the Court was likely to rebuff, NAACP lawyers would chip away at segregation in the area of education, showing in case after case that separate facilities could not possibly be equal.[21]

The NAACP campaign finally reached fruition in ***Brown v. Board of Education of Topeka*** (1954), probably the most famous Supreme Court decision of the twentieth century. Thanks to skillful leadership by the new chief justice, Earl Warren, the Court was unanimous in rejecting the separate but equal doctrine in the field of education. The claim in the *Plessy* decision that segregation did not stamp blacks as inferior was repudiated in Warren's opinion for the Court: "Segregation of white and colored children in public schools has a detrimental effect upon the colored children.... A sense of inferiority affects the motivation to learn." The chief justice's concluding words marked a historic watershed for the Court and for the nation: "In the field of public education the doctrine of 'separate but equal' has no place. Separate educational facilities are inherently unequal."[22] Although the case dealt only with public schools, the *Brown* decision, reclaiming the original promise of the Fourteenth Amendment, inflicted a mortal wound on racial segregation in America.

But the death of segregation would not be swift. And the Supreme Court had to share a portion of the blame for its agonizingly slow demise. When the Court considered how to implement its decision in a second *Brown* case a year later, it was fearful of a hostile and potentially violent response by southern whites. So rather than setting a firm timetable for school desegregation, the Court returned the problem to the lower federal courts with the instruction that desegregation proceed "with all deliberate speed." These ambiguous words did not accomplish the goal of heading off southern white hostility and violence; instead, they only seemed to invite southern strategies of delay. The stage for the historic drama of civil rights now shifted from the Supreme Court to the cities and small towns of the South, where the civil rights movement, encouraged by *Brown*, would have to finish off a dying—but still powerful and violent—segregationist system.

Ending Segregation

Up to the *Brown* decision in 1954, the primary focus of the civil rights movement had been litigation, and its leading group had been the NAACP. After *Brown*, new civil rights groups emerged and intensified the pace of the struggle for equality by turning from litigation to direct action. Direct-action campaigns began in 1955 with the Montgomery bus boycott, led by Martin Luther King Jr. Subsequent direct-action struggles were risky, both in their use of civil disobedience to break unjust segregation laws and in the violence with which they were met by southern mobs and southern police. But these struggles were increasingly effective in riveting the attention of the North on the brutal injustices of southern segregation and in pressuring northern politicians to do something about them.

The legislative triumphs for civil rights in the mid-1960s can be traced directly to the movement campaigns that inspired them. In response to the direct-action campaign of King's Southern Christian Leadership Conference in Birmingham, Alabama, President Kennedy proposed major civil rights legislation in 1963. Passed only after his death, the **Civil Rights Act of 1964** struck a powerful blow at segregation in many areas. Its most important provisions outlawed racial discrimination in public accommodations (such as hotels and restaurants) and in employment. In response to another direct-action campaign led by King and his organization in Selma, Alabama, President Johnson proposed landmark voting rights legislation early in 1965. Responding more promptly this time, Congress passed the **Voting Rights Act of 1965**. This act, removing the barriers that southern officials had placed in the way of potential black registrants, finally gave effective enforcement to the Fifteenth Amendment.[23]

As the pace of the struggle against segregation picked up in other areas, school desegregation lagged behind. By the end of the 1960s, the Supreme Court had had enough of "all deliberate speed" and was ready to order immediate desegregation. Given residential patterns that separated the races, however, significant desegregation could be accomplished only by busing schoolchildren. In the case of *Swann v. Charlotte–Mecklenburg Board of Education* (1971), a unanimous Court approved a massive busing plan for a sprawling urban/rural school district in North Carolina.

Ironically, court-ordered busing to end the perpetuation of all-white and all-black schools was more controversial in the North than in the South. Angry white parents in the North asked why their children should be bused to remedy patterns of discrimination for which they were not responsible. The limitations of busing as a remedy for racially separate schools became evident in a case from Detroit.

The phenomenon of "white flight" made the suburbs increasingly black city, combined with economic changes, left too few white children remaining in Detroit to achieve racial balance in the schools. So a federal judge ordered a busing plan that would have incorporated the city's suburbs as well as the city itself. In *Milliken v. Bradley* (1974), a five-to-four Supreme Court majority rejected the plan, arguing that suburban school districts that had not engaged in segregated practices could not be compelled to participate in a remedy for Detroit's segregation problem.

Since only interdistrict desegregation plans like that in Detroit were likely to achieve racial balance in the schools, the long-term result has been that African American children are now more likely to attend an all-black school in a big city in the North than they are in the once-segregated South. As an alternative to busing, some cities introduced plans that assigned students to schools partly on the basis of their race. But in 2007, in cases involving Seattle, Washington, and Louisville, Kentucky, Chief Justice Roberts proclaimed that their assignment systems were themselves racially discriminatory and thus unconstitutional.

Affirmative Action

As the controversy over busing receded, it was supplanted by an equally bitter debate over affirmative action. **Affirmative action** involves taking positive steps to award educational opportunities or jobs to racial minorities or women because these groups have been the victims of prior discrimination.

Supporters of affirmative action argue that simply adopting a color- or gender-blind approach won't overcome discrimination. Only a deliberate policy of preferential treatment for groups victimized by discrimination, they insist, can eliminate racial and gender inequities from our society; affirmative action will open the door of opportunity for those previously excluded, allowing them at last to show what they can do. Critics of affirmative action argue that it goes beyond "equal protection of the laws" to promote equal results regardless of merit. Affirmative action, they say, is "reverse discrimination" against white males. The debate over affirmative action has become partisan, with Democrats generally favoring it and Republicans opposed.

The Supreme Court has often seemed as divided and uncertain about affirmative action as the rest of American society. The first and most famous affirmative action case to reach the Court, *Regents of the University of California v. Bakke* (1978), had an inconclusive outcome. The University of California Medical School at Davis set aside 16 of the 100 slots in its entering class for members of racial minorities. Denied admission to the medical school although his grades and test scores were higher than those of the minority students admitted, Alan Bakke sued, claiming a violation of his civil rights. A split Court rejected the idea of a fixed quota of positions for minorities and ordered Bakke's admission to the medical school. Yet the Court also ruled that taking race into consideration as part of a school's admission process was legitimate as a way of enhancing diversity in the student body.

Affirmative action for women was first considered by the Supreme Court in the 1987 case of *Johnson v. Santa Clara County*. Two employees of the Santa Clara County Transportation Agency, Diane Joyce and Paul Johnson, sought promotion to a better-paying craft position as a road dispatcher. Both passed an agency test, with Johnson achieving a slightly higher score. Since women held none of the agency's 238 craft positions, Johnson was passed over, and the promotion was given to Joyce on affirmative action grounds. The Court upheld the agency, establishing that voluntary affirmative action plans can operate to end the underrepresentation of women in job categories traditionally dominated by men.

After the *Johnson* decision, affirmative action began to lose ground in the Supreme Court. In *Adarand Constructors v. Peña* (1995), a five-to-four majority ruled that government programs specifying preferential treatment for minority contractors are unconstitutional unless a pattern of prior discrimination can be demonstrated. The Court remained more supportive of affirmative action in higher education. In two important rulings announced in 2003, both of which involved affirmative action programs at the University of Michigan, it rendered a split verdict.

By a vote of six to three, the Court rejected the university's affirmative action program for undergraduate admissions, which awarded extra points to those from minority groups, on the grounds that such a mechanical approach violated the standard set a quarter century earlier in the *Bakke* decision. More important, however, the university law school's affirmative action program was upheld by a five-to-four vote in *Grutter v. Bollinger*. Writing for the majority, Justice O'Connor praised the law school's "individualized, holistic review" of applicants and harked back to the *Bakke* precedent in validating the consideration of race as one factor in admissions decisions in order to achieve a diverse student body.

Affirmative action has also been under fire in the states. Voters in California, Washington, and Michigan approved bans on affirmative action in state programs. Its future in the nation now hinges on shifting balances of power on the Supreme Court and between the political parties. In *Fisher v. University of Texas* (2013), the Court postponed any major shift in affirmative action for the time being.

Equal Rights for Women

The struggle for equal rights for women has taken a different course than the civil rights struggle of African Americans. During Reconstruction, drafters of the Fifteenth Amendment excluded women on the grounds that there was not enough political support to enfranchise black males and all females, an argument that infuriated pioneer feminist leaders Elizabeth Cady Stanton and Susan B. Anthony. It took several generations of struggle by the women's movement before women won the vote in 1920 with the Nineteenth Amendment. Having attained a goal denied for so long, the women's movement faded in strength for almost half a century.

Energized by the civil rights and New Left movements, a second women's movement sprang up in the 1960s. Modeling its strategy after the NAACP's historic campaign that led to the *Brown* decision, legal advocates from the new women's movement began to press test cases of women's rights on the Supreme Court in the early 1970s. They won some important victories. Yet there was no women's rights equivalent to *Brown*, no landmark case that established full-fledged equality for women. (The most important victory for women in the Supreme Court—*Roe v. Wade*—was decided on the grounds of a right of privacy rather than equal rights for women.)

The early women's rights cases were the easiest. In *Reed v. Reed* (1971), for example, argued before the Court by future justice Ruth Bader Ginsburg, the unanimous justices struck down an Idaho law favoring men over women as executors of estates. But what test should the

Court apply in cases of less blatant gender discrimination? Women's rights advocates hoped that the Court would apply the same strict scrutiny in cases of discrimination against women that it used in cases of discrimination against racial minorities. But advocates were pressing this argument before the Burger Court, not the Warren Court.

In *Craig v. Boren* (1976), the women's movement fell short of its objective. At issue was an Oklahoma law that allowed women to buy beer at age eighteen but required men to wait until age twenty-one. The Court struck down the law as a violation of equal protection. But Justice Brennan could not get a majority of the Court to base this holding on strict scrutiny toward gender classifications. The best he could obtain was the creation of a new, intermediate category: *heightened scrutiny*. A statute that classified by gender would pass muster with the Court, according to this new form of scrutiny, only if it aimed at an important government objective and substantially furthered that objective. Women's rights now have more constitutional protection than before but less than the protection enjoyed by racial minorities.

Equal Rights for Gays and Lesbians

The civil rights movement launched what many have called a "rights revolution" in the United States. Since the 1950s, racial minorities, women, and people with disabilities have won landmark victories in the courts and in Congress. But for Americans who are gay or lesbian, recognition of equal rights has been more problematic. Although public attitudes toward gays and lesbians have been growing more tolerant, legal affirmation of their equal rights has been slow in coming. At present, no other area of civil rights presents so many controversies.

President Bill Clinton was the first chief executive to be favorably disposed toward equal rights for gays and lesbians. Yet shortly after he took office, Congress and the Joint Chiefs of Staff forced him to back away from an executive order guaranteeing nondiscrimination against gays and lesbians in the military. Clinton compromised by announcing the policy of "Don't Ask, Don't Tell": The armed services would not inquire into the sexual orientation of recruits, but service members who disclosed by word or action that they were gay or lesbian would be discharged. With his reelection bid pending, Clinton signed the Defense of Marriage Act (DOMA), initiated by the Republican majority in Congress, in 1996. DOMA defined marriage in federal law as a union between one man and one woman, and proclaimed that no state had to recognize same-sex marriages that had been legalized in another state. Even if a same-sex couple could be married under the law of a state, that couple would not be entitled to the federal benefits (e.g., tax advantages or Social Security survivor payments) coming to heterosexual couples.

The U.S. Supreme Court has not always championed gay rights either. The Court began its consideration of gay and lesbian rights in *Bowers v. Hardwick* (1986). It ruled against Michael Hardwick, who had been arrested for homosexual conduct in his own bedroom and charged under Georgia's sodomy law. A five-to-four majority argued that he was not protected by a right of privacy: Prior privacy decisions, it said, involved "family, marriage, or procreation," thus excluding gays and lesbians.[24]

The Court was more favorable to gay and lesbian rights in the face of overt discrimination. In *Romer v. Evans* (1996), a six-to-three majority struck down an amendment that voters had added to the Colorado Constitution nullifying existing local ordinances prohibiting discrimination against homosexuals and barring the state or any of its municipalities from enacting any new antidiscrimination measures on behalf of gays and lesbians. Justice Anthony Kennedy's majority decision argued that the Colorado amendment singled out homosexuals in an unconstitutional fashion: "A state cannot so deem a class of persons a stranger to its laws."[25]

385

I now pronounce you man and property.

In *Boy Scouts of America v. Dale* (2000), a five-to-four majority ruled that the Boy Scouts could drop Dale, a scoutmaster, from the organization because he was a gay rights leader in college. Chief Justice William Rehnquist based the decision on the Boy Scouts' First Amendment right to "freedom of expressive association." The organization, he wrote, had the right to eject Dale from his post because his sexual orientation clashed with the Boy Scouts' promulgation of values for young people.[26]

Catching up a bit with evolving public attitudes, the Supreme Court reconsidered its *Bowers v. Hardwick* precedent in 2003. In *Lawrence v. Texas*, a six-to-three majority invalidated the Texas sodomy law under which two men had been prosecuted for engaging in a sexual act, finally bringing gays and lesbians under the protection of the privacy doctrine. In the majority opinion, Justice Anthony Kennedy wrote that gays and lesbians "are entitled to respect for their private lives. The state cannot demean their existence or control their destiny by making their private sexual conduct a crime."[27]

Despite some disheartening setbacks, the gay and lesbian movement continued to struggle for nondiscrimination in the armed services and in marriage law. In the first decade of the twenty-first century, public opinion moved significantly to its support. In a December 2010 *Washington Post-ABC News* poll, 77 percent of respondents agreed that gays and lesbians should be allowed to openly serve in the military. That month, Congress repealed the "Don't Ask, Don't Tell" policy, and sexual orientation no longer was an issue in military service.

The main front in the conflict over equal rights for gays and lesbians has become same-sex marriage. The same-sex marriage controversy erupted in 2003 after the Massachusetts

Supreme Court, in a four-to-three decision, ruled that same-sex couples have an equal right to marry under the state's constitution. Across the nation, social conservatives, defending "traditional" marriage, were outraged by the decision. In 2004, they succeeded in passing bans on same-sex marriage in all eleven states where the issue appeared on the ballot. By the end of 2011, thirty states had added amendments to their constitutions banning same-sex marriages.

Despite this backlash, a number of states followed the lead of Massachusetts, sometimes by court action, sometimes through legislation, and recently by popular votes. By August 2013, same-sex marriage had become legal in 13 states–California, Connecticut, Delaware, Iowa, Maine, Maryland, Massachusetts, Minnesota, New Hampshire, New York, Rhode Island, Vermont, and Washington, as well as in the District of Columbia.

Public opinion has been shifting in favor of same-sex marriage more rapidly than state laws have. In a 1996 Gallup Poll, only 27 percent supported same-sex marriage. By 2011, another Gallup Poll showed 53 percent support. One reason for the shift is a generation gap in attitudes toward same-sex marriage. In the 2011 Gallup Poll, 70 percent of those aged 18 to 34 favored legalizing same-sex marriages as compared to 39 percent of those aged 55 and older.[28]

The U.S. Supreme Court handed down two major decisions on same-sex marriage in June 2013. In *United States v. Windsor*, a five-to-four majority struck down a provision of the Defense of Marriage Act (1996) that, by defining marriage as between one man and one woman, denies federal benefits available to heterosexual couples to same-sex couples who wed in those states in which their marriage is legal. Writing for the Court, Justice Kennedy argued that the federal statute denied equal respect to same-sex spouses without serving any legitimate public purpose. In *Hollingsworth v. Perry*, the Court upheld a lower-court decision that invalidated a California proposition banning same-sex marriage, effectively establishing the right of same-sex couples to wed in the nation's largest state.

Conclusion: The Struggle Over Liberties and Rights

Americans can legitimately take pride in the civil liberties and civil rights they enjoy today. Yet these liberties and rights are the result of long struggles and quite recent landmark advances. The newness of the critical Supreme Court precedents and the political and legal backlash that they have produced indicate that the struggle over the definition of American liberties and rights is far from ended.

Both elite democrats and popular democrats have played checkered parts in this history. Elite democrats in positions of power, while mouthing rhetorical support for American liberties, have moved to limit them in times of crisis and challenge. Popular democrats have often backed and applauded the repressive measures that elites have instituted. Yet some elite democrats and some popular democrats have done better. Judicial champions of civil liberties and civil rights have understood how fundamental these freedoms and powers are to the creation and maintenance of a democratic society. Popular democratic forces (Anti-federalists, abolitionists, New Deal populists, blacks and Hispanics, feminists, and gays and lesbians) have fought to establish civil liberties and civil rights in the first place as well as to bring before the courts the cases that will broaden their definition and scope.

Given that a majority of ordinary Americans may not support civil liberties and civil rights when they protect unpopular individuals or groups, individuals committed to the values of popular democracy must recognize the responsibilities of democratic education. In the spirit of the tradition initiated by the Anti-federalists, they must remind others of the importance of an open and tolerant society, where new and unconventional ideas can circulate freely, where reigning elites can be challenged, where the spark of protest that launched the American revolutionary experiment can enlighten and revitalize American democracy. And with an emphasis on the importance of citizenship, popular democrats cannot rest content merely with the defense of American liberties and rights. They must also encourage other citizens to make active use of them.

Reader's Guide

Critical Thinking Questions

1. Do Americans place *too much* emphasis on civil liberties even when the individuals who are protected by them are doing harm to public morality and social order?

2. How far should freedom of speech extend in political matters? In artistic expression about sexuality?

3. Did the Supreme Court go too far in basing abortion rights on a "right to privacy" that cannot be found in the words of the Constitution or its amendments?

4. Should the exact same civil rights belong to racial minorities, women, and gays and lesbians? Or are there distinctions between these population groups that justify differential legal protections?

5. Will legalization of same-sex marriage do damage to the traditional meaning and values of marriage as a social institution? Or is it likely to have no impact or even a positive impact upon marriage as a social institution?

Key Word Definition

civil liberties   The basic freedoms embodied in the Bill of Rights, such as speech and religion, which individuals enjoy and government cannot invade.

civil rights   Constitutional guarantees, such as the right to vote and equal treatment under the law, that belong to people because of their status as citizens.

Civil War amendments   The Thirteenth, Fourteenth, and Fifteenth Amendments to the Constitution, which extended the Bill of Rights to and emphasized equality in the treatment of the former slaves.

footnote 4   A footnote in a 1938 Supreme Court decision that sets out three conditions under which the Court will not grant the presumption of constitutionality to government action: when the action falls under the prohibitions of the Bill of Rights or Fourteenth Amendment, when the action restricts the democratic process, or when the action is harmful to particular religions or national or racial minorities.

strict scrutiny   A Supreme Court standard in civil liberties or civil rights cases of striking down a law unless the government can demonstrate a "compelling interest" that necessitates such a law.

incorporation   The doctrine that the Supreme Court used to apply the Bill of Rights to the states under the 14th Amendment Due Process Clause.

clear and present danger test   A Supreme Court standard stating that the government can prohibit political speech only if it can bring about an immediate evil that Congress has a right to prevent.

McCarthyism   The practice, named after Senator Joseph McCarthy, of falsely accusing individuals of being disloyal or subversive in order to gain publicity or suppress opposition.

symbolic speech   Protected political expression that communicates with visual symbols instead of words.

unprotected speech   Communication that is not protected by the First Amendment either because its social value is insignificant or because it verges on conduct that is harmful to others.

obscenity   Sexually explicit material that lacks serious literary, artistic, political, or scientific value and that appeals to a "prurient" interest; one of the categories of unprotected speech.

prior restraint   The First Amendment prohibition against government officials preventing information from being published.

Establishment Clause   That part of the First Amendment that forbids Congress to make any law instituting a religion; the central component of the separation of church and state.

Lemon test   The standard used by the Supreme Court in cases involving government aid to religion, which states that government assistance is constitutional only if it has a secular purpose, its effect does not advance or inhibit religion, and it does not entangle government and religious institutions in each other's affairs.

Free Exercise Clause   The part of the First Amendment that states that Congress shall make no law prohibiting the practice of religion.

exclusionary rule   A doctrine, based on the Fourth Amendment's guarantee against unreasonable searches and seizures, in which the Supreme Court established that material seized in an illegal search cannot be introduced as evidence in a criminal case.

Miranda warnings   The requirement that police inform all criminal suspects of their rights before taking them into custody.

right of privacy   The freedom to be left alone implied in the Constitution.

Roe v. Wade   The 1973 Supreme Court case that established a woman's right to choose abortion and rendered unconstitutional all state laws that made abortion a crime.

separate but equal   The doctrine established by the Supreme Court in the 1896 case of *Plessy v. Ferguson*, that separate equivalent facilities for whites and blacks did not violate the Fourteenth Amendment's guarantee of equal protection of the laws, thereby providing the legal basis for segregation of the races.

National Association for the Advancement of Colored People (NAACP)   An organization that fights for the rights of black Americans.

Brown v. Board of Education of Topeka   The 1954 case in which the Supreme Court rejected the separate but equal doctrine in the field of education and thereby began the end of legal racial segregation.

Civil Rights Act of 1964   A law that made racial discrimination in public accommodations (e.g., hotels and restaurants) and employment illegal.

Voting Rights Act of 1965   The law that removed the barriers that southern officials had placed in the way of African Americans who sought to register to vote, and involved federal supervision of the voting process.

affirmative action   Positive steps taken to award educational opportunities or jobs to racial minorities or women because these groups have been the victims of prior discrimination.

Economic and Social Policy: The Democratic Connections

Ki Gulbranson is a hardworking owner of a logo apparel shop in Chisago County, northeast of Minneapolis, Minnesota.[1] After dealing in jewelry on the side and refereeing soccer games, Gulbranson is able to make about $39,000 a year. A conservative Tea Party sympathizer, Gulbranson favors cutting taxes and government spending. Government is on the brink of financial collapse, he says, because too many people have become dependent on government aid. "I don't feel like I need the government," he asserts.

Gulbranson's opposition to government aid, however, does not stop him from taking advantage of government programs to help support his family. Gulbranson, for example, pays no federal income taxes and instead gets several thousand dollars a year back from the government through the federal Earned Income Tax Credit (EITC) program. Without this money, Gulbranson would not be able to pay for his younger children to participate in sports or keep the older ones on his family's car insurance. He signed his three children up for free breakfast and lunch at school, paid for by the federal government, and Medicare twice paid for his 88-year old mother's hip surgery. Gulbranson cannot imagine retiring without Social Security and Medicare, at least "not the way we expect to live as Americans."

President Obama's victory in the 2012 election represented a qualified defense of a strong role for government in protecting citizens. Ki Gulbranson's story, however, is representative of where many Americans stand on social and economic policies in the early twenty-first century. Americans depend on government aid more than ever, but they often deny that dependence and even resent it. In 2009, government benefit programs provided an average of $6,583 for every man, woman, and child in the nation—a whopping 69 percent increase from 2000.[2] Many Americans seem blind to the fact that they rely on government. This is perhaps best exemplified by the man in South Carolina who warned his congressman in 2009: "Keep your government hands off my Medicare" (not recognizing that Medicare is a government program).[3] According to one survey, even though 91.6 percent of Americans benefit from some government social program, only 43.5 percent reported that they had used one.[4]

While denying their own dependence on government, many Americans are concerned that *other* people have become overly dependent on government programs, especially poor people and minorities, and that this will bankrupt the government and burden future generations.

Many Americans believe that they would be better off if the government would just "leave them alone." We celebrate the free market and increasingly view it as the epitome of freedom and democracy. The idea that taxes are unjust and government is oppressive has gone so far that Daniel Mitchell of the Heritage Foundation compared offshore tax evaders to civil rights protestors—to "Rosa Parks sitting in the back of the bus."[5]

In fact, the myth of the "self-made" man is just that—a myth. We all depend on government. Government is necessary for markets to operate effectively. Government defines property rights, enforces contracts, maintains a national money supply, and provides public goods such as roads and clean air that private actors could not provide alone. Without government social programs, we would all be much more vulnerable to unemployment, disease, and the infirmities of old age. Would we really want to live in a society where children starved in the streets or elderly died for lack of simple medical care? American social policies reduce economic insecurity and improve the quality of everyone's lives. As Supreme Court Justice Oliver Wendell Holmes once wrote: "Taxes are the price we pay for a civilized society."[6]

Having acknowledged that we need a social safety net, however, we must also acknowledge that American social programs are expensive and there are limits to what the government can do. The growth of social spending, especially government provided health care, has exceeded the growth of tax revenues, and this is not fiscally sustainable over the long run. But the reason we are in a fiscal crisis is not, as many Americans believe, because the poor have become dependent on a vast welfare state. Indeed, spending on the poor is declining as a proportion of social welfare spending. Welfare for the poor has become a lightning rod for attacks on government because it is highly visible and the poor lack political power. The major cause of our fiscal predicament is the rapid growth of a much larger "submerged" welfare state that benefits the middle and upper classes and large corporations—"the welfare state nobody knows."[7] In this chapter we bring the submerged welfare state to the surface to examine how it operates and who it benefits.

Finally, in this chapter we focus on the political effects of economic and social policies. Too often, government is viewed as another service provider, and public policies are judged on how they benefit us as consumers. Public policies, however, should also be evaluated on how they impede or enhance democratic participation and inclusiveness.

The Democratic Debate over the Money Supply

Governments are responsible for establishing the basic conditions for smooth-functioning markets; the decisions that establish these conditions are called **macroeconomic policy**. These policies are designed to fine-tune the national economy as a whole while not altering the distribution of economic activity across different sectors, classes, or places. Macroeconomic policies aim to moderate the booms and busts of capitalism, making sure that the economy expands while keeping inflation and unemployment low. There are two basic kinds of macroeconomic policies: **Fiscal policy** uses the government's taxing and spending policies to speed up or slow down the economy; **monetary policy** uses government's control over the money supply (the amount of money in circulation) to achieve the same results. We start with monetary policy, which in the United States is run by a secretive, elite-dominated institution with limited democratic accountability.

Throughout U.S. history, elite and popular democrats have debated the money supply. Elite democrats have favored *tight money policies*. With fewer dollars "chasing" a fixed or expanding supply of goods, prices remain stable or even fall. Falling prices—**deflation**, which characterized most of the late nineteenth century,[8] are good for those who are owed money (bondholders and bank lenders) because they are paid back in more valuable dollars. In the nineteenth century, farmers found themselves squeezed between falling prices for their crops and rising interest rates for the money they had to borrow to buy land and finance spring planting. Farmers agitated to increase the money supply by having the federal government issue "greenbacks," or use silver, in addition to gold, to back up the currency. To this day, the conflict between wealthy investors and the mass of debtors and businesspeople needing credit remains at the heart of the democratic debate over the money supply.

Popular democrats have generally favored *loose money policies*—not only because they make it easier on debtors but because these policies reduce unemployment. The big trade off in monetary policy is between **inflation** (rising prices) and unemployment. Tight money policies lower inflation but can cause higher unemployment. Economic elites are more concerned with fighting inflation, which eats away at their wealth, than they are with fighting unemployment, which hurts ordinary workers. Popular democrats favor loose money policies that reduce unemployment, even if that results in moderate inflation. (Very high rates of inflation can have disastrous effects, causing a lack of confidence in the dollar and an unwillingness to invest.) In short, popular democrats favor loose money policies that reduce unemployment, even if that leads to moderate inflation; by contrast, elite democrats favor tight money policies that keep inflation very low, even at a cost of higher unemployment.

The institution responsible for regulating the money supply is the **Federal Reserve**, created in 1913. President Woodrow Wilson compromised with the bankers to create a unique institution that combines the private powers of bankers with the public powers of government. In 1935, after criticism that contraction of the money supply had contributed to the Great Depression, the Federal Reserve—or "Fed," as it is called—expanded its mission and took full charge of controlling the nation's money supply.

The Federal Reserve is run by a seven-member board of governors appointed by the president for fourteen-year terms with the advice and consent of the Senate. The powerful chair serves a four-year term. To carry out its policies, the Fed relies on twelve regional banks, which are private institutions owned by the approximately 6,000 commercial banks that participate in the Federal Reserve system. The most important policy-making body at the Fed is the *Federal Open Market Committee* (FOMC), which basically determines the nation's money supply and powerfully influences interest rates. The FOMC is made up of the seven members of the Board of Governors, appointed by the president, and the presidents of five regional banks, who are appointed by the commercial banks. The key decision-making body, then, is controlled by a mixture of public and private. As Representative Lee H. Hamilton, an Indiana Democrat, put the matter in 1991, "Nowhere else in the Government are private individuals permitted to participate in decisions which have such an enormous influence over the prosperity and well-being of millions of Americans."[9]

The basic mechanisms by which the Fed controls the money supply are quite simple: The American economy can be thought of as a gigantic plumbing system, with money circulating through the pipes at various rates and pressures. The Fed is the hydraulic engineer who, by turning various valves, such as the interest rate they charge to loan money to banks, can either expand or contract the flow of money in the system.

Under the Federal Reserve system, the money supply in the United States is firmly under the control of elites. Proponents of this system argue that control over the money supply must be left in the hands of experts who understand how to protect the long-term interests of the American economy. Popular democrats reply that the interests of Wall Street are different from the interests of Main Street. The Fed's tight money policies primarily benefit a small financial elite. In 2009 the top 1 percent had an average net worth of almost $14 million whereas those in the bottom 20 percent actually had negative net worth (the value of assets minus debt). (See Chapter 4.) Tight money, popular democrats argue, acts like a regressive tax, redistributing wealth from debtors to creditors. The shortage of credit curbs business expansion, especially hurting small businesses and farmers, who depend on credit to see them through tough times. Above all, tight money policies increase unemployment.

Popular democrats object especially to keeping unemployment high to fight inflation. Many economists argue that there is a *nonaccelerating inflation rate of unemployment* (NAIRU). If the unemployment rate falls below a certain level—say, 5 percent—tight labor markets will enable workers to demand higher wages, causing inflation. Critics such as University of Texas economist James Galbraith argue that no one knows what the NAIRU is. NAIRU simply enables the Fed to shroud its political choices in technical mumbo jumbo.

Controversies at the Fed

Because of his leadership position in setting monetary policy, which is crucial to the performance of the economy, the chairman of the Federal Reserve Board has been called "the second most powerful man in the United States" (so far, all have been men). Alan Greenspan, who was appointed by President Reagan in 1987 and held the position until 2006, was one of the longest serving and most powerful Fed chairmen. With a reputation as the nation's premier inflation fighter, Greenspan was popular on Wall Street. In classic elite democratic fashion Greenspan's policies frequently sacrificed job growth to fight inflation. Many argue that Greenspan's slow-growth policies contributed to the defeat of President Bush in 1992.

In 2006 President Bush appointed Ben Bernanke as Greenspan's successor. A Princeton University economics professor, Bernanke is a Republican but is considered less doctrinaire than Greenspan. Bernanke faced a crisis early in his tenure when mounting mortgage foreclosures threatened the stability of the financial system. Many banks and investment firms held mortgage-backed securities that were rapidly losing value because homeowners could not repay the loans and were being forced into foreclosure (losing ownership of their home). Facing the prospect of a financial panic, the Fed took unprecedented actions that were controversial. Acting quickly in March 2008, Bernanke and the Federal Reserve took the surprising steps of brokering and partially paying, up to $29 billion, for JP Morgan to buy Bear Stearns, a major investment bank heavily invested in mortgage-backed securities, and for Bank of America to absorb Merrill Lynch. Essentially, the Fed insured the mortgage-backed securities acquired by these companies, and if they turned out to be worthless, the federal taxpayers would be on the hook for billions of dollars. Bernanke strongly supported the $700 billion Troubled Asset Relief Program (TARP), signed into law by President Bush in October 2008, which purchased questionable securities and other assets from banks in order to prevent them from collapsing.

Bernanke also used the usual tools of the Federal Reserve in order to stimulate the economy. The Fed aggressively cut short-term interest rates in 2008 to stimulate the economy and prevent it from falling into a recession. Short-term interest rates were cut to near zero in an effort to provide the banks with more money to loan out. Some critics argue the Fed could do more to reduce unemployment, such as buying more long-term government debt and committing to a higher inflation target in the years ahead. According to Paul Krugman, the absence of more expansionary policies, such as these, results in "mass suffering for American workers."[10] In the fall of 2012 the unemployment rate was still 7.9 percent.

Many criticized the Fed for rescuing Wall Street investment banks whose risky behavior was a major cause of the financial meltdown. Bernanke may have had no choice: if Bear Stearns had gone bankrupt it could have set in motion a financial panic that would have tumbled the U.S. economy into a deep recession. In any case, the Bear Stearns bailout shows the

People protesting home foreclosures.

incredible power of the Fed Chairman and lack of transparency within the Federal Reserve. The negotiations over a weekend in March 2008 risking billions in taxpayer funds were conducted behind closed doors by Bernanke, the New York Fed, and the executives of JP Morgan and Bear Stearns. The Wall Street investment firms may, indeed, have become "too big to fail," but there is something deeply wrong with a government willing to spend billions of dollars to help those who caused the crisis but unwilling to spend anywhere near that amount to help the homeowners who were victimized.

The power of the Fed depends, in part, on effective political leadership by the chair of the Board of Governors.[11] Like Greenspan, Bernanke seems to know how to use the levers of power. In a democracy, such power in the hands of unelected officials is dangerous. Various proposals have been put forward to make the Fed more accountable and transparent, but Congress and the president have always hesitated to put greater controls on the Fed for fear they will be accused of undermining the confidence of the financial markets.

Fiscal Policy: The Rise and Fall of the Keynesian Consensus

Besides regulating the money supply, governments can also use their taxing and spending powers to maximize economic growth. This is known as fiscal policy. As we will see, however, fiscal policy is not just about expanding the economic pie; it is also about how that pie will be divided up. Fiscal policy is inherently political and it can either enhance or undermine popular democracy.

English economist John Maynard Keynes (1883–1946) promoted the idea that the government can pull the economy out of a depression by deliberately engineering a deficit (spending more than it receives in tax revenues). His classic work *The General Theory of Employment, Interest, and Money* (1936) argued that capitalist economies do not have a natural tendency to employ all the nation's workers and achieve full productive capacity because consumers cannot buy all the products that a fully operating economy produces. At a certain stage of the business cycle, Keynes argued, the savings rate is too high, leaving too little money for consumption.

Keynes's solution was for the government to use fiscal policy, its control over taxing and spending, to make the economy perform at maximum capacity. When the economy begins to fall into a recession, the government stimulates consumer demand by spending *more* than it takes in through taxes. Deficit spending heats up the economy, putting people and productive capacity back to work. When demand is too high and an overheated economy begins to cause inflation, the government deliberately spends *less* than it takes in, cooling off the economy. (Keynes did not recommend, as some have alleged, that the government continue to run massive budget deficits during prosperous times, such as the United States did under President George W. Bush.)

Keynesianism dominated economic policy making in the major industrial countries after World War II. Although Keynes's theory encouraged governments to take an active role in smoothing out the business cycle, it did not require any direct interventions in markets. Keynes called for manipulating the overall level of consumer demand, but he said nothing about how that consumer demand should be distributed. Thus, Keynesianism was a theory that could be embraced by both the left and the right. European governments used Keynes's ideas to justify redistributing wealth through progressive taxes and social spending, a scheme based partly on the notion that giving more resources to those at the bottom would result in immediate increases in consumer spending because poor people save little.

In the United States, Keynesianism was applied in a less egalitarian manner to justify what has been called "military Keynesianism" or "business Keynesianism." Deficits were created by boosting military spending and by cutting taxes on business. The Kennedy tax cuts for investors, passed in 1964, were sold to the public, Congress, and the business community on Keynesian grounds. With the economy doing well in the 1960s, there was a broad consensus behind Keynesianism and an optimistic feeling that fiscal policy could be used to prevent disastrous economic downturns. In a 1971 *Newsweek* cover story, Republican President Richard Nixon famously proclaimed, "We are all Keynesians now."

Supply-Side Economics and the Debate over the Deficit

With the economic troubles of the 1970s, the Keynesian consensus began to crumble. The problems of the U.S. economy did not appear to be the result of too much saving. Indeed, the savings rate was tumbling, and the soaring trade deficit seemed to be caused in part by inadequate savings and investment in the latest production technologies. For the first time, increases in the productivity of American workers lagged behind those of other countries. The problem seemed to lie not in underconsumption but in underinvestment.

Many economists began to move from a demand-side explanation of economic troubles based on Keynesianism to a supply-side analysis. **Supply-side economics** argues that the cause of the economic problems is a capital shortage—that we need to reduce consumption and put more of our resources into productive investment. Supply-siders especially stress that we are consuming too much in the way of government services and that a bloated public sector serves as a drag on economic growth. High levels of taxation and government regulation reduce incentives to work hard, innovate, and invest.

Paradoxically, supply-siders stress that the best way to reduce the federal deficit is to *reduce* taxes, not increase them. This idea is based on the **Laffer curve**, named after economist Arthur B. Laffer. Above a certain point, Laffer argued, increasing tax rates actually decreases total tax revenues because of the disincentive effects on productive effort. Tax rates were so high in the United States, Laffer argued, that by decreasing tax rates the country could move down the Laffer curve, unleashing an explosion of productive effort that would increase tax revenues. Jude Wanniski, an editorial writer for the *Wall Street Journal*, upon seeing the Laffer curve first drawn on a cocktail napkin in a Washington restaurant, remarked that "it hit me as a wonderful propaganda device" for persuading policy makers to cut tax rates.[12] Supply-side economics has been effective at reducing taxes, but its claim that budget deficits can be reduced by cutting taxes is contradicted by the historical evidence.

The first experiment in supply-side economics took place under President Ronald Reagan (1981–1989). To illustrate the disincentive effects of high taxes Reagan was fond of telling how he stopped making movies when the marginal income tax rate hit 94 percent during World War II. His experiment with supply-side economics was a failure however, resulting in the largest budget deficits in history to that point (see Figure 17.1).

The experience of the Clinton administration casts more doubt on supply-side economics. In 1993 Clinton increased the top tax rate on high-income earners from 31 percent to 39.6 percent. Supply-siders predicted that the economy would go into a tailspin and tax revenues would shrink. Just the opposite happened: The economy boomed and so did tax revenues. In 1997 Clinton engineered a compromise tax increase, and in 1998 the federal

FIGURE 17.1 | Federal Budget Surpluses and Deficits, 1950–2012

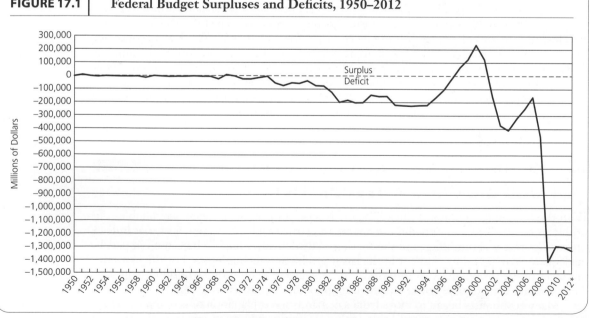

Source: Historical tables for the *Budget for Fiscal Year 2012*, created by the Office of Management and Budget and posted to the source URL: http://www.whitehouse.gov/omb/budget/Historicals/.

* projection for the year 2012

government enjoyed its first budget surplus in almost thirty years. Clinton can take some credit for the dramatic shift from deficits to surpluses, but most of the credit must go to the booming economy spurred by the tremendous productivity gains that resulted from investments in computer technology.

George W. Bush came to office in 2001 facing the pleasing prospect of huge budget surpluses almost as far as the eye could see. The Congressional Budget Office (CBO) projected they would total almost $10 trillion over ten years. Bush was determined to cut taxes, which he did in 2001 and 2003. Bush's first tax cut cost an estimated $2.1 trillion over a ten-year period. It cut rates at all income levels and phased out the estate tax over a ten-year period. In 2003 Bush and the Republicans pushed through another tax cut estimated to cost the federal treasury over $100 billion a year. Once again, the rosy predictions that they would boost the economy and expand government revenues proved false. The 2008 budget deficit hit a record $459 billion.

Under President Barack Obama annual deficits soared to unprecedented levels of more than a trillion dollars (see Figure 17.1), but according to estimates from the nonpartisan Congressional Budget Office (CBO) the deficit for fiscal year 2013 will shrink to $642 billion. Budget deficits have become more of a political issue than ever. Tea Party Republicans blame Obama for soaring deficits and burdening future generations with oppressive debt. In truth, Obama is only partially responsible for the soaring debt. First, Republicans in Congress refused to rescind the Bush tax cuts, which have cost the federal treasury trillions of dollars. But the most important reasons for the soaring deficits are the **automatic stabilizers** that increase government spending when the economy is in a downturn. Without any action by Congress or the president, tax revenues are designed to fall in a recession, and spending on certain programs, such as unemployment compensation and food stamps, automatically goes up. The idea behind automatic stabilizers is to stimulate the economy when it is shrinking (and cool off the economy when it gets overheated). The nonpartisan CBO estimated that automatic stabilizers caused the 2009 federal budget deficit to increase by $481 billion (more than one-third of the total deficit).[13]

Obama *can* be held responsible for the part of the deficit caused by his stimulus package, the **American Recovery and Reinvestment Act (ARRA) of 2009**. CBO estimated that ARRA would increase the budget deficit by $825 billion over a ten-year period. (President Bush had his own $152 billion stimulus act in 2008.) Besides new spending on "shovel-ready" infrastructure projects and other spending programs, ARRA also included $288 billion in tax cuts.[14] Following the principles of Keynesianism, the purpose of the stimulus was to boost the economy and reduce unemployment. According to the CBO, ARRA increased the number of people employed in 2012 by between 0.4 and 1.1 million.[15]

The economic downturn that began in 2008 divided the country between those who favor austerity, immediate deficit cutting, and those who advocated increasing deficits in the short term to stimulate the economy (and reduce deficits later when the economy is operating at full potential). The same issue, austerity versus stimulus, has divided the European Union. In the United States, the debate over the budget deficit has become tangled up in the issue of the size of government. Your answer to the question of the appropriate size of government depends on your political leanings. Libertarians, for example, would like to eliminate almost all federal social programs. As Figure 17.2 shows, however, the United States already has one of the smallest governments, relative to the private economy, of any advanced industrial economy.

Many who advocate cutting the deficit refuse to consider increasing any tax revenues, suggesting that their goal is not just to cut the deficit but to reduce the overall size of government. In the 112th Congress (2011–2012) 238 members of the House of Representatives and 41 members of the Senate signed the Taxpayer Protection Pledge, committing them to oppose any tax increases. Sponsored by Americans for Tax Reform, led by Grover Norquist, the Taxpayer Protection Pledge was signed by only three Democrats (one Senator and two members of the House). It is difficult to reduce the deficit by only cutting spending. As Figure 17.3 shows,

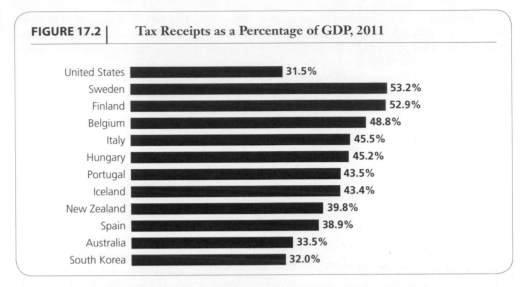

FIGURE 17.2 | Tax Receipts as a Percentage of GDP, 2011

United States — 31.5%
Sweden — 53.2%
Finland — 52.9%
Belgium — 48.8%
Italy — 45.5%
Hungary — 45.2%
Portugal — 43.5%
Iceland — 43.4%
New Zealand — 39.8%
Spain — 38.9%
Australia — 33.5%
South Korea — 32.0%

Source: U.S. Bureau of Census, *United States Statistical Abstract for 2012*, Table 1360, http://www.census.gov/compendia/statab/cats/international_statistics/government_receipts_expenditures_debt.html.

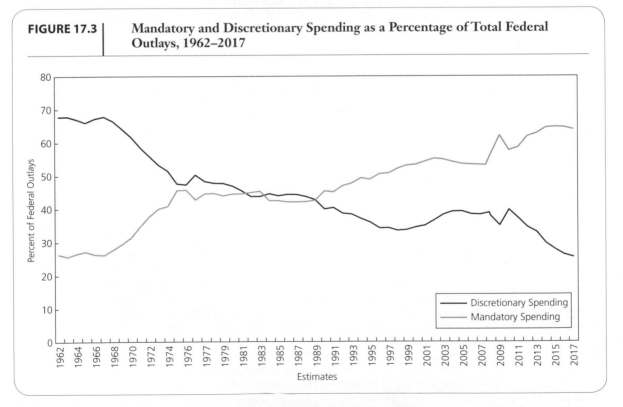

FIGURE 17.3 | Mandatory and Discretionary Spending as a Percentage of Total Federal Outlays, 1962–2017

Percent of Federal Outlays

Estimates

— Discretionary Spending
— Mandatory Spending

Source: Budget for Fiscal Year 2012 created by the Office of Management and Budget, Table 8.3—Percentage Distribution of Outlays by Budget Enforcement Act Category: 1962–2017; accessed at: http://www.whitehouse.gov/omb/budget/Historicals.

about two-thirds of federal spending is mandatory, such as interest on debt and obligatory payments owed to individuals for Social Security and Medicaid. Only about a third of the budget is **discretionary spending** that Congress can control and more than half of that is defense spending that is almost impossible to cut in a time of war.

The extreme polarization between Republicans, who refuse to consider any "revenue enhancements," and Democrats, most of whom insist on a mix of tax increases and spending cuts, has set up a dangerous game of political chicken. The political impasse over the deficit came to a head in 2011 when Republicans refused support an increase in the debt ceiling to authorize the government to borrow more money. In the past, the debt ceiling had been routinely approved by bipartisan majorities. This time, the Republican majority in the House demanded large cuts in spending before it would agree to increase the debt ceiling. Failure to increase the debt ceiling would mean that the government would not be able to meet some of its spending obligations required by law, resulting in a partial government shutdown. It could also lead to a default on U.S. sovereign debt, causing a crisis in international markets, and loss of confidence in American Treasury bonds.

The crisis was averted when President Obama and leaders of both houses agreed to a deal that increased the debt ceiling in exchange for large future cuts in the deficit. This is the so-called "fiscal cliff." If Congress fails to pass a bill with at least $1.2 trillion in cuts to the deficit, this would trigger major tax increases and across-the-board spending cuts ("sequestration"), split equally between defense and domestic spending. Four days after the deal was passed, for the first time in history, American debt was downgraded from AAA, a signal to investors that a political stalemate could cause the United States to default on its debt payments. The dispute caused public approval of Congress to fall, especially for Republicans, who lost seats in the 2012 election. The Democrats' strong showing in the 2012 election puts them in a better position to negotiate a budget deal. In January 2013, Obama signed a law that continued the Bush tax cuts for individuals making less than $400,000 and increased taxes on those making above that. It also continued extended unemployment insurance and delayed the sequester, or spending cuts, for two months. At the time of writing, a political deal on the spending cuts has not been reached.

What difference do large deficits make? Opinions polls have consistently shown that the voters do not rank deficits as a top concern. Nevertheless, very large deficits are harmful. Deficits force us to rely upon foreign investors to fund our federal budget. Nations such as Japan and China own trillions of dollars of Treasury Securities and if they should ever decide to stop investing, the United States might not be able to finance the government without greatly increasing interest rates.[16] Another negative effect of large deficits is generational inequity. The federal government and present taxpayers are living beyond their means. The living standards of young people today will suffer in the future when they have to pay back that debt, which now totals more than $50,000 for every man, woman, and child.

There is no painless way to bring the deficit under control. The evidence on supply-side economics is now in: cutting taxes does not lead to increased revenues. There is little evidence that the supply-side tax cuts significantly increase work effort, the savings rate, or investment.[17] Some argue that tax cutting is part of a "starve-the-beast" strategy, where huge deficits will finally force Democrats in Congress to cut spending, shrinking government to pre–New Deal size. Such an approach is irresponsible, assuming as it does that the democratic process is so broken that one side has to resort to subterfuge, risking the financial future of the country, in order to gets its way.

The democratic political process can get the deficit under control by passing a combination of tax increases and spending cuts that are fair. The popular democratic view is that taxes should be **progressive**, meaning that the tax rate should increase as income increases. A tax is called **regressive** if people in lower income brackets pay higher rates. The rationale behind progressive taxation is that the heaviest burden should be borne by those with the

A CLOSER LOOK

The Attack on the Estate Tax

The estate tax has a proud popular democratic history. First passed in 1916, the tax on inheritances was designed to break up the huge industrial fortunes that so often corrupted politics. Huge accumulations of wealth—what Teddy Roosevelt called "fortunes swollen beyond all healthy limits"—can corrupt our political system and beget a hereditary ruling class. The estate tax was the single most progressive tax. In 1999 it was imposed on only the top 2.3 percent of estates, with more than half of the revenue coming from the richest 7 percent of taxable estates.[19] In 2001 opponents of the estate tax almost succeeded in repealing it. They did succeed in weakening the estate tax so that it now applies to even fewer estates and at lower rates.

Clearly, opponents of the estate tax could not appeal directly to the interests of voters. They succeeded by skillfully combining disinformation, symbolic politics, and deceptive policy design. Assembled by Bush's chief political strategist, Karl Rove, the Tax Relief Coalition (TRC) ran a well-funded comprehensive campaign for President Bush's tax cuts. Generously funded by big business and wealthy individuals, the repeal effort worked to create the impression that the tax affected the vast majority of estates. They repeatedly claimed that large numbers of small-business owners and farmers would be forced to liquidate their family businesses to pay the tax—leaving nothing to pass on to their children.

Shunning statistics, repeal advocates relied upon emotional stories. Their most heart-wrenching story was told by Chester Thigpen, an 83 year-old Mississippi grandson of slaves who testified before Congress that he

supported estate tax reform because he wanted to pass his hard-earned tree farm on to his children. Thigpen's story was endlessly repeated by supporters of repeal. His son later reported that his estate was not taxable because it was below the minimum threshold.[20] The disinformation campaign worked: A 2003 poll found that 49 percent of Americans thought that most families would have to pay the estate tax.[21] The Congressional Black Caucus even supported repeal, persuaded by a handful of black entrepreneurs who opposed the tax.

Supporters of repeal were also masters at using language that framed the issue to their advantage. They always talked about tax "relief"—a metaphor implying that taxes were an "affliction" and anyone who opposed them was a hero.[22] Their key symbolic move was to label the estate tax the "death tax." The Republican leadership even issued a directive to its members in Congress to only use the term "death tax," and one Republican strategist recommended staging press conferences at the local mortuary. Remarkably, major networks, like CNN, began using the term "death tax."[23] Many Americans supported repeal because they came to view the "death tax" as cruel: The government should not take advantage of families during their time of grief.

Supporters of repeal turned it into a moral issue, not a political choice. First, they separated the tax cut from any connection to the spending cuts or increased debt that would necessarily follow. They framed the issue in dramatic moral terms that made defenders of the estate tax look like tyrants. In a radio interview, Grover Norquist, head of the powerful Americans for Tax Reform, compared the estate tax to the "morality of the Holocaust."[24]

Defenders of the estate tax kept repeating that the tax only affected 2 percent of estates but this had little effect because they had no effective way to counter the moral attack on estate taxes. They could have challenged their opponents by focusing not on those who earned fortunes by hard work but on the heirs, like Paris Hilton, who had done little to deserve fabulous wealth. Interestingly, Bill Gates, Sr., the father of Bill Gates, Jr., the Microsoft billionaire, pulled together a group of 120 of America's richest individuals to sign a petition in support of retaining the estate tax. Gates made the argument that repealing the estate tax would have a devastating impact by removing a powerful incentive to bequeath estates to charities. He also made the moral argument that the estate tax would inhibit "large fortunes passing from generation to generation forming ever larger pools of money and accretions of power."[25]

Bill Gates, the ultimate elite, however, was no match for the Chester Thigpens of the world and in 2001 Congress passed a temporary repeal of the estate tax. What is most disturbing about the movement to repeal the estate tax is how it used the symbols of popular democracy to achieve elite democratic ends. Two political scientists charged that "the temporary 2001 estate tax repeal may be the single most regressive change to a tax code passed by a democratic legislature in the history of the world."[26] In 2010 Congress passed an act that temporarily exempted individuals with estates of less than $5 million (married couples up to $10 million) and reduced the maximum tax rate to 35 percent (down from 55 percent in 2001).

Popular democrats must make the case for a progressive estate tax—not just because it is fair but because it can protect our democracy from the corrupting effects of concentrated wealth.

greatest ability to pay and who benefit the most from government. Bush's tax cuts were highly regressive. Overall, the two tax cuts provided an average tax savings for those in the bottom 20 percent of only $61 and an average saving for those in the top 1 percent of $66,601.[18] Such regressive tax cuts are not politically sustainable. Any popular democratic plan to control the deficit will require that the costs fall more on wealthy elites than on ordinary citizens who are having trouble making ends meet in tough economic times.

The Contours of Social Policy

Social policies are designed to protect people against market outcomes that society considers unacceptable. Individuals could take responsibility for insuring themselves against their own risks for illness, disability, or old age, but society has decided that it should provide a social safety net that guarantees a basic level of protection against these risks. Social policy also includes programs to guarantee equal opportunity for jobs, education, and other essential goods.

The conventional view is that the United States spends relatively little compared to other developed nations on social policies and the social policies it does fund, known as welfare, are targeted on the poor. In fact, including the entire array of spending and taxing programs that qualify as social policy, the U.S. has a relatively large welfare state. But that welfare state is not targeted on the poor; most of the benefits are delivered through the tax code, creating a "privatized" welfare state that mostly benefits the middle and upper classes. With some important exceptions, which we will discuss later, American social policies do not significantly reduce economic inequalities. Finally, we will discuss the effect of the design of social policies on democratic participation. Some policies discourage citizens, especially the poor, from participating in politics. Properly designed social policies, we will show, can enhance democratic participation.

American social policies are often divided into two tiers: In the first tier, based on individual contributions into a social insurance fund, people, mostly the elderly, are guaranteed benefits regardless of incomes. The second tier of "noncontributory" programs is targeted at children and the poor, and requires recipients to apply for benefits and meet a means-test (prove that you make below a certain income and own few assets).

As Table 17.1 shows, contributory social insurance programs, targeted to the elderly, have fared much better than noncontributory public assistance programs, targeted to the poor. Social Security started out modestly in 1935 as a contributory insurance program designed to guarantee a minimum standard of living in retirement. Over the years, however, it has expanded rapidly, both in benefit levels and in the number of people covered. Coverage

Table 17.1   U.S. Social Welfare Programs

Type of Program	Year Enacted	Number of Recipients in 2010 (in millions)	Federal and State Outlays in 2010 (in billions)
Contributory (Insurance) Programs			
Old Age, Survivors, and Disability Insurance (Social Security)	1935	54.0	$689.9
Medicare	1965	7.5	$521.1
Unemployment Compensation	1935	14.2*	$79.6*
Total			$1,290.6
Noncontributory (Public Assistance) Programs			
Medicaid	1965	61.8*	$318*
Food Stamps	1964	40.3	$64.7
Supplemental Security Income (cash assistance for aged, blind, disabled)	1974	7.7*	$46.6*
Housing Assistance to low-income families[a]	1937	11.1	$50.0
School Lunch Program	1946	32.0	$9.9
Temporary Assistance to Needy Families	1996	2*	$10.5*
Total			$499.7

a. Number of units, Section 8 Housing and low-cost public housing.

Source: U.S. Bureau of Census, *United States Statistical Abstract for 2012*, Tables 546, 146, 558, 152, 570, 563, 565, 447, 543, and 567.

*2009

was significantly expanded on three occasions: In 1939, widows were included; in 1956, the disabled were added; and in 1965, health insurance for the elderly was enacted (Medicare).

Many people believe that Social Security is not a public assistance program at all because it is paid for by contributions from beneficiaries. In fact, Social Security redistributes wealth across classes and across generations. The system is paid for by a payroll tax designated as FICA (Federal Insurance Contributions Act) on your paycheck. The Social Security tax is *regressive* because it is a flat rate, 6.2 percent on income up to $110,100 (2012). (Employers pay 6.2 percent as well.) Beyond that income, people pay nothing. (Medicare is funded by a tax of 1.45 percent with no income limits.) However, the benefits paid out for Social Security are *progressive*: low earners get about 54 percent of their previous income in retirement compared to high earners who get only 33 percent [27]

Social Security does not only redistribute income from high earners to low earners, it also redistributes income from present workers to present retirees. As life expectancy increased, it became clear that what people paid into the system would not be sufficient to maintain them at a dignified level through retirement. In 1972, Social Security pensions were indexed to inflation, removing the question of future benefit levels from politics and guaranteeing that payments will not be eroded by inflation. Today, most people exhaust the funds they paid into the system within four to eight years. After that, their pension is essentially paid for by the payroll taxes of the present generation of workers. The evolution of Social Security has made it, in the words of Harvard's Theda Skocpol, "America's most effective antipoverty program."[28] As Figure 17.4 shows, the poverty rate among the elderly fell from 28 percent in the late 1960s to only about 9 percent in 2009. Without Social Security, the poverty rate among the elderly would be about 50 percent.[29]

In contrast to Social Security programs for the elderly, means-tested welfare programs, which mostly benefit poor children, provide spotty coverage and inadequate benefits. The main program to provide cash assistance mainly to women and children who cannot support

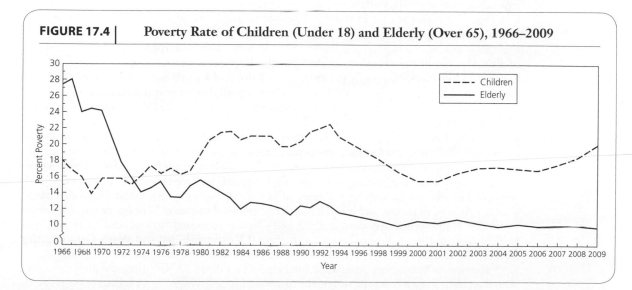

FIGURE 17.4 | **Poverty Rate of Children (Under 18) and Elderly (Over 65), 1966–2009**

Source: U.S. Bureau of Census, *United States Statistical Abstracts 2006*, Table 691; U.S. Bureau of Census, *United States Statistical Abstracts 2007*, Table 697; U.S. Bureau of Census, *United States Statistical Abstracts 2008*, Table 712; U.S. Bureau of Census, *United States Statistical Abstracts 2009*, Table 713; U.S. Bureau of Census, *United States Statistical Abstracts 2010*, Table 697; U.S. Bureau of Census, *United States Statistical Abstract 2012*, Table 712.

themselves, which used to be called "welfare," is now called Temporary Assistance for Needy Families (TANF). Between 1995 and 2010, TANF rolls fell 58 percent. Despite the recent recession, TANF enrollments are near an all-time low. Only 27 percent of families with children in poverty receive any sort of cash assistance.[30] At the same time that the elderly poverty rate fell, the child poverty rate rose (Figure 17.4). Child poverty is much lower (on average only 10.7 percent) in other developed countries, partly due to their social policies.[31] Most other developed countries have broad entitlement programs to address the needs of the nonelderly poor. The most important of these is health insurance. They also have child allowances in which every family, regardless of income, is entitled to a payment each year from the government for each child. These allowances are politically popular and have played a major role in reducing poverty rates.[32]

The question that arises is why spending programs targeted on those who need them the most have been cut, with a few exceptions, while other programs that benefit primarily the elderly have fared so well. One major reason is that the design of programs for the elderly has stimulated political participation while programs for the poor have suppressed political involvements.

The Successful Attack on Welfare

The 1935 Social Security Act created a program called Aid to Families with Dependent Children (AFDC), or what was known pejoratively as welfare. Based on a system of matching grants to the states, AFDC created a **means-tested benefit**, which meant that in order to obtain benefits, a person had to prove that he or she lacked adequate means of support. But it was also an **entitlement**, which meant that any family in the nation meeting the federal means test was entitled to get help. Although states could set benefit levels, they could not deny benefits to any eligible person. In the 1960s, welfare was supplemented with other means-tested programs, including food stamps and Medicaid.

During the 1960s, welfare expenditures grew rapidly, partly because of a militant welfare rights movement that encouraged people to apply for welfare.[33] As expenditures on welfare soared, taxes increased, and industrial jobs declined, a welfare backlash developed, especially among working-class white ethnics. A book on the flight of Jews and Italians of Brooklyn from the Democratic Party to the Republican Party quotes an enraged city worker: "These welfare people get as much as I do, and I work my ass off and come home dead tired. They get up late, and they can shack up all day long and watch the tube. With their welfare and food stamps, they come out better than me. . . . Let them tighten their belts like we have to."[34]

AFDC became an increasingly unpopular program. The key transformation in the image of welfare was when conservatives persuaded the public that welfare was not just failing to solve poverty, *it was actually a cause of poverty*. By enabling women to get by without working, getting married, or staying in school, they argued, welfare created a culture of dependency.[35] The claim that welfare is a cause of poverty is highly questionable but it resonated with the American people and it had a wonderful political message: "*The less we spend, the more we care!*"[36] Running for president in 1992, Bill Clinton promised "to end welfare as we know it."[37] In August 1996, Clinton signed the **Personal Responsibility and Work Opportunity Act**, ending the federal government's sixty-one-year-old guarantee of aid for the poor.

Known as Temporary Assistance for Needy Families (TANF), the new program converted welfare from a federal entitlement to a state block grant, with wide discretion given to states on who was eligible and how much they would get. Federal spending on welfare was cut $55 billion over six years and federal rules required that states place 50 percent of welfare recipients in private sector jobs within six years. In addition, no person can collect welfare for more than five years in a lifetime or two years in any one stretch.

Welfare reform represents one of the biggest social experiments in American history. The evidence is now in. Buoyed by a strong economy, welfare reform was initially deemed a success. By 2001 welfare rolls had fallen 63 percent and many former recipients had found jobs. But the economic downturn that began in 2007 exposed the flaws in welfare reform. As the unemployment rate rose, the number of poor and very poor households soared. Welfare reform gave states control over how the federal money was spent and despite dire needs, many states diverted TANF monies to plug budget gaps. Fearing that generous programs would cause them to become "welfare magnets," many states have engaged in a "race to the bottom" to cut benefits.[38] Arizona, for example, has cut its welfare caseloads by 50 percent since the start of the recession. One of the biggest beneficiaries of welfare reform has been fast-food restaurants, low-wage manufacturers, and retailers like Walmart (see Chapter 1) that will keep wages lower because of the influx of millions of poor women desperate for work.

Those who have been kicked off of welfare do whatever is necessary in order to survive. One journalist who interviewed them wrote, "They have sold food stamps, sold blood, skipped meals, shoplifted, doubled up with friends, scavenged in trash bins for bottles and cans and returned to relationships with violent partners—all with children in tow."[39] Above all, critics worry about the effect on children. With many women entering the workforce, the strain on relatives to provide child care is great.[40] One study found that when the wages of women who left welfare were supplemented with other policies, such as daycare and job training, the children did better in school. Without such supplements, most children are worse off after their mothers leave welfare.

The main reason why states have not hesitated to divert welfare monies away from the poor is because of the negative image of means-tested welfare programs. Because means-tested programs are narrowly targeted on poor, minority, female-headed households, they engender resentment from working poor, who do not qualify for public assistance. Many working families, just above the poverty line, are not eligible for any means-tested benefits and they resent the help poor, often minority, households get.

Welfare fails the popular democratic test of a public policy: Instead of encouraging civic participation, it discourages it. Normally, we think of policies as the result of the political process. But policies also shape the political process, encouraging or discouraging political participation in a process that political scientists call **policy feedback** (Figure 17.5).

Studies have shown that people who receive means-tested benefits vote at lower rates and are less likely to work in a campaign or join a protest than people who receive entitlements, such as Social Security.[41] People on welfare experience government very differently than people who collect Social Security. One former welfare mother described it this

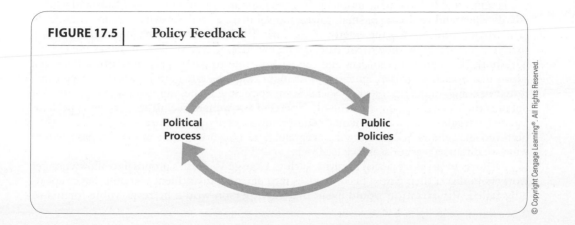

FIGURE 17.5 | **Policy Feedback**

way: "Unlike Social Security, [welfare] is distributed on a case-by-case basis, with enough strings to hang an elephant. It is meanly administered, hard to qualify for, hard to keep; it provides niggardly benefits and is tough to stomach with all its invasive attempts at behavior modification."[42] Welfare bureaucracies treat clients with disrespect, control their lives, and give them little opportunity for input. Welfare recipients generalize this experience to government as a whole.[43]

Not all public assistance programs for the poor discourage political participation. The Earned Income Tax Credit (EITC) program has expanded over the years and is now one of the most important programs targeted to the poor. The basic idea of EITC is to "make work pay." Under EITC, households earning below a certain amount (about $43,000 for families with three or more children) are given a credit, or a check from the government, instead of having to pay taxes. In 2011 the maximum credit for a single person or a married couple filing jointly with three or more children was $5,751. EITC started out modestly in 1975 but since then it has been the fastest growing social program in the United States, totaling over $36 billion in 2004.[44]

EITC is viewed as the antithesis of welfare. The term "earned" in the title of the program suggests that the government benefits are deserved because you must work to qualify. In contrast to traditional welfare, which reduced government aid when a recipient went to work, EITC rewards work. EITC is gradually phased out as your earnings rise but not on a dollar-for-dollar basis so that recipients have an incentive to work more. Republicans felt vulnerable to charges that they had made the income tax system biased toward the rich, and EITC gave them a way to address this political concern. President Ronald Reagan praised EITC. Democrats and Republicans have competed for the votes of the working poor, a growing group in the electorate, by supporting EITC. EITC payments pump money into disadvantaged communities. Local governments and community organizations often sponsor projects to encourage people to apply for the credit. President Clinton probably summed up the case for the EITC best: "those who work and play by the rules shouldn't be poor."[45]

The Successful Defense of Social Security

In contrast to welfare, Social Security is an example of a program that is consistent with the tenets of popular democracy and is able to defend itself from cuts. Unlike means-tested social policies, Social Security unites people instead of dividing them and encourages civic participation instead of discouraging it.

Benefiting more than 90 percent of the workforce, Social Security is a classic case of **majoritarian politics**, in which both the costs and the benefits are widely spread. Social Security is supported by a broad coalition uniting the poor and the middle class, blacks and whites, city dwellers and residents of small towns and suburbs. Social Security has also stimulated civic participation among the elderly. In the early 1950s, seniors participated at a lower rate than nonseniors. Now they participate at a higher rate. Social Security provides the elderly with both the material resources and the leisure time to participate in politics. Research shows that Social Security recipients vote at about twice the rate of those who receive means-tested benefits. And 31 percent of Social Security recipients belong to an organization that defends their benefits compared to only 2 percent for welfare recipients.[46] What is perhaps most remarkable is that low-income seniors now actually participate at higher rates than high-income seniors in defending the program. Social Security is one of the best examples of what we discussed earlier as policy feedback.

Efforts to privatize Social Security, such as George W. Bush's proposal to allow younger workers to divert their Social Security taxes into personal investment accounts, have repeatedly failed. Privatization would mean that each person would be responsible for his or

her retirement. By contrast, defenders of Social Security argue that by banding together Americans can insure each other against the risks of old age. In addition, we can build a better democracy by ensuring that senior citizens have the dignity, time, and resources to participate in politics.

Tax Expenditures: Welfare for the Middle and Upper Classes

The social policies we have talked about so far—public assistance, Social Security, Medicare, Medicaid—are all at least mildly redistributive, helping those at the bottom more than those at the top. But a whole range of other social polices run through the tax code work just the opposite, benefiting upper-income households more than the poor. These programs create a "privatized welfare state" that is largely hidden from public view. Once again, they show that policy design, how benefits are delivered to citizens, can affect political success.

Besides government payments to individuals, citizens also benefit from special provisions, known as **tax expenditures**. Tax expenditures are provisions in the tax code that reduce people's taxes in order to promote public objectives. Calling them tax *expenditures* highlights the fact that tax exemptions are essentially the same as spending programs. The government can either exempt certain income from taxes or it can tax income normally and write a check to the recipient for the value of the exemption. Either way, the government is spending resources to benefit certain taxpayers. In an effort to subject tax expenditures to public scrutiny, in 1968 the Treasury Department published the first budget for the United States that included tax expenditures. The Congressional Budget Act of 1974 made tax expenditures an integral part of the budget process. Misunderstood by most Americans, tax expenditures disproportionately benefit the middle class and especially the wealthy.

Tax expenditures are massive, and they have grown at an astounding pace, far outstripping the growth of conventional spending programs. By 2008 social tax expenditures, designed to promote desirable social outcomes, cost the federal treasury more than one

Table 17.2 Major Tax Expenditure Programs, Estimated Cost to the U.S. Treasury in 2013	
Homeowner tax breaks (deductibility of mortgage interest and state and local taxes, exclusion of capital gains, and net imputed rent)	$257.1 billion
Exclusion of employer contributions to health insurance	$228.0 billion
Exclusion of contributions to retirement (employer contributions, 401(k) plans, individual retirement accounts, and Keogh plans)	$159.1 billion
TOTAL	$644.2 billion

Source: Office of Management and Budget, *Analytical Perspectives, Budget of the United States Government, FY 2011* (2011), http://www.whitehouse.gov/sites/default/files/omb/budget/fy2011/assets/spec.pdf.

trillion dollars.[47] Table 17.2 lists some of the major tax expenditures and their costs to the U.S. Treasury. Tax expenditures go disproportionately to upper-income households. In 2004, 69 percent of the benefits of the Home Mortgage Interest Deduction and 55 percent of the tax-free benefits of retirement went to the richest 15 percent of households.[48] The working poor, who normally rent, do not benefit from the mortgage interest deduction and usually get no health insurance or retirement benefits through their jobs. The amount the federal government spends on tax benefits for homeowners is about *six times* greater than the entire Housing and Urban Development (HUD) budget (which includes almost all spending on low income housing).

Tax expenditures have distinct political advantages over conventional spending programs. First, they are buried in the tax code and therefore have low political visibility. Second, once enacted, they do not require annual congressional appropriations, like conventional spending programs. Third, there are no congressional committees with oversight responsibilities for tax expenditures, and hearings are rarely held to scrutinize their effectiveness—as happens for spending programs. Homeowner tax breaks are defended for increasing the homeownership rate, which has many public benefits. But homeowner tax deductions are remarkably inefficient at achieving that goal. It would be easy to design a program that targeted tax breaks on young families trying to purchase their first home. Instead, homeowner tax deductions go overwhelmingly to upper-income households who would almost certainly be homeowners without the deduction. Using homeowner tax breaks to promote homeownership is like using a shotgun to ring a doorbell—sure a few pellets will hit the target but the overwhelming majority miss.

Defenders of tax expenditures argue that the middle class already pays too much in taxes and they ought to get a break. But this begs the question of why people who rent an apartment or work for a small business should not get a similar tax break. The people who benefit from these tax breaks still enjoy all of the benefits of U.S. citizenship, but they don't pay their fair share of the costs. Tax expenditures for housing, retirement, and health care subsidize a privatized welfare state for the middle and upper classes.

Health Care Reform: The Big Fix?

When President Obama signed the **Patient Protection and Affordable Care Act** (PPACA) on March 23, 2010, a supersensitive microphone picked up Vice President Joe Biden, known for verbal gaffs, as saying this was "a big f...ing deal." In fact, PPACA *is* a big deal. It is one of the most significant pieces of social legislation in American history, comparable to the Social Security Act of 1935. PPACA touches on all aspects of social and economic policy—entitlements, means-tested benefits, tax expenditures, and economic regulation. For supporters, PPACA is the "big fix," a comprehensive effort to fix a broken health care system, control costs, and, above all, make it more fair and inclusive. For opponents, PPACA is a "big fix" of another sort—a government takeover of the American health care system that will empower government bureaucrats to institute "death panels" and take away our freedom by forcing us to purchase health insurance.

The overheated rhetoric about Obama's health care reform obscures what is really going on. You cannot understand health care reform by listening to sound bites and talking heads. Here we look inside the complicated health care machine and determine who will benefit and who will lose from reform as well as how this affects American democracy.

Few disagree that the American health care system needs fixing. Americans spend more than 16 percent of their total economic output on health care, more than twice the average for advanced industrial countries.[49] This percentage has been rising at an unsustainable rate for decades. What makes the rising cost of health care so troubling is that our health outcomes are relatively poor. In 2011, for example, we ranked 41st in infant mortality.[50] Americans with health insurance receive some of the most sophisticated health care in the world, but when Obama assumed office about 50 million Americans had no health insurance at all. We are the only developed nation without national health insurance. Moreover, the rising cost of health care is a drag on the economy. General Motors spends about $1,400 on health care for every car that rolls off the assembly line. Japanese and German automakers have a competitive advantage because the government pays for health insurance

Despite facing the most serious economic crisis since the Great Depression, President Obama made reforming the health care system a top priority during his first two years in office.[51] Learning from the failure of President Clinton to pass comprehensive health care reform in 1994, Obama articulated the general principles of reform and left the details to be hammered out in Congress. This political pragmatism enabled Obama to achieve what presidents Teddy Roosevelt, Franklin Roosevelt, Harry Truman, and Bill Clinton had all failed to achieve. But it also had its costs. The horse-trading and backroom deals necessary to pass complex legislation are troubling. As a quote popularly attributed to German Chancellor Otto von Bismarck puts it: "Laws are like sausages—it is best not to see them being made." With the 24-hour news cycle, the deals that were necessary to pass health care reform received glaring media attention, undermining public support.

Obama made every effort to turn powerful vested interests who previously had opposed reform into supporters of reform—or at least keep them on the sidelines. He and his supporters in Congress succeeded by cutting a series of deals with three powerful potential adversaries:

1. **Health care providers:** Under PPACA, the American Medical Association (AMA) and the American Hospital Association will receive new revenues from about 32 million new insured patients estimated at $399 billion. In return, they accepted reductions in payments from Medicare and Medicaid of about $235 billion. Both organizations supported reform.

2. **Big drug companies:** Led by former Congressman Billy Tauzin (see Chapter 10, the Pharmaceutical Research and Manufacturers of America (PhRMA) agreed to lower drug prices and fees totaling about $85 billion over ten years. In exchange, the government agreed to new subsidized drug payments for Medicare patients to the tune of tens of billions of dollars. Tauzin pumped $100 million into ads supporting reform.

3. **Private health insurance companies:** Buoyed by Obama's refusal to support a "public option" (government insurance competing with private insurance), the private insurance

industry largely supported reform because it would hugely expand the number of people purchasing private health insurance. Ironically, the private insurance industry took out ads attacking PPACA for giving government too much power at the same time that it was pushing for more government control—specifically, for stronger government sanctions to enforce the "individual mandate," requiring most Americans to purchase health insurance. Without the individual mandate, the insurance companies were concerned, with good reason, that people would only purchase insurance after they got sick, undermining insurance company profits.

Despite these powerful supporters, many doubted that health care reform could make its way through Congress. Despite the fact that Obama's health care proposal had many Republican ideas in it (Mitt Romney signed a similar law as governor of Massachusetts), Republicans early on decided they would oppose every aspect of reform, betting that they would have a better chance of defeating Obama in 2012 by stonewalling reform, even if it resulted in a law less to their liking. Not a single Republican voted for "Obamacare."

The Democrats had a clear majority in the House, but they barely had the 60 votes necessary in the Senate to stop the Republicans from filibustering the bill to death.[52] In January 2010, Democrats were shocked when Tea Party favorite Scott Brown won the Massachusetts Senate seat of Teddy Kennedy, longtime champion of universal health insurance. Suddenly, it looked like health care reform was dead because Democrats lacked a filibuster-proof majority. Democratic leaders, however, came up with a way to pass the law that did not require 60 votes in the Senate. Fiscal bills on taxes and spending are not subject to a filibuster. By combining previous bills passed by both houses with a sidecar bill that mandated the necessary taxes and spending, Democrats were able to pass the health care reform by a simple majority vote in the Senate.

Freed of the necessity of satisfying conservative Democrats in the Senate, health care reformers pushed for new taxes on the wealthy to pay for expanded health care coverage. In effect, PPACA places taxes on the wealthiest 3 percent of Americans (about $560 a year on average) to pay for expansion of health insurance for an additional 32 million people. Part of the insurance coverage comes from expansion of Medicaid. Everyone making up to 133 percent of the poverty level will now be eligible for Medicaid. Those above that income level who do not have health insurance will be subsidized by the government to purchase insurance at lower rates by pooling their purchasing power in state-run insurance exchanges. If those who can afford to purchase health insurance do not do so, they will be forced to pay a tax. This is the so-called "individual mandate" so hated by libertarian opponents. Other key elements of PPACA include:

1. Insurance companies will not be able to turn people down because they are sick—so-called "pre-existing conditions."

2. Young people will be able to stay on their parent's health insurance up to age 26.

3. A series of pilot programs was authorized to control health care costs.

The passage of PPACA in 2010 did not end the democratic debate on health reform, but ushered in a new phase of political maneuvering. Having lost in Congress, opponents turned to the courts, with 26 states joining other plaintiffs in a lawsuit challenging the constitutionality of the law. The Supreme Court announced its much-anticipated ruling on June 28, 2012 in the case of ***National Federation of Independent Businesses v. Sebelius***. By a narrow 5–4 majority, the Supreme Court upheld the constitutionality of the individual mandate on the grounds that the law did not command people to purchase health insurance but instead simply required them to pay a tax if they failed to purchase insurance. Chief Justice John Roberts, the surprising swing vote, argued that Congress clearly has the power to tax and therefore the individual mandate is constitutional. In a separate ruling, the Supreme Court struck down one aspect of PPACA, ruling that the federal government did not have the power to take away all Medicaid funding if a state refused to expand coverage as outlined in the law. Because the federal government will pay the entire cost for the first few years and at least 90 percent of the expenses after that, states will have to think twice before refusing to expand coverage.

Despite the Supreme Court approval of PPACA, Republicans have vowed to repeal it, charging that the law is a big government takeover of the American health care system. This charge is misleading. The law works within the present mixed system in which the government subsidizes health care provided by *private* insurance companies, in *private* hospitals, staffed by doctors who work for the *private* sector, not for government. As two political scientists put it, PPACA uses "conservative means to pursue progressive ends."[53] Despite charges that PPACA will balloon the deficit, the nonpartisan Congressional Budget Office estimates that it will reduce the federal deficit by $110 billion over ten years.

Ultimately, the fate of health care reform will depend on citizen support. When informed that powerful vested interests cut deals behind closed doors in Congress, many citizens concluded that the process was corrupt and they became receptive to the disinformation campaign conducted by opponents. In fact, PPACA is a progressive law in the popular democratic tradition that taxes the wealthy in order to enable more than 30 million people to obtain health insurance and live more dignified and stress-free lives. Obama's reelection in 2012 means that Obamacare will survive in the short run. However, Obama will need to do a better job of explaining its benefits. As the benefits for ordinary working Americans begin to kick in, such as people with pre-existing conditions finally getting health insurance, Obama's task should become easier.

Even though PPACA is a popular democratic law, the political process by which it was created was not popular democratic. Most Americans were spectators to the inside-the-beltway maneuvering that produced PPACA. That is why they have been susceptible to half-truths and outright lies about the law. Supporters of health reform need to find better ways to engage the American people in making decisions about health care to rebuild their trust in popular democratic government.

Conclusion: The Future of Economic and Social Policy

Economic policy is too important to be left in the hands of elites. Too often, economic elites ignore the social and political social ramifications of their policies. When the Federal Reserve ratchets up interest rates to stop inflation and throws 100,000 people out of work, they do not take into account the effects of unemployment on suicide, homicide, mental illness, crime, alcoholism, and domestic violence.[54] In the long run, economic policy will be more effective if it has democratic input so that it can balance the complex economic, social, and political trade-offs.

We live in an age when the market is worshipped as the solution to all of our problems. It is as if all tyranny and oppression comes from government, never from markets. In fact, market actors can exploit consumers and investors. If the reader doubts this, consider the foreclosure crisis. When the federal government withdrew from regulating the mortgage industry, predatory lenders stepped in to exploit homebuyers. Investors were also taken advantage of, purchasing mortgage-backed securities they had no idea were full of bad loans. Deregulation freed up predatory mortgage companies to, in effect, steal from unsuspecting homebuyers and investors. We all suffered from the resulting economic meltdown. As the economic historian R. H. Tawney once wrote: "Freedom for the pike is death for the minnows."[55] We need a strong federal government to check and balance the power of corporations.

Government can of course be a source of oppression. We need to be vigilant in holding government accountable. But government can also enhance our freedom. Consider Obama's health care reform. Before reform, those with health insurance were forced to pay for the medical care of those without insurance by paying for the cost of their emergency room care through higher hospital fees. Under health care reform, more people will buy insurance (or they will have to pay a tax) and, as a result, previously insured households will be freed from having to pay for the medical bills of the uninsured. The top 3 percent of households will see their freedom reduced by being forced to pay additional taxes, but this new revenue will help more than 30 million people obtain health insurance for the first time. These people will have new freedoms. They will be free from the anxiety that a sick child will suffer needlessly from a serious illness. They will be free to leave a job with health insurance, knowing that they will be guaranteed health insurance in their new job—even if they have a sick child.

Health care policy involves many difficult tradeoffs but any implication that government involvement is automatically oppressive is misleading in the extreme. The health care system in the United States is a complex partnership between public and private actors. A majority of Americans (60 percent) obtain health insurance through their employer. Many do not recognize that privately provided health insurance is deeply subsidized by government—to the tune of $228 billion under the federal government's tax expenditure for employer contributions to health insurance.

The attacks on social programs for the poor are driven by a fear of "dependency" on government. In fact, in our fast-moving, high-tech society, no one is independent or dependent; we are all *interdependent*. No one should be ashamed of this. In fact, human beings are social and political animals, and we find our identity and meaning by deliberating with our fellow citizens about how to create a more democratic and just society.

Reader's Guide ★ ★ ★

Critical Thinking Questions

1. In what ways is the quality of your life affected by government? What policy of the government affects you the most? How will you be affected by the Patient Protection and Affordable Care Act?

2. How do economic inequalities create political inequalities? Be specific.

3. How do we distinguish between tolerable and intolerable levels of inequality in a democracy?

4. Do you believe that government should provide a guaranteed annual income below which no one who works fulltime should fall? If so, approximately what should the minimum income be for a single person or a couple with children?

Key Word Definition

macroeconomic policy   Economic policy that influences the performance of the economy as a whole and is not designed to have direct effects on different sectors or on the distribution of economic opportunities among different groups in the population.

fiscal policy   The manipulation of components of the national budget, taxes, and spending to regulate the economy.

monetary policy   A method of economic management that regulates the supply of money in the economy.

deflation   A condition of falling prices and increased purchasing power for the dollar.

inflation   A condition of rising prices and reduced purchasing power for the dollar.

Federal Reserve   The main institution responsible for monetary policy in the United States. Created in 1913 to regulate banks and adjust the money supply, thus controlling inflation, its seven-member board of governors is appointed by the president with the consent of the Senate.

Keynesianism   The economic theory that the government needs to intervene into the economy to guarantee full employment and smooth out the ups and downs of the business cycle.

supply-side economics   The economic theory used by the Reagan administration to justify reducing taxes on investment, profits, and income and reducing government regulation of industry to promote economic prosperity.

Laffer curve   The representational graph that argues that decreasing tax rates below a certain point will actually increase total tax revenues.

automatic stabilizers   Declines in tax revenue and increases in spending that occur automatically without any action by Congress. They are designed to stabilize the economy by stimulating it in a downturn and cooling it off in periods of rapid growth.

American Recovery and Reinvestment Act of 2009   A combination of tax cuts and spending increases designed by the Obama administration to stimulate the economy.

discretionary spending   That part of the federal budget that is not committed and can be controlled by Congress each year. Discretionary spending is contrasted with mandatory spending, such as interest on debt and payments committed to individuals, such as Social Security.

progressive and regressive taxes   Progressive taxes take a higher proportion of income as income rises, whereas regressive taxes take a higher proportion of income from lower income earners.

means-tested benefit   The method of granting public assistance that forces people to prove their inability to support themselves in order to secure that assistance.

entitlement   A social benefit, such as Social Security, in which all who pay into it have a right to the benefits; you do not have to apply for the program or prove that you deserve help.

Personal Responsibility and Work Opportunity Act of 1996   The act passed by Congress and signed into law by President Clinton in August 1996 that did away with the federal entitlement to welfare and replaced it with a block grant to the states that required the states to move half of the people on welfare into jobs by 2002. The new program, called Temporary Assistance to Needy Families (TANF), replaced Aid for Families with Dependent Children (AFDC).

policy feedback   A situation where policies, after they are passed, influence future political participation, either undermining or reinforcing the coalition behind the original policies.

majoritarian politics   The politics of policy making in which all, or nearly all, citizens receive some benefits of the policy and pay the costs.

tax expenditures   Defined in the 1974 Budget Act as "revenue losses attributable to provisions of the federal tax laws which allow a special exemption, exclusion, or deduction." Tax expenditures are calculated by subtracting what the government actually collects in taxes from what it would have collected had the special exemptions not been in place.

Patient Protection and Affordable Care Act of 2010   Comprehensive reform of the American health care system, signed into law by President Obama, that increases taxes and regulations in order to improve private health insurance and extend health insurance to most Americans.

***National Federation of Independent Businesses v. Sebelius* (2012)**   Supreme Court decision that largely upheld the constitutionality of the Patient Protection and Affordable Care Act of 2010.

18

Foreign Policy in the National Security State

The Bush administration had enormous ambitions for its adventure in Iraq. Not only would the United States remove Saddam Hussein, a tyrannical ruler, from power, but it would reshape Iraq into an American-style capitalist democracy whose shining example would inspire reform throughout the Arab world. These ambitions, however, rapidly collided with stubborn realities. The people who planned the war or who were sent to Iraq to reconstruct its society understood little about the nation they were hoping to reshape. Indeed, they were largely unaware of how hard it is to fundamentally alter the ways of any culture.

To make matters worse, the Bush administration refused to send experts whose support for the invasion of Iraq was suspect. Instead, it gave preference to job applicants whose credential for a position in Iraq was simply that they were politically connected in the Republican Party. What flowed from the administration's illusions and mistakes in its effort to reconstruct Iraq was, in equal parts, tragic and comic.

In one of many examples, the Bush administration put Jay Hallen, a twenty-four-year-old working for a real-estate firm, in charge of reforming Iraq's stock market. Hallen was appalled by what he found at Baghdad's stock exchange: Brokers scrawled trades on pieces of paper and kept track of them on a blackboard. What was needed, he decided, was a total overhaul that would create an American-style stock market, with a computerized trading system and a supervising board of directors. He proceeded to order the computers and appoint the board, and he fired a majority of the stock exchange's existing staff (whom he concluded had been made unnecessary by the computerization). Then, Hallen was recalled to the United States. The head of the new board of directors rehired the fired staff members and ignored the computerization. Soon, Iraqi traders were again writing down their trades on paper and accounting for them on the blackboard.[1]

Elite democrats have long claimed that foreign policy, even more than domestic policy, requires the superior expertise and talent of elites. Ordinary citizens, they argue, are generally ignorant about events in other nations and are prone to emotional and fickle responses inconsistent with a realistic and stable foreign policy. Therefore, foreign policy should largely be left in the hands of the president and the diplomatic and military personnel who advise him. The Bush administration's blunders in Iraq should lead us to question this conventional wisdom about wise elites and ignorant masses. When foreign policy decisions are made by a handful of elite actors operating free of public scrutiny, the result can be folly rather than wisdom. And the cost can be great, both to America's true national security and to its most cherished democratic values.

This chapter considers the democratic debate over foreign policy. It is a debate that has been waged since the nation's founding and continues today with passionate and increasingly partisan disagreements. It is a debate not only about the stance the United States should take toward other nations, but about the consequences of how we define and decide that stance for our democracy at home.

Beginnings of the Democratic Debate over Foreign Policy

Elite democrats and popular democrats of the founding generation differed not only on how Americans should govern themselves but also on how the American nation should relate to the rest of the world. The former favored executive control and promoted professional armies, while the latter sought public control and favored citizen militias.

The strongest proponent of the original elite position on foreign policy was Alexander Hamilton. In *The Federalist Papers*, Hamilton called on Americans to recognize that they lived in a dangerous world, where nations would fight regularly over power, territory, and commerce. Hamilton argued that the new United States needed professional armies and navies like those of the major European powers, England and France. These forces would be required for defense and for the establishment of America as a great power, extending its influence throughout the western hemisphere.[2]

In Hamilton's conception of foreign and defense policy, the president was the dominant figure. Members of Congress lacked the information and experience to make wise decisions in foreign policy; furthermore, they could not act swiftly or keep diplomatic secrets. In contrast, the executive had the proper qualities for controlling foreign policy and using military might—in Hamilton's words, "decision, activity, secrecy, and dispatch."[3]

The Anti-federalists feared Hamilton's professional military forces. A standing army might overturn republican institutions and seize power for its commander (the example of Julius Caesar in ancient Rome was frequently cited). Or it might become a dangerous tool for the executive, tempting him to crush his domestic opponents or launch aggressive military adventures abroad. As an alternative to a professional military in times of peace, the Anti-federalists wanted to rely on state militias composed of armed citizens.

That citizen militias were capable only of defensive military operations reveals a great deal about the Anti-federalist view of foreign policy. The Anti-federalists did not want the new republic to become like the reigning great powers of the day. Rather than playing power politics, America should relate to the rest of the world as an example of how a people could flourish in freedom and self-government. A peaceful, commercial relationship with other nations could be governed as much by the people's representatives in Congress as by the executive. Foreign and defense policy of this kind would, the Anti-federalists believed, provide Americans with genuine security without endangering the republic's institutions and values.

In today's world of massive military forces and awesome technological destructiveness, some of the Anti-federalists' arguments are outdated. Yet the fundamental questions of the original democratic debate endure: Should American foreign and military policy be determined largely by a small elite acting often in secret and be directed toward the projection of American power abroad? Or should American foreign and defense policy be subject to greater popular democratic control and seek a form of national security that violates as little as possible the nation's professed values as a democratic society?

Isolation and Expansion

The foreign policies that nations pursue reflect in good part their distinctive cultural identities. American foreign policy has been marked from the outset by a belief in the exceptional character of the United States in world history. What historian Walter Hixson calls "the myth of America" is the idea that this nation is uniquely democratic and virtuous, no matter whether it is remaining aloof from foreign conflicts or using military force to prevail in them. For many, the myth has a religious basis, with Americans fulfilling a divine mission to reform the world.[4]

How should this mission be conducted? For much of American history, elite democrats who shared Hamilton's vision of the United States as a great power were frustrated. **Isolationism**, not power politics, was the core principle of American foreign and defense policy. Apart from commercial relations, the United States sought to stay isolated from the political and military quarrels of the rest of the world. Protected by two vast oceans, the young republic concentrated on its internal development. Since military threats were remote, the standing army remained small. Only when the United States actually became engaged in a war did the military swell in size; once war was over, the citizen-soldiers who composed the bulk of the forces were rapidly demobilized.

Even though isolationism characterized American relations with other nations until well into the twentieth century, American foreign policy was neither as defensive nor as passive as the term seems to imply. The American republic from its inception was engaged in a process of **expansion**, first on a continental scale and later into Latin America and Asia. American expansion drove the European powers from their remaining holdings on the continent. But it had a dark side: Expansion also drove Native Americans from their ancestral lands, often in brutal fashion. And later it extended American power over Latin Americans and Filipinos, speaking the language of benevolence but employing the instrument of armed force. The responsibility for this dark side of American expansion belonged to both elite democrats and popular democrats.

Removal of indigenous peoples, the initial pillar of American expansion, was the work of popular democrats. The central figure in this removal was popular democratic hero Andrew Jackson. He understood that many ordinary Americans hungered for the fertile lands that the Native American tribes occupied—and he shared their incomprehension at Indians' refusal to give up their way of life and adopt the white man's economic and social practices. Under Jackson's leadership, Native Americans were driven from their homes in the southeastern states. As historian Richard Barnet notes, "In 1820, 125,000 Indians lived

This Modern World.

east of the Mississippi; by 1844 there were fewer than 30,000 left. Most had been forcibly relocated to the west. About a third had been wiped out."[5]

If popular democrats had their shameful moments in the history of American expansion, so, too, did elite democrats. Consider, for example, the clique of elite expansionists in the 1890s, led by such avowed admirers of Hamilton as Massachusetts senator Henry Cabot Lodge and Assistant Secretary of the Navy Theodore Roosevelt. It was these elite expansionists, eager to project American power abroad, who prodded a wavering President William McKinley to fight a Spanish-American war and to extend the war from its ostensible focus, Cuba, halfway around the world to the Philippine Islands. The same men guided the subsequent American military campaign to crush Filipino nationalists, who wanted independence rather than American rule. A forerunner to the Vietnam conflict, the American war in the Philippines caused as many as 200,000 Filipino deaths.[6]

Although expansion drew support from both elites and masses, it always had its critics, who echoed the original Anti-federalist fear that America could become a great power only by violating its republican principles. America's role in the Mexican War, the war in the Philippines, and World War I was denounced by those who wanted the nation not to follow the path of European militarism and imperialism. These critics, among them Abraham Lincoln, were especially outraged by claims that American expansion was motivated by a desire to spread liberty to other lands; they detected the real desire for wealth and power that such rhetoric disguised.[7]

Even as the United States expanded across the continent (and into Latin America and the Philippines), even as it became the greatest industrial power in the world, the doctrine of isolationism remained strong. America came late to World War I—and recoiled after the war from the slaughter on the battlefield and the power politics of the victorious allies. Only with World War II did the nation begin to change its traditional foreign and defense policy, and it was in the immediate postwar years that the great transformation in American international relations occurred. Then, in the Cold War era, some of Hamilton's dreams were finally fulfilled, and some of the Anti-federalists' fears finally came true.

The Cold War

The **Cold War** was a forty-year struggle (lasting from the late 1940s to the late 1980s) between the United States and its allies, championing the cause of democracy and capitalism, and the Soviet Union (USSR) and its allies, championing the cause of communism. It was called a "cold" war because the two principal adversaries, the United States and the Soviet Union, armed themselves to the teeth yet never actually engaged in direct combat with each other. But the Cold War became a "hot" war in many places, with major armed conflicts in Korea and Vietnam, and numerous smaller armed conflicts around the globe. It was also waged with nonmilitary weapons ranging from political manipulation and economic pressure to propaganda and espionage.

The Cold War fundamentally transformed American foreign policy. With the Cold War, the United States became an active and interventionist global superpower. It developed an enormous peacetime military establishment, armed with weaponry of previously unthinkable destructiveness. Presidents became the overwhelmingly dominant factors in policy making and came to possess, among other resources, the capacity to operate in secret, employing new agencies of covert action such as the CIA. Meanwhile, Congress and the public were reduced to a marginal role, expected to support but not to question American actions abroad. These developments gave rise to a **national security state**, a complex of executive, military, and secret powers previously unknown in the American republic. Even after the Cold War ended, this national security state remained.

One of the principal justifications for the national security state was that the United States must be able to mount overpowering opposition to aggression by foreign nations. The mistake of the Western allies before World War II—appeasing Adolf Hitler at Munich in 1938—must never again be repeated. The United States organized a European alliance, the **North Atlantic Treaty Organization (NATO)**, to block any Soviet expansion in Europe. Aggression by Soviet allies and clients in the Third World also had to be halted, a rationale that involved the United States in wars in Korea and Vietnam. In this view, which survived the end of the Cold War, the United States had built a national security state not to secure military supremacy but to keep peace in the world.

A second justification for building and maintaining the national security state was to defend freedom around the globe. In advocating a global American struggle for the **containment** of communism, President Truman declared "I believe that it must be the policy of the United States to support free peoples who are resisting attempted subjugation by armed minorities or by outside pressures."[8] The strategy of containment, proclaimed in what came to be known as the Truman Doctrine, formed the basis of American policy throughout the Cold War.

For roughly the first half of the Cold War, almost all Americans believed in its ideas and institutions. But this "Cold War consensus" cracked during the Vietnam War of the 1960s and early 1970s. It was during the protests against American policy in Vietnam that the popular democratic tradition of opposing a foreign and defense policy based on unchecked executive power, militarism, and secret, unaccountable institutions was revived. This opposition was expressed chiefly through mass movements, first against the war in Vietnam and later against President Reagan's policy in Central America and his nuclear arms buildup.

The Cold War came to a sudden and surprising end in the late 1980s and early 1990s, first with the collapse of the Soviet empire in Eastern Europe and then with the disappearance of the Soviet Union itself. The United States and its allies exulted in the Cold War's demise. Indeed, the whole world breathed easier now that the frightening prospect of a third world war and a nuclear holocaust had been removed. However, the celebration was bound to be brief, for the post–Cold War world already contained new problems and violent conflicts. Within American government, the institutions of the national security state had to redefine their roles in an era that initially lacked the simplifying assumption of a single global enemy. It is time to describe these institutions.

Foreign and Defense Policy: Institutions

The presidency is the dominant institution in the making of foreign and defense policy, and in the first half of the Cold War era it controlled this area with few checks from anyone else. But the disastrous presidential war in Vietnam sparked Congress to reassert its constitutional role in shaping American policy abroad. Since Vietnam, foreign and defense policy has often been the subject of struggle between presidents and Congress (see Chapters 12 and 13).

Agencies of the executive branch are central to the formulation and implementation of national security policy. Presidents have considerable latitude to use these agencies as they see fit, so the role of each agency and the structure of the foreign policy process itself have varied from one administration to the next. National security agencies are subordinate units that advise and assist the president, yet they shape how the United States understands and operates in international affairs.

The National Security Council

The **National Security Council (NSC)** was created in 1947, at the dawn of the Cold War, to serve as a coordinating mechanism for foreign and defense policy at the highest level. The president, vice president, secretary of state, and secretary of defense are statutory members of the NSC; the Director of National Intelligence and the chair of the Joint Chiefs of Staff are statutory advisers (see Table 18.1).

Presidents have found NSC meetings to be a ponderous instrument. The importance of the NSC has come to reside, instead, in the head of its staff, the president's **national security adviser**. President Kennedy was the first to transform this position from bureaucratic assistant to the council to personal adviser to the president; his national security adviser, McGeorge Bundy, came to overshadow his secretary of state, Dean Rusk, in influence. Subsequent national security advisers expanded on Bundy's role. None dominated American foreign policy as thoroughly as Henry Kissinger. Under Presidents Nixon and Ford, Kissinger was the basic architect of American foreign policy and its most celebrated spokesperson in the media.

National security advisers are in a strong position to exert influence. They have an advantage over secretaries of state in physical proximity to the president, working in the White House and briefing the president frequently on developments around the globe. National security advisers and their staffs filter the massive amounts of information flowing into the White House from American diplomatic, military, and intelligence personnel throughout the world and can tailor what they report to fit the president's interests more effectively than the larger and more bureaucratic State Department can.[9]

Table 18.1 Composition of the National Security Council		
Statutory Members of the NSC	**Statutory Advisers to the NSC**	**Other Attendees**
President	Director of National Intelligence	Chief of staff to the president
Vice president	Chair, Joint Chiefs of Staff	Assistant to the president for national security affairs
Secretary of state		
Secretary of defense		Secretary of the treasury
		Attorney general
		Others as invited

Source: http://www.whitehouse.gov/nsc/.

However, criticism in the media and among foreign policy experts that NSC advisers had grown too powerful led recent presidents to downgrade the adviser's role somewhat. Occupants of the position are now expected to act mainly as coordinators and facilitators and not to compete with the secretary of state for public attention. Among recent national security advisers, Condoleezza Rice, who held the job during George W. Bush's first term, has been the most prominent. She was elevated to the position of secretary of state at the start of Bush's second term.

Department of State

The **Department of State** is the oldest department in the president's cabinet and the traditional organ of American diplomacy. For most of American history, the secretary of state was the president's principal foreign policy adviser. State Department personnel, stationed in embassies and consulates in nations with which the United States maintained diplomatic relations, were America's principal point of contact with the rest of the world.

During the Cold War, however, the Department of State was eclipsed in influence by other institutions. The national security adviser often had greater influence with the president than did the secretary of state. The Department of Defense grew vastly larger than the Department of State in budget and personnel, and played a more central role in overseas conflicts. The Department of State also suffered from its reputation as a rigidly bureaucratic institution whose recommendations to the president were overly cautious and uncreative.[10]

With the end of the Cold War, the Department of State made something of a comeback. However, with the initiation of President Bush's war on terror, the State Department fell back into the secondary role it had played during the Cold War. During the early years of the Iraq war, Bush's secretary of defense, Donald Rumsfeld, was notably more influential than his secretary of state, Colin Powell.

The stature of the department rose again in Bush's second term, chiefly because the new secretary of state, Condoleezza Rice, was a Bush loyalist who did not question the White House perspective on the world. It has been even higher under President Obama. During his first term, his secretary of state, Hillary Clinton, had star power at home and abroad second only to the president's own. John Kerry, secretary of state for Obama's second term, also brings unusual prestige to the position.

Below the top echelon of officials, who are appointed by the president, the state department is staffed by a unique government elite: the Foreign Service. The Foreign Service is highly selective: Rigorous written tests weed out the vast majority of applicants, and subsequent interviews and group simulations eliminate most of the remaining pool, leaving only 1–2 percent able to gain admission to the service. Yet, although the exclusivity of the Foreign Service bestows prestige, its members are not necessarily as influential as other actors in foreign and defense policy bureaucracies. Their rivals in the National Security Council, Defense Department, or the Central Intelligence Agency often possess the specialized academic expertise or the important political contacts that Foreign Service officers normally lack.[11]

Department of Defense

The end of the Cold War was more beneficial to the State Department than to the **Department of Defense**. During the Cold War, this umbrella organization for the armed forces, symbolized by its massive headquarters, the Pentagon, had been the most powerful agency of the national security state.

The Department of Defense has a dual leadership structure: civilian and military. The secretary of defense heads the department and maintains the American tradition of civilian control of the military. Below the secretary on the civilian side are several assistant secretaries for specialized functions, along with civilian secretaries for the army, navy, and air force. Each of the military services also has a commanding officer from among its ranks. The top uniformed leaders come together in the **Joint Chiefs of Staff (JCS)**, headed by a chair. The JCS conveys the military's point of view to the president and to the secretary of defense.

The enormous expansion of the American military during the Cold War was built on claims, at times deliberately exaggerated, of a communist campaign to take over the planet. Concealed beneath the rhetoric about the communist threat was a different fuel for military expansion: interservice rivalry. Each branch of the services was eager to grow larger, more powerful, and better armed; each was fearful that the others would encroach on its central missions (see Chapter 14 for an example). Each service pushed for its own preferred new weapons system, even when the result was overlap and duplication in weaponry. Every time the Air Force developed a new model fighter plane, for instance, the Navy had to have a new fighter plane to match, and vice versa.

Cold War expansion of the military was furthered by the growth of the **military-industrial complex**. Coined by President Eisenhower, the term refers to the potentially dangerous influence of the political alliance between the Pentagon and the corporations that manufacture its arms. Expensive new weapons systems are mutually rewarding to the armed forces and to companies, especially in such fields as aircraft, electronics, and shipbuilding, for which defense contracts can bring in billions of dollars a year in guaranteed sales. Defense contractors thus place their financial muscle and lobbying resources behind Pentagon budget requests.

The terrorist attacks of September 11, 2001, restored the Pentagon for a time to its dominant place in the national security state. However, the decade of war that followed, first in Afghanistan and then in Iraq, eventually produced weariness in the United States toward the global overextension of American military forces. Economic crisis and soaring deficits also sparked questions about the size of the defense budget.

The Intelligence Community

One of the central features of the national security state is a large and diverse *intelligence community*. A number of U.S. agencies gather intelligence (information) about military, political, and economic developments in other countries. Some of the institutions in this community specialize in high-tech intelligence gathering. Among these is the National Security Agency, which employs the most advanced computer technology and spy satellites to monitor communications around the world. Each branch of the armed forces maintains its own intelligence unit. But the preeminent force in the intelligence community has been the **Central Intelligence Agency (CIA)**.

When Congress created the CIA in 1947, it thought it was establishing an agency to gather intelligence by various means ranging from analyses of foreign newspapers to espionage. Yet a vague congressional phrase referring to "other functions and duties" was seized on by the CIA to establish a unit that had little to do with intelligence gathering.[12] This was the **covert action** wing of the CIA, which specialized in clandestine operations that could not be traced to the U.S. government. Covert action became a secret weapon for presidents, allowing them to conduct a hidden foreign policy by, for example, bribing foreign politicians, stirring up economic unrest in other nations, or pushing for military coups to overthrow governments considered unfriendly.

Covert action became the hallmark of the CIA and was usually supported by the argument that the nation's communist enemies were employing the same kinds of "dirty tricks" to advance their sinister objectives. Few covert operations, as it turned out, actually hurt the communists or furthered American national security. Many backfired, making more enemies than friends in the long run. For example, the CIA overthrew a nationalist government in Iran in 1953 and restored the autocratic shah to power. After a quarter-century of his repressive rule, he was overthrown not by communists but by Islamic fundamentalists, who invoked the interference by the CIA in their country as a justification for their fierce hostility to the United States.[13]

However, it is not the ineffectiveness of covert action that has made the CIA the national security agency that most disturbs popular democrats. They are even more worried about the incompatibility of covert action with American democracy. Political scientist Loch Johnson notes that whereas democracy requires open government, public debate, the rule of law, and ethical behavior, covert action requires "the use of tactics or 'dirty tricks' that are far removed from the accepted philosophical tenets of democratic theory—lying, sabotage, even clandestine warfare and assassination in times of peace."[14]

Revelations in the mid-1970s of CIA abuses, including spying on American citizens as well as assassination plots, led to the formation of intelligence committees in the House and Senate to monitor and occasionally veto covert operations. Through these congressional committees, there is now at least some measure of CIA public accountability.[15] Yet the CIA found ways to evade accountability during President Reagan's covert campaign to overthrow the left-wing government of Nicaragua.

The CIA again has been subjected to criticism in the new era of U.S. foreign policy that began on September 11, 2001. Failure to anticipate and prevent the terrorist attacks that destroyed the World Trade Center and damaged the Pentagon represents one of the greatest intelligence disasters in American history. Top CIA officials were more attuned to the threat posed by Al Qaeda than were others in the federal government, but they were unable to mobilize their organization to respond to it effectively.

CIA officials and analysts did not do much better in the aftermath of September 11 than they had done in the period prior to the terrorist strikes. In selling the American public on the need to invade Saddam Hussein's Iraq, President Bush, Vice President Cheney, and Secretary of State Powell claimed that the CIA had uncovered compelling evidence that Saddam possessed weapons of mass destruction (WMD) that could be used to threaten the security of the United States and its allies. Some CIA career personnel told reporters that they felt pressure from the administration to shape their intelligence analyses in accordance with the White House view. But at the top of the CIA, officials were vigorous in promoting the idea of Saddam as a menace to the world. The CIA's director, George Tenet, told the president that it was a "slam dunk" conclusion that the Iraqi regime possessed WMD.[16] Tenet was wrong: After the United States invaded and occupied Iraq, no WMD were ever found.

The CIA also was implicated in some of the more seamy episodes of the war on terrorism. CIA agents have been accused of involvement in the torture of detainees at prisons in Iraq and Afghanistan. The CIA operated a secret "rendition" program whereby individuals suspected of having information on terrorist activities were transported for interrogation to other countries, such as Egypt, Saudi Arabia, and Pakistan, where torture is commonly employed. Released later, without ever being charged with an offense, a number of these individuals have told tales of being drugged, beaten, or subjected to electric shocks by their captors.[17]

In response to its glaring failures, a major change was made in the U.S. intelligence community in 2004: a new position atop the intelligence bureaucracy, Director of National Intelligence, was established. This official is responsible for compelling the CIA and the other intelligence agencies of the U.S. government to coordinate their activities. Despite this organizational change, it remains uncertain whether the U.S. intelligence community will improve the quality of its advice about threats to American security or will simply do the bidding of its boss in the White House.

International Economics Agencies

As national security threats temporarily declined with the end of the Cold War, American foreign policy makers began to direct greater attention to the globalized economy (see Chapter 4). Officials with responsibilities for international economics have become more prominent on the global stage than previously, sometimes coming to rival diplomats, generals, and intelligence chiefs in their impact on American foreign policy.

Created in 1974, the *Office of the United States Trade Representative* was upgraded and raised to cabinet status under President Clinton. The head of this office leads the American team that participates in multilateral trade negotiations. The U.S. trade representative also negotiates bilateral agreements with important trading partners.

The new focus on international economics also brought greater influence and visibility to cabinet agencies previously associated primarily with domestic affairs. President Clinton's second secretary of the treasury, Robert Rubin, was arguably the most important American official in international affairs during the last half of the 1990s. When an Asian financial crisis threatened the global economy, it was Treasury Secretary Rubin and not Secretary of State Madeleine Albright who shaped and led the American effort to stabilize the situation.

In the wake of the global financial crash that began in 2008, U.S. officials in the field of international economics continue to play a critical role. The emergence of China as an economic superpower and as the chief rival to the United States in world affairs is also likely to enhance the importance of these officials in the making of American foreign policy.

Foreign Policy and Economic Power

Although military concerns were uppermost for American foreign policy makers during the Cold War, economic concerns were by no means forgotten. The United States emerged from World War II as an unchallenged economic giant, its superiority all the greater because its rivals had been physically or economically devastated by the war. To restore the shattered economies of Europe as trading partners (and to prevent European nations from falling prey to communist subversion), the United States undertook a massive program of economic aid, the Marshall Plan. During the first several decades of the Cold War, the United States was the hegemonic (predominant) power in the capitalist part of the world, setting the rules on international economic relations. American overseas investments and trade boomed during these decades.

This hegemonic power eventually weakened, eroded both by the economic resurgence of Western Europe and Japan, and by the heavy burden of the arms race against the Soviet Union (a burden that America's capitalist competitors largely escaped). Starting in 1971, the United States began to run up a trade deficit, importing more from other countries than it sold to them. The 1990s saw a partial restoration of American dominance in the global economy, as the United States regained the technological edge from Japan. By the next decade, however, China was challenging the United States for economic influence in many parts of the world. In sum, the global economy in the second decade of the twenty-first century is far more complex than it was after World War II, so America's economic power in the world is now more difficult to deploy.

Private interests have always played a significant role in American foreign economic policy. Labor unions are active, especially in seeking to restrict imports from low-wage nations because they eliminate American jobs. Farm groups press for greater government efforts to promote agricultural exports. But the most influential private force is the corporate sector. Research by political scientists Lawrence R. Jacobs and Benjamin I. Page finds that "internationally oriented business leaders exercise strong, consistent, and perhaps lopsided influence on the makers of U.S. foreign policy."[18]

Individuals in the top decision-making echelon of the national security state have often been recruited into temporary government service from large corporations, investment banks, and corporate law firms.[19] Regardless of economic background, American foreign policy makers have generally subscribed to the proposition that what advances the interests of American corporations and banks abroad advances the American national interest. In the globalized economy of the post–Cold War era, business interests have become even more important players in American foreign policy than before.

It is difficult to disentangle economic interests from political interests in the history of U.S. foreign policy. Consider two cases concerning the CIA: Iran and Chile. In Iran, the CIA's role in putting the shah in power not only established an anticommunist bastion in the Middle East; it also opened up Iran as a profitable field of operations for American oil companies. In Chile, American corporations were just as zealous as President Richard Nixon and National Security Adviser Henry Kissinger in getting rid of President Salvador Allende, a socialist. Fearful that Allende might nationalize their properties, the International Telephone and Telegraph Corporation and other American businesses offered the CIA $1.5 million for its covert campaign against him.[20]

That American foreign policy has often served corporate interests abroad leads critics to look for economic motives underneath the national security rationales advanced by government officials. Some opponents of President Bush's war in Iraq argued that it was not undertaken to protect the United States or to advance the cause of democracy in the Middle East, but rather was a war for oil.

Foreign Policy and Public Opinion

Until recently, scholars presented a picture of American public opinion in foreign policy that was closely in line with the perspective of elite democracy. Their studies suggested that the mass of Americans lacked interest in or knowledge of foreign affairs, were subject to emotional reactions to foreign events, and tended to defer to elites, especially presidents, in the determination of foreign policies. This view implied that it was fortunate for U.S. foreign policy that elites had the upper hand and that ordinary citizens had relatively little influence.

Further research by political scientists has altered this picture substantially.[21] The view of public opinion that has emerged is more favorable to the perspective of popular democracy. Although public knowledge of foreign affairs may fall short of the standard held by foreign policy experts, the newest research shows public opinion about foreign policy to be sensible and stable. The public responds rationally to the information it receives. It rallies behind a president who monopolizes the dissemination of information in a foreign crisis. But it may turn against the White House when alternative sources of information become available.

A CLOSER LOOK

Selling Wars

Survey research suggests that ordinary citizens are more cautious than are foreign policy elites in sending American forces to fight in wars overseas. Perhaps this is because it is the elite managers of the national security state who plan the wars, while it is ordinary citizens who pay for them with their money and their blood. The American public quickly rallies behind the government when the nation comes under attack, as happened after Pearl Harbor and September 11, 2001. But when the threat appears distant and the connection to vital American interests is murky, war has to be sold to the public.

In the Gulf War of 1991, the first President Bush mobilized Americans for war by pointing to the demonic nature of the enemy. Saddam Hussein, the Iraqi dictator, was a brutal leader who had committed an act of naked aggression against his neighbor, tiny but oil-rich Kuwait. However, the danger that Saddam posed to American national interests was unclear. To convince Americans that this was a righteous as well as a necessary war, the Bush administration stoked the public's sense of moral outrage. For this task, nothing was as useful as babies.

A shocking story of Iraqi brutality helped persuade many Americans that the nation had to go to war to rescue the suffering people of Kuwait. A fifteen-year-old Kuwaiti girl, identified only by her first name, Nayirah, appeared before a congressional caucus and related in a tearful voice how she had witnessed Iraqi soldiers take Kuwaiti babies out of their hospital incubators and leave them on the floor to die. The incubator story was widely repeated by President Bush and other advocates of war. After the war, it was revealed that Nayirah was in fact the daughter of Kuwait's ambassador to the United States and that the incubator story had been devised by an American public-relations firm in the pay of the

425

Kuwaiti government. Reporters seeking evidence of the incubator tragedy found none and concluded that this notorious Iraqi atrocity had never happened.

Eleven years later, the second President Bush confronted the same evil dictator. Having come under attack on September 11, Americans were now more receptive to fighting a large-scale war abroad. On the other hand, there was no obvious act of aggression to charge against Saddam this time. Weakened by United Nations sanctions, his military forces had not threatened anyone in a decade. To mobilize the American public for a second war against Saddam, the second President Bush needed stronger medicine than moral outrage; he needed to sell this war with fear.

The Bush administration's principal argument for war was that Saddam's regime already possessed terrible biological and chemical weapons and was frantically attempting to obtain nuclear weapons. These WMD, the administration claimed, must not be permitted to be distributed to terrorist groups or used by Saddam against the United States or its friends. To back up this argument, Bush and his aides made a number of dubious claims. For example, the president told the public that according to a report by the International Atomic Energy Agency (IAEA), Iraq was six months away from developing nuclear weapons, and then said, "I don't know what more evidence we need." What the IAEA actually reported was that there was no evidence that Iraq was currently manufacturing such weapons or even had the physical capability or materials to produce them. The president also told the nation that Iraq was developing unmanned aircraft that could deliver chemical or biological weapons against U.S. targets. He neglected to mention that the unmanned aircraft did not have the range to reach Europe, much less cross the Atlantic Ocean.

The Bush administration also tried to link Saddam, a secular leader, to Al Qaeda, the fanatical religious organization that had carried out the September 11 attacks. If these two evil forces were in cahoots, eliminating Saddam would be a major victory in the war on terror. The administration's prime piece of evidence for a connection was the allegation that Mohammed Atta, the ringleader for the September 11 plot, had met with an Iraqi intelligence officer in Prague, Czech Republic, in April 2001. However, when the FBI investigated the story, it found that Atta had been in Virginia at the time of the supposed meeting. Further, the president of the Czech Republic informed the U.S. government that his intelligence agents had also discredited the story. Nevertheless, Bush officials continued to use the allegation to suggest a link between Saddam and September 11, while carefully hedging their remarks with the claim that the veracity of the story had not yet been conclusively determined.

There is an old saying: "In war, truth is the first casualty." The same seems to be the case for selling the public on the war in the first place. No decision is as critical for a democracy as a decision on war or peace. Unless the military threat to the nation is imminent, no occasion so demands a genuine democratic debate. Instead, what Americans usually get from their leaders in this situation is more akin to false advertising.

Sources: John R. MacArthur, *Second Front: Censorship and Propaganda in the Gulf War* (New York: Hill and Wang, 1992); Sheldon Rampton and John Stauber, *Weapons of Mass Deception: The Uses of Propaganda in Bush's War on Iraq* (New York: Tarcher/Penguin, 2003); Louis Fisher, *Presidential War Power*, 2nd ed. revised (Lawrence: University Press of Kansas, 2004).

The public seldom has a direct impact on *specific* foreign policy decisions. But it can establish a climate of opinion that policy makers have to take into account. During the era of Cold War consensus, elites enjoyed a permissive climate for dispatching American troops to overseas conflicts. In the 1970s and 1980s, however, the majority of Americans were affected by a "Vietnam syndrome," an apprehension about sending troops abroad that constrained decision makers. President Reagan tried to overcome this syndrome with a guaranteed military victory in Grenada. Yet his efforts were not very successful: Public opinion constrained the Reagan administration from sending troops to attack the Sandinista government of Nicaragua and pressured the president to resume arms control negotiations with the Soviet Union.[22]

The first President Bush claimed that he had finally vanquished the Vietnam syndrome in the Persian Gulf War of 1991. Yet public fears about sending American forces "in harm's way" continued to restrict President Clinton's options abroad. For example, his decision to rely exclusively on air power in the Kosovo crisis of 1999 reflected his concern that public opinion would turn sharply against U.S. involvement should there be a significant number of American casualties.

Rather than always deferring to foreign policy elites, public opinion can, if it becomes intense, compel elites to change their policies. Neither the president nor Congress is likely to hold out long once public opinion moves sharply in a new direction. Political scientists Robert Shapiro and Benjamin Page found that when public opinion changed significantly, American foreign policy subsequently changed with it about two-thirds of the time. The more that public unhappiness over American casualties in the war in Vietnam mounted, the faster the president withdrew American forces from the conflict.[23] Growing public unhappiness over the war in Afghanistan similarly put pressure on President Obama to seek a more rapid exit from that conflict.

Foreign Policy and Partisanship

"Politics stops at the water's edge" used to be a popular saying in America. Divided on domestic issues, the two major political parties were expected to mute their differences and collaborate in defending American interests abroad. However, in an era of increasing partisan polarization, U.S. foreign policy is no more exempt than domestic policy from sharp disagreements between Republicans and Democrats.

With some notable exceptions (such as ex-Republican congressman Ron Paul of Texas), today's activists in the two parties hold contrary views on fundamental matters of international relations. Their differences can be summarized as follows:

1. Views of the U.S. role in world affairs: Republicans view American motives as uniquely virtuous and ascribe problems abroad as stemming from the evil motives of adversaries. While hailing American democratic values, Democrats believe that the United States has sometimes acted badly abroad and made matters worse by its own overreaching.

2. Military spending: Although critical of government spending in general, Republicans favor increasing spending on national security. Democrats try to restrain defense spending, believing that a bloated Pentagon budget takes funds away from domestic needs and encourages overreliance on the use of force in international relations.

3. Armed interventions: "Peace through strength" is a Republican motto and suggests that the active use of American military superiority is often the key to resolving problems in global hot spots. Democrats draw from the disasters of Vietnam and Iraq the lesson that military intervention is often an ineffective remedy for problems abroad and carries high costs in both lives and dollars.

4. Diplomacy and negotiations: Republicans are skeptical that talking to foreign adversaries or negotiating international agreements are realistic means to a successful foreign policy. Democrats favor diplomacy as an alternative to force wherever possible and see little risk in engaging diplomatically with even the most hostile regimes.

5. International institutions: Republicans are critical of international institutions, especially the United Nations, because they constrict the freedom of the United States to pursue its own course in international affairs. Democrats place greater hopes in international institutions as vehicles for enhancing global cooperation in addressing shared problems.

The electoral platforms, campaign slogans, and congressional rhetoric of the two parties reflect these fundamental disagreements. Partisan polarization also characterizes the differences in the initial foreign policy approaches of Republican and Democratic presidents. As we will see in the case of Barack Obama, however, the institutions of the national security state and the pressures of the global environment operate to reduce these differences. As a result, there is continuity as well as change in U.S. foreign policy when control of the White House shifts from one party to the other.[24]

Post–Cold War Foreign Policy

In one form or another, *containment* of communism was the U.S. strategy during the Cold War era. What should U.S. strategy be for a post–Cold War period in which no single adversary or problem towered over everything else? Many foreign policy elites and academic specialists proposed new doctrines, but no contender for the position of successor to containment managed to capture a dominant place. The post–Cold War world seemed too complex to be addressed through a single approach.

Compared to the Cold War era, foreign policy in its immediate aftermath seemed far less urgent to the majority of Americans. There was no longer a despised enemy against whom a president could easily rally Americans. There was no longer the threat of attack from a nuclear superpower that had given the subject of national security a life-and-death quality during the Cold War. Most Americans were now reluctant to commit American troops or resources abroad and preferred that the president concentrate instead on making life at home more prosperous and harmonious. The lack of an overarching national security strategy and the diminished public support for presidential activism in international relations were evident in the administration of Bill Clinton.

Critics frequently complained that President Clinton's foreign and defense policies were ad hoc and incoherent, devoid of any strategic vision.[25] Yet two consistent commitments characterized his approach to the world. First, Clinton sought to shift the emphasis of U.S. foreign policy from military power to economic power. Believing that the new measuring stick of national power in an age of globalization is economics, and that America's new rivals are market competitors rather than military adversaries, Clinton was a dedicated apostle of free trade as the key to American economic primacy.

Second, Clinton went further than Cold War predecessors in shaping a foreign policy of **multilateralism**, in which the United States prefers to work in combination with partners in its international endeavors. To Clinton, multilateralism was a matter of genuine belief in growing international interdependence. But it was also a political necessity: in the post–Cold War world, he recognized, the American people were increasingly eager to share with our allies the military and financial burdens of ensuring a peaceful world.

Initially, Clinton was reluctant to use military might in the absence of strong public support and clearly endangered American interests. But with Haiti in 1994, Bosnia in 1995, and Kosovo in 1999, Clinton overrode objections—some of them constitutional—and sent in American forces. These were small-scale military conflicts, primarily fought with air power; remarkably, there was not a single American combat death in Haiti, Bosnia, or Kosovo.

President Clinton also sought out a diplomatic role as a peacemaker. One of his signal foreign policy achievements was his part in fostering a peace agreement between the Catholic and Protestant militants who had long been warring with each other in Northern Ireland. The first president to venture into this thorny conflict, he was able to bring the two sides together in the Easter Sunday pact of 1998. Less successful were his repeated efforts to find a formula for a definitive settlement between Israel and the Palestinians.

September 11 and the Bush Presidency

The post–Cold War period proved to be brief, lasting only from the collapse of the Soviet Union in 1991 to the terrorist attacks on the World Trade Center and Pentagon on September 11, 2001. The horrific events of 9/11 catapulted national security back to the primacy in U.S. politics it had held during the Cold War period. Once again, Americans had a despised enemy in the world. Once again, international affairs took on a life-and-death quality for Americans.

Yet if in the post–September 11 period international affairs have taken on the same kind of urgency as during the Cold War era, U.S. foreign policy after 9/11 has not been marked by the consensus that prevailed during the early years of the Cold War. During the presidency of George W. Bush, views of American foreign policy were as polarized as views on domestic issues.

George W. Bush and American Foreign Policy

Unlike his father, George W. Bush entered the White House without much experience or expertise in international affairs. More than most modern presidents, he was highly dependent on his top foreign policy advisers. And most of these advisers held strongly partisan views of international relations.

From the day he entered the White House, President Bush opposed the multilateral approach that Clinton had favored. The most controversial early foreign policy actions of the new administration were its repudiation of international agreements. President Bush rejected the Kyoto Protocol on global warming, the Comprehensive Test Ban Treaty on nuclear weapons, and a Biological Weapons Protocol that enforced compliance with a treaty banning biological weapons. His administration also withdrew the United States from the Antiballistic Missile Treaty in order to develop a national missile defense program. Critics described the basis of Bush's foreign

429

policy as **unilateralism**—that is, the United States looks to its own interests and goes its own way regardless of the concerns of other nations.

September 11 and the War on Terror. The focus of Bush's foreign policy was altered by Al Qaeda's horrifying attacks on the American homeland on September 11, 2001. National security issues that had preoccupied the administration up to that date, such as the challenge of China, were shelved as Bush proclaimed a global war against terrorism as the defining purpose of his presidency. With overwhelming support at home and from many nations around the globe, the president launched a military campaign that toppled the Taliban regime in Afghanistan. However, relying primarily on Afghan fighters rather than American troops, Bush's Pentagon failed to capture the top leadership of Al Qaeda, including its chief, Osama bin Laden.

In his State of the Union address in January 2002, Bush called for an expansion of the war on terror beyond the fight against the Al Qaeda terror network, focusing on three nation-states—North Korea, Iran, and Iraq—that he depicted as "an axis of evil." This dramatic phrase signaled that the United States under President Bush would now take on the mission of ridding the world of its most immoral and dangerous regimes. Apart from Great Britain, most of America's traditional allies were disturbed by Bush's return to unilateralism. Their unease would only grow once the Bush administration prepared to turn its rhetoric into reality.

The Bush administration introduced a new national security doctrine in September 2002. According to this new doctrine, terrorist groups or the rogue nations that might assist them or use WMD on their own accord could not be contained in the old way.[26] Consequently, the United States had to be prepared to wage **preventive war**: "The greater the threat, the greater is the risk of inaction—and the more compelling the case for taking anticipatory action to defend ourselves—even if uncertainty remains as to the time and place of the enemy's attack. To forestall or prevent such hostile acts by our adversaries, the United States will, if necessary, act preemptively."[27]

War in Iraq. Al Qaeda had struck the United States on September 11, 2001, but it was Iraq that was to become the centerpiece of President Bush's war on terror. As the Bush administration geared up for an invasion of Iraq, U.S. allies such as France and Germany, and massive protest demonstrations at home and around the world, tried to head off war. Dismissing their objections, the president began the war in March 2003, and within a month American forces were in Baghdad and Saddam Hussein had gone into hiding. On May 1, 2003, a triumphant commander in chief, dressed in flight gear, appeared on the aircraft carrier USS *Lincoln* to announce that the military effort in Iraq was a "mission accomplished!"

However, the proclamation was premature, and the mission was far from accomplished. The first major problem that Bush faced in the occupation of Iraq was that his premises for this preventive war proved to be false. Despite extensive efforts by American search teams, no WMD were found in Iraq. Increasing evidence emerged in the United States that the Bush administration had exaggerated ambiguous intelligence data about WMD before the war in order to convince the American public that it was in danger.[28] (See this chapter's A Closer Look box.)

A second—and even larger—problem was that the occupation and reconstruction of Iraq proved far more difficult than the invasion had been. Members of the administration, especially Vice President Cheney, confidently predicted that American armed forces would be welcomed by the Iraqi people as liberators. Misled by this optimistic assumption, neither the civilian nor the military officials in charge of the war effort engaged in systematic planning for what the United States needed to do to put Iraq back together again. Expecting that American forces could be quickly withdrawn from Iraq, they were unprepared for what turned out to be one of the longest wars in American history.[29]

Former supporters of Saddam's secular regime joined with Islamic fundamentalists and nationalists in an insurgency whose size and ferocity stunned Americans. As the war in Iraq mushroomed, Iraqi civilians and soldiers, and American troops suffered heavy casualties. Efforts to persuade Iraqis that U.S. motives were benevolent were further undercut by revelations that American military personnel at the Abu Ghraib prison had sexually humiliated and tortured detainees.[30]

During Bush's second term, the conflict grew even grimmer, with a bloody civil war erupting between the major Islamic sects in Iraq, Sunnis and Shiites. A majority of Americans had come to believe that the war was a mistake, and President Bush's public approval

ratings sank. The security situation improved in 2007–2008, as an increase in American troops and a shift of former Sunni insurgents to the American side brought a reduction in violence. Yet after six years of war under Bush, the Iraqi government was still struggling to unite the country, while American military forces were severely overstretched. Meanwhile, with the bulk of U.S. armed forces committed to Iraq, the security situation worsened in Afghanistan, which the Bush administration had largely neglected since fall 2001.

Barack Obama and U.S. Foreign Policy

By the time of the 2008 presidential election, President Bush's national-security strategy was in tatters. His military venture in Iraq had been launched on misguided premises. Equally important, it was symptomatic of a deeper disorder, as international relations scholar Andrew Bacevich suggested. Bush had aimed to manage foreign affairs to American advantage by relying on the superiority of U.S. armed forces. Yet as Bacevich observed, the president was reluctant to ask Americans for the kinds of sacrifices—military service or higher taxes—that distant wars demanded. As the conflicts in Iraq and Afghanistan severely strained the armed forces and drove up the national debt, what were increasingly apparent were the limits rather than the extent of American global power.[31]

Barack Obama had been a critic of the war in Iraq from the beginning, and he was more clear-eyed than his predecessor in comprehending the limits on American power that Bush's war had revealed. Running for president, Obama spoke of a fundamental transformation in U.S. foreign policy. He pledged to set the United States on a new global course and restore American prestige, which Bush had squandered in Iraq. In office, however, Obama has encountered additional limits on U.S. foreign policy that he had not foreseen.

431

Obama's Worldview

Consistent with the contemporary partisan polarization in foreign-policy perspectives, Obama's worldview is, in many respects, the opposite of Bush's. Rejecting Bush's unilateralism, Obama favors multilateral partnerships with friendly nations and diplomatic dialogues with unfriendly ones. Rejecting Bush's emphasis on preventive war, Obama promotes a strategy that "skillfully uses, balances, and integrates all elements of American power—our military and diplomacy, our intelligence and law enforcement, our economy and the power of our moral example."[32] Rejecting Bush's near-exclusive focus on a global struggle against terrorism, Obama has insisted that the United States must move simultaneously to cope with a diverse array of global challenges.[33]

Despite his disagreements with Bush, Obama shares with his predecessor a belief that the United States has the responsibility to exercise global leadership. Moreover, as commander in chief, the safeguarding of the nation from military or terrorist threats remains his highest priority. Obama had little background in military affairs when he ran for president, a fact that his electoral opponents often used against him, but in office all eyes have been upon his attempt to convey the nation's—and his own—strength.

Obama as Commander in Chief

Contrary to the predictions of his opponents, Obama has enjoyed some success as commander in chief. His greatest accomplishment has been one that eluded President Bush: On May 1, 2011, a contingent of U.S. Navy Seals stormed Osama bin Laden's hideout in Pakistan and killed the leader of Al Qaeda. Obama has also outdone his predecessor in thinning the ranks of Al Qaeda leaders below bin Laden, chiefly through missile attacks by remote-controlled aerial drones.

President Obama has succeeded as well in bringing to a close America's long war in Iraq. Fulfilling one of his chief campaign promises, the president withdrew all American forces from that country by the end of 2011. This initial success may, however, prove fleeting if the Iraqi government cannot achieve political stability and the country falls back into sectarian warfare. An additional military success was scored in Libya in 2011, where American forces, working in collaboration with European allies, helped bring down the regime of dictator Muammar Qaddafi.

Obama's most problematic military undertaking has been in Afghanistan. Faced with urgent requests from his military commanders, the president increased the number of U.S. troops in Afghanistan late in 2009. This "surge" in American military strength led to gains in taking territory back from Taliban insurgents. Yet the deeper dilemmas for U.S. foreign policy, such as widespread corruption among Afghan government officials, were hardly resolved by Obama's fresh commitments of American support. From the start, the president had set an upper limit to the number of U.S. troops he would send to Afghanistan, and by 2012, with the situation stalemated on the battlefield and the conflict increasingly unpopular back home, the administration had announced plans for an American exit from the Afghan war.

Obama as Diplomat

Obama has attempted to shift the emphasis in U.S. foreign policy from armed force to diplomacy. Ironically, however, his successes have been fewer and his frustrations more abundant in his role as diplomat in chief than in his role as commander in chief.

Obama's diplomacy has won favor in the many countries that had been alienated by the belligerent unilateralism of the Bush administration. The president was a bit embarrassed when his new turn to diplomacy won him the Nobel Peace Prize in 2009 before he had actually accomplished much of anything on the world stage.

In his overseas travels, Obama has delivered a number of important speeches that highlighted changed priorities in U.S. foreign policy. In Prague, the Czech Republic, he laid out the visionary goal of a world without nuclear weapons. In Cairo, Egypt, he sought greater understanding between Americans and the Muslim world. In Africa, Latin America, and Russia as well, Obama has staked out the terms for more harmonious relationships.[34]

More often, however, there has been little to show, at least so far, for Obama's belief that diplomatic dialogue can produce significant progress in resolving global challenges. The president's diplomatic team has pursued engagement with such hostile regimes as Iran and North Korea, yet both have rebuffed American positions and continued to pursue their nuclear ambitions. The drive to make headway in solving a problem that has bedeviled a long string of American presidents—the Israel-Palestinian conflict—has stalled. On an issue that Obama highlighted in campaigning for the presidency—the threat to the planet of global warming—the United States has remained a laggard in joining international efforts, although in this case, a limitation on the president has been resistance from Republicans in Congress.[35]

The Limits of U.S. Foreign Policy

Observers have suggested that Obama has been less able to change the *practice* of U.S. foreign policy than the principles. Indeed, it is not hard to find continuities in practice between the foreign policies of Bush and Obama: "continuing indefinite detention [of suspected terrorists] and the use of military tribunals; citing 'state secrets' privileges to block judicial review of counterterrorism policies; continuing intrusive domestic surveillance programs; and authorizing the CIA and the U.S. military to execute extra-judicial targeted assassinations."[36] Although one of Obama's first executive orders as president was to close the prison at Guantanamo Bay in Cuba, which the Bush administration used to hold terrorist suspects, the order was never implemented due to opposition from Congress and the public.

Despite the frustrations that Obama has at times encountered in carrying out his foreign policy, the American public has viewed him more favorably in this area than it did his predecessor. In public opinion surveys, Obama earns higher marks for his national security policies than for his domestic policies. The public appears to care more about his successes in combating Al Qaeda than about his failures elsewhere. Some Americans simply may be relieved that at a time of economic crisis, and by contrast to Bush's disaster in Iraq, nothing terribly bad has happened in U.S. foreign policy during Obama's presidency.

Conclusion: A More Democratic Foreign Policy? ★ ★ ★

Frightened by the unprecedented vulnerability of the homeland to terrorist violence, most Americans initially looked to the White House for safety and security. However, once the war in Iraq became increasingly unpopular, habits of deference declined and the longstanding democratic debate over U.S. foreign policy was resumed.

Contrary to claims from some political elites that dissent gives comfort to America's enemies, it is all the more crucial at a moment of crisis that the popular democratic tradition, which questions elite dominance over foreign policy, be maintained. Popular democrats have long argued that American strength in the world depends on a healthy economy and society, and on the vigor of democratic life. They have believed that America should seek cooperative relations with other nations and support democratic progress around the globe. They have warned of aggressive uses of military force and emphasized the distortions it can introduce into the conduct of America's international relations.

Popular democrats seek to widen the democratic debate over foreign policy. To open up this debate, the secretive habits of the national security state, including excessive classification of information and covert action, must be challenged. Foreign policy experts in the executive branch and the Pentagon must not monopolize the discussion; voices in Congress and in citizen groups also must be heard. Because the United States must speak to the rest of the world in a clear fashion and must defeat the threat of terrorism, presidential leadership in foreign policy will remain necessary. But in the post–September 11 world, presidents should not be the sole masters of foreign policy. Their approach to the world should emerge from a democratic dialogue over the goals and instruments of American foreign policy.

Reader's Guide

Critical Thinking Questions

1. Looking at the history of American foreign policy, do you see a principled commitment to the promotion of democracy, a mythical belief in America's uniquely virtuous role in world politics, or a self-interested pursuit of national power and wealth?

2. How and why have the Pentagon and the intelligence agencies come to play a larger role in shaping U.S. foreign policy than the Department of State?

3. Is the American public too preoccupied with domestic affairs and too ignorant of developments abroad to play a significant part in determining U.S. foreign policy?

4. In coping with the international threat of terrorism, what are the advantages and disadvantages of unilateralist versus multilateral strategies?

Key Word Definition

isolationism   The idea that apart from commercial relations, the United States should stay out of the political and military quarrels of the rest of the world; the core principle of American foreign and defense policy from the founding until World War II.

expansion   Nineteenth-century activities by the United States to extend the nation to the Pacific Ocean and to gain influence in Latin America and Asia.

Cold War   A worldwide political, economic, and ideological struggle between the United States and the Soviet Union that lasted from 1945 to 1989.

national security state   A complex of executive, military, and secret powers that shaped American international relations in the Cold War and largely excluded Congress and the public from decisions about the country's security.

North Atlantic Treaty Organization (NATO)   The military alliance among the United States, Canada, and the Western European states, created to oppose Soviet aggression in the Cold War period.

containment   A Cold War policy, also known as the Truman Doctrine, of a global American struggle to restrict the spread of communism.

National Security Council (NSC)   A governmental body created in 1947 to advise the president and coordinate foreign and defense policy.

national security adviser   The personal counselor to the president in foreign policy and defense matters.

Department of State   The cabinet department that is the traditional organ of American diplomacy and is headed by a secretary.

Department of Defense   The cabinet department that coordinates and controls American military activities and is headed by a civilian secretary.

Joint Chiefs of Staff (JCS)   A body composed of the commanding officer of each military service, and headed by a chair, that conveys the military's point of view to the president and the secretary of defense.

military-industrial complex   The political alliance between the Pentagon and the corporations that manufacture its arms.

Central Intelligence Agency (CIA)   The chief government intelligence-gathering agency, which has two primary functions: espionage and covert action.

covert action   Secret CIA activities that cannot be traced to the U.S. government.

multilateralism   An approach to foreign policy in which the U.S. prefers to work in partnership with allies in its international endeavors.

unilateralism   An approach to foreign policy in which the U.S. goes its own way and looks to its own interests regardless of the concerns of other countries.

preventive war   A military conflict initiated against a potential future enemy in the absence of any immediate threat.

ENDNOTES

CHAPTER 1

1. Joseph A. Schumpeter, *Capitalism, Socialism and Democracy*, 3rd ed. (New York: Harper & Row, 1950), 269. In Part IV, Schumpeter makes one of the classic defenses of elite democracy. For critiques of the elite theory of democracy from a popular democratic viewpoint, see Jack L. Walker, "A Critique of the Elitist Theory of Democracy," *American Political Science Review* 60 (1966): 285–95; and Peter Bachrach, *The Theory of Democratic Elitism: A Critique* (Boston: Little, Brown, 1967).

2. The most influential political scientist who has written on the ideas of elite and popular democracy is Robert Dahl. Dahl began his career by defending a version of elite democracy in *A Preface to Democratic Theory* (Chicago: University of Chicago Press, 1956) and in *Who Governs? Democracy and Power in an American City* (New Haven, CT: Yale University Press, 1961). In his later works, Dahl shifted dramatically to a more popular democratic position. See *A Preface to Economic Democracy* (Berkeley and Los Angeles: University of California Press, 1985) and *Democracy and Its Critics* (New Haven, CT: Yale University Press, 1989).

3. See Frank M. Bryan, *Real Democracy: The New England Town Meeting and How It Works* (Chicago: University of Chicago Press, 2004).

4. See Ralph Ketcham, ed., *The Anti-Federalist Papers and the Constitutional Convention Debates* (New York: New American Library, 1986), 213.

5. We are not the first to present a cyclical view of American politics in which participatory upsurges are followed by periods of elite consolidation. See Arthur M. Schlesinger Jr., *Paths to the Present* (New York: Macmillan, 1949); Arthur M. Schlesinger Jr., *The Cycles of American History* (Boston: Houghton Mifflin, 1986); and Albert O. Hirschman, *Shifting Involvements: Private Interest and Public Action* (Princeton, NJ: Princeton University Press, 1982).

6. The views of the Tea Party are not simple or consensual. For a sophisticated discussion of what the Tea Party stands for, see Theda Scocpol and Vanessa Williamson, *The Tea Party and the Remaking of Republican Conservatism* (New York: Oxford University Press, 2012).

7. See Walter Dean Burnham, *Critical Elections and the Mainsprings of American Politics* (New York: W. W. Norton, 1970).

8. For an insightful argument that if Jefferson were alive today he would favor a strong federal government, see Lew Daly, "What Would Jefferson Do? How Limited Government Got Turned Upside Down," *Dissent* (Summer 2008): 59–66.

9. George Will, "In Defense of Nonvoting," *Newsweek* (October 10, 1983): 96.

CHAPTER 2

1. Gordon S. Wood, *The Radicalism of the American Revolution* (New York: Alfred A. Knopf, 1992), 11–92.

2. Jon Butler, *Becoming America: The Revolution Before 1776* (Cambridge, MA: Harvard University Press, 2000).

3. For an excellent account of this political dynamic, see Pauline Maier, *From Resistance to Revolution: Colonial Radicals and the Development of American Opposition to Britain, 1765–1776* (New York: Vintage, 1974).

4. Gary B. Nash, *The Unknown American Revolution: The Unruly Birth of Democracy and the Struggle to Create America* (New York: Viking, 2005), xvi.

5. Sidney Hook, ed., *The Essential Thomas Paine* (New York: New American Library, 1969), 33, 48.

6. On republicanism and the origins of the American Revolution, see Bernard Bailyn, *The Ideological Origins of the American Revolution* (Cambridge, MA: Harvard University Press, 1967); and Gordon S. Wood, *The Creation of the American Republic: 1776–1787* (New York: W. W. Norton, 1972), 3–124.

7. On the place of the Declaration of Independence in American political thought, see especially two books by Garry Wills: *Inventing America: Jefferson's Declaration of Independence* (New York: Vintage, 1978) and *Lincoln at Gettysburg: The Words That Remade America* (New York: Simon & Schuster, 1992).

8. Roy P. Basler, ed., *The Collected Works of Abraham Lincoln*, vol. 3 (New Brunswick, NJ: Rutgers University Press, 1953), 375.

9. The Declaration of Independence was creatively used by Elizabeth Cady Stanton to advance the cause of women and by Frederick Douglass, W. E. B. Du Bois, and Martin Luther King Jr. to promote equality for African Americans.

10. On the state constitutions of 1776, see Wood, *Creation of the American Republic*, 127–255.

11. On the economic legislation of the 1780s, see Merrill Jensen, *The New Nation: A History of the United States during the Confederation, 1781–1789* (New York: Vintage, 1950), 302–26.

12. Jackson Turner Main, "Government by the People: The American Revolution and the Democratization of the Legislatures," in *The Reinterpretation of the American Revolution, 1763–1789*, ed. Jack P. Greene (New York: Harper & Row, 1968), 322–38.

13. Marvin Meyers, ed., *The Mind of the Founder: Sources of the Political Thought of James Madison*, rev. ed. (Hanover, NH: University Press of New England, 1981), 62. For a penetrating analysis of Madison as an elite democratic thinker, see Richard K. Matthews, *If Men Were Angels: James Madison and the Heartless Empire of Reason* (Lawrence: University Press of Kansas, 1995). For an impressive presentation of the opposing position that Madison was something of a popular democrat, see Lance Banning, *The Sacred Fire of Liberty: James Madison and the Founding of the Federal Republic* (Ithaca, NY: Cornell University Press, 1995).

14. Among the many treatments of the Constitutional Convention and the political system it shaped, one of the richest in insights is Jack N. Rakove, *Original Meanings: Politics and Ideas in the Making of the Constitution* (New York: Alfred A. Knopf, 1996).

15. David Brian Robertson, *The Constitution and America's Destiny* (New York: Cambridge University Press, 2005).

16. Alfred A. Young, "Conservatives, the Constitution, and the 'Spirit of Accommodation,'" in *How Democratic Is the Constitution?*, eds. Robert A. Goldwin and William A. Schambra (Washington, DC: American Enterprise Institute, 1980), 118, 138.

17. Max Farrand, ed., *The Records of the Federal Convention of 1787*, vol. 1 (New Haven, CT: Yale University Press, 1937), 65, 66.

18. Charles A. Beard, *An Economic Interpretation of the Constitution* (New York: Macmillan, 1913).

19. Farrand, ed., *Records of the Federal Convention*, vol. 2, 370.

20. See Michael Allen Gillespie and Michael Lienesch, eds., *Ratifying the Constitution* (Lawrence: University Press of Kansas, 1989) and Pauline Maier, *Ratification: The People Debate the Constitution, 1787–1788* (New York: Simon & Schuster, 2010).

21. Saul Cornell, *The Other Founders: Anti-Federalism and the Dissenting Tradition in America: 1788–1828* (Chapel Hill, NC: University of North Carolina Press, 1999), 81.

22. Michael I. Meyerson, *Liberty's Blueprint: How Madison and Hamilton Wrote the Federalist Papers, Defined the Constitution, and Made Democracy Safe for the World* (New York: Basic Books, 2008).

23. Herbert J. Storing, *What the Anti-Federalists Were For* (Chicago: University of Chicago Press, 1981), 72.

24. Clinton Rossiter, ed., *The Federalist Papers* (New York: New American Library, 1961), 79.

25. Ibid., 346.

26. Ibid., 414.

27. On the Anti-federalist conception of virtue, see Storing, *What the Anti-Federalists Were For*, 19–23.

28. Ralph Ketcham, ed., *The Anti-Federalist Papers and the Constitutional Convention Debates* (New York: New American Library, 1986), 202.

29. Rossiter, ed., *Federalist Papers*, 83.

30. See Storing, *What the Anti-Federalists Were For*, 16–23.

31. Herbert J. Storing, ed., *The Anti-Federalist* (Chicago: University of Chicago Press, 1985), 116.

32. Rossiter, ed., *Federalist Papers*, 82.

33. Storing, *What the Anti-Federalists Were For*, 24.

34. Rossiter, ed., *Federalist Papers*, 322.

35. Ketcham, ed., *Anti-Federalist Papers*, 213.

36. Rossiter, ed., *Federalist Papers*, 78.

37. Ibid., 88.

38. Ketcham, ed., *Anti-Federalist Papers*, 207–8.

39. Rossiter, ed., *Federalist Papers*, 314.

40. Merrill D. Peterson, ed., *The Portable Thomas Jefferson* (New York: Penguin, 1975), 417.

41. Jackson Turner Main, *The Anti-Federalists: Critics of the Constitution, 1781–1788* (New York: W. W. Norton, 1974), 133.

42. On Madison and the Bill of Rights, see Robert A. Rutland, *James Madison: The Founding Father* (New York: Macmillan, 1987), 59–65.

43. Cornell, *The Other Founders*, 307.

CHAPTER 3

1. David Brian Robertson, *Federalism and the Making of America* (New York: Routledge, 2012), 34–35.

2. Edward S. Corwin, "The Passing of Dual Federalism," *Virginia Law Review* 36, 1 (1950): 4.

3. *Dred Scott v. Sandford*, 19 How. 393 (1857).

4. *Wabash, St. Louis and Pac. Ry. v. Illinois*, 118 U.S. 557 (1886).

5. *Wabash, St. Louis and Pac. Ry. v. Illinois*, 118 U.S. 557 (1886).

6. *Pollock v. Farmers' Loan and Trust Co.*, 157 U.S. 429 (1895).

7. *Cincinnati N.O. & T.P. Railway Co. v. Interstate Commerce Commission*, 162 U.S. 184 (1896).

8. *Hammer v. Dagenhart*, 247 U.S. 251 (1918).

9. James A. Maxwell, *The Fiscal Impact of Federalism in the United States* (Cambridge, MA: Harvard University Press, 1946), 135.

10. Josephine Chapin Brown, *Public Relief 1929–1939* (New York: Henry Holt, 1940), 14–15, as cited in Frances Fox Piven and Richard A. Cloward, *Regulating the Poor: The Functions of Public Welfare* (New York: Random House, 1971), 47.

11. In fact, in 1929 ten states authorized no outdoor relief at all. (Outdoor relief allows people to stay in their homes while they receive aid, like the present welfare system.) Advisory Commission on Intergovernmental Relations (ACIR), *The Federal Role in the Federal System: The Dynamics* *of Growth, Public Assistance: The Growth of a Federal Function* (Washington, DC: ACIR, 1980), 7.

12. Piven and Cloward, *Regulating the Poor*, 60.

13. Mark I. Gelfand, *A Nation of Cities: The Federal Government and Urban America 1933–1965* (New York: Oxford University Press, 1975), 32–33.

14. *Congressional Record*, vol. 75, 11597, as quoted in Maxwell, *Fiscal Impact*, 138.

15. *Schechter Poultry Corp. v. United States*, 295 U.S. 495 (1935).

16. David B. Robertson and Dennis R. Judd, *The Development of American Public Policy: The Structure of Policy Restraint* (Glenview, IL: Scott, Foresman, 1989), 105.

17. *The United States v. Butler et al.*, 297 U.S. 1 (1936).

18. *New State Ice Company v. Liebmann*, 285 U.S. 262 (1932).

19. *Massachusetts v. Mellon* (1923), as quoted in Robertson and Judd, *American Public Policy*, 138.

20. Maxwell, *Fiscal Impact*, 26.

21. The classic statement of American federalism as regulated by political processes is Herbert Wechsler, "The Political Safeguards of Federalism: The Role of the States in the Selection of the National Government," *Columbia Law Review* 54 (1954): 543–60.

22. Jeffrey L. Pressman and Aaron Wildavsky, *Implementation*, 3rd ed. (Berkeley: University of California Press, 1984).

23. Not all federal grant programs targeted the poor. Many large federal grants, such as those for interstate highways and the construction of sewer and water systems, primarily benefited the suburban middle class.

24. Pressman and Wildavsky, *Implementation*, 75–76.

25. Pew Research Center Survey available at: http://pewresearch.org/pubs/1569/trust-in-government-distrust-discontent-anger-partisan-rancor.

26. John Kincaid, "The Devolution Tortoise and the Centralization Hare," *New England Economic Review* (May–June 1998): 34.

27. Jason DeParle, "Welfare Limits Left Poor Adrift as Recession Hit," *New York Times* (April 8, 2012).

28. Sabrina Tavernise, "Food Stamps Helped Reduce Poverty Rate, Study Finds," *New York Times* (April 10, 2012).

29. Dale Krane, "The Middle Tier in American Federalism: State Government Policy Activism during the Bush Presidency," *Publius* 37, 3 (2007): 453–477. This issue of *Publius* is dedicated to an examination of federalism during the Bush administration.

30. John Dinan, "The State of American Federalism 2007–2008: Resurgent State Influence in the National Policy Process and Continued State Policy Innovation," *Publius* 38, 3 (2008): 389.

31. Charles Fried, "Federalism as a Right to Life, Too," *New York Times* (March 24, 2005).

32. Dick Armey and Matt Kibbe, *Give Us Liberty: A Tea Party Manifesto* (New York: Harper Collins, 2010).

33. We rely heavily in this section on Timothy J. Conlan and Paul L. Posner, "Inflection Point? Federalism and the Obama Administration," *Publius* 41, 3 (2011): 421–46.

34. Ibid., 424.

35. Ibid., 438.

36. For information on the Tenth Amendment Center, see http://tenthamendmentcenter.com/tag/federalism/.

37. For a critical analysis of *Bush v. Gore*, see Alan M. Dershowitz, *Supreme Injustice: How the High Court Hijacked Election 2000* (New York: Oxford University Press, 2001).

38. *United States v. Lopez*, 115 S. Ct. 1624 (1995).

39. David J. Barron, "A Localist Critique of the New Federalism," *Duke Law Journal* 51 (2001): 377–433.

40. National Conference of State Legislatures, Budgets and Revenues Committee, *Mandate Monitor* 6, 1 (April 8, 2008).

41. National Association of State Fiscal Officers, *2010 State Expenditure Report: Examining Fiscal 2009–2011 State Spending* (Washington, DC: Author, 2011), 45.

42. Christopher W. Hoene and Michael A. Pagano, "Fend-for-Yourself Federalism: The Impact of Federal and State Deficits on America's Cities," *Government Finance Review* (October 2003): 36–42.

43. Elizabeth C. McNichol and Iris Lay, "29 States Faced Total Budget Shortfall of at Least $48 Billion," Center on Budget and Policy Priorities; available at: www.cbpp.org/1-15-08sfp.htm (accessed October 8, 2008).

44. Robertson, *Federalism and the Making of America*, 2.

45. Barron, "A Localist Critique," 379.

46. Robert S. Erickson, Gerald C. Wright, and John P. McIver, *Statehouse Democracy: Public Opinion and Policy in the American States* (New York: Cambridge University Press, 1993).

47. V. O. Key Jr., *Southern Politics in State and Nation*, new ed. (Knoxville: University of Tennessee Press, 1984).

48. Steven Greenhouse, "Raising the Floor on Pay," *New York Times* (April 10, 2012).

49. Quoted ibid.

50. For an insightful analysis of how federal laws that require disclosure of information can empower citizens, see Archon Fung, Mary Graham, and David Weil, *Full Disclosure: The Perils and Promise of Transparency* (New York: Cambridge University Press, 2007).

51. Paul Peterson, *The Price of Federalism* (Washington, DC: The Brookings Institution, 1995), 144.

52. David B. Robertson and Dennis R. Judd, *The Development of American Public Policy* (Glenview, IL: Scott, Foresman, 1989), 380.

53. Gerald Frug, "Beyond Regional Government," *Harvard Law Review* 115 (2002): 1763–836.

54. Michael C. Dorf and Charles F. Sabel, "A Constitution of Democratic Experimentalism," *Columbia Law Review* 98, 2 (March 1998): 267–473.

CHAPTER 4

1. This is after taxes and including government payments such as Social Security and unemployment insurance. Congressional Budget Office: Trends in the Distribution of Household Income Between 1979 and 2007. October 2011, ix. Accessed March 21, 2012. http://www.cbo.gov/publication/42729.

2. "The World's Biggest Private Companies," *Forbes* (April 2011). Accessed March 21, 2012. http://www.forbes.com/global2000/list/.

3. Liza Featherstone, *Selling Women Short: The Landmark Battle for Workers' Rights at Wal-Mart* (New York: Basic Books, 2004), 218.

4. Michael Barbaro, "Wal-Mart's Latest Special: 6% Raises at Some Stores," *New York Times* (August 8, 2006).

5. Moira Herbst, "The Costco Challenge: An Alternative to Wal-Martization?" *Working Life* (July 5, 2005), Labor Research Association Online (www.workinglife.org).

6. Bob Ortega, *In Sam We Trust: The Untold Story of Sam Walton and How Wal-Mart Is Devouring America* (New York: Random House, 1998), 349.

7. Featherstone, *Selling Women Short*, 7, 128–9.

8. Ehrenreich's experiences in the underbelly of the American labor market are detailed in *Nickel and Dimed: On (Not) Getting By in America* (New York: Metropolitan Books, 2001).

9. Rebecca Blumenstein and Louis Lee, "The Changing Lot of the Hourly Worker," *Wall Street Journal* (August 28, 1997).

10. Featherstone, *Selling Women Short*, 147.

11. Sam Walton with John Huey, *Made in America: My Story* (New York: Bantam, 1992).

12. Featherstone, *Selling Women Short*, 10.

13. Ortega, *In Sam We Trust*, 236–40.

14. For information and advice on how to fight Walmart, go to the website http://www.sprawl-busters.com/.

15. See Larry M. Bartels, *Unequal Democracy: The Political Economy of the New Gilded Age* (New York: Princeton University Press, 2008).

16. Charles Lindblom, *Politics and Markets: The World's Political and Economic Systems* (New York: Basic Books, 1977), chap. 13.

17. Milton Friedman, *Capitalism and Freedom* (Chicago: University of Chicago Press, 1962), 23.

18. R. H. Tawney, *Equality* (London: Allen & Unwin, 1931).

19. The story of the Meyerses is taken from Gary Rivlin, *Broke, USA* (New York: Harper, 2010), Prologue.

20. U.S. Department of Housing and Urban Development, *Report to Congress on the Root Causes of the Foreclosure Crisis* (Washington, DC: Author, 2010).

21. Jan Hatzius and Michael A. Marschoun, "Home Prices and Credit Losses: Projections and Policy Options." Goldman Sachs Global Economics Paper 177 (2009).

22. For a synthesis of the research on the effects of foreclosures, see Thomas G. Kingsley, Robin Smith, and David Price, *The Impacts of Foreclosures on Families and Communities: A Report Prepared for the Open Society Institute* (Washington, DC: Urban Institute, 2009).

23. Our account of the causes of the foreclosure epidemic and financial meltdown is based on Daniel Immergluck, *Foreclosed: High-Risk Lending, Deregulation, and the Undermining of America's Mortgage Market* (Ithaca, New York: Cornell University Press, 2009) and Richard A. Posner, *A Failure of Capitalism: The Crisis of '08 and the Descent into Depression* (Cambridge, MA: Harvard University Press, 2009).

24. The Obama Administration did pass the $75 billion Home Affordable Modification Program (HAMP) that was designed to help 7–9 million households avoid foreclosure by modifying their mortgages. As of this writing, however, less than a million households had actually been helped and much of the money was unspent.

25. See Thomas Frank, *Pity the Billionaire: The Hard-Times Swindle and the Unlikely Comeback of the Right* (New York: Metropolitan, 2012).

26. Ted Nace, *Gangs of America: The Rise of Corporate Power and the Disabling of Democracy* (San Francisco: Berrett-Koehler, 2003), 16–17.

27. Ehrenreich, *Nickel and Dimed*, 210.

28. Lindblom, *Politics and Markets*, 356.

29. Lawrence Mishel, Jared Bernstein, and Sylvia Allegretto, *The State of Working America 2006/2007* (Ithaca, NY: Cornell University Press, 2007), 260–1.

30. See Jeremy Rifkin and Randy Barber, *The North Will Rise Again: Pensions, Power and Politics in the 1980s* (Boston: Beacon, 1979); Richard Ippolito, *Pensions, Economics and Public Policy* (Homewood, IL: Dow Jones–Irwin, 1986).

31. Quoted in Leslie Wayne, "Shareholders Who Answer to a Higher C.E.O.," *New York Times* (February 19, 2005).

32. For a survey of popular democratic ideas on corporate governance, see Lee Drutman and Charlie Cray, *The People's Business: Controlling Corporations and Restoring Democracy* (San Francisco: Berrett-Koehler, 2004), chap. 3.

33. Two of the most important works on the function of the modern corporation are Gardiner Means and Adolph Berle, *The Corporation and Private Property* (New York: Macmillan, 1948); and John Kenneth Galbraith, *The New Industrial State* (Boston: Houghton Mifflin, 1985).

34. Lindblom, *Politics and Markets*, 154–5.

35. *Advertising Age* (August 5, 2008); accessed at adage.com/datacenter/article?article_id=127791.

36. Drutman and Cray, *The People's Business*, 264.

37. Juliet B. Schor, *The Overspent American: Upscaling, Downshifting, and the New Consumer* (New York: Basic Books, 1998), 78. For a provocative critical analysis of our consumer culture, go to www.adbusters.org, or buy a copy of the magazine *Adbusters* (with no ads, of course).

38. Richard J. Barnet, *Global Reach: The Power of Multinational Corporations* (New York: Simon & Schuster, 1974).

39. William Greider, *One World, Ready or Not: The Manic Logic of Global Capitalism* (New York: Touchstone, 1997), 22.

40. See Louis Uchitelle and N. R. Kleinfield, "On the Battlefields of Business, Millions of Casualties," *New York Times* (March 3, 1996), A1; Jeremy Rifkin, *The End of Work: The Decline of the Global Labor Force and the Dawn of the Post-Market Era* (New York: G. P. Putnam Sons, 1995), part II.

41. As of July, 2008, according to the World Trade Organization website (www.wto.org).

42. For a vivid account of union decline, see Thomas Geoghegan, *Which Side Are You On?* (New York: Plume, 1991). See also Michael Goldfield, *The Decline of Organized Labor in the United States* (Chicago: University of Chicago Press, 1987).

43. According to a poll by Hart Research Associates, 2002, as reported in Margaret Levi, "Organizing Power: The Prospects for an American Labor Movement," *Perspectives on Politics* 1, 1 (March 2003): 51.

44. For a recent update, see Steven Greenhouse, "Labor Board's Detractors See a Bias against Workers," *New York Times* (January 2, 2005).

45. Steven Greenhouse, "Report Faults Laws for Slowing Growth of Unions," *New York Times* (October 24, 2000).

46. David Madland and Nick Bunker, "Unions Make Democracy Work for the Middle Class," Center for American Progress (January 2012).

47. Ibid., 3.

48. Robert B. Reich, *Locked in the Cabinet* (New York: Alfred A. Knopf, 1997), 280–1. For articles about the revival of unions, see David Moberg, "Can Labor Change?" *Dissent* (Winter 1996): 16. See also Steven Greenhouse, "A Union Comeback? Tell It to Sweeney," *New York Times* (June 6, 1997), 4; Roger Waldinger et al., "Justice for Janitors: Organizing in Difficult Times," *Dissent* (Winter 1997): 37–47.

49. All figures are based on data collected by Thomas Piketty and Emmanuel Saez as reported in Jacob S. Hacker and Paul Pierson, *Winner-Take-All Politics: How Washington Made the Rich Richer—And Turned Its Back on the Middle Class* (New York: Simon & Schuster, 2010).

50. See Michael W. Cox and Richard Alm, *Myths of Rich and Poor* (New York: Basic Books, 1999).

51. The human development, or "capabilities," approach provides an alternative to viewing human well being solely on the basis of income or wealth. For an overview, see Martha C. Nussbaum, *Creating Capabilities: The Human Development Approach* (Cambridge, MA: Harvard University Press, 2011).

52. For these reasons, even middle-class families often have trouble making ends meet. See Elizabeth Warren and Amilia Warren Tyagi, *The Two-Income Trap: Why Middle-Class Mothers and Fathers Are Going Broke* (New York: Basic Books, 2003).

53. See http://www.geargather.org/profiles/blogs/your-driving-costs-from-aaa.

54. For a synthesis of the considerable research on the negative effects of high levels of inequality, see Richard Wilkinson and Kate Pickett, *The Spirit Level: Why Greater Equality Makes Societies Stronger* (London: Allen Lane, 2009).

55. Deborah Lutterbeck, "Falling Wages," *Common Cause Magazine* (Winter 1995): 14; Herbert Stein and Murray Foss, *The New Illustrated Guide to the American Economy* (Washington, DC: American Enterprise Institute, 1995), 126, 130, 132; Steven Greenhouse, "Minimum Wage Maximum Debate," *New York Times* (March 31, 1996), 3.

56. The following account of Countrywide and Mozilo is based on Reuters, "A Losing Year at Countrywide, but Not for Chief," *New York Times* (April 25, 2008); Gretchen Morgenson, "Stock Sales by Chief of Lender Questioned," *New York Times* (October 11, 2007).

57. "Meet the 23,000% Stock," *Fortune* (September 2003).

58. Gretchen Morgenson, "Explaining (or Not) Why the Boss Is Paid So Much," *New York Times* (January 25, 2004).

59. Drutman and Cray, *The People's Business*, 102. In July 2008, the minimum wage increased to $6.55 an hour.

60. Ibid., 98.

61. Josh Funk, "Corporate Board Pay Soars as Directors' Tasks Grow," *New York Times* (May 8, 2008).

62. See Lawrence R. Jacobs and Theda Skocpol, eds., *Inequality and American Democracy: What We Know and What We Need to Learn* (New York: Russell Sage Foundation, 2005).

63. The political philosopher Michael Walzer calls this the "art of separation." See his *Spheres of Justice: A Defense of Pluralism and Equality* (New York: Basic Books, 1983).

64. David Card, Thomas Lemieux, and W. Craig Riddell, *Unionization and Wage Inequality: A Comparative Study of the U.S., the U.K., and Canada*, National Bureau of Economic Research, Working Paper 9473 (January 2003): http://www.nber.org/papers/w9473.

65. *Year-by-Year Analysis of the Bush Tax Cuts Shows Growing Tilt to the Very Rich*, Citizens for Tax Justice (June 12, 2002).

66. For a synthesis of the research on public opinion and the Bush tax cuts, see Larry M. Bartels, *Unequal Democracy: The Political Economy of the New Gilded Age* (New York: Russell Sage Foundation, 2008), 170–76.

67. Laura Langbein, "Money and Access: Some Empirical Evidence," *Journal of Politics* 48, 4 (1986): 1052–62.

68. Bartels, *Unequal Democracy*, 5.

69. Sidney Verba, Kay Lehman Schlozman, and Henry E. Brady, *Voice and Equality: Civic Voluntarism in American Politics* (Cambridge, MA: Harvard University Press, 1995).

70. Task Force on Inequality and American Democracy, American Political Science Association (APSA), *American Democracy in an Age of Rising Inequality*, APSA, 2004; available at www.apsanet.org.

71. See Peter Dreier, John Mollenkopf, and Todd Swanstrom, *Place Matters: Metropolitics for the 21st Century*, rev. ed. (Lawrence: University Press of Kansas, 2005).

72. In 1973, the U.S. Supreme Court ruled that there is no right to equal education under the Constitution (*San Antonio v. Rodriquez*, 1973). Since then, however, state courts have intervened in many states to order more equal funding of local schools. Kenneth K. Wong, *Funding Public Schools: Politics and Policies* (Lawrence: University Press of Kansas, 1999).

73. *State of Working America*; http://stateofworkingamerica.org/charts/median-real-earnings-by-gender-from-1973-2010/.

74. Randy Albelda, *Real World Macro*, 12th ed. (Somerville, MA: Dollars and Sense, 1995); Margery Turner et al., *Opportunities Denied, Opportunities Diminished: Racial Discrimination in Hiring* (Washington, DC: Urban Institute, 1992).

75. Jacob Hacker, *The Great Risk Shift: The Assault on American Jobs, Families, Health Care, Retirement and How You Can Fight Back* (New York: Oxford University Press, 2006).

76. See Robert Frank and Philip Cook, *The Winner-Take-All Society: Why the Few at the Top Get So Much More Than the Rest of Us* (New York: Penguin Books, 1995) and Jacob S. Hacker and Paul Pierson, *Winner-Take-All Politics: How Washington Made the Rich Richer—And Turned Its Back on the Middle Class* (New York: Simon & Schuster, 2010).

77. Peter Gosselin, *High Wire: The Precarious Financial Lives of American Families* (New York: Basic Books, 2008), 56–7.

78. Ibid., 9.

79. Ibid., 261.

80. Ibid., 264–6.

81. Ibid., 212.

82. Much of this section is based on Edward M. Gramlich, *Subprime Mortgages: America's Latest Boom and Bust* (Washington, DC: Urban Institute Press, 2007).

83. Two works argue persuasively that strong civil societies are necessary for effective democratic participation: Robert D. Putnam, *Bowling Alone: The Collapse and Revival of American Community* (New York: Simon & Schuster, 2000); and Verba, Schlozman, and Brady, *Voice and Equality*.

84. Verba, Schlozman, and Brady, *Voice and Equality*, chap. 3.

85. Putnam, *Bowling Alone*, 438.

86. Ibid., 46.

87. Ibid., 360–1.

88. Verba, Schlozman, and Brady, *Voice and Equality*, 315. The poor are defined as having family incomes below $15,000, the rich at $125,000 and over.

89. Putnam, *Bowling Alone*, 198–201.

90. Mishel, Bernstein, and Allegretto, *State of Working America, 2006–07*, 91.

91. Juliet B. Schor, *The Overworked American: The Unexpected Decline of Leisure* (New York: Basic Books, 1992), 34–8.

92. Higher Education Research Institute (HERI), *The American Freshman: National Norms for Fall 2004* (Los Angeles: HERI, 2005).

93. Vincent P. Bzdek, "The Ad Subtractors, Making a Difference," *Washington Post* (July 29, 2003); as reported in Drutman and Cray, *The People's Business*, 264.

94. Cornel West, *Democracy Matters: Winning the Fight Against Imperialism* (New York: Penguin, 2004), 5.

95. See Theda Skocpol, "Unraveling from Above," *The American Prospect* (March–April 1996): 22–3.

CHAPTER 5

1. Robert Nisbet, "Public Opinion versus Popular Opinion," in *Debating Democracy*, eds. Bruce Miroff, Raymond Seidelman, and Todd Swanstrom (Boston: Houghton Mifflin, 2001), 117; Phillip Converse, "The Nature of Belief Systems in Mass Publics," in *Ideology and Discontent*, ed. David Apter (New York: Free Press, 1964), 243–5; Hamilton is quoted in *The Federalist Papers*, ed. Clinton Rossiter (New York: New American Library, 1961), 432.

2. Robert Erikson and Kent Tedin, *American Public Opinion* (New York: Longman, 2000), 54. "Political Knowledge Update: Well Known: Twitter; Little Known: TARP," July 15, 2010, Pew Research Center, http://pewresearch.org/pubs/1668; "US Public Beliefs on Iraq and the Presidential Election," PIPA-Knowledge Networks Poll, April 22, 2004, www.pipa.org, 4, 5.

3. Benjamin Ginsberg, *The Captive Public* (New York: Basic Books, 1986). See also Walter Lippmann, *The Phantom Public* (New York: Harcourt Brace Jovanovich, 1925), 15, 155; Thomas Dye and Harmon Ziegler, *The Irony of Democracy* (Monterey, CA: Brooks/Cole, 1987), 145; Michael Delli Carpini and Scott Keeter, "The Public's Knowledge of Politics," in *Public Opinion, the Press, and Public Policy*, ed. David Kennamer (Westport, CT: Praeger, 1992).

4. C. Wright Mills, *The Power Elite* (New York: Oxford University Press, 1956), 298–304; John Dewey, *The Public and Its Problems* (Athens, Ohio: Swallow Press, 1954). For a discussion of Dewey's views on public opinion, see Robert Westerbrook, *John Dewey and American Democracy* (Ithaca, NY: Cornell University Press, 1991).

5. Robert Cirino, *Don't Blame the People* (New York: Basic Books, 1971). For a brilliant account of public opinion during the Vietnam War, see Godfrey Hodgson, *America in Our Time* (New York: Pantheon, 1976).

6. A more recent survey, done by the "branding consultancy" Reputation Institute and reported in *The Economist* magazine, ranked the U.S. 11th. Perhaps this reflected the harsh economic downturn and the unpopularity of the Bush administration. The survey and the institute's methodology weren't available for review; therefore its results are not included in the main text. See citation below. National Election Study, University of Michigan, 1988. Robert S. Erikson and Kent L. Tedin, *American Public Opinion: Its Origins, Content, and Impact*, Updated 8th Edition (New York: Longman, 2010), chap. 6; "American Exceptionalism Subsides: The American-Western European Values Gap, Updated February 29, 2012," http://www.pewglobal.org/2011/11/17; "Pride and Patriotism" and "Patriotism (general)," The Roper Center, CBS/*New York Times* poll, May 2011, www.ropercenter.uconn.edu; "What Polls Say about the State of American Patriotism," Karlyn Bowman and Andrew Rugg, AEIdeas: Freedom, Opportunity, Ideas: The Public Policy Blog of the American Enterprise Institute, July 3, 2012, http://www.aei-ideas.org/channel/politicsandpublicopinion/page/24/; "Proud Patriots—and Harsh Critics of Government," July 1, 2010, Pew Center for the People and the Press, http://pewresearch.org/pubs/1649/; Tom W. Smith, and Seokho Kim, "National Pride in Comparative Perspective: 1995/96 and 2003/04," *International Journal of Public Opinion Research* 18, no.1 (Spring 2006): 127–36; "National pride: Who Admires Their Country the Most?," *The Economist* (September 29, 2009), www.economist.com/node; and Andrew Main, "Aussies Top World List of National Pride," *The Australian* (October 2, 2009), www.news.com.au.

7. Kenneth Dolbeare and Linda Medcalf, *American Political Ideas in the 1980s* (New York: Random House, 1985); John Sullivan, James Pierson, and George Marcus, *Political Tolerance and American Democracy* (Chicago: University of Chicago Press, 1982).

8. See Robert Bellah et al., *Habits of the Heart* (New York: HarperCollins, 1995), chaps. 1, 10, 11; James Kluegel and Eliot Smith, *Beliefs About Inequality* (New York: Aldine De Gruyter, 1986), 135–43; Roper Center for Public Opinion Research, "Change and Persistence in American Ideas," *The Public Perspective* (April/May 1995): 14; Andrew Greeley, "The Other Civic America: Religion and Social Capital," *The American Prospect* (May/June 1997); Survey by Center for a New American Dream and Widmeyer Communications, July 2004; Survey by National Opinion Research Center, University of Chicago, March 10–August 7, 2006; Survey by Pew Research Center for the People & the Press, Council on Foreign Relations and Princeton Survey Research Associates International, Abt SRBI, September 9–14, 2008.

9. Robert Putnam, "Bowling Alone: America's Declining Social Capital," *Journal of Democracy* (January 1995): 34–35; "The Strange Disappearance of Civic America," *The American Prospect* (May 1996); Putnam's larger and monumental study is *Bowling Alone: The Collapse and Revival of American Community* (New York: Simon & Schuster, 2000). A refutation of Putnam's general thesis can be found in Everett Carll Ladd's article in *Public Perspective* (June/July 1996). See also Jason Kaufman, *For the Common Good* (New York: Oxford University Press, 2002); On how the professionalization of voluntary associations also undercuts their civic value, see Theda Skocpol and Morris Fiorina, eds., *Civic Engagement in American Democracy* (Washington, D.C.: Brookings Institution Press, 1999); and Theda Skocpol, *Diminished Democracy: From Membership to Management in American Civic Life* (Norman: University of Oklahoma Press, 2003).

10. Haya El Nasser, "Gated Communities More Popular, and Not Just for the Rich," *USA Today* (December 15, 2002), www.usatoday.com. On gated communities and their implications for American political culture and democracy, see Robert Reich, "Secession of the Successful," *New York Times Magazine* (January 20, 1992); Setha Low, *Behind the Gates: Life, Security and the Pursuit of Happiness in Fortress America* (New York: Routledge, 2004); Evan McKenzie, *Privatopia: Homeowner Associations and the Rise of Residential Private Government* (New Haven, CT: Yale University Press, 1996); Edward J. Blakely and Mary Gail Snyder, *Fortress America: Gated Communities in the United States* (Washington, D.C.: Brookings Institution Press, 1999); Rich Benjamin, "The Gated Community Mentality," *New York Times* (March 29, 2012), A27.

11. "Americans Say They Like Diverse Communities; Election, Census Trends Suggest Otherwise," December 2008, Pew Research Center, http://www.pewsocialtrends.org/2008/12/02/; Bill Bishop, *The Big Sort: Why the Clustering of Like-Minded Americans Is Tearing Us Apart* (New York: Houghton Mifflin, 2008).

12. See Jennifer Hochschild, *What's Fair: American Beliefs About Distributive Justice* (Cambridge, MA: Harvard University Press, 1981). See also William Jacoby, "Public Opinion and Economic Policy in 1992," in Barbara Norrander and Clyde Wilcox, *Understanding Public Opinion* (Washington, D.C.: Congressional Quarterly Press, 1997); Leslie McCall and Julian Brash, "What Do Americans Think About Economic Inequality?" Demos—A Network of Ideals and Action (May 2004), www.demos.org; Dennis Jacobe, "Home Ownership Hits Decade Low" (April 26, 2012), Gallup, at: http://www.gallup.com/poll/154124/u.s.-homeownership-hits-decade-low.aspx; "Impact of Institutions," (February 23, 2012), Pew Research Center for the People & the Press, http://www.people-press.org/2012/02/23/section-3; "72% Believe Small Business Owners Primarily Responsible for Their Own Success" (July 23, 2012), Rasmussen Reports, http://www.rasmussenreports.com/public_content/business/general_business/july_2012/72_believe_small_business_owners_primarily_responsible_for_their_own_success; "Values About Business, Wall Street and Labor" (June 4, 2012), Pew Center for the People & the Press, http://www.people-press.org/2012/06/04/section-5-values-about-business-wall-street-and-labor/.

13. See Gallup Poll (November 13, 2000), www.gallup.com. "Understanding the Partisan Divide over American

Values" (June 4, 2012), Pew Research Center, http://www.people-press.org/2012/06/04/. For an argument that polarization has not increased in American politics, see Morris P. Fiorina, Samuel J. Abrams, and Jeremy C. Pope, *Culture War: The Myth of a Polarized America*, Third Edition (White Plains, NY: Longman, 2011).

14. "Understanding the Partisan Divide over American Values" (June 4, 2012), Pew Research Center; Nate Silver, "As Swing Districts Dwindle, Can a Divided House Stand?" *New York Times* (December 27, 2012), http://fivethirtyeight.blogs.nytimes.com/2012/12/27/.

15. See John Zaller and Stanley Feldman, "A Simple Theory of the Survey Response: Answering Questions and Revealing Preferences," *American Journal of Political Science* 36 (1992): 579–616. See also John Zaller, *The Nature and Origins of Mass Opinion* (Cambridge: Cambridge University Press, 1992); Paul Sniderman et al., "Principle Tolerance and the American Mass Public," *British Journal of Political Science* (February 1989): 25–45; Herbert McClosky and Alida Brill, *Dimensions of Political Tolerance* (New York: Russell Sage, 1983); Dye and Ziegler, *The Irony of Democracy*, 137–43; Samuel Stouffer, *Communism, Conformity, and Civil Liberties* (New York: Doubleday, 1955); Erikson and Tedin, *American Public Opinion*, 163–73; For a critique arguing that some scholars overstate intolerance in ways that may serve an advocacy agenda, see Robert Weissberg, *Political Tolerance: Balancing Community and Diversity* (Thousand Oaks, CA: Sage, 1998).

16. James Gibson, "Political Intolerance During the McCarthy Red Scare," *American Political Science Review* (June 1988): 512–9; Michael Rogin, *The Intellectuals and McCarthy* (Cambridge, MA: MIT Press, 1970).

17. Weissberg, *Political Tolerance*, Conclusion.

18. Zachary Bell, "NDDA's Indefinite Detention Without Trial Returns," *Salon* (December 19, 2012), http://www.salon.com/2012/12/19/; "Americans on Detention, Torture and the War on Terrorism," PIPA/Knowledge Networks (July 22, 2004), www.pipa.org, 3; "War on Terrorism Has Not Made Public Feel Safer," PIPA/Knowledge Networks (September 9, 2004), www.pipa.org; Reg Whitaker, "After 9/11: A Surveillance State?" in *Lost Liberties: Ashcroft and the Assault on Personal Freedom*, ed. Cynthia Brown and Aryeh Neier (New York: New Press, 2003), 52–71.

19. Benjamin Page and Robert Shapiro, *The Rational Public* (Chicago: University of Chicago Press, 1992); Ted Halstead, "The Politics of Generation X," *Atlantic Monthly* (April 1999); Pew Research Center for the People and the Press, "2004 Political Landscape," Part 9, www.people-press.org; "Behind Gay Marriage Momentum, Regional Gaps Persist," Pew Research Center for the People & the Press, November 9, 2012, http://www.people-press.org/2012/11/09/; Pew Research Center for the People and the Press, "Democratic Leaders Face Growing Disapproval, Criticism on Iraq: Mixed Views on Immigration Bill" (June 7, 2007), www.pewresearch.org; Gallup Poll, June 5–July 6, 2008; NBC/*Wall Street Journal* Poll, December 14–17,

2007, June 8–11, 2007; *Los Angeles Times*/Bloomberg Poll, November 30–December 3, 2007; Associated Press/Ipsos Poll, May 15–17, 2006, www.pollingreport.com; "U.S. Public, Hispanics Differ on Arizona Immigration Law," Pew Hispanic Center (June 25, 2012), http://www.pewhispanic.org/2012/06/25/; Jeffrey M. Jones, "Americans More Positive About Immigration," *Gallup Politics* (June 16, 2012), www.gallup.com; "2012 Fox News Exit Polls," Fox News, http://www.foxnews.com/politics/elections/2012-exit-poll.

20. See, for example, Judith Miller, "Threats and Responses: Intelligence; Defectors Bolster U.S. Case Against Iraq, Officials Say," *New York Times* (January 24, 2003); and Michael R. Gordon and Judith Miller, "Threats and Responses: The Iraqis; U.S. Says Hussein Intensifies Quest for A-Bomb Parts," *New York Times* (September 8, 2002); Interview with Wolf Blitzer, September 8, 2002, reported in "Search for the Smoking Gun," by Wolf Blitzer, CNN.com, www.cnn.com/2003/US/01/10/wbr.smoking.gun/; "Vice President Appears on NBC's Meet the Press," The White House (December 9, 2001), www.whitehouse.gov/vicepresident/news-speeches/speeches/vp20011209.html; Hannah Allam and Laith Hammoudi, "Cheney Again Links Iraq Invasion to 9/11 Attacks," *McClatchy Newspapers* (March 18, 2000), www.mcclatchydc.com/100/story/30828.html.

21. Polling data from PIPA/Knowledge Networks poll, "Americans and Iraq on the Eve of the Presidential Elections" (October 28, 2004), A-40; and "The Separate Realities of Bush and Kerry Supporters" (October 21, 2004), www.pipa.org; "Iraq and Public Opinion: The Troops Come Home" (December 14, 2011), Pew Research Center, http://www.pewresearch.org/2011/12/14/.

22. Reason-Rupe Poll, September 2012, www.reason.com; Pew Research Center for the People & the Press Values Survey, April 2012; Public Religion Research Institute American Values Survey, September 2012; Allstate/National Journal Heartland Monitor Poll, September 2012; Pew Research Center for the People & the Press Political Survey, September 2012, iPoll, Databank, The Roper Center, www.ropercenter.uconn.edu. Gallup Poll, March 25–27, 2011, http://www.gallup.com/poll/5248/big-business.aspx#1; Jennifer Agiesta, "Voters' Vantage Point: The Economy" *Washington Post* (November 14, 2008), www.washingtonpost.com; 2012 Fox News Exit Polls, http://www.foxnews.com/politics/elections/2012-exit-poll; "Partisan Polarization Surges in Bush, Obama Years Trends in American Values: 1987–2012: Values About Government and the Social Safety Net," Pew Center for the People & the Press (June 4, 2012), http://www.people-press.org/2012/06/04/; Program on International Policy Attitudes (PIPA), "Americans on Globalization: A Summary of U.S. Findings," School of Public Affairs, University of Maryland, 1999, www.pipa.org; Ruy Teixeira and Joel Rogers, *America's Forgotten Majority: Why the White Working Class Still Matters* (New York: Basic Books, 2002), 147–60; Andrew Kohut, "Globalization and the Wage Gap," *New York Times* (December 3, 1999), A31.

23. Leon Baradat, *Political Ideologies: Their Origins and Impact* (Englewood Cliffs, NJ: Prentice-Hall, 1979), 30–7.

24. The General Social Survey changed its sample design in 2004, which required the use of sample weights. To obtain comparable figures for earlier years, it was necessary to weight those years as well, resulting in slight changes in previous results.

25. For an effort at typology, see "Beyond Red vs. Blue: The Political Typology," Pew Resarch Center (May 4, 2011), http://www.people-press.org/2011/05/04/; See, for example, Kathleen Knight and Robert Erikson, "Ideology in the 1990s," in Norrander and Wilcox, *Understanding Public Opinion*, 107–10. See also Pamela Conover and Stanley Feldman, "The Origins and Meanings of Liberal and Conservative Self-Identification," *American Journal of Political Science* (November 1981): 617–45. See also Teixeira and Rogers, *America's Forgotten Majority*, chaps. 2 and 3; Regarding the intensity of beliefs of independents see, "Partisan Polarization Surges," Pew Center, http://www.people-press.org/2012/06/04.

26. E. J. Dionne, *Why Americans Hate Politics* (New York: Simon & Schuster, 1993), 14.

27. See Robert Putnam, *Bowling Alone*. chap. 6; Alan Wolfe, *One Nation, After All* (New York: Penguin, 1999); Alan Wolfe, *The Transformation of American Religion* (New York: Free Press, 2003).

28. For an unconventional but important account, see Thomas Hine, *Rise and Fall of the American Teenager* (New York: Bard Books, 1999). see also William Finnegan, *Cold New World* (New York: Modern Library, 1999).

29. M. Kent Jennings, "Residuals of a Movement: The Aging of the American Protest Generation," *American Political Science Review* 81 (June 1987): 365–82.

30. Putnam, *Bowling Alone*, 259; Halstead, "The Politics of Gen X"; Daniel Yankelovich, "How Changes in the Economy Are Reshaping American Values," *Values and Public Policy*, eds. Henry Aaron, Thomas Mann, and Timothy Taylor (Washington, D.C.: Brookings Institution Press, 1994); Tyler Kingkade, "Youth Vote 2012 Turnout: Exit Polls Show Greater Share of Electorate Than in 2008," *The Huffington Post* (November 7, 2012), www.huffingtonpost.com.

31. See M. R. Jackman and R. W. Jackman, *Class Awareness in the United States* (Berkeley and Los Angeles: University of California Press, 1983); Jared Bernstein et al., *The State of Working America 2003* (White Plains, NY: M.E. Sharpe, 2003).

32. General Social Survey, 1998; AFL-CIO Survey of Young Workers, Peter Hart Associates, 1999, www.afl-cio.org.

33. All figures are from the General Social Survey (GSS), 2008, *except* aid to the poor, which is from GSS 2006, child care, which is from the American National Election Study (ANES) 2008, and AIDS research, which is from ANES 2000.

34. Michael Goldfield, *The Color of Politics* (New York: New Press, 1998); David Roediger, *The Wages of Whiteness* (London: Verso, 1991); Pew Research Center for the People and the Press, "2004 Political Landscape: Race," www.people-press.org.

35. Joshua J. Dyck and Laura S. Hussey, "The End of Welfare as We Know It?: Durable Attitudes in a Changing Information Environment," *Public Opinion Quarterly*, Volume 72, Issue 4 (2008), 589–618; Edward Carmines and James Stimson, *Issue Evolution: Race and the Transformation of American Politics* (Princeton, NJ: Princeton University Press, 1989); David Shipler, *A Country of Strangers* (New York: Alfred A. Knopf, 1997); Jeffrey M. Jones, "Record-High 86% Approve of Black-White Marriages," Gallup, (September 12, 2011), www.gallup.com.

36. 2010 Blair-Rockefeller Poll, http://blairrockefeller-poll.uark.edu/6107.php; "Public Backs Affirmative Action, but Not Minority Preferences," Pew Research Center (June 2, 2009), http://www.pewresearch.org/2009/06/02/; David Bositis, Joint Center for Political Studies, "2004 National Opinion Poll," www.jointcenter.org. Howard Schuman, Charlotte Steeh, Lawrence Bobo, and Maria Krysan, *Racial Attitudes in America* (Cambridge, MA: Harvard University Press, 1997); Steven Tuch and Lee Sigelman, "Race, Class, and Black-White Differences in Social Views," in Norrander and Wilcox, *Understanding Public Opinion*, 48–9. See also "Whites Retain Negative Views of Minorities," *New York Times* (January 14, 1991).

37. No figures on Republicans were given, presumably because of inadequate sample size when differentiated by racial/ethnic groups. See Pew Hispanic Center, "America's Immigration Quandary" (April 6, 2006).

38. Kluegel and Smith, *Beliefs*, 135–43; Lee Sigelman and Susan Welch, *Black Americans' Views of Racial Inequality* (Cambridge, MA: Harvard University Press, 1991), 589; Jennifer Hochschild, *Facing Up to the American Dream* (Princeton, NJ: Princeton University Press, 1995).

39. See Kristi Anderson, "Gender and Public Opinion," in Norrander and Wilcox, *Understanding Public Opinion*; John Judis and Ruy Teixeira, *The Emerging Democratic Majority* (New York: Scribner's, 2002); James Ceasar and Andrew Busch, *Red over Blue* (New York: Rowman & Littlefield, 2005); Lydia Saad, "Americans Still Split Along 'Pro-Choice,' 'Pro-Life' Lines," *Gallup Politics* (May 23, 2011) www.gallup.com; Frank Newport, "Sixty-Nine Percent of Americans Support Death Penalty," *Gallup* (October 12, 2007), www.gallup.com; Lydia Saad, "Before Recent Shootings, Gun-Control Support Was Fading," *Gallup* (April 8, 2009), www.gallup.com; "Attitudes Toward Spanking," Child Trends Data Bank (October 2012), www.childtrendsdatabank.org.

40. Amanda Marcotte, "The Religion of an Increasingly Godless America," Reuters (November 24, 2011), http://blogs.reuters.com/great-debate/2011/11/24/; "Unfavorable View of Jews and Muslims on the Increase in Europe, Chap. 2: Religiosity," Pew Global Attitudes Project (September 17, 2008), http://www.pewglobal.org/2008/09/17/; "The

Generation Gap and the 2012 Election: Section 1: How Generations Have Changed," Pew Research Center, http://www.people-press.org/2011/11/03/; "Nones" on the Rise, Pew Forum on Religion and Public Life (October 9, 2012), www.pewforum.org; Sara Diamond, *Not by Politics Alone* (New York: Guilford, 1999); Kenneth Wald, *Religion and Politics in the United States*, 3rd ed. (Washington, D.C.: Congressional Quarterly Press, 1997). See also Ted Jelen, "Religion and Public Opinion in the 1990s," in Norrander and Wilcox, *Understanding Public Opinion*, 19–36. For 2004, see Pew Center for the People and the Press, "2004 Political Landscape: Religion, Public Life," www.people-press.org. See also Wolfe, *The Transformation*; Jim Wallis, *God's Politics* (San Francisco: HarperCollins, 2005), A-41.

41. Pew Center for the People and the Press, "2004 Political Landscape: Religion," www.people-press.org; Peter Steinfels, "Catholics and Choice (in the Voting Booth)," *New York Times* (November 7, 2008), A21; "Election Results 2008: National Exit Polls Table," *New York Times* (November 5, 2008), www.nytimes.com.

42. Gallup quoted in Christopher Hitchens, "Voting in the Passive Voice," *Harpers* (April 1992), 46; Susan Herbst, *Numbered Voices* (Chicago: University of Chicago Press, 1993), 2; Michael Traugott and Paul Lavrakas, *The Voter's Guide to Election Polls*, 2nd ed. (New York: Chatham House, 2000), 129–30.

CHAPTER 6

1. While not rejecting the formal political institutional processes of liberal democracies, Philip Green gives a passionate defense of the idea that we need to look beyond them to a variety of forms of direct action. He writes, "The great moments of this democratic process are strikes, demonstrations, marches, occupations, even funerals." The "real history of democracy," he argues is "the history of popular struggle." "A Review Essay of Robert A. Dahl, Democracy and Its Critics," *Social Theory and Practice* 16 (Summer 1990): 217, 234–5.

2. For a complex discussion of receptivity and the "political arts of listening," see Romand Coles, *Beyond Gated Politics: Reflections for the Possibility of Democracy* (Minneapolis: University of Minnesota Press, 2005), esp. chap. 7.

3. Sidney Verba and Gary R. Orren, *Equality in America: The View from the Top* (Cambridge, MA: Harvard University Press, 1985), 9–17.

4. Steven J. Rosenstone and John Mark Hansen, *Mobilization, Participation, and Democracy in America* (New York: Macmillan, 1993), 43–44.

5. Kay Lehman Schlozman, Sidney Verba, and Henry E. Brady, *The Unheavenly Chorus: Unequal Political Voice and the Broken Promise of American Democracy* (Princeton, NJ: Princeton University Press, 2012) 197–98.

6. See Sidney Verba, Kay Scholzman, and Henry Brady, *Voice and Equality: Civic Voluntarism in American Politics* (Cambridge, MA: Harvard University Press, 1995), 532. See also Theda Skocpol and Morris Fiorina, eds., *Civic Engagement in American Democracy* (Washington, D.C.: Brookings Institution Press, 1999); Theda Skocpol, *Diminished Democracy: From Membership to Management in American Civic Life* (Norman, OK: University of Oklahoma Press, 2003).

7. The only exception to this seems to be engaging in protest activity, according to Schlozman, Verba, and Brady, *The Unheavenly Chorus*, 124.

8. Ruy Teixeira, *The Disappearing American Voter* (Washington, D.C.: The Brookings Institution, 1992), 3–4. See also Raymond Wolfinger and Steven Rosenstone, *Who Votes?* (New Haven, CT: Yale University Press, 1978), 61–88; Walter Dean Burnham, "The Appearance and Disappearance of the American Voter," in Burnham, ed., *The Current Crisis in American Politics* (New York: Oxford University Press, 1982).

9. For contemporary and historical voter turnout in countries throughout the world, see International Institute for Democracy and Electoral Assistance (IDEA), "Voting Turnout," http://www.idea.int/vt/. See also G. Bingham Powell, "Voter Turnout in Comparative Perspective," *American Political Science Review* (March 1986): 1.

10. Michael McDonald, United States Election Project, "Voter Turnout," http://elections.gmu.edu/voter_turnout.htm. These contemporary turnout figures are for the highest office rather than the total number of ballots counted. They are calculated as a proportion of the voter eligible population. See Box feature: How Should We Measure Voting Turnout; "2012 Presidential Nomination Contest Turnout Rates," http://elections.gmu.edu/Turnout_2012P.html.

11. Teixeira, *The Disappearing American Voter*, 8–9; Robert Wiebe, *Self-Rule* (Chicago: University of Chicago Press, 1996); Paul Kleppner, *Who Voted? The Dynamics of Electoral Turnout* (New York: Harper & Row, 1983).

12. In 2008, 66.4 percent (adjusted –4.5% for over-reporting) of those families with incomes from $50,000 to $74,999 voted, leaving a voting gap of 8.9 percent with the families earning $100,000 or more. Since the median income of $52,000 is just above the low end of this group where turnout would be lower than the group average, it is reasonable to conservatively estimate approximately a 10 percent gap between median earners and the high earners. "Voting and Registration in the Election of 2008: Population Characteristics," May 2010; Jessica Semega, "Median Household Income for States: 2007 and 2008," *American Community Survey*, U.S. Census Bureau, September 2009, 4, http://www.census.gov/prod/2009pubs/acsbr08-2.pdf; Thom File, "The Diversifying Electorate: Voting Rates by Race and Hispanic Origin in 2012 (and Other Recent Elections)," *Population Characteristics*, Current Population Survey, May 2013,

U.S. Census Bureau, pp. 3, 6, http://www.census.gov/prod/2013pubs/p20-568.pdf. See also "Gender Differences in Voter Turnout," Center for American Women and Politics (CAWP), Eagleton Institute of Politics, Rutgers University, http://www.cawp.rutgers.edu/fast_facts/voters/turnout.php.

13. See Schlozman, Verba, and Brady, *The Unheavenly Chorus*, 156 and Figure 1 on 153. We have to await Census turnout data available in 2014 to calculate the index of voting equality for 2012. However, based on exit polls showing lower income voters comprising a slightly *higher* proportion of voters than in 2008, the index may be relatively high for 2012 as well, in spite of the drop from 2008 in overall turnout. See 2008 and 2012 Fox News Exit Polls, www.foxnews.com.

14. Samuel P. Huntington, "The United States," in *The Crisis of Democracy*, eds. Michael Crozier, Samuel P. Huntington, and Joji Watanuki (New York: New York University Press, 1975); Samuel P. Huntington, *American Politics: The Promise of Disharmony* (Cambridge, MA: Belknap, 1981).

15. George F. Will, "In Defense of Nonvoting," *Newsweek* (October 10, 1996), 96.

16. George F. Will, *Statecraft as Soulcraft* (New York: Simon & Schuster, 1983).

17. Two founding studies in this tradition are Anthony Downs, *An Economic Theory of Democracy* (New York: Harper & Row, 1978); V. O. Key, *The Responsible Electorate* (New York: Cambridge University Press, 1966). One of the most well-known works is Morris Fiorina, *Retrospective Voting in American National Elections* (New Haven, CT: Yale University Press, 1981). See also Teixeira, *The Disappearing American Voter*.

18. Mark N. Franklin, "Electoral Participation," in *Comparing Democracies*, eds. Lawrence LeDuc, Richard G. Niemi, and Pippa Norris (Thousand Oaks, CA: Sage, 1996), 218; Frances Fox Piven and Richard A. Cloward, *Why Americans Don't Vote* (New York: Pantheon, 1988), 119. Sidney Verba, Kay Lehman Schlozman, and Henry E. Brady, *Voice and Equality: Civic Voluntarism in American Politics* (Cambridge, MA: Harvard University Press, 1995), 532.

19. Rosenstone and Hansen, *Mobilization, Participation, and Democracy in America*, 238.

20. Schlozman, Verba, and Brad, *The Unheavenly Chorus*, 481–2.

21. Rosenstone and Hansen, 243–4.

22. Rosenstone and Hansen, 229.

23. See Verba, Schlozman, and Brady, "Civic Participation and the Equality Problem," in *Civic Engagement in American Democracy*, eds. Skocpol and Fiorina, 427–60; Burnham, "The Appearance and Disappearance," 86.

24. See Ruy Teixeira and Joel Rogers, *America's Forgotten Majority* (New York: Basic Books, 2000).

25. The Bureau of the Census computes the voting age population from the pool of persons 18 or older (21 and older in most states before 1971) who live in the United States in noninstitutional settings. The "voter eligible population" is a phrase Michael McDonald's used to refer to all citizens eligible to vote. McDonald argues for the use of VEP because VAP *includes* those ineligible to vote such as noncitizens, felons (and in some states former felons), and mentally incapacitated persons, and *excludes* voters such as those in the military and those living abroad. Michael McDonald, United States Elections Project, "Voting Turnout" (elections.gmu.edu/Turnout), and "Voting Turnout: Frequently Asked Questions" (elections.gmu.edu/FAQ).

26. McDonald, "Voting Turnout."

27. This was not always so. For an excellent history of the long struggle for the right to vote, see Alexander Keyssar, *The Right to Vote: The Contested History of Democracy in the United States* (New York: Basic Books, 2000).

28. Orna Feldman, "Voting Procedures, Lessons from the 2000 Election, a Guide for 2008," *Spectrum*, Massachusetts Institute of Technology (Winter 2008), spectrum.mit.edu.

29. See Jim Morrill and Ted Mellnick, "Record N.C. Voter Rolls Might Help Dems," *The Charlotte Observer* (October 2, 2008), www.newsobserver.com. Eligible voter comparison computed from McDonald, "Voter Turnout." Deborah Charles, "Voter ID Laws Spark Heated Debate Before Election" Reuters, April 5, 2012, www.reuters.com; Scott Keyes, Ian Millhiser, Tobin Van Ostern, and Abraham White, "Voter Suppression 101: How Conservatives Are Conspiring to Disenfranchise Millions of Americans," Center for American Progress (April 4, 2012), http://www.americanprogress.org.

30. Keyssar, *The Right to Vote*, 311–4; Frances Fox Piven, personal communication with the author, July 17, 1996; Frances Fox Piven and Richard Cloward, "Northern Bourbons: A Preliminary Report on the National Voter Registration Act," PS (March, 1996): 39–41; Committee for the Study of the American Electorate, "2004 Election Report," www.fairvote.org.

31. Martin P. Wattenberg, "Elections: Turnout in the 2004 Presidential Election," *Presidential Studies Quarterly*, Volume 35, Issue 1 (March 2005), www3.interscience.wiley.com.

32. See, "Voting Irregularities in Florida During the 2000 Presidential Election," U.S. Commission on Civil Rights, July 2001.

33. The disputed section is known as "preclearance." It mandates that changes to election rules, procedures, and laws in "covered districts" be cleared by the Justice Department before they go into effect. Some argue that the law has served its purpose, especially given the election of an African American president. Some charge that it is unfairly applied, especially given that most covered states are in the South. In a prior ruling, the Supreme Court has strongly hinted sympathy with these arguments. However, with charges of voter suppression in the 2012 election, for example, by way of the numerous "voter identification" laws that have been passed, civil rights violations regarding elections is clearly still an issue that needs to be addressed either through continuation of this law, or through strengthening and modernizing it. See, Nathaniel Persily, "Is the Voting Rights Act Doomed?," *New York Times* (November 14, 2012), http://campaignstops. blogs.nytimes.com/2012/11/14/. The case is *Shelby County, Alabama v. Holder*. It will be decided in 2013.

34. Joann Wypijewski, "The Party's Over," *The Nation* (November 2004); "Ground War, 2004," *The Nation* (November 2004); Greg Palast, *The Best Democracy Money Can Buy* (New York: Plume Books, 2004); Mary Lu Carnevale, "Tight House Up in Ohio over Voting Procedures," Washington Wire, *Wall Street Journal* (September 22, 2008) blogs.wsj.com/washwire.

35. Christopher Uggen, Sarah Shannon, and Jeff Manza, "State-Level Estimates of Felon Disenfranchisement in the United States, 2010," The Sentencing Project, (July 2012), www.sentencingproject.org.

36. Mark Hugo Lopez, Seth Motel, and Eileen Patten, "A Record 24 Million Latinos Are Eligible to Vote, but Turnout Rate Has Lagged That of Whites, Blacks," Pew Research Hispanic Center (October 1, 2012), http://www. pewhispanic.org/2012/10/01/; "The Hispanic Population: 2010," United States Census Bureau (May 2011); "Democracy Denied," *Demos* (April 2004) www.demos.org; Steven Hill, *Fixing Elections* (New York: Routledge, 2002); Roberto Suro, Richard Fry, and Jeffrey Passel, "Hispanics and the 2004 Election," *Pew Hispanic Center*, 2005, www. pewhispanic.org; Paul Taylor and Richard Fry, "Hispanics and the 2008 Election: A Swing Vote?" *Pew Hispanic Center*, www.pewhispanic.org. 2012 Fox News Exit Polls, http:// www.foxnews.com/politics/elections/2012-exit-poll.

37. "Voter ID Laws Spark Heated Debate Before Election," Deborah Charles, Reuters, April 5, 2012. *Crawford v. Marion County Election Board*, 28 S. Ct. 1610 (2008).

38. Devin Dwyer, Emily Friedman, and Christina Ng, "Election 2012: The Campaigns by the Numbers," ABC News (November 6, 2012), www.abcnews.go.com. Susan Page, "Voter Turnout Higher in Swing States Than Elsewhere," *USA Today* (December 23, 2012), www.usatoday.com. The study that calculated a 7.4 percent difference in turnout between swing and non-swing states included the following states as "swing states": Colorado, Florida, Iowa, North Carolina, New Hampshire, Nevada, Ohio, Pennsylvania, Virginia, and Wisconsin. In this text, however, when we refer to swing or battleground states we exclude Pennsylvania.

39. "Reelection Rates over the Years," Center for Responsive Politics, OpenSecrets.org, http://www.opensecrets.org/bigpicture/reelect.php; Greg Giroux, "Voters Throw Bums in while Holding Congress in Disdain," *Bloomberg* (December 13, 2012), http://www.bloomberg.com.

40. According to the U.S. Census, Hispanics and the category "Asians-alone" both grew at roughly 43 percent in population from 2000–2010. The Hispanic population

in 2010, however, is far larger at 50.5 million compared to 14.7 million for Asians. United States Census Bureau, "2010 Census Shows America's Diversity" (March 24, 2011), http://2010.census.gov/news/releases/operations/cb11-cn125.html; Lopez et al., "A Record 24 Million Latinos Are Eligible to Vote."

41. The U.S. Census reports that 31.2 percent of Hispanic respondents said they voted. We would subtract 4.5 percent to account for over reporting. See the note under Table 6.2; "Voting and Registration in the Election of November 2010—Detailed Tables," "Hispanic," http:// www.census.gov/hhes/www/socdemo/voting/publications/ p20/2010/tables.html.

42. The growth in the number of Latinos who actually do vote is rising, but rising slightly more slowly than the number of Latinos who are eligible to vote. "A Record 24 Million Latinos Are Eligible to Vote, but Turnout Rate Has Lagged That of Whites, Blacks," *Pew Research Hispanic Center* (October 1, 2012), http://www.pewhispanic. org/2012/10/01.

43. Michael Goldfield, *The Color of Politics* (New York: New Press, 1998); John Dittmer, *Local People* (Champaign-Urbana: University of Illinois Press, 1995), chaps. 10–12.

44. Roman Hedges and Carl Carlucci, "The Implementation of the Voting Rights Act," unpublished paper, State University of New York, Albany.

45. Bureau of Labor Statistics, "Union Member Summary" (January 23, 2013), http://www.bls.gov/news.release/ pdf/union2.pdf; Gerald Mayer, "Union Membership Trends in the United States," *Congressional Research Service* (August 31, 2004), 23, Table A1.

46. Peter Hart Research Associates, "Survey on Labor Participation in 2000 General Election" (November 9, 2000); Harold Meyerson, "A Tale of Two Cities"; Meyerson, "Voters," *American Prospect* (July 2000). Frank Swoboda, "Labor Targets 71 House Districts in Watershed Year," *Washington Post* (February 16, 2000), A14; Alec MacGillis, "AFL-CIO Outlines Major Election Effort" *The Washington Post* (June 25, 2008) www.washingtonpost.com; "U.S. Elections: How Groups Voted in 2000: The Roper Center, www.ropercenter.uconn.edu; 2012 Election Exit Polls, Fox News, www.foxnews.com; "Labor: Long Term Contribution Trends," www.opensecrets.org, Center for Responsive Politics, www.opensecrets.org; Nancy Marshall-Genzer, "Citizens United Decision Boosts Union Canvassers," *Marketplace* (October 10, 2012), www.marketplace.org; Dave Jamieson, "Labor Unions Deliver for Obama with Post-Citizens United Ground Game," *The Huffington Post* (November 7, 2012), www.huffingtonpost.com.

47. "Tea Party Movement," *Encyclopedia Britannica*, www.britannica.com. Vanessa Williamson, Theda Skocpol, and John Coggin. "The Tea Party and the Remaking of Republican Conservatism," *Perspectives on Politics*, 9, 1 (2011): 25–43; Chris Good, "A Guide to the Six Major Tea Party

Groups," *The National Journal* (January 30, 2011), www. nationaljournal.com; "Tea Party Movement," Times Topics, *New York Times* (December 26, 2012); Alan Abramowitz, "Partisan Polarization and the Rise of the Tea Party Movement," American Political Science Association, 2011; "Topline Results of Oct. 9–10, 2011," TIME Poll, www. swampland.time.com; "Just 8 Percent Now Say They Are Tea Party Members," *Rasmussen Reports* (January 7, 2013), www.rasmussenreports.com; Ian Gray, "Tea Party Election Results: Conservative Movement of 2010 Takes Pounding in 2012," *The Huffington Post* (November 7, 2012) www. huffingtonpost.com; Thomas B. Edsall, "The Republican Autopsy Report," *The New York Times* (March 20, 2013) www.nytimes.com.

48. Alasdair S. Roberts, "Why the Occupy Movement Failed" (May 26, 2012). *Public Administration Review*, Vol. 72, p. 754, 2012; Joseph Goldstein, "Wall Street Demonstrations Test Police Trained for Bigger Threats," *New York Times* (September 26, 2011), www.nytimes.com.

49. "Occupy Movement (Occupy Wall Street)," Times Topics, *New York Times*, Updated (September 17, 2012), http://topics.nytimes.com/; Andy Kroll, "How Occupy Wall Street Really Got Started," *Mother Jones* (October 17, 2011), www.motherjones.com; Jessica Firger, "Occupy Groups Get Funding," *Wall Street Journal* (February 28, 2012), http://online.wsj.com; Max Read, "The Single Largest Benefactor of Occupy Wall Street Is a Mitt Romney Donor," *Gawker* (October 17, 2011), www.gawker.com; Costas Panogopoulos, "Occupy Wall Street Survey Results October 2011," Fordham University. Conducted October 14–18, 2011. Based on interviews with 301 respondents. Response rate: 78%; Ariel Kaminer, "Occupy Wall St Offshoot Aims to Erase People's Debts," *New York Times* (November 13, 2012), www.nytimes.com; Neal Caren and Sarah Gaby, "Occupy Online: Facebook and the Spread of Occupy Wall Street," Available at SSRN 1943168 (2011); Michael Billera, "Occupy Wall Street: The Major Problems with the Movement," *International Business Times* (November 3, 2011), www.ibtimes.com; Ross Sorkin, A. "Occupy Wall Street: A Frenzy That Fizzled, *The New York Times*, (September 17, 2012); Eliot Spitzer, "Eliot Spitzer Encourages the Occupy Movement to Rally Around Elizabeth Warren," *Current* (September 17, 2012), http:// current.com; Tom Watson, "Occupy Wall Street's Year: Three Outcomes for the History Books," *Forbes* (September 17, 2012), www.forbes.com; David Whitford, "The End of OWS or the Beginning of Something Else?" *Fortune* (November 16, 2011), http://finance.fortune.cnn.com; Andy Ostroy, "The Failure of Occupy Wall Street," *The Huffington Post* (May 31, 2012), www.huffingtonpost.com; See also, Sidney Tarrow, "Why Occupy Wall Street Is Not the Tea Party of the Left," *Foreign Affairs* (2011).

50. "Act Blue: 2008 PAC Summary Data," Center for Responsive Politics, www.opensecrets.org; for it's up-to-the-minute fundraising claims go to: https://secure.actblue.com/.

51. "Netroots Nation Strives to Keep Right Online Away from Next Year's Convention," TPM (Talking Points Memo), Evan McMorris-Santoro (June 22, 2011). See also the websites of RightOnline http://rightonline.com/beta/; and Netroots Nation http://www.netrootsnation.org/.

52. For additional information on these developments, see Lowell Feld and Nate Wilcox, *Netroots Rising: How a Citizen Army of Bloggers and Online Activists Is Changing American Politics* (Westport, CT: Praeger, 2008); Morley Winograd and Michael D. Hais, *Millennial Makeover: MySpace, YouTube, and the Future of American Politics* (Piscataway, NJ: Rutgers University Press, 2008); "Netroots Nation: Changing the Face of Progressive Politics," (October 3, 2008), www.Netrootsnation.org; Jerome Armstrong and Markos Moulitsas, *Crashing the Gate: Netroots, Grassroots, and the Rise of People-Powered Politics* (White River Junction, VT: Chelsea Green, 2006).

53. Stephen Moss, "Julian Assange: The Whistleblower," *The Guardian* (July 13, 2010), http://www.guardian.co.uk/ media/2010/jul/14/julian-assange-whistleblower-wikileaks.

54. Schlozman, Verba, and Brady, *Unheavenly Chorus*, 530.

55. Jeffrey Stonecash argues that the less affluent support the Democratic Party more, and the Republicans less, than they did in the 1950s and 1960s. *Class and Party in American Politics:* (Boulder, CO: Westview Press, 2000).

56. Ruy A. Teixeira, *The Disappearing American Voter*, 2–3.

57. Rosenstone and Hansen, *Mobilization, Participation, and Democracy in America*, 229.

CHAPTER 7

1. Joseph A. Schumpeter, *Capitalism, Socialism, and Democracy, 3rd ed.* (New York: Harper & Row), 264, 284–5.

2. William Mayer, ed., *In Pursuit of the White House* (Chatham, NJ: Chatham House, 2000).

3. William Mayer, "The Presidential Nominations," in *The Election of 1996*, ed. Gerald Pomper (Chatham, NJ: Chatham House, 1997).

4. Obama, however, remained popular with Democrats in spite of criticism within his party that his policies were too tepid and that he should not be so conciliatory to the Republican leadership because it would never compromise with him. Some people did make what amounted to symbolic efforts to run against Obama (see Chapter 8). When Ralph Nader tried to find a formidable opponent to Obama, he failed. See Daniel Strauss, "Nader: White House Presured Democrats not to Challenge Obama," *The Hill* (January 7, 2012), www.thehill.com.

5. "Analysis of Election Factors Points to Romney Win, University of Colorado Study Says" (August 22, 2012), and "Updated Election Forecasting Model Still Points to Romney Win, University of Colorado Study Says"

(October 4, 2012), both in "News," University of Colorado Boulder, www.colorado.edu. For a number of efforts by political scientists to forecast the 2012 election see "Symposium: Forecasting the 2012 American National Elections," *PS: Political Science & Politics*, 45(4), October 2012. For their own review of their forecasting after the election, see "Features Symposium: Recap: Forecasting the 2012 Election," *PS: Political Science & Politics*, 46(1), January 2013.

6. David A. Fahrenthold, "Mitt Romney Reframes Himself as a 'Severely Conservative' Governor," *The Washington Post* (February 16, 2012), http://articles.washingtonpost.com.

7. Chris Stirewalt, "The Rise of the Anti-Romney: Barbour Campaign Takes Shape," FoxNews.com (March 8, 2011), http://www.foxnews.com; "Gingrich Moves to Front-Runner in Republican Presidential Poll," *Bloomberg* (November 22, 2011), www.bloomberg.com; "Mitt Romney's 'Cadillac' Flub One of Many," *Politico* (February 24, 2012), www.politico.com; Colbert I. King, "Romney's Poor Image? Don't Blame That on Obama," *The Washington Post* (November 7, 2012), www.washingtonpost.com/blogs; Alex Roarty, "Romney Finally Gets His Title: Presumptive Republican Nominee," *National Journal* (May 14, 2012) (updated), www.nationaljournal.com.

8. Beth Fouhy, "Obama, Romney Pursue Divergent Ad Strategies," *AP* (August 23, 2012), www.bigstory.ap.org.

9. Glenn Kessler, "Fact checking the GOP Convention's Opening Night," *The Washington Post* (July 29, 2012), www.washingtonpost.com; Z. Byron Wolf, "Clint Eastwood Explains Empty-Chair Speech," *ABC NEWS* (September 7, 2012), www.abcnews.go.com; Russell Berman, "Romney: Voters 'Deserve Better' Than What Obama Has Delivered," *The Hill* (August 20, 2012), www.thehill.com; "Excerpts: Romney's Acceptance Speech," Political Ticker, *CNN* (August 30, 2012), http://politicalticker.blogs.cnn.com.

10. Hendrik Hertzberg, "We Built It," *The New Yorker* (August 29, 2012), www.newyorker.com; "'You Didn't Build That'; A Theme Out of Context," *CNN* (September 1, 2012); Greg Sargent, "Romney's 'You Didn't Build That' Attack: An Epic FAIL," *The Washington Post* (October 3, 2012), www.washingtonpost.com.

11. Karen Tumulty and Ed O'Keefe, "Michelle Obama's Convention Speech Proves to Be Shining Moment," *The Washington Post* (Sepbemer 5, 2012), http://articles.washingtonpost.com; Richard Wolf and David Jackson, "Analysis: Clinton Argues the Case for Re-election," *USA Today* (September 6, 2012), http://usatoday30.usatoday.com; David Firestone, "Joe Biden's Speech," *The New York Times* (September 6, 2012), http://takingnote.blogs.nytimes.com; Rebecca Sinderbrand, "Analysis: Obama Hit the Marks He Needed To," *CNN Politics* (September 7, 2012), www.cnn.com; Helen Cooper and Peter Baker, "Obama Makes Case for 2nd Term: 'Harder' Path to 'Better Place,'" *The New York Times* (September 6, 2012), www.nytimes.com.

12. Nate Silver, "Sept 8: Conventions May Put Obama in Front-Runner's Position," Five Thirty Eight, *The New York Times* (September 8, 2012), http://fivethirtyeight.blogs.nytimes.com.

13. Donovan Black, "RIP Postive Ads in 2012," *Politico* (November 4, 2012), www.politico.com.

14. John F. Harris and Alexander Burns, "The Verdict Is In: Obama Levels More Personal Attacks," *Politico* (September 6, 2012), www.politico.com; Evan McMorris-Santoro, "Romney Attacks Obama for Being a Socialist Without Calling Him a Socialist," *Talking Points Memo* (December 7, 2011), www.talkingpointsmemo.com.

15. For a good summary on a range of issues, see Peter Grier, "Obama vs. Romney 101: Where Are the Sharpest Divides?," *The Christian Science Monitor* (August 12, 2012), www.csmonitor.com; Tom Cohen, "Obama Administration to Stop Deporting Some Young Illegal Immigrants," CNN Politics (June 16, 2012), www.cnn.com; Philip Rucker, "Romney Repeats Sharp Criticism of Obama After Benghazi, Cairo Attacks," *The Washington Post* (September 12, 2012), www.washingtonpost.com.

16. "Transcript: Romney's Speech From Mother Jones Video," *The New York Times* (September 19, 2012), www.nytimes.com; "Mitt Romney, Class Warrior," *The New York Times* (September 18, 2012), www.nytimes.com; Nate Silver, "Sept. 27: The Impact of the '47 Percent,'" Five Thirty Eight, *The New York Times* (September 28, 2012), http://fivethirtyeight.blogs.nytimes.com.

17. Jeff Zeleny and Jim Rutenberg, "Obama and Romney, in First Debate, Spar over Fixing the Economy," *The New York Times* (October 3, 2012), www.nytimes.com; Elise Viebeck, "Obama Brought Up Planned Parenthood Four Times in Debate," Healthwatch, *The Hill* (October 16, 2012), www.thehill.com; "Barack Obama says Mitt Romney Opposes Contraception Mandate and Would Cut Planned Parenthood Funding," *PoliticFact.com*, *Tampa Bay Times*, www.politifact.com, accessed February 28, 2013.

18. Nate Silver, "Nov. 4: Did Hurricane Sandy Blow Romney Off Course?," Five Thirty Eight, *The New York Times* (November 4, 2012).

19. Spending is after April 11, when Romney's last Republican challenger, Rick Santorum, dropped out of the race. It includes the candidates' spending and that of parties and supporting outside groups. "Mad Money: TV Ads in the 2012 Presidential Campaign," *The Washington Post* (updated November 14, 2012), www.washingtonpost.com; Devin Dwyer, "Election 2012: The Campaigns by the Numbers," ABC News, http://abcnews.go.com; Marcus Stern and Tim McLaughlin, "Obama 2012: President's Ad Team Used Cable TV to Outplay Mitt Romney," *HuffingtonPost.com* (January 1, 2013), www.huffingtonpost.com; Scott Bomboy, "A Real TV Ad Bombshell to Drop on Swing States," *Constitution Daily* (October 25, 2012), http://blog.constitutioncenter.org.

20. Ben DiMiero and Eric Hananoki, "It's Official: Dick Morris Is 'Through,'" *Media Matters for America*, http://mediamatters.org/blog.

21. Aaron Blake, "Guess What? The Polls (and Nate Silver) Were Right," *The Washington Post* (November 7, 2012), www.washingtonpost.com; Aaron Blake, "Why Obama Won the 2012 Election (in One Chart)," *The Washington Post* (December 6, 2012), www.washingtonpost.com; Blake posts the conservative polling group Resurgent Republic's graphic, "The 2012 Enthusiasm Mirage"; Jan Crawford, "Adviser: Romney Shellshocked by Loss," CBS News (November 8, 2012), www.cbs.com; Noam Scheiber, "The Internal Polls That Made Mitt Romney Think He'd Win," *The New Republic* (November 30, 2012), www.newrepublic.com; "Exit polls 2012: How the Vote Has Shifted," *Washington Post* (November 8, 2012), www.washingtonpost.com.

22. It was only the second time since World War II that one party won control of the House while getting less overall votes than the other party. See, Griff Palmer and Michael Cooper, "How Maps Helped Republicans Keep an Edge in the House," *The New York Times* (December 14, 2012), www.nytimes.com.

23. Richard Viguerie, "10 Reasons Why Obama Won and Romney Lost—A Two Part Series," *Conservative HQ* (November 20, 2012), www.conservativehq.com; Linda Feldmann, "Election 2012: 12 Reasons Obama Won and Romney Lost," DC Decoder, *The Christina Science Monitor* (November 7, 2012), www.csmonitor.com; David Jackson, "How Obama Won Re-Election," *USA Today* (November 9, 2012); Maggie Haberman, "President Obama's Reelection: 12 Takeaways," *Politico* (November 7, 2012); Darrell M. West, "Communications Lessons from the 2012 Election," *Brookings* (November 6, 2012), www.brookings.edu; Mark Blumenthal, "Obama Campaign Polls: How the Internal Data Got It Right," *Huffington Post* (November 21, 2012), www.huffingtonpost.com.

24. Sasha Issenberg, "Obama Does It Better," *Slate* (October 29, 2012); Eric Siegel, "Team Obama Mastered the Science of Mass Persuasion—And Won" (January 22, 2013), http://www.truth-out.org/news/item/14026; Lois Becket, "Everything We Know (So Far) About Obama's Big Data Tactics," *ProPublica* (November 29, 2012), www.probulica.com (accessed on March 11, 2013); John Hayward, "Orca Aground: Romney's High-Tech 'Get Out the Vote' Failure," *Human Events: Powerful Conservative Voices* (November 21, 2012), www.humanevents.com; Robert Draper, "Can the Republicans Be Saved From Obsolescence?," *The New York Times* (February 13, 2013), www.nytimes.com.

25. Viguerie, "10 Reasons"; Feldmann, "Election 2012"; Jackson, "How Obama Won Re-Election"; Haberman, "President Obama's Reelection"; West, "Communications Lessons".

26. Albert R. Hunt, "Party's Base Is the Reason Romney Lost," *The New York Times* (November 18, 2012), www.nytimes.com; "Presidential Approval Ratings—George W. Bush," Gallup, www.gallup.com; "George W. Bush: Favorability Ratings," CNN/ORC Poll, *PollingReport.com* (May 29-31, 2012), www.pollingreport.com; "Democratic Party," "Republican Party," *PollingReport.com*, www.pollingreport.com; "Disapproval of Republicans in Congress Reaches Highest Level Ever," *Democracy Corps* (January 16, 2012), www.democracycorps.com; David Jackson, "Biden: Bin Laden Is Dead, General Motors Is Alive," *USA Today* (August 26, 2012), http://content.usatoday.com.

27. "How Groups Voted in 2008," "How Groups Voted in 2012," *Roper Center*, www.ropercenter.uconn.edu (accessed February 27, 2013); Thom File, "The Diversifying Electorate—Voting Rates by Race and Hispanic Origin in 2012 (and Other Recent Elections)," Population Characteristics, Current Population Survey, May 2013, U.S. Census Bureau, p. 3, 6, http://www.census.gov/prod/2013pubs/p20-568.pdf; Michael McDonald, "Voter Turnout," United States Election Project, http://elections.gmu.edu/voter_turnout.htm (accessed on March 24, 2013).

28. Alexander Keyssar, "Voter Suppression Returns: Voting Rights and Parisan Practices," *Harvard Magazine* (July-August 2012), www.harvardmagazine.com; Bill Fletcher, Jr., "Reflections on the 2012 Election," *The Progressive* (February 22, 2013), www.progressive.org.

29. See Martin Wattenberg, *The Rise of Candidate-Centered Politics* (Cambridge, MA: Harvard University Press, 1991); David Meneffee-Libey, *The Triumph of Campaign Centered Politics* (Chatham, NJ: Chatham House, 2000).

30. Sidney Blumenthal, *The Permanent Campaign* (New York: Harper & Row, 1981). See also David Mayhew, *Congress: The Electoral Connection* (New Haven, CT: Yale University Press, 1974).

31. On this theme, see Tom De Luca and John Buell, *Liars! Cheaters! Evildoers! Demonization and the End of Civil Debate in Politics* (New York: NYU Press, 2005).

32. "Politicians & Elections," "Historical Elections," Center for Responsive Politics, www.opensecrets.org; Tarini Parti, "$7 Billion Spent on 2012 Campaign, FEC says," *Politico* (January 31, 2013), www.politico.com; "Statement of Chair Ellen L. Weintraub," Federal Election Commission (January 31, 2013), http://www.fec.gov.

33. 2012 figures compiled from the Federal Election Commission. See Jay Costa, "What's the Cost of a Seat in Congress," Maplight, (March 13, 2013), http://maplight.org/content/73190.

34. Alan Abramowitz, "The Anti-Incumbent Election Myth," *Sabato's Crystal Ball* (December 22, 2011), www.centerforpolitics.org. Data on fundraising from "Historical Elections, Congress, The Dollars and Cents of Incumbency, Incumbent Advantage," Opensecrets.org, Center for Responsive Politics, www.opensecrets.org.

35. Nine switched from Democrat to Republican and nine from Republican to Democrat for a total of eighteen party changes. Open seats here refer to districts in which an incumbent retired, died or lost a primary election, but does not include new districts, or redistricting that prompted an incumbent to retire. "2012 House Election Results," House Press Gallery, http://housepressgallery.house.gov/2012-house-election-results.

36. David Plotz, "The House Incumbent: He Can't Lose," *Slate* (November 3, 2000), www.slate.com.

37. For an exhaustive review of the early period of the FECA, see Anthony Corrado, Thomas Mann, and Frank Sorauf, eds., *Campaign Finance Reform: A Sourcebook* (Washington, D.C.: Brookings Institution Press, 1997).

38. In 2012, the limit for coordinated expenditures with the presidential campaign was $21,684,200 for each party. "2012 Coordinated Party Expenditure Limits," Federal Election Commission, www.fec.gov. Political parties are also under some restrictions as to how they can spend money on their candidates. They may do so in three ways: By giving donations within campaign finance limits, which are low; by purchasing goods and services in coordination with the campaign, which has different limits depending on the place and on the year; by making independent expenditures, which must be uncoordinated but can be unlimited. See R. Sam Garrett and L. Paige Whitaker, "Coordinated Party Expenditures in Federal Elections: An Overview, for the Congressional Research Service Report for Congress," http://www.congressionalresearch.com.

39. *McConnell v. Federal Election Commission*, 540 U.S. 93 (2003), 123-4, and note 7, http://www.supremecourt.gov/opinions/boundvolumes.aspx; Jennifer Keen and John Daly, *Beyond the Limits: Soft Money in the 1996 Elections* (Washington, D.C.: Center for Responsive Politics, 1997); see also Anthony Corrado, "Financing," in *The Election of 2000*, ed. Gerald M. Pomper (New York: Chatham House), 152–57. For general accounts, see Elizabeth Drew, *The Corruption of American Politics* (Secaucus, NJ: Carol Publishing, 1999); and Michael Malbin and Thomas Gais, *The Day After Reform* (Albany, NY: Rockefeller Institute Press, 1998).

40. The bill also included "stand behind your ad" provision that requires candidates to take responsibility for ads that their campaigns broadcast. "Introduction to Bipartisan Campaign Reform Act of 2002 (BCRA)," Public Citizen, www.citizen.org/congress.

41. Adam Liptak, "Justices, 5-4, Reject Corporate Spending Limit," *New York Times* (January 21, 2010), www.nytimes.com; Citizens United v. Federal Election Commission (08-2050) 558 U.S. 310 (2010) (www.law.cornell.edu).

42. "527s—Frequently Asked Questions," Center for Public Integrity, www.publicintegrity.org.

43. Thomas B. Edsall, "New Routes for Money to Sway Voters," *Washington Post* (September 27, 2004); Edsall, "FEC Adopts Hands-Off Stance on '527' Spending," *Washington Post* (June 1, 2006), A4. For 527 spending in 2004 and 2008 see, "527s: Advocacy Group Spending in the 2008 Elections," Opensecrets.org, Center for Responsive Politics, www.opensecrets.org; "Soft Money Political Spending by 501(c) Nonprofits Tripled in 2008 Election," Campaign Finance Institute (February 25, 2009), www.cfinst.org. Sandy Johnson and Peter H. Stone, "New Ads Reflect Spending Power of Super PACs, 501(c)(4) Groups," The Center for Public Integrity (December 1, 2011), www.publicintegrity.org; Paul Blumenthal, "DISCLOSE Campaign Spending Act Blocked by Senate Republicans," The Huffington Post (July 17, 2012, www.huffingtonpost.com; "2012 Outside Spending, by Group," Non-Disclosing Groups, Center for Responsive Politics, www.opensecrets.org; "527: Advocacy Group Spending," Center for Responsive Politics, http://www.opensecrets.org/527/index.php.

44. Parti, "$7 Billion Spent on 2012 Campaign, FEC says"; The $950 million figure is from the FEC. The Sunlight Foundation and Center for Responsive Politics suggest lower expenditures. See, "Statement of Chair Ellen L. Weintraub," Federal Election Commission; "Super PACs," Sunlight Foundation; http://reporting.sunlightfoundation.com/outside-spending-2012/super-pacs/; "Super PACs," Center for Responsive Politics, http://www.opensecrets.org/pacs/superpacs.php?cycle=; "Independent Spending Totals," *The New York Times*, http://elections.nytimes.com/2012/campaign-finance/independent-expenditures/totals.

45. In 2003, most of BCRAs provisions had been upheld by the Supreme Court in McConnell v. Federal Election Commission (02-1674) 540 U.S. 93 (2003) (www.law.cornell.edu); "Campaign-Finance Excerpts, Remarks," The First Amendment Center, http://archive.firstamendmentcenter.org/news.aspx?id=12336. According to Mel Sembler, former finance chair of the Republican National Committee, "Much of those funds that used to flow to the national party committees as soft money have found their way to these c4s and super PACs for the electoral process." Sandy Johnson and Peter H. Stone, "New Ads Reflect Spending Power of Super PACs, 501(c)(4) Groups," The Center for Public Integrity (December 1, 2011), www.publicintegrity.org; "Follow the Unlimited Money," Sunlight Foundation Reporting Group.

46. "Groups Energized by Amendments to Overturn Citizens United, Bipartisan Support, Enthusiastic 'Netroots Response,'" Free-Speech-For-People.org (January 23, 2012), www.freespeechforpeople.org.

47. For the full text of the House Joint Resolution 20, go to Library of Congress, http://thomas.loc.gov/cgi-bin/query/z?c113:H.J.RES.20:/. For House Joint Resolution 21, go to http://thomas.loc.gov/cgi-bin/query/z?c113:H.J.RES.21:/.

48. Parti, "$7 Billion Spent on 2012 Campaign, FEC says"; "Top PACs," Opensecrets.org, Center for Responsive Politics, http://www.opensecrets.org/pacs/toppacs.php (accessed March 24, 2013); "About Us," http://www.northropgrumman.com/about_us/index.html; SIPRI Yearbook 2012, "Arms Production and Military Services," Stockholm International Peace Research Institute, http://www.sipri.org/yearbook/2012/05.

49. "2004 Election Overview: Business-Labor-Ideology Split," Opensecrets.org, Center for Responsive Politics, www.opensecrets.org; "Political Action Committees," and "Business-Labor-Ideology Split in PAC & Individual Donations to Candidates and Parties," Opensecrets.org, Center for Responsive Politics, www.opensecrets.org.

50. "Donor Demographics" for the years 2012, 2008, and 2004, Opensecrets.org, Center for Responsive Politics, www.opensecrets.org; "Political Involvement and Participation in Politics," Table 6B.5, "Gave Money to Help a Campaign," The American National Election Studies, www.electionstudies.org. For an earlier comprehensive study of the subject of political inequalities see, Sidney Verba, Kay Schlozman, and Henry Brady, *Voice and Equality: Civic Voluntarism in American Politics* (Cambridge, MA: Harvard University Press, 1995): 49–87.

51. "Political Parties Overview, 2012," Opensecrets. org, Center for Responsive Politics, www.opensecrets.org (accessed, February 11, 2013).

52. "State and County QuickFacts," "USA," United States Census Bureau, http://quickfacts.census.gov (accessed February 16, 2013).

53. "Top Overall Individual Contributors," and "Bundlers," Opensecrets.org, Center for Responsive Politics, www.opensecrets.org (accessed February 7, 2013); Michael Beckel, "Democratic Financier Cynthia Stroum Flames Out after Brief Stint as Barack Obama's Ambassador to Luxembourg," Opensecrets.org (February 4, 2011), www.opensecrets.org; Michael Barbaro, "For Wealthy Romney Donors, Up Close and Personal Access," *New York Times* (June 23, 2012), www.nytimes.com.

54. Thomas Edsall, "Study: Corporate PACs Favor GOP," *Washington Post* (November 25, 2004); Politicalmoneyline.org (November 2004); "Business-Labor-Ideology Split in PAC & Individual Donations to Candidates, Parties, Super PACs and Outside Spending Groups, 2012 Overview," *Opensecrets.org*, Center for Responsive Politics, www.opensecrets.org. According to the Center, "The broadest classification of political donors separates them into business, labor, or ideological interests. Whatever slice you look at, business interests dominate, with an overall advantage over organized labor of about 15 to 1. Even among PACs—the favored means of delivering funds by labor unions—business has a more than 3-to-1 fundraising advantage. In soft money, the ratio is nearly 17-to-1. An important caveat must be added to these figures: 'business' contributions from individuals are based on the donor's occupation/employer. Since nearly everyone works for someone, and since union affiliation is not listed on FEC reports, totals for business are somewhat overstated, while labor is understated. Still, the base of large individual donors is predominantly made up of business executives and professionals. Contributions under $200 are not included in these numbers, as they are not itemized."

55. See "Interest Groups," Opensecrets.org, The Center for Responsive Politics, www.opensecrets.org.

56. Lee Drutman, "The Political One Percent of the One Percent," The Sunlight Foundation (December 13, 2011), http://sunlightfoundation.com/blog/2011/12/13/.

57. Ibid.

58. Martin Gillens, "Inequality and Democratic Responsiveness," *Public Opinion Quarterly*, 69(5), http://poq.oxfordjournals.org/content/69/5/778.full; Jamelle Bouie, "Who Are the 1 Percent?" *The Nation* (December 15, 2011), http://www.thenation.com/blog/165176/who-are-1-percent#; John Sides, "The Politics of the Top One Percent," FiveThirtyEight, *New York Times* (December 14, 2011), http://fivethirtyeight.blogs.nytimes.com/2011/12/14.

59. Jonathan D. Salant, "Obama Outpaces Romney in Small-Donor Contributions," *Bloomberg* (August 28, 2012), www.bloomberg.com.

60. Michael Malbin, "Money vs. Money-Plus: Post-Election Reports Reveal Two Different Campaign Strategies," Campaign Finance Institute, Press Release (January 11, 2013), see Table 3, www.cfinst.org; Michael Malbin, "Obama's Long-Term Small-Donor Strategy Begins to Show Dividends against Romney in August," Campaign Finance Institute, Press Release (September 24, 2012), http://www.cfinst.org. For a discussion of which donor levels gave Obama his campaign contributions in 2008, see Michael Malbin, "CFI Analysis of Presidential Candidate's Donor Reports; REALITY CHECK: Obama Received about the Same Percentage from Small Donors in 2008 as Bush in 2004," Campaign Finance Institute, Press Release (November 24, 2008), www.cfinst.org.

61. Melanie Mason and Joseph Tanfani, "Obama, Romney Break Fundraising Records," *The Los Angeles Times* (December 7, 2012), http://articles.latimes.com; "Public Funding of Presidential Elections," Federal Election Commission, www.fec.gov. For an overview of money taken in for the presidential election by the candidate committees and the parties, see Malbin, "Money vs. Money-Plus: Post-Election Reports Reveal Two Different Campaign Strategies"; "2012 Election Spending Will Reach $6 Billion, Center for Responsive Politics Predicts," Center for Responsive Politics (October 31, 2012), www.opensecrets.org; "2012 Presidential Race," Center for Responsive Politics, http://www.opensecrets.org/pres12/#out (accessed March 24, 2013).

62. See James Moore and Wayne Slater, *Bush's Brain* (New York: Wiley, 2003); Dennis W. Johnson, *No Place for Amateurs: How Political Consultants Are Reshaping American Democracy* (New York: Routledge, 2001); Dick Morris, *Behind the Oval Office* (New York: Random House, 1997).

63. Johnson, *No Place for Amateurs*, p. 6; Larry Sabato, *The Rise of Political Consultants* (New York: Basic Books, 1981); Lou DuBose, *Boy Genius* (New York: Public Affairs, 2003).

64. "The Great Ad Wars," *New York Times* (November 1, 2004); Thomas Edsall and Derek Willis, "Fundraising Records Broken," *Washington Post* (December 3, 2004). For 2008 figures, see Campaign Media Analysis Group, *TNS Media Intelligence/CMAG*, www.tnsmi-cmag.com; Katharine Q. Seelye, "About $2.6 Billion Spent on Political Ads in 2008," The Caucus, *New York Times* (December 2, 2008), http://thecaucus.blogs.nytimes.com.

65. Script adapted from *P2012: Race for the White House*, http://www.p2012.org/ads3/obamaad100912bb.html; Devin Dwyer, "Obama TV Ad Uses 'Big Bird' to Mock Romney," *ABC News* (October 19, 2012), www.abcnews.go.com; see also Stephen Ansolabehere and Shanto Iyengar, *Going Negative* (New York: Free Press, 1995); Darrell West, *Air Wars: Television Advertisements in Election Campaigns* (Washington, D.C.: Congressional Quarterly Press, 1997). To watch the ad go to http://www.youtube.com/watch?v=bZxs09eV-Vc&feature=em-uploademail-new.

66. José Antonio Vargas, "Obama Raised Half a Billion Online," *The Washington Post* (November 20, 2008), http://voices.washingtonpost.com; Glen Justice, "Kerry Kept Money Coming with Internet," *New York Times* (November 6, 2004). See Joe Trippi, *The Revolution Will Not Be Televised* (New York: Regan Books, 2004); Michael Cornfield, *Politics Moves Online* (New York: Century Foundation, 2004); Richard Viguerie, *America's Right Turn: How Conservatives Used New and Alternative Media* (Santa Monica, CA: Bonus Books, 2004); Michael Scherer, "Exclusive: Obama's 2012 Digital Fundraising Outperformed 2008," *Time* (November 15, 2012), http://swampland.time.com.

67. For an early defense of these practices, see James Carville and Mary Matalin, *All's Fair* (New York: Random House, 1994); Timothy Cook, Marion Just, and Ann Crigler, *Crosstalk: Campaigns, Candidates, Citizens, and the Press* (Chicago, IL: University of Chicago Press, 1996).

68. The term "science of mass persuasion" is taken from Eric Siegel, "Team Obama Mastered the Science of Mass Persuasion—And Won."

69. Adam Nagourney, "Bush Campaign Manager Views the Electoral Divide," *New York Times* (November 19, 2004); Katherine Seelye, "How to Sell a Candidate to a Porsche-Driving Leno-Loving Nascar Fan," *New York Times* (December 6, 2004); Matt Bai, "The Multi-Level Marketing of the President," *New York Times Magazine* (April 25, 2004); Nicole Mellow, "Republicans," in Nelson, ed., *The Elections of 2004*; Ronald Brownstein and Richard Rainey, "GOP Plants Flag on New Voting Frontier," *Los Angeles Times* (November 22, 2004): A1.

70. Siegel, "Team Obama Mastered the Science of Mass Persuasion—And Won." Robert L. Mitchell, "Election 2012: Obama for America's 'Moneyball' Moment," *Computerworld* (November 6, 2012), http://blogs.computerworld.com; "KXEN's Predictive Analytics Helps Drive a Smarter Obama Campaign," Press Release, KXEN (January 29, 2013), www.marketwatch.com.

71. Mitchell, "Campaign 2012: Mining for Voters" (October 29, 2012), www.computerworld.com; Sasha Issenberg, "Obama's White Whale: How the Campaign's Top-Secret Project Narwhal Could Change This Race, and Many to Come," *Slate* (February 15, 2012), www.slate.com.

72. Siegel, "Team Obama Mastered the Science of Mass Persuasion—And Won"; Mitchell, "Election 2012: Obama for America's 'Moneyball' Moment" (November 6, 2012), http://blogs.computerworld.com. See also West, "Communications Lessons from the 2012 Elections."

73. Leslie Wayne, "Democrats Take Page From Their Rival's Playbook," *New York Times* (October 31, 2008), www.nytimes.com.

74. Dennis J. McGrath and Dane Smith, *Professor Wellstone Goes to Washington: The Inside Story of a Grassroots U.S. Senate Campaign* (Minneapolis, MN: University of Minnesota Press, 1995); Richard Berke, "Several Won Big by Spending Less," *New York Times* (November 2, 1990).

75. Martha T. Moore, "Obama Volunteers Plan to Keep in Touch," *USA Today* (November 21, 2008), www.usatoday.com. For a discussion of Obama's efforts see, for example, Sarah Lai Stirland, "Inside Obama's Surging Net-Roots Campaign," *Wired* (March 3, 2008), www.wired.com.

76. See American Political Science Association Standing Committee on Civic Education and Engagement, "Democracy at Risk," Electoral Processes chapter, 2005, www.apsa.org.

CHAPTER 8

1. Lawrence Goodwyn, *The Populist Moment in America* (New York: Oxford University Press, 1976); Thomas B. Edsall and Mike Allen, "Bush Fundraisers," *Washington Post* (July 14, 2003).

2. There are a number of classic works on political parties. They include Maurice Duverger's *Political Parties* (New York: Wiley and Sons, 1954); and Max Weber, "Politics as a Vocation," in *From Max Weber*, eds. Hans Gerth and C. Wright Mills (New York: Oxford University Press, 1958), 77–128. See also E. E. Schattschneider, *Party Government* (New York: Holt, Rinehart and Winston, 1942).

3. See Walter Dean Burnham, "The End of American Party Politics," *Transaction* 7 (December 1969): 16–36; Samuel Huntington, "The Visions of the Democratic Party," *Public Interest* (Spring 1985): 64.

4. See Burnham, "The End of American Party Politics."

5. Huntington, "The Visions of the Democratic Party."

6. Walter Dean Burnham and William Nisbet Chambers, *The American Party Systems* (New York: Oxford University Press, 1976); Paul Kleppner, *Who Voted? The Dynamics* *of Electoral Turnout, 1870–1950* (New York: Harper & Row, 1983).

7. This is now somewhat less true of European parties, as there are "Americanizing" tendencies. See Joel Krieger and Mark Kesselman, *European Politics in Transition* (Boston: Houghton Mifflin, 2003).

8. See the discussion in Walter Dean Burnham, *The Current Crisis in American Politics* (New York: Oxford University Press, 1983).

9. See Ted Lowi, "Toward a Responsible Three Party System," in *A Republic of Parties?*, eds. Theodore Lowi and Joseph Romance (Lanham, MD: Rowman & Littlefield, 1998).

10. See Stephen Hill, *Fixing Elections: The Failure of America's Winner Take All Politics* (New York: Routledge, 2002): 82.

11. Dan Cantor and J. W. Mason, "Inside, Outside, or Somewhere In Between?: Fusion Voting," Working Families Party paper, 2003, www.wfp.org. See also L. Sandy Maisel and John Bibby, *Two Parties or More?* (Boulder, CO: Westview Press, 1998); and Micah Sifry, *Spoiling for a Fight: Third Party Politics in America* (New York: Routledge, 2002).

12. See George Edwards III, *Why the Electoral College Is Bad for America* (New Haven, CT: Yale University Press, 2004); and Alexander Keyssar, "The Electoral College Flunks," *New York Review of Books* (March 24, 2005).

13. Brian Montopoli, "Do the debates unfairly shut out third parties?," *CBS News* (October 15, 2012), www.cbsnews.com.

14. See Hill, *Fixing Elections*; Jeffrey Toobin, "The Great Election Grab," *The New Yorker* (December 8, 2003); "Drawing Lines: A Public Interest Real Redistricting Reform," Demos (2005), www.demos-usa.org. Every ten years, after the census, state legislatures must redraw both congressional and state legislative district lines to ensure that each one has roughly equal populations to the others, according to the constitutional principle of "one person, one vote."

15. "Presidency2012: Ballot Access," www.politics1.com (accessed March 14, 2013); "2012 Presidential Form 2 Filers," Federal Election Commission, March 15, 2013, http://www.fec.gov/press/press2011/presidential_form2nm.shtml; Harriet Rowan, "Meet a Few Other Presidential Candidates on the Ballot This Fall," PRWatch, Center for Media and Democracy (October 9, 2012), www.prwatch.org; Montopoli, "Do the Debates Unfairly Shut Out Third Parties?"; David Boaz, "First Woman," *Cato Institute* (August 29, 2008), www.cato.org.

16. We thank Tim Price for originally calculating the relative power of voters in these two states for the fifth edition of this text.

17. On how battleground states absorb the bulk of TV advertising see, for example, Steve Rabinowitz, "Pres. TV advertising spending continues to grow; Over $28 million spent from September 28–October 4," *Wisconsin Ad Project* (October 8, 2008), http:// wiscadproject.wisc.edu.

18. For the Reform Party, see Lowi, "Toward a Responsible Three Party System"; for the Greens, see Ruth Conniff, "On the Road with Ralph Nader," *The Nation* (July 17, 2000); Ralph Nader, "Parties to Injustice; Democrats Will Do Anything to Keep Me Off the Ballot," *Washington Post* (September 5, 2004). Frank Newport, "Americans Split on Need for Third Party," *Gallup* (September 12, 2012). www.gallup.com.

19. Giovanni Sartori, *Parties and Party Systems* (Cambridge, UK: Cambridge University Press: 1976): 42.

20. Walter Dean Burnham, *Critical Elections and the Mainsprings of American Politics* (New York: W. W. Norton, 1967). See also John Aldrich, *Why Parties?* (Chicago: University of Chicago Press, 1995).

21. See Jerome Clubb, Nancy Zingale, and William Flanigan, *Partisan Realignment: Voters, Party, and Government in American History* (Beverly Hills, CA: Sage, 1980). See Richard Jensen, *The Winning of the Midwest: Social and Political Conflict, 1888–1896* (Chicago: University of Chicago Press, 1971). See also Walter Dean Burnham, "The Appearance and Disappearance of the American Voter," in Burnham, ed., *The Current Crisis in American Politics*, 142–60. There are many outstanding accounts of this period. See Michael McGerr, *The Decline of Popular Politics* (New York: Oxford University Press, 1986); Robert Wiebe, *The Search for Order* (New York: Hill & Wang, 1967); V. O. Key, *Southern Politics* (New York: Alfred A. Knopf, 1967); Michael Goldfield, *The Color of Politics* (New York: New Press, 1998).

22. See Steve Fraser and Gary Gerstle, eds., *The Rise and Fall of the New Deal Order* (Princeton, NJ: Princeton University Press, 1989); Stephen Skowronek, *The Politics Presidents Make* (Cambridge, MA: Harvard University Press, 1993); Sidney Milkis, *The Modern Presidency and the Transformation of the American Party System* (New York: Oxford University Press, 1993).

23. A perceptive account of racial and cultural divides is Thomas and Mary Edsall, *Chain Reaction* (New York: W. W. Norton, 1991). See also James Davison Hunter, *Culture Wars: The Struggle to Define America* (New York: Basic Books, 1990).

24. Two good accounts of this are to be found in Goldfield, *The Color*, chap. 8; and Godfrey Hodgson, *America in Our Time* (New York: Pantheon, 1976). See the classic accounts by Norman Mailer, *Miami and the Siege of Chicago* (New York: Harper & Row, 1970); and Garry Wills, *Nixon Agonistes* (New York: Pantheon, 1970). See also Terry Anderson, *The Movement and the Sixties* (New York: Oxford University Press, 1995); and Rick Perlstein, *Before the Storm* (New York: Hill & Wang, 2002).

25. See Hodgson, *America in Our Time*.

26. A good account of Democratic economic policy is Barry Bluestone and Bennett Harrison, *The Great U-Turn* (New York: Basic Books, 1985).

27. Nicole Mellow, "Voter Behavior: The 2004 Election and the Roots of Republican Success," in *The Elections of 2004*, ed. Michael Nelson (Washington, D.C.: Congressional Quarterly Press, 2005), chap. 4; David Greene, "Architect of a Re-Election," *Newsday* (November 8, 2004); Todd Purdum and David Kirkpatrick, "Campaign Strategist Is in Position to Consolidate Republican Majority," *New York Times* (November 5, 2004).

28. For a defense of Clinton and his policies, see Sidney Blumenthal, *The Clinton Wars* (New York: Farrar, Straus, & Giroux, 2003). For analysis of the move to the "[illegible]" and a "[illegible]," see [illegible], *[illegible] Democrats* (Lawrence: University Press of Kansas, 2000). See also Morris Fiorina, *Culture War: Myth of a Polarized America* (New York: Longman, 2004).

29. Thomas Frank, *What's the Matter with Kansas?* (New York: Metropolitan Books, 2004): 6–7, 245. For more on dealignment characteristics, see *The End of Realignment*, ed. Byron Shafer (Madison: University of Wisconsin Press, 1991); and Martin Wattenberg, *The Decline of American Political Parties* (Chicago: University of Chicago Press, 1990).

30. Christopher Lasch, *The True and Only Heaven* (New York: W.W. Norton, 1991), 515.

31. Ross Douthat, "The Obama Realignment," *The New York Times* (November 7, 2012), www.nytimes.com; Bruce N. Gyory, "Democratic Realignment in the Making If Republicans Don't Adapt," *The Hill* (November 12, 2012), www.thehill.com.

32. Jeffrey M. Jones, "In U.S., Views of Obama, Democrats Improve After Election," Gallup Politics (November 16, 2012), www.gallup.com; Lydia Saad, "GOP Takes Another Image Hit Post-Election," Gallup Politics (November 20, 2008), www.gallup.com.

33. Phillip Klinkner, "Red and Blue Scare," *The Forum* 2 (1), (2004); Gerald Pomper, "The Presidential Election," and Mellow, "Voting Behavior," in *The Election*, ed. Nelson, chap. 3.

34. "2012 Fox News Exit Polls," *Fox News*, www.foxnews.com (accessed on March 14, 2013); "Election Results 2008: Exit Polls," *New York Times*, http://elections.nytimes.com; "The 2004 Election Exit Poll," www.cnn.com.

35. Larry M. Bartels, "What's the Matter with *What's the Matter with Kansas?*" unpublished paper prepared for presentation at the annual meeting of the American Political Science Association, (Washington, D.C., September 1–4), 2005, www.princeton.edu/~bartels/kansas.pdf; Bartels, "What's the Matter with *What's the Matter with Kansas?*" *Quarterly Journal of Political Science*, 2006, 1:201–226, see especially pp. 205–211, http://www.princeton.edu/~bartels/kansasqjps06.pdf; Jeffrey M. Stonecash, *Class and Party in American Politics* (Boulder, CO: Westview Press, 2000): 117. "Exit Poll" NBC News (2004), www.nbcnews.com; "Election Results 2008," Exit Polls, *New York Times*, http://elections.nytimes.com; Lisa Wade, "Presidential Candidates' Share of White Votes, 1968-2008," *Sociological Images*, http://thesocietypages.org/socimages/2008/12/05/; The Roper Center, www.ropercenter.uconn.edu/; "Election Polls—Vote by Groups, 1960-1964," Gallup, www.gallup.com. See also Ruy Teixeira and Joel Rogers, *America's Forgotten Majority: Why the White Working Class Still Matters* (New York: Basic Books, 2000): 31–34. 2008. Some of these points are discussed in Rick Perlstein et al., "Symposium on the Democrats," *Boston Review* (June 2004).

36. Simon Rios, "Lesser-Known Candidates Bring Colorful Campaigns to St. Anselm," *New Hampshire Union Leader* (December 19, 2011), www.unionleader.com; Pat Griffin, "Vermin Reins Supreme," *The Granite Column* (December 21, 2012), www.thegranitecolumn.com.

37. [illegible], "[illegible] Raising, [illegible] [illegible], [illegible] Raisers," *Washington Post* (January 22, 2004): E1; Glen Justice, "Young Bush Fundraisers Are Courted by the GOP," *New York Times* (January 22, 2005): A11; Jeremy W. Peters, "Limited Convention Broadcasts Shuts Out Ann Romney," *The New York Times* (August 22, 2012), www.nytimes.com.

38. David Brock, *Republican Noise Machine* (New York: Crown, 2004), chap. 2; Trudy Lieberman, *Slanting the Story: The Forces That Shape the News* (New York: New Press, 2000); "Buying a Movement: Right Wing Foundations," People for the American Way, www.pfaw.org.

39. Brock, *Republican Noise Machine*, chap. 2.

40. Daniel Galvin, "Why the Republican Party Is So Critical to McCain," *Britannica Blog* (June 12, 2008), www.britannica.com/blogs.

41. Matthew Creamer, "Obama Wins!…Ad Age's Marketer of the Year, *Advertising Age* (October 17, 2008), www.adage.com; Leslie Wayne, "Democrats Take Page from Their Rival's Playbook," *New York Times* (October 31, 2008), www.nytimes.com; Sasha Issenberg, "Obama Does It Better," *Slate* (October 29, 2012).

42. Robert Draper, "Can the Republicans Be Saved from Obsolescence?," *The New York Times* (February 13, 2013), (www.nytimes.com); Zachary Roth, "Strong for the Future? The Democratic Party After Obama," MSNBC (January 22, 2013), http:///tv.www.msnbc.com; Cameron Joseph, "Rebranded Obama Campaign Group Causes Frustration for DNC," *The Hill* (January 22, 2013), www.thehill.com.

43. Robert Reich, "Movement Politics," *Boston Review*, Summer 2004.

CHAPTER 9

1. PIPA/Knowledge Networks Poll, "Americans and Iraq on the Eve of the Presidential Election" (October 28, 2004); PIPA/Knowledge Networks Poll, "The Separate Realities of Bush and Kerry Supporters" (October 21, 2004), www.pipa.org.

2. The Project for Excellence in Journalism, "The State of the News Media 2011: An Annual Report on American Journalism," www.stateofmedia.org; National Directory of Magazines 2010; Benn's Media 2004, 152nd edition.

3. "Demographics of Internet Users," Pew Internet and American Life Project (August 2012), www.pewinternet.org.

4. While Disney owns ABC, Comcast has 51% of NBC, while GE owns 49%.

5. Thomas Leonard, *The Power of the Press* (New York: Oxford University Press, 1986).

6. Michael Schudson, *Discovering the News* (New York: Basic Books, 1978).

7. Frank Luther Mott, *American Journalism 1660–1960* (New York: Macmillan, 1962), 529. For an account of Hearst's life, see W. A. Swanberg, *Citizen Hearst* (New York: Scribner's, 1961). Richard Niemi and Harold Stanley, *Vital Statistics on American Politics, 2003–2004* (Washington, D.C.: Congressional Quarterly Press, 2004); "Media," Pew Research Center for the People and the Press (January 2005), www.people-press.org; Suzanne M. Kirchhoff, "The U.S. Newspaper Industry in Transition," Congressional Research Service (September 9, 2010), http://www.fas.org/sgp/crs/misc/R40700.pdf; "Newspapers by the Numbers," State of the News Media 2012, The Pew Research Center's Project for Excellence in Journalism, http://stateofthemedia.org/2012/.

8. See the account in Ronald Berkman and Laura Kitch, *The Politics of Mass Media* (New York: St. Martin's Press, 1990): 42.

9. On TV coverage of the 1960s, see Edward Epstein, *News from Nowhere* (New York: Random House, 1973); Michael Arlen, *The Living Room War* (New York: Viking, 1969).

10. For recent data on the decline of network news viewing, see: The Project for Excellence in Journalism, "Audience," The State of the News Media 2012: An Annual Report on American Journalism, http://stateofthenewsmedia.org/2012.

11. Louisa Ada Seltzer, "Nightly News Viewers Are Aging Faster: Median Age for the Big Three Rises to 62.3 Years," *Medialife* (April 29, 2010), http://www.medialifemagazine.com/nightly-news-viewers-are-aging-faster/; "Average Age of Old Media Users/Viewers," *Stephen's Lighthouse*, http://stephenslighthouse.com/2010/08/16/; National Annenberg Election Survey, "*Daily Show* Viewers Knowledgeable About Presidential Campaign" (September 21, 2004), www.naes04.org.

12. "In Changing News Landscape, Even Television Is Vulnerable: Trends in News Consumption 1991–2012," Pew Research Center for the People and the Press (September 27, 2012), http://www.people-press.org/2012/09/27/.

13. "NAVIGATING NEWS ONLINE: Facebook Is Becoming Increasingly Important," Journalism.org (May 9, 2011), www.journalism.org; "What Is Digg?", digg.com/about; David Carr, "Muckraking Pays, Just Not in Profit," *New York Times*, (December 10, 2007), www.nytimes.com; Amy Mitchell, Tom Rosenstiel, and Leah Christian, "What Facebook and Twitter Mean for News" and "Mobile Devices and News Consumption: Some Good Signs for Journalism," *The State of the News Media 2012*, The Pew Research Center's Project for Excellence in Journalism, http://stateofthemedia.org/2012/; Joanna Brenner, "Internet: Mobile," Pew Internet (December 4, 2012), http://pewinternet.org.

14. Carr, "Muckraking Pays, Just Not in Profit."

15. Cass Sunstein, "The Daily We," *Boston Review*, Summer 2001; Cass Sunstein, *Republic.com* (Princeton, NJ: Princeton University Press, 2002).

16. "Americans Spending More Time Following the News," Pew Research Center (September 12, 2010), http://www.people-press.org/2010/09/12/americans-spending-more-time-following-the-news/. For 1940s media studies, see Paul Lazarsfeld, Bernard Berelson, and Hazel Gaudet, *The People's Choice* (New York: Columbia University Press, 1948). For the 1970s, see Thomas Paterson and Robert McClure, *The Unseeing Eye* (New York: G. P. Putnam, 1976): 90.

17. Shanto Iyengar and Donald Kinder, *News That Matters: The Agenda-Setting Function of the Press* (Chicago: University of Chicago Press, 1987); S. Iyengar, M. Peters, and D. Kinder, "Experimental Demonstrations of the Not-So-Minimal Consequences of Television News Programs," *American Political Science Review* (Winter 1982): 848–58.

18. Robert McChesney, *The Problem of the Media: U.S. Communications Politics in the 21st Century* (New York: Monthly Review Press, 2004), chap. 5; Gina Keating and Robert MacMillan, "TIMELINE: NBC, Universal Through the 20th Century and Beyond," Reuters (December 3, 2009), www.reuters.com; "Jan. 10, 2000, AOL and Time Warner Announce Merger," The Learning Network (January 10, 2012), http://learning.blogs.nytimes.com/2012/01/10/.

19. "The Big Six," *freepress*, www.freepress.net; Robert McChesney, *Rich Media, Poor Democracy* (New York: The New Press, 2001), chap. 2; Peter Golding and Phil Harris, eds., *Beyond Cultural Imperialism: Globalization, Communication and the New International Order* (London: Sage, 1997); McChesney, *Problem of the Media*, 178. See also Mark Crispin Miller, "Big Media, Bad News," *The Nation* (January 7, 2002).

20. "Who Owns What," *Columbia Journalism Review*, 2012, www.cjr.org.

21. Peter Philips, *Censored 2000* (New York: Seven Stories Press, 2001); "Project Censored 2005," Sonoma State University, www.projectcensored.org.

22. On labor and the media, also see: "Media Ignoring Labor Union Successes." BeyondChron (February 17, 2010), http://www.beyondchron.org/news/index.php?itemid=7820; Stephen Franklin, "Where Have All the Labor Writers Gone?" *In These Times* (December 10, 2009), www.inthesetimes.com; Todd Gitlin, "What Was Gained at WTO?," *Los Angeles Times* (December 7, 1999): 9; Janet Thomas, *The Battle in Seattle* (Eugene, OR: Fulcrum, 2001). See also "Protesting the Piece," National Public Radio, *On the Media* (November 1, 2002); Michael Frome, "The 21st Century Economy," *The American Writer* (Winter 2000), 14.

23. McChesney, *Rich Media*, chap. 2; Golding and Harris, *Beyond Cultural Imperialism*.

24. Carr, "Muckraking Pays, Just Not in Profit."

25. McChesney, *Problem of the Media*, p. 82 and chap. 5. See Ken Auletta, "Sign Off," *The New Yorker* (March 7, 2005); Doug Underwood, *When MBAs Rule the Newsroom* (New York: Columbia University Press, 1996).

26. Paul Farhi, "Olympics Coverage by NBC News Questioned" *The Washington Post* (July, 26, 2012), www.washingtonpost.com; Paul Farhi, "NBC News Tout?" Playback: The Games on NBC (August 21, 2008), http://voices.washingtonpost.com.

27. McChesney, *Problem of the Media*, 84; Joe Strupp, "New Advertorials Raise Old Ethical Questions," *Editor and Publishers* (November 17, 2003;) Mark Jurkowitz, "When Journalists Become Pitchmen," *Boston Globe* (February 10, 2000); Lance Bennett, *News: The Politics of Illusion* (New York: Longman, 2004).

28. Richard Pérez-Peña, "Times to Sell Display Ads on the Front Page," *New York Times* (January 5, 2009), www.nytimes.com.

29. Douglas Rushkoff, "The Internet: Coercion in Cyberspace?" in Bruce Miroff, Raymond Seidelman, and Todd Swanstrom, *Debating Democracy. A Reader in American Politics*, 3rd ed. (Boston, MA: Houghton Mifflin, 2001), 205.

30. See www.savetheinternet.com for an example of a website devoted to maintaining "net neutrality."

31. "Internet Freedom Law Will Keep Internet Open for Future Innovators: Rep. Markey Introduces Internet Freedom Legislation with Rep. Pickering" (February 13, 2008), http://markey.house.gov. Peter Voskamp, "GOP Attempt to Overturn FCC's Net Neutrality Rules Fails in Senate," Reuters (November 10, 2011), www.reuters.com.

32. "A Digital Cold War?" *The Economist* (December 14, 2012), http://www.economist.com/blogs/babbage/2012/12/internet-regulation; Elise Ackerman. "The U.N. Fought the Internet and the Internet Won; WCIT Summit in Dubai Ends," *Forbes* (December 14, 2012), www.forbes.com.

33. See Martha Honey, "Contra Coverage: Paid for by the CIA," *Columbia Journalism Review* (March/April 1987): 31–32.

34. David Barstow, William J. Broad, and Jeff Gerth, "How the White House Embraced Disputed Arms Intelligence," *New York Times* (August 3, 2004), www.nytimes.com.

35. Michael Massing, "Now They Tell Us," *New York Review of Books* (February 26, 2004), www.nybooks.com; Massing, "The Unseen War," *New York Review of Books* (May 29, 2003); Sheldon Rampton and John Stauber, *Weapons of Mass Deception* (Boston: Common Courage Press, 2004).

36. "Judith Miller Goes to Jail," *New York Times* (July 7, 2005): A22.

37. Amy Goodman and Juan Gonzalez, "Is WikiLeaks' Julian Assange a Hero? Glenn Greenwald Debates Steven Aftergood of Secrecy News," *Democracy Now!* (December 3, 2010), www.democracynow.org; Bill Keller, "WikiLeaks, a Postscript," *New York Times* (February 19, 2012), www.nytimes.com; Bradley Bennett, "Bradley Manning Trial in WikiLeaks Case Delayed by Military Judge," *Los Angeles Times* (January 10, 2013), www.latimes.com; Alasdair Roberts, "The WikiLeaks Illusion," *The Wilson Quarterly* (September 2011), www.wilsonquarterly.com.

38. Naomi Wolf, "WikiLeaks, Revolution, and the Lost Cojones of American Journalism," *Huffington Post* (February 4, 2011), www.huffingtonpost.com; Charlie Beckett, "WikiLeaks Symptomatic of a Trend That's Going to Accelerate," Editors Weblog, World Association of Newspapers and Publishers (September 21, 2011), www.editorsweblog.org; Bill Dedman, "U.S. v. WikiLeaks: Espionage and the First Amendment," MSNBC legal panel, www.msnbc.com (last accessed June 24, 2013); Päivikki Karhula, "What Is the Effect of WikiLeaks for Freedom of Information?" *IFLA Journal* (January 19, 2011), http://www.ifla.org/publications/what-is-the-effect-of-wikileaks-for-freedom-of-information.

39. For excellent accounts of the corrosive effects of celebrity journalism on the political agenda, see James Fallows, *Breaking the News: How the Media Undermine American Democracy* (New York: Pantheon, 1995). See also Martin Lee and Norman Solomon, *Unreliable Sources* (New York: Carol, 1991); Jim Drinkard, "President Criticizes Education Dept.'s Payout to Williams," *USA Today* (January 14, 2005).

40. See also Robert McChesney, *Telecommunications, Mass Media, and Democracy* (New York: Oxford University Press, 1993), chaps. 1, 6; Joshua Rosenkranz, "Free TV Speech for Candidates," *The Nation* (June 8, 1998): 31; Christopher Stern, "Broadcast Loan Has Xmas Wrapping," *Variety* (April 4, 1997): 24; Robert McChesney, "The Digital TV Scandal: How a Powerful Lobby Stole Billions in Public Property," *Public Citizen News* (Fall 1997).

41. McChesney, *Problem of the Media*, final chapter; Robert Siegel, "Federal Appeals Court Tosses Out Set of FCC Regulations Regarding the Number of Media Properties That a Single Company Can Own," National Public Radio, *All Things Considered*, June 24, 2004.

42. Daniel Weaver and C. Cleveland Wilhoit, *The American Journalist in the 1990s: U.S. News People at the End of an Era* (Mahwah, NJ: Erlbaum, 1996): 7; David Croteau, "Examining the Liberal Media Claim: Journalists' Views on Politics, Economic Policy, and Media Coverage," Fairness and Accuracy in Reporting (FAIR) (June 1998), www.fair.org/reports; Pew Center for the People and the Press and Project for Excellence in Journalism, *State of the Media, 2004*, Journalists' Survey, www.journalism.org; "State of Journalism," Pew Center for the People and the Press and Project for Excellence in Journalism, *State of the Media*, 2008, http://www.people-press.org/2008/03/17/.

43. Bob Papper, "RTDNA/Hofstra Survey Finds Mixed News for Women and Minorities in TV, Radio News," RTDNA/Hofstra Survey (2011), http://www.rtdna.org/uploads/files/div11.pdf; "Total and Minority Newsroom Employment Declines in 2011 but Loss Continues to Stabilize," ASNE: 2012 Census (April 4, 2012), www.asne.org; Fallows, *Breaking the News*, 33, 80.

44. Bennett, *News*, chap. 4. According to a 2009 Associated Press report the military spends at least $4.7 billion on "winning hearts and minds" in the United States and abroad, a 63 percent increase from five years before. $1.6 billion goes into recruitment and advertising; over $1 billion goes into "public affairs" to reach American audiences and what are called "psychological operations" that target foreign audiences; $2.1 billion goes into staffing all of these areas. "Pentagon Spending Billions on PR to Sway World Opinion," Associated Press (February 5, 2009), www.foxnews.com.

45. Robert Entman, *Democracy Without Citizens: Media and the Decay of American Politics* (New York: Oxford University Press, 1989).

46. See David Okrent, "Weapons of Mass Destruction? Or Mass Distraction?" *New York Times* (May 30, 2004), Opinion-Editorial section; Judith Miller, "Illicit Arms Kept Till Eve of War," *New York Times* (April 23, 2003): A1; John R. MacArthur, "The Lies We Bought," *Columbia Journalism Review* (May/June 2003). Massing, "The Unseen War," 16; Bennett, *News*, 37, 120; Sally Covington, *Moving a Public Agenda: The Strategic Philanthropy of Conservative Foundations* (Washington, D.C.: The National Committee for Responsive Philanthropy, 1997).

47. See Jarol Manheim, *All of the People, All of the Time* (Armonk, NY: M.E. Sharpe, 1991), chap. 3; W. Lance Bennett and Timothy Cook, "Journalism Norms and News Construction," *Political Communication* (Winter 1996); Doris Graber, *The Mass Media in American Politics* (Washington, D.C.: Congressional Quarterly Press, 1996), 44–45; Ray Suarez, *Talk of the Nation*, National Public Radio (March 13, 1997); Bennett, *News*, 173–77.

48. Peter Hart, "Re-Establishing the Establishment," *Extra!* (April 2004); Eric Boehlert, "Dean," *Salon* (January 6, 2004), www.salon.com; Bryan Keefer, "Spin Buster," Campaign Desk, *Columbia Journalism Review*, www.campaigndesk.org; Dana Milbank, *Smashmouth* (New York: Basic Books, 2001). See also, for material on framing, Shanto Iyengar, *Is Anyone Responsible? How Television Frames Political Issues* (Chicago: University of Chicago Press, 1991).

49. Jim Rutenberg, "Fox Portrays a War of Good and Evil, and Many Applaud," *New York Times* (December 3, 2001). See for this general point, Tom Rosenstiel and Bill Kovach, *Warp Speed: America in the Age of Mixed Media* (New York: The Century Foundation, 1999).

50. Manheim, *All of the People*, chap. 3.

51. Maisa Guthrie, "Election 2008: News Media Get Trampled by Their Own Horse Race," *Broadcasting & Cable* (October 14, 2008), www.broadcastingcable.com. On how the candidates rather than issues were the centerpiece of the 2008 campaign see, "Winning the Media Campaign: Top Storylines," Pew Research Center's Project for Excellence in Journalism (October 22, 2008); Bennett, *News*, 43–44; Christina Alsina, Philip John Davies, and Bruce Gronbeck, "Preference Poll Stories in the Last Two Weeks of Campaign 2000," *American Behavioral Scientist* (August 2001); "The Debate Effect," Project for Excellence in Journalism (October 27, 2004), www.journalism.org.

52. Michael Schudson and Danielle Haas, "Getting Bit: When Sound Bites Get Snack-Sized," *Columbia Journalism Review* (May/June 2008), www.cjr.org; Erik P. Bucy and Maria Elizabeth Grabe, "Taking Television Seriously: A Sound and Image Bite Analysis of Presidential Campaign Coverage, 1992–2004," *Journal of Communication* (December 2007), Volume 57, Issue 4, 652–675. Bucy and Grabe report that "image-bites" of candidates, however, are increasing in duration, and we need to study more such aspects of "nonverbal communication." Marjorie Randon Hershey, "The Campaign and the Media," in *The Election of 2000*, ed. Gerald Pomper (New York: Chatham House, 2001): 46–72; Erika Falk and Sean Aday, "Candidate Discourse on Network Evening News Programs," Annenberg Public Policy Center, University of Pennsylvania; Scott Neuman, "Don't Confuse Us With Facts: Why Debates Are All About Style," Political News From NPR (October 4, 2012), www.npr.org; "Both Candidates Received More Negative Than Positive Coverage in Mainstream News, but Social Media Was Even Harsher," Pew Research Center's Project for Excellence in Journalism (November 2, 2012), www.journalism.org.

53. James Boylan, "Where Have All the People Gone?" *Columbia Journalism Review* (May/June 1991): 31–38.

54. Project for Excellence in Journalism, "E-Politics 2004" (October 2004), www.journalism.org; Cass Sunstein, "The Daily We." For data on Jon Stewart's *Daily Show* viewers, see "No Joke: Daily Show Viewers Follow Presidential Race," *Business Journal* (September 21, 2004).

CHAPTER 10

1. As reported by the Center for Responsive Politics in http://www.opensecrets.org/revolving/index.php (accessed May 21, 2012).

2. Based on the median household income from the American Community Survey, 2005–2009; http://www.bloomberg.com/news/2010-12-14/u-s-median-income-by-county-sorted-by-highest-income-table-.html (accessed May 23, 2012).

3. Jeffrey N. Birnbaum, "The Road to Riches Is Called K Street," *Washington Post* (June 22, 2005). According to a recent study by the nonpartisan Congressional Budget Office (CBO), less educated workers make more working for the federal government, but highly educated workers make significantly less. See http://www.cbo.gov/publication/42921 (accessed May 23, 2012).

4 The legal definition of a lobbyist is contained in the 1995 Lobbying Disclosure Act. There is evidence that Gingrich did lobby members of Congress to pass the Medicare drug benefit plan. Timothy P. Carney, "Gingrich Was a Lobbyist, Plain and Simple," *Washington Examiner* (November 20, 2011); http://campaign2012.washingtonexam-iner.com/article/newt-gingrich-was-lobbyist-plain-and-simple (accessed May 23, 2012).

5. Jeffrey H. Birnbaum, "Mickey Gets a Washington," *Washington Post* (February 17, 2008).

6. See David Truman, *The Governmental Process* (New York: Alfred A. Knopf, 1951); Robert Dahl, *A Preface to Democratic Theory* (Chicago: University of Chicago Press, 1956); and Dahl, *Who Governs? Democracy and Power in an American City* (New Haven, CT: Yale University Press, 1961). Since *Who Governs?* Dahl has shifted from an elite democratic to a more popular democratic analysis of American politics. See his *A Preface to Economic Democracy* (Berkeley: University of California Press, 1985).

7. Jeffrey Berry, *The Interest Group Society*, 2nd ed. (Glenview, IL: Scott, Foresman, 1989), 16.

8. Data compiled from the *Washington Representatives* directory by Kay Lehman Schlozman, Sidney Verba, and Henry E. Brady, *The Unheavenly Chorus: Unequal Political Voice and the Broken Promise of American Democracy* (Princeton, NJ: Princeton University Press, 2012), 349. Our analysis of inequality in the interest group system relies heavily on this valuable volume.

9. Ibid., 270.

10. E. E. Schattschneider, *The Semi-Sovereign People: A Realist's View of Democracy in America* (New York: Holt, Rinehart and Winston, 1960), 35. For critiques of pluralist theory as a form of democratic elitism, see Jack Walker, "A Critique of the Elitist Theory of Democracy," *American Political Science Review* 60 (1966): 285–95; and Peter Bachrach, *The Theory of Democratic Elitism: A Critique* (Boston: Little, Brown, 1967).

11. Schlozman, Verba, and Brady, *The Unheavenly Chorus*, 330–31.

12. Ibid., 328.

13. Ibid., 332.

14. For a provocative account of how cultural issues have displaced basic economic issues in one state, see Thomas Frank, *What's the Matter with Kansas?: How Conservatives Won the Heart of America* (New York: Henry Holt and Company, 2004).

15. Schlozman, Verba, and Brady, *The Unheavenly Chorus*, 129.

16. Ibid., 442. Unless otherwise noted, these figures are based on 2001 data.

17. Ibid., 14.

18. Laura Langbein, "Money and Access: Some Empirical Evidence," *Journal of Politics* 48 (1986): 1052–62.

19. Mike McIntire and Michael Luo, "White House Welcomes Donors, and Lobbyists Slip in Door, Too," *New York Times* (April 15, 2012).

20. Frank R. Baumgartner, Jeffrey M. Berry, Marie Hojnacki, David C. Kimball, and Beth L. Leech, *Lobbying and Policy Change: Who Wins, Who Loses, and Why* (Chicago: University of Chicago Press, 2009), 20.

21. Darrell M. West and Burdett A. Loomis, *The Sound of Money: How Political Interests Get What They Want* (New York: W. W. Norton, 1998).

22. Steven E. Schier, *By Invitation Only: The Rise of Exclusive Politics in the United States* (Pittsburgh, PA: University of Pittsburgh Press, 2000).

23. Jose Antonio Vargas, "Obama Raised a Half a Billion Online," *Washington Post Online* (November 20, 2008); http://voices.washingtonpost.com/44/2008/11/20/obama_raised_half_a_billion_on.html (accessed May 26, 2012).

24. Schlozman, Verba, and Brady, *The Unheavenly Chorus*, 504.

25. Karen Mossberger, Caroline J. Tolbert, and Mary Stansbury, *Virtual Inequality: Beyond the Digital Divide* (Washington, D.C.: Georgetown University Press, 2003).

26. Theda Skocpol, *Diminished Democracy: From Membership to Management in American Life* (Norman: University of Oklahoma Press, 2003), 153.

27. Ibid., 162 63.

28. Robert Putnam, *Bowling Alone: The Collapse and Revival of American Community* (New York: Simon & Schuster, 2000), 49.

29. Theda Skocpol, "Government Activism and the Reorganization of American Civic Democracy," in *The Transformation of American Politics: Activist Government and the Rise of Conservatism*, eds. Paul Pierson and Theda Skocpol (Princeton, NJ: Princeton University Press, 2007), 39–67.

30. Theda Skocpol, "Advocates without Members: The Recent Transformation of American Civic Life," in *Civic Engagement in American Democracy*, eds. Theda Skocpol and Morris P. Fiorina (Washington, D.C.: Brookings Institution Press, 1999), 461–509.

31. The distinction between insider and outsider lobbying strategies is discussed in Jack L. Walker, *Mobilizing Interest Groups in America: Patrons, Professions and Social Movements* (Ann Arbor: University of Michigan Press, 1991).

32. Quoted in Jeffrey H. Birnbaum and Alan S. Murray, *Showdown at Gucci Gulch: Lawmakers, Lobbyists, and the Unlikely Triumph of Tax Reform* (New York: Random House, 1987), 178–79.

33. Kay Lehman Schlozman and John T. Tierney, "More of the Same: Washington Pressure Group Activity in a Decade of Change," *Journal of Politics* 45 (1988): 351–75.

34. Quoted in Kay Lehman Schlozman and John T. Tierney, *Organized Interests and American Society* (New York: Harper & Row, 1986), 85.

35. Public Citizen, *Congressional Revolving Door: The Journey from Congress to K Street* (Washington, D.C.: Public Citizen, 2005).

36. See Mancur Olson Jr., *The Logic of Collective Action: Public Goods and the Theory of Groups* (New York: Schocken Books, 1968).

37. Schlozman, Verba, and Brady, *The Unheavenly Chorus*, 321.

38. Ralph Nader, *Unsafe at Any Speed: The Designed-in Dangers of the American Automobile* (New York: Grossman, 1966).

39. Our discussion of the Powell memo is based on Jerry M. Landay, "The Powell Manifesto: How a Prominent Lawyer's Attack Memo Changed America" (August 20, 2002); available at www.mediatransparency.org/storeis/powell.htm.

40. Public Citizen, "Eleven to One" (May 18, 2010); http://www.citizen.org/documents/Derivatives Lobbyist-sReport.pdf (accessed May 27, 2012).

41. See Samuel Huntington's article "The United States" in *The Crisis of Democracy: Report on the Governability of Democracies to the Trilateral Commission*, eds. Michel J. Crozier, Samuel Huntington, and Joji Watanuki (New York: New York University Press, 1975), 59–118.

42. For a popular democratic effort to debunk the exaggerated claims of business, see the "Cry Wolf Project": http://crywolfproject.org/.

43. See Thomas Frank, *Pity the Poor Billionaire: The Hard-Times Swindle and the Unlikely Comeback of the Right* (New York: Metropolitan Books, 2012).

44. Schlozman and Tierney, *Organized Interests*, 94–95.

45. Cited in Ibid., 22.

46. Hugh Heclo, "Issue Networks and the Executive Establishment," in *The New American Political System*, ed. Anthony King (Washington, D.C.: American Enterprise Institute, 1978), 87–124.

47. John C. Stauber and Sheldon Rampton, *Toxic Sludge Is Good for You: Lies, Damn Lies, and the Public Relations Industry* (Monroe, ME: Common Courage Press, 1995), 79.

48. As reported in Ken Silverstein, "Hello. I'm Calling this Evening to Mislead You," *Mother Jones* (November/December 1997).

49. Quoted in Greider, *Who Will Tell The People: The Betrayal of American Democracy* (New York: Simon & Schuster, 1993), 38.

50. See West and Loomis, *The Sound of Money*.

51. Schlozman and Tierney, *Organized Interests*, 115.

52. Charles Murray, *Losing Ground: American Social Policy, 1950–1980* (New York: Basic Books, 1984), 227.

53. For a critique of Murray's analysis, see William Julius Wilson, *The Truly Disadvantaged: The Inner City, the Underclass, and Public Policy* (Chicago: University of Chicago Press, 1987), chap. 4.

54. James G. McGann, *Think Tanks and Policy Advice in the United States: Academics, Advisers, and Advocates* (New York: Routledge, 2007). See also James A. Smith, *The Idea Brokers: Think Tanks and the Rise of the New Policy Elite* (New York: Free Press, 1991), and Andrew Rich, *Think Tanks, Public Policy, and the Politics of Expertise* (New York: Cambridge University Press, 2004).

55. Schlozman, Verba, and Brady, *The Unheavenly Chorus*, 547.

56. West and Loomis, *The Sound of Money*, 240.

57. Bruce Ackerman and James Fishkin, *Deliberation Day* (New Haven, CT: Yale University Press, 2004). For a discussion of deliberative polling, see Bruce Ackerman, *We the People*, Vol. 2 (Cambridge, MA: Beklnap Press, 1998).

58. Jean Stefancic and Richard Delgado, *No Mercy: How Conservative Think Tanks and Foundations Changed America's Social Agenda* (Philadelphia: Temple University Press, 1996), 53.

CHAPTER 11

1. Michael Lipsky, *Protest in City Politics: Rent Strikes, Housing and the Power of the Poor* (Chicago: Rand McNally, 1970), 2. We draw freely in this chapter on Lipsky's analysis of protest as a political resource.

2. Charles C. Euchner, *Extraordinary Politics: How Protest and Dissent Are Changing American Democracy* (Boulder, CO: Westview Press, 1996).

3. The following account of Occupy Wall Street is based on a number of different sources, including Christopher Ketcham, "The New Populists: The Rise and Fall of Zuccotti Park—and the Future of the Movement It Birthed," *The American Prospect* (January/February 2012) and Nathan Schneider, "Some Assembly Required: Witnessing the Birth of Occupy Wall Street," *Harper's* (February 2012).

4 As reported in Ketcham, "The New Populists," 21.

5. Peter Dreier, "Will Occupy Wall Street Be Co-opted?" *Huffington Post* (October 11, 2011); http://www.huffingtonpost.com/peter-dreier/occupy-wall-street_b_1005708.html (accessed June 7, 2012).

6. The following account of the Montgomery bus boycott is based on Taylor Branch, *Parting the Waters: America in the King Years 1954–63* (New York: Simon & Schuster, 1988); and Juan Williams, *Eyes on the Prize: America's Civil Rights Years 1954–1965* (New York: Penguin, 1987).

7. Quoted in Williams, *Eyes on the Prize*, 78.

8. Euchner, *Extraordinary Politics*; Craig A. Rimmerman, *The New Citizenship: Unconventional Politics, Activism, and Service* (Boulder, CO: Westview Press, 1997).

9. Paul Kleppner, *Who Voted? The Dynamics of Electoral Turnout* (New York: Praeger, 1982), 116, as cited in Frances Fox Piven and Richard A. Cloward, *Why Americans Don't Vote* (New York: Pantheon, 1989), 144.

10. Martin Luther King Jr. sermon, delivered at Ebenezer Baptist Church, Atlanta, Georgia, on July 4, 1965.

11. T. R. Gurr, *Why Men Rebel* (Princeton, NJ: Princeton University Press, 1970).

12. John D. McCarthy and Mayer N. Zald, "Resource Mobilization and Social Movements: A Partial Theory," *American Journal of Sociology* 82, 6 (1977): 1212–41.

13. Sara M. Evans and Harry C. Boyte, *Free Spaces: The Sources of Democratic Change in America* (Chicago: University of Chicago Press, 1992).

14. For an insightful account of the populist movement that stresses the formation of a movement culture, see Lawrence Goodwyn, *The Populist Moment* (New York: Oxford University Press, 1978).

15. Quoted in Sara Evans, *Personal Politics: The Roots of Women's Liberation in the Civil Rights Movement and the New Left* (New York: Vintage, 1980), 87.

16. Quoted in Williams, *Eyes on the Prize*, 76.

17. The concepts of transactional and transformational leaders are developed in James MacGregor Burns, *Leadership* (New York: Harper & Row, 1978).

18. For an analysis of Stanton as a dissenting movement leader, see Bruce Miroff, *Icons of Democracy: American Leaders as Heroes, Aristocrats, Dissenters, & Democrats* (New York: Basic Books, 1993), chap. 4.

19. Saul D. Alinsky, *Reveille for Radicals* (New York: Random House, 1969), 132.

20. Henry David Thoreau, "Civil Disobedience," in *Thoreau: People, Principles, and Politics*, ed. Milton Meltzer (New York: Hill & Wang, 1963), 38.

21. Frances Fox Piven and Richard A. Cloward, *Poor People's Movements: Why They Succeed, How They Fail* (New York: Pantheon, 1977).

22. *Report of the National Advisory Commission on Civil Disorders* (New York: Bantam Books, 1968).

23. Murray Edelman, *The Symbolic Uses of Politics* (Urbana: University of Illinois Press, 1967); see also Edelman's *Constructing the Political Spectacle* (Chicago: University of Chicago Press, 1988).

24. See Alan Wolfe, *The Seamy Side of Democracy* (New York: David McKay, 1978); David Caute, *The Great Fear* (New York: Simon & Schuster, 1978); and Robert Justin Goldstein, *Political Repression in Modern America* (Cambridge, MA: Schenkman, 1978).

25. Quoted in William Greider, *Who Will Tell the People? The Betrayal of American Democracy* (New York: Simon & Schuster, 1992), 17.

26. For an elite democratic critique of mass politics, see Samuel P. Huntington, *American Politics: The Promise of Disharmony* (Cambridge, MA: Harvard University Press, 1981).

27. For a critique of the Populist/Progressive movements along these lines, see Richard Hofstadter, *The Age of Reform: From Bryan to F.D.R.* (New York: Vintage, 1955).

28. Tom Wolfe, *Radical Chic and Mau-Mauing the Flak Catchers* (New York: Bantam, 1971), 117–18.

29. Merrill D. Peterson, ed., *The Portable Thomas Jefferson* (New York: Penguin, 1975), 417.

30. Thomas R. Dye and Harmon Ziegler, *The Irony of Democracy: An Uncommon Introduction to American Politics*, 9th ed. (Belmont, CA: Wadsworth, 1993), 17.

31. In 1977, a federal district court ordered all tapes, transcripts, and other FBI information on King's private life to be impounded for fifty years under the seal of secrecy. See Branch, *Parting the Waters*, 872.

32. Euchner, *Extraordinary Politics*, 221.

33. Jeffrey M. Berry, Kent E. Portney, and Ken Thomson, *The Rebirth of Urban Democracy* (Washington, D.C.: The Brookings Institution, 1993).

34. Our account of the Tea Party relies heavily on Theda Skocpol and Vanessa Williamson, *The Tea Party and the Remaking of Republican Conservatism* (New York: Oxford University Press, 2012).

35. Ibid., 22.

36. According to a 2010 national survey, only 7 percent of Tea Party supporters "approve of the way Barack Obama is handling his job." Reported in Kate Zernike, *Boiling Mad: Inside Tea Party America* (New York: Times Books, 2010), 197.

37. Skocpol and Williamson, *The Tea Party*, 11.

38. See Kevin Mattson, "Goodbye to All That," *The American Prospect* (April 5, 2005), 32–37; and Christina Larson, "Postmodern Protests," *Washington Monthly* (March 2005), 12–14.

39. For evidence on the personal effects of participation in protests, see Euchner, *Extraordinary Politics*, 232–33.

40. Rufus P. Browning, Dale Rogers Marshall, and David H. Tabb, *Protest Is Not Enough: The Struggle of Blacks and Hispanics for Equality in Urban Politics* (Berkeley: University of California Press, 1984).

CHAPTER 12

1. Gallup Poll, "Congress Ends 2011 with Record-Low 11% Approval," December 19, 2011.

2. The classic works on congressional individualism are David R. Mayhew, *Congress: The Electoral Connection* (New Haven, CT: Yale University Press, 1974); Richard E. Fenno Jr., *Home Style: House Members in Their Districts* (Boston: Little, Brown, 1978); and Morris P. Fiorina, *Congress: Keystone of the Washington Establishment*, 2nd ed. (New Haven, CT: Yale University Press, 1989).

3. Gary C. Jacobson, *The Politics of Congressional Elections*, 4th ed. (New York: Longman, 1997), 19–28.

4. John W. Kingdon, *Congressmen's Voting Decisions*, 3rd ed. (Ann Arbor: University of Michigan Press, 1989).

5. See Burdett Loomis, *The New American Politician: Ambition, Entrepreneurship, and the Changing Face of Political Life* (New York: Basic Books, 1988).

6. For a rational-choice explanation of this problem, see Kenneth R. Mayer and David T. Canon, *The Dysfunctional Congress? The Individual Roots of an Institutional Dilemma* (Boulder, CO: Westview, 1999).

7. Michael J. Malbin, *Unelected Representatives: Congressional Staff and the Future of Representative Government* (New York: Basic Books, 1980).

8. Richard L. Hall, *Participation in Congress* (New Haven, CT: Yale University Press, 1996), 37–48.

9. Norman J. Ornstein, Thomas E. Mann, and Michael J. Malbin, *Vital Statistics on Congress, 1993–1994* (Washington, D.C.: Congressional Quarterly Press, 1994), 201–2.

10. John R. Hibbing and Elizabeth Theiss-Morse, *Congress as Public Enemy: Public Attitudes Toward American Political Institutions* (New York: Cambridge University Press, 1995), 49.

11. John C. Berg, *Unequal Struggle: Class, Gender, Race, and Power in the U.S. Congress* (Boulder, CO: Westview, 1994), 37–47.

12. See Barbara Sinclair, "The Emergence of Strong Leadership in the 1980s House of Representatives," *Journal of Politics* 54 (August 1992): 657–84.

13. Ronald M. Peters Jr., "The Republican Speakership," paper delivered at the annual meeting of the American Political Science Association, San Francisco, August–September 1996.

14. For the party unity scores, see *CQ Weekly*, January 3, 2004.

15. Janet Hook, "Conservative Freshman Class Eager to Seize the Moment," *Congressional Quarterly* (January 7, 1995): 47–9.

16. Quoted in Sheryl Gay Stolberg, "Quietly but Firmly, Hastert Asserts His Power," *New York Times* (January 3, 2005).

17. Lou Dubose and Jan Reid, *The Hammer: Tom DeLay, God, Money, and the Rise of the Republican Congress* (New York: Public Affairs, 2004).

18. Jonathan Allen, "Effective House Leadership Makes the Most of Majority," *CQ Weekly* (March 29, 2003).

19. Derek Willis, "Republicans Mix It Up When Assigning House Chairmen for the 108th," *CQ Weekly* (January 11, 2003); Allen, "Effective House Leadership."

20. David Firestone, "Frist Forsakes Deal-Making to Focus on Party Principles," *New York Times* (March 13, 2003).

21. Charles Stewart III, "Congressional Committees in a Partisan Era: The End of Institutionalization as We Know It?" in *New Directions in Congressional Politics*, ed. Jamie L. Carson (New York: Routledge, 2012), 106–8.

22. Lawrence A. Becker and Vincent G. Moscardelli, "Congressional Leadership on the Front Lines: Committee Chairs, Electoral Security, and Ideology," *PS: Political Science & Politics* (January 2008): 77–82.

23. Tracy Roof, "Can the Democrats Deliver for the Base? Partisanship, Group Politics, and the Case of Organized Labor in the 110th Congress," *PS: Political Science & Politics* (January 2008): 83–87.

24. Barbara Sinclair, "Leading the New Majorities," *PS: Political Science & Politics* (January 2008): 89–93.

25. See Gregory Koger, "The Rise of the 60-Vote Senate," *Extensions* (Winter 2012): 10–15.

26. Jennifer Steinhauer, "Fervent G.O.P. Freshmen Ignite Budget Fight," *New York Times* (February 17, 2011).

27. David A. Farenthold and Paul Kane, "Gingrich Campaign Brings Up Comparison of Republican Revolutions," *Washington Post* (January 27, 2012).

28. "Can I Scream?" *Politico* (November 20, 2011).

29. Barry C. Burden, *Personal Roots of Representation* (Princeton, NJ: Princeton University Press, 2007).

30. Sean M. Theriault, *Party Polarization in Congress* (New York: Cambridge University Press, 2008).

31. Barbara Sinclair, *Party Wars: Polarization and the Politics of National Policy Making* (Norman: University of Oklahoma Press, 2006), 351.

32. Juliet Eilperin, *Fight Club Politics: How Partisanship Is Poisoning the House of Representatives* (Lanham, MD: Rowman & Littlefield, 2007), 6.

33. James A. Thurber, "The Impact of Budget Reform on Presidential and Congressional Governance," in *Divided Democracy: Cooperation and Conflict Between the President and Congress*, ed. James A. Thurber (Washington, D.C.: CQ Press, 1991).

34. William G. Howell and Jon C. Pevehouse, *While Dangers Gather: Congressional Checks on Presidential War Powers* (Princeton, NJ: Princeton University Press, 2007), 75.

35. Andrew J. Polsky, "Collective Inaction: Presidents, Congress, and Unpopular Wars," *Extensions* (Spring 2008), 4–8.

36. Eileen Burgin, "Assessing Congress's Role in the Making of Foreign Policy," in *Congress Reconsidered*, eds. Lawrence C. Dodd and Bruce I. Oppenheimer, 6th ed., (Washington, D.C.: Congressional Quarterly Press, 1997), 293–324.

37. See Stephen R. Weissman, *A Culture of Deference: Congress's Failure of Leadership in Foreign Policy* (New York: Basic Books, 1995).

38. See Benjamin Ginsberg and Martin Shefter, *Politics by Other Means: Politicians, Prosecutors, and the Press from Watergate to Whitewater* (New York: W. W. Norton, 1999), 39–46.

CHAPTER 13

1. Alexander Hamilton et al., *The Federalist Papers* (New York: New American Library, 1961), 423.

2. Ibid., 424.

3. Ralph Ketcham, ed., *The Anti-Federalist Papers* (New York: New American Library, 1986), 211. Support for Henry's suspicions can be found in William E. Scheuerman, "American Kingship? Monarchical Origins of Modern Presidentialism," *Polity* 37 (January 2005): 24–53.

4. Max Farrand, ed., *The Records of the Federal Convention of 1787*, vol. 1 (New Haven, CT: Yale University Press, 1937), 112.

5. James David Barber, *The Presidential Character: Predicting Performance in the White House*, 4th ed. (Englewood Cliffs, NJ: Prentice Hall, 1992).

6. Precise numbers for White House staff are difficult to determine. See John Hart, *The Presidential Branch: From Washington to Clinton* (Chatham, NJ: Chatham House, 1995), 112–25.

7. Richard L. Berke, "Bush Is Providing Corporate Model for White House," *New York Times* (March 11, 2001).

8. Ibid.

9. See Thomas E. Cronin, *The State of the Presidency*, 2nd ed. (Boston: Little, Brown, 1980), 223–51.

10. David Gergen, *Eyewitness to Power: The Essence of Leadership* (New York: Simon & Schuster, 2000), 85.

11. See George E. Reedy, *The Twilight of the Presidency* (New York: New American Library, 1971).

12. See Hugh Heclo, "OMB and the Presidency: The Problem of 'Neutral Competence,'" *The Public Interest* 11 (1975): 80–98.

13. Quoted in George C. Edwards III and Stephen J. Wayne, *Presidential Leadership: Politics and Policy Making*, 5th ed. (New York: St. Martin's Press, 1999), 208.

14. James Traub, "After Cheney," *New York Times Magazine* (November 29, 2009).

15. Cronin, *State of the Presidency*, 276–78.

16. For a hilarious and insightful view of life in President Clinton's outer cabinet, see Robert B. Reich, *Locked in the Cabinet* (New York: Alfred A. Knopf, 1997).

17. See Mary Anne Borrelli, *The President's Cabinet: Gender, Power, and Representation* (Boulder, CO: Lynne Rienner Publishers, 2002); and Janet M. Martin, *The Presidency and Women: Promise, Performance, and Illusion* (College Station: Texas A&M University Press, 2003).

18. Quoted in Richard E. Neustadt, *Presidential Power and the Modern Presidents* (New York: Free Press, 1990), 10.

19. See Kenneth Mayer, *With the Stroke of a Pen: Executive Orders and Presidential Power* (Princeton, NJ: Princeton University Press, 2001); and William G. Howell, *Power Without Persuasion: The Politics of Direct Presidential Action* (Princeton, NJ: Princeton University Press, 2003).

20. Anne Farris, Richard P. Nathan, and David J. Wright, *The Expanding Administrative Presidency: George W. Bush and the Faith-Based Initiative* (Albany, NY: Rockefeller Institute of Government, 2004).

21. Hamilton et al., *Federalist Papers*, 322. For a view of legislative-executive relations that stresses cooperation as well as conflict, see Mark A. Peterson, *Legislating Together: The White House and Capitol Hill from Eisenhower to Reagan* (Cambridge, MA: Harvard University Press, 1990).

22. See William W. Lammers and Michael A. Genovese, *The Presidency and Domestic Policy: Comparing Leadership Styles from FDR to Clinton* (Washington, DC: Congressional Quarterly Press, 2000).

23. Paul C. Light, "Domestic Policy Making," *Presidential Studies Quarterly* 30 (March 2000): 109–32.

24. Edwards and Wayne, *Presidential Leadership*, 330–31.

25. James P. Pfiffner, "George W. Bush and the Abuse of Executive Power," paper delivered at the American Political Science Association Annual Meeting, Chicago, August 2007.

26. On presidential resources and constraints in economic policy making, see M. Stephen Weatherford and Lorraine M. McDonnell, "Clinton and the Economy: The Paradox of Policy Success and Political Mishap," *Political Science Quarterly* 111 (Fall 1996): 403–36.

27. Robert Reich, "Why Business Should Love Gore," *The American Prospect* (July 31, 2000), 56.

28. "No Love Lost: Barack Obama and Corporate America," *The Economist* (September 23, 2010); Chris Cillizza, "What Bill Daley Taught the White House," *Washington Post* (January 9, 2012),

29. Arthur Schlesinger Jr., *The Imperial Presidency* (Boston: Houghton Mifflin, 1973).

30. *United States v. Curtiss-Wright Corp.*, 299 U.S. 304 (1936).

31. David Gray Adler, "The Clinton Theory of the War Power," *Presidential Studies Quarterly* 30 (March 2000): 163.

32. Charlie Savage and Mark Landler, "White House Defends Continuing U.S. Role in Libya Operation," *New York Times* (June 15, 2011).

33. Bruce Ackerman, "Obama's Unconstitutional War," *Foreign Policy* (March 24, 2011).

34. See Christopher Andrew, *For the President's Eyes Only: Secret Intelligence and the American Presidency from Washington to Bush* (New York: HarperCollins, 1996).

35. For a vivid account of repression in the Nixon administration, see Jonathan Schell, *The Time of Illusion* (New York: Vintage, 1976).

36. For a good analysis of the framers' view of the president, see Jeffrey K. Tulis, *The Rhetorical Presidency* (Princeton, NJ: Princeton University Press, 1987), 25–45.

37. Samuel Kernell, *Going Public: New Strategies of Presidential Leadership*, 2nd ed. (Washington, DC: Congressional Quarterly Press, 1993), 90–1.

38. Richard J. Ellis, *Presidential Travel: The Journey from George Washington to George W. Bush* (Lawrence: University Press of Kansas, 2008), 221–27.

39. See George C. Edwards III, *On Deaf Ears: The Limits of the Bully Pulpit* (New Haven, CT: Yale University Press, 2003).

40. See B. Dan Wood, *The Myth of Presidential Representation* (New York: Cambridge University Press, 2009).

41. Lawrence R. Jacobs and Robert Y. Shapiro, *Politicians Don't Pander: Political Manipulation and the Loss of Democratic Responsiveness* (Chicago: University of Chicago Press, 2000), 121–54.

42. Martha Joynt Kumar, *Managing the President's Message: The White House Communications Operation* (Baltimore: Johns Hopkins University Press, 2007), 4–6.

43. See John Anthony Maltese, *Spin Control: The White House Office of Communications and the Management of Presidential News,* 2nd ed. (Chapel Hill: University of North Carolina Press, 1994).

44. Jeffrey E. Cohen, *The Presidency in the Era of 24-Hour News* (Princeton, NJ: Princeton University Press, 2008).

45. Bruce Miroff, "Monopolizing the Public Space: The President as a Problem for Democratic Politics," in *Rethinking the Presidency,* ed. Thomas E. Cronin (Boston: Little, Brown, 1982), 218–32.

46. Rick Perlstein, *Nixonland: The Rise of a President and the Fracturing of America* (New York: Scribner, 2008), 477–99.

47. See Sidney M. Milkis and Daniel J. Tichenor, "Reform's Mating Dance: Presidents, Social Movements, and Racial Realignments," *The Journal of Policy History* 23 (2011): 451–90.

CHAPTER 14

1. Monica Davey and Steven Greenhouse, "Angry Demonstrations in Wisconsin as Cuts Loom," *New York Times* (February 18, 2011).

2. Andy Kroll, "What's Happening in Wisconsin Explained," *Mother Jones* (March 17, 2011).

3. Sabrina Tavernise, "Ohio Turns Back a Law Limiting Unions' Rights," *New York Times* (November 8, 2011).

4. Quoted in James A. Morone, *The Democratic Wish: Popular Participation and the Limits of American Government* (New York: Basic Books, 1990), 87.

5. Matthew A. Crenson, *The Federal Machine: Beginnings of Bureaucracy in Jacksonian America* (Baltimore: Johns Hopkins University Press, 1975), 4.

6. On late nineteenth-century state builders, see Stephen Skowronek, *Building a New American State: The Expansion of National Administrative Capacities, 1877–1920* (New York: Cambridge University Press, 1982), esp. 42–45.

7. Morone, *Democratic Wish,* 98.

8. George McJimsey, *Harry Hopkins* (Cambridge, MA: Harvard University Press, 1987).

9. Quoted in Charles T. Goodsell, *The Case for Bureaucracy,* 2nd ed. (Chatham, NJ: Chatham House, 1985), 166.

10. Quoted in Paul Singer, "By the Horns," *National Journal* (March 26, 2005), 899.

11. Lyndsey Layton, "Obama's Appointees Are Flexing Their Regulatory Powers," *Washington Post* (October 12, 2009).

12. Michael Lipsky, *Street-Level Bureaucracy: Dilemmas of the Individual in Public Service* (New York: Russell Sage Foundation, 2010).

13. Charles T. Goodsell, *The Case for Bureaucracy: A Public Administration Polemic,* 4th ed. (Washington, D.C.: Congressional Quarterly Press, 2004), 101.

14. Ibid., 24–41.

15. See James Q. Wilson, *Bureaucracy: What Government Agencies Do and Why They Do It* (New York: Basic Books, 1989), 179–95.

16. Kenneth J. Meier and Laurence J. O'Toole, Jr., *Bureaucracy in a Democratic State: A Governance Perspective* (Baltimore: Johns Hopkins University Press, 2006).

17. See John A. Rohr, *To Run a Constitution: The Legitimacy of the Administrative State* (Lawrence: University Press of Kansas, 1986), 59–89.

18. Francis E. Rourke, *Bureaucracy, Politics, and Public Policy,* 2nd ed. (Boston: Little, Brown, 1976), 16.

19. Kenneth J. Meier, *Politics and the Bureaucracy: Policymaking in the Fourth Branch of Government,* 3rd ed. (Pacific Grove, CA: Brooks/Cole, 1993), 68–72.

20. Barry Bozeman, *Bureaucracy and Red Tape* (Upper Saddle River, NJ: Prentice-Hall, 2000).

21. Quoted in William T. Gormley, Jr., and Steven J. Balla, *Bureaucracy and Democracy: Accountability and Performance* (Washington, D.C.: Congressional Quarterly Press, 2004), 164.

22. Rourke, *Bureaucracy, Politics, and Public Policy,* 46.

23. Wilson, *Bureaucracy,* 251.

24. David J. Garrow, *The FBI and Martin Luther King, Jr.* (New York: Penguin, 1983), 125–34.

25. Charles H. Levine, B. Guy Peters, and Frank J. Thompson, *Public Administration* (Glenview, IL: Scott, Foresman, 1990), 52–53.

26. Morton H. Halperin, *Bureaucratic Politics and Foreign Policy* (Washington, D.C.: Brookings Institution Press, 1974), 43.

27. Wilson, *Bureaucracy,* 257. For a historical account of this rivalry, see Skowronek, *Building a New American State,* 165–292.

28. Michael D. Reagan, *Regulation: The Politics of Policy* (Boston: Little, Brown, 1987), 15.

29. See Gabriel Kolko, *The Triumph of Conservatism* (Chicago: Quadrangle Books, 1967).

30. John Atlas and Peter Dreier, "The Conservative Origins of the Sub-Prime Mortgage Crisis," *American Prospect Online* (December 18, 2007).

31. Carrie Budoff Brown and Kendra Marr, "Obama Signs Wall Street Reform Bill," *Politico* (July 21, 2010); Daniel Carpenter, "The Contest of Lobbies and Disciplines: Financial Politics and Regulatory Reform," in *Reaching for a New Deal: Ambitious Governance, Economic Meltdown, and Polarized Politics in Obama's First Two Years,* eds. Theda Skocpol and Lawrence R. Jacobs (New York: Russell Sage Foundation, 2011), 139–88.

32. Joel Brinkley, "Out of Spotlight, Bush Overhauls U.S. Regulations," *New York Times* (August 14, 2004).

33. Jia Lynn Yang, "Does Government Regulation Really Kill Jobs? Economists Say Overall Effect Minimal," *The Washington Post* (November 13, 2011).

34. CNN Poll, "Trust in Government at All Time Low," September 28, 2011; Gallup Poll, "Americans Say Federal Gov't Wastes over Half of Every Dollar," September 19, 2011.

35. Paul C. Light, *A Government Ill Executed: The Decline of the Federal Service and How to Reverse It* (Cambridge, MA: Harvard University Press, 2008), 102.

36. Ibid., 139.

37. Ibid., 102–30.

38. See E. S. Savas, *Privatizing the Public Sector: How to Shrink Government* (Chatham, NJ: Chatham House, 1982).

39. See Elliott D. Sclar, *You Don't Always Get What You Pay For: The Economics of Privatization* (Ithaca, NY: Cornell University Press, 2000).

40. Matthew A. Crenson and Benjamin Ginsberg, *Downsizing Democracy: How America Sidelined Its Citizens and Privatized Its Public* (Baltimore: Johns Hopkins University Press, 2004), 210–11.

41. Donald F. Kettl, *System Under Stress: Homeland Security and American Politics* (Washington, D.C.: Congressional Quarterly Press, 2004), 45–7.

CHAPTER 15

1. David G. Savage, "Obama-Alito Tensions Surface at State of the Union Address," *Los Angeles Times* (January 29, 2010).

2. The Constitution, ostensibly an expression of the will of the people, has become a lawyers' document. See John Brigham, *The Cult of the Court* (Philadelphia: Temple University Press, 1987).

3. For an illuminating treatment of the conflicting theories of democracy that have been used by different justices on the modern Supreme Court, see Martin Edelman, *Democratic Theories and the Constitution* (Albany: State University of New York Press, 1984).

4. Antonin Scalia, *A Matter of Interpretation* (Princeton, NJ: Princeton University Press, 1997), 3–47.

5. Stephen Breyer, *Active Liberty: Interpreting Our Democratic Constitution* (New York: Alfred A. Knopf, 2005).

6. David Kairys, ed., *The Politics of Law: A Progressive Critique*, 3rd ed. (New York: Basic Books, 1998).

7. *Marbury v. Madison*, 1 Cranch 137 (1803).

8. Robert G. McCloskey, *The American Supreme Court* (Chicago: University of Chicago Press, 1960), 57.

9. *Dred Scott v. Sandford*, 60 U.S. (19 How.) 393 (1857).

10. Michael Les Benedict, "History of the Court: Reconstruction, Federalism, and Economic Rights," in *The Oxford Companion to the Supreme Court of the United States*, eds. Kermit L. Hall et al. (New York: Oxford University Press, 1992), 388.

11. Thomas M. Keck, *The Most Activist Supreme Court in History: The Road to Modern Judicial Conservatism* (Chicago: University of Chicago Press, 2004).

12. Linda Greenhouse, "The Court Rules, America Changes," *New York Times* (July 2, 2000).

13. Charles Lane, "Narrow Victories Move Roberts Court to Right," *Washington Post*, (June 29, 2007); Linda Greenhouse, "At Supreme Court, 5-to-4 Rulings Fade, but Why?," *New York Times* (May 23, 2008).

14. David M. O'Brien, *Storm Center: The Supreme Court in American Politics*, 3rd ed. (New York: W. W. Norton, 1993), 107.

15. Linda Greenhouse, "Rock Bottom," *New York Times* (December 15, 2011).

16. Jesse J. Holland, "Obama Judicial Nominations Set Record for Women, Minorities," *HuffingtonPost.com* (September 13, 2011).

17. See Laurence H. Tribe, *God Save This Honorable Court: How the Choice of Supreme Court Justices Shapes Our History* (New York: New American Library, 1986), 36–48.

18. David M. O'Brien, *Storm Center: The Supreme Court in American Politics*, 5th ed. (New York: W. W. Norton, 2000), 55.

19. See Tribe, *God Save This Honorable Court*, 60–92.

20. See John Massaro, *Supremely Political: The Role of Ideology and Presidential Management in Unsuccessful Supreme Court Nominations* (Albany: State University of New York Press, 1990).

21. David A. Yalof, "Obama and the Law: Judicial Restraint at the Crossroads," in *The Obama Presidency: Appraisals and Prospects*, eds. Bert A. Rockman, Andrew Rudalevige, and Colin Campbell (Washington, D.C.: CQ Press, 2012), 226–29.

22. *Brown v. Allen*, 344 U.S. 443 (1953).

23. Mark Silverstein, *Judicious Choices: The Politics of Supreme Court Confirmations*, 2nd ed. (New York: W. W. Norton, 2007), 211–13; Jeffrey Rosen, "Roberts's Rules," *The Atlantic* (January/February 2007); Lane, "Narrow Victories Move Roberts Court to Right."

24. See Walter Murphy, *Elements of Judicial Strategy* (Chicago: University of Chicago Press, 1964).

25. See Phillip J. Cooper, *Battles on the Bench: Conflict Inside the Supreme Court* (Lawrence: University Press of Kansas, 1995).

26. Lawrence Baum, "Membership Change and Collective Voting Change in the United States Supreme Court," *Journal of Politics* 54, no. 1 (February 1992): 3–24; Jeffrey A. Segal and Harold J. Spaeth, *The Supreme Court and the Attitudinal Model Revisited* (New York: Cambridge University Press, 2002).

27. Lawrence Baum, *The Supreme Court*, 4th ed. (Washington, D.C.: Congressional Quarterly Press, 1992), 144–56.

28. Stephen L. Wasby, *The Supreme Court in the Federal Judicial System*, 4th ed. (Chicago: Nelson-Hall, 1993), 349.

29. Keith E. Whittington, *Political Foundations of Judicial Supremacy: The Presidency, the Supreme Court, and Constitutional Leadership in U.S. History* (Princeton, NJ: Princeton University Press, 2007), 22–25, 71–81.

30. See Gregory A. Caldeira, "Neither the Purse nor the Sword: Dynamics of Public Confidence in the Supreme Court," *American Political Science Review* 80, no. 4 (December 1986): 1209–26.

CHAPTER 16

1. *West Virginia State Board of Education v. Barnette*, 319 U.S. 624 (1943).

2. *Texas v. Johnson*, 491 U.S. 397 (1989).

3. See Samuel Walker, *In Defense of American Liberties: A History of the ACLU* (New York: Oxford University Press, 1990).

4. Actually, twelve amendments passed Congress. One was rejected by the states; the other, which required that congressional pay raises not take effect until after an election, was not ratified by enough states. Resurrected in the early 1980s, this amendment finally became the Twenty-seventh Amendment in 1992—over 200 years after it was originally proposed!

5. *United States v. Carolene Products Co.*, 304 U.S. 144 (1938).

6. On the double standard, see Henry J. Abraham and Barbara A. Perry, *Freedom and the Court: Civil Rights and Liberties in the United States*, 6th ed. (New York: Oxford University Press, 1994), 9–29.

7. See Alan Wolfe, *The Seamy Side of Democracy: Repression in America* (New York: David McKay, 1973).

8. *Schenck v. United States*, 249 U.S. 47 (1919).

9. *Brandenburg v. Ohio*, 395 U.S. 444 (1969).

10. *Tinker v. Des Moines Independent Community School District*, 393 U.S. 503 (1969).

11. *Roth v. United States*, 354 U.S. 476 (1957).

12. *Miller v. California*, 413 U.S. 15 (1973).

13. *F.C.C. v. Pacifica Foundation*, 438 U.S. 726 (1978).

14. Garry Wills, *Under God: Religion and American Politics* (New York: Simon & Schuster, 1990), 16.

15. See the classic account by Anthony Lewis, *Gideon's Trumpet* (New York: Vintage, 1964).

16. *Jencks v. United States*, 353 U.S. 657 (1957).

17. *Olmstead v. United States*, 277 U.S. 438 (1928).

18. *Griswold v. Connecticut*, 381 U.S. 479 (1965).

19. See Barbara Hinkson Craig and David M. O'Brien, *Abortion and American Politics* (Chatham, NJ: Chatham House, 1993), 35–68.

20. *Plessy v. Ferguson*, 163 U.S. 537 (1896).

21. For the story of the NAACP campaign against school segregation, see Richard Kluger, *Simple Justice* (New York: Alfred A. Knopf, 1976).

22. *Brown v. Board of Education of Topeka*, 347 U.S. 483 (1954).

23. See Juan Williams, *Eyes on the Prize: America's Civil Rights Years, 1954–1965* (New York: Penguin, 1988).

24. *Bowers v. Hardwick*, 478 U.S. 186 (1986).

25. *Romer v. Evans*, 517 U.S. 620 (1996).

26. *Boy Scouts of America v. Dale*, 520 U.S. 640 (2000).

27. *Lawrence v. Texas*, 539 U.S. 558 (2003).

28. Gallup Poll, "For First Time, Majority of Americans Favor Legal Gay Marriage," May 20, 2011.

CHAPTER 17

1. Gulbranson profile is from Binyamin Appelbaum and Robert Gebeloff, "Even Critics of Safety Net Increasingly Depend on It," *New York Times* (February 12, 2012).

2. Ibid. The increase controls for inflation.

3. Suzanne Mettler, *The Submerged State: How Invisible Government Policies Undermine American Democracy* (Chicago: University of Chicago Press, 2011), 2.

4. Ibid., 37.

5. Quoted in Peter G. Peterson, *Running on Empty: How the Democratic and Republican Parties Are Bankrupting Our Future and What American Can Do About It* (New York: Farrar, Straus and Giroux, 2004), 143.

6. These words are inscribed over the entrance to the Internal Revenue Service Headquarters at 1111 Constitution Avenue in Washington, D.C.

7. Christopher Howard, *The Welfare State Nobody Knows: Debunking Myths About U.S. Social Policy* (Princeton, NJ: Princeton University Press, 2007). For insightful analysis of the submerged welfare state, see Mettler, *The Submerged State*.

8. The wholesale price index dropped an astonishing 65 percent between 1864 and 1890. Robert B. Reich, *The Work of Nations* (New York: Vintage, 1992), 27.

9. Quoted in David E. Rosenbaum, "Critics Want Fed's Power Under More Accountability," *New York Times* (November 14, 1991).

10. Paul Krugman, "Earth to Ben Bernanke," *New York Times Magazine* (April 29, 2012), 18.

11. Donald F. Kettl, *Leadership at the Fed* (New Haven, CT: Yale University Press, 1986).

12. Quoted in Alfred L. Malabre, *Lost Prophets: An Insider's History of the Modern Economists* (Boston: Harvard Business School Press, 1994), 183. See Jude Wanniski, *The Way the World Works* (New York: Basic Books, 1978).

13. Congressional Budget Office, *The Effects of Automatic Stabilizers on the Federal Budget Deficit* (Washington, D.C.: Congressional Budget Office, May 2010).

14. Even though 95 percent of all working Americans received tax cuts, a survey conducted one year after the law was passed found that only 12 percent of Americans believed that their taxes had been reduced. As reported in Mettler, *The Submerged State*, 1.

15. Congressional Budget Office, *Estimated Impact of the American Recovery and Reinvestment Act on Employment and Economic Output from April 2011 through July 2011* (Washington, D.C.: Congressional Budget Office, August 2011), 3.

16. For a summary of the damage that large deficits could inflict on the economy, see Peterson, *Running on Empty*.

17. See Barry Bosworth, *Tax Incentives and Economic Growth* (Washington, D.C.: The Brookings Institution, 1984); Charles R. Hulten and Isabel V. Sawhill, eds., *The Legacy of Reaganomics: Prospects for Long-Term Growth* (Washington, D.C.: Urban Institute Press, 1984).

18. Lawrence Mishel, Jared Bernstein, and Sylvia Allegretto, *The State of Working America 2006/2007* (Ithaca, NY: Cornell University Press, 2007) 85.

19. Michael J. Graetz and Ian Shapiro, *Death by a Thousand Cuts: The Fight over Taxing Inherited Wealth* (Princeton, NJ: Princeton University Press), 6. Our account of the fight over the estate tax relies heavily on Graetz and Shapiro's comprehensive study.

20. Ibid., 65.

21. Reported in Paul Krugman, "The Tax-Cut Con," *New York Times Magazine* (September 14, 2003), 59.

22. Geoerge Lakoff, *Don't Think of an Elephant! Know Your Values and Frame the Debate* (White River Junction, VT: Chelsea Green Publishing, 2004), 3–4.

23. Graetz & Shapiro, *Death by a Thousand Cuts*, 76.

24. Ibid., 213.

25. Quoted in ibid., 170.

26. Mayling Birney and Ian Shapiro, "Death and Taxes: The Estate Tax Repeal and American Democracy," Department of Political Science, Yale University, October 5, 2003. Our account of estate tax repeal relies heavily on this article.

27. Christopher Howard, *The Welfare State Nobody Knows: Debunking Myths About U.S. Social Policy* (Princeton, NJ: Princeton University Press, 2007), 37.

28. Theda Skocpol, "Targeting Within Universalism: Politically Viable Policies to Combat Poverty in the United States," in *The Urban Underclass*, eds. Christopher Jencks and Paul E. Peterson (Washington, D.C.: The Brookings Institution, 1991), 425.

29. Theda Skocpol, *The Missing Middle: Working Families and the Future of American Social Policy* (New York: W. W. Norton, 2000), 76.

30. Danilo Trisi and LaDonna Pavetti, *TANF Weakening as a Safety Net for Poor Families* (Washington, D.C.: Center on Budget and Policy Priorities, March 13, 2012).

31. Mishel, Bernstein, and Allegretto, *The State of Working America 2006/2007*.

32. Arnold J. Heidenheimer, Hugh Heclo, and Carolyn Teich Adams, *Comparative Public Policy: The Politics of Social Choice in America, Europe, and Japan*, 3rd ed. (New York: St. Martin's, 1990), 249.

33. See Frances Fox Piven and Richard A. Cloward, *Regulating the Poor: The Functions of Public Welfare* (New York: Random House, 1971).

34. Quoted in Jonathan Rieder, *Canarsie: The Jews and Italians of Brooklyn Against Liberalism* (Cambridge, MA: Harvard University Press, 1985), 102.

35. The most influential statement that welfare is a cause of poverty is in Charles Murray, *Losing Ground: American Social Policy, 1950–1980* (New York: Basic Books, 1984). For an effective critique of Murray, see William Julius Wilson, *The Truly Disadvantaged: The Inner City, the Underclass, and Public Policy* (Chicago: University of Chicago Press, 1987).

36. Jason DeParle, *American Dream: Three Women, Ten Kids, and a Nation's Drive to End Welfare* (New York: Viking, 2004), 131.

37. Quoted in Gwen Ifill, "Clinton Offers Plan for Overhaul of Welfare, with Stress on Work," *New York Times* (September 10, 1992).

38. Paul E. Peterson and Mark C. Rom, *Welfare Magnets: A New Case for a National Standard* (Washington, D.C.: The Brookings Institution, 1990); Sanford F. Schram and Samuel H. Beer, eds., *Welfare Reform: A Race to the Bottom?* (Washington, D.C.: Woodrow Wilson Center Press, 1999).

39. Jason DeParle, "Welfare Limits Left Poor Adrift as Recession Hit," *New York Times* (April 8, 2012).

40. Andrew C. Revkin, "Welfare Policies Alter the Face of Food Lines," *New York Times* (February 26, 1999); Jason De Parle, "As Welfare Rolls Shrink, Load on Relatives Grows," *New York Times* (February 21, 1999).

41. Andrea Louise Campbell, *How Policies Make Citizens: Senior Political Activism and the American Welfare State* (Princeton, NJ: Princeton University Press, 2003), 128.

42. Ibid., 268.

43. Quoted in Joe Soss, "Lessons of Welfare: Policy Design, Political Learning, and Political Action," *American Political Science Review* 93, no. 2 (June 1999), 367.

44. Howard, *The Welfare State Nobody Knows*, 99.

45. Quoted in ibid., 106.

46. Andrea Louise Campbell, *How Policies Make Citizens: Senior Political Activism and the American Welfare State* (Princeton, NJ: Princeton University Press, 2003), 129–30.

47. Mettler, *The Submerged State*, 20.

48. U. S. Bureau of the Census, "Annual Social and Economic (ASEC) Supplement," 2005, http://pubdb3.census.gov/macro/032007/hhinc/new06_000.htm; as reported in Mettler, *The Submerged State*, 23.

49. Mettler, *The Submerged State*, 98.

50. CIA, *The World Fact Book*, https://www.cia.gov/library/publications/the-world-factbook/rankorder/2091rank.html.

51. Our account of the politics of health care reform relies heavily on Lawrence R. Jacobs and Theda Skocpol, *Health Care Reform and American Politics: What Everyone Needs to Know* (New York: Oxford University Press, 2010), 21.

52. The 58 Senate Democrats needed the support of two independent senators, Bernie Sanders of Vermont and Joseph Lieberman of Connecticut.

53. Jacobs and Skocpol, *Health Care Reform and American Politics*, 130.

54. Dean Baker and Kevin Hassett, "The Human Disaster of Unemployment," *New York Times* (May 13, 2012).

55. Famously quoted in Isaiah Berlin, *Four Essays on Liberty* (London: Oxford University Press, 1969).

CHAPTER 18

1. Rajiv Chandrasekaran, *Imperial Life in the Emerald City: Inside Iraq's Green Zone* (New York: Vintage Books, 2007), 107–12, 258–62.

2. See especially Hamilton's arguments in *Federalist No. 6* and *No. 11*.

3. Clinton Rossiter, ed., *The Federalist Papers* (New York: New American Library, 1961), 424.

4. Walter L. Hixson, *The Myth of American Diplomacy: National Identity and U.S. Foreign Policy* (New Haven, CT: Yale University Press, 2008).

5. Richard J. Barnet, *The Rockets' Red Glare: When America Goes to War—The Presidents and the People* (New York: Simon & Schuster, 1990), 82.

6. Ibid., 111–15, 125–38; Bruce Miroff, *Icons of Democracy: American Leaders as Heroes, Aristocrats, Dissenters, and Democrats* (Lawrence: University Press of Kansas, 2000), 182–87.

7. Roy P. Basler, ed., *The Collected Works of Abraham Lincoln* (New Brunswick, NJ: Rutgers University Press, 1953–55), vol. 3, 357.

8. Quoted in Ralph B. Levering, *The Cold War, 1945–1987* (Arlington Heights, IL: Harlan Davidson, 1988), 30.

9. James M. McCormick, *American Foreign Policy and Process*, 2nd ed. (Itasca, IL: Peacock, 1992), 377–80.

10. Ibid., 361–69.

11. Ibid., 152–54.

12. Loch K. Johnson, *America's Secret Power: The CIA in a Democratic Society* (New York: Oxford University Press, 1989), 16–17.

13. See Tim Weiner, *Legacy of Ashes: The History of the CIA* (New York: Doubleday, 2007).

14. Johnson, *America's Secret Power*, 10.

15. Ibid., 107–10, 118–29, 207–33.

16. Mark Leibovich, "George Tenet's 'Slam Dunk' into the History Books," *Washington Post* (June 4, 2004).

17. Douglas Jehl and David Johnston, "Rules Change Lets C.I.A. Freely Send Suspects Abroad to Jails," *New York Times* (March 6, 2005).

18. Lawrence R. Jacobs and Benjamin I. Page, "Who Influences U.S. Foreign Policy?" *American Political Science Review* 99 (February 2005): 120.

19. Richard J. Barnet, *Roots of War* (New York: Penguin, 1973), 179–82.

20. Weiner, *Legacy of Ashes*, 306–17.

21. See Thomas W. Graham, "Public Opinion and U.S. Foreign Policy Decision Making," in *The New Politics of American Foreign Policy*, ed. David A. Deese (New York: St. Martin's, 1994), 190–215.

22. McCormick, *American Foreign Policy and Process*, 498–505.

23. Robert Y. Shapiro and Benjamin I. Page, "Foreign Policy and Public Opinion," in Deese, *New Politics*, 229–33.

24. These paragraphs are drawn from Bruce Miroff, "Partisan Polarization, the Presidency, and U.S. Foreign Policy," a paper delivered at Global Leadership Workshop, Yale University, March 2011.

25. Emily O. Goldman and Larry Berman, "Engaging the World: First Impressions of the Clinton Foreign Policy Legacy," in *The Clinton Legacy*, eds. Colin Campbell and Bert A. Rockman (New York: Chatham House, 2000), 226–30.

26. Ivo H. Daalder and James M. Lindsay, "Bush's Foreign Policy Revolution," in *The George W. Bush Presidency: An Early Assessment*, ed. Fred I. Greenstein (Baltimore: Johns Hopkins University Press, 2003), 125–29.

27. Quoted in Benjamin R. Barber, *Fear's Empire: War, Terrorism, and Democracy* (New York: W. W. Norton, 2003), 79.

28. Thomas E. Ricks, *Fiasco: The American Military Adventure in Iraq* (New York: Penguin Books, 2007), 46–95.

29. Ibid., 96–111, 149–58.

30. Ibid., 149–297, 378–80.

31. Andrew J. Bacevich, *The Limits of Power: The End of American Exceptionalism* (New York: Henry Holt and Company, 2009).

32. Quoted in "Charting a New World Order," *Boston.com* (December 2, 2008).

33. Robert S. Singh, "Continuity and Change in Obama's Foreign Policy," in *The Obama Presidency: Appraisals and Prospects*, eds. Bert A. Rockman, Andrew Rudalevige, and Colin Campbell (Washington, D.C.: CQ Press, 2012), 269–72.

34. James M. McCormick, "The Obama Presidency: A Foreign Policy of Change?," in *Transforming America: Barack Obama in the White House*, ed. Steven E. Schier (Lanham, MD: Rowman & Littlefield, 2011), 237–38.

35. Jackson Diehl, "Obama's Foreign Initiatives Have Been Failures," *Washington Post* (January 8, 2012).

36. Singh, "Continuity and Change in Obama's Foreign Policy," 288.

DEMOCRATIC DEBATE INDEX

N